FAITHS AND
FOLKLORE

A SUPERSTITION OF THE MONTH OF DECEMBER.

On Christmas Eve it is reputed in some districts that cocks crow all night, and thus scare away evil spirits for future days.

FAITHS AND
FOLKLORE

Of the British Isles

A DESCRIPTIVE AND
HISTORICAL DICTIONARY

of the superstitions, beliefs, and popular customs
of England, Scotland, Wales, and Ireland,
from Norman times to the end of the nineteenth century,
with Classical and foreign analogues.

By

W. CAREW HAZLITT

(Based on "The Popular Antiquities of Great Britain"—by John Brand and Sir Henry Ellis)

VOLUME I

Benjamin Blom

BIBLIOGRAPHICAL NOTE

The nucleus of the present work was first published in London 1813 as Brand's *The Popular Antiquities Of Great Britain*, originally compiled by John Brand and posthumously revised and enlarged by Sir Henry Ellis. This work was republished in London 1870, considerably revised, enlarged, and corrected by W. C. Hazlitt.

In 1905 the book was again revised by Hazlitt. By that time his revisions and additions were so extensive that the authorship in large measure is that of W. C. Hazlitt.

The present edition is a reprint of the 1905 edition, with a new introduction by Dr. Decherd Turner, Bridwell Librarian, Southern Methodist University.

L.C. Catalog Card Number: 64-18758

Printed in U.S.A. by
NOBLE OFFSET PRINTERS, INC.
NEW YORK 3, N. Y.

LETTER TO THE PUBLISHER

January 11, 1965

It was my intention, as you know, to write an extensive introduction to FAITHS AND FOLKLORE, and to add footnotes throughout the text. I spent months working toward that goal, but the more deeply I delved into the book, the more acutely aware I became of the problems inherent in such an undertaking.

From its inception, FAITHS AND FOLKLORE was never intended as the definitive survey of the subject. This is all to the good, for any attempt to be definitive in a field as vast as this is doomed to failure. How can one summarize almost fifteen centuries of British popular customs and beliefs, superstitions and mores, religious celebrations and secular festivities (etc. etc. etc.), within the confines of two, or even twenty, volumes? The miracle of it all is that Hazlitt was able to compress the fantastic amount of information he did gather into the confines of two volumes.

I envy Hazlitt! Only by reviewing his work did I begin to realize the boundless amounts of energy, time, and knowledge that must have gone into the making of this text. How few of us today have the leisure to devote decades to "revising" a book? That's how long it took Hazlitt to do *his* "latest revised edition," and that is how long it would take me to do a revised edition of his revised edition.

But that's only half the reason for my reticence. The other half is that FAITHS AND FOLKLORE is a personal book, very much in the tradition of Samuel Johnson, the lexicographer-moralist of "Dictionary" fame. Hazlitt, like Johnson, doesn't hesitate to inject his own views, likes and dislikes. And what a wonderful Victorian/Edwardian moralist he is! I can picture him standing on the banks of the Thames, crying "shame," "shame," at the *vaccinated* citizens mumbling incantations in their effort to locate a drowned body. But he undoubtedly rushed home, there to record still another of those "barbaric" customs. I suspect he derived some pleasure from his task (did he ever get paid for all his labors?); how else explain the many delightful passages?

To us, Twentieth Century man, such moralizing seems quite inappropriate in a "descriptive dictionary." At times, FAITHS AND FOLKLORE smacks of Colonel Blimp. We smile at Hazlitt, not with him, when he takes such a homiletic stance. But we must remember that he wrote at a time when so many of these "barbaric" customs still prevailed in "The Empire" (the new Empire, i.e.). And such hang-overs of yesterday were to be rooted from the domain, making way for the triumph of modern rational man. When Hazlitt uses FAITHS AND FOLKLORE as the polemic weapon to exorcise the evils of ignorance from the land, his role takes on a patriotic fervor.

There are not many such direct confrontations throughout the book. Generally, the attack is implicit, subtle, and by indirection. Hazlitt works by commission and omission. How else could we explain this extraordinary work, with not a semblance of "balance" by modern critical standards? Obviously, Hazlitt, like Samuel Johnson before him, felt free to in- and ex-clude at will: Or rather, by design, for there is rationality behind the seeming imbalance. The rationality is Hazlitt's: it is he, the great authority, who would decide what was to go into the columns of print, and how much space was to be assigned to each entry. The reader, at times, is left high and dry and, at others, stands in awe and amazement at the erudition and fullness of Hazlitt's documentation, observations, and analyses.

No reputable scholar would dare to compile such a work today, even if some foolhardy publisher would agree to publish it. The folklorist of our time is the product of an Academy which demands "objectivity-above-everything." We must not consciously project our personalities (or, still worse, our opinions) into descriptive dictionaries. Our attack on such a project unquestionably would be to assemble a committee of scholars to act as advisors, and to compose our ode within the confines and standards approved by the Foundation, with the appropriate sabbatical leaves and boost of Fellowship to propel the work to its ultimate destination.

I have no quarrels with our modern method and, if I did, this would not be the time and place to air them. What does concern me is that we must not delude ourselves into believing that we produce a truly "objective" or scientifically sound "final" entity, devoid of the biases and limits of men like Hazlitt. Behind our golden encyclopedias and mightily self-touted definitive dictionaries lie the limits of our age, and its prejudices, biases, polemics, homilies.

Perhaps that is why I respond so to Hazlitt. There is an honesty that pervades the work. One knows where he stands. Even his methodology is honest. How many of today's encyclopedists would dare to reveal the source of their erudition? How many would, and do, tell us where, and from whom, they obtained their data? Would we expose ourselves in a modern encyclopedia by unblushingly revealing that we base some of our account upon a secondary hack author? (Not that Hazlitt relies upon second-rate hacks; but he's not afraid to quote them if nothing else serves the purpose as well.) Wouldn't it sound so much more "right" if Hazlitt had simply resorted to a pastiche, taking from all and sundry, and rephrased and restyled it all?

The question is not entirely rhetorical. I'm afraid that Hazlitt, for our tastes, did make the fatal error of too much honesty. True, his book is recommended in the Winchell *Guide*, but the fact remains that, whereas a great many of the reference books listed by Winchell have been reprinted, Hazlitt's has not been. The oversight becomes blatant if we keep in mind that some of these reprints are of strictly secondary importance, both in their scholarship and subject matter. Furthermore, some of the "ancient" books which have been reprinted today, have been, by every standard, superseded by one or many later works. None of this holds true for Hazlitt.

Who was this man Hazlitt anyway? I won't duplicate the information in the "Dictionary Of National Biography" and elsewhere, but I do believe it is pertinent to conjecture that, to all but the most limited circle, his name means nothing today. And if the name does have meaning, it is probably only because William Carew Hazlitt is confused with his illustrious grandfather, the English critic and author, William Hazlitt. Well, *our* Hazlitt may not warrant the accolades of his progenitor, but neither should he be relegated to the dustbin. Just look at his bibliography of English literature which he published over the course of decades in an edition (I believe) limited to one hundred and fifty copies. Its double-columns encompass more pages than the *Cambridge Bibliography Of English Literature*. But it's not only the quantity that impresses one (although, God knows, that, in and of itself, would evoke astonishment.) His annotations for thousands of books, and his exact bibliographical notes, are the fruits of the work of a man of exceptional knowledge, taste, and perception. This was no second-rate cataloguer, but a brilliant pioneer in a field which we, today, are only beginning to utilize to the fullest.

It was such a man, and such a scholar, who produced FAITHS AND FOLKLORE, and it is such a man who has earned the right to have his life's work presented without additions, emendations, excisions, and revisions.

When I first accepted your commission to re-edit Hazlitt, I plunged ahead, convinced that such additions could retain the spirit of his book, and secondly, that such additions must be made to make it acceptable to the modern reader. I felt that, without re-editing, FAITHS & FOLKLORE would have little meaning except as an antiquarian curiosity or, at best, a work restricted to the specialist. After months of work, I am convinced that both premises were false: FAITHS AND FOLKLORE must not be revised, but revived. Revived in the sense that you, the publisher, must convince the readers that upon perusing Hazlitt, they will be in for an exceptionally enriching experience. And if Hazlitt is, as I believe him to be, in the tradition of Samuel Johnson (mind you, I do not declare him to be a latter-day Johnson!), then let your readers partake of Hazlitt, the ethnologist-lexicographer-moralist-and-man-of-culture, unencumbered by the opinions of still another editor, and the clutter of footnotes to pages already bursting with sound information.

Proceed without me! The book *should* be reprinted, and the sooner the better.

Decherd Turner
Bridwell Librarian
Southern Methodist University

PREFACE.

It is very rarely indeed that a book on Popular Antiquities or any other analogous topic so commends itself to the public, and so maintains its rank and estimation, as to continue to be the recognised source of reference in successive editions during more than a century and a half.

The present work, from its first appearance under the auspices of the Rev. Henry Bourne in 1725, and under the title of *Antiquitates Vulgares*, has so largely and essentially partaken of the anecdotal character, and so much depends on detail, not only for the confirmation of statements, but for the maintenance of interest, that an Editor, whatever he may do in the withdrawal of positive redundancies, is scarcely able to emulate the judicial conciseness of Buckle in his *History of Civilization* or the rhetorical and imposing periods of Macaulay. A compiler of a picture of Ancient Manners and Opinions on a documentary and lexicographical principle or basis, besides a bare statement of facts, has, as it were, to call witnesses, and record their depositions for the benefit of the reader. His personal views and experience are apt to be of service in chief measure in the choice of authorities and in the arrangement of evidence. Much of the charm in a book of the present class must necessarily lie in more or less copious and varied illustration, and its value and use would be impaired by lending to it the character of a summary or digest. The reader in this case prefers to form his own conclusions, and to linger over descriptive passages.

JOHN BRAND, as Secretary to the London Society of Antiquaries, and as a zealous collector of old and curious books during a long series of years, while such things remained within the reach of persons of moderate resources, enjoyed the opportunity of selecting extracts illustrative of the subject, which he had made his own in the character of successor to the author of *Antiquitates Vulgares;* and so far as an amplified republication of Bourne went, he lived to bring out in 1777 a more complete edition, yet on the same narrow and imperfect lines. During the latter years of his life, however, he proceeded to accumulate material for an undertaking on a larger and more comprehensive scale, and at the time of his death was in possession of a large body of MSS. collectanea of unequal value, eventually secured by a firm of publishers, and placed for editorial purposes in the hands of Sir Henry Ellis, of the British Museum. Ellis found, no doubt, amid the pressure of official work, considerable difficulty in reducing the whole to anything like method and form; but he accomplished what he could, and presented the world with the result in two large quarto volumes in 1813.

When I in 1869 entered on an examination of this text, I was disposed to exercise a free hand in every way; but I remember that I was dissuaded from going so far as my own feeling prompted me by the idea on the part of some of my advisers that to interfere with the work of such eminent antiquaries too drastically was little less than sacrilege. I have only once regretted the course, which I actually took thirty-five years ago—and that is ever since.

As material Brand's extracts had, and have, their undoubted worth, nor is the text of Ellis much more than rough copy; but it was found requisite on the former occasion to rearrange and collate the whole, and in once more re-editing the volumes on a new principle certain matter, from the discovery of better information and other causes, proved superfluous or undesirable.

The sectional arrangement, which has hitherto prevailed in regard to the book, unavoidably interfered with its use as a ready means of acquiring the desired particulars about any given subject, more especially as it constituted one of the exigencies of such a method to repeat in substance, even in the laboriously revised text of 1870, certain statements and, which was yet more inconvenient, to make it necessary for the referrer to collect the full detail, of which he might be in search, from two or three divisions of the three-volume work, under which they were perhaps not inappropriately ranged.

The new plan has been one of Disintegration and Redistribution, and will have, it is trusted, the effect of bringing more promptly and handily within reach the details connected with the enormous number of subjects, with which the Dictionary deals. At the same time, an excess in the way of subdivisions of matter or entries has been, so far as possible, avoided, as such a course has a necessary tendency to scatter references up and down the volume, and to interfere with the view of a subject in all its bearings.

By reason of the new lexicographical form, which the *Popular Antiquities* takes, a very considerable body of additional matter has been introduced from a wide variety of sources, sometimes, in justice to those authorities, in an abbreviated form with a reference. But, as a rule, the accounts of customs and other topics, where they occurred in the Editor's Brand of 1870, were already more copious and satisfactory. Nothing, however, has been taken from other works, unless it was directly connected with the subject-matter of the present undertaking.

In the edition of 1870 I thought it desirable to intersperse occasional quotations and extracts from modern sources, in order to shew the survival of customs and beliefs, and this feature has now been considerably developed, as it seemed of importance and interest as establishing the two-sided aspect of these matters in a large number of instances and the fact, not always realized, that we have not yet, after all these centuries and in the face of our boasted education and enlightenment, outlived the prejudices of our ancestors.

Numerous cross-references will be observed to the Glossary of Nares, 1859, the Dictionary of Halliwell, 1860, and Davis's *Supplementary Glossary*, 1881. The Editor did not see the utility of repeating or borrowing information elsewhere so readily accessible, and in some cases of a glossarial character rather than cognate to the immediate object. The value of this class of entry lies in its collateral service as a sort of index to the body of facts or statements readable elsewhere.

Two other publications by the present writer run on very parallel lines: his edition of Blount's *Jocular Tenures*, 1874, and of Ray's *Proverbs* (second and improved edition), 1882. Many collateral illustrations of the topics embraced in the volume before us occur in those two works, to which I must frequently content myself with directing the reader.

Since the first recension of the archæological labours of Blount, Bourne, Brand, and Ellis was published by me, the critical and comparative study of Popular Mythology has, under the auspices of the Folk-Lore Society, been elevated into a science. It was impracticable, even had it been expedient and proper, to incorporate with these pages facts and opinions based on this higher and deeper view of the topics before me, and my volume has to recommend itself to attention and favour mainly as a repository, more or less methodically assorted, of all the substantive information, which it has been in my power to collect and to reduce, in this second essay, to a reformed system.

There may be said perhaps to be three periods or stages of development in the case of our national popular archæology: 1. the early school of lexicography and writing, when philology and etymology were very imperfectly understood: 2. the age of the more modern antiquaries and glossarists when this study was placed on a very improved footing, but was still limited to superficial or *prima facie* evidence : and 3. the quite recent Folk-Lore movement, when in all these matters a latent sense is sought and *sometimes* found.

Whatever view may be taken of a large proportion of the obsolete or moribund usages and superstitions, of which the following pages attempt to constitute a record, it is certain that on two broad and solid grounds they deserve and demand commemoration. For in the first place they very importantly illustrate the writings and policy of our ancestors alike in their absolute and in their relative aspects, and secondly they render it more possible for us to judge the amount and degree of progress in knowledge and culture, which have been attained in the intervening time, and of which we are in actual enjoyment.

It is quite a moot question indeed, if not something more, whether the stricter scientific platform will ever extinguish or indeed seriously affect the public interest in this class of antiquities as described in the ordinary fashion on more or less uncultured lines.

In reference to some of the authorities quoted it may be desirable to meet the allegation that they are too slight and untrustworthy, by pointing out that for the immediate and special purpose, authenticity and *bona fides* being presumed and granted, the minor popular writers are precisely the class of witnesses and vouchers, which we require to assist us in elucidating the statements and views of those of a higher reach.

The authors quoted naturally and necessarily often belong to the school brought up side by side with the notions and beliefs, of which I am treating, and in not a few cases were partakers of them. It is necessary, however, to guard against accepting secondary or unscientific testimony for more than it is in its nature worth, and it is on that account that I have endeavoured, so far as it lay in my power, to arrange the text of this recension agreeably to the principle of proportion or degree of contributory weight.

The governing aim has been to accumulate and arrange to the best advantage and in the most convenient shape as large a body as possible of real or supposed matters of fact on all branches of the subject, with which I deal; and in re-editing the 1870 book, to adapt it to an improved state of knowledge, I trust I have been fairly successful.

It is to be remarked that the moral and conclusion derived from a perusal of the following pages are not perhaps likely to be of a very flattering nature, so far as regards either the opinions and intelligence of former ages or their educational progress. Amid a vast amount of material and detail, which can hardly fail to prove entertaining and valuable, there is much, too much, even as we draw near to our own epoch, which bespeaks a prevalence of low mental development arising, no doubt, in great measure from a faulty system of teaching both in a secular and clerical direction. Modern principles of instruction will gradually extinguish most, if not all, of the foolish prejudices and superstitions recorded here, and while it will be an unquestionable blessing, that such a change should occur, it also seems desirable that we should possess in a tolerably complete shape the means of comparison between the Older and the Newer Life of this Empire.

It is hardly too much to say that, in scrutinizing many of the headings in the Dictionary, the average reader may have to reflect, before he is assured that the views or accounts contained under them refer to the country known as Great Britain; yet how many of these customs and corruptions yet survive!

W. C. H.

Barnes Common, Surrey,
September, 1904.

NATIONAL FAITHS
AND POPULAR CUSTOMS.

Abbot of Bon Accord. — The Aberdeen name for the *Lord of Misrule*.

Abbot of Unreason. — The Scotish name for the *Lord of Misrule*, q.v. In Scotland, where the Reformation took a more severe and gloomy turn than in England, the *Abbot of Unreason*, as he was called, with other festive characters, was thought worthy to be suppressed by the Legislature as early as 1555. Jamieson seems to have thought, however, that the abolition of these sports was due rather to the excesses perpetrated in connection with them than to the Reformation. Perhaps this may be considered almost as a distinction without a difference.

Abingdon, Berks. — For a custom after the election of a mayor here, see the *Gentleman's Magazine* for Dec., 1782.

Abraham-Men, itinerant beggars, who ranged town and country after the Dissolution of Monasteries and the absence of any other system of poor-relief. There is some illustration of this subject in *Hazlitt's Popular Poetry*, 1864-6, iv, 17 *et. se.*, in Harman's *Caveat*, 1567, &c., Compare *Tom of Bedlam*.

Advertisements and Bills. — The Poster for a wide variety of purposes is known to have been in use in England, no less than in France and Germany, at an early period, and shared with the Cry and Proclamation the function of notifying approaching events or official ordinances. Hazlitt's *Shakespear: The Man and the Writer*, 2nd ed. 1903, pp. 102-3. This method of notification also prevailed toward the latter end of the reign of Elizabeth in respect to theatrical performances, which were announced on advertisements affixed to conspicuous places; but the modern play-bill was a much later comer. There is an Elizabethan broadside recently discovered among some old MSS., setting forth the particulars of a tilting match at Westminster, to be held in honour and vindication of a certain lady, whose beauty and accomplishments the challenger was prepared to defend against all opponents. Hazlitt's *Collections and Notes*, 1903, v. *Gallophisus*.

Adventurer. — A partner in a voyage of discovery or colonization. *Adventurers on return* were persons who lent money before they started on one of these enterprizes, on condition that they should receive so much profit, if they returned home.

Admiral of the Blue, a sobriquet for a tapster, from his blue apron. Compare, as to the blue apron, Hazlitt's *Garden Literature*, 1887, pp. 9-10. The gardener and fruit-grower, however, still cling to blue paper, as a material for covering their baskets of produce.

Adoption. — Several of our sovereigns adopted children offered to them, and then contributed toward their maintenance, but did not necessarily, or indeed usually, remove them from their parents' roof. Very numerous illustrations of this custom might be afforded. In the "Privy Purse Expenses of Elizabeth of York," May, 1502, we have, for instance, this entry: "Item the xijth day of May to Mawde Hamond for keping of hire child *geven* to the Quene for half a yere ended at Estre last past. . . . viijs."

Æpiornis or **Epiornis.** — An extinct bird of Madagascar, of which an egg was discovered in an alluvial deposit in 1850, by M. d'Abbadie. It is said to be 13 or 14 inches long, and to have six times the capacity of that of the ostrich. The Epiornis seems to be identifiable with the *Roc* or *Rukh*, which is mentioned by Marco Polo. But it is doubtful whether this enormous creature really exceeded in size the great apteryx or moa of New Zealand, also extinct. A specimen of the egg was sold in London (November, 1899) for £44, described as about a yard in circumference, a foot in length, and of the capacity of 150 hens' eggs. Compare *Roc*.

Aërolites, the modern name and view given to the mediæval and ancient fire-balls, firedrakes, *dracones volantes*, thunderbolts, &c. Their nature is at present generally better understood, although we have yet to learn their exact origin. A very intelligent writer says, speaking of the matter of falling stars: "Amongst ourselves, when any such matter is found in the fields, the very countrey-men cry it fell from Heav'n and the starres, and as I remember call it the *Spittle of the Starres*." He adds: "An Ignis fatuus has been found fallen down in a slippery viscous substance full of white spots. They stay upon military ensigns and spears; because such are apt to stop and be tenacious of them. In the summer and hot regions they are more frequent, because the good concoction produces fatnesse." *White's Peripatetical Institutions*, 1656, p. 148. Compare *Fire-drake*. In an official account of Bendothey, co. Perth, written in 1797, it is said : "The substance called shot stars is nothing else than frosted potatoes. A night of hard frost, in the end of autumn, in which those meteors called fallen stars are seen, reduces the potatoe to the consistence of a jelly or soft pulp having no resemblance to a potato, except when parts of the skin of the potato adhere below undissolved. This pulp remains soft and fluid, when all things else in Nature are consolidated by frost : for which reason it is greedily taken up by crows and other fowls when no other sustenance is to be had, so that it is often found by man in the actual circumstance of having fallen from above, having its parts scattered and dispersed by the fall, according to the law of falling bodies. This has given rise to the name and vulgar opinion concerning it." *Stat. Acc. of Scotl.*, xix., 351.

Ætites.—The *Ætites*, or Eagle Stone, was regarded as a charm of singular use to parturient women. Lemnius says : "It makes women that are slippery able to conceive, being bound to the wrist of the left arm, by which from the heart towards the Ring Finger, next to the little Finger, an artery runs : and if all the time the woman is great with child, this jewel be worn on those parts, it strengthens the child, and there is no fear of abortior or miscarrying."—*Occult Miracles of Nature*, 1658. p. 270. Lemnius tells us elsewhere, that "the jewel called Ætites, found in an eagle's nest, that has rings with little stones within it, being applied to the thigh of one that is in labour, makes a speedy and easy delivery ; which thing I have found true by experiment." Lupton speaks of "*Ætites*, called the Eagle's stone, tyed to the left arm or side ; it brings this benefit to women with child, that they shall not be delivered before their time : besides that, it brings love between the man and the wife : and if a woman have a painfull travail in the birth of her child, this stone tyed to her thigh, brings an easy and light birth." Elsewhere he says : "Let the woman that travels with her child, (is in labour) be girded with the skin that a serpent or snake casts off, and then she will quickly be delivered."

Agatha's Letters, St.—Bishop Pilkington observes : "They be superstitious that put holiness in *S. Agathes Letters* for burning houses, thorne bushes for lightnings." *Burnynge of Paules Church* in 1561, 88, 1563, I. 8 and G. i.

Afternoon Music. — In Brooke's "Epithalamium," inserted in *England's Helicon*, 1614, we read :
"Now whiles slow Howres doe feed the Times delay,

Confus'd Discourse, *with Musicke mixt among*,
Fills up the Semy-circle of the Day."
In the margin opposite is put "*Afternoone Musicke*."

Agnes Day or **Eve, St.**—(Jan. 21.) St. Agnes was a Roman virgin and martyr, who suffered in the tenth persecution under the Emperor Diocletian, A.D. 306. In the office for St. Agnes' Day in the "Missale ad usum Sarum," 1554, this passage occurs : "Hec est Virgo sapiens quam Dominus *vigilantem invenit*." The Gospel is the parable of the Virgins. The "Portiforium ad usum Sarum" declares that Agnes was the daughter of immaculate parents. — *Cujus mater Virgo est, cujus pater fœminam nescit*, and that she was so deeply versed in magic, that it was said that Christ was her spouse. The festival of St. Agnes was not observed with much rigour in Germany in the time of Naogeorgus ; but he describes the celebration at Rome on this anniversary as very solemn. It was customary to offer two lambs in remembrance of the legend at the high altar ; these were taken by the priest and kept till shearing time, when their fleeces were used for palls. The same practice was noticed by Jephson the traveller in Italy in 1794. The life of this Saint was written by L. Sherling (*i.e.,* Daniel Pratt), in prose and verse, and printed in 1677. On the eve of her day many kinds of divination are practised by virgins to discover their future husbands. It is called fasting St. Agnes' Fast. The following lines of Ben Jonson allude to this :
"And on sweet St. Agnes' night
    Please you with the promis'd sight,
    Some of husbands, some of lovers,
    Which an empty dream discovers."
She was condemned to be debauched in the public stews before her execution ; but her virginity was miraculously preserved by lightning and thunder from Heaven. About eight days after her execution, her parents going to lament and pray at her tomb, they saw a vision of angels, among whom was their daughter, and a lamb standing by her as white as snow, on which account it is that in every graphic representation of her there is a lamb pictured by her side.

Burton, in his "Anatomy," also speaks of this sort of divination, and Aubrey, in his "Miscellanies," directs that "Upon St. Agnes' Night you take a row of pins, and pull out every one, one after another, saying a Pater Noster, sticking a pin in your sleeve, and you will dream of him or her you shall marry." This anniversary is known in connection with the celebrated poem by Keats. In the bishopric of Durham, the country people have the following address in use :

"Fair St. Agnes, play thy part,
And send to me my own sweetheart,
Not in his best nor worst array,
But in the clothes he wears every day:
That to-morrow I may him ken,
From among all other men."

I have observed that in Cornwall, where we should speak of St. Agnes, they say *St. Anne*, as if the two names, if not persons, were the same. Yet females are sometimes christened *Agnes Anne*.

Agues.—Aubrey furnishes an infallible receipt for the cure of an ague: Write this following spell in parchment, and wear it about your neck. It must be writ triangularly:

ABRACADABRA
ABRACADABR
ABRACADAB
ABRACADA
ABRACAD
ABRACA
ABRAC
ABRA
ABR
AB
A

With this the writer affirms that one at Wells in Somersetshire had cured above a hundred of the disease. He gives another specific for the same purpose a little further on: "Gather cinquefoil in a good aspect of ♃ to the ☽ and let the moone be in the mid-heaven, if you can, and take ——— of the powder of it in white wine. If it be not thus gathered according to the rules of astrology, it hath little or no virtue in it." Other superstitious cures follow for the thrush, the toothache, the jaundice, bleeding, &c.—*Miscellanies*, ed. 1857, 133, 134, 137, where farther information may be found. Blagrave prescribes a cure of agues by a certain writing which the patient weareth, as follows: "When Jesus went up to the Cross to be crucified, the Jews asked Him, saying, Art thou afraid? or hast thou the ague? Jesus answered and said, I am not afraid, neither have I the ague. *All those which bear the name of Jesus about them shall not be afraid, nor yet have the ague.* Amen, sweet Jesus, Amen, sweet Jehovah, Amen." He adds: "I have known many who have been cured of the ague by this writing only worn about them; and I had the receipt from one whose daughter was cured thereby, who had the ague upon her two years." To this charact, then, may be given, on the joint authority of the old woman and our doctor, "*Probatum est*." — *Astrological Practice d'Physic*, p. 135. In Ashmole's Diary, 11 April, 1681, is preserved the following curious incident: "I took early in the morning a good dose of elixir, and hung three spiders about my neck, and they drove my ague away. Deo Gratias!"

Ashmole was a judicial astrologer, and the patron of the renowned Mr. Lilly. *Par nobile fratrum.* In Pope's Memoirs of P. P. Clerk of the Parish, is the following :— "The next chapter relates how he discovered a thief with a Bible and key, and experimented verses of the Psalms that had cured agues." Douce notes that, in his day, it was usual with many persons about Exeter, who had the ague, "to visit at dead of night the nearest cross road five different times, and there bury a new-laid egg. The visit is paid about an hour before the cold fit is expected; and they are persuaded that with the egg they shall bury the ague. If the experiment fail, (and the agitation it occasions may often render it successful) they attribute it to some unlucky accident that may have befallen them on the way. In the execution of this matter they observe the strictest silence, taking care not to speak to any one, whom they may happen to meet.— *Gentleman's Magazine*, 1787, p. 719. I shall here note another remedy against the ague mentioned as above, viz., by breaking a salted cake of bran and giving it to a dog, when the fit comes on, by which means they suppose the malady to be transferred from them to the animal." Compare *St. Germanus.*

Aldate, St.—Hearne, in his *Diary*, informs us that this personage was a bishop of Gloucester, living in the time of Hengist, whom he slew; and a part of Oxford is still named after him. But his existence is questionable. *Diary*, 1869, ii., 285.

Ale.—*Ale*, or *eale*, A.-S. (a form not yet obsolete) seems to be considered as significant in the present connection of nothing, more or less, than a merry-making. "That ALE is *festival* appears from its sense in composition," says Warton; "as amongst others, in the words Leet-ale, Lamb-ale, Whitsun-ale, Clerk-ale, and Church-ale. Leet-ale, in some parts of England, signifies the dinner at a court-leet of a manor for the jury and customary tenants. Lamb-ale is still used at the village of Kirtlington in Oxfordshire, for an annual feast or celebrity at lamb-shearing. Clerk-ale occurs in Aubrey's 'History of Wiltshire,' printed in 1847. Church-ale was a feast celebrated for the repair of the church, or in honour of the church saint. In Dodsworth's Manuscripts, there is an old indenture, made before the Reformation, which not only shews the design of the Church-ale, but explains this particular use and application of the word ale. . . But Mr. Astle had a curious record about 1575, which proves the Bride-ale synonymous with the Weddyn-ale.* . . . . Among Bishop Tanner's MSS. additions to Cowel's 'Law Glossary,' in the Bodleian Library, is the following note from his own collections : 'A.D. 1468. Prior Cant. et Commissarii visitationem fecerunt (Diocesi Cant. vacante per mortem archipiscopi) et ibi publicatum erat, quod potationes factæ in ecclesiis, vulgariter dictæ Yelealys, vel Bredealys, non essent ulterius in usu sub pœna excommunicationis majoris.'". For Scot-ales, give-ales, leet-ales, bride-ales, clerk-ales, &c., see " Archæol," vol. xii. p. 11-77. In the MSS. Papers of Aubrey, under date of 1678, it is said that " in the Easter Holidays, was the Clerk's ale for his private benefit and the solace of the neighbourhood." " Antiquarian Repertory." No. 26. Mr. Denne, in his " Account of stone figures carved on the porch of Chalk Church," (" Archæol." vol. xii. p. 12,) says : " the Clerks' ale was the method taken by the Clerks of parishes to collect more readily their dues ." In the *Church Times* about twenty years ago, appeared the following account of the matter by Mr. Pope, which may be considered worth preservation :—" We read of Scotales and give-ales, appellations thought to be used synonymously ; but their meanings are distinct. Scotales, as the word imports, were maintained by contribution of those resorting to them. Thus the tenants of South Malling in Essex, which belonged to the Archibishop of Canterbury, were at keeping of a court to entertain the lord or his bailiff with a feast, or an ale, and the stated quotas toward the charge were, that a man should pay 3½d. for himself and his wife, and a widow 1¼d. In Terring, Sussex, it was the custom to make up a Scot-ale of sixteen pence halfpenny, and allow out of each sixpence three halfpence to find drink for the bailiff. There were also feasts in which the prefix Scot was omitted, and instead thereof, leet-ale, bride - ale, clerk - ale, and Church - ale, To the first contributed all the residents the second was defrayed by the relatives of the happy pair, who were too poor to buy a wedding dinner. The Clerk's-ale was at Easter, and was the method taken to enable clerks of parishes to collect the more readily their due. (Aubrey's Hist., Wilts). From an old indenture, before the Reformation, is seen the design for a church-ale. " The parishioners of Elveston and Okebrook (Derbyshire) agree jointly to brew four ales, and every ale of one quarter of malt betwixt this and the feast of St. John the Baptist next coming. That every inhabitant of Okebrook be there. That every husband and his wife shall pay twopence, and every cottager one penny, and all profits and advantages shall be and remain to the use of the church of Elveston. And the inhabitants of Elveston shall brew eight ales betwixt this and the said feast of St. John, at which feasts or ales the inhabitants of Okebrook shall

come and pay as before rehearsed." These different contributions were mostly, in a greater or less degree, compulsory. But the giveales were the legacies of individuals and differed from the Scotales in that they were entirely gratuitous ; though some might be in addition to a common giveale before established in the parish. The history of Kent gives many instances in the parishes of Hoo, Snodland, Cowling, Wateringbury, and others, *e.g.*, : — " St. Mary's, Hoo, Test. Will Hammond, ' Also I will that specially my feoffees and exors. see that the Yeovale of St. James's be kept for ever, as it hath bin here aforetime.'" Hoo, Alhallows, Test. John Devell. ' Allsoe I will that the geavalle of Alhalows in Hoo have one acre of land after my wife's decease to maintain it withall, called Pilchland, and that it be done after the custom of olde time." At Cowling, Test. Tho. Love and Tho. Tomys. " I will that my wife Joane shall have house and my daur [? daywere] land to keep or doe a yevall on St. James's day, to which yevall I bind it (the land) whosoever have it without end." Giveales differ also materially from Scotales in their having been blended with notions of a superstitious tendency ; for the bequest was often to the light or altar of a saint, with directions to sing masses at the obit, trental, or anniversary of the testator's death. Lands were settled for the perpetual payment of the legacies thus appropriated. The parish of St. John, Thanet, is possessed of 15 acres acquired by a legacy bequeathed for a giveale by Ethelred Banen in 1513, who willed that " such a yearle yeovale should be maintayned while the world endureth." It was evident that a man in high glee over " a stoup of strong liquor " was not an unusual sight within the precincts of a church. At St. Mary's, Chalk, near Gravesend, William May, in his will, 1512, gave, *inter alia*, To every godchild he had in Kent 6 bushels of barley ; if 4 of them could bear him to the church 6d. each ; his executors to buy 2 new torches for his burial, 2d. each to men to bear them. That his wife make every year for his soull an obit in bread 6 bushels of wheat, in drink 10 bushels of malt, in cheese 20d., to give poor people for the health of his soull. His wife to continue the obit before rehearsed for evermore, These give-ales on obsequies, as on dedications, allowed great freedom in sports, dissolute dances in churches and churchyards, and this is particularly instanced in the churchyard of St. Mary, Chalk. " The porch has a grotesque carving in the portrait of a jester grasping a jug, while his principal is exercising his talents as a posture maker, and two other faces appear on whom the sculptor seems to have bestowed such an indelible smirk, that in spite of corrosion by time and weather, to the almost loss of features, the smile is yet visible. In the centre is a niche formerly occupied by the figure of the Blessed Virgin. The whole subject is doubtless intended to realise a feast in the precincts of the church on the dedication carried on whilst a private Mass was being performed at the altar." (*Archœologia*, 1794). At many other churches grotesque figures are mixed up with sacred subjects. At St. Mary's Church, Chalk, her statue was demolished by the iconoclasts of the 17th century; although possibly there might not be at that time a parishioner aggrieved, or in whose mind the image would have excited an idolatrous propensity. But the grotesque figures escaped the hammers of those pious reformers, whose tender feelings were not hurt with the view of a toper and hideous contortionist carved on the front of a house of prayer, notwithstanding, in their own conceits, they held purer doctrines, were sanctimonious in their devotions and stricter in their morals than other men. Compare *Whitsuntide.*

Ale-House.—Ale-houses are at present licensed to deal in tobacco; but it was not so from the beginning; for so great an incentive was it thought to drunkenness, that it was strictly forbidden to be taken in any ale-house in the time of James I. There is an ale-house licence extant, which was perhaps *circâ* 1630 granted by six Kentish justices of the peace: at the bottom the following item occurs: "Item, you shall not utter, nor willingly suffer to be uttered, drunke, or taken, any tobacco within your house, celler, or other place thereunto belonging." See Hazlitt's *Bibl. Coll.*, General Index, 1893. v. *Alehouse*, and Lemon's *Cat. of the Soc. of Antiquaries' Broadsides*, 1866.

Ale-Stake, or **Bush.**—The former term is found in very early use, as in 1375 the Mayor and Aldermen of London imposed restrictions on the extent to which alestakes might project over the highway. Riley's *Memorials*, 1868, p. 386. Bansley, in his "Treatise on the Pride and Abuse of Women," *circâ* 1550, says:

"For lyke as the jolye ale house
 Is alwayes knowen by the good ale
   stake,
So are proud Jelots sone perceeved to
 By theyr proude foly, and wanton
   gate."

Comp. *Bush.*

Allhallow Even, *vulgarly Hall E'en* or *Nutcrack Night.* Hallow Even is the vigil of All Saints' Day, which is on the first of November. In the Roman Calendar I find under November 1: "The feast of *Old Fools* is removed to this day." This was also known as Soulemass Day, or corruptly, *Salmes Day*, which latter form occurs in the "Plumpton Correspondence," under 1502. Comp. *Hallowe'en.*

All Fours.—A game at cards, said in the *Compleat Gamester*, 1680, to be very much played in Kent. But in the time of Queen Anne it appears from Chatto (*Facts and Speculations*, 1848, p. 166), to have shared with Put, Cribbage, and Lanterloo the favour of the lower orders. Comp. Davis, *Suppl. Glossary*, 1881, p. 11. (ii.) A sport for the amusement of children, where a grown-up person goes *a quatre pattes*, and allows a child to ride on his back. Masson, in his *Napoléon et les Femmes*, describes that great man doing this to please his nephew, the future Emperor.

All-Hallows.—See *Hallowe'en* and *Hallowmass.*

All-Hid. — See Levins' *Manipulus*, 1570, p. 293. In *Love's Labour Lost*, written, before 1598, iv., 3, this is called "An infant play." In *Hamlet, Act* iv., sc. ii., the Prince of Denmark says: ". . . The King is a thing," upon which Guilderstein rejoins, "A thing, my lord?" whereupon Hamlet adds: "Of nothing. Bring me to him. Hide, fox, and all after." This is supposed to be an allusion to the sport called *All Hid.* Steevens tells us that it is alluded to in Decker's "Satiromastix:" "Our unhandsome-faced poet does play at bo-peep with your Grace, and cries *All-hid* as boys do." In "A Curtaine Lecture," 1637, p. 206, is the following passage: "A sport called *All-hid*, which is a mere children's pastime."

All in the Well, a juvenile game described by Halliwell (*Dict.* 1860, in v.) as played in Newcastle and the neighbourhood.

All Saints. — See *Hallow-e'en* and *Hallowmass.*

Alsatia, a popular name for Whitefriars, while it enjoyed the privilege of a sanctuary. Shadwell's *Squire of Alsatia*, Scott's *Fortunes of Nigel*, and Ainsworth's *Whitefriars*, illustrate this point.

Altar.—Selden remarks: "The way of coming into our great churches was anciently at the west door, that Men might see the Altar, and all the Church before them; the other Doors were but posterns." *Table Talk*, ed. 1860, p. 131. Moresin tells us that altars in Papal Rome were placed toward the east, in imitation of ancient and heathen Rome. *Papatus*, 117. Thus we read in Virgil's Eleventh Æneid:

"Illia ad surgentem conversi lumina
   Solem
Dant fruges manibus salsas."

Comp. *Bowing.*

Ambassador. — A trick to duck some ignorant fellow or landsman, frequently played on board ships in the warm latitudes. It is thus managed: a large tub is filled with water, and two stools placed on each side of it. Over the whole is thrown a tarpaulin, or old sail: this is kept tight by two persons, who are to represent the King and Queen of a foreign country and are seated on the stools. The person intended to be ducked plays the Ambassador, and after repeating a ridiculous speech dictated by him, is led in great form up to the throne, and seated between the King and Queen, who rising suddenly as soon as he is seated, he falls backward into the water.

Ampoule, St.—See *Graal.*

Amulets.—There appears to be some ground for supposing that the most ancient amulets, sentences from Scripture, originated in the usage of burying portions of the sacred writings with holy men. A paper on the subject is printed in the *Antiquary* for 1896. Burton has the following passage: "Amulets, and things to be borne about, I find prescribed, taxed by some, approved by others: looke for them in Mizaldus, Porta, Albertus, &c. A ring made of the hoofe of an asse's right fore-foot carried about, &c. I say with Renodeus they are not altogether to be rejected. Piony doth help epilepsies. Pretious stones, most diseases. A wolf's dung carried about helps the cholick. A spider, an ague. &c. . . . Such medicines are to be exploded that consist of words, characters, spells and charms, which can do no good at all, but out of a strong conceit, as Pomponatius proves, or the Divel's policy that is the first founder and teacher of them." *Anatomy*, 1621, 476. Among Mr. Cockayne's "Saxon Leechdoms," there are some, as it may be supposed, for *bewitched* persons, in the form of amulets held to be efficacious. One is as follows: "Against every evil rune lay, and one full of elvish tricks, write for the bewitched man this writing in Greek, alfa, omega, Ivesum, Beronike [Veronica]." Another is: "Take a bramble apple, and lupins, and pulegium, pound them, then sift them, put them in a pouch, lay them under the altar, sing nine masses over them, put the dust into milk, drip thrice some holy water upon them, administer this in drink at three hours, at nine in the morning. etc." From the middle ages gems and rings have been regarded and employed as amulets and charms. The belief in their virtues, which were numerous and varied, was fostered by the churches, and a rich store has descended to our times. The gems bearing the effigy or figure of Pegasus or Bellerophon was held to confer courage, and was prized by soldiers. Those engraved with Andromeda reconciled differences between men and women. The image of Mercury rendered the possessor wise and persuasive, and so on. Roach Smith's

Richborough, 1850, p. 90-92. The ruby was supposed to be an amulet against poison. plague, sadness, evil thoughts, and wicked spirits; and, most wonderful of all, it warned its wearer of evil by becoming black or obscure. Brahman traditions describe the abode of the gods as lighted by enormous rubies and emeralds. The magical properties of the sapphire are rated as high as those of the ruby. It was sacred to Apollo, and was worn by the inquirer of the oracle at his shrine. During the Middle Ages it continued in high estimation, because it was supposed to prevent evil and impure thoughts. and it was worn by priests on account of its power to preserve the chastity of the wearer. St. Jerome affirmed that it procures favour with princes, pacifies enemies, and obtains freedom from captivity; but one of the most remarkable properties ascribed to it was the power to kill any venomous reptile that was put into the same glass with it. *H. B. Wheatley.* The turquoise was believed to be a protection from falls, and the amethyst against intoxication. Jasper cured madness, and agate was an antidote to the poison of scorpions and spiders, besides being beneficial to the eyes. Lemnius remarks, "So coral, piony, misseltoe, drive away the falling sicknesse, either hung about the neck or drank with wine. Rosmary purgeth houses, and a branch of this, hung at the entrance of houses, drives away devils and contagions of the plague, as also ricinus, commonly called Palma Christi, because the leaves are like a hand opened wide. Corall bound to the neck takes off turbulent dreams and allays the nightly fears of children. Other jewells drive away hobgoblins, witches, nightmares, and other evill spirits, if we will believe the monuments of the Antients."—*Occult Secrets of Nature*, 1658, p. 270. But coins with the effigies of saints, such as the gold *angels*, and the *George noble*, or the touch-pieces in gold and silver, in the English series, were also credited with the power of guardianship against sickness and casualties. The George noble. with its legend taken from a hymn by Prudentius *Tali Dicata Signo Mens Fluctuare Nequit*, was supposed to protect the wearer who suspended it round his neck, against accidents in riding; and perhaps the peculiar rarity of the half noble of this type may indicate its more general uses for the purpose aforesaid. A curious gold florin, with the Madonna and Child on reverse. struck by one of the Dukes of Gueldres, is still preserved in the original gold box, and is supposed to have been carried on the person as a charm. Hazlitt's *Coins of Europe*, 1893, p. 200. In cases of trepanning for epilepsy, the portions excised were formerly employed as amulets against the disease. Hering has the following: "Perceiving many in this citie to weare about their necks, upon the region of the heart, certaine placents or amulets, (as preservatives against the pestilence), confected with arsenicke, my opinion is that they are so farre from effecting any good in that kinde, as a preservative, that they are very dangerous and hurtfull, if not pernitious, to those that weare them."—*Preservative against the Pestilence*, 1625, sign. B. 2 *verso.* Cotta inserts "A merrie historie of an approved famous spell for sore eyes. By many honest testimonies, it was a long time worne as a jewell about many necks, written in paper and enclosed in silke, never failing to do soveraigne good when all other helps were helplesse. No sight might dare to reade or open. At length a curious mind, while the patient slept, by stealth ripped open the mystical cover, and found the powerful characters Latin: 'Diabolus effodiat tibi oculos, impleat foramina stercoribus.'"—*Short Discoverie*, 1612, p. 49. In Wiltshire, a lemon stuck with pins, and in Lincolnshire the heart of an animal similarly treated, were, so lately as 1856, treated as amulets against witchcraft. — *Notes and Queries*, 2nd S., i., 331, 415. It was a supposed remedy against witchcraft to put some of the bewitched person's water, with a quantity of pins, needles, and nails into a bottle, cork them up and set them before the fire, in order to confine the spirit: but this sometimes did not prove sufficient, as it would often force the cork out with a loud noise, like that of a pistol, and cast the contents of the bottle to a considerable height. In one of the Essays of Montaigne, where he refers to the marriage of Madame de Gurson, we see that the fear of a spell being cast upon the couple, when they had retired to their chamber, was met, when the company had assembled in the room, and the bride and bridegroom had partaken of the spiced wine, by Jacques Pelletier producing his amulet, which defeated the enchantment. Douce has given wood engravings of several Roman amulets: these were intended against fascination in general, but more particularly against that of the evil eye. Such, he observes, are still used in Spain by women and children, precisely in the same manner as formerly among the Romans.—*Illustr. of Shakespear*, 1807, i., 493. Mungo Park, in his Travels, speaking of "certain charms or amulets called Saphies, which the negroes constantly wear about them," says: "These saphies are prayers or sentences from the Koran, which the Mahometan priests write on scraps of paper and sell to the natives, who suppose them to possess extraordinary virtues. Some wear them to guard against the attack of snakes and alligators: on such an occasion the saphie is enclosed in a snake or alligator's skin, and tied round the ancle. Others have recourse to them in time of war, to protect their persons from hostile attacks: but the general use of these amulets is to prevent or cure bodily diseases, to preserve from hunger and thirst, and conciliate the favour of superior powers." He informs us in another place, that his landlord requested him to give him a lock of his hair to make a saphie, as he said he had been told it would give to the possessor all the knowledge of white men. Another person desired him to write a saphie · Mr. Park furnished him with one containing the Lord's Prayer. He gave away several others. These saphies appear to have corresponded with the "chartes of health," mentioned in some of our own early writers. The same, speaking of a Mahometan negro who, with the ceremonial part of that religion, retained all his ancient superstition, says that, "in the midst of a dark wood he made a sign for the company to stop, and, taking hold of an hollow piece of bamboo that hung as an amulet round his neck, whistled very loud three times; this, he said, was to ascertain what success would attend the journey. He then dismounted, laid his spear across the road, and, having said a number of short prayers, concluded with three loud whistles; after which he listened for some time as if in expectation of an answer, and receiving none. said. the company might proceed without fear, as there was no danger. — See *Caracts, Charms, Magic,* &c

Anagram. — An anagram has been defined to be "a divination by names, called by the ancients Onomantia. The Greeks referre this invention to Lycophron, who was one of those they called the Seven Starres or Pleiades; afterwards (as witnesses Eustachius) there were divers Greek wits that disported themselves herein, as he which turned Atlas for his heavy burthen in supporting Heaven, into *Talas*,. that is, wretched. Some will maintain, that each man's fortune is written in his name, which they call anagramatism or metragramatism: poetical liberty will not blush to use E. for Æ., V. for W., S. for Z. That amorous youth did very queintly sure, (resolving a mysterious expression of his love to Rose Hill.) when in the border of a painted cloth he caused to be painted as rudely as he had devised grossly, a rose, a hill, an eye, a loaf, and a well, that is if you spell it, 'I love Rose Hill well.'" Worcester, in his "Dictionary," gives a somewhat more satisfactory account of the meaning of the word and thing. "An Anagram," he says, "is a word or sentence of apt significance, formed by transposing the letters of another word or sentence as *Est vir qui adest*, formed from Pilate's question *Quid est Veritas?*" Mr. Wheatley's monograph "Of Anagrams," 1862, should also be consulted, as well as the Editor's extensive *Additions* in the *Antiquary*.

Ancients.—The governing body at Gray's Inn corresponding to the Benchers of the two Temples and Lincoln's Inn.

Andrew's Day, St. — (November 30). The patron saint of Scotland. The legend of St. Andrew, with that of St. Veronica, in Anglo-Saxon, has been edited for the Cambridge Antiquarian Society (8vo. series) by Mr. Goodwin. A Life of St. Andrew, from a MS. in the Bibliothéque Imperiale at Paris, is given in "Chronicles of the Picts and Scots," 1867. It is a mere summary or sketch. A second and more lengthy narrative, from Harl. MS., 4628, occurs in the same volume. The reduction to nudity in this case must not be supposed to have been intended (primarily, at least) as an act of indecency, but rather as a relict of paganism. The ancients, our own Saxon forefathers not excepted, seem to have made an absence of clothing in some instances part of their religious rites, and the same idea was found by early travellers prevailing among the inhabitants of the American continent.—See *Ourselves in Relation to a Deity and a Church*, by the present Editor 1897, pp. 92, 97. Luther says, that on the evening of the Feast of St. Andrew, the young maidens in his country strip themselves naked; and, in order to learn what sort of husbands they shall have, they recite a prayer.—*Colloquia Mensalia*, part i. p. 232. The prayer was: "Deus Deus meus, O Sancte Andrea, effice ut bonum pium acquiram virum: hodie mihi ostende qualis sit cui me in uxorem ducere debet." Naogeorgus probably alludes to the observances noticed above as to nudity, when he says:

"To Andrew all the lovers and the lustie wooers come,
Beleeving, through his ayde. and certain ceremonies done,
(While as to him they presentes bring, and conjure all the night.)
To have good lucke, and to obtaine their chiefe and sweete delight."

We read, that many of the opulent citizens of Edinburgh resort to Duddingston parish, about a mile distant, in the summer months to solace themselves over one of the ancient homely dishes of Scotland, for which the place has been long celebrated. The use of singed sheeps' head boiled or baked, so frequent in this village, is supposed to have arisen from the practice of slaughtering the sheep fed on the neighbouring hill for the market, removing the carcases to the town, and leaving the head, &c., to be consumed in the place. Singed sheeps' heads are borne in the procession before the Scots in London on St. Andrew's Day. Hasted, speaking of the parish of Easling, says, that, "On St. Andrew's Day, Nov. 30, there is yearly a diverson called squirril-hunting in this and the neighbouring parishes, when the labourers and lower kind of people, assembling together, form a lawless rabble, and being accoutred with guns, poles, clubs, and other such weapons spend the greatest part of the day in parading through the woods and grounds, with loud shoutings; and, under the pretence of demolishing the squirrils, some few of which they kill, they destroy numbers of hares, pheasants, partridges, and in short whatever comes in their way, breaking down the hedges, and doing much other mischief, and in the evening betaking themselves to the alehouses, finish their career there, as is usual with such sort of gentry."—"Hist. of Kent," folio ed. vol. ii. p. 757. At Stratton, in Cornwall, on this anniversary, at a very early hour a number of youths pass through the different parts of the town to the accompaniment of the blowing of a remarkably unmelodious horn, the fearful strumming of tin pans, &c., driving out, presumably, any evil spirits which haunt the place—greed. fraud, drunkenness, gluttony, and their companions. The hand-bell ringers follow, gently inviting more acceptable spirits—content, fair play, temperance, chastity, and others. After a suitable pause, the church bells ring out, in peals of eight, a hearty welcome to these latter.

Andrew's Well, St. — Martin, speaking of the Isle of Lewis, says that, "St. Andrews' Well, in the village of Shadar, is by the vulgar natives made a test to know if a sick person will die of the distemper he labours under. They send one with a wooden dish, to bring some of the water to the patient, and if the dish, which is then laid softly upon the surface of the water, turn round sun-ways, they conclude that the patient will recover of that distemper: but if otherwise, that he will die." — *Western Islands of Scotland*, p. 7. In a French version of the romance of *Bevis of Hampton* there is an allusion to the pilgrimage on foot to St. Andrew's Well as of equal efficacy to that to Mont St. Michel in Brittany for the removal of certain physical troubles. This was St. Andrew's, in Fifeshire. Michel, *Les Ecossais en France*, 1862, ii., 498.

Angelica. — See Nares, *Glossary*, 1859, in v.

Angels or **Genii.** — Bourne says: The Egyptians believed that every man had three angels attending him: the Pythagoreans, that every man had two; the Romans, that there was a good and evil genius."—Butler's "Angel bad or tutelar." "Every man," says Sheridan in his notes to "Persius," (2d. edit. 1739, p. 28) "was supposed by the ancients at his birth to have two Genii, as messengers between the gods and him. They were supposed to be private monitors, who by their insinuations disposed us either to good or evil actions; they were also supposed to be not only reporters of our crimes in this life, but registers of them against our trial in the next, whence they had the name of Manes given them." Few are ignorant that Apollo and Minerva presided over Athens, Bacchus and Hercules over Bœotian Thebes, Juno over Carthage, Venus over Cyprus and Paphos, Apollo over Rhodes; Mars was the tutelar god of Rome, as Neptune of Tænarus; Diana presided over Crete, &c., &c. St. Peter succeeded to Mars at the revolution of the religious Creed of Rome. He now presides over the castle of St. Angelo, as Mars did over the the ancient Capitol. Hereupon Symmachus, Against the Christians, says: "The divine Being has distributed various Guardians to cities, and that as souls are communicated to infants at their birth, so particular genii are assigned to particular societies of men." Moresin tells us that Papal Rome, in imitation of this tenet of Gentilism, has fabricated such kinds of genii for guardians and defenders of cities and people. Thus she has assigned St. Andrew to Scotland, St. George to England, St. Denis to France, St. Egidius to Edinburgh, St. Nicholas to Aberdeen. Popery has in many respects closely copied the heathen mythology. She has the supreme being for Jupiter, she has substituted angels for genii, and the souls of saints for heroes, retaining all kinds of dæmons. Against these pests she has carefully provided her antidotes. She exorcises them out of waters, she rids the air of them by ringing her hallowed bells, &c. The Romanists have similarly assigned tutelar gods to each member of the body: as, for instance, the arms were under the guardianship of Juno, the breast, of Neptune, the waist, of Mars, the reins, of Venus; and so on." The following extract from "Curiosities, or the Cabinet of Nature," by Robert Basset, 1637, p. 228, informs us of a very singular office assigned by ancient superstition to the good Genii of Infants. The book is by way of question and answer: "Q. Wherefore is it that the childe cryes when the absent nurses brests doe pricke and ake?" 'A. That by dayly experience is found to be so, so that by that the nurse is hastened home to the infant to supply the defect: and the reason is that either at that very instant that the infant hath finished its concoction, the breasts are replenished, and, for want of drawing, the milke paines the breast, as it is seen likewise in milch cattell: or rather the good genius of the infant seemeth by that means to sollicite or trouble the nurse in the infants behalfe: which reason seemeth the more firme and probable, because sometimes sooner, sometimes later, the child cryeth, neither is the state of nurse and infant alwayes the same." The Negroes believe that the concerns of the world are committed by the Almighty to the superintendence and direction of subordinate spirits, over whom they suppose that certain magical ceremonies have great influence. A white fowl suspended to the branch of a particular tree, a snake's head, or a few handsful of fruit, are offerings to deprecate the favour of these tutelary agents.

Aneling.—Among the articles of expense at the funeral of Sir John Rudstone, Mayor of London, 1531, given by Strutt, we find the following charges: "Item to the priests at his ennelling, 9s. 0d.: to poor folke in almys, £1 5s. 0d.; 22 days to 6 poor folke, 2s. 0d.: 26 days to a poore folke, 8d." *Ennelling* is the extreme unction. Comp. Nares, *Glossary*, 1859, in v.

Anne's Well, near Nottingham, St.—Deering says: "By a custom time beyond memory, the Mayor and Aldermen of Nottingham and their wives have been used on Monday in Easter week, morning prayers ended, to march from the town to St. Anne's Well, having the town waits to play before them, and attended by all the Clothing and their wives, *i.e.*, such as have been Sheriffs. and ever after wear scarlet gowns, together with the officers of the town, and many other burgesses and gentlemen," &c.— *Hist. of Nottingham*, 125.

Anthony of Egypt or Thebes, St. — This eminent man, sometimes called *The Great*, has been occasionally confounded with his namesake of Padua, and the error appears to be of old standing, as there are early representations, where the Egyptian saint is exhibited with a firebrand in his hand, with flames beneath him, and a black hog, the symbol of gluttony and sensuality, under his feet, so that he may have been regarded as the archenemy of the qualities characteristic of the animal, rather than as the patron or protector of it. In the "Memoirs of Arthur Wilson," the historian and dramatist, written by himself, the erysipelas is called St. Anthony's fire, and such continues to be its common or vulgar name;

it has received certain others; *Ignis sacer, rual des artus, ergot*, &c., and it was not unknown to the ancients. In the Cleveland country, the disease, instead of St. Anthony's fire, is known as Wildfire. The alleged reason was that the people of Dauphiny, cured by the saint of this complaint, gave it his name; but the real fact seems to be, that the disease sprang from his penury and physical under-nourishment. and that the sufferers in this province were apt to be cured by being received into the Abbey of St. Antoine at Vienne, where they were properly fed. Sir John Bramston notes the death of his daughter-in-law Elizabeth Mountford, 9th December, 1689, and describes this complaint, to which she seems to have succumbed. "She had been very ill," he says, "with a distemper called St. Anthonie's fier, her eyes, nose, face, and head swelled vastly; at length it took her tongue and throat."—*Autobiography*, p. 348.

A writer in the *Globe* newspaper, March 6th, 1899, observes: "One of the most picturesque customs in Mexico is that of blessing animals, called the blessings of San Antonio. The poorer class take their domestic animals of all kinds, dogs, cats, parrots, sheep, horses, burros, &c., to be sprinkled with holy water, and to receive through the priest St. Anthony's blessing. It is the custom of the common class to clean and bedeck their animals specially for this blessing. Dogs are gaily decorated with ribbons tied around their necks. Sheep are washed thoroughly until their fleece is as white as snow, and then taken to the father to be blessed. The beaks of the parrots are gilded. Horses and burros are adorned with garlands.

Anthony of Padua, St., *Abbot and Confessor.* — Riley furnishes the substance of the oath exacted in 1311, 4. Edward III., from the Renter as to the swine of the House of St. Anthony or Antonine, whereby that official was restrained from making the privilege enjoyed by such animals a cover for begging or alms, and from putting bells round their necks, or suffering others to do so in regard to their property to the extent of his power. *Memorials of London Life,* 1868, p. 83. Davis, *Suppl. Glossary,* 1881, p. 19. The exemption from the ordinary regulations in regard to vagrant swine also prevailed in mediæval times with perhaps greater latitude. Hazlitt's *Venetian Republic,* 1900, ii., 352. Bale, in his "Kynge Johan," says: "Lete Saynt Antoynes hogge be had in some regarde." There is an early notice of the legend of St. Anthony and the pigs to be found in the "Book of Days" under January 17. In

"The World of Wonders," translated from Stephanus, p. 57, is the following translation of an epigram :

> "Once fed'st thou, Anthony, an heard of swine,
> And now an heard of monkes thou feed'st still ;
> For wit and gut alike both charges bin :
> Both loven filth alike : both like to fill
> Their greedy paunch alike. Nor was that kind
> More bestly, sottish, swinish, then this last.
> All else agrees : one fault I onely find,
> Thou fedest not thy monkes with oaken mast."

The author mentions before persons "who runne up and downe the country. crying, "Have you anything to bestow upon my lord S. Anthonies swine?"

Apostle Spoons.—It was anciently the custom for the sponsors at christenings to offer gilt spoons as presents to the child: these spoons were called Apostle spoons, because the figures of the twelve Apostles were chased or carved on the tops of the handles. Opulent sponsors gave the whole twelve. Those in middling circumstances gave four ; and the poorer sort contented themselves with the gift of one, exhibiting the figure of any saint in honour of whom the child received its name. It is in allusion to this custom that when Cranmer professes to be unworthy of being sponsor to the young Princess, Shakespear makes the King reply, "Come, come, my lord, you'd spare your spoons." In the year 1560, we find entered in the books of the Stationers' Company : "A spoyne, the gyfte of Master Reginold Wolfe, all gylte, with the pycture of St. John." Ben Jonson also, in his "Bartholomew Fair," mentions spoons of this kind : "And all this for the hope of a couple of Apostle spoons and a cup to eat caudle in." So, in Middleton's "Chaste Maid in Cheapside," 1630 : "Second Gossip : What has he given her? What is it, Gossip?—Third Gossip : A faire high-standing cup and two great postle spoons, one of them gilt." Again, in Davenant's "Wits," 1636 :

> "My pendants, carcanets, and rings,
> My christening caudle-cup and spoons,
> Are dissolved into that lump."

Again, in the "Noble Gentleman," by Beaumont and Fletcher :

> "I'll be a gossip. Bewford,
> I have an odd Apostle spoon."

Shipman, in his "Gossips," is pleasant on the failure of the custom of giving Apostle spoons, &c., at christenings:

" Especially since Gossips now
  Eat more at christenings than bestow.
  Formerly, when they us'd to troul
  Gilt bowls of sack, they gave the bowl ;
  Two spoons at least ; an use ill kept ;
  'Tis well now if our own be left."

Comp. Nares, *Glossary*, 1859, and Halliwell's *Dict.*, 1860, in vv.

Apparitions. — " The Chylde of
Bristowe," the romances of " Sir Amadas " and " The Avowynge of King
Arthur," Shakespear's " Hamlet," the
ballad of " William and Margaret," Dryden's " Cymon and Iphigenia " (a very
ancient fiction in a comparatively modern
dress), may be mentioned in passing, as
fair samples of the various shapes which
the inhabitants of the Land of Shadows
have taken from time to time at the bidding of poets, playwrights, novelists, and
balladmongers. Scott has sufficiently demonstrated, in his " Letters on Demonology and Witchcraft," that the appearance of spectres to persons in their sleep,
and even otherwise, can in most cases be
explained on the most common-place
medical principles, and originates in mental illusions engendered by undue indulgence or constitutional debility. A great
deal of learning in connection with our
popular superstitions generally is in that
work most entertainingly conveyed to us ;
but I do not feel that I should be rendering any substantial service by transplant-
ing thence to these pages detached
passages illustrative of the immediate
subject. The " Letters " should be read
in their full integrity, for they are
among the most admirable things Scott
has left. In connection with the subject
of apparitions, may be cited the visions of
the Holy Maid of Kent, and the vision of
John Darley, a Carthusian monk. The history of the former is perhaps too familiar
to need any recapitulation here. Darley
relates that, as he was atending upon the
death-bed of Father Raby, in the year
1534, he said to the expiring man : " Good
Father Raby, if the dead can visit the
living, I beseech you to pay a visit to me
by and by : " and Raby answered, " Yes,"
immediately after which he drew his last
breath. But on the same afternoon about
five o'clock, as Darley was meditating in
his cell, the departed man suddenly appeared to him in a monk's habit, and said
to him, " Why do you not follow our
father?" " And I replied," Darley tellse
us, " ' Why? ' He said, ' Because he is a
martyr in heaven next to the angels.'
Then I said," says Darley : " ' Where are all
our other fathers who did like him?' He answered and said ' They are all pretty well.
but not as well as he is.' And then I asked
him how he was, and he said
' Pretty well.' And I said, ' Father,

shall I pray for you?' To which he
replied, ' I am as well as need be, but
prayer is at all times good,' and with
these words he vanished." On the following Saturday, at five o'clock in the morning, Father Raby reappeared, having this
time a long white beard and a white staff
in his hand. " Whereupon, says Darley,
" I was afraid, but he, leaning on his
staff, said to me, ' I am sorry that I did
not live to become a martyr ;' and I answered, that I thought he was as well as
though he had been a martyr. But he
said, ' Nay, for my Lord of Rochester and
our father were next to the angels.' I
asked ' What else?' He replied, ' The
angels of peace lamented and mourned un-
ceasingly' ; and again he vanished." The
" Lord of Rochester " was, of course,
Bishop Fisher. A curious and interesting
account of the pretended visions of Elizabeth Barton, whose case excited so strong
a sensation in the reign of Henrv VIII.,
will be found in Mr. Thomas Wright's
Collection of Original Letters. On the
Suppression of the Monasteries, 1843. In
" The Death of Robert Earl of Hunting-
ton," 1601, Matilda feels the man who has
been sent by King John to poison her and
the abbess, and says :

" Are ye not fiends, but mortal bodies,
    then?"

The author of the popular ballad of " William and Margaret " (quoted in the
" Knight of the Burning Pestle," 1613),
in describing Margaret's ghost, says :

" Her face was like an April morn,
    Clad in a wintry cloud :
  And clay-cold was her lily hand,
    That held her sable shroud."

In Aubrey's Miscellanies, 1696, there
is the well-known tradition of Lady
Diana Rich, daughter of the Earl of Holland, beholding her own apparition, as
she walked in her father's garden at Kensington, in the day-time, shortly before
her death, and of her sister experiencing
the same thing prior to her decease. The
former lady was in bad health at the time,
a fact which may partly account for the
circumstance. It may be recollected that
at an abbey not far from the residence of
Sir Roger de Coverley was an elm walk,
where one of the footmen of Sir Roger saw
a black horse without a head, and accordingly the butler was against anyone going
there after sunset. In this legend have
we the germ of Captain Mayne Reade's
Headless Horseman? Gay has left us a
pretty tale of an apparition. The golden
mark being found in bed is indeed after
the indelicate manner of Swift, or rather
is another instance of the obligation of our
more modern writers to the ancient story-
books), but yet is one of those happy

strokes that rival the felicity of that dash of the sponge which (as Pliny tells us) hit off so well the expression of the froth in Protogenes' dog. It is impossible not to envy the author the conception of a thought which we know not whether to call more comical or more pointedly satirical. Comp. *Ghosts, Spirits,* &c.

Apollonia's Day, St. (Feb 9.)—In the *Comedy of Calisto and Meliboea,* circâ 1520, in Hazlitt's Dodsley, i.:

"It is for a prayer mestres my de-
    mandyng,
That is sayd ye haue of Seynt Appolyne
For the toth ake wher of this man is in
    pyne."

In the *Conflict of Conscience,* by N. Woodes, 1581, this "virgin and martyr," it is said, should be invoked in cases of toothache.

Apple-Howling.—In several counties the custom of apple-howling (or Yuling), to which Herrick refers in his "Hesperides," is still in observance. A troop of boys go round the orchards in Sussex, Devonshire, and other parts, and forming a ring about the trees, they repeat these doggerel lines:

"Stand fast root, bear well top,
Pray God send us a good howling crop;
Every twig, apples big:
Every bough, apples enou;
Hats full, caps full,
Full quarter sacks full."

Hasted says: "There is an odd custom used in these parts, about Keston and Wickham, in Rogation Week; at which time a number of young men meet together for the purpose, and with a most hideous noise run into the orchards, and incircling each tree, pronounce these words:

"Stand fast root; bear well top;
God send us a youling sop,
Every twig apple big,
Every bough apple enow."

For which incantation the confused rabble expect a gratuity in money or drink, which is no less welcome: but if they are disappointed of both, they with great solemnity anathematize the owners and trees with altogether as significant a curse. "It seems highly probable that this custom has arisen from the ancient one of perambulation among the heathens, when they made prayers to the gods for the use and blessing of the fruits coming up, with thanksgiving for those of the preceding year; and as the heathens supplicated Eolus, god of the winds, for his favourable blasts, so in this custom they still retain his name with a very small variation; this ceremony is called Youling, and the word is often used in their invo-

cations." Comp. *Twelfth Day, Wassail* and *Yule.*

Appleton-Thorn. — Mr. Wilbraham, in his "Cheshire Glossary," 1826, says: "At Appleton, Cheshire, it was the custom at the time of the wake to clip and adorn an old hawthorn which till very lately stood in the middle of the town. This ceremony is called the Bawming (dressing) of Appleton Thorn."

April Fools.—Maurice, speaking of "the First of April, or the ancient Feast of the Vernal Equinox, equally observed in India and Britain," tells us: "The first of April was anciently observed in Britain as a high and general festival, in which an unbounded hilarity reigned through every order of its inhabitants; for the sun, at that period of the year, entering into the sign Aries, the New Year, and with it the season of rural sports and vernal delight, was then supposed to have commenced. The proof of the great antiquity of the observance of this annual festival, as well as the probability of its original establishment in an Asiatic region, arises from the evidence of facts afforded us by astronomy. Although the reformation of the year by the Julian and Gregorian Calendars, and the adaptation of the period of its commencement to a different and far nobler system of theology, have occasioned the festival sports, anciently celebrated in this country on the first of April, to have long since ceased: and although the changes occasioned, during a long lapse of years, by the shifting of the Equinoctial points, have in Asia itself been productive of important astronomical alterations, as to the exact era of the commencement of the year; yet on both continents some very remarkable traits of the jocundity which then reigned, remain even to these distant times. Of those preserved in Britain, none of the least remarkable or ludicrous is that relic of its pristine pleasantry, the general practice of making April-Fools, as it is called, on the first day of the month; but this Colonel Pearce proves to have been an immemorial custom among the Hindoos, at a celebrated festival holden about the same period in India, which is called 'the Huli Festival.' During the Huli, when mirth and festivity reign among the Hindoos of every class, one subject of diversion is to send people on errands and expeditions that are to end in disappointment, and raise a laugh at the expense of the person sent. The Huli is always in March, and the last day is the general holiday. I have never yet heard any account of the origin of this English custom; but it is unquestionably very ancient, and is still kept up even in great towns, though less in them than in the country. With us, it is chiefly confined to the lower class of people; but in India high and low join in it; and the late Suraja Doulah, I am told, was very fond of making Huli Fools, though he was a Mussulman of the highest rank. They carry the joke here so far, as to send letters, making appointments in the name of persons who, it is known, must be absent from their house at the time fixed upon; and the laugh is always in proportion to the trouble given.' The least inquiry into the ancient customs of Persia, or the minutest acquaintance with the general astronomical mythology of Asia, would have taught Colonel Pearce that the boundless hilarity and jocund sports prevalent on the first day of April in England, and during the Huli Festival of India, have their origin in the ancient practice of celebrating, with festival rites the period of the Vernal Equinox, or the day when the new year of Persia anciently began." *Ind. Antiq.*, vi., 71. Cambridge tells us that the first day of April was a day held in esteem among the alchemists, because Basilius Valentinus was born on it. In the North of England persons thus imposed upon are called "April gowks." A gouk or gowk is properly a cuckoo, and is used here metaphorically in vulgar language for a fool. The cuckoo is indeed everywhere a name of contempt. *Gauch*, in the Teutonic, is rendered *stultus*, fool, whence also our Northern word, a goke or a gawky. In Scotland, upon April Fool Day, they have a custom of "hunting the gowk," as it is termed. This is done by sending silly people upon fools' errands from place to place by means of a letter, in which is written:

"On the first day of April
Hunt the Gowk another mile."

A custom, says "the Spectator," prevails everywhere among us on the first of April, when everybody strives to make as many fools as he can. The wit chiefly consists in sending persons on what are called "sleeveless errands, for the "History of Eve's Mother," for "pigeon's milk," with similar ridiculous absurdities. He takes no notice of the rise of this singular kind of anniversary. But Dr. Pegge, in the "Gentleman's Magazine" for 1766, has a tolerably plausible conjecture that the first of April ceremonies may be deducible from the old New Year's Day rejoicings. New Year's Day formerly falling on the 25th March, the first of April would have been the octaves on which the proceedings may have terminated with some such mummeries as these. A writer in one of the papers, under date of April 1, 1792, advances a similar theory, not aware

that he had been anticipated. In "The Parson's Wedding," the Captain says: "Death! you might have left word where you went, and not put me to hunt like Tom Fool." So, in Defoe's "Memoirs of the late Mr. Duncan Campbel," 1732, p. 163: "I had my labour for my pains; or, according to a silly custom in fashion among the vulgar, was made an April-Fool of, the person who had engaged me to take these pains never meeting me." In the "British Apollo," 1708, is the following query: — "Whence proceeds the custom of making April Fools? Answer. — It may not improperly be derived from a memorable transaction happening between the Romans and Sabines, mentioned by Dionysius, which was thus: the Romans, about the infancy of the city, wanting wives, and finding they could not obtain the neighbouring women by their peaceable addresses, resolved to make use of a stratagem; and accordingly Romulus instituted certain games, to be performed in the beginning of April (according to the Roman Calendar), in honour of Neptune. Upon notice thereof, the bordering inhabitants, with their whole families, flocked to Rome to see this mighty celebration, where the Romans seized upon a great number of the Sabine virgins, and ravished them, which imposition we suppose may be the foundation of this foolish custom." This solution is ridiculed in No. 18 of the same work as follows:

" Ye witty sparks, who make pretence
To answer questions with good sense,
How comes it that your monthly Phœbus
Is made a fool by Dionysius?
For had the Sabines, as they came,
Departed with their virgin fame,
The Romans had been styl'd dull tools,
And they, poor girls! been April Fools.
Therefore, if this ben't out of season,
Pray think, and give a better reason."

Poor Robin, in his "Almanack for 1760," alludes to All Fools' Day, and to the practice of sending persons "to dance Moll Dixon's round," and winds up with the query—Which is the greatest fool, the man that went, or he that sent him? The following verses are hardly perhaps worth quoting:

" While April morn her Folly's throne
exalts:
While Dob calls Nell, and laughs because she halts;
While Nell meets Tom, and says his tail is loose,
Then laughs in turn, and calls poor Thomas goose;

Let us, my Muse, thro' Folly's harvest
range,
And glean some Moral into Wisdom's
grange,
Verses on several Occasions, 1782, p. 50

Hone, in his *Every Day Book,* of course
mentions this custom, and illustrates it by
the urchin pointing out to an old gentleman that his handkerchief is falling out of
his tail-pocket. The French, too, have
their All-Fools' Day, and call the person
imposed upon "an April Fish," *Poisson
d'Avril.* Minshew renders the expression,
"Poisson d'Avril," a young bawd; a page
turned pandar; a mackerell; which is thus
explained by Bellingen: "Je sçay que la
plus part du monde ignorant cette raison,
l'attribue à une autre cause, & que par-
ceque les marchands de chair humaine, ou
courtiers de Venus, sont deputez a faire
de messages d'Amour & courent de part
et d'autre pour faire leur infame traffic;
on prend aussy plaisir à faire courir ceux
qu'on choisit á ce jour-lá pour objet de
raillerie, comme si on leur vouloit faire
exercer ce mestier honteux." *Ibid.* He
then confesses his ignorance why the
month of April is selected for this purpose,
unless, says he, "on account of its being
the season for catching mackerell, or that
men, awaking from the torpidity of the
winter season, are particularly influenced
by the passions, which, suddenly breaking
forth from a long slumber, excite them to
the pursuit of their wonted pleasures."
This may perhaps account for the origin
of the word "macquereau" in its obscene
sense. Leroux, "Dictionnaire Comique,"
tom. 1., p. 70, quotes the following:—

"Et si n'y a ne danger ne peril
Mais j'en feray votre poisson d'Avril."

Poesies de Pierre Michault. Goujet, Bib-
lioth. Franç. tom. ix., p. 351. The Festival of Fools at Paris, held on this day,
continued for two hundred and forty
years, when every kind of absurdity and
indecency was committed. This was probably a legacy from Pagan times, when,
according to the authorities presently
cited, the Calends of January were set
apart by all the early Christians for a
species of loose festival. Conf. "Monta-
cut. Orig. Eccles." pars prior, p. 128.
"Maeri Hiero-lexicon," p. 156; "Joannes
Boemus Aubanus," p. 265 (all quoted by
Brand). One of the Popes prohibited these
unholy rites on pain of anathema, as appears from a Mass inserted in some of the
old missals, "ad prohibendum ab Idolis."
The French appear to have had an
analogous usage on another occasion:
envoit au Temple les Gens un peu
"A la Saint Simon et St. Jude on
simple demander de Nefles (Medlars)
a fin de les attraper & faire noircir

par des Valets."—*Sauval Antiq. de Paris,*
vol. ii., p. 617.—Douce. The Quirinalia
were observed in honour of Romulus on
the 11th of the kal. of March; that is, the
19th of February. "Why do they call
the Quirinalia the Feast of Fools? Either
because they allowed this day (as Juba
tell us) to those who could not ascertain
their own tribes, or because they permitted those who had missed the celebration of the Fornacalia in their proper
tribes, along with the rest of the people,
either out of negligence, absence, or ignorance, to hold their festival apart on this
day." Plu. Quæst. Rom.; Opera, cum
Xylandri notis, fol. Franc. 1599, tom. ii.,
p. 285. The translation was communicated to Mr. Brand by the Rev. W. Walter, of Christ's College, Cambridge. The
custom of making fools on the 1st of April
prevails among the Swedes and Spaniards.
In Toreen's "Voyage to China," he says:
"We set sail on the 1st of April, and the
wind made April Fools of us, for we were
forced to return before Shagen, and to
anchor at Riswopol." For a similar
practice at Venice see Hazlitt's *Venetian
Republic,* 1900, ii., 793.

Apprentices.—We are to infer that
it was anciently usual for apprentices to
collect presents at Christmas in the form
of what we call Christmas-boxes, for Aubrey, speaking of an earthern pot dug up
in Wiltshire in 1654, tells us that it
resembled an apprentice's earthern
Christmas-box. — *Miscellanies,* ed. 1857,
p. 212. In "Pleasant Remarks on
the Humours of Mankind," we read:
"'Tis common in England for Prentices,
when they are out of their time, to make
an entertainment, and call it the Burial of
their Wives." This remains a common
expression.

Arbor Judæ.—See *Elder.*

Archery.—With the history of this
exercise as a military art we have no concern here. Fitzstephen, who wrote in the
reign of Henry II., notices it among the
summer pastimes of the London youth:
and the repeated statutes from the 13th
to the 16th century, enforcing the use of
the bow, usually ordered the leisure time
upon holidays to be passed in its exercise. Sir T. Elyot, in his "Governor,"
1531, terms shooting with or in a long
bow "principall of all other exercises,"
and he adds, "in mine opinion, none may
bee compared with shooting in the long
bowe, & that for sundry vtilities, yt come
theroff, wherein it incomparably excelleth
all other exercise. For in drawing of a
bowe, easy and congruent to his strength,
he that shooteth, doth moderately exercise his armes, and the other part of his
body: and if his bowe be bigger, he must
adde too more strength wherin is no lesse

valiant exercise then in any other. In shooting at buttes, or broade arrowe markes, is a mediocritie of exercise of the lower partes of the bodye and legges, by going a little distaunce a measurable pace. At couers or pryckes, it is at his pleasure that shoteth, howe faste or softly he listeth to goo, and yet is the praise of the shooter, neyther more ne lesse, for as farre or nigh the marke is his arrow, whan he goeth softly, as when he runneth." No one requires to be told, that a few years after the appearance of Elyot's "Governor," the learned Ascham devoted an entire treatise to this peculiarly national subject. His "Toxophilus" was published in 1545, and is still justly celebrated and admired. The regulations connected with the practice of archery constantly underwent alteration or modification. The common "Abridgement of the Statutes" contains much highly curious matter under this, as under other heads. It is sufficiently remarkable that by the Act, 12 Edw. IV. c. 2 (1472), each Venetian merchant, importing wine into England, was required to give in with each butt "four good bowstaves," under the penalty of a fine of 6s. 8d. for each default. This demand was enlarged, 1 Richard III. c. 11, in the case, at any rate, of Malvoisin or Tyre wine, with every butt of which ten bowstaves were to be reckoned in, under pain of 13s. 4d. By 19 Hen. VII. c. 2, all bowstaves of the length of six feet and a half were admitted into England free of duty. The price of a bow, by 22 Edw. IV. c. 4, was not to exceed 3s. 4d. under pain of 20s. fine to the seller. In the Robin Hood collection, printed in Hazlitt's *Tales and Legends*, 1892, p. 312, there is an account of a shooting at Nottingham. under the greenwood shade, to which all the bowmen of the North were freely invited to repair, and the prize to the winner was a silver arrow, feathered with gold. Robin won the award. We are to regard this narrative of a fourteenth century incident as one edited by a late-fifteenth century writer, namely the compiler of the *Little Gest*. By 6 Hen. VIII. cap. 13, it was ordered : "That non Shote in any crosebow nor handgon excepte he haue possessyons to the yerely valew of ccc. marke or els lycence from hensforth by the kynges placard vnder payne of .x li. ye one halfe to the kynge and the other halfe to hym that wyll sew for it / and ye forfetour of the same crosbow or handgonne to hym that wyll sease hit by accyon of det / and yt non kepe any crosebowe or hand gonne in his house on payne of iprisonment & of forfetour to the kynge .x li. . . prouydyd alway that this acte extend not to crosebow makers / nor to dwellers i wallyd townes within vii. myle of the see / and other holders on

the see costes or marchis for agayns Scotlad/kepyng crosebows for theyr defence/ nor to no marchautes hauyng crosebowes & handgonnys to sel only/nor to non host loggyng any ma bryngyng them in to his house, but the forfetur to be onely vpon the brynger." Among the Churchwardens' accounts of St. Laurence Parish, Reading, 1549, is the following entry :— "Paid to Will'm Watlynton, for that the p'ishe was indetted to hym for makyng of the Butts, xxxvis." Ibid. St. Mary's Parish, 1566: "Itm. for the makyng of the Buttes, viijs." Ibid. 1622 : "Paid to two laborers to playne the grounde where the Buttes should be, vs. vjd." 1629 : "Paid towards the butts mending, ijs. vjd." Among the accounts of St. Giles's Parish, 1566, we have : "Itm. for carrying of turfes for the buttes, xvjd." 1605 : "Three labourers, two days work aboute turfes for the butts, iiijs." "Carrying ix. load of turfes for the butts, ijs." "For two pieces of timber to fasten on the railes of the buttes, iiijd." 1621 : "The parishioners did agree that the Churchwardens and Constables should sett up a payre of buttes called shooting butts, in such place as they should think most convenient in St. Giles Parish, which butts cost xivs. xjd." Wood, in his "Bowman's Glory," 1682, has republished some of the statutes relating to archery ; but the earliest which he gives is of the 29 Hen. VIII. A remarkably curious tract is printed by Wood in the same volume, called "A Remembrance of the Worthy Show and Shooting of the Duke of Shoreditch (a man named Barlow, whom Henry VIII. jocularly so entitled) and his Associates, &c., 1583." Queen Elizabeth was fond of this sport, and indulged in it, as Henry Machyn the Diarist informs us, during her visit to Lord Arundel at Nonsuch, in the autumn of 1559. "The v day of August," says Machyn, "the Queens grace removyd from Eltham unto Non-shyche, my lord of Arundells, and ther her grace had as gret chere evere nyght and bankettes. . . . . as ever was sene. . . . . On monday the Quens grace stod at her standyng in the further park, and there was corse after—." Upon which Mr. Nichols quotes Hunter's "New Illustrations of Shakespeare," to show that shooting with the cross-bow was a favourite amusement then and afterward among ladies of rank. But this fact had been already sufficiently demonstrated by Strutt, who has shown that in England women excelled and delighted in the use of the common bow and cross-bow from a very early date. "In the sixteenth century we meet with heavy complaints," says Strutt, "respecting the disuse of the long-bow, and especially in the vicinity of London." Stow informs us that before his time it had been customary at Bartholomew-tide for the Lord Mayor, with the Sheriffs and Aldermen, to go into the fields at Finsbury, where the citizens were assembled, and shoot at the standard with broad and flight arrows for games; and this exercise was continued for several days: but in his time it was practised only one afternoon, three or four days after the festival of Saint Bartholomew. Stow died in 1605. After the reign of Chas. I., archery appears to have fallen into disrepute. Davenant, in a mock poem, entitled "The long Vacation in London," describes the attorneys and proctors as making matches in Finsbury Fields:

"With Loynes in canvas bow-case tied,
Where arrows stick with mickle pride;
Like ghosts of Adam Bell and Clymme;
Sol sets for fear they'll shoot at him!"

A correspondent of the "Gentleman's Magazine" for August, 1731, notices the ancient custom among the Harrow boys, of shooting annually for a silver arrow of the value of £3; this diversion, he states, was the gift of the founder of the school, John Lyon, Esq. About 1753, a society of archers appears to have been established in the Metropolis, who erected targets on the same spot during the Easter and Whitsun holidays, when the best shooter was styled captain, and the second lieutenant for the ensuing year. Of the original members of this society, there were only two remaining when Barrington published his Observations on the Statutes in the "Archæologia." It is now incorporated in the Archers' Division of the Artillery Company. In the latter half of the 18th century, the taste remained dormant; in the earlier part of the next one the Toxophilite Society started at Old Brompton, Robert Cruikshank being one of the members; and of late years the movement has exhibited symptoms of new vitality, and archery-clubs are established in almost every part of the country. The bow, however, has ceased for ever to be a weapon of offence. It has been resigned entirely to the ladies, who form themselves into Toxophilite associations. Archery forms one of the subjects of a series of papers on our Sports and Pastimes, contributed to the *Antiquary*.

Arches, Court of, the original Consistory Court of the see of Canterbury, held in Bow Church, or St. Mary *De Arcubus.* See Nares, *Glossary,* in v.

Arles, earnest money, given to servants at hiring as a retainer. See Halliwell in v.

Armorial Bearings in Inns.— See Pegge's *Curialia,* 1818, p. 349.

Arthur, King. — "A game used at sea, when nearing the Line, or in a hot latitude. It is performed thus: a man who is to represent King Arthur, ridiculously dressed, having a large wig, made out of oakum, or some old swabs, is seated on the side, or over a large vessel of water. Every person in his turn is to be ceremoniously introduced to him, and to pour a bucket of water over him, crying. Hail, King Arthur! If, during this ceremony, the person introduced laughs or smiles, (to which his Majesty endeavours to excite him, by all sorts of ridiculous gesticulations), he changes place with, and then becomes King Arthur, till relieved by some brother tar, who has as little command over his muscles as himself."— *Arthur O'Bradley.* See Nares, Glossary, 1859, in v.

Arthur O'Bradley..—See Nares, Glossary, 1859, in v.

Arthur's Show.—A sort of dramatic spectacle presented before Queen Elizabeth at Mile-End Green, in 1587-8. See Black's *History of the Leathersellers' Company,* 1871, p. 65, and Hazlitt's Monograph on Shakespear, second edition, 1903.

Arvals. — In the North of England, at funerals, a particular sort of loaf, called arvel-bread, is distributed among the poor.—Brockett, *N.C. Gloss.,* 1825, p. 7. Mr. Atkinson notices a special kind of bread formerly made at Whitby, for use at the arval-suppers; he describes it as "a thin, light, sweet cake." It has occurred to me that the game of hot cockles, of which Aubrey has left us a tolerably good description, originated in the practice of kneading one of these funeral loaves, as the rhyme with which the girls used to accompany the supposed moulding of cockle-bread, begins—

"My dame is sick and gonne to bed,
And Ile go mould my cockle-bread—"

And it is not an unreasonable supposition that, in course of time, the reason of the thing was lost, and the practice degenerated into a stupid and indelicate female sport. At the funeral of John Bagford, 1716, Mr. Clifton, a vintner, gave four bottles of sack to be drunk by the guests. Moresin, *Papatus,* tells us that in England in his time they were so profuse on this occasion, that it cost less to portion off a daughter, than to bury a dead wife. These burial feasts are still kept up in the North of England, and are there called arvals or arvils. The bread distributed on these occasions is called arvil bread. The custom seems borrowed from the ancients, amongst whom many examples of it are collected by Hornman. *De miraculis Mortuorum,* c. 36. This word occurs in "The Praise of Yorkshire Ale":

"Come, bring my jerkin, Tibb, I'll to
the Arvil,
Yon man's ded seny scoun, it makes me
marvill."
—P. 58.

Hutchinson thus mentions the Arval
Dinner : "On the decease of any person possessed of valuable effects, the
friends and neighbours of the family
are invited to dinner on the day of
interment, which is called the arthel
or arvel dinner. Arthel is a British
word, and is frequently more correctly
written arddelw. In Wales it is written
arddel, and signifies, according to
Dr. Davies' Dictionary, *asserere*, to
avouch. This custom seems of very distant antiquity, and was a solemn festival,
made at the time of publicly exposing the
corps, to exculpate the heir and those entitled to the possessions of the deceased,
from fines and mulcts to the Lord of the
Manor, and from all accusation of having
used violence : so that the persons then
convoked might avouch that the person
died fairly and without suffering any personal injury. The dead were thus exhibited by antient nations, and perhaps the
custom was introduced here by the
Romans.—*Northumberland*, ii. 20. Compare *Funeral Customs*.

These funeral entertainments are of
very old date. Cecrops is said to have instituted them for the purpose of renewing
decayed friendship amongst old friends,
&c.

Ascension Eve. — By his will,
proved in December, 1527, John Cole, of
Thelnetham, Suffolk, directed that a certain farm-rent should be applied yearly
to the purpose of providing "a busshell
and halffe of malte to be browne and a
bushelle of whete to be baked to fynde a
drinkinge upon Ascension Even everlast-
inge for ye parishe of Thelnetham to
drinke at the crosse of Trappetes."

Ascension Day.—It was a general
custom formerly, and is still [1903] observed in some country parishes, to go
round the bounds and limits of the parish,
on one of the three days before Holy Thursday, or the Feast of our Lord's Ascension,
when the minister, accompanied by his
churchwardens and parishioners, were
wont to deprecate the vengeance of God,
beg a blessing on the fruits of the earth,
and preserve the rights and properties of
the parish. It is the custom in many villages in the neighbourhood of Exeter to
'hail the Lamb,' upon Ascension morn.
That the figure of a lamb actually appears
in the east upon this morning is the popular persuasion : and so deeply is it rooted,
that it hath frequently resisted (even in
intelligent minds) the force of the strongest argument. The following supersti-

tion relating to this day is found in Scot's
"Discovery of Witchcraft," 1584 : "In
some countries they run out of the doors
in time of tempest, blessing themselves
with a cheese, whereupon was a cross
made with a rope's-end upon Ascension
Day."—"Item, to hang an egg laid on
Ascension day in the roof of the house,
preserveth the same from all hurts."
"Yesterday being Ascension Day, work
was entirely suspended at Lord Penrhyn's
extensive slate quarries near Bangor. The
cessation of work is not due to any religious regard for the day, but is attributable
to a superstition, which has long lingered
in the district, that if work is continued
an accident is inevitable. Some years ago
the management succeeded in overcoming
this feeling and in inducing the men to
work. But each year there was a serious
accident, and now all the men keep at a
distance from the quarries on Ascension
Day."—*Times*, April 11, 1888. Ascension
Day is thus described in Googe's Naogeorgus, 1570 :—

"Then comes the day when Christ ascended to his fathers seate,
Which day they also celebrate, with store
of drink and meate.
Then every man some birde must eate, I
know not to what ende,
And after dinner all to Church they come,
and there attende.
The blocke that on the aultar still till then
was seene to stande,
Is drawne vp hie aboue the roofe, by ropes
and force of hande :
The Priests aboute it rounde do stande,
and chaunte it to the skie,
For all these mens religion great in sing-
ing most doth lie.
Then out of hande the dreadfull shape of
Sathan downe they throw
Oft times, with fire burning bright, and
dasht asunder tho,
The boyes with greedie eyes do watch, and
on him straight they fall
And beate him sore with rods, and breake
him into peeces small.
This done, the wafers downe doe cast, and
singing Cakes the while,
With Papers rounde amongst them put,
the children to beguile.
With laughter great are all things done :
and from the beames they let
Great streames of water downe to fall, on
whom they meane to wet.
And thus this solemne holiday, and hye
renowmed feast,
And all their whole deuotion here is ended
with a ieast."
The unique Venetian pageant, La Sensa,
commenced on this day, and lasted a fortnight. It was a fair, where every description of property, including pictures by
Titian and Tintoretto, were offered for

sale. Its attractions were as multifarious as those at Nijny Novgorod, and more elegant and refined.—Hazlitt's *Venetian Republic*, 1900, ii., 355, 756.

Ash.—Gilbert White, writing at the end of the eighteenth century, informs us that "In a farm yard near the middle of this village (Selborne) stands, at this day, a row of pollard-ashes, which by the seams and long cicatrices down their sides, manifestly shew that in former times they have been cleft asunder. These trees, when young and flexible, were severed and held open by wedges, while ruptured children, stripped naked, were pushed through the apertures, under a persuasion that by such a process the poor babes would be cured of their infirmity. As soon as the operation was over, the tree, in the suffering part, was plastered with loam, and carefully swathed up. If the parts coalesced, and folded together, as usually fell out, where the feat was performed with any adroitness at all, the party was cured; but, where the cleft continued to gape, the operation, it was supposed, would prove ineffectual. Having occasion to enlarge my garden not long since, I cut down two or three such trees, one of which did not grow together. We have several persons now living in the village, who in their childhood were supposed to be healed by this superstitious ceremony, derived down perhaps from our Saxon ancestors, who practiced it before their conversion to Christianity. At the south corner of the Plestor or area, near the Church, there stood, about twenty years ago, a very old grotesque hollow pollard-ash, which for ages had been looked upon with no small veneration as a shrew-ash. Now a shrew-ash is an ash whose twigs or branches, when gently applied to the limbs of cattle, will immediately relieve the pains which a beast suffers from the running of a shrew mouse over the part affected : for it is supposed that a shrew-mouse is of so baneful and deleterious a nature, that wherever it creeps over a beast, be it horse, cow or sheep, the suffering animal is afflicted with cruel anguish, and threatened with the loss of the use of the limb. Against this accident, to which they were continually liable, our provident fore-fathers always kept a shrew-ash at hand, which, when once medicated, would maintain its virtue for ever. A shrew-ash was made thus : (for a similar practice see Plot's Staffordshire) : Into the body of the tree a deep hole was bored with an auger, and a poor devoted shrew-mouse was thrust in alive, and plugged in, no doubt, with several quaint incantations long since forgotten. As the ceremonies necessary for such a consideration are no longer understood, all succession is at an end, and no such tree is known to subsist in the manor or hundred. As to that on the Plestor, ' the late Vicar stubb'd and burnt it,' when he was Way-warden, regardless of the remonstrances of the bystanders, who interceded in vain for its preservation, urging its power and efficacy, and alledging that it had been

' Religione patrum multos servata annos.' "

The sap of the ash, a powerful astringent, was formerly given to the Highland children, not only as a medicine, but because it was supposed to be efficacious as a preservative against witchcraft and its allied influences. The ash itself was thought to be possessed of certain virtues by the herd-boys of the same district, who entertained an idea, that they might throw a stick of it at their cattle without injury. Comp. *Charms*.

Ash Wednesday.—Durandus, in his "Rationale" tells us, Lent was counted to begin on that which is now the first Sunday in Lent, and to end on Easter Eve; which time, saith he, containing forty-two days, if you take out of them the six Sundays (on which it was counted not lawful at any time of the year to fast), then there will remain only thirty-six days : and, therefore, that the number of days which Christ fasted might be perfected, Pope Gregory added to Lent four days of the week before-going, viz. that which we now call Ash Wednesday, and the three days following it. So that we see the first observation of Lent began from a superstitious, unwarrantable, and indeed profane, conceit of imitating our Saviour's miraculous abstinence. Lent is so called from the time of the year wherein it is observed : Lent in the Saxon language signifying Spring, being now used to signify the Spring-Fast, which always begins so that it may end at Easter to remind us of our Saviour's sufferings, which ended at his Resurrection. Ash Wednesday is in some places called "Pulver Wednesday," that is, *Dies pulveris*. The word Lentron, for Lent, occurs more than once in the edition of the "Regiam Majestatem," 1609. Sir H. Ellis mentions that Lenten-tide for spring, when the days lengthen, occurs in the Saxon "Heptateuch," 1698. Exod. xxxiv. 18. There is a curious clause in one of the Romish Casuists concerning the keeping of Lent; it is "that beggars which are ready to affamish for want, may in Lent time eat what they can get." This, which is the first day of Lent, *Caput Jejunii*, is called Ash Wednesday, as we read in the Festa Anglo-Romana, p. 19, from the ancient ceremony of blessing ashes on that day, and therewith the priest signeth the people on the forehead, in the form of a cross. The ashes used this day in the Church of Rome, are made of the palms blessed the Palm Sunday before. In the "Festyvall," 1511, fol. 15, it is said: "Ye shall begyn your faste upon Ashe Wednesdaye. That daye must ye come to holy chirche and take ashes of the Preestes hondes, and thynke on the wordes well that he sayeth over your hedes, (*Memento, homo, quia cinis es; et in cinerem reverteris*), have mynde thou man, of ashes thou art comen, and to ashes thou shalte tourne agayne." In a convocation held in the time of Henry the Eighth, mentioned in Fuller's "Church History," p. 222, "Giving of ashes on Ash Wednesday, to put in remembrance every Christian man in the beginning of Lent and Pennance, that he is but ashes and earth, and thereto shall return &c., is reserved with some other rites and ceremonies, which survived the shock that at that remarkable era almost overthrew the whole pile of Catholic superstitions. In a proclamation, dated 26th Feb. 30 Henry VIII., we read: "On Ashe Wenisday it shall be declared, that these ashes be gyven, to put every Christian man in remembraunce of penaunce, at the begynnynge of Lent, and that he is but erthe and ashes." On the 9th March, 1550-1, a proclamation was published against the use of flesh on "ymberyng days," as well as in Lent, &c. "Mannerlye to take theyr ashes devoutly," is among the Roman Catholic customs censured by John Bale in his "Declaration of Bonner's Articles," 1554, signat. D 4 verso, as is, ibid. D 2 verso, "to conjure ashes." In "The Doctrine of the Masse Book," 1554, fig. B 3 verso, we find translated the form of "The hallowing of the ashes." The Masse Book saith, that upon Ash-Wedensdaye, when the prieste hath absolved the people, &c., then must there be made a blessynge of the ashes, by the Prieste, being turned towards the East. In the first prayer is this passage: "Vouchsafe to blesse and sanctifie these ashes, which because of humilitie and of holy religion for the clensyng out of our trespaces, thou hast appointed us to cary upon our heades after the manner of the Ninivites." And after directions to sprinkle the ashes with holy water, and another prayer, this Rubric is added: "Then let them distribute the ashes upon the heades of the Clarckes and of the lay people: the worthier persons makyng a sygne of the Crosse with the ashes, saying thus: 'Memento, homo, quod cinis,' &c." In Bp. Bonner's "Injunctions," 1555, signat. A 1 verso, we read, "that the hallowed ashes gyven by the Priest to the people upon Ashe Wednisdaye, is to put the people in remembrance of penance at the begynnynge of Lent, and that their bodies ar but earth,

dust, and ashes." In Howes's edition of Stow's "Annales," 1631, 1547-8, occurs: "The Wednesday following, commonly called Ash Wednesday, the use of giving ashes in the Church was also left throughout the whole Citie of London." Lord North, in his "Forest of Varieties," 1645, p. 165, in allusion to this custom, styles one of his essays, "My Ashewednesday Ashes." The ancient discipline of sackcloth and ashes, on Ash Wednesday, is at present supplied in our Church by reading publicly on this day the curses denounced against impenitent sinners, when the people are directed to repeat an Amen at the end of each malediction. Enlightened as we now think ourselves there are many who consider the general avowal of the justice of God's wrath against impenitent sinners as cursing their neighbours : consequently, like good Christians, they keep away from church on the occasion.

"The peasantry of France," says the *Morning Chronicle*, March 10th, 1791, "distinguish Ash Wednesday in a very singular manner. They carry an effigy of a similar description to our Guy Faux round the adjacent villages, and collect money for his funeral, as this day, according to their creed, is the death of good living. After sundry absurd mummeries, the corpse is deposited in the earth." This may possibly be a relic of the same usage. Armstrong, in his "History of Minorca," says, "During the carnival, the ladies amuse themselves in throwing oranges at their lovers : and he who has received one of these on his eye, or has a tooth beat out by it, is convinced, from that moment, that he is a high favourite with the fair one who has done him so much honour. Sometimes a good hand-full of flour is thrown full in one's eyes, which gives the utmost satisfaction, and is a favour that is quickly followed by others of a less trifling nature."—"We well know that the holydays of the antient Romans were, like these carnivals, a mixture of devotion and debauchery." — "This time of festivity is sacred to pleasure, and it is sinful to exercise their calling until Lent arrives, with the two curses of these people, abstinence and labour, in its train." Aubanus tells us of a custom in Franconia on Ash Wednesday, when such young women, he says, as have frequented the dances throughout the year are gathered together by young men, and, instead of horses, are yoked to a plough, upon which a piper sits and plays : in this maner they are dragged into some river or pool. He suspects this to have been a kind of self-enjoined voluntary penance for not having abstained from their favourite diversion on holidays, contrary to the injunctions of the Church.

Ashton Fagot.—At Lidiard Lawrence, between Bishop's Lidiard and Stokegomer, Somersetshire, it has been a custom at Christmas to burn what is known as the Ashton Fagot, perhaps a designation or name derived from Long Ashton in the same county. A quart of cyder was originally provided for those—a limited company—who witnessed the ceremony, as the fagot, in reality a bundle of sticks hooped together, disappeared in the flames, the hoops successively bursting with the heat. The cyder seems to have developed into a carouse at the local inn, and as lately as 1902, one of the spectators was brought before the magistrates for disorderly conduct, and the Bench pronounced the custom a bad one. It has the aspect of being a form of the Yule-log.

Ass.—There is a superstition remaining among the vulgar concerning the ass, that the marks on the shoulders of that useful and much injured animal were given to it as memorials that our Saviour rode upon an ass. "The Asse," says Sir Thomas Browne, "having a peculiar mark of a Crosse made by a black list down his back, and another athwart, or at right angles down his shoulders, common opinion ascribes this figure unto a peculiar signation : Since that beast had the honour to bear our Saviour on his back." In the "Athenæum," about forty years ago, appeared the following :—"The popular belief as to the origin of the mark across the back of the ass is mentioned by Sir Thomas Browne, in his ' Vulgar Errors,' and from whatever cause it may have arisen it is certain that the hairs taken from the part of the animal so marked are held in high estimation as a cure for the hooping-cough. In this metropolis, at least so lately as 1842, an elderly lady advised a friend who had a child dangerously ill with that complaint, to procure three such hairs, and hang them round the neck of the sufferer in a muslin bag. It was added that the animal from whom the hairs are taken for this purpose is never worth anything afterwards, and, consequently, great difficulty would be experienced in procuring them : and, further, that it was essential to the success of the charm that the sex of the animal, from whom the hairs were to be procured, should be the contrary to that of the party to be cured by them."

Assumption of the Virgin Mary (August 15). — Naogeorgus describes the consecration of the herbs on this festival by the priests of Germany, and laments the nourishment of popular ignorance and prejudice by such means, as the herbs when blessed or sanctified were held to be efficacious in witchcraft and magic, and if cast into the fire, to afford protection from malignant influences : " far otherwise," as the writer says truly enough, " than nature of the Worde of God doth tell."—*Pop. Kingdom*, by Barnaby Googe, 1570, p. 55. Bishop Hall, in his *Triumphs of Rome*, p. 58, also tells us, " that upon this day it was customary to implore blessings upon herbs, plants, roots, and fruits."

Aston, Birmingham.—A writer in the " Gentleman's Magazine " for February, 1795, gave the following account of a custom which took place annually on the 24th of December, at the house of a gentleman residing at Aston juxta Birmingham : " As soon as supper is over, a table is set in the hall. On it is placed a brown loaf, with twenty silver threepences stuck on the top of it, a tankard of ale, with pipes and tobacco : and the two oldest servants have chairs behind it, to sit as judges if they please. The steward brings the servants, both men and women, by one at a time, covered with a winnow-sheet, and lays their right hand on the loaf, exposing no other part of the body. The oldest of the two judges guesses at the person, by naming a name, then the younger judge, and lastly the oldest again. If they hit upon the right name, the steward leads the person back again ; but, if they do not, he takes off the winnow-sheet, and the person receives a threepence, makes a low obeisance to the judges, but speaks not a word. When the second servant was brought, the younger judge guessed first and third ; and this they did alternately till all the money was given away. Whatever servant had not slept in the house the preceding night forfeited his right to the money. No account is given of the origin of this strange custom, but it has been practiced ever since the family lived there. When the money is gone, the servants have full liberty to drink, dance, sing, and go to bed when they please. Can this be what Aubrey, in a passage elsewhere quoted from his " Natural History of Wiltshire," calls the sport of " Cob-loaf stealing ? "

Astrologer. — Fuller has this passage : " Lord, hereafter I will admire thee more and fear astrologers lesse : not affrighted with their doleful predictions of dearth and drought, collected from the Collections of the planets. Must the earth, of necessity be sad, because some ill-natured starr is sullen ? As if the grass could not grow without asking it leave. Whereas thy power, which made herbs before the stars, can preserve them without their propitious, yea, against their malignant aspects." *Good thoughts in Bad Times*, ed. 1669, p. 37. A prose writer of the same period observes : " Surely all astrolgers are Erra Pater's disciples, and the Divil's professors, telling their opinions in spurious ænigmatical doubtful tearmes, like the Oracle at Delphos. What a blind dotage and shamelesse impudence is in these men, who pretend to know more than saints and angels? Can they read other men's fates by those glorious characters the starres, being ignorant of their owne? Qui sibi nescius, cui præscius? Thracias the sooth-sayer, in the nine years drought of Egypt, came to Busiris the Tyrant and told him that Jupiter's wrath might bee expiated by sacrificing the blood of a stranger: the Tyrant asked him whether he was a stranger: he told him he was,

"Thou, quoth Busiris, shalt that stranger bee,
Whose blood shall wet our soyle by Destinie."

If all were served so, we should have none that would relye so confidently on the falshood of their Ephemerides, and in some manner shake off all divine providence, making themselves equal to God, between whom and man the greatest difference is taken away, if man should foreknow future events. — Browne's *Map of the Microcosme,* 1646, sign. D 8 *verso.* Sir Aston Cokain, in his *Poems,* 1658, has a quip for the astrologers:

To Astrologers.

Your Industry to you the Art hath given
To have great knowledge in th' outside of Heaven:
Beware lest you abuse that Art, and sin,
And therfore never visit it within."

The quack astrologer has been thus portrayed: "First, he gravely inquires the business, and by subtle questions pumps out certain particulars which he treasures up in his memory; next, he consults his old rusty clock, which has got a trick of lying as fast as its master, and amuses you for a quarter of an hour with scrawling out the all-revealing figure, and placing the planets in their respective pues; all which being dispatch'd you must lay down your money on his book, as you do the wedding fees to the parson at the delivery of the ring: for 'tis a fundamental axiome in his art, that, without crossing his hand with silver no scheme can be radical: then he begins to tell you back your own tale in other language, and you take that for divination which is but repetition. . His groundless guesses he calls resolves, and compels the stars (like Knights o' th' Post) to depose things they know no more than the man i' the moon: as if Hell were accessory to all the cheating tricks Hell inspires him with. . . . He impairs God's universal monarchy, by making the stars sole keepers of the liberties of the sublunary world, and, not content they should domineer over naturals, will needs promote their tyranny in things artificial, too, asserting that all manufactures receive good or ill fortunes and qualities from some particular radix, and therefore elects a time for stuing of pruins, and chuses a pisspot by its horoscope. Nothing pusles him more than fatal necessity: he is loth to deny it, yet dares not justify it, and therefore prudently banishes it from his theory, but hugs it in his practice, yet knows not how to avoid the horns of that excellent dilemma, propounded by a most ingenious modern Poet:

"If fate be not, how shall we ought fore-see,
Or how shall we avoid it, if it be?
If by free-will in our own paths we move,
How are we bounded by decrees above?'"

—*Character of a Quack Astrologer.* 1675. He, we are told, "offers, for five pieces, to give you home with you a talisman against flies; a sigil to make you fortunate at gaming; and a spell that shall as certainly preserve you from being rob'd for the future; a sympathetical powder for the violent pains of the toothache." *Ibid.* sign. C. *verso.* Some years ago, a periodical entitled *The Astrologer* was set up in London, for the purpose of casting the horoscopes of correspondents, and furnishing intelligence connected with astrology. Its success was great; but in fact that very success it was, which killed it. The pressure of applicants was so enormous, it is said, that the post brought the letters for the editor in sacks, and the undertaking had to be given up. It is diffiuclt to say when the belief in divination by the stars will be extinguished or expire: at present that belief is entertained by a numerous body of people, educated and uneducated, whose enthusiasm and credulity remain unabated. Henry, speaking of astrology, tells us, "Nor did this passion for penetrating into futurity prevail only among the common people, but also among persons of the highest rank and greatest learning. All our kings, and many of our earls and great barons had their astrologers, who resided in their families, and were consulted by them in all undertakings of great importance. Of this," he says, "we meet with a very curious example in the account given by Matthew Paris of the marriage of Frederick Emperor of Germany and Isabella sister of Henry III. A.D. 1235. The great man kept these to cast the horoscopes of his children, discover the success of his designs, and the public events that were to happen." "Their predictions," he adds, "were couched in very general and artful terms."—*History of Great Britain,* iii., 515, and iv., 577. "Nocte vero prima qua concubit Imperator cum ea, noluit eam carnaliter cognoscere, donec competens hora ab astrologis ei nunciaretur." M.

Paris, p. 285, ad ann. 1235. Bishop Hall says :—

"Thou damned mock-art, and thou brain-sick tale
Of old astrologie"—
"Some doting gossip 'mongst the Chaldee wives
Did to the credulous world thee first derive :
And superstition nurs'd thee ever sence,
And publisht in profounder arts pretence :
That now, who pares his nailes, or libs his swine,
But he must first take counsell of the signe."

—*Virgidemiarum*, lib., ii., sat. 7. Astrology is ridiculed in a masterly manner in *King Lear*, 1608. Mason mentions in his list of the then prevailing superstitions : "erecting of a figure to tell of stolne goods. Philip Henslowe has a receipt "To know wher a thinge is that is stolne :—Take vergine waxe and write upon yt ✠ Jasper ✠ Melchisor ✠ Balthasar ✠ and put yt under his head to whome the good partayneth, and he shall knowe in his sleape wher the thinge is become." — *Diary*, ed., 1845. Johnson, speaking of *Hudibras*, says : "Astrology, however, against which so much of the satire is directed, was not more the folly of the Puritans than of others. It had at that time a very extensive dominion. Its predictions raised hopes and fears in minds which ought to have rejected it with contempt. In hazardous undertakings care was taken to begin under the influence of a propitious planet; and, when the King was prisoner in Carisbrook Castle an astrologer was consulted as to what hour would be found most favourable to an escape." "Astrology," says "a person of honour," "imagines to read in the constellations, as in a large book, every thing that shall come to pass here below, and figuring to itself admirable rencounters from the aspects and conjunctions of the planets, it draws from thence consequences as remote from truth as the stars themselves are from the earth. I confess I have ever esteemed this science vain and ridiculous : for indeed it must be either true or false; if true, that which it predicts is infallible and inevitable, and consequently unuseful to be foreknown. But, if it is false, as it may easily be evinced to be, would not a man of sense be blamed to apply his mind to and lose his time in, the study thereof? It ought to be the occupation of a shallow Braine, that feeds itself with chimerical fancies, or of an impostor who makes a mystery of every thing which he understands not, for to deceive women and credulous people.— *Courtier's Calling*, 1675, p. 241. Agrippa exposes astrology as the mother of heresy,

and adds : "Besides this same fortune-telling astrology not only the best of moral philosophers explode, but also Moses, Isaias, Job, Jeremiah, and all the other prophets of the ancient law : and among the Catholick writers, St. Austin condemns it to be utterly expelled and banish'd out of the territories of Christianity. St. Hierome argues the same to be a kind of idolatry. Basil and Cyprian laugh at it as most contemptible. Chrysostome, Eusebius, and Lactantius utterly condemn it. Gregory, Ambrose, and Severianus inveigh against it. The Council of Toledo utterly abandon and prohibit it. In the Synod of Martinus and by Gregory the younger and Alexander III. it was anathematized and punished by the civil laws of the Emperors. Among the ancient Romans it was prohibited by Tiberius, Vitellius, Diocletian, Constantine, Gratian, Valentinian, and Theodosius, ejected also, and punish'd. By Justinian made a capital crime, as may appear in his Codex."—*Vanity of Sciences*, p 98. He pleasantly observes of astrologers, that "undertaking to tell all people most obscure and hidden secrets abroad, they at the same time know not what happens in their own houses and in their own chambers. Even such an astrologer as Henry More laught at them in his epigram :

"The Stars, ethereal bard, to thee shine clear,
And all our future fates thou mak'st appear.
But that thy wife is common all men know,
Yet what all see, theres not a star doth show.
Saturn is blinde, or some long journey gone,
Not able to discern an infant from a stone.
The moon is fair, and as she's fair she's chast,
And wont behold thy wife so leudly embrac't,
Europa Jove, Mars Venus, she Mars courts,
With Daphne Sol, with Hirce Hermes sports.
Thus while the stars their wanton love pursue,
No wonder, Cuckold, they'll not tell thee true."

It appears that figures were often erected concerning the voyages of ships from London to Newcastle, &c.—Gadbury's *Nauticum Astrologicum*, 1710, pp. 93, 123, &c. We are told in one place that the prediction was verified; the ship, though not lost, had been in great danger thereof, having unhappily run aground at Newcastle, sprung a shroud, and wholly lost her keel. In another, there is a figure given of a ship that set sail from London towards Newcastle, Aug. 27, 11 p.m., 1669. This proved a fortunate voyage. "As indeed," saith Gadbury, "under so auspicious a position of Heaven it had been strange if she had missed so to have done; for herein you see Jupiter in the ascendant in sextile aspect of the sun; and the moon, who is Lady of the Horoscope, and Governess of the Hour in which she weighed anchor, is applying ad Trinum Veneris. She returned to London again very well laden, in three weeks time, to the great content as well as advantage of the owner." I have to observe here that the shipowners in the Newcastle trade are now much wiser than to throw away money on such fooleries, and, with much greater propriety, when things augur ill, apply to the assurance office, in preference to that of the diviner or fortuneteller.

Dallaway tells us that astrology was a favourite folly with the Turks. "Ulugh-bey," he says, "amongst very numerous treatises is most esteemed. He remarks the 13th, 14th, and 15th of each month as the most fortunate; the Ruznameh has likewise its three unlucky days. to which little attention is paid by the better sort. The Sultan retains his chief astrologer, who is consulted by the Council on state emergencies. When the treaty of peace was signed at Kainargi in 1774, he was directed to name the hour most propitious for that ceremony. The Vizier's Court swarms with such impostors It was asserted that they foretold the great fire at Constantinople in 1782. There was likewise an insurrection of the janissaries which they did not foretel, but their credit was saved by the same word bearing two interpretations of *Insurrection* and *Fire*. It may now be considered rather as a state expedient to consult the astrologer, that the enthusiasm of the army may be fed and subordination maintained by the prognostication of victory.— *Tour to Constantinople*, p. 390.

There are even literary gentlemen who seeks counsel of their astrologer before they undertake a new venture, and when they desire to know the most propitious time for publication. A lady informed the present writer that, before she was married, she consulted Professor Wilson, of the Caledonian Road, who asked her the hour of her birth and other questions, and after elaborate calculations mentioned certain circumstances which were untrue. He then made a second experiment, placing her nativity half an hour later, and then related some matters which had really occurred to her, and others which had not, and never did—particularly, that she would have plenty of money.

Astrology, Judicial, or Astronomy.—In "Dives and Pauper," 1493, Signat. E 2, we meet with the following: "Or take hede to the Judicial of Astronomy—or dyvyne a mans lyf or deth by nombres and by the Spere of Pyctagorus, or make any dyvyning therby, or by Songuary or Sompnarye, the Boke of Dremes, or by the boke that is clepid the Apostles lottis." The author adds: "And alle that use any manner wichecraft or any misbileve. that all suche forsaken the feyth of holy Churche and their Cristendome, and bicome Goddes enmyes and greve God full grevously and falle into dampnacion withouten ende, but they amende theym the soner." Zouch says, mentioning Queen Mary's reign: "Judicial astrology was much in use long after this time. Its predictions were received with reverential awe: and men, even of the most enlightened understandings, were inclined to believe that the conjunctions and oppositions of the planets had no little influence in the affairs of the world. Even the excellent Joseph Mede disdained not to apply himself to the study of astrology."— Ed. of *Walton's Lives*, 1796, p. 131.

Auctions.—The earliest Roman auctions were held *sub hastâ*, to indicate that the proceedings were carried on under public or official authority.—Smith's *Dict. of Gr. and Rom. Antiq.* 2nd ed., v. *Hasta*. During the middle ages, and down to comparatively modern times, the auctioneer continued to be known as the *subhastator*, and an auction as the *Asta*. —Lacroix, *Mœurs et Usages*, 1872. p. 337. But the trumpet and bell also came into use, as well as the crier. At Venice, in the fourteenth century, we find the bell and the cry (*campanella* and *incanto*), and there it was said that a sale was held by the bell, as in England in the 17th century the parallel expression was "to sell at the candle." Among the Anglo-Saxons time-candles appear to have been known. The Venetians, in the case at all events of official or Government sales, required guarantees for the payment of the money offered by the highest bidder.— Hazlitt's *Venetian Republic*, 1900. ii., p. 355. The system of selling by inch of candle is still retained at Broadway, Dorsetshire, when the annual lease of a meadow is sold in this way. The biddings started at £3. and the candle expired at £8 4s. 0d.—*Daily Mail*, Jan. 10. 1903. Comp. Davis. *Suppl. Glossary*, 1881, p. 100. A Dutch Auction has become a mere phrase rather than an usage. It signifies the practice of quoting an upset price, and descending by bids, until a customer occurs, whose maximum has been reached.

Augrim Stones.—Counters formerly used in arithmetic. See Halliwell in v.

Avenor.—From Fr. *avoine*, the person who, in great towns, formerly had the superintendence of the horse-meat. See Halliwell in v.

Babies in the Eyes.. See Nares, *Glossary*, 1859, in v. In Braithwaite's "Two Lancashire Lovers," 1640, p. 19, in Camillus' speech to Doriclea, in the Lancashire dialect, he tells her, in order to gain her affections, "We han store of goodly cattell; my mother, though shee bee a vixon, shee will blenke blithly on you for my cause; and we will ga to the dawnes and slubber up a sillibub; and I will looke babbies in your eyes, and picke silly-cornes out of your toes: and we will han a whiskin at every rush-bearing, a wassel cup at Yule, a seed-cake at Fastens, and a lusty cheese-cake at our sheepe-wash; and will not aw this done bravely, Jantlewoman?" In her answer to this clown's addresses, she observes, among other passages, "What know you but I may prove untoward, and that will bring your mother to her grave; make you, pretty babe, put finger ith' eye, and turne the door quite off the hinges." The above romance is said to have been founded on a true history; the costume appears to be very accurate and appropriate.

Bachelor's Buttons.—There is a rustic species of divination by bachelor's buttons, a plant so called. There was an ancient custom, says Grey, amongst the country fellows, of trying whether they should succeed with their mistresses by carrying the bachelor's buttons, a plant of the lychnis kind, whose flowers resemble also a button in form, in their pockets: and they judged of their good or bad success by their growing or not growing there. *Notes on Shakespear*, i., 108. Bachelor's buttons are described as having been worn also by the young women, and that too under their aprons. "Thereby I saw the batchelors butons, whose vertue is to make wanton maidens weepe, when they have worne it forty weekes under their aporns for a favour."—Greene's *Quip*, 1592, reprint *Collier*, p. 10.

Backgammon.—See *Tables*.

Badger-in-the-Bag. — In the tale of *Pwyll Prince of Dyved*, in the *Mabinogion*, an account is furnished of the alleged circumstances under which this game was first played, where Rhiannon persuades Gnawl, the son of Clud, to put his feet into the bag to tread down the food within, and he finds himself overhead in it, whereupon all present kicked the bag with their foot, or struck it with a staff. Every one as he came in asked, "What game are you playing at thus?" "The game of Badger-in-the Bag." said they. And then was the game of Badger-in-the-Bag first played." Ed. 1877, p. 350.

Badger-the-Bear.—A rough game played by boys, and described by Halliwell in v.

Bagatelle. — A well-known game played with one black and eight coloured or white balls, and a cue and mallet, and somewhat following the lines of billiards, but without pockets in the table. It is said to have been well established in 1827. Its origin is uncertain, but it is said not to be French, although the name is so. It is played with variations.

Baker's Clem..—At Cambridge the bakers have an annual supper, which is called "The Bakers' Clem." A correspondent of "Notes and Queries" (Cuthbert Bede) testifies to its celebration in 1863.

Baker's Dozen. — Originally a *Devil's Dozen*. Comp. Nares, *Glossary*, 1859, in v., and see *Numbers*.

Ballad - Monger. — Braithwaite, describing a ballad-monger, in his *Whimzies*, 1631, writes: By this time they (his ballads) are cashiered the City, and must now ride poast for the countrey: where they are no lesse admir'd than a gyant in a pageant: till at last they grow so common there too, as every poore milk-maid can chant and chirpe it under her cow, which she useth as an harmlesse charme to make her let downe her milke."

Ball-Money. — See *Nuptial Usages*.

Ball. — In the *Odyssey*, Nausicaa, daughter of the King of Phœacia, is represented playing at this game with her handmaidens; and there are Greek coins where a girl is seen engaged in the same sport. At a period posterior to Homer, it was known as Phœninda. Sophocles the tragedian, in his play of *Nausicaa*, distinguished himself in the performance by his skill at the game. Playing at ball, as early as the fourteenth century, is denounced by a bishop of London as one of the ways in which the precincts of St. Paul's Church, London, were then desecrated (1385); and this disorderly and licentious condition of affairs continued during centuries. There used to be a practice of rolling a ball down the table after dinner; it is thought that this was, when a match had been recently played, where the ball was used, and the victorious party, to whom it belonged, thus exhibited it as a trophy.

Balloon.—This was played with an inflated ball of leather, which was struck by the arm, the latter being protected by a bracer of wood. In "Eastward Hoe," 1605, Sir Pretonel Flash is represented as having a match at balloon with my lord Whackham for four crowns. Donne also mentions it:

"'Tis ten a clock and past; all whom the mues,
Baloun, tennis, diet, or the stewes

Had all the morning held, now the second
Time made ready, that day, in flocks are
found."

And in a writer of somewhat later date
it is coupled with several other diversions
of the period: "also Riding the Great
Horse, Running at a ring, Tilts and Tour-
naments, are noble exercises as well as
healthy, and becoming his (the gentleman's) grandeur. In like manner, Balon,
Quintan, Stop-Ball, Pitching of a Bar,
Casting of a Weight, are healthy and laudable." — *The Gentleman's Companion,*
1676, p. 136-7. Randolph, in his eclogue
on the revival of the Cotswold Games by
Dover, seems to speak of balloon as a sort
of football. The whole passage is curious:

"Colin, I once the famous Spain did see,
A nation famous for her gravity.
Yet there a hundred knights on warlike
    steeds
Did skirmish out a fight arm'd but with
    reeds;
At which a thousand ladies' eyes did gaze,
Yet 'twas no better than our prison-base.
What is the barriers but a worthy way
Of our more downright sport, the cudgel-
    play?
—*Works,* 1875, 621.

Balls, Three.—The three blue balls
prefixed to the doors and windows of
pawnbrokers' shops, (by the vulgar humorously enough said to indicate that it is
two to one that the things pledged are
ever redeemed) were is reality the arms of
the Medici family, a branch of whom, with
many other Lombard houses, settled in
London at an early date, and concen-
trated themselves chiefly in a quarter
which was called after them Lombard
street. But in the Medici cognizance
there are six balls. On a Brabantine coin
anterior to the rise of the Medici appear
nine balls.

Ballock.—See Halliwell in v.

Bally-bleeze. — Speaking of the
Cleveland word Bally-bleeze (a bonfire),
in his Glossary of that dialect, 1868, Mr.
Atkinson remarks: "It need scarcely be
added that any assumption of an etymological connection between the name Baal
and this word bally-bleeze must be groundless. Even in the Gaelic form *baltein,*
while *tein* is equivalent to our bleeze, Dan.
blysse, Sw. *blosse,* &c., I doubt if *bal* be
radically distinct from E. *bale,* Sw. *bal,*
&c. In other words, I do not for a moment
suppose the worship of Baal, any more
than that of Balder, or Apollo. or Phœbus, considered as persons with distinct
ethnic names, was intended in these bale-
fires. It was the worship of the Sun-god
simply, and his name not even hinted at
in that of the fire-rites involved."

Banbury Cross.—Halliwell, in his
Nursery Rhymes, prints two versions of
"Ride a Cock-horse," but does not give
the following. which was often repeated to
the present Editor, while he was on his
nurse's or mother's knee, with an action
suited to the words:

'Ride a cock-horse
To Banbury-Cross,
To see an old woman
Ride on a white horse.
Rings on her fingers,
And bells on her toes,
And she shall have music
Wherever she goes."

Which appears to indicate some custom in
cidental to Banbury Mop or Michaelmas
Statute Fair, where perhaps some female
character on horseback was one of the performers in a procession or sport. The suggestion is offered, that there was some
local imitation of the Godiva pageant.

Banks's Horse.—See Halliwell in
v. At Hereford Midsummer Fair, in 1640,
there was, it seems, a fellow, a second
Bankes, who exhibited a dancing horse;
for in the account book of Mrs. Joyce
Jeffries under this year occurs a payment
to him.—*Archæologia,* xxxvii.

Banns. — The following account of
this subject is derived from the information of my friend Mr. Yeowell: *Notes and
Queries,* 4th S. i., 149-50. "We learn
from Tertullian, *Ad Uxorem,* De Pudici-
tiâ, c. 4, that the Church, in the primitive
ages, was forewarned of marriages. The
earliest existing canonical enactment on
the subject, in the English Church, is that
in the 11th canon of the synod of Westminster or London, A.D. 1200, which en-
acts that 'no marriage shall be contracted
without banns thrice published in the
church, unless by the special authority of
the bishop.' Wilkins' *Concilia,* i., 507.
It is supposed by some that the practice
was introduced into France as early as the
ninth century; and it is certain that Odo,
Bishop of Paris, ordered it in 1176. The
council of Lateran, in 1215, prescribed it
to the whole Latin Church. Before pub-
lishing the banns, it was the custom for
the curate anciently to affiance the two
persons to be married in the name of the
Blessed Trinity; and the banns were sometimes published at vespers, as well as during the time of mass. In the early ballad
of *Robin Hood and Allen a Dale* we have a
curious reference to the banns, where the
bishop says, in answer to Robin:

"That shall not be, the bishop he said:
For thy word shall not stand;
They shall be three times askt in the
    church,
As the law is of our land."

Banyan Day.—See Davis, *Suppl.
Glossary,* 1881, in v.

Barbara, St.—(December 4). Although Nicholas, in his "Chronology of

History," on the authority of Arundel MS. 155, seems to indicate the existence of two saints of this name, I doubt if he is not in the present case making two persons out of one, and if St. Barbara of Heliopolis in Egypt, who is mentioned in the "Anniversary Calendar" as martyred in A.D. 306, and whose life is in the "Golden Legend," as well as in a separate biography printed by Julian Notary in 1518, where she is styled virgin and martyr, is not, in reality, the only canonized lady of this name. It was formerly the usage at York to preach a sermon in St. William's Chapel on St. Barbara's Day, and Davies, in his "Extracts from the Municipal Records of York," 1843, mentions a payment of two shillings to a Bachelor of Divinity for this purpose in 18 Edw. IV. "In time of thunder," remarks Aubrey (1678), "they invoke St. Barbara. So Chaucer, speaking of the great hostess, says that her guests would cry St. Barbara, when she let off her gun."

Barbers. — The sign of a barber's shop being singular, has attracted much notice. It is generally distinguished by a long pole, with coloured bandages depicted on it, instead of a sign. The true intention of that party-coloured staff, it is explained correctly in the "Antiquarian Repertory," was to shew that the master of the shop practiced surgery, and could breathe a vein as well as mow a beard: such a staff being to this day, by every village practitioner, put into the hand of a patient undergoing the operations of phlebotomy. The white band, which encompasses the staff, was meant to represent the fillet thus elegantly twined about it. In confirmation of this opinion the reader may be referred to the cut of the barber's shop in Comenii "Orbis pictus," where the patient under phlebotomy is represented with a pole or staff in his hand. And that this is a very ancient practice appears from an illumination in a missal of the time of Edward I. I find the following odd passage in Gayton: "The barber hath a long pole elevated; and at the end of it a labell, wherein is in a fair text hand written this word Money. Now the pole signifies itself, which joined to the written word makes Pole-money. There's the rebus, that Cut-bert is nobody without Pole-money. — *Festivous Notes*, 1654, p. 111. Lord Thurlow in his speech for postponing the farther reading of the Surgeons' Incorporation Bill, July 17th, 1797, to that day three months, in the House of Peers, stated " that by a statute still in force, the barbers and surgeons were each to use a pole. The barbers were to have theirs blue and white, striped, with no other appendage; but the surgeons', which was the same in other respects, was likewise to have a galley-pot and a red rag to denote the particular nature of their vocation."

Stephanus ridicules the " grosse ignorance " of the barbers: "This puts me in minde of a barber who after he had cupped me (as the physician had prescribed) to turn away a catarrhe, asked me if I would be sacrificed. Sacrificed? said I. Did the Phisition tell you any such thing? No (quoth he) but I have sacrificed many, who have bene the better for it. Then musing a little with myself I told him, Surely, Sir. you mistake yourself, you mean scarified. O Sir, by your favour (quoth he) I have ever heard it called sacrificing, and as for scarifying I never heard of it before. In a word I could by no means perswade him, but that it was the barber's office to sacrifice men. Since which time I never saw any man in a barber's hands, but that sacrificing barber came to my mind."— *World of Wonders*, transl. by R. C., 1607, p. 125. Rowlands, in his "Pair of Spy-Knaues," 1619, describes the humours of "A Fanatical Knaue," and pictures him giving directions to his servant:

" First to my barber, at his bason signe,
Bid him be heere to-morrow about nine."

As to the barber's chair and basin, see Nares, *Glossary*, 1859, in v., and under *Basin*, where it is shown that barbers' basins were hired by the mob, when any infamous person was carted, in order, by beating them ahead of the procession, to draw the attention of spectators. "The Barbers' Chaire," says Gabriel Harvey, in the *Trimming of Thomas Nash*, 1597, " *is the verie Royall-Exchange of newes*, barbers the head of all trades." He adds, a little farther on: "if they be happie, whom pleasure, profit, and honor make attaine to happiness. . . . if at home and happie, then barbers with great facilitie at worke, they are in pleasing conference; if idle, they pass that time in life-delighting musique." The beating down the barbers' basins on Shrove Tuesday, I have not found elsewhere than in Fennor's *Pasquils Palinodia*, 1619 :—

" It was the day of all deys in the yeare,
That unto Bacchus hath his dedication,
When mad-brained prentices, that no men feare,
O'erthrow the dens of bawdie recreation:
When tylors, cobblers, plaist'rers, smiths, and masons
And every rogue will beat down Barbers' basons,
Whereat Don Constable in wrath appeares,
And runs away with his stout halbardiers.

"It was the day whereon both rich and
poore
Are chiefly feasted with the self-same
dish,
When every paunch, till it can hold no
more,
Is fritter-fill'd, as well as heart can wish;
And every man and maide doe take their
turne,
And tosse their pancakes up for feare they
burne,
And all the kitchen doth with laughter
sound,
To see the pancakes fall upon the ground.

"It was the day when every kitchen
reekes,
And hungry bellies keepe a Jubile,
When flesh doth bid adieu for divers
weekes,
And leaves old ling to be his deputie.
It was the day when Pullen goe to block,
And every spit is fill'd with bellie timber,
When cocks are cudgel'd down with many
a knock,
And hens are thrasht to make them
short and tender;
When country wenches play with stoole
and ball,
And run at barly breake untill they fall."

The subsequent is from Greene's "Quip
for an upstart Courtier," 1592 : "Barber,
. . . when you come to poore Cloth-
breeches, you either cut his beard at your
own pleasure, or else, in disdaine, aske
him if he will be trimd with Christs cut,
round like the half of a Holland cheese,
mocking both Christ and us." In "Wits,
Fits, and Francis," 1595, we read : "A
gentleman gave a gentlewoman a fine
twisted bracelet of silke and golde, and
seeing it the next day upon another gentle-
womans wrist, said it was like a Barber's
girdle soon slipt from one side to
another." Steevens remarks : "It was
formerly part of a barber's occupation to pick the teeth and ears. So
in the "Trimming of Thomas Nashe,
Gentleman," 1597, Gabriel Harvey
says to his antagonist, who taunted
him (Harvey) with being the son of
a barber : "for thoughe (as I am a
ci urgian) I could pick your teeth for the
other stinkinge breath, yet this I durst
not meddle with"; and in Herod and
Antipater," 1622, Tryphon the barber
enters with a case of instruments, to each
of which he addresses himself separately :

"Toothpick, dear tooth-pick : ear-pick,
both of you
Have been her sweet companions !" &c.

Austin, in his poem entitled *Urania*, 1629,
seems to suggest that barbers sold books—
at all events popular ones ; for, speaking
of a volume of amatory or satirical productions, he writes that in either case :

" — this would take,
Eu'n like Tobacco, each Barbours shop
would make
A sale of it ——."

Gay, in his fable of the goat without a
beard, thus describes a barber's shop :

"His pole with pewter basons hung
Black rotten teeth in order strung,
Rang'd cups, that in the window stood,
Lin'd with red rags to look like blood,
Did well his threefold trade explain,
Who shav'd, drew teeth, and breath'd a
vein."

In the *British Apollo*, 1708, there is a
solution of the custom of combining the
two trades of barber and surgeon, which
has, perhaps, more humour than weight :

"In antient Rome, when men lov'd
fighting,
And wounds and scars took much de-
light in,
Man-menders then had noble pay,
Which we call surgeons to this day.
'Twas order'd that a huge long pole,
With bason deck'd, should grace the hole
To guide the wounded, who unlopt
Could walk, on stumps the others hopt : —
But, when they ended all their wars,
And men grew out of love with scars,
Their trade decaying ; to keep swimming,
They joyn'd the other trade of trimming ;
And on their poles to publish either
Thus twisted both their trades together."

In the North of England, within living
memory, the two callings of barber and
bookseller were occasionally united. Although it does not strictly belong to the
province of popular antiquities, it may be
useful to refer to the paper in Pegge's
Curialia, 1818, "on the Barber for the
King's most High and Dread Person."
There used to be in barbers' shops, hung
up against the wall, a thrift-box, into
which each customer was supposed to put
a trifle. Comp. *Curfew*.

Barguest, The or **Great Dog-
fiend.**—In Beaumont and Fletcher's
Thierry and Theodoret, i., 1, we have : —

"—— Let night-dogs tear me,
And goblins ride me in my sleep to jelly,
Ere I forsake my sphere."

In the North of England ghost is pronounced "guest." This appears to be an
offshoot or side-growth of the Nature-cult
prevalent among the Romans, and after
them among the Spaniards (*Current
Notes*, August, 1856, p. 72), and the word
barguest is evidently synonymous with the
Celtic baarge, which is still used for a sow
(the Roman *numen porcinum*), by the
peasantry of Exmoor. The streets of Newcastle-upon-Tyne were formerly, according to vulgar tradition, haunted by a
nightly guest, which appeared in the

shape of a mastiff dog, &c., and terri
fied such as were afraid of shadows.
This word is a corruption of the Anglo-
Saxon ᚱᚪᚾ, *spiritus*, *anima*. Brand heard,
when a boy, many stories concerning it.
The bar-guest is the "Rongeur d'Os" of
Norman folk-lore, and the boggart of Lancashire, both great dog-spirits, which
prowl about in the night time, dragging
heavy chains behind them. The authors
of "Lancashire Folk Lore," 1867, say:
"Near Blakeley, in Lancashire, is a
romantic spot, still known as the 'Boggart Hole,' the position of which may seem
to militate somewhat against Drake's etymology of Barguest—burh, a town, and
gast, a ghost, that is, a spirit haunting
towns. The fact is, however, that this
derivation is not at all likely to be correct
on other grounds, for the Lancashire and
Yorkshire boggart or barguest was, from
all the evidence we have, an ubiquitous
goblin, who did not restrict himself to any
particular localities." The appearance
of the barguest is still considered in Lancashire a "certain death sign," and "has
obtained the local names of Trash and
Skriker," say the authors of "Lancashire
Folk Lore." This dog-spirit may be the
malignant influence referred to under the
name of Fray-bug, in a curious extract
from a letter of Master Saunders to his
wife, 1555, printed in the "Dialect of
Craven," 1828. Under the name of boggle
this incubus or spirit is introduced into
the "Flyting Betwixt Montgomery and
Polwart," written about 1580. Sir Patrick Hume of Polwart is made to say
to Montgomery:

"Leaue boggles, brownies, gyr-carlings,
　　　and gaists;
Dastard, thou daffes, that with such
　　　divilrie mels."

Perhaps the Cleveland beeagle (a
scarecrow), the Whitby beagle (the
same), and the other Yorkshire forms
boggle, bogle, or bogill (same as bogie?)
boc, *beggar*, *bull beggar*, are merely
varieties of the boggart or barguest.
　　Gibbon says, in reference to Hun-
niades, Regent of Hungary, 1441-52. "By
the Turks, who employed his name to
frighten their perverse children, he was
constantly denominated Jancus-Lam, or
the Wicked. See farther, Lucas, *Studies
in Nidderdale*, pp. 145, *et seqq*; and Davis,
Suppl. Glossary, 1881, p. 39, and comp.
Richard Coeur de Lion.
　　Barley-break. — Jamieson, in his
"Etymological Dictionary," calls this "A
game generally played by young people in
a corn-yard. Hence called Barlabracks
about the stacks, S. B." (*i.e.* in the North
of Scotland.) "One stack is fixed on as
the dule or goal; and one person is appointed to catch the rest of the company

who run out from the dule. He does not
leave it till they are all out of his sight.
Then he sets off to catch them. Any one,
who is taken, cannot run out again with
his former associates, being accounted a
prisoner, but is obliged to assist his captor in pursuing the rest. When all are
taken, the game is finished; and he, who
was first taken, is bound to act as catcher
in the next game. This innocent sport
seems to be almost entirely forgotten in
the South of S. It is also falling into desuetude in the North." The following description of Barley Break, written by Sir
Philip Sidney, is taken from the Song of
Lamon in the "Arcadia," where he relates the passion of Claius and Strephon
for the beautiful Urania, and shews the
English practice:—

—"She went abroad, thereby,
At barley brake her sweet, swift foot to
　　try.
　　　*　　*　　*　　*　　*
A field they goe, where many lookers be.
　　　*　　*　　*　　*　　*
Then couples three be streight allotted
　　there,
They of both ends, the middle two doe flie:
The two that in mid-place Hell called
　　were,
Must striue with waiting foot and watch-
　　ing eye,
To catch of them, and them to Hell to
　　beare,
That they, as well as they Hell may
　　supplye;
Like some which seeke to salue their
　　blotted name
With others blot, till all doe taste of
　　shame.

There may you see, soon as the middle
　　two
Doe coupled towards either couple make,
They false and fearfull do their hands
　　vndoe;
Brother his brother, friend doth friend
　　forsake,
Heeding himselfe, cares not how Fellow
　　doe,
But if a stranger mutuall helpe doth take:
As periur'd cowards in aduersitie,
With sight of feare from friends to
　　fremb'd doe flie."

Another description of the sport occurs in
Barley-breake, or a Warning for Wantons,
1607:
"To barley-breake they roundly then 'gan
　　fall:
Raimon, *Euphema* had unto his mate:
For by a lot he won her from them all:
Wherefore young Streton doth his fortune
　　hate.

But yet ere long he ran and caught her
　　out,

And on the backe a gentle fall he gaue her.
It is a fault which iealous eyes spie out,
A maide to kisse before her iealous father.

Old Elpin smiles, but yet he frets within,
Euphema saith, she was vniusly cast,
She striues, he holds, his hand goes out,
    and in :
She cries, Away, and yet she holds him
    fast.

Till sentence giuen by another maid,
That she was caught, according to the law :
The voice whereof this ciuill quarrell staid,
And to his make each lusty lad 'gan draw.

Euphema now with Streton is in hell :
(For so the middle roome is alwaies cald)
He would for euer, if he might, there
    dwell ;
He holds it blisse with her to be inthrald.

The other run, and in their running
    change :
Streton 'gan catch, and then let goe his
    hold,
Euphema, like a Doe, doth swiftly range,
Yet taketh none, although full well she
    could.

And winkes on Streton, he on her 'gan
    smile,
And faine would whisper something in
    her eare.
She knew his mind, and bid him vse a wile,
As she ran by him, so that none did heare.

Some other pastimes then they would
    begin ;
And to locke hands one doth them all
    assummon.
Varietie is good in euery thing,
Excepting only Gods and earthly
    women."

Drayton introduces fairies playing at
this :

    " At barly-breake they play
    Merrily all the day,
    At night themselues they lay
    Vpon the soft leaues—"

This was perhaps rather a stretch of poetic licence. Suckling also has given the following description of this pastime with allegorical personages :

    " Love, Reason, Hate did once bespeak
    Three mates to play at barley-break.
    Love Folly took, and Reason Fancy ;
    And Hate consorts with Pride, so dance
        they ;
    Love coupled last, and so it fell
    That Love and Folly were in Hell.

    The break ; and Love would Reason
        meet,
    But Hate was nimbler on her feet ;
    Fancy looks for Pride, and thither
    Hies, and they two hug together :
    Yet this new coupling still doth tell
    That Love and Folly were in Hell.

The rest do break again, and Pride
Hath now got Reason on her side ;
Hate and Fancy meet, and stand
Untouch'd by Love in Folly's hand ;
Folly was dull, but Love ran well,
So Love and Folly were in Hell."

Barly-break is several times alluded to in Massinger's Plays. The subsequent is from Herrick, p. 34 :

    " *Barly-Break* ; or, *Last in Hell.*
    We two are last in hell : what may we
        feare
    To be tormented, or kept pris'ners here :
    Alas, if kissing be of plagues the worst,
    We'll wish, in hell we had been last and
        first."

Comp. Nares, *Glossary*, 1859, in v. *Barli-break.*

Barnabas, St. — In the Churchwardens' account of St. Mary at Hill, London, 17 and 19 Edward IV., the following entry occurs : " For Rose-garlondis and woodrove garlondis on St. Barnebes' Daye, xjd." And, under the year 1486 : " Item, for two doss' di bocse garlands for prestes and clerks on Saynt Barnabe daye, js. xd." Under 1512 occurs : " Recd. of the gadryng of the Maydens on St. Barnabas' Day, vi. s. viijd." And among the disbursements of 1512 we have : " Rose-garlands and lavender, St. Barnarbas, i.s. vjd." In the same accounts, for 1509, i.s. the following : " For bred, wine, and ale, for the singers of the King's Chapel, and for the clarks of this town, on St. Barnabas, i.s. iijd." Collinson, speaking of Glastonbury, tells us, that, " besides the Holy Thorn, there grew in the Abbey Church-yard, on the north side of St. Joseph's Chapel, a miraculous walnut tree, which never budded forth before the feast of St. Barnabas, viz. the eleventh of June, and on that very day shot forth leaves, and flourished like its usual species. This tree is gone, and in the place thereof stands a very fine walnut tree of the common sort. It is strange to say how much this tree was sought after by the credulous ; and, though not an uncommon walnut, Queen Anne, King James, and many of the nobility of the realm, even when the times of monkish superstition had ceased, gave large sums of money for small cuttings from the original." The original tree was mentioned in the metrical Life of Joseph of Arimathea, 1520 :

    " Great meruaylles men may se at
        Glastenbury
    One of a walnot tree that there doth
        stande
    In the holy grounde called the semetery
    Hard by ye place where Kynge Arthur
        was foude
    South fro Iosephs Chapell it is walled
        in roude

It bereth no leaues tyll the day of Saynt
  Barnabe,
And than that tree that standeth in the
  grounde
Sproteth his leaues as fayre as any other
  tree."

And Manningham, in his *Diary*, May 2,
1602, speaking of Glastonbury, says:
"There is a walnut-tree which hath no
leaues before Barnabies Day in June, and
then it beginns to bud, and after becomes
as forward as any other." The diarist
was indebted for this piece of intelligence
to a friend. According to the old style,
this was Midsummer Day, and hence came
the proverb:

"Barnaby bright, Barnaby bright
The longest day and the shortest night."

Barnaby bright is the popular name of
the lady-bird in some localities, probably
from this insect being seen more about St.
Barnabas' Day than at any other. For
two other curious particulars relative to
this day the reader may be referred to the
"Book of Days (June 11)."

Barnacles. — Suaverius refers to
barnacles in his MS. Diary (1535), giving
an account of English and Scotish
customs, &c. : There are trees (he
says) in Scotland from which birds
are produced : he is told it is undoubtedly true ; those birds which fall
from the trees into water become animated, but those which fall to the ground
do not ; the figures of birds are found in
the heart of the wood of the trees and on
the root ; the birds themselves (which are
very delicate eating) do not generate.
"There are," (says Gerarde, in his
"Herbal," edit. 1597, p. 1391) "in the
North parts of Scotland certaine trees,
whereon do grow shell-fishes, &c., &c.,
which, falling into the water, do become
fowls, whom we call Barnakles, in the
North of England Brant Geese, and in
Lincolnshire Tree Geese," &c. It seems
hardly conceivable that so gross an error
in natural history could so long have prevailed, as that the barnacle, a well known
kind of shell-fish, which is found sticking
on the bottom of ships, should when
broken off become a species of goose. Yet
old writers of the first credit in other respects have fallen into this mistaken and
ridiculous notion : and we find no less an
authority than Holinshed gravely declar-
ing that with his own eyes he saw the
feathers of these barnacles "hang out of
the shell at least two inches."

"That Scottish barnacle, if I might
  choose,
That of a worme doth waxe a winged
  goose."
                    Hall's *Virgid.* iv. 2.

"———Like your Scotch barnacle, now
  a block,
Instantly a worm, and presently a great
  goose."
                    Marston's *Malcontent*, 1604.

"My meal hath done. Avoided for the
  nonce :
I wrong the devil should I lick their
  bones.
That fall is his ; for when the Scots
  decease,
Hell, like their nation, feeds on
  barnacles.
A Scot, when from the gallows-tree got
  loose,
Drops into Styx, and turns a Scotland
  goose."
                    Cleveland's *Rebel Scot*, 1647.

The best account of these mythical
creatures is to be found in Drayton's
Polyolbion, Song xxvii.

Barnwell Fair.—The reputation of
this Fair does not seem to have been very
good in Heywood's time, for in his "If
you know not me," &c., 1605, that writer
makes Hobson say :

"Bones a me, knave, thou'rt welcome.
  What's the news
At bawdy Barnwell, and at Stourbridge
  fair?"

The place was so called, says the editor of
"England's Gazeteer," 1751, (enlarged
from Adams' "Index Villaris," 1690),
"from the wells of children or bearns, because they used to meet here for sport on
St. John's Eve ; so that it came at last to
be what is now called Midsummer Fair."
It is to be concluded that the deplorable
fire which, in 1727, committed dreadful
havoc among the spectators at a puppet-
show in a barn, happened at this season.
The scene of one of Scogin's jests is laid
at Barnwell Fair.

Barring Out.—See *Bromfield* and
Eton. But the usage does not seem to
have been limited to these places.

Bartholomew Baby.——In describing "a zealous brother," Braithwaite
says : "No season through all the yeere
accounts hee more subject to abhomina-
tion than Bartholomew faire : their drums,
hobbihorses, rattles, babies, iewtrumps,
nay pigs and all, are wholly Iudaicall."
The roasted pigs at St. Bartholomew's
Fair are also noticed in "Poor Robin's
Almanack" for 1677. "Poor Robin" for
1695 has this passage : "It also tells farmers what manner of wife they shall
choose, not one trickt up with ribbens and
knots like a Bartholomew Baby, for such
an one will prove a Holy-day wife, all
play and no work,

And he who with such kind of wife is
sped,
Better to have one made of ginger-
bread."
—*Whimzies*, 1631, p. 300.

In Nabbes's "Totenham Court," 1638, p.
47, is the following: "I have pack't her
up in't, like a Bartholomew-babie in a
boxe. I warrant you for hurting her."

**Bartholomew, St., the
Apostle.**—(August 24).

[⁴ "Ða wæs ſe eahtoða dæg þæs kalendes
Septembres, þe man au þa tid wurðað Sæ
Bartholomei þæs apoſtoles, þa ſe eadiga mer
Guðlac com to þære foreſprecenan ſtowe, to
Cruwlande."—*Anglo-Saxon Verſion of the Life
of St. Guthlac*, ed. Goodwin, p. 22-4.]

Gough mentions an ancient custom at
Croyland Abbey, of giving little knives to
all comers on St. Bartholomew's Day.
This abuse, he says, "was abolished by
Abbot John de Wisbech, in the time of
Edward the Fourth, exempting both the
abbot and convent from a great and need-
less expence. This custom originated in
allusion to the knife, wherewith St. Bartholomew was flayed. Three of these knives
were quartered with three of the whips so
much used by St. Guthlac in one coat
borne by this house. Mr. Hunter had
great numbers of them, of different sizes,
found at different times in the ruins of the
abbey and in the river. We have engraved
three from drawings in the Minute Books
of the Spalding Society, in whose drawers
one is still preserved. These are adopted
as the device of a town-piece, called the
'Poores Halfepeny of Croyland,' 1670."—
History of Croyland Abbey, p. 73. In
Stephens' "Essayes and Characters,"
1615, we read: "Like a booksellers shoppe
on Bartholomew Day at London: the stalls
of which are so adorn'd with Bibles and
Prayer-bookes, that almost nothing is left
within, but heathen knowledge."

Bartholomew Fair.—In a tract
entitled, "Bartholomew Faire or variety
of fancies," 1641, occurs this account:
"Bartholomew Faire begins on the twenty-
fourth day of August, and is then of so
vast an extent, that it is contained in no
less than four several parishes, namely
Christ Church, Great and Little St. Bar-
tholomewes, and St. Sepulchres. Hither
resort people of all sorts and conditions.
Christ Church cloisters are now hung full
of pictures. It is remarkable and worth
your observation to beholde and heare
the strange sights and confused noise in
the faire. Here, a knave in a fooles coate,
with a trumpet sounding, or on a drumme
beating, invites you to see his puppets:
there, a rogue like a wild woodman, or in
an antick shape like an Incubus, desires
your company to view his motion: on the
other side, hocus pocus, with three yards
of tape, or ribbin, in's hand, showing his
art of legerdemaine, to the admiration and
astonishment of a company of cocko-
loaches. Amongst these, you shall see a
gray goose-cap, (as wise as the rest), with
a what do ye lacke, in his mouth, stand in
his boothe, shaking a rattle, or scraping
on a fiddle, with which children are so
taken, that they presentlie cry out for
these fopperies: and all these together
make such a distracted noise, that you
would thinck Babell were not comparable
to it. Here there are also your gamesters
in action: some turning of a whimsey,
others throwing for pewter who can
quickly dissolve a round shilling into a
three halfepeny saucer. Long Lane at
this time looks very faire, and puts out her
best cloaths, with the wrong side outward,
so turn'd for their better turning off:
and Cloth Faire is now in great request:
well fare the alehouses therein, yet better
may a man fare, (but at a dearer rate)
in the Pig-Market, alias Pasty-Nooke, or
Pye-Corner, where pigges are al houres of
the day on the stalls piping hot, and would
cry (if they could speak), ' come eate me.'
The fat greasy hostesse in these houses instructs Nick Froth, her tapster, to aske
a shilling more for a pig's head of a
woman big with child, in regard of her
longing. than of another ordinary cumer.
Some of your cutpurses are in fee with
cheating costermongers, who have a trick,
now and then, to throw downe a basket of
refuge peares, which prove choake-peares
to those that shall loose their Hats or
Cloakes in striving who shall gather
fastest.

Now farewell to the Faire: you who are
wise,
Preserve your purses, whilst you please
your eyes."

The pickpockets and cutpurses did not
spare anyone. In "A Caveat for Cutpurses," a ballad of the time of Charles
I., there is the following illustration:

"The players do tell you, in Bartholomew
Faire,
What secret consumptions and rascals
you are;
For one of their actors, it seems had the
fate
By some of your trade to be fleeced of
late."

Gayton says in his *Art of Longevity*, 1659,
p. 3:
—"(As if there were not Pigg enough)
Old Bartholomew with purgatory fire,
Destropes the Babe of many a doubtfull
Sire."

And speaking of plums, he adds:
"If eaten as we use at Barthol'mew tide,
Hand over head, that's without care or
guide,
There is a patient sure."

Pepys, under date of August 25, 1663, says: "It seems this Lord Mayor (Sir John Robinson) begins again an old custome, that upon the three first days of Bartholomew Fayre, the first. there is a match of wrestling, which was done, and the Lord Mayor there and the Aldermen in Moorfields yesterday: second day. shooting; and to-morrow hunting. And this officer of course is to perform this ceremony of riding through the City. I think to proclaim or challenge any to shoot. It seems that the people of the fayre cry out upon it, as a great hindrance to them." Sir John Bramston, in his *Autobiography*, p. 315, under the date of 1688, refers to the annual custom by which the Lord Mayor proclaimed St. Bartholomew Fair on that Saint's Eve, and riding past Newgate was accustomed to receive from the keeper or governor a cup of sack. In *Wit and Drollery*, 1682, p. 227, we have:

"Now London Mayor, in Saddle new :
Rides into fair of Bartholomew :
He twirles his Chain, and looketh big,
As he would fright the head of Pig :
Which gaping lies on greasy stall —"

Ladies were fond of attending Bartholomew Fair. In a little work printed in 1688, it is observed: "Some women are for merry-meetings, as Bessus was for duck; they are ingaged in a Circle of Idleness, where they turn round for the whole year, without the interruption of a serious hour, they know all the players names & are intimately acquainted with all the booths in Bartholomew Fair. — *The Lady's New Year's Gift, or Advice to a Daughter*, p. 187. In 1711, an attempt was made without success to extend the duration of the fair to fourteen days. and a tract was published and specially addressed by the author to the civic authorities, to oppose and denounce the project. It is said, on the authority of Mrs. Piozzi, that, during a whole year, Andrew Johnson, the doctor's uncle, kept the ring here, where the boxing and wrestling took place, and was not once beaten. Perhaps his nephew inherited from him his burly appearance. In *Current Notes* for February. 1851. are some memoranda by Theodore Hook, from a copy of Ackermann's *Microcosm of London*, in one of which he notes the occupation of the site of Bartholomew Fair by *Billingsgate Market*. Charles Lamb, in one of his letters to Coleridge, speaks of the Wordsworths being in town, and of his having been their guide over the Fair. in September. 1802. Rimbault, in his "Book of Songs and Ballads," 1851, has printed from rare musical works two or three ballads illustrative of the old usages and scenes at Bartholomew Fair. The entertainments appear, from all accounts, to have been of

the most various description, with a view, doubtless, to the satisfaction of every taste. The puppet-shows and drolls included St. George and the Dragon, Guy of Warwick, Judith and Holofernes, Robin Hood (an opera). the Quaker's Opera, Susanna and the Elders, Dives and Lazarus, Punchinello, The Devil and the Pope, and the Whore of Babylon. The character of the performances at Bartholomew Fair, a little later on, seems to have been singularly heterogeneous; for Strutt quotes a bill of the beginning of the eighteenth century. which announces that, "at Heatly's booth, over against the Cross Daggers, will be presented a little opera, called The old creation of the world, newly reviv'd, with the addition of the glorious battle obtained over the French and Spaniards by his Grace the Duke of Marlborough." During the reign of George II., the class of entertainment changed somewhat, if we are to judge from the contents of the "Stroler's Pacquet Opened," 1741, which purports to be a collection of the drolls played at Southwark and other fairs at that time. These pieces, sufficiently contemptible in their construction, were. in most cases, formed out of old dramas. Down to the year 1854 it was customary for the representative of the Merchant Taylors' Gild to proceed to Cloth Fair, which immediately joined Bartholomew Fair, and test the measures used for selling cloth there by the Company's silver yard. This very ancient practice expired with the institution. Hazlitt's *Livery Companies of London*, 1892, p. 280, where a facsimile of the yard is engraved. For a more particular account of this fair the reader may be referred to *Memoirs of Bartholomew Fair*, by the late Professor Morley, 8v., 1859. with illustrations by Fairholt. Also see Hone's *Every Day Book*, i., 1572. *Robin Hood* and the *Quaker's Opera* were printed in 1730 and 1728 respectively with the music.

Basil.—In the second part of the *Secrets of Alexis of Piedmont*, translated by W. Warde, 1563, there is this entry: "*To make that a woman shall eate of nothing that is set vpon the table.* "Take a little grene Basil. & when men bring the dishes to the table, pvt it vnderneth them, yt the woman perceiue it not: for men saye that she will eate of none of that which is in the dishe where vnder the Basill lieth." The family of aromatic plants, so-called, has long been recognized among the Hindoos as of virtue in protection from malaria, like the Australian eucaliptus, and from the attack of the mosquito, and their great or supposed efficacy in either case was naturally very important in tropical regions unprovided with other safeguards from contagion with masses of decayed animal and vegetable refuse.

Basilisk.—See *Cockatrice.*

Basset.—In a MS. song purporting to proceed from a lady of honour in Queen Flizabeth's days, the supposed speaker, enumerating her virtues and claims to respectful remembrance, says:

"I never bought cantharides,
Ingredient good in Passett,
Nor ever stript me to my stayes
To play ye Punt att Bassett."

Sir Samuel Tuke, in the *Adventures of Five Hours*, 1671, an adaptation from Calderon, speaks of the chairmen as engaged *a las pintas*, the same game as this, where Diego is made to say:

They are deeply engaged
A las pintas, and will not leave their game,
They swear, for all the dons in Seville.
—Hazlitt's Dodsley, xv. 265.

Bastard.—A species of wine. Compare examples from old writers in Nares, *Glossary*, 1859, in v.

Bats.—Willsford supplies this item of intelligence: "Bats, or flying mice, come out of their holes quickly after sunset, and sporting themselves in the open air, premonstrates fair and calm weather." *Nature's Secrets*, 1658, p. 134. Compare *Weather Omens.*

Battledore or **Shuttle-cock.**—It is as old as the fourteenth century. Skelton has the expression, "Not worth a shyttle cocke." Strutt, in his "Sports and Pastimes," illustrates it by a drawing of that period lent to him by Douce. Manningham, in his Diary, Feb. 1602-3, notes: "The play at shuttlecocke is become soe much in request at Court, that the making shuttlecocks is almost growne to a trade in London." Manningham relates an odd anecdote in connection about Lady Effingham. Armin, in the "Two Maids of More-Clacke," 1609, says: "To play at shuttlecock methinkes is the game now." It was a favourite amusement with Prince Henry, who died in 1612. In his "Horæ Vacivæ," 1646, Hall observes: "Shittle-Cock requires a nimble arme, with a quick and waking eye; 'twere fit for students, and not so vehement as that waving of a stoole, so commended by Lessius." A somewhat similar amusement is mentioned in the *Journal of the Asiatic Society* for 1835, as followed in Bengal. The game is now known as Battledore and Shuttlecock, and is almost exclusively a juvenile recreation, though it is sometimes played by grown-up persons in the country on wet indoor days. Stevenson, in his *Twelve Months*, 1661, under October, says: "The Shuttle-cock and Battledore is a good house exercise,

and occupies the Lady before she be drest."

Battle Royal.—See *Cock-Fighting.*

Bawdry..—Wallis, in his essays on the Privileges of the University of Oxford," printed in "Collectanea Curiosa," notices that by a charter of 37 Hen. VI. the Chancellor had the power of banishing to a distance of not more than ten miles all whores, and of imprisoning them if they returned. The subsequent extract from a proclamation of Henry VIII., April 13, year 37, will be thought curious: "Furthermore his Majesty straightlie chargeth and commandeth that all such Householders as, under the name of Baudes, have kept the notable and marked Houses, and knowne Hosteries, for the said evill disposed persons, that is to saie, such Householders as do inhabite the Houses whited and painted, with Signes on the front, for a token of the said Houses, shal avoyd with bagge and baggage, before the feast of Easter next comyng, upon paine of like punishment, at the Kings Majesties will and pleasure." The punishment for this offence was riding in a cart through the parish where it was committed, and sometimes through the adjoining ones also, with a paper attached to the back or front of the dress, descriptive of the particulars, and a basin ringing before them to draw the attention of the people to their disgrace. Occasionally the culprit went on horseback. The examples given by Stowe and others of this class of chastisement are not only very numerous; but we cannot fail to be struck by the great frequency of cases, where parents were guilty of the crime towards their own offspring, and of the respectable position of many of those who were implicated. The publication of the delinquency on a sheet of paper pinned to the person was common to many other crimes, such as perjury, &c., but then it seems to have been more usually fixed over the culprit's head. In 1560-1 a woman who had sold fish contrary to law, was led about London on horseback by the beadle of Bridewell with a garland on her head, strung with these fish, and others hanging from the saddle, both before and behind her. In Strype's edition of Stow, 1720, Book i. p. 258, we read, that in the year 1555, "An ill woman, who kept the Greyhound in Westminster, was carted about the city, and the Abbot's servant (bearing her good will) took her out of the cart, as it seems, before she had finisht her punishment, who was presently whipped at the same cart's tail for his pains." In 1556, "were carted two men and three women. One of these men was a bawd, for bringing women to strangers. One of the women kept the Bell in Gracechurch

Bull beside London-stone; both bawds and whores." In 1559, "The wife of Henry Glyn, goldsmith, was carted about London for "being bawd to her own daughter." It is remarked with much probability in a Note upon Dekker's "Honest Whore," that it was formerly a custom for the Peace-officers to make search after women of ill-fame on Shrove-Tuesday, and to confine them during the season of Lent. So, Sensuality says in Nabbes' masque of "Microcosmus," act 5: "But now welcome a Cart or a Shrove-Tuesday's tragedy." Overbury, in his "Characters," speaking of "a *Maquerela*, in plaine English, a bawde," says: "Nothing daunts her so much as the approach of Shrove-Tuesday." *Ibid.*, speaking of "a roaring boy," he observes, that "he is a supervisor of brothels, and in them is a more unlawful reformer of vice than prentices on Shrove-Tuesday." In Dekker's play of "Match Me in London," Bilbo says, "I'll beate down the doore, and put him in mind of Shrove-Tuesday, the fatall day for doores to be broke open." The punishment of people of evil fame at this season seems to have been one of the chief sports of the apprentices. In a *Satyre against Separatists*, 1642, we read :

"——— ——— The Prentises—for they
Who, if upon Shrove-Tuesday, or May-
    Day,
Beat an old Bawd or fright poor Whores
    they could,
Thought themselves greater than their
    Founder Lud, . . .
They'r mounted high, contemn the humble
    play.
Of Trap or Football on a Holiday
In Finesbury-fieldes—"

Bay-Tree. — Parkinson writes: "The Bay-leaves are necessary both for civil uses and for physic, yea, both for the sick and for the sound, both for the living and for the dead. It serveth to adorne the House of God as well as man — to crowne or encircle, as with a garland, the heads of the living, and to sticke and decke forth the bodies of the dead: so that, from the cradle to the grave, we have still use of it, we have still need of it." *Paradisus Terrestris*, 1629, p. 426. In "A strange Metamorphosis of Man," &c., 1634, it is observed, that "hee (the Bay) is fit for halls and stately roomes, where if there be a wedding kept, or such like feast, he will be sure to take a place more eminent then the rest. He is a notable smell-feast, and is so good a fellow in them, that almost it is no feast without him. He is a great companion with the Rosemary, who is as good a gossip in all feasts as he is a trencher-man." Among death omens the withering of bay trees was, according to

Shakespear, reckoned one. Thus in Richard II :
    "'Tis thought the King is dead; we
        will not stay.
The bay trees in our country are
        all wither'd—"
Upon which Steevens observes that "Some of these prodigies are found in Holinshed, 'In this yeare, in a manner throughout all the realme of England, old Baie Trees withered, &c.'" This we also learn from Lupton, "Neyther falling sycknes, neyther devyll, will infest or hurt one in that place whereas a bay tree is. The Romaynes calle it the Plant of the good Angell," &c. Sir Thomas Browne observes that the Christian custom of decking the coffin with bay is a most elegant emblem. It is said that this tree, when seemingly dead, will revive from the root, and its dry leaves resume their wonted verdure. William Browne, in a sonnet to Cœlia, evidently alludes to some ancient love-omen or portent, still current in his time, in connexion with the rind of the laurel :

"Fair Laurell, that the onelye witnes
    art
To that discourse, which vnderneath thy
    shade
Our griefe swolne brests did lovinglie
    impart
With vowes as true as ere Religion
    made :
If (forced by our sighs) the flame shall
    fly
Of our kinde love, and get within thy
    rind,
Be warye, gentle Baye, & shrieke not
    bye,
When thou dost such vnusuall feruor
    finde."
Hazlitt's edit. ii., 288.

Beadsmen.—See *Blue-Gowns*.
Beans, Religious use of.—The choosing of a person King or Queen by a bean found in a piece of a divided cake, was formerly a common Christmas gambol at the English and Scotish Courts, and in both English Universities. "Mos inolevit et viget apud plurimas nationes, ut in profesto Epiphaniæ, seu trium Regum, in quaque familia seu alia Societate, sorte vel alio fortuito modo eligant sibi Regem, et convivantes unà ac genialiter viventes, bibente rege, acclamant: Rex, bibit, bibit Rex, indicta multa qui non clamaverit." See the "Sylva Sermonum jucundissimorum," 8vo. Bas. 1568, pp. 73, 246.— *Douce*. In Ben Jonson's "Masque of Christmas," the character of Baby-Cake is attended by "an Usher bearing a great cake with a bean and a pease." These beans, it should seem from the following passage in Burton's "Anatomy of Melancholy" were hallowed. He is enumerat-

ing Popish superstitions: "Their Breviaries, Bulles, hallowed beans, Exorcisms, Pictures, curious Crosses, Fables, and Bables." Democritus to the Reader, p. 29. edit. fol. Oxf. 1632. Bale, in his "Yet a Course at the Romysh Foxe," &c. Signat. L. 11, attributes to Pope Euticianus, "the blessynge of Benes upon the Aultar."

In the "Anniversary Calendar," there is an amusing extract from Teonge's "Diary" (1676), giving an account of a cake they made on board his ship off the Morea. He (Teonge) says: "The cake was cut into several pieces, and all put into a napkin, out of which every one took his piece, as out of a lottery, then each piece was broken to see what was in it, which caused much laughter to see our lieutenant prove the cuckold." Probably the piece which contained the bean is referred to. In "A World of Wonders," 1607, a translation by R. C from H. Stephanus, "Apologie d'Herodote," there are some curious extracts from the "Quadragesimale Spirituale," 1565. Thus, chap. 2: "After the sallad (eaten in Lent at the first service) we eate fried Beanes, by which we understand confession. When we would have beanes well sodden, we lay them in steepe, for otherwise they will never seeth kindly. Therefore, if we purpose to amend our faults, it is not sufficient barely to confesse them at all adventure, but we must let our confession lie in steepe in the water of Meditation." "And a little after: We do not use to seeth ten or twelve beanes together, but as many as we mean to eate: no more must we let our confession steepe, that is, meditate, upon ten or twelve sinnes onely, neither for ten or twelve dayes, but upon all the sinnes that ever we committed, even from our birth, if it were possible to remember them." Chap. 3: "Strained Pease (Madames) are not to be forgotten. You know how to handle them so well, that they will be delicate and pleasant to the tast. By these strained pease our allegorizing flute pipeth nothing else but true contrition of heart." "River-water, which continually moveth, runneth, and floweth, is very good for the seething of pease. We must (I say) have contrition for our sins and take the running water, that is, the teares of the heart, which must runne and come even into the eyes." The soft beans are much to our purpose: why soft, but for the purpose of eating? Thus our peas on this occasion are steeped in water. In the "Roman Calendar," I find it observed on this day, that "a dole is made of soft beans." I can hardly entertain a doubt but that our custom is derived hence. It was usual amongst the Romanists to give away beans in the doles at funerals: it was also a rite in the funeral ceremonies of heathen Rome. Why we have substituted peas I know not, unless it was because they are a pulse somewhat fitter to be eaten at this season of the year. They are given away in a kind of dole at this day. Our popish ancestors celebrated (as it were by anticipation) the funeral of our Lord on Care Sunday, with many superstitious usages, of which this only, it should seem, has travelled down to us. Durandus tells us, that on Passion Sunday "the Church began her public grief, remembering the mystery of the Cross, the vinegar, the gall, the reed, the spear," &c. Among the "Cries of Paris," a poem composed by Guillaume de Villeneuve in the thirteenth century, and printed at the end of the poem printed by Barbazan. *Ordene de Chevalerie*, beans for Twelfth Day are mentioned: "Gastel à feve orrois crier." There is a very curious account in Le Roux, *Dictionnaire Comique*, tom. ii., p 431, of the French ceremony of the "Roi de la Feve," which explains Jordaen's fine picture of "Le Roi boit." Bufalde de Verville "Palais des Curieux," edit. 1612, p. 90. See also Pasquier, Recherches de la France, p. 375. To the account given by Le Roux of the French way of choosing King and Queen, may be added, that in Normandy they place a child under the table, which is covered in such a manner with the cloth that he cannot see what he is doing; and when the cake is divided, one of the company, taking up the first piece, cries out, "Fabe Domini pour qui?" The child answers, "Pour le bon Dieu:" and in this manner the pieces are allotted to the company. If the bean be found in the piece for the "bon Dieu," the King is chosen by drawing long or short straws. Whoever gets the bean chooses the King or Queen, according as it happens to be man or woman. Urquhart of Cromarty says, ("Discovery of a most exquisite jewel, &c." 1651, p. 237): "Verily, I think they make use of Kings—as the French on the Epiphany-day use their Roy de la fehve, or King of the Bean; whom after they have honoured with drinking of his health, and shouting aloud "Le Roy boit, Le Roy boit," they make pay for all the reckoning; not leaving him sometimes one peny, rather than that the exorbitancie of their debosh should not be satisfied to the full." And elsewhere (Stephan. , World of Wonders, transl. by R. C. p. 189), we read of a Curate, "who having taken his preparations over evening, when all men cry (as the manner is) the King drinketh, chanting his Masse the next morning, fell asleep in his Memento: and when he awoke, added with a loud voice, The King drinketh."

There is a great deal of learning

in Erasmus's Adages concerning the religious use of beans, which were thought to belong to the dead. An observation which he gives us of Pliny, concerning Pythagoras's interdiction of this pulse, is highly remarkable. It is "that beans contain the souls of the dead." For which cause also they were used in the Parentalia. Plutarch also, he tells us, held that pulse to be of the highest efficacy for invoking the manes. Ridiculous and absurd as these superstitions may appear, it is yet certain that our Carlings deduce their origin thence. Erasmi Adag. in "A fabis abstineto, Edit. fol. Aurel. Allob. 1606, p. 1906; and Spencer "De Legibus Hebræorum," lib. i. p. 1154. But the latter seems to have thought that the reason for the Pythagorean doctrine was the use of beans and other vegetables at funeral repasts, and their consequent pollution. In the Lemura, which was observed the 9th of May, every other night for three times, to pacify the ghosts of the dead, the Romans threw beans on the fire of the altar to drive them out of their houses. There were several religious uses of pulse, particularly beans, among the Romans. Hence Pliny says, "in eâdem peculiaris Religio." Thus in Ovid's "Fasti," B. v. l. 435, where he is describing some superstitious rites for appeasing the dead:

"Quumque manus puras fontana pro-
 luit unda;
Vertitur, et nigras accipit ore fabas.
Aversusque jacit: sed dum jacit, Hæc-
 ego mitto
His, inquit, redimo meque meosque
 fabis."

Thus also in Book ii. l. 575:

"Tum cantata ligat cum fusco licia
 plumbo:
Et septem nigras versat in ore fabas."

Bear the Bell, To.—A writer in the "Gentleman's Magazine" says: "A bell was a common prize: a little golden bell was the reward of victory in 1607 at the races near York; whence came the proverb for success of any kind, 'to bear away the bell.'" Lord North alludes to this custom:

"Jockey and his horse were by their
 Master sent
To put in for the Bell——
Thus right, and each to other fitted
 well,
They are to run, and cannot misse the
 Bell."

Forest of Varieties, 1645, p. 175. Another old writer remarks: "Whoever bears the bell away, yet they will ever carry the clapper." *Paradoxical Assertions*, by R. H., 1664, p. 4.

Bear-Baiting. — Bear-baiting appears anciently to have been one of the Christmas sports with our nobility. "Our nobility," says Pennant, in the "Zoology," "also kept their bear-ward. Twenty shillings was the annual reward of that officer from his lord, the fifth Earl of Northumberland, 'when he comyth to my Lorde in Cristmas, with his Lordshippes beestes for making of his Lordschip pastyme the said twelve days.'" Gilpin, in his "Life of Cranmer," tells us: "Bear baiting, brutal as it was, was by no means an amusement of the lower people only. An odd incident furnishes us with the proof of this. An important controversial manuscript was sent by Archbishop Cranmer across the Thames. The person entrusted bade his waterman keep off from the tumult occasioned by baiting a bear on the river before the King; he rowed however too near, and the persecuted animal overset the boat by trying to board it. The manuscript, lost in the confusion, floated away, and fell into the hands of a priest, who, by being told that it belonged to a Privy Counsellor, was terrified from making use of it, which might have been fatal to the head of the Reformed Party." In a Proclamation "to avoyd the abhominable place called the Stewes," dated April 13, 37 Hen. 8, we read as follows: "Finallie to th' intent all resort should be eschued to the said place, the Kings Majestie straightlie chargeth and comaundeth that from the feast of Easter next ensuing, there shall noe beare-baiting be used in that Rowe, or in any place on that side the Bridge called London Bridge, whereby the accustomed assemblies may be in that place clearly abolished and extinct, upon like paine as well to them that keepe the beares and dogges, whych have byn used to that purpose, as to all such as will resort to see the same." Accompanying Lily the grammarian's *Antibossicon*, an attack on Whittinton the grammarian, printed in 1521, is a woodcut, three times repeated, of a bear worried by six dogs. Maitland, in his *Early Printed Books at Lambeth*, 1843, pp. 316-18, has done his best to explain the allegory and the origin of the terms. In Laneham's "Letter from Kenilworth," 1575, we have the following curious picture of a bear-baiting, in a letter to Mr. Martin, a mercer of London:—

"Well, syr, the Bearz wear brought foorth intoo the Coourt, the dogs set too them, too argu the points eeuen face to face; they had learned counsell allso a both partz: what may they be counted parciall that are retaind but to a syde? I ween no. Very feers both ton and toother & eager in argument: if the dog in pleadyng woold pluk the bear by the throte, the bear with trauers woold claw him again by the skalp ; confess & a list, but a voyd a coold not that waz bound too the bar : And hiz coounsell tolld him that it coold bee too him no pollecy in pleading. Thearfore thus with fending and proouing, with plucking and tugging, skratting and byting, by plain tooth & nayll a to side & toother, such exspés of blood & leather waz thear between them, az a moonths licking I ween wyl not recoouer ; and yet remain az far oout az euer they wear.

"It was a Sport very pleazaunt of theez beastz ; to see the bear with his pink nyez leering after hiz enmiez approoch, the nimbleness & wayt of ye dog to take hiz auauntage, and the fors & experiens of the bear agayn to auoyd the assaults : if he war bitten in one place, hoow he woold pynch in an oother to get free : that if he wear taken onez, then what shyft, with byting, with clawyng, with rooring, tossing & tumbling, he woold woork to wynd hym self from them : and when he waz lose, to shake his earz twyse or thryse wyth the blud and the slauer aboout his fiznamy, waz a matter of a goodly releef." In Vaughan's "Golden Grove," 1600, we are told : "Famous is that example which chanced neere London, A.D. 1583, on the 13th Daye of Januarie being Sunday, at Paris Garden, where there met together (as they were wont) an infinite number of people to see the beare-bayting, without any regard to that high Day. But, in the middest of their sports, all the scaffolds and galleries sodainely fell downe, in such wise that two hundred persons were crushed well nigh to death, besides eight that were killed forthwith." In *The Merry Wives of Windsor*, Shakespear makes Slender speak of a bear-baiting as "meat and drink" to him, while Anne Page says she is afeard of it. In "The Life of the reverend Father Bennet of Canfilde," Douay, 1623, p. 11, is the following passage : "Even Sunday is a day designed for beare bayting and even the howre of theyre (the Protestants) service is allotted to it, and indeede the tyme is as well spent at the one as at the other." R. R. was at least an honest Catholic ; he does not content himself with equivocal glances at the erroneous Creed, but speaks out plainly.

Bear's Cubs.—Thomas Vaughan, otherwise *Eugenius Philalethes*, observes : "I shall here gainsay that gross opinion, that the whelps of bears are, at first littering, without all form or fashion, and nothing but a little congealed blood on lump of flesh, which afterwards the dam shapeth by licking, yet is the truth most evidently otherwise, as by the eye-witenss

of Joachimus Rheticus, Gesner and others, it hath been proved. And herein, as in many other fabulous narrations of this nature (in which experience checks report) may be justly put that of Lucretius thus rendered by Vaughan :—

" ' What can more certain be than sense Discerning truth from false pretence.' "

Brief Natural History, 1669, p. 87. Browne places this among his "Vulgar Errors ;" but Ross, in his "Medicus Medicatus," affirms that "the bears send forth their young ones deformed and unshaped to the sight, by reason of the thick membrane in which they are wrapt, which also is covered over with so mucous and flegmatick matter, which the dam contracts in the winter time, lying in hollow caves, without motion, that to the eye it looks like an unformed lump. This mucosity is licked away by the dam, and the membrane broken, and so that which before seemed to be informed, appears now in its right shape. This is all that the antients meant, as appears by Aristotle, who says that in some manner the young Bear is for a while rude and without shape."

Beaulieu, Witch of.— See *Mary Dore*.

Beaver. "The Bever," observes Vaughan, "being hunted and in danger to be taken, biteth off his stones, knowing that for them his life only is sought, and so often escapeth : hence some have derived his name, Castor, *a castrando seipsum ;* and upon this supposition the Egyptians in their hierogliphics, when they will signify a man that hurteth himself, they picture a bever biting off his own stones, though Alciat in his emblems turns it to a contrary purpose, teaching us by that example to give away our purse to theeves, rather than our lives, and by our wealth to redeem our danger. But this relation touching the bever is undoubtedly false, as both by sense and experience, and the testimony of Dioscorides, lib. iii. cap. 13, is manifested. First, because their stones are very small, and so placed in their bodies as are a bore's, and therefore impossible for the bever himself to touch or come by them : and secondly, they cleave so fast unto their back, that they cannot be taken away, but the beast must of necessity lose his life, and consequently most ridiculous is their narration who likewise affirm that when he is hunted, having formerly bitten off his stones, he standeth upright, and sheweth the hunters that he hath none for them, and therefore his death cannot profit them, by means whereof they are averted, and seek for another."—*Brief Natural History*, p. 89. An early essayist refers to this belief without seeming to question the accuracy of it. "The beauer, when hee heares the houndes, he knows for what they hunt, and immediately to secure his skinne, he biteth of his stones. Nature hath taught both it and vs how to preserve ourselves—." —Tuvill's *Essays*, 1609, I. 3 *verso*.

Bed.—Ady says: "It appeareth still among common silly country people, how they had learned charms by tradition from Popish times, for curing cattel, men, women, and children; for churning of butter, for baking their bread, and many other occasions; one or two whereof I will rehearse only, for brevity. An old woman in Essex, who was living in my time, she had also lived in Queen Maries time, had learned thence many Popish charms, one whereof was this; every night when she lay down to sleep she charmed her bed, saying:

'Matthew, Mark, Luke, and John,
The bed be blest that I lye on;'

and this would she repeat three times, reposing great confidence therein, because (as she said) she had been taught it, when she was a young maid, by the Church-men of those times. — *Candle in the Dark*, 1659, p. 58. This idea may have had its germ in St. John's Gospel, xx., 12. In Cornwall, an experiment was once made on some poor, who were coaxed with great difficulty into confessing what they said the last thing before they got into bed, and it was a varied and extended form of the above, namely:

"Matthew, Mark, Luke, and John,
Bless the bed that I lie on.
Four Angels around my bed.
One to foot, and one to head,
And two to carry me when I'm dead."

Bede's-Well.—About a mile to the west of Jarrow (near Newcastle-upon-Tyne), there is a well still called Bede's Well, to which, as late as the year 1740, it was a prevailing custom to bring children troubled with any disease or infirmity; a crooked pin was put in, and the well laved dry between each dipping. My informant has seen twenty children brought together on a Sunday, to be dipped in this well, at which also, on Midsummer Eve, there was a great resort of neighbouring people, with bonfires, music, &c.—Brand's *Newcastle*, ii., 54.

Bedfellow.—Men used formerly to sleep together, even those of rank, as Henry V. and Lord Scroop, and it was so abroad. We find Charles VIII. of France and the Duke of Orleans occupying the same bed. See Hazlitt's *Venetian Republic*, 1900, ii., 43. Compare an interesting note in Nares, 1859 in v., Halliwell's *Dict.*, 1860, in v. and *Span Counter*, *infrâ*.

Bedlamer.—Bedlamer was a name for a Fool. He used to carry a horn. Quære, if thence the expression "hornmad." See Braithwaite's "Boulster Lecture," 1640, p. 242. Comp. *Tom of Bedlam*.

Bedlam Beggars.—See Halliwell in v.

Beer. — "A booke howe to brewe all sortes of beere,' was licensed at Stationers' Hall in 1591, but is not at present known. See Hazlitt's *Bibl. Coll.* Gen. Index, *Beer*, *Gallobelgicus*, *Wine*, *and Y-Worth*. Three halfpenny beer and single beer are mentioned in the Churchwardens' and Chamberlain's Accounts of Kingston, Surrey, 24 Hen. VII., and provided for the entertainment at the King-Game and Robin Hood. A kilderkin of each cost together 2s. 4d. The term *Doctor Double Ale* is applied to a dissolute person in a poem printed by Hazlitt (*Popular Poetry*, iii., 296, *et seqq.*) The subjoined passage seems to be nothing more than an alliteration intended to convey a complete devotion to beer—he wants nothing but the ale-tap and toast, till he is laid under the turf:

"Call me the sonne of Beere, and then confine
Me to the tap, the tost, the turfe; let wine
Ne'er shine upon me."

Hesperides, 1648, p. 87. Comp. Halliwell's *Dict.* in v. Putting a cold iron bar upon the barrels, to preserve the beer from being soured by thunder, has been noticed in another section. This is particularly practiced in Kent and Herefordshire.

Bees.—A vulgar prejudice prevails in many places of England that when bees remove or go away from their hives, the owner of them will die soon after. A clergyman in Devonshire informed Mr. Brand, about 1790, that when a Devonian makes a purchase of bees, the payment is never made in money, but in things, corn for instance, to the value of the sum agreed upon. And the bees are never removed but on a Good Friday. In "The Living Librarie," translated by John Molle, 1621, we read: "Who would beleeve without superstition (if experience did not make it credible), that most commonly all the bees die in their hives if the master or mistress of the house chance to die, except the hives be presently removed into some other place. And yet I know this hath hapned to folke no way stained with superstition." Hilman observes, respecting bees: "The tinkling after them with a warming pan, frying pan, or kettle, is of good use to let the neighbours know you have a swarm in the air, which you claim wherever it lights; but I believe of very little purpose to the reclaiming the bees, who are thought to delight in no noise but their own."—*Tusser Redivivus*, 1710, ed. 1744, p. 42. I found the followin the "Argus," a London newspaper, Sept. 13, 1790: "A superstitious custom prevails at every funeral in Devonshire, of turning round the beehives that belonged to the deceased, if he had any, and that at the moment the corpse is carrying out of the house. At a funeral some time since at Cullompton, of a rich old farmer, a laughable circumstance of this sort occurred: for just as the corpse was placed in the herse, and the horsemen, to a large number, were drawn up in order for the procession of the funeral, a person called out, 'Turn the bees,' when a servant who had no knowledge of such a custom, instead of turning the hives about, lifted them up, and then laid them down on their sides. The bees, thus hastily invaded, instantly attacked and fastened on the horses and their riders. It was in vain they galloped off, the bees as precipitately followed, and left their stings as marks of their indignation. A general confusion took place, attended with loss of hats, wigs, &c., and the corpse during the conflict was left unattended; nor was it till after a considerable time that the funeral attendants could be rallied, in order to proceed to the interment of their deceased friend." The necessity of inviting bees to the funeral of their late owner, having previously apprised them of his decease, and of clothing the hive in mourning, is a very common and familiar superstition still, or at least very recently, cherished in many parts of England. The correspondents of "Notes and Queries" have contributed to assemble very numerous examples of its existence. The bees are thought to have a prescience of the death of their master; but formal notice of the event, and a summons or request to serve his successor, are thought to be essential to the preservation and welfare of the insects.

Beggar my Neighbour. — A well-known simple game at cards, where the two players divide the pack, and the winner is the one, who succeeds in getting the majority of court cards, especially knaves. Whether Taylor, the water-poet, intended the allusion to it in his *Motto*, 1621, seriously, he cites it there. And see Davis, *Suppl. Glossary*, 1881, in v.

Beggar's Bush Fair.—This was a fair held at Rye in Sussex on St. Bartholomew's Day, by virtue of a charter granted in 1290 by Edward I. It was not originally appointed for that date, but was altered to it in 1305; the mayor used to be chosen on the same anniversary. Beggar's Bush lay just above the hospital grounds; the fair was limited to stalls kept by small pedlars, and has been long discontinued. While it lasted the lord of the manor of Brede claimed, through his steward, a trifling fee from each stall-keeper by way of nominal rent; but he ceased to attend in consequence of having been once roughly handled, and driven out of the place. A ring which, so late as 1878, was still to be seen in a field near the King's Head Inn, was the last memento of the practice of bull-baiting, formerly usual on this occasion. The last bull-baiting is said to have been about 1808. It seems very probable that Beaumont and Fletcher's play of *Beggar's Bush*, printed in the folio of 1647, but acted as early as 1622, was so called from the locality near Rye, as Fletcher was a Rye man.

Beggar's Clack-Dish. — The beggars, it is observable, two or three centuries ago, used to proclaim their want by a wooden dish with a moveable cover, which they clacked, to shew that their vessel was empty. This appears from a passage quoted on another occasion by Grey. Grey's assertion may be supported by the following passage in Middleton's "Family of Love," 1608:—

"*Ger.* —can you think I get my living by a bell and a clack-dish?

Dryfat. By a bell and a clack-dish? How's that?

Ger. Why, by begging, Sir," &c.

And by a stage direction in the second part of Heywood's "Edward IV." 1600: "Enter Mrs. Blague, poorly drest, begging with her basket and clap-dish."

Belfry.—Election of a mayor there. See *Brightlingsea*.

Bell, Book, and Candle. — The solemn form of excommunication under the Romish Church.—See Nares, 1859, in v.

Bell Corn.—A small perquisite belonging to the clerk of certain parishes in North Wales. Pennant's *Whiteford and Holywell*, 1796, p. 100. It seems to have been connected with the service for ringing the Passing and other bells.

Bellman.—See Nares, *Glossary*, 1859, in v., where his function in blessing sleepers as he passed their doors on his round, is noticed.

Bellman of the Dead.—Till the middle of the 18th century, a person called the Bell-man of the Dead went about the streets of Paris, dressed in a deacon's robe, ornamented with deaths' heads, bones, and tears, ringing a bell, and exclaiming, "Awake, you that sleep! and pray to God for the dead!" This custom prevailed still longer in some of the provinces, where they permitted even the trivial parody, "Prenez vos femmes, embrassez-les."— *Voyageur à Paris*, i., 71.

Bells.—It is well known that before the present principles of horology were established, a clock was nothing more than a piece of striking machinery, moved first by hydraulic pressure, and afterward by the action of a bell. Hence in German, Anglo-Saxon, French, and other languages the same word stood, and still stands, for a bell and for a clock. Hazlitt's *Venetian Republic*, iv., 344-6. The ancients had some sort of bells. I find the word "Tintinnabula," which we usually render bells, in Martial, Juvenal, and Suetonius. The Romans appear to have been summoned by these, of whatever size or form they were, to their hot baths, and to the business of public places. In the account we have of the gifts made by St. Dunstan to Malmesbury Abbey, it appears that bells were not very common in that age, for he says the liberality of that prelate consisted chiefly in such things as were then wonderful and strange in England, among which he reckons the large bells and organs he gave them. An old bell at Canterbury took twenty-four men to ring it; another required thirty-two men *ad sonandum*. The noblest peal of ten bells, without exception, in England, whether tone or tune be considered, is said to be in St. Margaret's Church, Leicester. When a full peal was rung, the ringers were paid *pulsare Classicum*. Durandus tells us that, "when any one is dying, bells must be softly tolled, that the people may put up their prayers: twice for a woman and thrice for a man: if for a clergyman, as many times as he had orders, and at the conclusion a peal on all the bells, to distinguish the quality of the person for whom the people are to put up their prayers. A bell, too, must be rung while the corpse is conducted to church, and during the bringing it out of the church to the grave." This seems to account for a custom still preserved in the North of England, of making numeral distinctions at the conclusion of this ceremony: *i.e.*, nine knells for a man, six for a woman, and three for a child, which are undoubtedly the vestiges of this ancient injunction of popery.—*Rationale*, lib. i., c. 4. It appears from an account of Killin parish, co. Perth, printed in the end of the 18th century, in Sinclair's *Statistical Account*, that at that time there was a bell "belonging to the Chapel of St. Fillan, that was in high reputation among the votaries of that Saint in old Times. It seems" (says the writer) "to be of some mixed metal. It is about a foot high, and of an oblong form. It usually lay on a grave-stone in the Church-yard. When mad people were brought to be dipped in the Saint's Pool, it was necessary to perform certain ceremonies, in which there was a mixture of Druidism and Popery. After remaining all night in the Chapel, bound with ropes, the bell was set upon their head with great solemnity. It was the popular opinion that, if stolen, it would extricate itself out of the thief's hands, and return home, ringing all the way." It is added: "For some years past this bell has been locked up, to prevent its being used for superstitious purposes. It is but justice to the Highlanders to say that the dipping of mad people in St. Fillan's pool and using the other ceremonies, was common to them with the Lowlanders. "The origin of the bell," pursues the author of the above narrative, "is to be referred to the most remote ages of the Celtic Churches, whose ministers spoke a dialect of that language. Ara Trode, one of the most antient Icelandic historians, tells us, in his second chapter, that when the Norwegians first planted a colony in Ireland, about the year 870, 'Eo tempore erat Islandia silvis concreta, in medio montium et littorum: tum erant hic viri Christiani, quos Norwegi Papas appellant: et illi peregre profecti sunt ex eo quod nollent esse hic cum viris Ethnicis, et relinquebant post se Nolas et Baculos: ex illo poterat discerni quod essent viri Christiani.' Nola and Bajula both signify handbells. Far in the 19th century it is curious to meet with things which astonished Giraldus, the most credulous of mortals, in the 12th. St. Fillan is said to have died in 649. In the tenth year of his reign, Robert the Bruce granted the Church of Killin in Glendochart, to the Abbey of Inchaffray, on condition that one of the canons should officiate in the Kirk of Strathfillan." The bell of St. Mura, or Muranus, which long belonged to the Abbey of Mabian, near Innisbowen, c. Donegal, founded in the 7th century, during the reign of Abodle Slaine, was said to have descended from Heaven, ringing loudly, but that as it approached the earth, the tongue detached itself, and returned whence it came, till the bronze object was deposited in some holy receptacle. This bell was regarded with peculiar veneration by the local peasantry, and especially as a medium for mitigating the pains of childbirth. It was eventually sold to the late Lord Londesborough, and is figured (the size of the original) in *Miscellanea Graphica*, 1857, plate xxx. See some curious particulars upon the subject of bells in Spelman's "History of Sacrilege," p. 284, *et seq*. I find the following monkish rhymes on bells in "A Helpe to Discourse," edit. 1633, p. 63:

"En ego Campana, nunquam denuntio vana,
Laudo Deum verum, Plebem voco, congrego Clerum,
Defunctos plango, vivos voco, fulmina frango,
Vox mea, vox vitæ, voco vos ad sacra venite.
Sanctos collaudo, tonitrua fugo, funera claudo,
Funera plango, fulgura frango, Sabbatha pango:
Excito lentos, dissipo ventos, paco cruentos."

Misson, in his "Travels," says: "Ringing of bells is one of their great delights, especially in the country. They have a particular way of doing this; but their chimes cannot be reckoned so much as of the same kind with those of Holland and the Low Countries." By the will of a mercer of London, named Donne, deposited in the Hustings Court, the tenor bell of Bow Church, Cheapside, used long to be rung every day at six o'clock in the morning and eight in the evening. Mr. Tanswell has furnished the following extracts from the Churchwardens' Books of Lambeth:—"1579. Payd for making the great clapper to a smithie in White Chapel, it waying xxxi. lb. et dim. at vid. the pounde, 15s. 9d. 1598. Item, the olde great belle that was broken in the time of Roger Wynslo, Rychard Sharpe, and John Lucas, churchwardens, in 1598, did contain in weighte xiiii. cwt. one quarter, and xxii. lb. 1623. Payd for ryngynge when the Prince came from Spain, 12s. 1630. June 27. To the ryngers the day the Prince was baptized, 3s. 1633. October 15. Payd for ryngynge on the Duke's birthday, 7s 1705. Ap. 10. Gave the ringers when the siege of Gibraltar was raised, 15s."—*History of Lambeth*, p. 108. Du Cange quotes an authority to shew that in the time of Charles IV. of France, 1378, the ringing of bells was recognized as a royal salutation, and Kennett seems to establish that in this country it used, in the fifteenth century at least, to be looked upon as an affront to a bishop if the bells were not set in motion on his approach to any town within his diocese. — *Continuator Nangii*, Anno 1378, Kennett MS., A.D., 1444, quoted by Ellis. In "Articles to be inquired of within the Archdeaconry of Yorke (any year till 1640), I find the following: "Whether there be any within your parish or chapelry that use to ring bells superstitiously upon any abrogated holiday, or the eves thereof." The custom of rejoicing with bells on high festivals, Christmas Day, &c., is derived to us from the times of popery. The ringing of bells on the arrival of emperors, bishops, abbots, &c., at places under their own jurisdiction was also an old custom. Whence we seem to have derived the modern compliment of welcoming persons of consequence by a cheerful peal. In the Churchwardens' Account of Waltham, 34 Hen. VIII. there is this: "Item. paid for the ringing at the Prince his coming, a Penny." In similar accounts for St. Laurence's Parish, Reading, is the following article under 1514. "It. payd for a galon of ale, for the ryngers, at the death of the Kyng of Scots, ijd." The rejoicing by ringing of bells at marriages of any consequence, is every where common. On the fifth bell at the church of Kendal in Westmoreland is the following inscription, alluding to this usage:

"In Wedlock bands,
All ye who join with hands
Your hearts unite;
So shall our tuneful tongues combine
To laud the nuptial rite."

Nicolson and Burn's *Westmoreland and Cumberland*, i., 620. "I remember once that in the dead time of the night there came a country-fellow to my uncle in a great haste, intreating him to give order for knocking the bells, his wife being in labour, (a thing usual in Spain), my good curate then waked me out of a sound sleep, saying, Rise, Pedro, instantly, and ring the bells, for child-birth, quickly quickly. I got up immediately, and as fools have good memories, I retained the words quickly, quickly, and knocked the bells so nimbly, that the inhabitants of the town really believed it had been for fire."—*The Lucky Idiot*, transl. from Quevedo, 1734, p. 13. The small bells which are seen in ancient representations of hermitages were most probably intended to drive away evil spirits. On the ringing of bells for this purpose, much may be collected from Magius "de Tintinnabulis." Brand writes: "Durandus would have thought it a prostitution of the sacred utensils, had he heard them rung, as I have often done, with the greatest impropriety, on winning a long main at cock-fighting. He would, perhaps, have talked in another strain, and have represented these aërial enemies as lending their assistance to ring them. In 1461 is a charge in the Churchwardens' Accounts of Sandwich for bread and drink for "ryngers in the gret Thanderyng." In "The Burnynge of Paules Church in London," 1561, we find enumerated, among other Popish superstitions: "ringing the hallowed belle in great tempestes of lightninges." Aubrey says: "At Paris when it begins to thunder and lighten, they do presently ring out the great bell at the Abbey of St. Germain, which they do believe makes it cease. The like was wont to be done heretofore in Wiltshire. When it thundered and lightened, they did ring St. Adhelm's bell at Malmesbury Abbey. The curious do say that the ringing of bells exceedingly disturbs spirits." *Miscellanies*, p. 148. Our forefathers, however, did not entirely trust to the ringing of bells for the dispersion of tempests, for in 1313 a cross, full of reliques of divers saints, was set on St. Paul's steeple to preserve from all danger of tempests. In 1783, Frederic II. of Prussia prohibited the ringing of bells on such occasions.—*News-letter* of Nov. 3, 1783, cited by Brand.—Hering advises that "the bells in cities and townes be rung often, and the great ordnance discharged; thereby the aire is purified.—*Certain Rules for this time of Pestilential Observance*, 1625. In Googe's translation of Naogeorgus, we have the following lines on the subject:

" If that the thunder chaunce to rore, and
    stormie tempest shake,
A wonder is it not for to see the wretches
    how they quake,
Howe that no fayth at all they have, nor
    trust in any thing,
The Clarke doth all the bells forthwith at
    once in steeple ring:
With wond'rous sound and deeper farre,
    than he was wont before,
Till in the loftie heavens dark, the thunder bray no more.
For in these christned belles they thinke,
    doth lie such powre and might
As able is the tempest great, and
    storme to vanquish quight.
I sawe myself at Naumburg once, a towne
    in Toring coast,
A belle that with this title bolde hirself
    did proudly boast:
By name I Mary called am, with sound I
    put to flight
The thunder-crackes and hurtfull stormes,
    and every wicked spright.
Such things when as these belles can do,
    no wonder certainlie
It is, if that the Papistes to their tolling
    alwayes flie.
When haile, or any raging storme, or tempest comes in sight,
Or thunder boltes, or lightning fierce, that
    every place doth smight."
The popular rhyme of *Oranges and*

Lemons, in connection with church bells is too well known for repetition; but we are told that there was in the eighteenth century a notice at Chiswick that from the music of the bells there could be made out " My dun cow has just calved." Sir Richard Phillips, *Walk from London to Kew*, 1817, p. 212. The bells of our early churches, as well as the general

fabrics, were under the supervision of the consistory court of the diocese. On the 24th October, 1617, the parochial authorities at Stratford-on-Avon were cited to appear at Worcester to answer a charge of having allowed the Church of the Holy Trinity and its bells to fall out of repair. *Extracts by J. O. Halliwell from the Vestry Book of the Church of the Holy Trinity*, 1865, p. 19.

The large kind of bells, now used in churches, are said to have been invented by Paulinus, Bishop of Nola, in Campania, whence the *Campana* of the lower Latinity, about the 400th year of the Christian æra. Two hundred years afterwards they appear to have been in general use in churches. Mr. Bingham, however, thinks this a vulgar error; and at the same time he informs us of an invention before bells of convening religious assemblies in monasteries: it was going by turns to every one's cell, and with the knock of a hammer calling the monks to church. This instrument was called the Night Signal and the Wakening Mallet. In many of the colleges at Oxford, the Bible-clerk knocks at every room door with a key to waken the students in the morning, before he begins to ring the chapel bell. A vestige, it should seem, of the ancient monastic custom. The Jews used trumpets for bells. The Turks do not permit the use of them at all: the Greek Church under their dominion still follows their old custom of using wooden boards, or iron plates full of holes, which they hold in their hands and knock with a hammer or mallet, to call the people together to church. Durandus tells us, " In festis quæ ad gratiam pertinent, Campanæ tumultuosius tinniunt et prolixius concrepant."—*Rationale*, lib. i. cap. 4, p. 12. At Venice and elsewhere, in the beginning of the fourteenth century, we find bells employed in lieu of clocks, and the hours of the day and night were divided and notified by this process. A decree of the Venetian Council of Ten in 1310, ordered, " that no person whosoever shall be suffered without special licence to walk abroad *after the third bell of the night*. Hazlitt's *Venetian Republic*, 1900, ii., 606. But this was part of an exceptional restriction, as it was during an acute political crisis.

China has been remarkably famous for its bells. Father Le Comte tells us, that at Pekin there are seven bells, each of which weighs one hundred and twenty thousand pounds. Comp. Ditchfield's *Old English Customs*, 1896, ch. xv.

Bells, Baptism of.—Bells were a great object of superstition among our ancestors; each of them was represented to have its peculiar name and virtues, and many are said to have retained great affection for the churches to which they belonged and where they were consecrated. When a bell was removed from its original and favourite situation, it was sometimes supposed to take a nightly trip to its old place of residence, unless exercised in the evening, and secured with a chain or rope.—Warner's *Hampshire*, ii., 162. In an Italian *Ordinale* of the fifteenth century, one of the miniatures represents the blessing of the bell by the bishop, or prelate, attended by his clergy, and by a person who wears a beard, and carries his cap in hand—apparently a lay attendant. The bell is laid on a cushion or ottoman and is apparently of large dimensions. The presiding dignitary holds the service-book before him, and reads from it the service, which follows in the text; he invokes the divine blessing on the water with which the bell is to be baptised. Egelrick, Abbot of Croyland, about the time of King Edgar, cast a ring of six bells, to all which he gave names, as Bartholomew, Bethlehem, Turketul, &c. The Historian tells us his predecessor Turketul had led the way in this fancy. The superstition is one which we find indicated in the "Beehive of the Romish Church," a compilation by George Gilpin, 1579, and which was followed in many other places at a later period, particularly at Winchester and at Christ-Church, Oxford. In the churchwardens' accounts of St. Laurence's Parish Reading, anno 14 Hen. VII., is the following article: "It. payed for halowing of the bell named Harry, vjs. viijd. and ovir that Sir Willm Symys, Richard Clech, and Maistres Smyth, beyng Godfaders and Godmoder at the Consecracyon of the same bell, and beryng all oth' costs to the Suffrygan." Coates, *Hist. of Reading*, i., 214. Pennant, speaking of St. Wenefride's Well, (in Flintshire), says: "A bell belonging to the Church was also christened in honour of her. I cannot learn the names of the gossips, who, as usual, were doubtless rich persons. On the ceremony they all laid hold of the rope; bestowed a name on the bell; and the priest, sprinkling it with holy water, baptized it in the name of the Father, &c., &c.; he then cloathed it with a fine garment. After this the gossips gave a grand feast, and made great presents, which the priest received in behalf of the bell. Thus blessed it was endowed with great powers, allayed (on being rung) all storms; diverted the thunder-bolt: drove away evil spirits. These consecrated bells were always inscribed." The inscription on that in question ran thus:

"Sancta Wenefreda, Deo hoc commendare memento,
Ut pietate sua nos servet ab hoste cruento."
And a little lower was another address:
"Protege prece pia quos convoco, Virgo Maria."

"The following ceremonies," observes Mr. Tanswell, "were formerly used at the baptism of bells:—1, the bell must be first baptized before it may be hung in the steeple; 2, the bell must be baptized by a bishop or his deputy; 3, in the baptism of the bell there is used holy water, oil, salt, cream, &c.; 4, the bell must have godfathers, and they must be persons of high rank; 5, the bell must be washed by the hand of a bishop; 6, the bell must be solemnly crossed by the bishop, 7, the bell must be anointed by the bishop: 8, the bell must be washed and anointed in the name of the Trinity; 9, at the baptism of the bell they pray literally for the bell. The following is part of the curious prayers used at the above ceremony:

"'Lord, grant that whatsoever this holy bell, thus washed and baptized and blessed, shall sound, all deceits of Satan, all danger of whirlwind, thunder and lightning, and tempests, may be driven away, and that devotion may increase in Christian men when they hear it. O Lord, pour upon it thy heavenly blessing, that when it sounds in thy people's ears they may adore thee; may their faith and devotion increase; the devil be afraid and tremble, and fly at the sound of it. O Lord, sanction it by thy Holy Spirit, that the fiery darts of the devil may be made to fly backwards at the sound thereof, that it may deliver us from the danger of wind, thunder, &c., and grant, Lord, that all that come to the church at the sound of it may be free from all temptations of the devil.'"—*History of Lambeth*, 1858, p. 105. In the *Diary* of the Abbé Legrix of Saintes, under 1781, we read:—January 4. After High Mass, the blessing of a bell, weighing about 6 cwt., took place. M Delaage, the Dean, performed the ceremony, at which all the Canons and the under-choir assisted. M. le Marquis de Monconseil and Madame la Comtesse de la Tour du Pin were *godfather and godmother.—Antiquary* for 1898, p. 268. The following is from the programme of the ceremony of the blessing of the new bells in St. Mary's Roman Catholic Church, Newport:—"The ancient and solemn rite of blessing bells is full of meaning, and very expressive. The Bishop, vested with mitre and crozier, begins by intoning the l. Psalm, 'Miserere mei Deus,' followed by the liii., lvi., lxvi., lxix., lxxxv. and cxxix. Psalms, which he recites aloud together with his clergy These psalms are expressive of confidence in obtaining the protection of Almighty God when invoked by prayer, and it is especially the object of the benediction service to ask of God to manifest his power against the spirits of wickedness, whenever these bells shall be sounded. The Bishop next proceeds to bless water, with which, according to apostolic tradition, salt is mingled; and with this water the bells are washed inside and out, and wiped afterwards with a linen cloth—hence, no doubt, has arisen the incorrect expression of baptism of bells. While this is being done, seven psalms of praise are recited, and then the bells are anointed, first with the oil used for the sick and dying, and afterwards with holy chrism, such as is used to anoint bishops, priests and kings. After anointing each bell the bishop prays: 'Grant, we beseech Thee, O Lord, that this vessel, moulded for Thy Church, be sanctified by the Holy Suirit, so that the faithful may by its tolling be invited to their reward. And when its melodious notes sound in the ears of the people, let their faith and devotion increase; let every snare of the enemy, rattling hail, rushing whirlwinds, &c.—be driven to a distance; let Thy mighty right hand lay the powers of the air low,' &c. When the bells have been blessed, the Bishop places a burning thurible with incense underneath each bell, whilst the lxxxxvi. Psalm is recited. The whole ceremony is concluded by a deacon chanting a portion of the holy Gospel." Baronius informs us that Pope John XIII., in 968, consecrated a very large new cast bell in the Lateran Church, and gave it the name of John. This would be almost contemporary with the case in England above-mentioned.

Ringing the bells backwards was anciently a practice to which the authorities of towns, &c., resorted as a sign of distress, or as an alarm to the people. Hazlitt's *Popular Poetry*, 1864-6, ii., 153, note. The custom has escaped the notice of our popular antiquaries. Cleveland, in his "Poems," 1669, employs the term metaphorically. It was also the usage in some districts of Italy, and in other parts of the Continent, to ring the church-bells backward, when a fire broke out, in order to summon assistance, as every one on such an occasion was formerly, and is indeed still, in many places (particularly in Switzerland and Sweden) bound to lend his aid. That the practice is of considerable antiquity may be inferred from the fact that it is mentioned in the "Gesta Romanorum," and in the old ballad-poem of "Adam Bel, Clym of the Clough," &c., when the outlaws came to Carlisle to release Cloudesley, it is said:

"There was many an oute horne in Carlyll blowen,
And the belles bacewarde did they ring."

Beltein.—In Sinclair's "Statis. Acc. of Scot." vol. iii. p. 105, the Minister of Loudoun in Ayrshire tells us: "The custom still remains amongst the herds and young people to kindle fires in the high grounds, in honour of Beltan. Beltan, which in Gaelic signifies Baal, or Bels Fire, was anciently the time of this solemnity. It is now kept on St Peter's Day. The minister of Callander in Perthshire reported in 1794, as follows: "The people of this district have two customs, which are fast wearing out, not only here, but all over the Highlands, and therefore ought to be taken notice of, while they remain. Upon the first day of May, which is called Beltan, or Bàl-tein-day, all the boys in a township or hamlet meet in the moors. They cut a table in the green sod, of a round figure, by casting a trench in the ground of such a circumference as to hold the whole company. They kindle a fire, and dress a repast of eggs and milk in the consistence of a custard. They knead a cake of oatmeal, which is toasted at the embers against a stone. After the custard is eaten up, they divide the cake into so many portions, as similar as possible to one another in size and shape, as there are persons in the company. They daub one of these portions all over with charcoal, until it be perfectly black. They put all the bits of the cake into a bonnet. Every one, blindfold, draws out a portion. He who holds the bonnet is entitled to the last bit. Whoever draws the black bit is the devoted person, who is to be sacrificed to Baal, whose favour they mean to implore, in rendering the year productive of the sustenance of man and beast. There is little doubt of these inhuman sacrifices having been once offered in this country as well as in the East, although they now pass from the act of sacrificing, and only compel the devoted person to leap three times through the flames; with which the ceremonies of the festival are closed." Sinclair's *Statis. Acc. of Scotland*, vol. xi. The minister of Logierait, in Perthshire, says: "On the first of May, O.S. a festival called Beltan is annually held here. It is chiefly celebrated by the cowherds, who assemble by scores in the fields to dress a dinner for themselves, of boiled milk and eggs. These dishes they eat with a sort of cakes baked for the occasion, and having small lumps, in the form of nipples, raised all over the surface, The cake might, perhaps, be an offering to some deity in the days of Druidism." Pennant's account of this rural sacrifice is more minute. He tells us that, on the first of May, in the Highlands of Scotland, the herdsmen of every village hold their bel-tein. "They cut a square trench in the ground, leaving the turf in the middle; on that they make a fire of wood, on which they dress a large caudle of eggs, butter, oatmeal, and milk, and bring, besides the ingredients of the caudle, plenty of beer and whisky: for each of the company must contribute something. The rites begin by spilling some of the caudle on the ground, by way of libation: on that, every one takes a cake of oatmeal, upon which are raised nine square knobs, each dedicated to some particular being, the supposed preserver of their flocks and herds, or to some particular animal, the real destroyer of them. Each person then turns his face to the fire, breaks off a knob, and, flinging it over his shoulders, says:—'This I give to thee, preserve thou my horses;' 'This to thee, preserve thou my sheep;' and so on. After that, they use the same ceremony to the noxious animals. 'This I give to thee, O fox! save thou my lambs'; 'this to thee, O hooded crow;' 'this to thee, eagle!' When the ceremony is over, they dine on the caudle; and, after the feast is finished, what is left is hid by two persons deputed for that purpose; but on the next Sunday they re-assemble, and finish the reliques of the first entertainment." Comp. *Ireland* and *St. John's Eve.*

Benchers.—The designation of the governing bodies or committees at Lincoln's Inn and the two Temples. At Gray's Inn they are termed Ancients, and at Clifford's Inn they were known as Rules. The Bench was originally and formerly, and is still by strict right, an elective assembly chosen from the whole constituency; but of recent years it has gradually and tacitly converted a merely temporary and fiduciary power into an absolute one, and spends the revenue of the Inn, and controls its hospitality without any reference to the Barristers' Table. It is a signal abuse and usurpation of long standing, which there might be a considerable difficulty in correcting or removing.

Bene (or Bean) House.—In the *Owl's Almanac*, 1618, mention is made of "a tapstering or *bene* house," evidently a place of common entertainment, and possibly the germ of the modern bean-feast, or workmen's holiday.

Benedictio Menscæ. — The grace before meat, as well as, though not so properly, that after it. Furnivall's *Babees Book; Antiquary* for January, 1895. In the latter place a knife, preserved at the Louvre, and belonging to the 16th century, bears the former upon it with the musical notation; the words are:

Quæ sumpturi benedicat trinus & unus, Amen. A very full account of the graces pronounced at the Oxford Colleges will be found in Hearne's *Diary*, 1869, Appendix V. Other forms are found in the printed collections (Hazlitt's *Bibl. Coll,* vv. *Graces* and *Seager*); and doubtless there were many no longer known.

Benedictio Panis. — The blessing on the consecrated bread used in the Communion; it is printed in the service-books for Salisbury and other uses, with the other forms of a similar character.

Benedictio Salis et Aquæ. — A form of prayer found in the Romish service-books, including those for English use. It is inferrible from the Durham Ritual that this blessing was pronounced when the salt was poured into the water, for the rubric is: "Hic mittatur sal in aquâ, Benedictio salis et Aquæ. Gratia Domini vobiscum." In the Durham Ritual (Surtees Society, 1840, pp. 97-104), a remarkable series of forms of benediction are given, dating from the ninth or tenth century. It seems to have been an ancient practice to bless objects of use and comsumption under a variety of circumstances; and we here find: *Benedictio super vasa reperta in locis antiquis, Benedictio quorunlibet vasorum, Benedictio Arborum, Benedictio Pomorum, Benedictio Panis, Benedictio ad omnia quæ volueris, Benedictio Domus, Benedictio quando judicium exituri sunt homines, Exorcismus aquæ ad Furtum Requirendum, Benedictio Aquæ, Benedictio Vestium virginum,* and *Benedictio Lac et Mel.* This frequent and habitual resort to adjuration and prayer led to the introduction of the liturgical *Benedictional.*

Benediction-Posset.—See *Sack Posset.*

Benefit of Clergy.—This privilege was abolished by 7 & 8 Geo. IV. Before that time, it appears that a felon could plead benefit of clergy, and be saved by what was aptly enough termed the neck-verse, which was very usually the *miserere mei* of Psalm 51, but was at the judge's discretion. At a period when capital punishment was inflicted on what would now be considered terribly slight grounds, such a means of evasion was perhaps not improperly connived at. In our old jest books, however, the practice was one of the themes selected for derision and satire. Machyn the diarist points to a provision in this obsolete usage, which I do not see noticed elsewhere. He tells us that, on the 8th March, 1559-60, an old man, who was a priest, was hanged for cutting a purse, "but," adds Machyn, "he was burnt in the hand afore, or elles ys boke would have saved hym." In the Year

Book of 30 Edward I. it seems to be intimated that, in order to claim benefit of
clergy, a technical denial of the charge
was then considered absolutely an essential condition.

Benski, or **The Fairy's Wife.**—
See *Wraith.*

Beryl.—Aubrey, in his Miscellanies,
1696-1721, ed. 1857, pp. 1547, devotes a
section to this subject, with an illustration
of one of these mirrors. They were formerly used by magicians in their superstitious and diabolical operations. Delrio
informs us that the Emperor Julian made
use of a mirror for this purpose, and refers us to his life by Spartianus. *Disquis.
Magicæ,* lib. iv., c. v. "Lilly," says
Grose, "describes one of these berryls or
crystals. It was as large as an orange, set
in silver, with a cross at the top, and
round about engraved the names of the
angels, Raphael, Gabriel, and Uriel. A
delineation of another is engraved in the
frontispiece to Aubrey's Miscellanies.
This mode of inquiry was practised by Dr.
Dee, the celebrated mathematician. His
speculator was named Kelly. From him,
and others practising this art, we have a
long muster-roll of the infernal host, their
different natures, tempers, and appearances. Reginald Scot has given us a
list of some of the chiefs of these devils or
spirits. Aubrey's had the name of
Gabriel, Uriel, Raphael, and Michael.
"Another mode," Grose remarks, "of
consulting spirits was by the berryl, by
means of a speculator or seer, who, to have
a complete sight, ought to be a pure virgin, a youth who had not known woman,
or at least a person of irreproachable life,
and purity of manners. The method of
such consultation is this : the conjuror,
having repeated the necessary charms and
adjurations, with the Litany, or Invocation peculiar to the spirits or angels he
wishes to call, (for every one has his particular form), the seer looks into a chrystal or berryl, wherein he will see the answer, represented either by types or
figures : and sometimes, though very
rarely, will hear the angels or spirits
speak articulately. Their pronunciation
is, as Lilly says, like the Irish, much in
the throat." In Andrews's Continua
tion of Henry, we read : "The Conjurations of Dr. Dee having induced his
familiar spirit to visit a kind of talisman,
Kelly (a brother adventurer) was appointed to watch and describe his ges-
tures." The stone used by these impostors was formerly in the Strawberry Hill
collection. It appears to be a polished
piece of cannel coal. To this Butler refers
when he writes,

"Kelly did all his feats upon
The Devil's looking-glass, a stone."

I do not know whether this is the same
stone which was in the possession of the
late Mr. Henry Huth. The latter is said,
at any rate, to have been Dr. Dee's. Did
he employ it, when Queen Elizabeth came
to Mortlake, to consult him? In Lodge's
"Wits Miserie," 1596, in the Epistle to
the Reader, are the following quaint allusions to sorcerers and magicians : "Buy
therefore this chrystall, and you shall see
them in their common appearance : and
read these exorcismes advisedly, and you
may be sure to conjure them without
crossings; but if any man long for a
familiar for false dice, a spirit to tell fortunes, a charme to heale diseased, this
only booke can best fit him."

This species of divination has still
its believers, and a case occurred
about forty years ago, from which it
transpired that the beryl or mirror
was consulted by some among our con-
temporaries who ought to have been superior to so silly a superstition.

Betrothal.—See *Handfasting and
Troth-Plight.*—Harl. MS. 980, cited by
Strutt, states that, "by the Civil Law,
whatsoever is given ex sponsalitia Largi-
tate, betwixt them that are promised in
marriage, hath a condition (for the most
part silent) that it may be had again if
marriage ensue not; but if the man should
have had a kiss for his money, he should
lose one half of that which he gave. Yet
with the woman it is otherwise, for, kissing or not kissing, whatsover she gave,
she may ask and have it again. However,
this extends only to gloves, rings, bracelets, and such like small wares." To the
betrothing contract under consideration
must be referred, if I mistake not, and not
to the marriage ceremony itself (to which
latter, I own, however, the person who
does not nicely discriminate betwixt them
will be strongly tempted to incline) the
well-known passage on this subject in the
last scene of Shakespear's play of "Twelfth
Night." The priest, who had been privy
to all that had passed, is charged by
Olivia to reveal the circumstances, which
he does, reciting the ceremonies of joining
the hands, kissing, and interchanging
rings, as preliminaries which had taken
place in the usual course. The same drama
affords an example of the old English
practice of lovers plighting their troth in
the chantry, in the presence of their
minister. It is where Olivia and Sebastian accompany the priest with this object
in view. It appears to have been formerly
a custom also for those who were betrothed
to wear some flower as an external and
conspicuous mark of their mutual engagement : the conceit of choosing such short-
lived emblems of their plighted loves cannot be thought a very happy one. That

such a custom, however, did certainly prevail, we have the testimony of Spenser:

"Bring coronations and sops in wine
Worn of paramours."

This passage is illustrated by the following extract from Gunning's "Reminiscences of Cambridge.": "The Dean (of St. Asaph), who appeared very desirous to clear up the matter, asked him, amongst other questions, if he had never made her any presents? He replied that he never had, but, recollecting himself, added, 'except a very choice bunch of flowers, which I brought from Chirk Castle.'" "This explains the whole matter," said the Dean; "in Wales, a man never sends a lady a bunch of flowers, but as a proposal of marriage, and the lady's acceptance of them is considered the ratification." This was in 1788. Fletcher the dramatist says:

"I knit this lady handfast, and with
this hand
The heart that owes this hand, ever
binding
By force of this initiating contract
Both heart and hand in love, faith,
loyalty,
Estate, or what to them belongs."
Wit at Several Weapons, act v. sc. i.

In "Witt's Recreations," 1640, the annexed passage belongs to a piece called "Abroad with the Maids"; it was written by Herrick:

"Next we will act how young men wooe;
And sigh, and kisse, as lovers do,
And talk of brides, and who shall make
That wedding-smock, this bridal-cake:
That dress, this sprig, that leafe, this
vine;
That smooth and silken columbine.
This done, we'l draw lots, who shall buy
And guild the bayes and rosemary:
What posies for our wedding-rings;
What gloves we'l give and ribbanings."

Strutt, in his "Manners and Customs," has illustrated this by an extract from the old play of the "Widow." From this it also appears that no dry bargain would hold on such occasions. For on the Widow complaining that Ricardo had artfully drawn her into a verbal contract, she is asked by one of her suitors, "Stay, stay,—you broke no gold between you?" To which she answers, "We broke nothing, Sir." And, on his adding, "Nor drank to each other?" she replies "Not a drop, Sir." Whence he draws this conclusion: "that the contract cannot stand good in law." The latter part of the ceremony seems alluded to in the following passage in Middleton's "No Wit like a Woman's" (written before 1626):

"E'en when my lip touch'd the contracting cup."

Thiers quotes passages from three ritualistic works apposite to this portion of the nuptial process, as practised in France. *Rituel de Bordeaux*, 98-9. Both the Synodal Statutes of Sens, in 1524, and the Evreux Ritual (1621) refrained from prescribing betrothal, merely leaving it permissive and optional; and the same may be said of the Provincial Council of Rheims, in 1583; but all these authorities laid down the rule that, where the espousal was solemnized, the ceremony must take place openly and in the church.

Beverage, Beverege, or Beveridge, reward, consequence. 'Tis a word now in use for a refreshment between dinner and supper; and we use the word when any one pays for wearing new clothes, &c. Hearne's Glossary to Robert of Gloucester's Chronicle in v. It is at present employed in the general sense of any liquid refreshment.

Bible Omens.—The superstitious among the ancient Christians practised a kind of divination by opening the Old and New Testament. Gibbon speaks of Clovis who, "marching (A.D. 507) from Paris, as he proceeded with decent reverence through the holy diocese of Tours, consulted the shrine of St. Martin, the sanctuary and oracle of Gaul. His messengers were instructed to remark the words of the psalm which should happen to be chaunted at the precise moment when they entered the church. These words, most fortunately, expressed the valour and victory of the champions of heaven, and the application was easily transferred to the new Joshua, the new Gideon, who went forth to battle against the enemies of the Lord." He adds: "This mode of divination by accepting as an omen the first sacred words which in particular circumstances should be presented to the eye or ear, was derived from the Pagans, and the Psalter or Bible was substituted for the poems of Homer and Virgil. From the fourth to the fourteenth century, these *Sortes Sanctorum*, as they are styled, were repeatedly condemned by the decrees of councils, and repeatedly practised by Kings, Bishops, and Saints." Willis of Gloucester bears testimony to this point: "As I was to passe through the roome where my little grand-childe was set by her grandmother to read her morning's chapter, the 9th of Matthew's Gospell, just as I came in she was uttering these words in the second verse, 'Jesus said to the sicke of the palsie, Sonne, be of good comfort, thy sinnes are forgiven thee': which words sorting so fitly with my case, whose whole left side is taken with that kind of disease, I stood at a stand at the uttering of them, and could not but conceive some joy and comfort in those blessed words, though by the childe's reading, as if the Lord by her had spoken them to my-selfe, a paralytick and a sinner, as that Sicke man was," &c. This may be called a Bible omen. *Mount Tabor*, 1639, pp. 199-200. It appears that Arise Evans, in the time of the Commonwealth, used this species of divination by the Bible, and also that one of the Earls of Berkeley had recourse to the then prevailing superstition. His lordship's words are : " I being sick, and under some dejection of spirit, opening my Bible to see what place I could first light upon, which might administer comfort to me, casually I fixed upon the sixth of Hosea : the first three verses are these. [Here follows the quotation.] I am willing to decline superstition upon all occasions, yet think my self obliged to make this use of such a providential place of Scripture : First, by hearty repenting me of my sins past : Secondly, by sincere reformation for the time to come."—*Eccho to the Voice from Heaven*, 1652, p. 227. Martin, speaking of the Isle of Collonsay, says, that in confidence of curing the patient by it, the inhabitants had an antient custom of fanning the face of the sick with the leaves of the Bible. *Descr. of the West of Scotland*, 248. A correspondent of "Notes and Queries," in the number for October 19, 1861, states that he met with the custom of dipping into the Bible on New Year's Day before noon in the county of Oxford, and that it was believed that the tenor of the first passage which caught the eye of the dipper, was a prognostication of the person's good or bad luck for the year.

Bicker-rade, The.—This is a practice among reapers in some parts. A correspondent of Notes and Queries described it, so far as its indelicate character would allow, in the columns of that periodical in 1857. The writer seems to consider the custom as belonging chiefly to Berwickshire. At the harvest-dinner " each band-wun, consisting of six shearers and a bandster, had the use of a bicker (a small round wooden vessel, composed of staves or staps, and neatly bound with willow girths or girds) ; sometimes more than one bicker was used by the bandwun. After the dinner repast was finished, any of the men of the boun, who felt disposed to inflict on any female the bicker-rade, extende her upon her back on the ground and reclining upon her commenced a series of operations, which are too indelicate to be minutely described." It seems further, that resistance was useless, and that serious injuries were sometimes suffered by the victims of this barbarous process. It has probably become entirely obsolete by this time : it was nearly so forty years ago.

Bid-Ale.—There was an ancient custom called Bid-ale or Bidder-ale, from the Saxon word *biddan*, to pray or supplicate, when any honest man, decayed in his estate, was set up again by the liberal benevolence and contributions of friends at a feast, to which those friends were bid or invited. It was most used in the West of England, and in some counties called a help-ale. A writer in "The Gentleman's Magazine" for May, 1784, mentions this custom in some parts of South Wales, peculiar, he thinks, to that country, and still practised at the marriages of servants, tradesfolks, and little farmers, " Before the wedding an entertainment is provided, to which all the friends of each party are bid or invited, and to which none fail to bring or send some contribution, from a cow or calf down to half-a-crown or a shilling. An account of each is kept, and if the young couple do well, it is expected that they should give as much at any future bidding of their generous guests. I have frequently known of £50 being thus collected, and have heard of a bidding, which produced even a hundred." The *Cambrian Register*, 1796, p. 450, adds : "Some time previous to these weddings, where they mean to receive contributions, a herald with a crook or wand, adorned with ribbons, makes the circuit of the neighbourhood, and makes his ' bidding ' or invitation in a prescribed form. The knight-errant cavalcade on horseback, the carrying off the bride, the rescue, the wordy war in rhythm between the parties, &c. which formerly formed a singular spectacle of mock contest at the celebration of nuptials, I believe to be now almost, if not altogether, laid aside every where through the Principality." The following is from the "Gentleman's Magazine" for 1789 :—

" Bidding.—As we intend entering the nuptial state, we propose having a bidding on the occasion on Thursday the 20th day of September, instant, at our own house on the Parade : where the favour of your good company will be highly esteemed ; and whatever benevolence you pleased to confer on us, shall be gratefully acknowledged and retaliated on a similar occasion by your most obedient humble servants, William Jones, Ann Davies ; Caermarthen, Sept. 4, 1787. N.B.— The young man's father (Stephen Jones) and the young woman's aunt (Ann Williams) will be thankfull for all favours conferred on them that day." Another writer in the "Gentleman's Magazine" for 1784 mentions a similar custom in Scotland called Penny Weddings. In the *Penny Magazine* for January, 1835, an improved and more ambitious form of communication (among the humbler classes) to the friends of the parties, is given. A couple belonging to Caermarthenshire are represented as addressing a circular to guests as follows :—

"Carmarthenshire, February 1, 1834.

"Dear Friend,—We take this convenience to inform you that we confederate such a design as to enter under the sanction of matrimony on the 19th of February inst. And as we feel our hearts inclining to regard the ancient custom of our ancestors, *sef Hiliogaeth Gomer*, we intend to make a wedding-feast the same day at the respective habitation of our parent; we hereby most humbly invite your pleasing and most comfortable fellowship at either of which places; and whatever kindness your charitable hearts should then grant will be accepted with congratulation and most lovely acknowledgment, carefully recorded and returned with preparedness and joy, whenever a similar occasion overtake you, by your affectionate servants,

DAVID JOSHUA.
MARY WILLIAMS.

In this case the parents of both parties entertained; but in another example of 1830, belonging to Glamorganshire, the hospitality was limited to the bride's family. "Some of the Cumbrians," observes the compiler of the "Westmoreland and Cumberland Dialect," 1839, "particularly those who are in poor circumstances, have, on their entrance into the married state, what is called a bidding, or bidden-wedding, over which a sort of master of the revels, called a birler, presides, and at which a pecuniary collection is made among the company for the purpose of setting the wedded pair forward in the world. It is always attended with music and dancing, and the fiddler, when the contributions begin, takes care to remind the assembly of their duties by notes imitative of the following couplet:

'Come, my friends, and freely offer;
Here's the bride who has no tocher (dowry)."

Bidding to Funerals.—From an early date it was customary among the gilds of the City of London to summon all the brethren to attend the obsequies of a departed member, and in more modern times a form of invitation on a small broadsheet, enclosed in a mourning border with the usual emblems of mortality was prepared and distributed. A facsimile of one of these notices is given in Hazlitt's *Livery Companies*, 1892. At South Shields, co. Durham, the bidders, *i.e.*, the inviters to a funeral never use the rapper of the door when they go about, but always knock with a key, which they carry with them for that purpose. I know not whether this custom be retained any where else. The following form of inviting to burials by the public bellman of the town was, in Brand's time, 'u use at Hexham, Northumberland: "Blessed are the dead which die in the Lord. Joseph Dixon is departed, son of Christopher Dixon was. Their company is desired to-morrow at five o'clock, and at six he is to be bu—ri—ed. For him and all faithful people give God most hearty thanks." A writer in the *Penny Magazine* for 1837, in reference to Northumbrian manners and customs, says: "In many places it is usual to invite not only the friends, but also the neighbours of a deceased person to his funeral. This is done by bidders, dressed in black silk scarfs, going round formally. The bidders never used the rapper of the door, but always knocked with a key, which they carried with them for that purpose. In the town of Hexham, until within the last few years, the public bellman went round publicly to invite attendance at a deceased's funeral; on such occasions a notice somewhat similar to the following was used : 'Blessed are the dead which die in the Lord. John Robson is departed, son of Richard Robson that was. Company is desired to morrow at five o'clock, and at six he is to be buried. For him and all faithful people give God most hearty thanks." See *Funeral Customs*.

Bidding Prayer.—See Nares, *Glossary*, 1859, in v.

Billiards.—At what date this game was introduced into England is uncertain. It occurs in Spenser's *Mother Hubbard's Tale*, among his *Complaints*, 1591, and is named by Shakespear in *Antony and Cleopatra*, iii., v., where the Queen, referring to music, says: "Let it alone, let us to billiards." This drama was licensed in 1608. Even in the poet's day, *barring* was understood, as Mr. Symon points out. *Shakespear Quotation*, 1901, p. 49. The game is thus mentioned in the Book of Expenses of James Masters, Esq., of Yotes Court, Mereworth, co. Kent :—"December 21, 1661. For 4 yards & ½ of Greene Cloath to cover my Billyard table at 10s. ye yard, 02. 05. 00." "Feb 12, 1661/2. For 2 Billyard Sticks, 2 balls, Ring & porch, 00. 18. 00." The *cannon* at billiards is taken to be a corruption of *carom*, itself an abbreviation of *carambole*, the French term for the red ball, which was neutral, and which was a form of the game formerly played with three balls it was the object of each of the two players to strike, as well as his adversary's. The name of this amusement is apparently derived from Fr. *bille*, for a ball, and hence *billard*. Cotton, in the *Compleat*

Gamester, 1676, refers to it in company with bowls, chess, cards, and dice. It is among the amusements described in a small volume entitled: "Games most in use in England, France and Spain," printed about 1710, and purporting to be regulated by the most experienced masters. The principal or largest monograph on the subject is that of Edwin Kentfield, of Brighton, folio, 1839, with a curious folding frontispiece and a series of diagrams, shewing the various stages of the game, and the modes of playing it in different places. Kentfield was himself a very expert hand, and was patronised by the then Duke of Devonshire, who, when he came to Brighton, used to play with him. It is said that Carter, at one time landlord of the Blue Posts, Brydges Street, Drury Lane, was a very successful player at this game from the length of his arms.

Bird of Paradise.

In *A Short Relation of the River Nile*, 1669, is is said: "The Bird of Paradise is found dead with her bill fixed in the ground, in an island joyning to the Maluccos not far from Macaca; whence it comes thither, is unknown, though great diligence hath been imployed in the search, but without success. One of them dead came to my hands. I have seen many. The tayle is worn by children for a penashe, the feathers fine and subtile as a very thin cloud. The body not fleshy, resembling that of a thrush. The many and long feathers (of a pale invivid colour, nearer white than ash colour), which cover it, make it of great beauty. Report says of these birds, that they alwaies flie from their birth to their death, and are not discovered to have any feet. They live by flyes they catch in the ayr, where, their diet being slender, they take some little repose. They fly very high, and come falling down with their wings displayed. As to their generation, Nature is said to have made a hole in the back of the male, where the female laies her eggs, hatcheth her young, and feeds them till they are able to fly: great trouble and affection of the parent! I set down what I have heard. This is certainly the bird so lively drawn in our maps." This beautiful creature is almost confined in its habitat to New Zealand and Southern Australia, once parts of the same continent. The account given above is of no value, except to shew the ignorance of the earlier travellers and naturalists. There are in fact several varieties. The *Paradisea apoda*, however, was not one of these, but merely a supposed footless genus, the specimens sent to Europe having lost their feet. This error produced a second, namely, that the bird was perpetually on the wing.

Bird and Fowl Augury.

These Fowl omens are probably derived to us from the Romans, at whose superstitions on this account Butler laughs:

> "A flamm more senseless than the Rog'ry
> Of old Aruspicy and Aug'ry,
> That out of Garbages of Cattle
> Presage'd th' events of truce or battel;
> From flight of birds or chickens pecking
> Success of great'st attempts would reckon."

The ancient augurs foretold things to come by the chirping or singing of certain birds, the crow, the pye, the chough, &c.: hence perhaps the observation, frequent in the mouths of old women, that when the pie chatters we shall have strangers. Horace, in his "Ode to Galatea," has this thought:

> "Teque nec lævus vetet ire picus,
> Nec vaga cornix."

Pennant, speaking of the hoopoe, tells that the country people in Sweden look on the appearance of this bird as a presage of war: Facies armata videtur. And formerly the vulgar in our country esteemed it a forerunner of some calamity, which has probably occasioned its growing scarcity. The same writer tells us that the great auk, a species of penguin, is a bird observed by seamen never to wander beyond soundings, and according to its appearance they direct their measures, being then assured that land is not remote. Moresin and Gaule rank the unseasonable crowing of the cock among omens. As also the sudden fall of hens from the housetop. *Papatus*, 1594, p. 21 *Mag-Astromancer posed*, p. 181. Bartholomæus says of the crow: "Divynours tell, that she taketh hede of spienges and awaytynges, and teacheth and sheweth wayes, and warneth what shal fal. But it is ful unleful to beleve, that God sheweth his prevy Counsayle to Crowes as Isidore sayth. Amonge many divynacions divynours meane that crowes token reyne with gredynge and cryenge, as this verse metneth:

> 'Tum Cornix plena pluviam vocat improba voce.'"

that is to understonde,

> 'Nowe then the crowe calleth reyne with an eleynge voyce.'"

In the Earl of Northampton's "Defensative," 1583, signat. T 2 verso, we read: "The Flight of many crowes uppon the left side of the campe, made the Romans very much afrayde of somme budde lucke: as if the great God Jupiter had nothing else to doo (sayd Carneades) but to dryve Jacke Dawes in a flocke together." Gaule particularizes among omens, "A crow lighting on the right hand or on the left."

Mag-Astromancer posed, p. 181. Another early author says: "If a crow fly but over the house and croak thrice, how do they fear, they, or some one else in the family shall die?" Ramsey's *Elmintho-logia*, 1668, p, 271. We are informed that "people prognosticate a great famine or mortality, when great flocks of jays and crows forsake the woods; because these melancholy birds, bearing the characters of Saturn the author of famine and mortality, have a very early perception of the bad disposition of that planet. *Athenian Oracle.* p 271. And Defoe writes: "Some will defer going abroad, tho' called by business of the greatest consequence, if, happening to look out of the window, they see a single crow." *Mem. of Duncan Campbel*, 60. Willsford has much to say on this branch of his subject: "Ravens and crows, when they do make a hoarse, hollow, and sorrowful noise, as if they sobbed, it presages foul weather approaching. Crows flocking together in great companies, or calling early in the morning with a full and clear voice, or at any time of the day gaping against the sun, foreshews hot and dry weather : but if at the brink of ponds they do wet their heads, or stalk into the water, or cry much towards the evening, are signs of rain." He adds : "The woodpecker's cry denotes wet. Buzards, or kites, when they do soar very high and much to lessening themselves, making many plains to and agin, foreshows hot weather, and that the lower region of the air is inflamed, which for coolnesse makes them ascend. Cranes soaring aloft, and quietly in the air, foreshows fair weather; but if they do make much noise, as consulting which way to go, it foreshows a storm that's neer at hand. Herons in the evening, flying up and down as if doubtful where to rest, presages some evill approaching weather." *Nature's Secrets*, 1658, p. 133. Pennant, speaking of the carrion crow, tells us Virgil says that its croakings foreboded rain. It was also thought a bird of bad omen, especially if it happened to be seen on the left hand.

"Ante sinistra cava monuisset ab ilice Cornix."

—*Zoology*, i. 220. In *Dives et Pauper*, ch. 46, we read : "Some bileve that yf the kyte or the puttock fle ovir the way afore them that they shuld fare wel that daye, for sumtyme they have farewele after that they see the puttock so fleynge; and soo they falle in wane by leve and thanke the puttocke of their welfare and nat God, but suche foles take none hede howe often men mete with the puttok so fleynge and yet they fare nevir the better: for there is no folk that mete so oft with the put-toke so fleynge as they that begge their mete from dore to dore." Hall in his "Characters," 1608, declares that in his time it was enough to induce the superstitious man to make his will, if a bittern flew over his head ; but in these statements one may fairly suspect a tincture of hyperbole or exaggeration. Dr. Leyden observes of the magpie, that "it is, according to popular superstition, a bird of unlucky omen. Many an old woman would more willingly see the devil, who bodes no more ill luck than he brings, than a magpie perching on a neighbouring tree." Leyden also informs us that "in the South and West of Scotland, this bird is much detested, though not reckoned ominous. As it frequents solitary places, its haunts were frequently intruded upon by the fugitive Presbyterians, during the persecution which they suffered in the disgraceful and tyrannical reign of Charles II. and James II., when they were often discovered by the clamours of the lapwing." *Glossary to the Complaynt of Scotland*. 1801, vv. *Piett and Thriasneck*. The notes of the night-crow, or night-jar, have always been regarded as portentous, and significant of death in a household, where they are heard. Mary, Countess of Pembroke, in her poem on the passion, written perhaps about 1590, says :

"The night crowes songe, that soundeth nought but death."

And Shakespear himself alludes to the superstition. In the "Parlyament of Byrdes" (circâ 1550), the popular superstition relating to this creature is referred to by the Hawk :

" — The crowe hath no brayne,
For to gyue counsell but of the rayne."

So, again, in "Tottel's Miscellany," 1557, one of the Uncertain Authors says :

"Thou dunghyll crowe that crokest agaynst the rayne,
Home to thy hole."

The modern sailors pay respect to auguries in the same manner as Aristophanes in his *Aves*, line 597, tells us those of Greece did above two thousand years ago. Pennant farther observes, that the stormy petrol presages bad weather, and cautions the seamen of the approach of a tempest by collecting under the sterns of the ships. *Zoology*, i., 258; ii., 508, 554. Werenfels says : "If the superstitious man has a desire to know how many years he has to live, he will inquire of the cuckow." In 1609, Thomas Dekker printed his "Raven's Almanack," which expressly purported to be a prognostication of calamities in store for this kingdom; and in 1620 Rowlands produced his *Night Raven* with the following distich on the title :

"All those whose deeds doe shun the Light,
Are my companions in the night."

Gay, too, in his pastoral called "The Dirge," has noted this omen :

"The boding raven on her cottage sat,
And with hoarse croakings warn'd us of our fate."

Its being accounted unlucky to destroy swallows is probably a pagan relique. We read in Ælian that these birds were sacred to the penates or household gods of the ancients, and therefore were preserved. They were honoured anciently as the nuncios of the spring. The Rhodians are said to have had a solemn anniversary song to welcome in the swallow. Anacreon's Ode to that bird is well known.

The ancients were firm believers— as it is scarcely necessary to observe —in auguries derived from the flight of birds. Willsford speaks of the low flight of the swallow as indicative of rain; but this is doubtful (*Nature's Secrets*, 1658, p. 134), and Gaule, (*Mag-Astromancers posed*, 181) says that a swallow falling down the chimney was thought in his day to be an inauspicious symptom. The former observes generally that birds which frequent trees and bushes, "if they do fly often out, and make quick returns, expect some bad weather to follow soon after." Rosse, in allusion to the English Civil Wars in the seventeenth century, declares that these misfortunes were foretold by the appearance of unusual flights of birds, seen in the air fighting on opposite sides. *Arcana Microcosmi*, 1652, App. 219. It was considered a bad omen if a swallow died in one's hand, and from some remains of proverbial law it appears that a degree of sanctity, which it has since lost, was formerly attached to this bird. Every one must be familiar with the adage (of which there is more than one version, however) :

"The martin and the swallow
Are God Almighty's birds to hollow " ;

where hollow is the old form of hallow, or keep holy. Parker, in his "Philomela," 1632, says, in allusion to the swallow :

"And if in any's hand she chance to dye,
'Tis counted ominous, I know not why."

There was also a belief that whoever stole a swallow's eggs, or a robin's or wren's young ones, would be punished by some domestic calamity. Lupton observes, that the peacock, by his loud and harsh clamour, prophesies and foretells rain,

and the oftener they cry, the more rain is signified." Theophrastus and Mizaldus are cited :—"and Paracelsus saies, if a peacock cries more than usual, or out of his time, it foretells the death of some in that family to whom it doth belong."— *Notable Things,* 1579, ed. 1660, p. 311. Willsford enters into a somewhat elaborate catalogue of omens of this description. His words are these : "The offspring or aliance of the Capitolian Guard, when they do make a gaggling in the air more than usual, or seem to fight, being over greedy at their meat, expect then cold and winterely weather. Peacocks crying loud and shrill for their lost Io, does proclaim an approaching storm. Doves coming late home to their houses than they are accustomed to do, presages some evil weather approaching. Jack-daws, if they come late home from forraging, presages some cold or ill weather neer at hand, and likewise when they are seen much alone. Finally, that duck, mallards, and all water-fowls, when they bathe themselves much, prune their feathers, and flicker, or clap themselves with their wings, it is a sign of rain or wind. The same with cormorants and gulls. Sea-mews, early in the morning making a gaggling more than ordinary, foretoken stormy and blustering weather." This superstition was entertained in Scotland in the 18th century. A person writing from Holywood, co. Dumfries, about 1790, says : "During the whole year the sea gulls, commonly called in this parish seamaws, occasionally come from the Solway Firth to this part of the country; their arrival seldom fails of being followed by a high wind and heavy rain, from the southwest, within twenty-four hours; and they return to the Firth again as soon as the storm begins to abate." *Nature's Secrets,* 1658, 132-4. The same notion appears to have prevailed in other parts. "The seagulls," says a writer from Arbilot, co. Forfar, "are considered as ominous. When they appear in the fields, a storm from the south-east generally follows; and when the storm begins to abate, they fly back to the shore." *Stat. Acc.,* i., 32. Such after all has always been, and is, pretty much the belief and experience all along our English coasts. We still attach credit to the symptoms of hard weather at sea, when the gulls fly landward, and are seen up the Thames. A traveller of the 18th century remarked that a bird, which he calls caldelia, appeared on the coasts of Corsica and Sardinia just before a storm, like the petrel with us. Smith's *Travels,* 1792, p. 11 Dallaway, when he visited the Bosphorus, was struck by the large flocks of seabirds, like swallows, but, says he, "because they are never known to rest, they are called halcyons, and by the French *ames damnées,*" which flew in a train from one sea to the other, and were looked upon as ominous by the inhabitants. It is held extremely portentous, says Grose, to kill a cricket, a ladybug, a swallow, martin, robin redbreast, or wren; perhaps from the idea of its being a breach of hospitality; all these birds and insects alike taking refuge in houses. Grose enumerates among unlucky things the killing of any of these birds or insects; and Park mentions that when he was a boy, he remembered a different version of a familiar distich :

"Tom Tit and Jenny Wren,
Were God Almighty's cock and hen."

Persons killing any of the above-mentioned birds or insects, or destroying their nests, will infallibly within the course of the year break a bone, or meet with some other dreadful misfortune. On the contrary, it is deemed lucky to have martins or swallows build their nests in the eaves of a house, or in the chimneys. Compare *Divination* and *Wren*.

Bishop in the Pan.—Tyndale, in his *Obedyence of a Christian Man,* 1528, p. 109, says: "When a thynge speadeth not well, we borrowe speach and saye the byshope hath blessed it, because that no-thynge speadeth well that they medyll wythall. If the podech be burned to, or the meate ouer rosted, we saye the byshope hath put his fote in the pote, or the bishope hath played the coke, because the bishopes burn who they lust and whosouer displeaseth them." In Tusser's "Husbandry," under April, are the following lines :

"Blesse Cisley (good Mistress) that Bushop doth ban,
For burning the milke of hir cheese to the pan."

On which Hillman has the following note : "When the Bishop passed by (in former times) every one ran out to partake of his blessing, which he plentifully bestow'd as he went along: and those who left their milk upon the fire, might find it burnt to the pan when they came back, and perhaps ban or curse the Bishop as the occasion of it, as much or more than he had blessed them : hence it is likely it grew into a custom to curse the bishop when any such disaster happen'd, for which our author would have the mistress bless, *Anglice* correct, her servant, both for her negligence and unmannerliness." Bishops were in Tusser's time still much in the habit of burning heretics.

Bishopping.—This is what is now generally known as Confirmation, a term which was not understood in early times. In the Privy Purse Expenses of the Prin-

cess Mary, under December, 1536, we have : "Itm Payed for the fascion of a Tablet geven to my lady Carowes (Carew's) Doughter beeng my ladyes goddoughter at the byshoppyng . . . . vjs." There is another and very different process, known technically as bishopping. In the printing business it used, before the introduction of the roller, to be the duty of the pressman to see to the bishopping of the balls, made of sheepskin attached to a stock, which are used to ink the type before printing. These balls, which are of considerable size, must be kept soft and moist to receive the ink, and this result is, or used to be, obtained by wrapping them after employment, against the following occasion, in a blanket dipped in urine. The practice was a sort of christening, and the term perhaps owed itself to the resentment of the printer at the old animosity of the episcopal order against the typographical art.

Bishops Stortford.—The following very extraordinary septennial custom at Bishops Stortford, Herts, and in the adjacent neighbourhood, on Old Michaelmas Day. I find in a London newspaper Oct. 18, 1787: "On the morning of this day, called Ganging Day, a great number of young men assemble in the fields, when a very active fellow it nominated the leader. This person they are bound to follow, who, for the sake of diversion, generally chooses the route through ponds, ditches, and places of difficult passage. Every person they meet is bumped, male or female ; which is performed by two other persons taking them up by their arms, and swinging them against each other. The women in general keep at home for this period, except those of less scrupulous character, who, for the sake of partaking of a gallon of ale and a plumb-cake, which every landlord or publican is obliged to furnish the revellers with, generally spend the best part of the night in the fields, if the weather is fair; it being strictly according to ancient usage not to partake of the cheer any where else."

Bisley, Surrey.—See *St. John the Baptist's Well.*

Black Belly and Bawsy Brown.—See *Browny.*

Black Knight of Ashton. — See Hazlitt's *Proverbs,* 1882.

Black Monday. — Easter Monday, 1360, when the cold was so intense, that the English troops before Paris, under Edward III., suffered severely. The expression must have been subsequently employed in a somewhat vague sense, and among other uses, by schoolboys, as it was an usual day for returning from the holidays. Compare Nares, 1859, in v.

Black Veil.—Prior to the assumption of this in the Romish Church, the recluse goes through on an appointed day all the forms of ordinary marriage, the physical or fleshly husband excepted: she is attired in white satin, wears a wreath of flowers, receives a wedding ring, and presides at a breakfast, where there is bride-cake. During the day she receives her girl-friends, and all is gaiety. It is her final experience of the world and those whom she knows. She has already taken the white veil, which is regarded as the Betrothal, as distinguished from this —the wedding. The two services usually occupy an hour and a half to two hours.

Blank.—This is no doubt the same as *La Blanque* of the early French drama and poetry, and was a game of hazard, at which even the lower orders in both countries were fond of playing, and in which serious losses were sometimes incurred. In the *Interlude of Youth*, printed two or three times about 1550, there is the following highly curious enumeration :

> Sir, I can teach you to play at the dice,
> At the queen's game and at the Irish ;
> The treygobet and the hazard also,
> And many other games mo ;
> Also at the cards I can teach you to play,
> At the triump and one-and-thirty,
> Post, pinion, and also aums-ace,
> And at another they call dewce-ace.
> Yet I can tell you more, and ye will con
> me thank,
> Pink, and drink, and also at the blank,
> And many sports mo.

Hazlitt's Dodsley, ii., 34-5. It is, as will appear, somewhat uncertain whether the writer intended to include blank among the games at cards or not, as he catalogues subject to the exigencies of rhyme.

Blaze's Day, St.—(February 3.) Hospinian describes this Saint as a Cappadocian Bishop who, in the persecution under Diocletian and Maximian, fled to a cavern and led the life of a hermit. He also followed the medical profession, and healed both men and animals. He was discovered, however, and cast into prison, from which, after enduring many tortures, he was led to the place of execution. After his martyrdom and canonization, candles were offered at his altar, which were said to possess the unusual property of curing diseases in human and other creatures. Minshew, in his "Dictionary," under the word Hock-tide, speaks of "St. Blaze his day, about Candlemas, when country women goe about and make good cheere, and if they find any of their neighbour women a spinning that day, they burn and make a blaze of fire of the distaffe, and thereof called S. Blaze his Day." Percy tells us "The anniversary of St. Blasius is the 3rd of February, when it is still the custom in many parts of England to light up fires on the hills on St. Blayse night : a custom antiently taken up, perhaps for no better reason than the jingling resemblance of his name to the word Blaze." *Notes to Northumb. Household Book*, 1770, p. 333. Scot, in his "Discovery of Witchcraft," gives us a charm used in the Romish Church upon St. Blaze's Day that will fetch a thorn out of any place of one's body, a bone out of the throat, etc, to wit, "Call upon God and remember St. Blaze." The following is the account of St. Blaze in the "Popish Kingdome," fol. 47 b. :

> "Then followeth good Sir Blaze, who
> doth a waxen candell give,
> And holy water to his men, whereby they
> safely live.
> I divers barrels oft have seene, drawne
> out of water cleare,
> Through one small blessed bone of this
> same Martyr heare :
> And caryed thence to other townes and
> cities farre away,
> Ech superstition doth require such earnest kinde of playe."

The following lines occur in an early MS. among Coles's MSS. in the British Museum :—

> "Imber si datur, Virgo dum purificatur,
> Inde notatur quod hyemps abinde
> fugatur :
> Si sol det radium, frigis, erit nimium."

A village in North Cornwall is called after this saint.

Blessing of Clouts.—The leaving of rags at wells was a singular species of popular superstition. Grose tells us that "Between the towns of Alten and Newton, near the foot of Rosberrye Toppinge there is a well dedicated to St. Oswald. The neighbours have an opinion that a shirt or shift taken off a sick person and thrown into that well, will show whether the person will recover or die ; for if it floated it denoted the recovery of the party ; if it sunk, there remained no hope of their life : and to reward the Saint for his intelligence, they tear off a rag of the shirt, and leave it hanging on the briars thereabouts ; where," says the writer, "I have seen such numbers as might have made a fayre rheme in a paper myll." Pennant tells us, "They visit the Well of Speye, in Scotland, for many distempers, and the Well of Drachaldy for as many, offering small pieces of money and bits of rags." Pinkerton, speaking of the River Fillan in the Vale of Strathfillan, says, "In this river is a pool consecrated by the antient superstition of the inhabitants of this country. The pool is formed by the eddying of the stream round a rock. Its waves were many years since consecrated by Fillan, one of the saints who converted the antient inhabitants of Caledonia from Paganism to the belief of Christianity. It has ever since been distinguished by his name, and esteemed of sovereign virtue in curing madness. About two hundred persons afflicted in this way are annually brought to try the benefits of its salutary influence. These patients are conducted by their friends, who first perform the ceremony of passing with them thrice through a neighbouring cairn; on this cairn they then deposit a simple offering of clothes, or perhaps a small bunch of heath. More precious offerings used once to be brought. The patient is then thrice immerged in the sacred pool. After the immersion, he is bound hand and foot, and left for the night in a chapel which stands near. If the maniac is found loose in the morning, good hopes are conceived of his full recovery. If he still remains bound, his cure is doubtful. It sometimes happens that death relieves him, during his confinement, from the troubles of life." Heron's *Journey through part of Scotland*, i., 282. In the "Statistical Account of Scotland," we read:— "A spring in the Moss of Melshach, Aberdeenshire, of the chalybeate kind, is still in great reputation among the common people. Its sanative qualities extend even to brutes. As this spring probably obtained vogue at first in days of ignorance and superstition, it would appear that it became customary to leave at the well part of the clothes of the sick and diseased, and harness of the cattle, as an offering of gratitude to the divinity who bestowed healing virtues on its waters. And now, even though the superstitious principle no longer exists, the accustomed offerings are still presented." (This was in or about 1794.) *Stat. Acc.* xiii., 76. We read " of a well called Craiguck, co. Ross, issuing from a rock near the shore of Bennetsfield, resorted to in the month of May by whimsical or superstitious persons, who, after drinking, commonly leave some threads or rags tied to a bush in the neighbourhood." *Stat. Acc. of Scotland*, xv., 613. Macaulay, speaking of a consecrated well in St. Kilda, called Tobirnimbuadh, or the spring of diverse virtues, says, that " near the fountain stood an altar, on which the distressed votaries laid down their oblations. Before they could touch sacred water with any prospect of success, it was their constant practice to address the Genius of the place with supplication and prayers. No one approached him with empty hands. But the devotees were abundantly frugal. The offerings presented by them were the poorest acknowledgments that could be made to a superior Being, from whom they had either hopes or fears. Shells and pebbles,

rags of linen or stuffs worn out, pins, needles, or rusty nails, were generally all the tribute that was paid; and sometimes. though rarely enough, copper coins of the smallest value. Among the heathens of Italy and other countries, every choice fountain was consecrated, and sacrifices were offered them, as well as to the deities that presided over them. *Hist. Acct.*

In the " Marriage of Wit and Wisdom," circâ 1570, Indulgence says to Wit:

" Well, yet before the goest, hold heare
   My blessing in a clout;
Well fare the mother at a neede,
   Stand to thy tackling stout."

The first allusion to this old belief and usage is, so far as I know, in John Heywoods "Dialogue," originally printed as early as 1546. The passage is as follows in the edition of 1562:

" Ye haue had of me all that I might make.
And be a man neuer so greedy to wyn,
He can haue no more of the foxe but the skyn.
Well (quoth he) if ye list to bring it out,
Ye can geue me your blessing in a clout
Ye can geue me your blessing in a clout."

Davies of Hereford seems to allude to the usage, where in his " Scourge of Folly," (1611), he gives the proverb:

" God-fathers oft give their blessings in a clout."

The only other example of this usage which I can find occurs in Lovelace:

  " *To a Lady with Child that asked an old Shirt.*"
" And why an honour'd ragged shirt, that shows
Like tatter'd ensigns, all its bodies blows?
Should it be swathed in a vest so dire,
It were enough to set the child on fire.
But since to ladies 't hath a custome been
Linnen to send, that travail and lye in:
To the nine sempstresses, my former friends,
I su'd; but they had nought but shreds and ends.
At last, the jolli'st of the three times three,
Rent th' apron from her smock, and gave it me.
'Twas soft and gentle, subtly spun, no doubt;
Pardon my boldness, Madam; here's the Clout."

Bishop Hall, in his " Triumphs of Rome." ridicules a superstitious prayer of the

Popish Church for the blessing of clouts in the way of cure of diseases. Can it have originated thence? This absurd custom (observed Mr. Brand) is not extinct even at this day : 1 have formerly frequently observed shreds or bits of rag upon the bushes that overhang a well in the road to Benton, a village in the vicinity of Newcastle-upon-Tyne, which, from that circumstance, is now or was very lately called the Rag-Well. This name is undoubtedly of long standing : probably it has been visited for some disease or other, and these rag-offerings are the relics of the then prevailing popular superstition. It is not far from another holy spring at Jesmond, at the distance of about a mile from Newcastle. Pilgrimages to this well and chapel at Jesmond were so frequent, that one of the principal streets of the great commercial town aforesaid is supposed to have its name partly from having an inn in it, to which the pilgrims that flocked thither for the benefit of the supposed holy water used to resort. St. Mary's Well, in this village (Jesmond), which is said to have had as many steps down to it as there are Articles in the Creed, was lately inclosed by Mr. Coulson for a bathing place ; which was no sooner done than the water left it. This occasioned strange whispers in the village and the adjacent places. The well was always esteemed of more sanctity than common wells, and therefore the failing of the water could be looked upon as nothing less than a just revenge for so great a profanation. But alas ! the miracle's at an end, for the water returned a while ago in as great abundance as ever. Thus far Bourne. Brand's *Newcastle*, i., 339 and *Appendix*, 622.

Using rags as charms, it seems, was not confined to England or Europe, for I read the following passage in Hanway's "Travels into Persia," vol. i., p. 177 : "After ten days' journey we arrived at a desolate caravanserai, where we found nothing but water. I observed a tree with a number of rags tied to the branches : these were so many charms, which passengers coming from Ghilan, a province remarkable for agues, had left there, in a fond expectation of leaving their disease also on the same spot." Mungo Park, in his "Travels," observes : "The company advanced as far as a large tree, called by the natives Neema Taba. It had a very singular appearance, being covered with innumerable rags or scraps of cloth, which persons travelling across the wilderness had at different times tied to its branches : a custom so generally followed, that no one passes it without hanging up something." Park followed the example, and suspended a handsome piece of cloth on one of the boughs."

Blindman's Buff. — This sport is found among the illuminations of the Missal, cited by Strutt in his "Manners and Customs." It is known to be an amusement with which the ancients were familiar. It is the Muinda and *Kollabismos* of the Greeks ;and it is supposed to have originated in the traditional story of Polyphemus. Taylor, the water-poet, nevertheless, maintains in his *Great Eater of Kent*, 1630, that the invention was due to Gregory Dawson, an Englishman ! See Levin's *Manipulus*, 1570, p. 293. Jamieson, in his Dictionary, gives us a very curious account of this game, which in Scotland appears to have been called belly-blind. In the Suio-Gothic it is called blind-hoc, i.e. blind goat ; and, in German, blind kuhe, i.q. blind cow. The French call it *Clignemusset*, from *cligner*, to wink, and *mussé* hidden ; also, *Colin-maillard*, equivalent to " Collin the buffon," and the old Greek *Kollabismos* is their *Capifolèt*.

"This game," says Jamieson, "is thus defined : Ludi genus qui hic quidem manibus expansis oculos suos tegit, ille vero postquam percussit, quærit num verberavit." Pollux ap. Scapul. It was also used among the Romans. But compare St. John's *Manners and Customs of Ancient Greece*, 1842, i., 149-50. Jamieson adds, under Blind Harie, (another name for Blindman's-buff in Scotland) : " It may be observed that this sport in Isl. is designated kraekis-blinda. Verelius supposes that the Ostrogoths had introduced this game into Italy ; where it is called *giuoco della cieca*, or the play of the blind." Chacke-blynd man and Jockie-blind man are other Scotish appellations for the same game. " We are told that the great Gustavus Adolphus, at the very time that he proved the scourge of the house of Austria, and when he was in the midst of his triumphs, used in private to amuse himself in playing at Blindman's Buff with his Colonels." "*Cela passoit*," says the *Dict. Trav. v. Colin Maillard, pour une galanterie admirable*." Day, in his *Humour out of Breath*, 1608, introduces one of his characters playing at the game, which one of them says that he learned when a student at Padua. A lady is told, when she is caught, that she must be hoodwinked or give a kiss to her captor as a ransom. Wodroephe, in his *Spared Hours of a Soldier*, 1623, says that it is " to winke and strike." Dr. Walker, in his *Parœmiologia*, 1672, gives the form " Blindman's buffet." Gay says concerning it :
" As once I play'd at Blindman's Buff,
    it hap't
About my eyes the towel thick was
    wrapt.

I miss'd the swains, and seiz'd on
Blouzelind,
True speaks that antient proverb. 'Love
is blind.' "

Blood-letting. — In the margin of
Harl. MS. 1772, fol. 115, verso, is written
the following caution in an early hand:
"Beware of letting blood, drinking, or
eating goose, on these three days, nono
k'lis Aprilis die lunis: intrante Augusto
die lunis xx: exeunte Decembris die
lunis." In the poem, "How the goode
Wife thaught hir Doughter." occurs the
line:

"For aftir the wrenne hathe veynes,
men schalle late hir blode"

which puzzled even Sir Frederic Madden. Edit. 1838. It seems almost to
refer to the hunting of the wren on St.
Stephen's Day (Dec. 26), when it was
deemed a propitious season for phlebotomy. In another (more modern) copy of
the poem, the line stands thus:

"After the wren has vaines men may
let blood—"

which has its signification, to be sure, but
it is a reading of doubtful genuineness.
Hazlitt's *Popular Poetry*, 1864, i., 187.
Among the "Receipts and disbursements
of the Canons of St. Mary, in Huntingdon," 1517, we have the following entry:
"Item, for letting our horses blede in
Chrystmasse weke, iiijd." Douce says the
practice of bleeding horses on St.
Stephen's Day is extremely ancient and
appears to have been brought into this
country by the Danes. In Tusser's "Husbandry," 1580, under December, are the
following lines:

"Yer Christmas be passed, let horsse be
let blood,
For manie a purpose it doth them much
good:
The day of S. Steeven, old fathers did
use,
If that do mislike thee, some other day
chuse."

On which is this note in "Tusser Redivivus," 1710: "About Christmas is a very
proper time to bleed horses in, for then
they are commonly at house, then spring
comes on, the sun being now come back
from the winter solstice, and there are
three or four days of rest, and if it be upon
St. Stephen's Day, it is not the worse,
seeing there are with it three days of rest,
or at least two." The following is from
Copley's "Wits, Fits and Fancies, 1595":
" "On S. Stevens Day it is the custome
for all horses to be let bloud and drench'd.
A gentleman being (that morning) de-
maunded whether it pleased him to have
his horse let bloud and drencht, according

to the fashion? He answered with a poor
quibble on the well-known malady among
horses (the farcin or equine scrofula), No,
sirra, my horse is not diseased of the
fashions." Aubrey, in the "Remains of
Gentilisme," says: "On St. Stephen's
Day the farrier came constantly and
blouded all our cart-horses.

Hospinian quotes a notion from Naogeorgus that it is good to gallop
horses till they are all over in a
sweat, and then bleed them, on Stephen's Day, to prevent their having
any disorders for the ensuing year. Hospinian "De Orig. Fest. Christianor," fol.
160:

"Then followeth St. Stephens Day
whereon doth every man
His horses jaunt and course abrode, as
swiftly as he can,
Until they doe extreemely sweate, and
than they let them blood,
For this being done upon this day, they
say doth do them good,
And keepes them from all the maladies
and sicknesse through the yeare,
As if that Steven any time took charge
of horses heare."

Googe's translation of Popish Kingdome,
fol. 45. Brand also quoted under this head
Hildebrandus "De Diebus Festis," SS.
Antiquitat. Epitome, p. 33.

Blood of Hales, The.—Perhaps to
the number of miraculous agencies to
which credit was given by our forefathers
may be added the holy blood of Christ in
Hales. This was a phial alleged to contain
some of the Saviour's blood, brought from
Palestine by Edmund, Earl of Cornwall,
and presented to the Cistercian brotherhood at Hales, Gloucestershire. There are
occasional allusions to this relic in our
household books, periodical oblations being
made to it, and Thomas Baker, of St.
John's College, Cambridge, states that
there was a short poetical narrative of the
prodigy, from the press of Wynkyn de
Worde. At the dissolution we find the
Abbot of Hales himself writing to Cromwell, and suggesting the demolition of the
shrine (worth, according to him, scarcely
£30 for the gold and silver about it), where
"the faynyd relycke called the Bloode"
was exhibited in order, as the abbot says,
that it may not "mynistre occasyon to any
weke person, loking thereupon, to abuse
his conscyens therewith!" In a subsequent letter from Bishop Latimer to Cromwell the whole trick is laid bare. Ellis's
Orig. Letters, 3rd Series, iii., 249.

Latimer, in his seventh Lent sermon
before Edward VI., 1549, says:—"What
became of his blud that fell downe trowe
ye? Was the bloude of Hales of it (wo
worthe it). What ado was it to brynge

thys out of the Kynges heade, thys greate abhominacion of the bloud of hales could not be taken a great whyle out of his mynde. . . . . Vnpreacheynge Prelates haue bene the cause, that the bloud of Hales did so long blynd the Kynge."

Blood Portents, &c.—Scot, in his "Discovery," 1584, says, "I have heard by credible report, that the wound of a man murthered, renewing bleeding at the presence of a dear friend, or of a mortal enemy. Divers also write that if one pass by a murthered body (though unknown) he shall be stricken with fear, and feel in himself some alteration by nature." "Three loud and distinct knocks at the bed's head," says Grose, "of a sick person, or at the bed's head or door of any of his relations, is an omen of his death." King James, in his "Dæmonology," 1597, says, "In a secret murther, if the dead carkasse be at any time thereafter handled by the murtherer, it will gush out of blood, as if the blood were crying to Heaven for revenge of the murtherer." In the narrative by Sir Simonds D'Ewes of the Babb murder at Kingston, in Somersetshire, 1613, there is a reference to this common belief.

In the prose *Merlin* we get the incident of the supposed miraculous power of the blood of the child "born without father," to stay the destruction of King Vortiger's strong tower. This is to be regarded as an early example of the belief in charms, which was unquestionably far more ancient in this country than any existing records shew. In *Five Philosophical Questions Disputed*, 1650, one is: "Why dead bodies bleed in the presence of their murtherers," and the writer accounts for the phenomenon on scientific grounds, arising from the tendency of blood to liquefy after death by the heat generated by corruption. The air being heated by many persons coming about the body, is the same thing to it as motion is. 'Tis observed that dead bodies will bleed in a concourse of people, when murtherers are absent as well as present, yet legislators have thought fit to authorize it, and use this tryal as an argument at least, to frighten though 'tis no conclusive one to condemn them.". It was part of the system of witchcraft that drawing blood from a witch rendered her enchantments ineffectual. This curious doctrine is very fully investigated in Hathaway's Trial, published in the "State Trials." In Glanville's "Account of the Dæmon of Tedworth," speaking of a boy that was bewitched, he says, the "Boy drew towards Jane Brooks, the woman who had bewitched him, who was behind her two sisters, and put his hand upon her, which his father perceiving, immediately scratched her face and drew blood from her. The

youth then cry'd out that he was well." *Blow at Modern Sadducism*, 1668, p. 148. Compare *Witchcraft*. The following passage is in a tract by Arise Evans: "I had heard some say, that when a witch had power over one to afflict him, if he could but draw one drop of the witches blood, the witch would never after do him hurt." *Eccho to the Voice from Heaven*, 1652, p. 34. In the first part of "Henry the Sixth," act i. sc. 10, Talbot says to the Pucelle d'Orleans :

—" I'll have a bout with thee,
Devil or Devil's dam, I'll conjure thee,
Blood will I draw on thee, thou art a witch."

Thus also in Butler's "Hudibras" :
" Till drawing blood o' the dames like witches,
They're forthwith cur'd of their capriches."

And in Cleveland's "Rebel Scot :"
" Scots are like witches, do but whet your pen,
Scratch till the blood come, they'll not hurt you then."

Park here refers to a passage in Bastard's "Chrestoleros," 1598 :
" Phisition Lanio neuer will forsake,
His golden patiente while his head doth ake :
When he is dead, farewell, he comes not there.
He hath nor cause, nor courage to appeare.
He will not look vpon the face of death,
Nor bring the dead vnto her mother earth.
I will not say, but if he did the deede,
He must be absent lest the corpse should bleed."

This notion is illustrated by the ballad of "Young Redin :"
" O white, white were his wounds washen,
As white as a linen clout;
But as the traitor she came near,
His wounds they gushed out."

Kinloch's *Ancient Scottish Ballads*, 1827, p. 1. And the Editor remarks, that he recollects "this ordeal having been practiced at Aberdeen about twenty years ago (this was written in 1827), on the occasion of the body of a pregnant woman having been found in the neighbouring canal." Blood flowed from her nostrils, it is said, directly the suspected murderer touched her; but this proof, though accepted by the populace, was not thought conclusive by the lawyers. There is a pretty little anecdote, which may be regarded as an illustration of the present matter by the way in Copley's, *Wits, Fits, and Fancies*,

1595, ed. 1614, p. 85:—" A gentlewoman went to church so concealed, that shee thought no body could know her. It chanced that her louer met her, and knewe her, and spake vnto her: Sir (shee answered) you mistake me, how know yee me? All too well (reply'd the gentleman) for so soone as I met you, beholde my wounds fell fresh a bleeding: Oh heereof you onely are guilty."

The superstition still prevails in some parts of the country. At the Warwick Winter Assizes for 1867, John Davis, a maltster. formerly residing at Stratford-on-Avon, was charged with having wounded Jane Ward, and on this occasion the following extraordinary particulars were divulged. "The prisoner, with his family, up to the time of his arrest, had resided in Sheep-street, Stratford-upon-Avon, and they had laboured under an impression that the prosecutrix, who occupied an adjoining house, had bewitched them. In spite of the efforts of friends to the contrary, they persisted in the delusion, and frequently narrated, with singular circumstantiality, visits which had been paid them in the night time by spirits. Some of these, they stated, entered the dwelling by descending the chimney, and when they landed in the room they went through a variety of capers such as seizing the furniture, and pitching it about the apartment, pulling the clothes off the bed, and even tossing the inmates up into the air. One young girl, who was an invalid, and was obliged to recline upon the sofa, solemnly declared that a man and woman came down the chimney on one occasion, both being headless, and taking her by the body, cast her violently upon the ground, then tossed her up into the air, and performed similar feats with the sofa. The statement created so great a stir in the town that the police were called in to investigate the matter, and although they pointed to the accumulated dust around the feet of the sofa in proof that no such thing could have happened the prisoner and his family declared their firm belief that witches had been there, and the only way to break the spell was to draw blood from the body of the prosecutrix, who was suspected of having bewitched them. A day or two after, the prisoner rushed into the house occupied by Jane Ward the complainant, and inflicted a frightful gash in her cheek. He inflicted a wound half an inch in width and two and a half inches deep When he saw the blood flowing down her face, he exclaimed, ' There, you old witch, I can do anything with you now.' At the station, he said, in answer to the charge, ' Serve her right: she can do no more for me now. I have drawn first blood.' "

Blow-point.—Blow-point appears to have been a relatively advanced game. Procter, in his book "Of the Knowledge and Conducte of Warres," 1578, observes: "Lycurgus, the politique Prince, amonge his lawes and customes, which hee established theare (in Lacedæmon) ordayned that all spare tyme shoulde be expended in vertuous exercises, and principallye in the noble practyses of armes, to gett honour, and soueraynetye of the enemyes, cleane cuttinge of vnthriftye wastfull ryott, abandoninge delycate nycenesse, and banishinge idle, and chyldishe games, as commen cardplaye, cayles, coytes, slyde-bourde, bowles, and blowepoynt, which weare throwen oute of the commen-wealthe. From whence also bee dyscarded and expelled ianglers, iesters iuglers, puppetplayers, pypers, and suche like vnprofitable persons, in steade of which weare mayntayned menne of valure, frequentynge and exercisynge actiuitye of wrastelinge, dartynge, throwinge the barre, the sledge, vsinge the weapons of warre," &c. Marmion, in his "Antiquary," 1641, act i. says: "I have heard of a nobleman that has been drunk with a tinker, and a Magnifico that has plaid at Blow-point." Among the old proverbs is, " to leave boy's play, and fall to blowpoint." Hazlitt's *Proverbs*, 1882, p. 437. So, in "Lingua," 1607, act iii. sc. 2, Anamnestes introduces Memory as telling " how he plaid at Blowe-point with Jupiter when he was in his side-coats."

Blue Gowns, or Beadsmen, an order of privileged mendicants in Scotland, of which the latest trace did not expire till 1863. The first appellation was due to the distribution among these persons of a gown of blue cloth, to which were added a loaf of bread, a bottle of ale, and a leathern purse containing a penny for every year of the ruling sovereign's age ;and annually a new beadsman or Blue Gown was elected. Each member of the body bore a pewter badge, on which were inscribed his name and the words *Past and Repast* The usage, which had had its origin in the ancient practice of vicarious prayer, resolved itself into a public charity, of which the sources were forgotten, and in 1833 sixty Beadsmen were on the roll. No appointments were made after that date, and the last survivor drew his allowance from the Exchequer at Edinburgh in May, 1863.

Boar's Head.—Holinshed says that, in the year 1170, upon the day of the young Prince's coronation, King Henry the Second "served his son at the table as sewer, bringing up the bore's head, with trumpets before it, according to the manner." It is probable that Chaucer alluded to the above custom in the following passage, in his Franklin's Tale:

" Janus sitteth by the fire with double
   berd,
And he drinketh of his bugle-horne the
   wine,
Before him standeth the brawne of the
   tusked swine."

Dugdale, speaking of the Christmas Day
Ceremonies in the Inner Temple, says:
" Service in the church ended, the gentlemen presently repair into the hall to
breakfast, with brawn, mustard, and
malmsey." At dinner, "at the first course
is served in a fair and large Bores Head,
upon a silver platter, with minstralsye."
Orig. Jurid., p. 155. Aubrey tells us (1678)
that, before the Civil Wars, it was customary in gentlemen's houses to bring in at
the first dish at Christmas a boar's head,
with a lemon in its mouth. Morant says
that the inhabitants of Horn Church, in
the Liberty of Havering, when they paid
the great tithes on Christmas Day, were
treated with a bull and brawn, and the
boar's head was wrestled for. The ceremony was long observed, as Hearne tells
us. at Queen's College, Oxford, with the
improvement that the boar's head was
neatly carved in wood. Ritson printed the
Carol sung in bringing in the head from
a collection published in 1521. *Ancient
Songs*, ed. 1877, p. 158. In later times the
words were greatly altered. In Dekker's
" Wonderful Yeare, 1603," signat. D 2,
our author, speaking of persons apprehen-
sive of catching the plague, says, "they,
went (most bitterly) miching and muffled
up and downe, with rue and wormewood
stuft into their eares and nosthrils, looking like so many bores heads stuck with
bianches of rosemary, to be served in for
brawne at Christmas." In the " Gothamite Tales," 1630, No. 18 is an anecdote of
a Scot, who ordered of a carver a boar's
head for a sign to his inn at Gotham.
"Hee did come to a carver or a joyner,
saying in his mother tongue : I say, speake,
canst thou make me a bare-head? Yea,
said the carver. Then said the Scottish-
man : make me a bare-head anonst Youle,
and thouse have twenty pence for thy hire.
I will doe it, said the carver. On S. An-
drewes day before Christmas the which is
named Youle in Scotland (and in England
in the North), the Scottish man did come
to London for the boreshead to set it at
the doore for a signe." This is alluded to
in King's " Art of Cookery," p. 75 :

" At Christmas time—
Then if you wou'd send up the brawner's
   head,
Sweet rosemary and bays around it
   spread ;
His foaming tusks let some large pippin
   grace,
Or, 'midst these thundring spears an
   orange place ;

Sauce, like himself, offensive to its foes,
The roguish mustard, dang'rous to the
   nose.
Sack, and the well-spic'd Hippocras the
   wine,
Wassail the bowl with antient ribbands
   fine,
Porridge with plumbs, and turkeys with
   the chine."

Boat-Show.—An annual ceremony
formerly practised at Cambridge, when the
College boats assembled at a certain point,
and were decorated with flags, flowers, &c.

Bodmin Riding.. — The late Mr.
Thomas Quiller Couch of Bodmin, one
of our best informed Cornish antiquaries, permitted me, in 1870, to
introduce here a full account of this
little-understood subject, communicated
by him some years before to the "Journal of the Penzance Society " : "Whilst
the material remains of the past, with
which our county abounds, have occupied
many an able pen and pencil, the curious
memorials of old forms of faiths and modes
of life, hardly less ancient and fully as
interesting, have been singularly neglected
by the Cornish antiquary. Modified in
the course of their long descent, until but
faint traces of their origin and intention
remain, there is frequently enough left unaltered to shew that they are in their form
as old as those relics which the ever-during
granite has preserved to us. It is quite
time, however, that a record should be
made of them, since the rapid fluctuations
and changes of the last fifty years have
done more to alter and efface them than
many previous centuries of stagnation, or
of very gradual progress. I shall begin
with a festival of which the remembrance
lingers only among people past middle-age,
and which is never likely to be revived. It
was kept at Bodmin on the Sunday and
Monday after St. Thomas à Becket's Day,
July 7. A puncheon of beer having been
brewed in the previous October, and duly
bottled in anticipation of the time, two or
three young men were entrusted with the
chief management of the affair, and who
represented the wardens of Carew's church
ales, went round the town attended
by a band of drums and fifes or other instruments. The crier saluted each house
with : ' To the people of this house, a prosperous morning, long life, health, and a
merry riding !' The musicians then struck
up the Riding Tune, a quick and inspirit-
ing measure, said by some to be as old as
the feast itself. The householder was solicited to taste the riding ale, which was
carried round in baskets. A bottle was
usually taken in, and it was acknowledged
by such a sum as the means or humour of
the townsman permitted, to be spent on
the public festivities of the season. Next

morning, a procession was formed, (all who could afford to ride mounted on horse or ass), first to the Priory, to receive two large garlands of flowers fixed on staves, and then in due order through the principal streets to the town-end, where the games were formally opened. The sports, which lasted two days, were of the ordinary sort; wrestling, foot-racing, jumping in sacks, &c. It is worthy of remark that a second or inferior brewing, from the same wort, was drunk at a minor merry-making at Whitsuntide. The description of the ceremony has been obtained from those who took part in its latest celebration. No one who compares this account of the riding with Carew's description of Church-ales, can doubt that the two were originally identical in their meaning. That the custom of keeping Church-ales on a Sunday was a common one, appears from a sermon preached by William Kethe, at Blandford Forum, in 1570; and in which he tells us that his holyday 'the multitude call their revelyng day, which day is spent in bull-baitings, beare-baitings, bowlings, dicying,' &c. In the accounts which are preserved relative to the rebuilding of Bodmin parish church, 'the stewards of the Ridyng-Gild' are mentioned as contributors. In an order, dated Nov. 15, 1583, regulating the business of shoemakers, (a class which seems for ages to have been more than usually numerous in Bodmin), it is directed by the Mayor and the masters of the occupation, 'that at the riding every master and journeyman shall give their attendance to the steward, and likewise bring him to the church, upon pain of 12d. for every master, and 6d. for every journeyman, for every such default, to the discretion of the masters of the occupation.' Polwhele gives an imperfect account of the Bodmin Riding. He is inclined to deduce it from the Floralia of Roman times; and he thinks that the Goddess Flora was, in later ages, superseded by St. Thomas of Canterbury, at whose shrine the garlands of flowers were presented. I have heard an opinion that the feast was in celebration of the restitution of St. Petrock's bones, which were stolen from the Priory of Bodmin about the year 1177, and carried to the Abbey of St. Mevennus in Brittany, but were restored at the powerful intercession of Henry II. Heath says, without giving any authority, that 'this carnival is said to be as old as the Saxons.' Several attempts have been made to resuscitate this festival, but it is now hopelessly dead. I have a deprecatory pamphlet, dated 1825, entitled: 'A leter to a Friend, relative to the approaching games commonly called Bodmin riding.' At this bright season, when field and wood put on their gayest green, and even tongueless things seem full of praise and thankfulness, it is not strange that the heart of man should be moved to joy and thanksgiving, even though the gratitude due to the Giver of all good may often be misdirected. The feast of the Summer Solstice modified by circumstances of time and place, but almost universally observed, is probably as old as the gratitude which the season's profusion naturally inspires; so that, instead of deriving our midsummer games from the floral festivities of the Romans, we should more rightly consider them as similar in meaning and coeval in origin. I have heard some doubts expressed as to the antiquity of the Riding Tune (appended to this account); and I have asked the opinion of William Sandys, Esq., F.S.A., a well-known antiquary, and an excellent authority on such a subject. He says: 'It struck me as having a similarity to some tunes of the last century, or perhaps the end of the 17th, and of which there are examples in 'The Dancing Master,' of which so many editions were published, although now not common. The tune, therefore, does not appear to be of very high antiquity; but, at the same time, there is something about it which might induce one to suppose it might be founded on an older tune.' Mr. Sandys kindly submitted it to Mr. Chappell, author of the excellent work on the Popular Music of England; and his opinion on such a point is especially valuable. Mr. Chappell considers it not more than thirty or forty years old, and founded on 'The Fall of Paris.' 'But even if this were so,' says Mr. Sandys, 'The Fall of Paris' is founded on, and almost identical with, the celebrated French revolutionary air 'Ça ira,' which is more than seventy years old.' I have direct proof of its being in use at this festival for a century past. Heath (and almost all our guide-books follow him) makes the Bodmin Riding identical with the Halgaver Sports; but with insufficient reason. He says: "A carnival is kept every year, about the middle of July, on Halgaver Moor, near Bodmin, resorted to by thousands of people; the sports and pastimes of which were so well liked by King Charles II., when he touched there in his way to Scilly, that he became a brother of the jovial society.' The MM. Lysons doubt the story of Charles's participation in these games, since the time of the Prince's journey to Scilly does not accord with the period of the festival. I know of no author, besides Carew, who makes independent mention of the Halgaver sports, and, from the account in the Survey, it would seem that Halgaver was the scene of perennial jokes; nor is it anywhere said that its usages and immunities were confined to any season. The Bodmin Riding is evidently quite distinct; though proably, at a time of great merry-making in the neighbourhood of the Moor, the 'ungracious pranks' may have been more than usually rife. No remembrance of Halgaver Court exists among people now resident in the neighbourhood. "Now and then,' says Carew, 'they extend this merriment, to the prejudice of overcredulous people persuading them to fight with a dragon lurking in Halgaver, or to see some strange matter there, which concluded at last with a training them into the mire.' This also is an interesting illustration of the social life of our forefathers. It was a custom, which the existence of good parish maps now renders less necesary, on one of the days of Rogation week to make a yearly renewal of the ancient landmarks :

' Our fathers us'd in reverent processions
(With zealous prayers and with praise-
    ful cheere),
To walke their parish-limits once a
    yeare :
And well-knowne marks (which sacri-
    legious hands
Now cut or breake) so bord'red out their
    lands,
That ev'ry one distinctly knew his own,
And many brawles, now rife, were then
    unknowne."

"In this procession, when clergy and people went round to beat the bounds of the parish, praying here and there at certain wonted spots, (frequently marked by a cross), it was usual to drag round an effigy of a dragon, representing the Spirit of evil. The Dragon usually came to some ignominous end, and the place where he finished his career is still known in many places by the name of Dragon Rock, Dragon Well, Dragon Pit. An excavation called 'Dragon Pit' still exists on Halgaver Moor."

The BODMIN "RIDING TUNE."

Boe Bullbagger.—See *Barguest* and *Bull-beggar.*

Bogane (Manx)..—See *Antiquary* for December, 1886.

Bo-Peep.—The best account of this child's amusement, which, however, grew into a proverb and an exclamation, is in Halliwell's *Popular Rhymes and Nursery Tales*, 1849, p. 109, *et seqq.* Compare Halliwell in v., *All - Hid* suprâ, and Davis, *Suppl. Glossary*, 1881. The fullest text is to be found. I think, in *Nursery Rhymes of England*, Percy Soc. ed. p. 75.

Boneshave.—The boneshave, a word perhaps nowhere used or understood in Devonshire but in the neighbourhood of Exmoor, means the sciatica ; and the Exmoorians, when affected therewith, use the following charm to be freed from it. The patient must lie upon his back on the bank of the river or brook of water, with a straight staff by his side between him and the water, and must have the following words repeated over him, viz. :

    Boneshave right,
    Boneshave straight,
    As the water runs by the stave
    Good for Boneshave."

They are not to be persuaded but that this ridiculous form of words seldom fails to give them a perfect cure. *Exmoor Scolding*, p. 8, note.

Bonfire.—

Hickes defines a Bonefire to be a feftive or triumphant fire. In the Iflandic language, he fays, *Baal* fignifies a burning. In the Anglo-Saxon, Bael-rẏp, by a change of letters of the fame organ, is made Baen-rẏp, whence our *Bonefire.*

In the Tinmouth MSS. cited so often in the History of Newcastle, " Boon-er," and " Boen-Harow," occur for ploughing and harrowing gratis, or by gift. There is a passage also, much to our purpose, in Ashton's Translation of Aubanus, p. 282 :— ' Common fires (or as we call them heere in England bonefires.)" I am therefore strongly inclined to think that bone-fire means a contribution fire, that is, a fire to which everyone in the neighbourhood contributes a certain portion of materials. The contributed Ploughing Days in Northumberland are called "Bone-daags." See also a letter from Pegge in the "Gent. Mag." for 1774, p. 315.

The third Council of Constantinople, A.D. 680, by its 65th canon, has the following interdiction: — "Those bonfires that are kindled by certaine people on new moones before their shops and houses, over which also they use ridiculously and foolishly to leape, by a certaine antient custome, we command them from henceforth to cease. Whoever therefore shall doe any such thing; if he be a clergyman, let him be deposed; if a layman, let him be excommunicated. For, in the Fourth Book of the Kings, it is thus written: "And Manasseh built an altar to all the hoast of heaven, in the two courts of the Lord's house, and made his children to passe through the fire,' &c." Prynne observes upon this: "Bonefires therefore had their originall from this idolatrous custome, as this Generall Councell hath defined; therefore all Christians should avoid them." And the Synodus Francica under Pope Zachary, A.D. 742, inhibits "those sacrilegious fires which they call *Nedfri* (or bonefires), and all other observations of the Pagans whatsoever." Bourne tells us, that it was the custom in his time, in the North of England, chiefly in country villages, for old and young people to meet together and be merry over a large fire, which was made for that purpose in the open street. This, of whatever materials it consisted, was called a bonefire. In Newton's "Observations upon the Prophecies of Daniel and the Apocalypse of St. John," the author observes, that "the heathens were delighted with the festivals of their gods, and unwilling to part with those ceremonies; therefore Gregory, Bishop of Neo-Cæsarea in Pontus, to facilitate their conversion, instituted annual festivals to the saints and martyrs: hence the keeping of Christmas with ivy, feasting, plays, and sports, came in the room of the Bacchanalia and Saturnalia, the celebrating May Day with flowers, in the room of the Floralia; and the festivals to the Virgin Mary, John the Baptist, and divers of the Apostles, in the room of the solemnities at the entrance of the Sun into the Signs of the Zodiac in the old Julian Calendar."—*Gent. Mag.* for 1733, and *Antiq. of Cornwall*, p. 130. Leaping over the fires is mentioned among the superstitious rites used at the Palilia in Ovid's *Fasti*. The Palilia were feasts instituted in honour of Pales, the goddess of shepherds (though Varro makes Pales masculine), on the calends of May. In order to drive away wolves from the folds, and distempers from the cattle, the shepherds on this day kindled several heaps of straw in their fields, which they leaped over. Borlase says sensibly: "Of the fires we kindle in many parts of England, at some stated times of the year, we know not certainly the rise, reason, or occasion; but they may probably be reckoned among the relicks of the Druid superstitious fires. In Cornwall the festival fires, called bonfires, are kindled on the eve of St. John Baptist and St. Peter's Day; and midsummer is thence, in the Cornish tongue, called 'Goluan,' which signifies both light and rejoicing. At these fires the Cornish attend with lighted torches, tarr'd and pitch'd at the end, and make their perambulations round their fires, and go from village to village carrying their torches before them, and this is certainly the remains of the Druid superstition, for 'faces præferre,' to carry lighted torches, was reckoned a kind of Gentilism ,and as such particularly prohibited by the Gallick Councils: they were in the eye of the law 'accensores facularum,' and thought to sacrifice to the devil, and to deserve capital punishment." Over and about this fire they frequently leap, and play at various games, such as running, wrestling, dancing, &c.; this, however, is generally confined to the younger sort; for the old ones, for the most part, sit by as spectators only of the vagaries of those who compose the

"Lasciva decentius ætas,"

and enjoy themselves over their bottle, which they do not quit till midnight, and sometimes till cock-crow the next morning.

In the play of "Sir Thomas More" (circâ 1590), Doll Williamson is made to say: "I, for we maye as well make bonefiers on Maye daye as at midsommer." "Leaping o'er a midsummer bonefire" is mentioned amongst other games in Tompson's "Garden of Delight," 1658. Torreblanca, in his "Demonology," has a passage, in which he tells us how the ancients were accustomed to pass their children of both sexes through the fire for the sake of securing them a prosperous and fortunate lot, and he adds that the Germans imitated this profane usage in their midsummer pyres in honour of the anniversary of St. John's Day. He, too, cites, among others, Ovid, where the poet says:—

"Certe ego transilii positas ter in ordine
 flammas."

Comp. *St. John's Eve* and *Midsummer*.

Books. — Books, by way of funeral tokens, used to be given away at the burials of the better sort in England. In my Collection of Portraits (notes Mr. Brand) I have one of John Bunyan, taken from before an old edition of his works,.

which I bought at Ware, in Hertfordshire. It is thus inscribed on the back in MS.: "Funeral Token in remembrance of Mr. Hen. Plomer, who departed this life Oct. 2, 1696, being 79 years of age, and is designed to put us that are alive in mind of our great change. Mr. Daniel Clerk the elder his book, Oct. 23, 1696." A writer in the "Athenian Oracle," considers that "a book would be far more convenient, more durable, and more valuable a present, than what are generally given, and more profitably preserve the memory of a deceased friend."

Boossenning.—See *Holy Wells.*

Booting. — Miss Baker, in her "Northamptonshire Glossary," 1854, describes this harvest usage of Booting, where any of the men has misconducted himself in the field. The culprit is brought up for trial at the harvest-home feast, and adjudged to be booted. The booting is also described by Clare the poet in his "Village Minstrel." A long form being placed in the kitchen, the good workers place themselves along it in a row, with their hands laid on each other's backs, so as to make a sort of bridge, over which the hog (so the delinquent is called, and there may be more than one) has to pass, running the gauntlet of a boot-legging, with which a fellow bastes him lustily as he scrambles over. The country people in Warwickshire use a sport at their harvest home, where one sits as a judge to try misdemeanors committed in harvest, and the punishment of the men is, to be laid on a bench and slapped on the breech with a pair of boots. This they call giving them the boots.

Borrowed or **Borrowing Days.** —There is a proverb: "April borrows three days of March, and they are ill." April is pronounced with an emphasis on the last syllable, so as to make a kind of jingling rhyme with "ill," the last word in the line. I have taken notice of this, because I find in the Roman Calendar the following observations on the 31st of March: "The rustic fable concerning the nature of the month. The rustic name of six days which shall follow in April, or may be the last in March." There is no doubt but that these observations in the Calendar, and our proverb, are derived from one common origin; but for want of more lights I am unable at present to trace them any farther. The Borrowed Days are common to many European countries, and M. Michel notices in his work on the Basques, that the idea prevails among that singular people. The Borrowing Days occur in "The Complaynt of Scotland." "There eftir i entrit in ane grene forest, to contempil the tendir zong frutes of grene treis, because the borial blastis of the thre

borouing dais of Marche hed chaissit the fragrant flureise of evyrie frut-tree far athourt the feildis."

"March said to Aperill,
I see three hogs upon a hill ;
But lend your three first days to me,
And I'll be bound to gar them die.
The first, it sall be wind and weet ;
The next, it sall be snaw and sleet ;
The third, it sall be sic a freeze
Sall gar the birds stick to the trees.
But when the Borrowed days were gane
The three silly hogs came hirplin hame."

The "Glossary" (in verbo) explains "Borrouing days, the three last days of March," and adds, "concerning the origin of the term, the following popular rhyme is often repeated :

"March borrowit fra Averill
Three days, and they were ill."

Speaking of the death of King James I., in 1625, at a time when a furious storm was raging along the Scotish coast, Chambers remarks : "This was long after remembered as the storm of the Borrowing Days. . . . It is a proverbial observation of the weather, which seems to be justified by fact, the bad weather being connected with the vernal equinox." *Domestic Annals of Scotland,* 2nd edit., i., 553. These days had not escaped the observation of Sir. T. Browne, who, however, gives no explanation. In the "Country Almanack" for 1676, among the "remarques upon April," are the following :

"No blust'ring blasts from March needs April borrow :
His own oft proves enow to breed us sorrow.
Yet if he weep (with us to sympathise), His trickling tears will make us wipe our eyes."

A clergyman in Devonshire informed Mr. Brand, about 1795, that the old farmers in his parish called the three first days of March "Blind Days," which were anciently considered as unlucky ones, and upon which no farmer would sow any seed. This superstition, however, was even then wearing out apace.

Bowed, or Crooked Money.— Bowed money appears anciently to have been sent as a token of love and affection from one relation to another. Thus we read in the "Third Part of Conny-Catching," by R. Greene, 1592, sign. b 2, verso : "Then taking fourth a bowed groat, and an olde pennie bowed, he gave it her as being sent from her uncle and aunt." In "The Country Wake," by Dogget, 1696, act v. sc. 1. Hob, who fancies he is dying, before he makes his last will and testimony, as he calls it, when his mother desires him to try to speak to Mary, " for she is thy wife, and no other," answers, " I know I'm sure to her—and I do own it before you all; I ask't her the question last Lammas, and at Allhollows'-tide we broke a piece of money; and if I had liv'd till last Sunday we had been ask'd in the church." Douce says:— " Analogous to the interchangement of rings seems the custom of breaking a piece of money." An example of this occurs in " Bateman's Tragedy," a well-known penny history, founded on Sampson's tragedy of the Vow Breaker," 1636, where the incident may be found. We find in *Hudibras* that the piece broken between the contracted lovers must have been a crooked one:

" Like Commendation Ninepence crook't, With to and from my Love it look't " ;

a circumstance confirmed also in " The Connoisseur," No. 56, with an additional custom, of giving locks of hair woven in a true lover's knot. " If, in the course of their amour, the mistress gives the dear man her hair wove in a true lover's knot, or breaks a crooken ninepence with him, she thinks herself assured of his inviolate fidelity." This " bent token " has not been overlooked by Gay:

" A ninepence bent,
A token kind, to Bumkinet is sent."

A crooked sixpence is probably yet regarded as lucky.

Bowing *towards the Altar or Communion Table on Entering the Church.*—This custom, which was prevalent when Bourne wrote (*Antiq. Vulg.* ch. v.), he deduces from the ancient practice of the Church of worshipping towards the east. This, says he, they did that, by so worshipping they might lift up their minds to God, who is called the Light, and the Creator of Light, therefore turning, says St. Austin, our faces to the east, from whence the day springs, that we might be reminded of turning to a more excellent nature, namely the Lord. As also, that as man was driven out of Paradise, which is towards the east, he ought to look that way, which is an emblem of his desire to return thither. St. Damascen therefore tells us that because the Scripture says that God planted Paradise in Eden towards the east, where he placed the man which he had formed, whom he punished with banishment upon his transgression, and made him dwell over against Paradise in the western part, v.) therefore pray (says he) being in quest of our ancient country, and, as it were, panting after it, do worship God that way.

It is almost superfluou· to observe that bowing toward the altar is a vestige of the ancient Ceremonial Law. Concession must be made by every advo-

cate for manly and rational worship, that there is nothing more in the east, than in the belfry at the west end, or in the body of the church. We wonder, therefore, however this custom was retained by Protestants. The cringes and bowings of the Roman Catholics to the altar are in adoration of the corporal presence, their wafer God, whom their fancies have seated and enthroned in this quarter of the East. *Durandus Rat.* 226. One who has left a severe satire on the retainers of those forms and ceremonies that lean towards popish superstiton, tells us: " If I were a Papist or Anthropo-morphite, who believes that God is enthroned in the East like a grave old King, I profess I would bow and cringe as well as any limber-ham of them all, and pay my adoration to that point of the compass (the East): but if men believe that the Holy One who inhabits Eternity, is also omnipresent, why do not they make correspondent ceremonies of adoration to every point of the compass?" Hickeringill's *Ceremony-Monger*, 15. " The maner of turnyng our faces to the Easte when wee praie, is taken of the old Ethnikes, whiche as Apuleius remembreth, used to loke Eastwarde and salute the sonne: we take it as a custom to put us in remembraunce that Christe is the sonne of Righteousnes, that discloseth all Secretes." Langley's *Polydore Virgil*, 1546, fol. 100, verso. Among the charges brought by Peter Smart, in 1628, against Bishop Cosin are the following: " Fifthly. He hath brought in a new custome of bowing the body downe to the ground before the altar (on which he hath set candlesticks, basons, and crosses, crucifixes, and tapers which stand ther for a dumb shew) : hee hath taught and enjoyned all such as come neere the altar to cringe and bow unto it: he hath commanded the choresters to make low leggs unto it, when they goe to light the tapers that are on it in the winter nights; and in their returne from it, hee hath enjoined them to make low leggs unto it againe, going backwards with their faces towards the East, till they are out of the inclosure where they usually stand. Sixthly: Hee enjoynes them all that come to the Cathedrall Church to pray with their faces towards the East, scoulding and brawling with them, even in time of divine service, which refuse to do it, and bidding them either to pray towards the East, or to be packing out of the church, so devoted is hee to this Eastern superstition." *Vanitie and Downfall of Superstitiovs Popish Ceremonies*, 1628. This was re-printed in 1640. We are informed by Crofton that " The late Archbishop Laud was the first that ever framed a canon for bowing to, towards, or before the Communion Table." *Altar-Worship*,

1661, pp. 60, 116. This shrewd writer adds: "For which, reason will require some symbol of divine nature and presence. Its being an holy instrument of divine service, being of no more force for the altar, than for the tongs, or snuffers of the tabernacle, or Aaron's breeches under the law, or for surplices, organs, chalices, patens, and canonical coates and girdles, which are made instruments of holy service, by our altar-adorers: and if on that reason they must be bowed unto, we shall abound in cringing not only in every church, but in every street. On Maundy Thursday, 1636, Mrs. Charnock, &c. went to see the King's Chapel, where they saw an altar, with tapers and other furniture on it, and a crucifix over it: and presently came Dr. Brown, one of his Majesties chaplaines, and his curate, into the Chappel, and turning themselves towards the altar, bowed three times: and then performing some private devotion departed: and immediately came two seminarie priests and did as the doctor and his curate had done before them." *Altar-worship*, 1661, pp. 60, 116. In the "Lincoln Articles of Enquiry," 1641, the following occurs: "Do you know of any parson, vicar, or curate that hath introduced any offensive rites or ceremonies into the Church, not established by the lawes of the land: as namely, that make three courtesies towards the Communion Table, that call the said table an altar, that enjoyne the people at their coming into the Church to bow towards the East, or towards the Communion-table?" Mr. Brand tells us that he observed this practice in College Chapels at Oxford. But in 1813 Sir H. Ellis remarks: "The practice of bowing to the altar, the Editor believes, is now entirely left off at Oxford. That of turning to it at the repetition of the Creed is pretty generally retained, and certainly has its use, in contributing very often to recall the wandering thoughts of those who attend the Chapel service."

Mede tells us that whatever reverential guise, ceremony, or worship they used at their ingress into churches, in the ages next to the apostles (and some he believes they did) is wholly buried in silence and oblivion. The Jews used to bow themselves towards the mercy-seat. The Christians, after them, in the Greek and Oriental Churches, have, time out of mind, and without any known beginning, used to bow in like manner. They do it at this day. Gregory tells us, that the holy men of Jerusalem held a tradition generally received from the ancients that our Saviour himself was buried with his face and feet towards the east. Bourne quotes Bede as his authority for saying, "that as the holy women entered at the eastern part into the circular house hewn out in the rock, they saw the Angel sitting at the south part of the place, where the body of Jesus had lain, i.e., at his right hand: for undoubtedly his body, having its face upwards and the head to the west, must have its right hand to the south." I find the following in "A Light Shining out of Darknes, or Occasional Queries," 1659, p. 26: "This reason likewise the common people give for their being buryed with their feet towards the east, so that they may be in a fitter posture to meet the Sun of Righteousness when he shall appear with healing in his wings, viz. at the Resurrection." The subsequent remark is found at p. 30, "Whether it be not a pretty foundation for the Oxford doctors to stand booted and spurred in the Act? because there is mention made in the Scripture of being shod with the preparation of the Gospel?"

"'Tis in the main allowed," says Selden, "that the heathens did, in general, look towards the East, when they prayed, even from the earliest ages of the World." Asplin's *Al Kibla*, 1728-31, quoted by Ellis. Comber says, "Some antient authors tell us that the old inhabitants of Attica buried thus before the days of Solon, who, as they report, convinced the Athenians that the Island of Salamis did of right belong to them by shewing them dead bodies looking that way, and sepulchres turned towards the east, as they used to bury." And the Scholiast upon Thucydides says it was the manner of all the Greeks to bury their dead thus. Again, it was used when they were baptized: they first turned their faces to the west, and so renounced the Devil, and then to the east, and made their covenant with Christ. Lastly, those of the ancient Church prayed that way, believing that our Saviour would come to judgment from that quarter of the heavens, St. Damascen asserting that when he ascended into Heaven, he was taken up eastward, and that his disciples worshipped him that way; and therefore chiefly it was, that in the ancient Church they prayed with their faces to the east.

Bowing at the Name of Jesus.—Several arguments against this usage were published in a tract "by a learned author" in 1660. Both as regards bowing to the altar and in this other act, it is to be remarked that the conventional usage of women curtseying is a solecism.

Bowl or Bowling Alley.—A covered space for the game of bowls instead of a green. See Halliwell in v. Stevenson, in his *Twelve Months*, 1661, (taken from Breton's Fantasticks, 1626), says under July: "Bowling (however tearmed like cards and dice unlawfull) I am sure is an healthfull exercise, and good for the body, and hath been prescribed for a recreation to great persons by the learned Physitians in which is a great deale of art and judgment to be seen especially in the expert bowler in choosing out his ground, ... whether it be in open wide places, or in Allies, and in this sport the choosing of the Bowles is not the least of the cunning belongs to it; your flat bowles being well for close Allies, your round byassed bowles for open ground of advantage, and your round bowles like a ball for green swarths that are plaine and levell." Braithwaite, in his "Rules for the Government of the house of an Earle," (circâ 1640) describes it as one of the duties of the gardener, "to make faire bowling alleys, well banked, and soaled; which being well kepte in many howses are very profitable to the gardiners."

The Bowling Green House was an old establishment under that name on Putney Heath, on the site of the residence of the younger Pitt. It is presumably the establishment to which John Locke alludes in his *Journal* under 1679, stating that during the whole summer several persons of quality might be seen bowling there two or three times a week. It was taken in 1693 by Edward Locket, keeper of an ordinary in Whitehall, and had originally, no doubt, been a small and stealthy incroachment on the common, due to the negligence or complicity of the authorities. "The Bowling Green House at Putney," observes a writer in 1761, "is pleasantly situated, and affords a fine prospect. It is now turned into one of those fashionable summer breakfasting-places, which level all distinction, and mingle the sexes together in company." Marylebone and Islington were also formerly celebrated for their bowling greens, which were also found in the centre of the Metropolis, as we know it. Locke mentions Marylebone in 1679. One was attached to Shaver's Hall in the Haymarket. The reader may be referred to an interesting paper on bowling-greens in *Notes and Queries* for January 15, 1887. See also "A description of a Bowling Alley" in the "Compleat Gamester," 1674, and compare Nares, *Glossary*, 1859, in v. and under *Skittles*.

Half-Bowl.—What was termed the Half-Bowl is mentioned in a tract of 1580. "It was my chance," says the writer, "to be at John Crokes, where there is a bowling alley of the half bowle, whether doth repaire many merchants and sundry gentlemen, and in a chamber above divers were at play." The half-bowl was sufficiently celebrated to induce Francis Coules, the popular bookseller of Charles the First and Second's times, to adopt it as part of his sign, which formed a rather singular compound—"The Lamb and the Half-Bowl." In an edition of the "History of Tom a Lincoln," 1655, however, the imprint bears the latter only.

Bowls.—It is rather difficult to determine whether the game, which was to console the Princess of Hungary in her despondency, was the same as our bowls: if so, it was surely an indifferent prescription. In the "Squyr of Lowe Degre," the following passage is found:

" An hundreth Knightes truly tolde,
Shall play with bowles in alayes colde,
Your disease to driue awaie."

A fair account of this diversion is given in Strutt's "Sports and Pastimes," and probably the best early one is in Taylor the Water-Poet's *Wit and Mirth*, 1629: "This wise game of bowling," says he, "doth make the fathers surpasse their children in apish toyes and delicate dog-trickes. As first for the postures: first handle your bowle: secondly, aduance your bowle; thirdly, charge your bowle: fourthly, ayme your bowle: fifthly, discharge your bowle: sixthly, plye your bowle: in which last posture of plying your bowle you shall perceiue many varieties and diuisions as wringing of the necke, lifting vp of the shoulders, clapping of the hands, lying downe of one side, running after the bowle, making long dutifull scrapes and legs (sometimes bareheaded), with entreating him to flee, flee, flee: and though the bowler bee a gentleman, yet there hee may meet with attendant rookes, that sometimes will bee his betters six to four or two to one. . . . A bowler, although the allye or marke bee but thirty or forty paces, yet sometimes I haue heard the bowler cry, Rub, rub, rub, and sweare and lye that hee was gone an hundred miles, when the bowle hath beene short of the blocke two yards. The marke which they ayme at hath sundry names and epithites, as a blocke, a jacke, and a mistris." Perhaps the foregoing passage may serve to elucidate the rather obscure title (as it has been regarded) of Freeman's Epigrams," 1614 — "Rubbe and a Great Cast." Our ancestors pursued it with peculiar ardour and delight, and it is still a favourite amusement. Stow seems to say that, in his time, the open ground about London was being gradually built upon, and that the archers encroached upon the bowling alleys. Sir Nicholas Carew was playing at bowls with Henry VIII., when by some retort to an offensive remark by Henry, he gave umbrage to the latter, and was disgraced, and ultimately executed in 1539 on Tower Hill. In the Privy Purse Expenses of the Princess Mary, under April, 1538-9, there is a highly-curious entry:— "Itm. payd for a brekefaste loste at Bolling by my lady maryes gce.

. . . xs." It appears also from passages in "Wit at Several Weapons," and other dramas, that the small ball, which is now called the Jack, was sometimes known as the mistress."

It may be recollected that, in the feuds of the great families of Scotland in the sixteenth century, the murderer of George Drummond came upon him while he and his friends were playing at the game. See a letter in the *Antiquary* for January, 1886. While Charles I. was at Holmby in 1647, he frequented the bowling green at Althorp. One of the pleasanter traits in the personal history of Charles is the recourse of the King to the country seat of Mr. Richard Shute, a Turkey merchant, at Barking in Essex, for the purpose of playing with him at this game. Shute used to be called by his majesty *Satin* Shute, from the material of which his doublet was made. Sometimes one won, sometimes the other; but on one occasion Charles lost so frequently, that he gave up. His entertainer begged him to try another turn—another £1,000; but the King, laying his hand on his shoulder, said : "I must remember I have a wife and children to keep." In the story of *The King and a Poor Northern Man*, 1640, the latter, coming up to London to seek redress, does not believe that it is the King, whom they point out to him at the Court, playing at bowls in his shirt-sleeves. We have all heard how the poet Suckling, living at the same time:

"Prized black eyes and a lucky hit
At bowls above all the trophies of wit."

Charles's successor in the Stuart line, the merry monarch, is reported to have played at the same diversion with his select set for an East—a watch made by the early master of the craft so-named. A game at bowls or ninepins was formerly at least a favourite diversion for the rowing parties up the Thames between Putney and Teddington, and the riverside places of entertainment were usually provided with accommodation for this purpose.

Boxing. — Misson, in his *Travels in England*, toward the close of the 17th century, speaking of sports and diversions, says: "Anything that looks like fighting is delicious to an Englishman. If two little boys quarrel in the street, the passengers stop, make a ring round them in a moment and set them against one another, that they may come to fisticuffs. When 'tis come to a fight, each pulls off his neckcloth and his waistcoat, and gives them to hold to the standers-by; (some will strip themselves quite naked to their wastes;) then they begin to brandish their fists in the air; the blows are aim'd all at the face, they kick one another's shins, they tug one another by the hair, &c. He

that has got the other down, may give him one blow or two before he rises, but no more; and let the boy get up ever so often, the other is obliged to box him again as often as he requires it. During the fight the ring of by-standers encourage the combatants with great delight of heart, and never part them while they fight according to the rules: and these by-standers are not only other boys, porters, and rabble, but all sorts of men of fashion; some thrusting by the mob, that they may see plain, others getting upon stalls; and all would hire places if scaffolds could be built in a moment. The father and mother of the boys let them fight on as well as the rest, and hearten him that gives ground or has the worst. These combats are less frequent among grown men than children; but they are not rare. If a coachman has a dispute about his fare with a gentleman that has hired him, and the gentleman offers to fight him to decide the quarrel, the coachman consents with all his heart: the gentleman pulls off his sword, lays it in some shop, with his cane, gloves, and cravat, and boxes in the same manner as I have described above. If the coachman is soundly drubb'd, which happens almost always, (a gentleman seldom exposes himself to such a battle without he is sure he's strongest) that goes for payment; but if he is the beater, the beatée must pay the money about which they quarrell'd." Brand once saw the Duke of Grafton at fisticuffs, in the open street, with such a fellow, whom he lamb'd most horribly. It was in the very widest part of the Strand. The Duke was big and extremely robust. He had hid his Blue Ribband, before he took the coach, so that the coachman did not know him. Compare *Bartholomew Fair* for a curious anecdote of Dr. Johnson's uncle. "In France," adds Misson, "we punish such rascals with our cane, and sometimes with the flat of our sword: but in England this is never practis'd; they use neither sword nor stick against a man that is unarm'd : and if an unfortunate stranger (for an Englishman would never take it into his head) should draw his sword upon one that had none, he'd have a hundred people upon him in a moment, that would, perhaps, lay him so flat that he would hardly ever get up again till the Resurrection."

Boy-Bishop. — It is uncertain at what period the custom of electing boy bishops on St. Nicholas's Day commenced in England; but there is little doubt that after it had been established on the continent, it would soon be imported hither. The association of this saint with the rite was, of course, due to his patronage of children. Warton thought he found traces of the religious mockery of the boy bishop as early as 867 or 870, in the Greek Church. *H.E.P.*, by Hazlitt, 1871, ii., 228-32, where farther particulars may be found. The ceremony has been traced to Canterbury, Eton (1441), St. Paul's, London, Colchester, Norwich, Winchester (1380), Exeter, Salisbury, Wells, Westminster, Lambeth, York, Beverley, Rotherham, Newcastle-upon-Tyne, and to several places abroad; there can be little doubt that it was almost universal. Gregory thought that the boy bishop was peculiar to Salisbury, perhaps because he met with the usage in the Sarum service book, and Warton supposed that the custom was confined to collegiate churches. It seems to be thought that this character was originally known as *Episcopus Choristarum* merely. In the archives of Norwich, down to 1521, are sundry entries relevant to the expenses incurred here on this anniversary, and notices of moneys left to support the institution. Aubrey's *Letters, &c.,* 1813, i. 302-4. In the statutes of Salisbury Cathedral, enjoined anno 1319, Tit. 45, it is ordered that the boy bishop shall not make a feast. The boy bishop, as it should seem from the Register of the capitulary Acts of York Cathedral under the date 1367 was to be *corpore formosus*, or the election to be void; and as in the same church, under a regulation of 1390, every chorister was bound to possess "claram vocem puerilem," such a quality was as justly imperative in the *episcopus puerorum*. Hazlitt's Warton, 1871, iv., 237 The Boy Bishop at Salisbury is actually said to have had the power of disposing of such prebends there as happened to fall vacant during the days of his episcopacy.

Edward I., in the 28th year of his reign, being near Newcastle-upon-Tyne, gave forty shillings to the Boy-Bishop and his companions for singing before him on St. Nicholas's Eve. It was during the King's passage through Newcastle on this occasion that a boy-bishop said vespers before him in his chapel at Heton. It appears that at Canterbury in 1464 there was no election of a boy bishop in the Grammar-school owing to the default or negligence of the masters. *Liber Johannis Stone, monachi eccl. Cant. de Obitibus, &c. sui Cenobii* (1415-67), a MS. in the library of C. C. C. Camb. One of the original rules drawn up for the scholars of Dean Colet's Foundation, in 1510, was: "Your chylde shal, on Chyldermas Daye, wayte vpon the boy byshop at Paules, and offer there—.' In the Statutes of St. Paul's, 1518, the following clause occurs: "All these children shall every Childermas Daye come to Paulis Churche and hear the Childe Bishop sermon: and after be at the hygh masse, and each of them offer a 1d. to the Childe Bishop, and with them the Maisters and Surveyors of the Scole." A tract by Hugh Rhodes, one of the children of the chapel

under Henry VIII., appeared, according to Herbert, in 1555, containing, in thirty-six 6-line stanzas, the "Song of the Child-Bishop of St. Paul's," as it was sung before the queen at her manor of St. James in the Fields in her privy chamber on St. Nicholas's Day and Innocents' Day that year. It is described as a fulsome panegyric, in which the queen is compared to Judith, Esther, the Queen of Sheba, and the Virgin.

In cathedrals this Boy Bishop seems to have been elected from among the children of the choir. After his election, being completely apparelled in the episcopal vestments, with a mitre and crozier, he bore the title and state of a Bishop, and exacted ceremonial obedience from his fellows, who were dressed like priests. Strange as it may appear, they took possession of the Church, and, except mass, performed all the ceremonies and offices. Northumb. Househ. Book, ed. 1827, p. 439, for an 'Inventory of the Robes and Ornaments of a Boy or Bearn Bishop." In Hearne's "Liber Niger Scaccarii, 1728, vol. ii., pp. 674, 686, we find that Archbishop Rotheram bequeathed "a myter for the Barnebishop, of cloth of gold, with two knopps of silver gilt and enamyled." But in the ordinary churches the appointments were almost equally sumptuous and costly. The Churchwardens' accounts of St Mary at Hill, 10 Henry VI., mention two children's copes, also a mitre of cloth of gold, set with stones. In 1523, 2s. 8d. are charged for the Bishop's dinner and his company on St. Nicholas's Day in the same accounts at Lambeth. Even posterior to the Proclamation of 33 Henry VIII., in the St. Mary at Hill books, 1549, is: "For 12 oz. silver, being clasps of books and the Bishop's mitre, at vs. viijd. per oz. vjl. xvis. jd." These last were sold. In the "Inventory of Church Goods" belonging to the same parish, at the same time, we have: "Item, a mitre for a Bishop at St. Nicholas-tyde, garnished with silver, and enamyled, and perle, and counterfeit stone." Maskell pointed out that, from the services to be said by the Boy Bishop and his choristers, as laid down in the Sarum Processional, it appears that "not only upon the Innocents' or Childermass Day did the 'Episcopus Puerorum' claim his rights, and perform all the ecclesiastical duties of his temporary rank, except the mass, but from the feast of St. Nicholas to Innocents' Day, a period of nearly a month. Whence it does not seem so extraordinary, as it otherwise might, that during this time the Boy Bishop might die, in which case he would be buried with the due honours: and the tomb at Salisbury is explained." *Selected Centuries of Books,* 1843, pp. 15-16, *note.* On the eve of Innocents' Day, the Boy Bishop was to go in solemn procession with his fellows, to the altar of the Holy Trinity and All Saints, or (as the Pie directs) to the altar of Holy Innocents or Holy Trinity in their copes, and burning tapers in their hands. The Bishop beginning, and the other boys following: "Centum quadraginta quatuor," &c. Then the verse, "Hi emti sunt ex omnibus,' &c. and this was sung by three of the boys. Then all the boys sang the "Prosa sedentem in supernâ majestatis arce," &c. The Chorister Bishop, in the mean time, fumed the altar first, and then the image of the Holy Trinity. Then the Bishop said *modestâ voce* the verse "Lætamini," and the response was, "Et gloriamini," &c. Then the prayer which we yet retain: "Deus cujus hodierna die," &c. In their return from the altar Præcentor puerorum incipiat, &c., the chanter-chorister began "De Sancta Maria," &c. The response was "Felix namque," &c., et "sic processio," &c. The procession was made into the quire, by the west door, in such order that the dean and canons went foremost: the chaplains next: the Bishop, with his little Prebendaries, in the last and highest place. The Bishop took his seat, and the rest of the children disposed themselves upon each side of the quire, upon the uppermost ascent, the canons resident bearing the incense and the book: and the petit canons the tapers, according to the Rubrick. And from this hour to the full end of the next day's procession no clerk is accustomed (whatever his condition may be) to take place above his superiors. Then the Bishop on his seat said the verse: "Speciosus forma, &c. diffusa est gratia in labiis tuis," &c. Then the prayer, "Deus qui salutis æternæ," &c., "Pax vobis," &c. Then after the "Benedicamus Domino," the Bishop, sitting in his seat, gave the Benediction to the people in this manner: "Princeps Ecclesiæ Pastor ovilis cunctam plebam tuam benedicere digneris," &c. Then, turning towards the people, he sang or said: "Cum mansuetudine & charitate humiliate vos ad benedictionem" : the chorus answering, "Deo gratias." Then the cross-bearer delivered up the crozier to the Bishop again, *et tunc Episcopus puerorum primò signando se in fronte sic dicat*, "Adjutorium nostrum," &c. The chorus answering "Qui fecit Cœlum & Terram." Then, after some other like ceremonies performed, the Bishop began the Completorium or Complyn; and that done, he turned towards the quire, and said, "Adjutorium," &c., and then, last of all, he said, "Benedicat Vos omnipotens Deus, Pater, and Filius, & Spiritus Sanctus." All this was done with solemnity of celebration, and under pain of anathema to any that should interrupt or press upon these children. See

Gregory's Works, 1649, p. 114. The show of the Boy Bishop, rather on account of its levity and absurdity, than of its superstition, was formally abrogated by a Proclamation, July 22, 1542. But it had been interdicted abroad, a century before, by the Council of Basle, 1431, as appears from a citation in Prynne's "Histriomastix," 1633, and the later statutory prohibition was more or less disregarded in England. The conclusion of Henry VIII.'s Proclamation is: "And whereas heretofore dyvers and many superstitious and chyldysh observauncies have be used, and yet to this day are observed and kept, in many and sundry partes of this Realm, as upon Saint Nicholas, the Holie Innocents, and such like, children be strangelie decked and apparayled to counterfeit Priests, Bishops, and Women, and to be ledde with songes and dances from house to house, blessing the people, and gathering of money ; and boyes do singe masse and preache in the pulpitt, with such other unfittinge and inconvenient usages, rather to the derysyon than anie true glorie of God, or honour of his sayntes. The Kynges Majestie wylleth and commaundeth that henceforth all such superstitious observations be left and clerely extinguished throwout all this Realme and Dominions." Bishop Tanner, in a letter to Hearne, says in allusion to the abuse of the ancient custom, that the choristers chose a bishop and waited on him in procession to several houses in the city, where the little rogues took great liberties. And Tanner traces to this circumstance the bye-name of St. Nicholas's Clerks conferred on them.

In Hall's "Triumphs of Rome" (Triumphs of Pleasure) he equally animadverts on the licence, which had crept into this Romish Observance, when he says, "What merry work it was here in the days of our holy fathers (and I know not whether, in some places, it may not be so still), that upon St. Nicholas, St. Katherine, St. Clement, and Holy Innocents' Day, children were wont to be arrayed in chimers, rochets, surplices, to counterfeit bishops and priests, and to be led, with songs and dances, from house to house, blessing the people, who stood girning in the way to expect that ridiculous benediction. Yea, that boys in that holy sport were wont to sing masses and to climb into the pulpit to preach (no doubt learnedly and edifyingly) to the simple auditory. And this was so really done, that in the cathedral church of Salisbury (unless it be lately defaced) there is a perfect monument of one of these Boy Bishops (who died in the time of his young pontificality) accoutred in his episcopal robes, still to be seen. Strype, however, in his "Memorials," speaking of the Boy

Bishop, among scholars, says: "I shall only remark that there might be this at least be said in favour of this old custom, that it gave a spirit to the children, and the hopes that they might at one time or other attain to the real mitre, and so made them mind their books."

With the Catholic Liturgy, all the pageantries of popery were restored to their ancient splendour by Queen Mary. Among these, the procession of the Boy Bishop was too popular a mummery to be overlooked. In Strype we read that, Nov. 13, 1554, an edict was issued by the Bishop of London to all the Clergy of his Diocese, to have a Boy Bishop in procession. In the same volume, however, we read, "The which was St. Nicholas Eve, at even-song time came a commandment that St. Nicholas should not go abroad nor about. But, notwithstanding, it seems, so much were the citizens taken with the mock of St. Nicholas, that is, a Boy Bishop, that there went about these St. Nicholases in divers parishes, as in St. Andrew's, Holborn, and St. Nicolas Olaves in Bread-street. The reason the procession of St. Nicolas was forbid, was, because the Cardinal had this St. Nicolas Day sent for all the Convocation, Bishops, and inferior Clergy, to come to him to Lambeth, there to be absolved from all their perjuries, schisms and heresies." In the accounts of St. Mary-at-Hill, London, 1554, is the following entry: "Paid for makyng the Bishops myter, with staff and lace that went to it, iiis. Paid for a boke for St. Nicholas, viijd." Strype says, that in 1556, on St. Nicholas' Even, "St. Nicholas, that is a boy habited like a bishop in pontificalibus, went abroad in most parts of London, singing after the old fashion, and was received with many ignorant but well-disposed people into their houses, and had as much good cheer as ever was wont to be had before, at least in many places." The Boy Bishop would naturally be put down again when Queen Elizabeth came to the crown: and yet, by Puttenham's account, it was exhibited in the country villages after her accession. Puttenham wrote his "Art of English Poesy" many years before it was published in 1589. He says: "Methinks this fellow speaks like Bishop Nicholas: for on St. Nicholas's night, commonly, the scholars of the country make them a bishop, who, like a foolish boy, goeth about blessing and preaching with such childish terms as make the people laugh at his foolish counterfeit speeches." The special service for Innocents' Day, in an early printed copy of it, is described as "In die innocentium sermo pro episcopo puerorum." It commences with the words: "Laudate, pueri, domi-

num, psalmo centesimo xii° et pro buius colacionis fundamento."

In the Posthumous Works of John Gregory, 1650, there is a monograph on this subject with three engravings; it is called: Episcopus Puerorum, In die Innocentium; or a Discoverie of an Antient Custom in the Church of Sarum, making an Anniversarie Bishop among the Choristers." In 12 Edward III., while the King was at Antwerp, the Boy-Bishop there received 13s. 6d. for singing before his majesty in his chamber. Hazlitt's Warton, 1871, ii., 229.

Aubanus tells us, that scholars on St. Nicholas's Day used to elect three out of their numbers, one of whom was to play the bishop, the other two the parts of Deacons. The Bishop was escorted by the rest of the boys, in solemn procession, to church, where with his mitre on, he presided during the time of divine worship: this ended, he and his deacons went about singing from door to door, and collected money, not begging it as alms, but demanding it as the Bishop's subsidy. On the eve of this day the boys were prevailed upon to fast, in order to persuade themselves that the little presents which were put that night for them into shoes (placed under the table for that purpose), were made them by St. Nicholas: and many of them kept the fast so rigorously on this account, that their friends, in order to prevent them from injuring their healths, were under the necessity of forcing them to take some sustenance. Bowle says, that in Spain formerly, on this commemoration-day, a chorister being placed with solemnity in the midst of the choir, upon a scaffold, there descended from the vaulting of the ceiling a cloud, which stopping, midway, opened. Two angels within it carried the mitre, and descended just so low as to place it on his head, ascending immediately in the same order in which they came down. This came to be an occasion of some irregularities; for till the day of the Innocents, he had a certain jurisdiction, and his prebendaries took secular offices, such as alguasils, catchpoles, dog-whippers and sweepers. From a paper in the St. James's Chronicle," for Nov. 16-18, 1797, it appears that at Zug, in Switzerland, the ceremonies of this day were suppressed in that year in consequence of the complaint addressed to the authorities against the exactions of the Boy Bishop and his attendants, who visited all the booths, &c., and demanded money.

Bragot Sunday.—In Lancashire, or some parts of it, a spiced ale, called Braget or Bragot, used to be drunk very largely on Palm Sunday, which was thence called Bragot Sunday.

Branks.—"They have an artifice at Newcastle under Lyme and Walsall," says Plot, "for correcting of scolds, which it does, too, so effectually and so very safely, that I look upon it as much to be preferred to the cucking stoole, which not only endangers the health of the party, but also gives the tongue liberty 'twixt every dipp; to neither of which this is at all liable: it being such a bridle for the tongue as not only quite deprives them of speech, but brings shame for the transgression and humility thereupon, before 'tis taken off: which being put upon the offender by order of the magistrate, and fastened with a padlock behind, she is led round the town by an officer, to her shame, nor is it taken off till after the party begins to shew all external signes imaginable of humiliation and amendment." *Staffordshire*, p. 389. In a plate annexed, he gives a representation of a pair of branks. They still preserve a pair in the Town Court at Newcastle-upon-Tyne, where the same custom once prevailed. Gardner's *England's Grievance*, 1656, and Brand's *History*, ii., 292. A fuller description of the brank occurs in Willis's "Current Notes" for May, 1854, where several engravings accompany and illustrate the letter-press. The writer says: It may be described as an iron skeleton helmet, having a gag of the same metal, that by being protruded into the mouth of an inveterate brawler, effectually branked that unruly member, the tongue. As an instrument of considerable antiquity at a time when the gag, the rack, and the axe were the *ratio ultima Romæ*, it has doubtless been employed, not unfrequently for purposes of great cruelty, though in most examples, the gag was not purposely designed to wound the mouth, but simply to restrain or press down the tongue. Several of these instruments are yet extant, though their use has now, thanks to more considerate civilization, become obsolete. . . . The earliest use of the brank in England is not antecedent to the reign of Charles." A curious variety of this old mode of penance is noticed in the same miscellany for October, 1854.

Brawl.—A dance introduced from France in or about the middle of the sixteenth century. See Halliwell in v.

Bread.—In Craven, in the West Riding of York, those who knead dough for baking are in the habit of making the sign of the cross, both when they knead or stiffen the material, and when they elt or moisten it with additional milk or milk and water, as a precaution against the sinister action of any witch or evil-eyed person at hand. Douce, in his interleaved copy of Brand's "Antiquities," pointed out that M. Thiers (in his *Traitè des Superstitions*) mentioned a belief as prevalent in France that bread baked on Christmas Eve would not turn mouldy.

Bread and Cheese Land.—Hasted, speaking of Biddenden, tells us that "twenty acres of land, called the Bread and Cheese Land, lying in five pieces, were given by persons unknown, the yearly rents to be distributed among the poor of this parish. This is yearly done on Easter Sunday, in the afternoon, in 600 cakes, each of which have the figures of two women impressed on them, and are given to all such as attend the church; and 270 loaves, weighing three pounds and a half a-piece, to which latter is added one pound and a half of cheese, are given to the parishioners only at the same time. There is a vulgar tradition in these parts, that the figures on the cake represent the donors of this gift, being two women twins, who were joined together in their bodies, and lived together so till they were between twenty and thirty years of age. But this seems without foundation. The truth seems to be, that it was the gift of two maidens, of the name of Preston; and that the print of the women on the cakes has taken place only within these fifty years, and was made to represent two poor widows, as the general objects of a charitable benefaction." "At Biddenden, Kent, yesterday, there was observed a curious Easter custom of distributing cakes bearing the impressed figures of the "Biddenden Maids." Their names were Eliza and Mary Chulkhurst, and they are said to have lived to the age of 34 years, when one died, and the other followed within six hours. They bequeathed land in the parish which produces about forty guineas a year, and from this the cost of the distribution is defrayed. The custom always attracts a very considerable number of visitors from the surrounding villages, and it is among these that the cakes, having a quaint representation of the maids, stamped with a boxwood die, are distributed, bread and cheese being given to the poor of the parish." *Globe*, April, 8 1890. There is a similar custom at Paddington, near London, where the gifts are thrown from the church steeple.

Breakfasting.—A Sussex custom. *Sussex Arch. Coll.*, xiv., 135.

Briaval's, St.—At St. Briaval's, Gloucestershire, a very strange quasi-jocular custom formerly prevailed on Whit-Sunday. Several baskets full of bread and cheese, cut very small, were brought into church, and immediately after service were thrown by the churchwardens from the galleries among the congregation, who scrambled for them. The custom was kept up, and may be still, in order to secure to the poor of St. Briaval's and Havelfield the right of cutting and carrying wood from 3,000 acres of coppice in Hudknoll and the Meend. Every householder was assessed 2d. towards defraying the cost of the bread and cheese.

In 1687, the "Orders and Rules of the Court of St. Briavells in the Forest of Dean, in the County of Gloucester," were printed in a volume with similar regulations for the miners in the Forest.

Bridal Bed.—In the papal times no new-married couple could go to bed together till the bridal bed had been blessed. In a MS. cited by Blakeway, it is stated that "the pride of the clergy and the bigotry of the laity were such that new married couples were made to wait till midnight, after the marriage day, before they would pronounce a benediction, unless handsomely paid for it, and they durst not undress without it, on pain of excommunication." Blomefield's *Norfolk*, iv. 221.

Bride-Ale. — In Ihre's "Glossarium Suio-Gothicum," 1769, we read : v. *Brudskal.* Gifwa i Brudskålen dicitur de Erano vel munere collectitio, quod Sponsæ diæ Nuptiarum a Convivis in pateram mittitur, habito antea brevi Sermone a præsente Sacerdote. Nescio, an huc quicquam faciat Tributum illud, quod in Gallia Sponsæ dabatur Escuellatta dictum, et de quo Du-Fresne in Gloss. Lat." Ibid. v. *Jul* p. 1005 : "Hemkomol, *Convivium quod novi Conjuges in suis œdibus instruunt.*" In the "Christen State of Matrimony," 1543, fol. 48, verso, we read : "When they come home from the church, then beginneth excesse of eatyng and dryncking—and as much is waisted in one daye, as were sufficient for the two newe married folkes halfe a year to lyve upon." The following is from the Court Rolls of Hales-Owen Borough, Salop, of the 15th Elizabeth : — *Custom of Bride-Ale* : "Item, a payne is made that no person or persons that shall brewe any weddyn ale to sell, shall not brewe above twelve strike of mault at the most, and that the said persons so married shall not keep nor have above eight messe of persons at his dinner within the burrowe : and before his brydall daye he shall keep no unlawfull games in hys house, nor out of hys house, on pain of 20 shillings." In Harrison's "Description of Britain," it is remarked : "In feasting also the husbandmen do exceed after their manner, especially at bridales, &c., where it is incredible to tell what meat is consumed and spent ; ech one brings such a dish, or so manie with him, as his wife and he doo consult upon, but alwaies with this consideration, that the leefer friend shall have the better provision." Thus it appears that among persons of inferior rank a contribution was expressly made for the purpose of assisting the bridegroom and bride in their

new situation. This custom must have doubtless been often abused : it breathed, however, a great deal of philanthropy, and would naturally help to increase population by encouraging matrimony. This custom of making presents at weddings seems also to have prevailed amongst those of the higher order. From the account of the nuptials of the Lady Susan with Sir Philip Herbert, in the reign of James I. it appears that the presents of plate and other things given by noblemen were valued at £2,500, and that the king gave £500 for the bride's jointure. His majesty gave her away, and, as his manner was, archly observed on the occasion that "if he were unmarried he would not *give her*, but *keep her* for himself." Bride-ales are mentioned by Puttenham in his "Arte of Poesie" : "During the course of Queen Elizabeth's entertainments at Kenilworth Castle, in 1575, a bryde-ale was celebrated with a great variety of shews and sports." From a passage in Jonson's "Silent Woman," Andrews infers that it seems to have been a general custom to make presents to the married pair, in proportion to the gay appearance of their wedding. Newton, speaking of rushes, says "Herewith be made manie pretie imagined devises for bride-ales, and other solemnities as little baskets, hampers, paniers, pitchers, dishes, combes, brushes, stooles, chaires, purses with strings, girdles. and manie such other pretie, curious, and artificiall conceits, which at such times many do take the paines to make and hang up in the houses, as tokens of good-will to the new married bride : and after the solemnitie ended, to bestow abroad for bridegifts or presents." In reference to the rose, he says : "At bride-ales the houses and chambers were woont to be strawed with these odoriferous and sweet herbes : to signifie that in wedlocke all pensive sullennes and lowring cheer, all wrangling strife, jarring, variance, and discorde, ought to be utterly excluded and abandoned ; and that in place thereof al mirth, pleasantnes, cheerfulnes, mildnes, quietnes, and love should be maintained, and that in matters passing betweene the husband and the wife all secresie should be used." Herbal from the Bible, 1587, p. 92. Compare *Bid-ale* and *Bride-Wain*.

Bride-Cake.—The connection between the bride-cake and wedding is strongly marked in the following custom still retained in Yorkshire, where the former is cut into little square pieces, thrown over the bridegroom's and bride's head, and then put through the ring. The cake is sometimes broken over the bride's head, and then thrown away among the crowd to be scrambled for.

This is noted by Aubanus in his description of the rites of marriage in his country and time. "Peractâ re divinâ Sponsa ad Sponsi domum deducitur, indeque Panis projicitur, qui a pueris certatim rapıtur," fol. 68. To break the cake over the head of the bride appears to have been sometimes usual in Drayton's time, for that writer, in his "Nimphidia, or the Court of Fairy," 1627, applies the custom, with the licence habitual to poets, to the fairy Tita :

"*Mertilla*. But coming back when she is wed,
Who breaks the cake above her head?
Claia. That shall Mertilla."

Thus Smollett, in his *Humphrey Clinker*, 1771: "A cake being broken over the head of Mrs. Tabitha Lismahago, the fragments were distributed among the bystanders, according to the custom of the antient Biitons, on the suppotion that every person who ate of this hallowed cake, should that night have a vision of the man or woman whom Heaven designed should be his or her wedded mate." In the North, slices of the bride-cake are put through the wedding ring: they are afterwards laid under pillows, at night, to cause young persons to dream of their lovers. Douce pointed out that this custom is not peculiar to the North of England, it seems to prevail generally. The pieces of the cake must be drawn nine times through the wedding ring. But it appears that the cake was not necessarily a wedding-cake. The "Spectator" observes also: "The writer resolved to try his fortune, fasted all day, and that he might be sure of dreaming upon something at night, procuied an handsome slice of bride cake, which he placed very conveniently under his pillow." The "Connoisseur" says: "Cousin Debby was married a little while ago, and she sent me a piece of bride-cake to put under my pillow, and I had the sweetest dream: I thought we were going to be married together. The following occurs in the *Progress of Matrimony*, 1733 :

"But, Madam, as a present take
This little paper of bride-cake:
Fast any Friday in the year,
When Venus mounts the starry sphere,
Thrust this at night in pillowber,
In morning slumber you will seem
T' enjoy your lover in a dream."

In the "St. James's Chronicle," April 16-18, 1799, are some lines on the "Wedding Cake."

Bride-Cup.—This custom has its traces in Gentilism. It is of high antiquity, says Malone, for it subsisted among our Gothic ancestors. "Ingressus domum convivalem Sponsus cum pronubo suo, sumpto poculo, quod maritale vocant, ac paucis a Pronubo de mutato vitæ genere prefatis, in signum constantiæ, virtutis, defensionis et tutelæ, propinat Sponsæ et simul Morgennaticam (Dotalitium ob virginitatem) promittit, quod ipsa grato animo recolens, pari ratione et modo, paulo post mutato in uxorium habitum operculo Capitis, ingressa, poculum, ut nostrates vocant, uxorium leviter delibans, amorem, fidem, diligentiam, et subjectionem promissum."—Stiernhook *De Jure Suecorum et Gothorum vetusto*, 1672, p. 163. quoted by Malone. In the Workes of John Heiwood, the following passage occurs :

"The drinke of my brydecup I should have forborne,
Till temperaunce had tempred the taste beforne.
I see now, and shall see while I am alive
Who wedth or he be wise shall die or he thrive."

Edit. 1576, sign. B. 4.

Bride Favours.—In "The Fifteen Comforts of Marriage," a conference is introduced, concerning bridal colours in dressing up the bridal bed by the bridemaids—not, say they, with yellow ribbands, these are the emblems of jealousy—not with "Fueille mort," that signifies fading love—but with true blue, that signifies constancy, and green denotes youth—put them both together, and there's youthful constancy. One proposed blew and black, that signifies constancy till death; but that was objected to, as those colours will never match. Violet was proposed as signifying religion; this was objected to as being too grave: and at last they concluded to mingle a gold tissue with grassgreen, which latter signifies youthful jollity. For the bride's favours, top-knots, and garters, the bride proposed blew, goldcolour, popingay-green, and limon-colour—objected to, gold-colour signifying avarice—popingay-green, wantonness. The younger bridemaid proposed mixtures—flame-colour, flesh-colour, willow, and milk-white. The second and third were objected to, as flesh-colour signifies lasciviousness, and willow forsaken. It was settled that red signifies justice, and seagreen inconstancy. The milliner, at last, fixed the colours as follows : for the favours, blue, red, peach-colour, and orangetawney: for the young ladies' top-knots, flame-colour, straw-colour, (signifying plenty), peach-colour, grass-green, and milk-white: and for the garters, a perfect yellow, signifying honour and joy. To this variety of colours in the bride favours used formerly, the following passage, wherein Lady Haughty addresses Morose, in Jonson's "Silent Woman," evidently alludes:

"Let us know your bride's colours and
yours at least."

The bride favours have not been omitted in
"The Collier's Wedding":
"The blithsome, bucksome country
maids,
With knots of ribbands at their heads,
And pinners flutt'ring in the wind,
That fan before and toss behind," &c.

And, speaking of the youth, with the
bridegroom, it says:
"Like streamers in the painted sky,
At every breast the favours fly."

Bride Knives.—Strange as it may
appear, it is however certain that knives
were formerly part of the accoutrements of
a bride. This perhaps will not be difficult
to account for, if we consider that it anciently formed part of the dress for women
to wear a knife or knives sheathed and suspended from their girdles: a finer and
more ornamented pair of which would very
naturally be either purchased or presented
on the occasion of a marriage. Among the
women's trinkets, about 1540, in the Four
P's of John Heywood, occur:
"Silke swathbonds, ribands, and sleeve-
laces,
Girdles, knives, purses, and pin-cases."

From a passage in the "Raigne of Edward
the third," 1596, there appear to have
been two of them. So in the Lottery for
1601, No. xi. is:
"*A Pair of Knives.*"
Fortune doth give these paire of knives
to you,
To cut the thred of love if't be not
true."

In Rowlands' "Well met, Gossip" (first
printed in 1602) the Widow says:
"For this you know, that all the wooing
season,
Sutors with gifts continuall seeke to
gaine
Their mistresse loue —"

The wife answers:
"That's very true ——
In conscience I had twenty pair of gloues
When I was maid, giuen to that effect;
Garters, kniues, purses, girdles, store of
rings,
And many a hundred dainty, pretty
things."

A bride says to her jealous husband, in
Dekker's "Match me in London," 1631:
"See at my girdle hang my wedding
knives!
With those dispatch me."

Bride-Laces.—These are noticed in
Laneham's *Letter from Kenilworth*, 1575.

In Jonson's *Tale of a Tub* Turf is introduced as saying: "We shall all ha' bride-
laces or points I zee." In the Lottery of
1601, the three following occur, in a list
of prizes for ladies: A dozen of points, a
scarfe, and a lace. Herrick, in his "Epi-
thalamie on Sir Clipseby Crew and his
Lady," thus cautions the bridegroom's
men against offending the delicacy of the
new-married lady:
"We charge ye that no strife
(Farther than gentleness tends) get
place
Among ye, striving for her lace:"

And it is observed, in the account
of the marriage of Jack of Newbury, that
his bride was led to church between two
sweet boys, "with bride-laces and rosemary tied about their silken sleeves." In
the second part of Dekker's "Honest
Whore," 1630, signat. K 3 verso, we read:
"Looke yee, doe you see the bride-laces
that I give at my wedding will serve to tye
rosemary to both your coffins when you
come from hanging." Heywood's *Woman
Killed with Kindness*, 1607, alludes to the
nosegays and bride-laces worn by the country lasses on this occasion in their hats.

Bridegroom Men.—These appear
anciently to have had the title of bride-
knights. "Paranymphi ejusmodi seu
Sponsi amici appellantur etiam
(Matt. ix. 15) filii thalami nuptialis; quâ
de re optimè vir præstantissimus Hugo
Grotius. Singulare habetur et apud nos
nomen ejusmodi eorum quos Bride-Knights
id est, Ministros Sponsalitios qui Sponsam
deducere solent, appellitamus." Seldeni
"Uxor Hebraica"; Opera, tom. iii. p.
638. He gives, ibid. a chapter "de Para-
nymphis Hebreorum Sponsi Amicis, in
utroque Fœdere dictis et in Novo Filiis
Thalami nuptialis." Those who led the
bride to church by the arms, as if committing an act of force, were always bachelors; Fletcher's "Scornful Lady," 1616,
(Dyce's B. and F. vol. iii. p. 16). But she
was to be conducted home by two married
persons. Polydore Vergil informs us that
a third married man, in coming home
from church, preceded the bride, bearing,
instead of a torch, a vessel of silver or gold.
"In Anglia servatur ut duo pueri, velut
Paranymphi, id est, Auspices, qui olim pro
nuptiis celebrandis Auspicia capiebant,
nubentem ad Templum—et inde domum
duo viri deducant, et tertius loco facis
Vasculum aureum vel argenteum præ-
ferat." In "A Pleasant History of the
First Founders," we read: "At Rome the
manner was that two children should lead
the bride, and a third bear before her a
torch of white-thorn in honour of Ceres,
which custome was also observed here in
England, saving that, in place of the torch,
there was carried before the bride a bason

of gold or silver; a garland also of corn eares was set upon her head, or else she bare it on her hand, or, if that were omitted, wheat was scattered over her head in token of fruitfulness; as also before she came to bed to her husband, fire and water were given her, which, having power to purifie and cleanse, signified that thereby she should be chast and pure in her body. Moresin relates that to the bachelors and married men who led the bride to and from church, she was wont to present cloves for that service during the time of dinner. It was part of the bridegroom man's office to put him to bed to the bride, after having undressed him.

Bride Maids.—The use of bride maids at weddings appears as old as the time of the Anglo-Saxons: among whom, as Strutt informs us, " The bride was led by a matron, who was called the bride's woman, followed by a company of young maidens, who were called the bride's maids." The bride's maids and bridegroom men are both mentioned by the author of the " Convivial Antiquities " in his description of the rites of marriages in his country and time. " Antequam eatur ad Templum Jentaculum Sponsæ et invitatis apponitur, Serta atque Corollæ distribuuntur. Postea certo ordine Viri primum cum Sponso, deinde Puellæ cum Sponsa, in Templum procedunt." — *Antiquitat. Convivial*, fol. 68.

Bride-Stake.—Around this bridestake the guests were wont to dance as about a may-pole. Thus Jonson :

" With the phant'sies of hey-troll
Troll about the bridal bowl,
And divide the broad bride cake
Round about the bride's stake."

Bride-Wain. — In Cumberland the Penny Wedding of the earlier Scots and the Bid-Ale of Wales had the appellation of a bride-wain, a term which will be best explained by the following extract from the Glossary, 1710, to Douglas's Virgil, v. Thig: " There was a custom in the Highlands and North of Scotland, where new married persons, who had no great stock, or others low in their fortune, brought carts and horses with them to the houses of their relations and Friends, and received from them corn, meal. wool, or whatever else they could get. The subsequent is extracted from the " Cumberland Packet," a newspaper :

" *Bride Wain.*

There let Hymen oft appear
In saffron robe and taper clear,
And pomp and feast and revelry,
With mask and antient pageantry.

" George Hayton, who married Ann, the daughter of Joseph and Dinah Collin of Crossley Mill, purposes having a bride wain at his house at Crossley near Mary Port on Thursday, May 7th, next, (1789), where he will be happy to see his friends and wellwishers, for whose amusement there will be a saddle, two bridles, a pair of gands d'amour gloves, which whoever wins is sure to be married within the twelve months, a girdle (Ceinture de Venus) possessing qualities not to be described, and many other articles, sports, and pastimes, too numerous to mention, but which can never prove tedious in the exhibition, &c." A short time after a match is solemnized, the parties give notice as above, that on such a day they propose to have a bride-wain. In consequence of this, the whole neighbourhood for several miles round assemble at the bridegroom's house, and join in all the various pastimes of the country. This meeting resembles our wakes and fairs: and a plate or bowl is fixed in a convenient place, where each of the company contributes in proportion to his inclination and ability, and according to the degree of respect the parties are held in : and by this very laudable custom a worthy couple have frequently been benefited at setting out in life, with a supply of money of from ten to fourscore pounds. Eden, in " The State of the Poor," 1797, observes " The custom of a general feasting at weddings and christenings is still continued in many villages in Scotland, in Wales, and in Cumberland : Districts, which, as the refinements of legislation and manners are slow in reaching them, are most likely to exhibit vestiges of customs deduced from remote antiquity, or founded on the simple dictates of Nature : and indeed it is not singular, that marriages, births, christenings, housewarmings, &c., should be occasions in which people of all classes and all descriptions think it right to rejoice and make merry. In many parts of these districts of Great Britain as well as in Sweden and Denmark, all such institutions, now rendered venerable by long use, are religiously observed. It would be deemed ominous, if not impious, to be married, have a child born, &c., without something of a feast. And long may the custom last : for it neither leads to drunkenness and riot, nor is it costly ; as alas ! is so commonly the case in convivial meetings in more favoured regions. On all these occasions, the greatest part of the provisions is contributed by the neighbourhood : some furnishing the wheaten flour for the pastry ; others, barley or oats for bread or cakes ; some, poultry for pies ; some, milk for the frumenty ; some eggs ; some bacon ; and some, butter ; and, in short, every article necessary for a plentiful repast. Every neighbour, how high or low soever, makes it a point to contribute something. " At a daubing (which is the erection of a house of clay), or at a bride-wain, (which is the carrying of a bride home) in Cumberland, many hundreds of persons are thus brought together, and as it is the custom also, in the latter instance, to make presents of money, one or even two hundred pounds are said to have been sometimes collected. A deserving young couple are thus, by a public and unequivocal testimony of the goodwill of those who best know them, encouraged to persevere in the paths of propriety, and are also enabled to begin the world with some advantage. The birth of a child, also, instead of being thought or spoken of as bringing on the parents new and heavy burthens, is thus rendered, as it no doubt always ought to be, a comfort and a blessing: and in every sense an occasion of rejoicing." "I own," adds this honourable advocate in the cause of humanity, "I cannot figure to myself a more pleasing, or a more rational way of rendering sociableness and mirth subservient to prudence and virtue." Vol. i.. p 598. In Cumberland, among the lower but not poorest, class, the entertainment consists of cold pies, furmety, and ale. "At the close of the day," says the author of the "Westmoreland and Cumberland Dialect," 1839, "the bride and bridegroom are placed in two chairs, in the open air or in a large barn, the bride with a pewter dish on her knee, half covered with a napkin; into this dish the company put their offerings, which occasionally amount to a considerable sum."

Bride's Pie.—The bride's pie should also be noticed as an important part of the wedding-feast, at least in some places or districts. It is thus referred to by Carr, in the "Dialect of Craven," 1828: "The bride's pie was so essential a dish on the dining-table, after the celebration of the marriage, that there was no prospect of happiness without it. This was always made round, with a very strong crust ornamented with various devices. In the middle of it was a fat laying hen, full of eggs, probably intended as an emblem of fecundity. It was also garnished with minced and sweet meats. It would have been deemed an act of neglect and rudeness, if any of the party omitted to partake of it." In the old song of "Arthur of Bradley," we read:

"And then did they foot it and toss it,
Till the cook had brought up the posset;
The bride-pye was brought forth,
A thing of mickle worth,
And so all, at the bed-side,
Took leave of Arthur and his bride."

Bridget, St. — (July 23). The "Roman Martyrology," 1627, observes under this date: "The departure out of this life of St. Bridget widdow, who, after many peregrinations made to holy places,

full of the Holy Ghost, finally reposed at Rome: whose body was after translated into Suevia. Her principal festivity is celebrated upon the seaventh of October." According to Porter's "Flowers of the Lives of the Saincts," 1632, p. 118, Brigitt's Day (Virgin of Kildare, in Ireland), was February the first. Her *Most Devout Prayers* were printed at Antwerp in 1659. See also Moore's "Diarium Historicum," 1590, p. 111, where we read under 23º, Julii, "Emortualis Dies S. Brigittæ Reg. Sueciæ, 1372." In the "Fifteen O's" the first O is introduced by a large woodcut representing a man crowned delivered out of purgatory by an angel, through the mediation of St. Bridget, who is kneeling at a small altar before him. Vallancey, speaking of Ceres, tells us: "Mr. Rollin thinks this deity was the same Queen of Heaven to whom the Jewish women burnt incense, poured out drink offerings, and made cakes for her with their own hands"; and adds: "This Pagan custom is still preserved in Ireland on the Eve of St. Bridget, and which was probably transposed to St. Bridget's Eve from the festival of a famed poetess of the same name in the time of Paganism. In an ancient glossary now before me she is described: 'Brigit, a poetess, the daughter of Dagha; a goddess of Ireland.' On St. Bridget's Eve every farmer's wife in Ireland makes a cake, called bairin-breac, the neighbours are invited, the madder of ale and the pipe go round, and the evening concludes with mirth and festivity."

Bridling Cast, The.—This seems to have been rather more common in Scotland than among the Southerners; it was the cup of drink offered to a visitor, at the gate, after mounting to depart. Skelton refers to it in the "Bowge of Courte," printed before 1500:

"What, loo, man, see here of dyce
    a bale !
A brydelynge caste for that is in thy
    male."

Weber says, in a note to his edition of Beaumont and Fletcher, "A bridling cast was probably similar to what is at present in Scotland, and particularly in the Highlands, called the door-drink, which is often administered after the guest is seated upon his horse, or while the horse is bridling." In Fletcher's "Scornful Lady," 1616, Young Loveless says:

"Let's have a bridling cast before you
    go —
Fill's a new stoop."
It is more generally known as the stirrup-cup.

Brightlingsea, Essex. — "Yesterday the ancient custom of electing a mayor in the belfry of Brightlingsea.

NATIONAL FAITHS

Church was observed, Mr. Miall Green, a yacht owner and resident of Kensington, being chosen for the second year in succession. The regalia, consisting of a truncheon and a handsome chain formed of gold models of oysters and silver models of sprats, was carried by a yacht captain. It was incidentally mentioned by the new mayor that according to an ancient statute the freedom of certain of the Cinque Ports, which included Brightlingsea, were entitled to wreck the house of any freeman who refused mayoral honours. *Daily Telegraph*, Tuesday, December 2, 1902.

Bring the Basket.—See *More Sacks to the Mill.*

Bromfield School.—Hutchinson tells us: "Till within the last twenty or thirty years, it had been a custom, time out of mind, for the scholars of the Free-School of Bromfield, about the beginning of Lent, or in the more expressive phraseology of the country, at Fasting's Even, to bar out the Master; i.e., to depose and exclude him from his school, and keep him out for three days. During the period of this expulsion, the doors of the citadel, the school, were strongly barricadoed within: and the boys, who defended it like a besieged city, were armed, in general, with bore-tree or elder pop-guns. The Master, meanwhile, made various efforts, both by force and stratagem, to regain his lost authority. If he succeeded, heavy tasks were imposed, and the business of the school was resumed and submitted to; but it more commonly happened that he was repulsed and defeated. After three days' siege, terms of capitulation were proposed by the Master and accepted by the boys. These terms were summed up in an old formula of Latin Leonine verses stipulating what hours and times should, for the year ensuing, be allotted to study, and what to relaxation and play. Securities were provided by each side for the due performance of these stipulations: and the paper was then solemnly signed by both Master and scholars. "One of the articles always stipulated for and granted, was, the privilege of immediately celebrating certain games of long standing; viz. a foot-ball match and a cock-fight. Captains, as they were called, were then chosen to manage and preside over these games: one from that part of the parish which lay to the westward of the school; the other from the east. Cocks and foot-ball players were sought for with great diligence. The party, whose cocks won the most battles, was victorious in the cock-pit; and the prize, a small silver bell, suspended to the button of the victor's hat, and worn for three successive Sundays. After the cock-fight was ended, the football was thrown down in the churchyard; and the point then to be contested was,

which party could carry it to the house of his respective captain; to Dundraw, perhaps, or West-Newton, a distance of two or three miles: every inch of which ground was keenly disputed. All the honour accruing to the conqueror at foot-ball was that of possessing the ball. Details of these matches were the general topics of conversation among the villagers, and were dwelt on with hardly less satisfaction than their ancestors enjoyed in relating their feats in the Border Wars. "Our Bromfield sports were sometimes celebrated in indigenous songs: one verse only of one of them we happen to remember:

" At Scales, great Tom Barwise gat the
    Ba' in his hand,
And t' wives aw ran out, and shouted,
    and bann'd :
Tom Cowan then pulch'd and flang him
    'mang t' whins,
And he bledder'd, Od-white-te, tou's
    broken my shins."

History of Cumberland, ii., 322. The writer thought this might be the basis of the (now obsolete) institution of the *Terræ Filius* at Oxford. It was a practice common to Eton.

Bromfield Sports.—Hutchinson, speaking of the parish of Bromfield, and a custom in the neighbourhood of Blencogo, tells us: — "On the common, to the east of that village, not far from Ware - Brig, near a pretty large rock of granite, called St. Cuthbert's Stane, is a fine copious spring of remarkably pure and sweet water, which (probably from its having been anciently dedicated to the same St. Cuthbert), is called Helly-Well, i.e. Haly or Holy Well. It formerly was the custom for the youth of all the neighbouring villages to assemble at this well early in the afternoon of the second Sunday in May, and there to join in a variety of rural sports. It was the village wake, and took place here, it is possible, when the keeping of wakes and fairs in the churchyard was discontinued. And it differed from the wakes of later times chiefly in this, that though it was a meeting entirely devoted to festivity and mirth, no strong drink of any kind was ever seen there; nor anything ever drank, but the beverage furnished by the Naiad of the place. A curate of the parish, about the year 1770, on the idea that it was a profanation of the Sabbath, saw fit to set his face against it; and having deservedly great influence in the parish, the meetings at Helly-Well have ever since been discontinued." *Cumberland*, ii., 323.

Broom.—An usage connected with marriage, and also with the broom, and of which the origin and significance do not appear to be very obvious, existed some years ago, it seems, in some parts of England. A man, when his wife left home for a short time, hung out a broom from one of the windows. Now a broom hung from the mast of a ship has a very different meaning from the one that must have been here intended—that the mistress of the establishment was away. An old woman in the Isle of Thanet adopted an odd method, so recently as 1850, of signifying her disapproval of her nephew's choice of a wife. She pronounced an anathema on the newly-married pair at the church-gate, procured a new broom, swept her house with it, and then hung it over the door. This was intended to be equivalent to cutting off with a shilling.

Broose.—Compare *Riding*.

Brougham, Westmoreland.—Every year, on the 2nd of April, the rector and churchwardens distribute the Countess of Pembroke's charity upon a stone tablet near the pillar, about two miles from Penrith. It and the pillar date from 1656, having been instituted and raised, the latter in the park at Whitfield, as a permanent memorial for the last parting of the Countess of Dorset, Pembroke, and Montgomery on that site with her mother, the Countess Dowager of Cumberland, April 2, 1616. The charity consists of a sum of £4 distributed here to the poor of Brougham. This custom was still observed in Beckwith the Elder's day; he died in 1799; and the monument is engraved in Pennant's *Journey to Alston Moor*, 1801.

Browny.—There were thought to have been a sort of domestic fairies, called *brownies*, who were extremely useful, and were said to have performed all sorts of domestic drudgery. The early Scotish poet, Dunbar, who died about 1515, in his *Dance of the Seven Deadly Sins*, speaks of two spirits called Black-Belly and Bawsy Brown. Warton thought it not unlikely that the latter might be identical with Brownie. "The spirit called Brownie," (says King James) "appeared like a rough man, and haunted divers houses without doing any evill, but doing as it were necessarie turnes up and downe the house; yet some were so blinded as to beleeve that their house was all the sonsier as they called it, that such spirits resorted there." *Demonology*, 127. Martin, speaking of the Shetland Isles, says: "It is not long since every family of any considerable substance in those Islands was haunted by a spirit they called Browny, which did several sorts of work: and this was the reason why they gave him offerings of the various products of the place. Thus some, when they churned their milk, or brewed, poured some milk and wort through the hole of a stone called Browny's Stone." He also says:—"A spirit by the country people called Browny, was

frequently seen in all the most considerable families in these Isles and North of Scotland, in the shape of a tall man: but within these twenty or thirty years past, he is seen but rarely." Speaking of three chapels in the Island of Valay, he says: "Below the chappels there is a flat thin stone, called Brownie's Stone, upon which the antient inhabitants offered a cow's milk every Sunday: but this custom is now quite abolished." *Western Islands*, p. 391. Johnson, in his *Tour to the Hebrides*, observes, that of Browny mentioned by Martin nothing has been heard for many years. Browny was a sturdy fairy who, if he was fed and kindly treated, would as they say do a great deal of work. They now pay him no wages, and are content to labour for themselves." We are told by Pinkerton that "The Brownie was a very obliging spirit, who used to come into houses by night, and for a dish of cream to perform lustily any piece of work that might remain to be done: sometimes he would work, and sometimes eat till he bursted: if old clothes were laid for him, he took them in great distress, and never more returned." Heron's *Journey*, 1799, ii., 227. Borlase informs us that in his time (a century since) the Cornish invoked a spirit whom they called Browny (a sort of Robin Goodfellow), when their bees began to swarm, thinking that "their crying Browny, Browny, will prevent their returning into their former hive, and make them pitch and form a new colony." *Antiquities of Cornwall*, 1769, p. 168. Milton, in a passage of his *Allegro*, seems to depict Browny rather than Robin Goodfellow:—

"Tells how the druging Goblin swet,
To earn his cream-bowl duly set,
When in one night 'ere glimpse of morn,
His shadowy flaile hath thresh'd the corn
That ten day-lab'rers could not end;
Then lays him down the lubbar-fiend,
And stretch'd out all the chimney's length
Basks at the fire his hairy strength,
And crop-full out of doors he flings,
Ere the first cock his matin rings."

Buckler-Play.—The following order was made by the Government of James I. in 1609: "That all plaies, bear-baitings, games, singing of ballads, buckler-play, or such like causes of assemblies of people be utterly prohibited, and the parties offending severely punished by any Alderman or Justice of the Peace." Misson says: "Within these few years you should often see a sort of gladiators marching thro' the streets, in their shirts to the waste, their sleeves tuck'd up, sword in hand, and preceded by a drum, to gather spectators. They gave so much a head to see the fight, which was with cutting swords, and a kind of buckler for defence. The edge of the sword was a little blunted, and the care of the prize-fighters was not so much to avoid wounding one another, as to avoid doing it dangerously; nevertheless, as they were obliged to fight, till some blood was shed, without which nobody would give a far-thing for the show, they were sometimes forc'd to play a little ruffly. I once saw a much deeper and longer cut given than was intended. These fights are become very rare within these eight or ten years. Apprentices, and all boys of that degree, are never without their cudgels, with which they fight something like the fellows before-mention'd, only that the cudgel is nothing but a stick; and that a little wicker basket, which covers the handle of the stick, like the guard of a Spanish sword, serves the combatant instead of defensive arms."

Bug, Welsh *Bwg*, a goblin. We now use bugbear without much recollection, perhaps, of the etymology. Boggle-bo, says Coles, (now corruptly sounded Buga-bow), signified "an ugly wide-mouthed picture carried about with May-games." It is perhaps nothing more than the dimi-nutive of Bug, a terrifying object. *Lat. Dict.*, 1678, in v. In Mathew's Bible, Psalm xci., v. 5, is rendered, "Thou shalt not nede be afraied for any bugs by night," this is hence known as the *Bug Bible*. In the Hebrew it is "terror of the night"; a curious passage, evidently alluding to that horrible sensation the night-mare, which in all ages has been regarded as the opera-tion of evil spirits. Compare Douce's *Illustr.*, i., 328. Boh, Warton tells us, was one of the most fierce and formidable of the Gothic Generals, and the son of Odin: the mention of whose name only was suffi-cient to spread an immediate panic among his enemies. The s me was the case with that of Narses among children. Com-pare *Richard-Cœur-de-Lion.*

Boe Bulbagger, as he is there called, in "Jacke of Dover, his Quest of Inquirie for the Veriest Foole in Eng-land," 1604, is mentioned as a sort of bogie or bugbear. Taylor the water-poet, in his "Great Eater of Kent," 1630, says of his hero, Nicholas Wood: ". . . he is a maine enemy to Ember weekes, he hates Lent worse than a butcher or a Puritan, and the name of Good Friday affrights him like a Bull-beggar." In Rowley's *Woman never Vext*, 1632, mine host says of his disorderly guests: "The bull-beggar comes when I show my head." Compare *Bar-guest.*

Bull-Baiting. — Fitzstephen men-tions the baiting of bulls with dogs as a diversion of the London youths on holidays in his time. *Descr. of London, temp.* Henry II., apud *Antiq. Reper.* v., 1807, vol. i. Hentzner, who visited England in

Elizabeth's reign, says: "There is a place built in the form of a theatre, which serves for the baiting of bulls and bears; they are fastened behind, and then worried by great English bull-dogs; but not without great risk to the dogs, from the horns of the one and the teeth of the other: and it some-times happens they are killed on the spot. Fresh ones are immediately supplied in the place of those that are wounded or tired. To this entertainment there often follows that of whipping a blinded bear, which is performed by five or six men, standing cir-cularly, with whips, which they exercise upon him without any mercy, as he cannot escape from them because of his chain. He defends himself with all his force and skill, throwing down all who come within his reach, and are not active enough to get out of it, and tearing the whips out of their hands and breaking them. At these spec-tacles, and every where else, the English are constantly smoking tobacco." *Itiner-ary*, 1612, transl. 1757. When Robert Chamberlaine published in 1637 his *New Book of Mistakes*, there seems from the preface to have been a white bull at the Bear garden in Southwark, "who tosseth up Dogges," he says, "like Tennis-balles," and catch-ing them again upon his hornes, makes them to garter their Legges with their owne guts." Misson, in his *Travels in England*, trans. by Ozell, 1734, describes bul-baiting as it was practised in the time of William III.

A considerable body of authentic tes-timony exists to shew that this ap-parently cruel amusement was due to a theory on the part of our ancestors, that the process rendered the flesh more tender, and some of the Leet Courts in England imposed a fine of 3s. 4d. on every butcher, who killed a bullock unbaited. Bull-rings were established for this pur-pose, and at Carlisle it is mentioned that the Butchers' Gild had charge of the chain used in the operation. *Antiquary* for April-May, 1893. We still deem a coursed hare, somewhat on the same principle, tenderer than a shot one. Bull-baiting was still carried on in the Midlands and in the North down to the second half of the nineteenth century; and the women en-joyed the sport as keenly as the men. At Leigh, near Preston, according to a story told me by a Leigh man, a fellow, in a room with his wife and a dog trained to this exercise, laid his head on a table; the dog rushed at his nose, the husband cried out from the pain, and would have got up, but, says the woman, ' lie still, man, he must draw blood, or he will be just ruined.' —Hazlitt's *Four Generations of a Literary Family*, 1897, ii., 296.

M. Michel, in "Le Pays Basque," 1857, traces back this diversion in that country to the year 1385. There is no want of material for the history of the sport on the other side of the Pyrenees subsequently to that date. Most of the Spanish princes appear to have encouraged it by their countenance and support.

At Stamford, in Lincolnshire, an annual sport used to be celebrated, called bull-running: of which the following account is taken from Butcher: "It is performed just the day six weeks before Christmas. The butchers of the town at their own charge against the time, provide the wildest bull they can get: this bull over night is had into some stable or barn belonging to the Alderman. The next morning proclamation is made by the common bellman of the town, round about the same, that each one shut up their shop-doors and gates, and that none, upon pain of imprisonment, offer to do any violence to strangers, for the preventing whereof (the town being a great thoroughfare and then being in Term Time) a guard is appointed for the passing of travellers through the same without hurt. That none have any iron upon their bull-clubs or other staff which they pursue the bull with. Which proclamation made, and the gates all shut up, the bull is turned out of the Alderman's house, and then hivie skivy, tag and rag, men, women, and children of all sorts and sizes, with all the dogs in the town promiscuously running after him with their bull-clubs spattering dirt in each other's faces, that one would think them to be so many Furies started out of Hell for the punishment of Cerberus, as when Theseus and Perillus conquered the place (as Ovid describes it):

Bull-Running.
"A ragged troop of boys and girls
Do pellow him with stones :
With clubs, with whips, and many raps,
They part his skin from bones."

And (which is the greater shame) I have seen both senatores majorum gentium and matrones de eodem gradu, following this bulling business." "I can say no more of it, but only to set forth the antiquity thereof, (as the tradition goes). William Earl of Warren, the first Lord of this town, in the time of King John, standing upon his castle-walls in Stamford, viewing the fair prospects of the river and meadow, under the same, saw two bulls a fighting for one cow; a butcher of the town, the owner of one of those bulls, with a great mastiff dog accidentally coming by, set his dog upon his own bull, who forced the same bull up into the town, which no sooner was come within the same but all the butchers' dogs, both great and small, follow'd in pursuit of the bull, which by this time made stark mad with the noise

of the people and the fierceness of the dogs, ran over man, woman, and child, that stood in the way; this caused all the butchers and others in the town to rise up as it were in a tumult, making such an hideous noise that the sound thereof came into the Castle unto the ears of Earl Warren, who presently thereupon mounted on horseback, rid into the town to see the business, which then appearing (to his humour) very delightful, he gave all those meadows in which the two bulls were at the first found fighting, (which we now call the Castle Meadows) perpetually as a common to the butchers of the town, (after the first grass is eaten) to keep their cattle in till the time of slaughter: upon this condition, that as upon that day on which this sport first began, which was (as I said before) that day six weeks before Christmas, the butchers of the town should from time to time yearly for ever, find a mad bull for the continuance of that sport." *Survey of Stamford*, 1775-76. In the "Antiquarian Repertory," an account is extracted from Plot of a similar bull-running at Tutbury, in Staffordshire, which occasioned much disorder annually, until it was abolished by the Duke of Devonshire, lay-prior of Tutbury, in the eighteenth century. This practice seems to have dated from ancient times, as it was usual, before the Dissolution, for the Prior of Tutbury to give the minstrels, who attended matins on the feast of the Assumption, a bull, if they would convey him on the side of the river Dove next the town or failing the bull, forty pence, of which a moiety went by custom to the lord of the feast. I believe that the practice of bull-running, and also of bull-baiting, is universally obsolete in this country, and has long been so.

Bull Week.—In Sheffield, this is the name given to the week before Christmas. The men work overtime, and often do not leave off till one or two in the morning, in order that they may earn money to spend in celebrating the great Christian festival. Their festive enjoyment chiefly consists in brutal drunkenness.

Bumpers.—Bumpers are of great antiquity. Paulus Warnefridus is cited in Du Cange's "Glossary," telling us in lib. v. "De Gestis Langobard." cap. 2, "Cumque ii qui diversi generis potiones ei a Rege deferebant, de verbo Regis eum rogarent, ut totam fialam biberet, ille in honorem Regis se totam bibere promittens, parum aquæ libabat de argenteo Calice." Vide Martial, lib. i. Ep. 72; lib. viii. 51, &c Comp. *Drinking Customs.*

Bundling used to be a widely diffused Welsh custom before marriage: the betrothed or engaged pair went to bed, or more frequently lay together in their clothes. It seems to have been intended as a method by which, without any detrimental result, the parties might form some idea of each other. It was by no means restricted to the lower orders. The mischievous consequences arising from such a practice are sufficiently obvious. It was formerly customary in Cumberland and Westmoreland, and produced similarly unfortunate and immoral consequences in the majority of cases. The usage was, however, growing obsolete there in 1839, when the author of the " W. and C. Dialect " wrote. According to a writer in the *Penny Magazine*, this practice was well known in Northumberland in or about 1830; but he does not seem to have heard that it was attended by very serious evils. It is not confined to this country. Such a practice was obviously prone to abuse, and more or less of mischief. But its localization seems to be an ill-founded hypothesis. Even among families of good position it is tacitly recognized and tolerated, and it was at the outset the product of the clothed state, where touch had to play the part of sight in the unclothed. It is a rigorous condition that no liberty is taken with the dress.

Burford.—Plot mentions a custom at Burford, in Oxfordshire (within memory) of making a dragon yearly, and carrying it up and down the town in great jollity on Midsummer Eve; to which, he says, not knowing for what reason, they added a giant. *Hist. of Oxfordshire*, p. 349. But a farther account of this usage may be found in Blount's *Tenures*, ed. Hazlitt, p. 49. The inhabitants of Burford formerly enjoyed the right of hunting deer in Whichwood Forest on Whitsunday. The Corporation still possesses the letter, directed to them in 1593, to stay the privilege for that year, and accept two bucks from the keepers in lieu thereof, without prejudice to the future.

Burial.—A paper on the Burial of the Britons forms part of his *Notes on Ancient Britain*, by W. Barnes, 1858. Strutt tells us, "that before the time of Christianity it was held unlawful to bury the dead within the cities, but they used to carry them out into the fields hard by, and there deposited them. Towards the end of the sixth century, Augustine obtained of King Ethelbert a Temple of Idols (where the King used to worship before his conversion) and made a burying place of it: but St. Cuthbert afterwards obtained leave to have yards made to the churches, proper for the reception of the dead." Comp. *Bidding, Deaths, Flowers, Gloves, Funeral Customs,* &c.

Burial Fees.—It is customary to give the clergy double fees where a person is buried not belonging to the parish.

Burlesque.—The antiquity of this practice is shown by the curious relics printed in *Reliquæ Antiquæ*, 1841-6, *et alibi*. At a very early date, the incantations of wizards and sorcerers appear to have been reduced to a burlesque sort of gibberish by those who either were unable to comprehend their meaning, or desired to ridicule their folly. See "Remains of Early Pop. Poetry of England," vol. i. p. 26 and vol. iv. p. 358. Dunbar, in his "Testament of Andro Kennedy," has parodied some of the rites which, in his day (he died about 1515), were observed at the interment of the dead. But the old Scotish Makar had less sympathy than the Southerners with this class of solemnity, for he belonged to a church, which treated the burial service lightly enough. Bishop Bale, writing in 1538, mentions the following burlesque charms:

" For the coughe take Judas Eare
Wth the parynge of a peare
And drynke them without feare
　　If ye will have remedy :

Thre syppes are fore the hyckocke
And six more for the chyckocke
Thus, my prety pyckocke,
　　Recover by and by.

If ye can not slepe but slumber,
Geve otes unto Saynt Uncumber
And beanes in a certen number
　　Unto Saynt Blase and Saint Blythe.

Give onyons to Saynt Cutlake
And garlycke to Saynt Cyryake
If ye wyll shunne the heade ake :
　　Ye shall have them at Quene hyth."

—*Comedy of Three Laws*, ed. 1562, sign. C 3 *verso*. And again :

" With blessynges of St. Germayne
I wyll me so determyne
That neyther fox nor vermyne
　　Shall do my chyckens harme.
For your gese seke Saynt Legeared,
And for your duckes Saynt Leonarde,
For horse take Moyses yearde,
　　There is no better charme.

Take me a napkyn folte
With the byas of a bolte
For the healyng of a colte
　　No better thynge can be :
For lumpes and for bottes
Take me Saynt Wilfrides knottes,
And Holy Saynt Thomas Lottes,
　　On my lyfe I warrande ye.

A dram of a shepes tyrdle,
And good Saynt Frances Gyrdle,
With the hamlet of a hyrdle,
　　Are wholsom for the pyppe :

Besydes these charmes afore
I have feates many more
That kepe styll in store,
Whom nowe I over hyppe."

So, in Heywood's Works, ed. 1598, sign.
C i. :

"I clawed her by the backe in way of a
charme,
To do me not the more good, but the less
harme."

In "Musarum Deliciæ," 1656, there is the
following incantation :

"—Or I to plague thee for thy sin,
Should draw a circle, and begin
To conjure, for I am, look to't,
An Oxford scholar, and can doe't.
Then with three sets of mops and mowes,
Seaven of odd words, and motley showes,
A thousand tricks that may be taken
From Faustus, Lambe, or Frier Bacon ;
I should begin."

Nash, in his ' Notes on Hudibras," says.
"Cato recommends the following as a
charm against sprains : ' Haut, haut, his-
ta, pista, vista.'" Andrews, the continuator of Henry, quoting Reginald Scot,
says : "The stories which our facetious
author relates of ridiculous charms which,
by the help of credulity, operated wonders,
are extremely laughable. In one of them
a poor woman is commemorated who cured
all diseases by muttering a certain form
of words over the party afflicted ; for which
service she always received one penny and
a loaf of bread. At length, terrified by
menaces of flames both in this world and
the next, she owned that her whole conjuration consisted in these potent lines,
which she always repeated in a low voice
near the head of her patient :

"Thy loaf in my hand,
And thy penny in my purse,
Thou art never the better—
And I am never the worse."

Melton tels us : "That a man may know
what's a clocke only by a ring and a silver
beaker." *Astrologestis*, 1620, p. 45. This
seems equally probable, with what we read
in Hudibras :

"And wisely tell what Hour o' th' Day
The clocke does strike by Algebra."

From Ravenscroft's *Deuteromelia*, 1609,
Dr. Rimbault has extracted the humorous
effusion of this class, entitled : *Martin said
to his Man*, where the second stanza runs :

I see a sheepe shearing corne,
Fie ! man, fie !
I see a sheepe shearing corne,
Who's the foole now ?
I see a sheepe shearing corne,
And a cuckold blow his horne ;
Thou hast well drunken, man,
Who's the foole now ?

And the rest is in a similar strain. *A
Little Book of Songs and Ballads*, 1851,
pp. 115-17. See *Prevaricator*.

Burning the Dead Horse.—A
nautical ceremony performed with a
wooden horse suspended from the shrouds
on crossing the line. See a representation
of it in *Black and White*, January 9, 1892.
Its origin and meaning are explained on p.
36, and come from the prepayment of a
month's wages, which are usually squan-
dered on shore, so that a sailor works, as
he thinks, for nothing during what is
termed the Horse or first month, at the
conclusion of which this imaginary animal
is burnt, and Jack is really on his legs
again.

Burning Shame.—A custom said
to be peculiar to Newport, Isle of Wight.
See Mr. T. Nicholls's publication, 1812.

Burying Old Tom.—The labourers
in Herefordshire usually indulge in an extra glass or two on New Year's Eve, and
call this burying Old Tom. The festivities
usually include considerable uproar and
confusion, and the assistants at these peculiar funeral obsequies rarely quit the tavern parlour, till mine host makes a clear-
ance. They have some verses adapted for
the occasion, which they sing on their way
homeward through the streets, not always,
as it may be supposed, in the best time or
with the clearest accents. Mr. T. H. Pat-
tison communicated a copy to "Current
Notes" for January, 1856 :—

"I wish you a merry Christmas,
And a happy New Year ;
A pocket full of money ,
And a cellar full of beer ;
And a good fat pig,
To serve you all the year.
Ladies and gentlemen sat by the fire,
Pity we, poor boys, out in the mire."

Bush.—There is a well known proverb,
"Good wine needs no bush" ; i.e. nothing
to point out where it is to be sold. Dickenson, in his "Greene in Conceipt," 1598,
has it : "Good wine needes no Ivie Bush."
The subsequent passage in Rowlands'
"Good Newes and Bad Newes," 1622,
seems to prove that anciently tavern keepers kept both a bush and a sign : a host is
speaking :

"I rather will take down my bush and
sign
Then live by means of riotous expence."
In the same author's "Knave of Harts,"
1612, "the drunken knave exclaims :

"What claret's this ? the very worst in
towne :
Your taverne-bush deserves a pulling
downe."

In "England's Parnassus," 1600, the first
line of the address to the reader runs
thus : "I have no ivie out to sell my

wine ": and in Braithwaite's "Strappado for the Divell," 1615, there is a dedication to Bacchus, 'sole soveraigne of the Ivy-bush, prime founder of Red-Lettices," &c. In Dekker's "Wonderful Yeare," 1603, signat. F, we read: "Spied a bush at the ende of a pole (the auncient badge of a countrey ale-house)." Sir William Vaughan of Merioneth, in his "Golden Grove," 1600, says: "Like as an ivy-bush put forth at a vintrie, is not the cause of the wine, but, a signe that wine is to bee sold there; so, likewise, if we see smoke appearing in a chimney, wee know that fire is there, albeit the smoke is not the cause of the fire." Elsewhere we find: "Nay if the house be not worth an ivie-bush, let him have his tooles about him; nutmegs, rosemary, tobacco, with other the appurtenances, and he knowes how of puddle-ale to make a cup of English wine." In the preface to Braithwaite's *Laws of Drinking*, 1617, keeping a publichouse is called "the known trade of the ivy-bush, or red lettice." There is a wedding sermon by Whateley of Banbury, entitled, "A Bride-Bush," as is another preached to a newly-married couple at Œsen in Norfolk. See "Wedding Sermons," 12mo. Lond. 1732. Coles says: "Box and ivy last long green, and therefore vintners make their garlands thereof: though perhaps ivy is the rather used, because of the antipathy between it and wine." Poor Robin, in his *Perambulation from Saffron Walden to London*, 1678, says:

"Some alehouses upon the road I saw,
And some with bushes shewing they wine did draw."

Nash, speaking of the head dresses of London ladies, says: "Even as angels are painted in church windowes, with glorious golden fronts, besette with sunne-beames, so beset they their foreheads on either side with glorious borrowed gleamy bushes; which rightly interpreted, should signify beauty to sell, since a bush is not else hanged forth, but to invite men to buy. And in Italy, when they sette any beast to sale, they crowne his head with garlands and bedeck it with gaudy blossoms, as full as ever it may stick." *Christ's Teares over Jerusalem*, 1593, ed. 1613, p. 145.

Butter.—St. Hascka is said by her prayers to have made stinking butter sweet. See the Bollandists under January 26, as cited by Patrick in his "Devot. of the Romish Church," p. 37. Ady speaks of an old woman who came into an house when the maid was churning of butter, and having laboured long and could not make her butter come, the old woman told the maid what was wont to be done when she was a maid, and also in her mothers young time, that if it happened their butter would not come readily, they used a charm to be said over it, whilst yet it was in beating, and it would come straight ways, and that was this:

"Come, butter, come,
Come butter, come,
Peter stands at the gate,
Waiting for a buttered cake,
Come, butter, come."

This, said the old woman, being said three times, will make your butter come, for it was taught my mother by a learned Church man in Queen Maries days, when as church men had more cunning, and could teach people many a trick, that our Ministers now a days know not." *Candle in the Dark*, 1659, p. 58. Jamieson, the editor of the *Scottish Ballads*, relates that when he was travelling on foot across the mountains from Fort Augustus to Fort Inverness, about the end of the 18th or beginning of the 19th century, he came to a dwelling, where the woman prepared the food to the accompaniment of song, and made him personally sing "like a mavis," to the bottle holding some cream, to make the butter come. She did the same in milking the cow, and searching in the hens' roost for some new-laid eggs.

Buzza, or **to Buzza One.**—I know nothing of the meaning of this word. I have been told that it is a college expression, and contains a threat, in the way of pleasantry, to black the person's face with a burnt cork, should he flinch or fail to empty the bottle. Possibly it may have been derived from the German "buzzen," *sordes auferre*, q.d. "Off with the lees at bottom." Grose explains this as signifying to challenge a person to pour out all the wine in the bottle into his glass, undertaking to drink it, should it prove more than the glass would hold. It is commonly said to one who hesitates to empty a bottle that is nearly out. To buzz a bottle of wine is usually understood in the sense of finishing it, which, if there is no more, is left to a guest.

Cakes and Salt were used in religious rites by the ancients. The Jews probably adopted their appropriation from the Egyptians: 'And if thou bring an oblation of a meat-offering baken in the oven, it shall be unleavened cakes of fine flour,' &c., *Levit.* ii. 4.—'With all thine offerings thou shalt offer salt.'"

Calendar.—There is a prevailing theory that the year was calculated prior to 1753 from the 25th of March, and only after that date from the 1st January. But, as a matter of fact, not only has wide diversity of practice existed everywhere in this respect, but even continues to do so, as well in Great Britain as abroad. Nicolas, *Chronology of History*, p. 40 *et seqq.* A writer from Sealby, near Scarborough,

Yorkshire, in a letter to the *Daily Graphic*, May 15, 1899, observes:—" In this part of England the new style has not yet been adopted in its entirety. With few exceptions rents become due and farms are entered or left on the 6th of April and 11th of October, called Lady Day and Michaelmas Day respectively. Midsummer Day is supposed to fall on the — July; and even in Scarborough and the larger towns of the district the 23rd of November is styled Martinmas. I know a few old inhabitants who firmly believe that May Day falls on the 13th of May.''

Camp.—See *Football*.

Canaries.—A quick and lively dance. See Halliwell in v. and authorities cited by him.

Candlemas Bleeze. — Colonel Alexander Fergusson writes in *Notes and Queries*:—" My father, sometime Governor and Captain General of the colony of Sierra Leone, was born about 1804. As a very small child he attended a parish school in the 'Redgauntlet' country, hard by the Solway. It was then the custom, as I have been informed, on Candlemas Day for every scholar to carry, as an offering to the schoolmaster, a gift of peats, varying in number according to the distance to be traversed and the strength of the pupil. This duty was known by the name of the " Candlemas bleeze, (i.e., blaze).'' Any one acquainted with the incomparable nature of the peats from the Lochar Moss —that terror to English troops and sanctuary for Border reivers—cut from a jetty soil as black as ink and smooth and soft as butter, and, when dried in the sun, the thin slices approaching coal in hardness, will understand what a welcome addition to the master's winter store of fuel was thus pleasantly provided. Probably this was about the last of an ancient custom; for in looking over, many years ago, some old accounts of the expenses connected with my father's education, there occurs an item of money paid to the schoolmaster " in lieu of the Candlemas bleeze.'' I have heard of a similar contribution being made to the parish schoolmaster in other parts of Scotland, where peat was not so common nor so good. It took the form of an offering of candles. I am sorry I can give no date for this latter instance of the survival of what was probably a custom dating from early Popish days.''

Candlemas Day.—(February 2). The name is evidently derived from the candles, which are then carried in procession; it is otherwse known as the Purification of the Virgin. The word " Purification '' itself carries in its original meaning the idea of cleansing by fire or light, and hither, rather perhaps than to Jesus Christ being the Spiritual Light, we ought to refer the connection of candles with this festival. The idea of celebrating the Purification of the Virgin on the same day strikes us as being an aftergrowth or graft, and was a piece of questionable clerical diplomacy, since it was apparently inconsistent with the Immaculate Conception. Fosbrooke (*British Monarchism*, i., 28) says: " The candles at the Purification were an exchange for the lustration of the Pagans, and candles were used " from the parable of the wise virgins.''—' Alcuinus de divinis Officiis, p. 231. " This feast is called by the Greeks υπαπαντα, which signifies a meeting, because Simeon and Anna the prophetess met in the Temple at the presentation of our Saviour.'' L'Estrange's " Alliance of Divine Offices,'' p. 147. See Luke ii. In the " Roman Calendar,'' I find the subsequent observations on the 2nd of February, usually called Candlemas Day:

" Torches are consecrated.
Torches are given away for many days.''
" Feb. 2. " Purificatio Virginis
Faces consecrantur.
Faces dantur multis diebus.''

" To beare their candels soberly, and to offer them to the Saintes, not of God's makynge, but the carvers and paynters,'' is mentioned among the Roman Catholic customs censured by John Bale in his " Declaration of Bonners Articles,'' 1554, signat. D 4 b.; as is, Ibid. fol. 18 b. " to conjure candels.'' " There is a canon,'' says Bourne, " in the Council of Trullus, against those who baked a cake in honour of the Virgin's lying-in, in which it is decreed, that no such ceremony should be observed, because she suffered no pollution, and therefore needed no purification.'' Pope Sergius, says Becon, in his " Reliques of Rome,'' 1563, commanded that all the people "shuld go on procession on Candlemas Day, and carry candels about with them brenning in their hands in the year of our Lord 684.'' How this candle-burning on Candlemas Day came first up, the author of the *Festival* declareth in this manner: " Sometyme,'' saith he, " when the Romaines by great myght and royal power, conquered all the world, they were so proude, that they forgat God, and made them divers gods after their own lust. And so among all they had a god that they called Mars, that had been tofore a notable knight in battayle; and so they prayed to hym for help, and for that they would speed the better of this knight, the people prayed and did great worship to his mother, that was called Februa, after which woman much people have opinion that the moneth February is called. Wherefore the second daie of thys moneth is Candlemass Day. The Romaines this night went about the city of Rome with torches and candles brenning in worship of this woman Februa, for hope to have the more helpe and succoure of her sonne Mars. Then there was a Pope that was called Sergius, and when he saw Christian people draw to this false maumetry and untrue belief, he thought to undo this foule use and custom, and turn it onto Gods worship and our Ladys, and gave commandment that all Christian people should come to church and offer up a candle brennyng, in the worship that they did to this woman Februa, and do worship to our Lady and to her sonne our Lord Jesus Christ. So that now this feast is solemnly hallowed thorowe all Christendome. And every Christian man and woman of covenable age is bound to come to church and offer up their candles, as though they were bodily with our Lady hopyng for this reverence and worship, that they do to our Ladye, to have a great rewarde in Heaven." The Festyvall adds: "A candell is made of weke and wexe; so was Christ's soule hyd within the manhode: also the fyre betokeneth the Godhede: also it betokeneth our Ladyes moderhede and maydenhede, lyght with the fyre of love."

In Dunstan's "Concord of Monastic Rules" it is directed that, "on the Purification of the Virgin Mary the monks shall go in surplices to the Church for candles, which shall be consecrated, sprinkled with holy water, and censed by the Abbot.—Let every monk take a candle from the sacrist, and light it. Let a procession be made, thirds and Mass be celebrated, and the candles, after the offering, be offered to the priest." In some of the ancient illuminated calendars a woman holding a taper in each hand is represented in the month of February.

In a proclamation dated 26th of February, 30 Henry VIII., "concernyng Rites and Ceremonies to be used in due fourme in the Churche of England," we read as follows: "On Candlemas Daye it shall be declared, that the bearynge of candels is done in the memorie of Christe the spirituall lyghte, whom Simeon dyd prophecye as it is redde in the Churche that daye." The same had been declared by a decree of Convocation. Fuller's "Church History," p. 222. We read in Woodde's "Dialogue," cited more particularly under Palm Sunday, signat. d. 1, "Wherefore serveth holye candels? (Nicholas.) To light up in thunder, and to bless men when they lye a dying." See on this subject Duprè's "Conformity between ancient and modern ceremonies," p. 96, and Stopford's "Pagano-Papismus," p. 238. Moresin gives us his conjecture on the use of the candle upon this occasion: "It was an Egyptian hieroglyphic for Life,

meant to express here the ardent desire of having had the life of the deceased prolonged." *Papatus*, pp. 26 - 89. In the "Doctrine of the Masse Book," &c., 1554, signat. A 8, we find: "The hallowing of candles on Candlemas Day." The prayer. "O Lord Jesu Christ, ✠ blesse thou this creature of a waxen taper at our humble supplication, and, by the vertue of the holy crosse, poure thou into it an heavenly benediction; that as thou hast graunted it unto mans use for the expelling of darknes, it may receave such a strength and blessing, thorow the token of thy holy crosse, that in what places soever it be lighted or set, the Divil may avoid out of these habitacions, and tremble for feare, and fly away discouraged, and presume no more to unquiete them that serve thee, who with God," &c. There follow other prayers, in which occur these passages: "We humbly beseech thee, that thou wilt vouchsafe to ✠ to blesse and ✠ sanctifie these candels, prepared unto the uses of men, and health of bodies and soules, as wel on the land as in the waters." "Vouchsafe ✠ to blesse and sanctifye, and with the Candle of heavenly benediction, to lighten these tapers, which we thy servants taking in the honour of thy name (whan they are lighted) desire to beare, &c. "Here let the candles be sprinkled with holy water." Concluding with this rubrick: "When the halowyng of the candels is done, let the candels be lighted and distributed." Queen Mary, when princess, was a scrupulous observer of the custom of offering tapers, &c., peculiar to this day, as repeated entries in her "Privy Purse Expenses" testify, and in Bishop Bonner's "Injunctions," 1555, signat. A i. we read, "that bearyng of candels on Candlemasse Daie is doone in the memorie of our Saviour Jesu Christe, the spirituall lyght, of whom Sainct Symeon dyd prophecie, as it is redde in the Church that day." This ceremony, however, had been previously forbidden in the metropolis: for in Stowe's "Chronicle," edit. 1631, p. 595, we read, "On the second of February, 1547-8, being the Feast of the Purification of our Lady, commonly called Candlemasse Day, the bearing of candles in the Church was left off throughout the whole citie of London;" and, in fact, King Edward VI. had declared, by royal proclamation, that no man was to be subject to imprisonment for omitting the Popish ceremonies incidental to the day. At the end of Smart's "Vanitie and Downefall of superstitious Popish ceremonies," 1628, I find, in "a briefe but true historicall Narration of some notorious Acts and Speeches of Mr. John Cosens" (Bishop of Durham), the following: "Fourthly, on Candlemass Day last past, Mr. Cozens in renuing that Popish ceremonie of burning candles to the honour of our Ladye, busied himself from two of the clocke in the afternoone till foure, in climbing long ladders to stick up wax candles in the said Cathedral Church: the number of all the candles burnt that evening was two hundred and twenty, besides sixteen torches : sixty of those burning tapers and torches standing upon and near the high altar (as he calls it), where no man came nigh." Herrick, in his "Hesperides," has two or three passages illustrating curiously enough the usages peculiar to this season. In the "Country Almanack" for 1676, under February, we read—

"Foul weather is no news; hail, rain, and snow
Are now expected, and esteemed no woe ;
Nay, 'tis an omen bad the yeomen say,
If Phœbus shews his face the second day."

Martin, in his "Description of the Western Islands," mentions an ancient custom observed on the second of February : "The mistress and servants of each family take a sheaf of oats and dress it up in women's apparel, put it in a large basket, and lay a wooden club by it, and this they call a Briid's Bed ; and then the mistress and servants cry three times, "Briid is come, Briid is welcome." This they do just before going to bed, and when they rise in the morning they look among the ashes, expecting to see the impression of Briid's club there ; which if they do, they reckon it a true presage of a good crop and prosperous year, and the contrary they take as an ill omen." There is a proverb :

"If Candlemas day be fair and bright,
Winter will have another flight ;
If on Candlemas day it be shower and rain,
Winter is gone and will not come again."

Which appears to point to the deceptive character of a premature season. The heavy winds which visit us during February and March are sometimes called "Candlemas-eve winds." Hospinian's account of this festival is remarkbaly brief ; but as Naogeorgus in Googe's paraphrase is a little more explicit, his account may be here inserted.

"Then comes the day wherein the Virgin offred Christ unto
The Father chiefe, as Moyses law commaunded hir to do.
Then numbers great of Tapers large, both men and women beare
To Church, being halowed there with pomp, and dreadful words to heare.
This done eche man his candell lightes where chiefest seemeth hee,
Whose taper greatest may be seene, and fortunat to bee ;
Whose candell burneth cleare and bright a wondrous force and might

Doth in these candels lie, which if at any time they light,
They sure beleve that neyther storme or tempest dare abide,
Nor thunder in the skies be heard, nor any Devils spite,
Nor fearefull sprites that walke by night nor hurts of frost or haile."

Comp. *Candles, God's Sunday,* and *Wives' Feast-Day.*

Candle Omens.—In the "Knight of the Burning Pestle," 1613, in a sort of dirge, which Luce sings, there is this passage :

"Come, you whose loves are dead,
And whiles I sing,
Weep and wring
Every hand, and every head
Bind with cypress and sad yew ;
Ribands black and candles blue
For him that was of men most true."

Melton says that "if a candel burne blew, it is a signe that there is a spirit in the house, or not farre from it." *Astrologaster,* 1620, p. 45. In "Ovid Travestie, 1673, the whimsical author makes Hero describe her alarm to her lover in consequence of an omen she had seen in the candle :

"For last night late to tell you true
My candel as I sate burnt blew,
Which put poor me in horrid fright,
And expectation of black spright,
With sawcer eyes, and horns and tail."

But, in "A New Tricke to cheat the Divell," by Robert Davenport, 1639, the blue in the candle seems to be regarded as a portent of something different :

Constable. My watch is set, charge given and all in peace,
But by the burning of the candel blew,
Which I by chance espyed through the lanthorne,
And by the dropping of the Beadles nose,
I smell a frost—"

Goldsmith, in his "Vicar of Wakefield," "speaking of the waking dreams of his hero's daughters, says, "The girls had their omens too, they saw rings in the candle." Willsford tells us : "If the flame of a candle, lamp, or any other fire does wave or wind itself, where there is no sensible or visible cause, expect some windy weather. When candles or lamps will not so readily kindle as at other times, it is a sign of wet weather neer at hand. When candles or lamps do sparkle and rise up with little fumes, or their wicks swell, with things on them (like mushrums) are all signs of ensuing wet weather." *Nature's Secrets,* 120. Boyle makes his 10th Meditation "upon a thief in a candle "—"which by its irregular way of making the flame blaze, melts down a good part of the tallow, and will soon spoil the rest, if the remains are not rescued by the removal of the Thief (as they call it) in the candle." *Occasional Reflections*, 1665, p. 218. The fungous parcels, as Browne calls them, about the wicks of candles are commonly thought to foretell strangers. See *Stranger*.

In the North, as well as in other parts of England, they are called letters at the candle, as if the forerunners of some strange news. These, says Browne, with his usual pedantry of style, which is so well atoned for by his good sense and learning, only indicate a moist and pluvious air, which hinders the avolation of the light and favillous particles, whereupon they settle upon the snast. That candles and lights, he observes also, burn blue and dim at the apparition of spirits, may be true, if the ambient air be full of sulphureous spirits, as it happens often in mines." The innkeepers and owners of brothels at Amsterdam are said to account these "fungous parcels" lucky, when they burn long and brilliant, in which case they suppose them to bring customers. But when they soon go out, they imagine the customers already under their roofs will presently depart. They call these puffs of the candle "good men." *Putanisme d'Amsterdam*, 1681, p. 92. A spark at the candle is held to import that the party opposite to it will shortly receive a letter.

Candle Rent.—A due or impost payable at Cambridge in ancient times. *Hist. of C. C. C.*, by Stokes, 1898, p. 29. But see Davies, *Suppl. Glossary*, 1881, p. 100, where the candle-rent seems to be satisfactorily explained.

Candle (Corpse), or Winding Sheet.—Corpse candles, says Grose, are very common appearances in the counties of Cardigan, Caermarthen, and Pembroke, and also in some other parts of Wales: they are called candles from their resemblance not to the body of the candle, but the fire; because that fire, says the honest Welchman, Mr. Davis, in a letter to Mr. Baxter, doth as much resemble material candle lights as eggs do eggs: saving that, in their journey, these candles are sometimes visible and sometimes disappear, especially if any one comes near to them, or in the way to meet them. On these occasions they vanish, but presently appear again behind the observer, and hold on their course. If a little candle is seen, of a pale bluish colour, then follows the corpse, either of an abortive, or some infant: if a larger one, then the corpse of some one come to age. If there be seen two, three, or more, of different sizes, some big, some small, then shall so many corpses pass together and of such ages or degrees. If two candles come from different places, and be seen to meet, the corpses will do the same; and if any of these candles be seen

to turn aside through some by-path leading to the church, the following corpse will be found to take exactly the same way. Sometimes these candles point out the places where persons shall sicken and die. They have also appeared on the bellies of pregnant women, previous to their delivery, and have predicted the drowning of persons passing a ford.

Candle (Religious Use of).— It appears from "Scogin's Jests," 1626, that in Henry the Eighth's time it was the custom to set two burning candles over the dead body. The passage is curious, as illustrative of more customs than one : "On Maundy-Thursday, Scogin said to his chamber-fellow, we wil make our maundy, and eate and drink with advantage. Be it, said the scholar. On Maundy-Thursday at night they made such cheere that the scholler was drunke. Scogin then pulled off all the schollers clothes, and laid him stark naked on the rushes, and set a forme over him, and spread a coverlet over it, and set up two tallow candles in candlesticks over him, one at his head, the other at his feet, and ran from chamber to chamber, and told the fellowes of that place that his chamber-fellow was dead : and they asked of Scogin if he died of the pestilence ? Scogin said : no I pray you go up, and pray for his soule ; and so they did. And when the scholler had slept his first sleepe, he began to turne himselfe, and cast down the forme and the candles. The fellowes of the house seeing that Scogin did run first out of the chamber, they and all that were in the chamber, one running and tumbling down on anothers neck, were afraid. The scholler, seeing them run so fast out of the chamber, followed them starke naked ; and the fellowes seeing him runne after them like a ghost, some ran into their chambers, and some ran into one corner, and some into another. Scogin ran into the chamber to see that the candles should doe no harme, and at last fetcht up his chamber-fellow, which ran about naked like a madman, and brought him to bed ; for which matter Scogin had rebuke." Hazlitt's *Old English Jestbooks*, ii., 55. In Herbert's "Country Parson," 1675, third impression, p. 157, he tells us, "Another old custom (he had been speaking of processions) there is, of saying, when light is brought in, God send us the light of Heaven ; and the parson likes this very well. Light is a great blessing, and as great as food, for which we give thanks : and those that think this superstitious, neither know superstition nor themselves." The following is from Copley's "Wits, Fits and Fancies," 1595 : " A gentlewoman in extremitie of labour sware that if it pleasęd God she might escape death for that once, she would never in all her life after hazard herselfe to the like daunger again; but being at last safely delivered, she then said to one of the midwives, 'So, now put out the holy candle, and keepe it till the next time.'' Comp. *Churching* and *Funeral Customs.*

Candles (Time).—There were no clocks in England in King Alfred's time. He is said by his biographer Asser, who is supposed to have died in 910, to have measured his time by wax candles, marked with circular lines to distinguish the hour.

Capon-Bell.—The following passage is in Dekker's "Strange Horse-Race," 1613. Speaking of "rich curmudgeons" lying sick, he says: "Their sonnes and heires cursing as fast (as the mothers pray) until the great capon-bell ring out." If this does not mean the passing bell, I cannot explain it.

Cappy-Hole. — This occurs, with other contemporary Scotish amusements, in the *Scotch Rogue,* 1722. It is also mentioned in the Notes to "Ancient Scotish Poems" from the Bannatyne MS. 1770, p. 251.

Cards, or the *Books of the Four Kings.* See Chatto's *Facts and Speculations on the History of Playing Cards,* 1848, Introductory Section. Cards seem to have evolved from chess, known in ancient times as *Chaturanga,* or the *Four Rajas,* which Edward I. learned to play in the Holy Land, and for which, in his wardrobe account, 8s. 5d. is delivered to him by Walter Sturton in 1278. The Arabians doubtless borrowed chess, if not cards, from India. Ducange cites card-playing as known to the modern Greeks in 1498; but it was familiar to Venice at a far earlier date, as in 1441 the Government of the Republic prohibited, on the prayer of the Painters' Gild, the importation of foreign cards, which paralysed the national trade. 1493 is the point of time fixed for their introduction into France in consequence of the necessity, after the King's seizure by sunstroke, for some amusement. This theory, however, is no doubt equally erroneous, since the cards described as being supplied to Charles VI. were evidently products belonging to a fairly advanced stage in the art, and, again, the French would have most probably received the idea from the Spanish Moors. The games alluded to in Benedictus Abbas, under the date 1190, did not include cards, which did not then exist in any shape, and were an accomplishment unknown to the ancient Greeks and Romans. But they may very well have played during the Crusades at various forms of dice. Cards are mentioned in the statute 11 Henry VII., c. 2 (1496). At a court held at Edgeware in 1551 two men were fined for playing at cards and draughts (*ad pictas cartas et tabulas*),

which is a curious notice for so early a date, considering the presumed station of the offenders. Lysons' *Environs,* 1st edit., ii., 244. Richard Rice, in his *Invective,* 1579, has a curious passage on this subject: "Is the waie to attain godliness," he inquires, "by plaiyng, and sportyng, or resting of the wearie bones, with the bones of a paire of dice, or with a paire of cardes (otherwise nowe called the bookes of life) and though it be spoken but in iestyng, yet is it not altogether for naught, for the nature of some is to reste more in theim, and are more at quiete with the ace, kyng, queene, or varlet of spades, then thei can be with a spade to digge or delue honestly after Goddes preceptes for

CARD-PLAYING.
(*From an ancient MS.*)

their hiryng: yea, and delighte quietlier in the ace, king, queene, or varlette of the hartes, then thei dooe in the booke of life." Sir David Lyndsay, in his *Complaint,* enumerates cards among the amusements of the Scotish Court under James IV. and V., even of a bishop, and in 1503, when the former prince waited on his consort in the Castle of Newbattle, it is said: "The Kynge came prively to the said castell, and entred within the chamber with a small cumpany, whar he founde the quene playing at the cardes." Hazlitt's *Warton,* 1871, iii., 243. Warton, in a note to Lyndsay's Works, observes: "In our Author's tragedie of Cardinal Betoun, a soliloquy spoken by the cardinal, he is made to declare that he played with the

King (James IV.) for three thousand crowns of gold in one night, at cartis and dice." They (cards) are also mentioned in an old anonymous Scotish poem of Covetice. Dalrymple, *Anc. Scot. Poems*, 168. Lyndsay, in his *Satire of the Three Estates* (1535) makes the parson say that at various amusements, including *cartis*, he may above all others bear the prize. Cards were, from numerous references, in great vogue both in Scotland and on the Borders, even among the lower classes, in the sixteenth and seventeenth centuries. The stakes in the case of the humbler players were placks or hardheads, two coins of very small value in the old Scotish currency. Hall, of Cambridge, says: " For cardes, the philologie of them is not for an essay. A man's fancy would be sum'd up in cribbidge; gleeke requires a vigilant memory and a long purse; maw, a pregnant agility; pichet, a various invention; primero, a dextrous kinde of rashnesse, &c. *Horæ Vacivæ*, 1646, p. 150. Lord Worcester includes in his " Century of Inventions," 1663, two which may be thought to have been as well omitted. They refer to cheating tricks with cards and dice. " White silk," says his lordship, " knotted in the fingers of a pair of white gloves, and so contrived without suspicion, that playing at primero at cards, one may without clogging his memory keep reckoning of all sixes, sevens and aces, which he hath discarded." Again, the writer says: " A most dexterous dicing box, with holes transparent, after the usual fashion, with a device so dexterous, that with a knock of it against the table the four good dice are fastened, and it looseneth four false dice made fit for his purpose." Urquhart of Cromarty observes : " Verily, I think they make use of Kings, as we do of Card-Kings in playing at the Hundred; any one whereof, if there be appearance of a better game without him, (and that the exchange of him for another incoming card is like to conduce more for drawing of the stake), is by good gamesters without any ceremony discarded." *Discovery*, 1657, p. 237. Mr. W. H. Allnutt, of Oxford, found in a MS. diary of 1629 the following list : " Games at Chartes.—Ruffe, trumpe, slam'e, gleeke, Newcut, swigg, loadam, putt, primifisty, post and pair, bone-ace, anakin, seven cardes one and thirty, my sow has pig'd."

The earliest English example of an attempt to treat cards as an apologue appears to have been in the lost comedy of the *Play of Cards*, mentioned by Sir John Harington in his *Apologie of Poetrie*, accompanying his English *Ariosto*, 1591, in which, he tells us, is showed in Four Parasitical Knaves Four Principal Vocations of the Realme, videl. The vocation of soldiers, schollers, marchants, and husbandmen. The popular character of cards was the inducement to certain publishers to make them a vehicle of instruction in history and other topics; and we have from the time of James II. nearly to our own packs illustrated in a variety of ways, shewing historical episodes, leading points in geography, and even the outlines of grammar.

Card-tricks began at a very early date to be a deviation from the original and legitimate application of the objects, and Reginald Scot, in his *Discovery*, 1584, dedicates a section to the exposure of the frauds of sharpers of various types, among whom he tells us that there were some who affected, for the purpose of cosenage, to be drunk. In *A Notable Discovery of Cosenage*, 1592, *Dequoy, Mumchance, Catchdolt*, or *Irish One-and-Thirty, Non est possible, Dutch Noddy*, are quoted as the names of cheating games of cards then in vogue. In the margin of the text a note describes them as " the names of such games as Conycatchers vse."

Since Brand and Ellis wrote, several important works on this subject have appeared, particularly Singer's *Researches*, 1816, and Chatto's still more valuable work in 1848. See also P. Boiteau D'Ambly, *Cartes a Jouer et la Cartomancie*, 1854, and the late Lady Charlotte Schreiber's monumental illustrated work. Copious notices of the different games will be found under their several heads and in the authorities there cited. In the 15th c. Italy had, besides chess, tables or backgammon, and triumphs or *tarocchi*, cards, running in suits like ours. These were usually *Cups, Swords, Coins, and Clubs*. Of these the *Tarrochi* were the most modern, and were composed of a series of 22 painted or engraved figures. The gambling tables were universally frequented, and reckless speculation on the part of both sexes prevailed. At Venice dice were introduced at a very remote date—perhaps the twelfth century—and chess was a favourite game among the higher classes. Hazlitt's *Venetian Republic*, 1900, i., 560, 758; ii., 456.

Care-Cloth. — Among the Anglo-Saxons the nuptial benediction was performed under a veil or square piece of cloth, held at each corner by a tall man, over the bridegroom and bride, to conceal her virgin blushes: but if the bride was a widow, the veil was esteemed useless. Strutt's *Manners and Customs*, i., 76. The most rational explanation of the meaning of *Care* here is that suggested in the last edition of Nares, 1859, making it equivalent to the Fr. *carré*. But I am afraid that Palsgrave, 1530, is wrong, as he and the author of the " Promptorium " (ed.

Way. in voce) intend an altogether different thing when they speak of Carde. See Scheller's Lex. art. Discerpiculum. According to the Sarum use, when there was a marriage before mass the parties kneeled together and had a fine linen cloth (called the care cloth) laid over their heads during the time of mass, till they received the benediction, and then were dismissed. In the Hereford Missal it is directed, that at a particular prayer the married couple shall prostrate themselves, while four clerks hold the pall, i.e., the care cloth over them. The rubric in the Sarum Missal is similar: "Prosternant se sponsus et sponsa in Oratione ad gradum Altaris: et tento pallio super eos, quod teneant quatuor Clerici in superpelliciis at quatuor cornua." — *Missale ad Usum Sarum*, 1494. The York Manual differs here:—" Missa dein celebratur, illis genuflectentibus sub Pallio super eos extento, quod teneant duo Clerici in Superpelliceis." In the Appendix to Hearne's "Hist. and Antiq. of Glastonbury," p. 309, is preserved "Formula antiqua nuptias in iis partibus Angliæ (occidentalibus nimirum) quæ Ecclesiæ Herfordensis in ritibus Ecclesiasticis ordine sunt usi, celebrandi." The care-cloth seems to be described in the following passage: "Hæc Oratio 'S. propiciare Domini,' semper dicatur super Nubentes sub pallio prosternentes."

Careing Fair.—In the "Gentleman's Magazine" for 1785, p. 779, an advertisement, or printed paper, for the regulation of Newark Fair, is copied, which mentions that: "Careing Fair will be held on Friday before Careing Sunday"; and Mr. Nichols remarks on this passage, that he has heard an old Nottinghamshire couplet in the following words:

"Care Sunday, Care away,
    Palm Sunday, and Easter-day."

Carling, Carle or Care Sunday.—See *Passion Sunday*.

Carlings.—The vulgar, in the North of England, and also in the Midland Counties, give the following names to the Sundays of Lent, the first of which is anonymous:

"Tid, Mid, Misera,
    Carling, Palm, Paste Egg day."

This couplet is differently given by a writer in the "Gentleman's Magazine," for 1788, as follows:

"Tid, and Mid, and Misera,
    Carling, Palm, and Good-Pas-day."

The abbreviated form here found may present the commencing words of the Psalms: *Te Deum, Mi Deus*, and *Miserere mei*. In the "Festa Anglo-Romana," 1678, we are told that the first Sunday in Lent is called Quadragesima or *In-*vocavit; the second, *Reminiscere*; the third, *Oculi*; the fourth *Lætare*; the fifth *Judica*; and the sixth *Dominica Magna. Oculi*, from the entrance of the 14th verse of the 25th Psalm. "Oculi mei semper ad Dominum," &c. *Reminiscere*, from the entrance of the 5th verse of Psalm 25, "Reminiscere Miserationum," &c., and so of the others. At Newcastle-upon-Tyne, and many other places in the North of England, and also in Lancashire and other counties, and in Scotland grey peas, after having been steeped a night in water, are fried with butter, given away, and eaten at a kind of entertainment on the Sunday preceding Palm Sunday, which was formerly called Care or Carle Sunday, as may be yet seen in some of our old almanacks. They are called carlings, probably, as we call the presents at fairs, fairings. In Yorkshire, as a clergyman of that county informed Brand, the rustics go to the publichouse of the village on this day, and spend each his carling-groat, i.e., that sum in drink, for the carlings are provided for them gratis; and, he added, that a popular notion prevails there that those who do not do this will be unsuccessful in their pursuits for the following year. So in the popular old Scotish song, "Fy! let us all to the Briddel":

"Ther'll be all the lads and the lasses
    Set down in the midst of the ha,
With Sybows, and Risarts, and Carlings
    That are both sodden and ra."

Sybows are onions; and risarts radishes. The practice was a very ancient one; it is mentioned by Skelton in his *Colin Clout* (about 1520):

"Men call you therfor prophanes,
Ye pycke no shrympes, nor pranes;
Salt-fyshe, stoc-fyshe, nor heryng,
It is not for your werynge.
Nor, in holy Lenton season,
Ye will netheyr benes ne peason.
But ye loke to be let lose,
To a pygge or to a gose."

The above writer, in the "Gentleman's Magazine" for 1788, also gives a more particular account of the carlings or grey peas, and of the manner of dressing and eating them. See also "Gent. Mag." vol. lvi. p. 410, and Davis, *Suppl. Glossary*, 1881.

Carol (Christmas).—Dr. Furnivall thinks that the word Carol is derived from *Corolla* or *Chorolla*. Bishop Taylor observes that the "Gloria in Excelsis," the well-known hymn sung by the angels to the shepherds at our Lord's Nativity, was the earliest Christmas Carol. Bourne cites Durandus, to prove that in the earlier ages of the churches the bishops were accustomed on Christmas Day to sing carols among their clergy. This species of pious song is undoubtedly of most ancient date. Compare *Hagmena.* In 1521 was printed a set of Christmas Carols. These, remarks Warton, were festal chansons for enlivening the merriments of the Christmas celebrity; and not such religious songs as are current at this day with the common people, under the same title, and which were substituted by those enemies of innocent and youthful mirth, the Puritans. The boar's head soused was anciently the first dish on Christmas Day, and was carried up to the principal table in the hall with great state and solemnity. For this indispensable ceremony there was a carol. "This carol," Warton adds, "yet with many innovations, is retained at Queen's College in Oxford," nor has it been discontinued since Warton's day. At present, it is usual for two atendants to bear aloft into the hall on Christmas Day the boar's head, on a large platter, preceded by a fellow of the College in surplice; but the head is fictitious, being merely a painted counterfeit with a brawn enclosed. Compare *Boar's Head.* William Cornish received at Christmas, 1502, the sum of 13s. 4d. "for setting of a carralle upon Christmas Day, in reward." In the "Paradyce of Daynty Devises," 1578, are hymns by Jasper Heywood and Francis Kinwelmersh for Christmas Day, Whitsunday, and Easter Day; and in the *Christmas Prince,* 1607, occurs the carol sung by him who brought into the hall the boar's head at the celebration in St. John's College, Oxford, in 1607. It is a species of burlesque. *The Christmas Prince,* ed. 1816, p. 24. These older pious chansons were sometimes borrowed from the early Christian poets, and the early Scotish writers did not scruple to set their *guid and godly ballates* to secular tunes. In the Churchwardens' accounts of St. Mary-at-Hill, London, 1537, is the tantalizing entry:— "To Sr. Mark for carolls for Christmas and for 5 square Books. iijs. iiijd." Here is a specimen from the first known impression of the *Dundee Psalms,* 1578 :

"ANE SANG OF THE BIRTH OF CHRIST.
[*To be sung with the tune of Balulalow.*]
(*Angelus, ut opinor, loquitur.*)

" I come from heuin to tell
The best nowellis that euer befell;
To yow the tythings trew I bring,
And I will of them say and sing.

This day to yow is borne ane Chylde
Of Mary meik and Virgin mylde;
That blyssit bairne, bening and kynde,
Sall yow reioyce bath hart and mynde.

It is the Lord Christ, God and man,
He will do for yow what he can;
Himself your Sauiour will be,
Fra sin and hell to mak yow fre.

He is your richt saluatioun,
From euerlasting dampnatioun,
That ye may ring in gloir and blis,
For euer mair in heuin with his.

Ye sall him find but mark or wying ,
Full sempill in ane cribe lying;
Sa lyis he quhilk yow hes wrocht,
And all this warld maid of nocht.

Let us reioyce and be blyith,
And with the Hyrdis go full swyith,
And se quhat God of his grace hes done,
Throw Christ to bring vs to his throne.

My saull and lyfe, stand vp and se
Quha lys in ane cribe of tre,
Quhat Babe is that, so gude and fair?
It is Christ, Goddis Sone and air.
[.   .   .   .   .   .]

O God that maid all creature,
How art thow now becummin sa pure,
That on the hay and stray will ly
Amang the assis, oxin and ky?
[.   .   .   .   .   .]

O my deir hart, young Jesus sweit,
Prepair thy creddill in my spreit,
And I sall rocke the in my hart,
And neuer mair fra the depart.

But I sall praise the euer moir ,
With sangis sweit vnto thy gloir,
The kneis of my hart sall bow
And sing that richt Balulalow."
[.   .   .   .   .   .]

Lamb, in his Notes on the poem on the " Battle of Flodden Field," 1774, tells us that the Nurse's Lullaby Song, Balow (or " He balelow "), is literally French, " He bas ! la le loup." "Hush ! there's the wolf."

At the end of Wither's " Fair Virtue," 1622, is a " Christmas Carroll," in which the customs of that season are not overlooked. Among Herrick's " Noble Numbers," is a " Christmas Carol sung to the King in the presence at White Hall." The musical part composed by Mr. Henry Lawes. Warmstrey, in his "Vindication of Christ's Nativity, 1648, observes: " Christmasse Kariles, if they be such as are fit for the time, and of holy and sober composures, and used with Christian sobriety and piety, they are not unlawfull, and may be profitable, if they be sung with grace in the heart. New Yeares Gifts, if performed without superstition, may be harmless provocations to Christian love and mutuall testimonies thereof to good purpose, and never the worse because the heathens have them at the like times." In " Batt upon Batt," a poem attributed to John Speed, of St. John's College, Oxford, 1694, p. 4.

speaking of Batt's carving knives, &c., the author tells us:

"Without their help, who can good Christmas keep?
Our teeth would chatter, and our eyes would weep.
Batt is the cunning engineer, whose skill
Makes fools to carve the goose and shape the quill:
Fancy and wit unto our meals supplies:
Carols, and not minc'd-meat, makes Christmas pies.
'Tis mirth, not dishes, sets a table off;
Brutes and phanaticks eat, and never laugh."

In Goldsmith's time, as he tells us in his "Vicar of Wakefield," the rustics held the Christmas Carol in careful observance." "In the Scilly Islands they have a custom of singing carols on a Christmas Day at church, to which the congregation make contribution by dropping money into a hat carried about the church when the performance is over." Heath's *Account of the Scilly Islands*, p. 125.

A writer in the "Gentleman's Magazine" for May, 1811, says: "About six o'clock on Christmas Day, I was awakened by a sweet singing under my window; surprized at a visit so early and unexpected, I arose, and looking out of the window, I beheld six young women, and four men, welcoming with sweet music the blessed morn." In "Doctour Doubble Ale," a satire on the irregularities of the clergy in the time of Henry VIII., there is an anecdote of a parson who had a Christmas carol sung at a funeral. In a satirical tract, which was printed in 1642, the author, among other proposals made for the consideration of the Parliament, suggested that, "instead of carols, which farmers sonnes, and servants sing on Christ's Birth-day before they may eate or drink, you take order, that by some of your best City-Poets (who will write certainly to their capacity) there be some songs made of the great deeds that his Excelencie did at Worcester and Edgehill." *Antiq. Repert.*, 1807, iii., 32.

Several collections of old Christmas carols have been made since Mr. Brand's time. Among them may be mentioned the volume edited by Mr. Wright for the Percy Society, Mr. Sandys's book, and a little quarto volume edited by Dr. Rimbault, in which the carols are accompanied by the tunes. For a notice of all the early printed collections known to exist see my "Handbook of E. E. Lit." and *Bibl. Coll.* Art. Christmas. There are carols in many other books of usual occurrence, such as Tusser's "Points of Husbandry," Aylet's "Wife not Ready Made but Bespoken," 1653, Herrick's "Hesperides," 1648, Furnivall's *Babees Book*, 1863, &c.

Carpet Knights, or Trencher Knights. — See Nares, *Glossary*, ed. 1859, in v. There is a scarce poetical volume, called *Pendragon, or the Carpet Knight, his Calendar*, 1698.

Carps (Ludus Carparum). — In a letter from Hearne to Dr. Richard Rawlinson, 1733, the former observes: "I am inquiring what sort of a game *Ludus Carparum* was. It is prohibited in some statutes, and is joined with cards, and reckoned as a kind of *alea*. . . . 'Twas, without doubt, call'd carps in English, and perhaps might be a sort of backgammon. The play was used in Oxford much; but being not mentioned in the New College statutes, I take it to have been brought up here since the foundation of that College." Nares and Halliwell render us no help here, nor Ducange.

Cartomancy. — The divination by cards, supposed to have been brought by the gypsies into Europe, and to have been familiar in the fifteenth century. See P. Boiteau D'Ambly, *Les Cartes À Jouer et la Cartomancie*, 1854.

Casting of Stones. — This is a Welsh custom, practised as they throw the blacksmith's stone in some parts of England. There is a similar game in the north of England called Long Bullets. The prize is to him that throws the ball furthest in the fewest throws. Compare *Quoits*.

Castor and Pollux. — Gregory observes: "Sailors have learned by experience that in great storms very frequently flames are seen upon the sails of ships, flashing hither and thither; these, if they appear double, portend the approach of a calm: if otherwise, sure and imminent shipwreck." He adds that through the superstition of ancient sailors the signs of Castor and Pollux were placed on the prows of ships. "Hoc certum satis, cum ejusmodi faculæ ardentes olim insidissent super capita Castoris & Pollucis ad Expeditionem Argonauticam, exinde Dioscuri in Deos indigites relati, et tanquam solida & sola Maris numina ab omnibus Navigantibus summa in veneratione habiti, cumque procellis suborientibus Tempestas immineat, astraque illa ab olim ominosa Antennis incubent, Castorem et Pollucem in auxilium adesse nemo dubitat." Pliny, in the second book of his *Natural History*, calls these appearances stars; and tells us that they settled not only upon the masts and other parts of ships, but also upon men's heads. Two of these lights forbode good weather and a prosperous voyage; and drive away the single one, which wears a threatening aspect. This the sailors call

Helen, but the two they call Castor and Pollux, and invoke them as gods. These lights do sometimes about the evening rest on men's heads. These appearances are called by the French and Spaniards inhabiting the coasts of the Mediterranean, St. Helmes or St. Telmes fires: by the Italians the fires of St. Peter and St. Nicholas, and are frequently taken notice of by the writers of voyages. Erasmus, in his dialogue entitled *Naufragium*, observes: "Nox erat sublustris et in summo malo stabat quidam e Nautis in Galea, circumspectans si quam terram videret: huic cœpit adsistere Spæra quædem ignea: id Nautis tristissimum ostentum est, si quando solitarius ignis est; felix, cum gemini. Hos Vetustas credidit Castorem et Pollucem. Mox globus igneus delapsus per funes devolvit sese usque ad Nauclerum: ubi paullisper commoratus, volvit se per margines totius Navis: inde per medios foros dilapsus evanuit. Fori sunt Tabulata Navis, ac veluti Tectum, sub meridiem cœpit magis ac magis incrudescere Tempestas." Cotgrave confirms what has already been said: "Feu d'-Helene, or Feu de S. Herme—St. Helens or S. Hermes fire; a meteor that often appears at sea. *Dictionary*, 1650, vv. *Feu d'Heléne* and *Furote*. Among the apothegms at the end of Herbert's Remains, 1652, p. 194, is the following: "After a great fight there came to the camp of Gonsalvo the great Captain, a gentleman, proudly horsed and armed; Diego de Mendoza asked the great captain, who's this? who answered, 'Tis St. Ermyn that never appears but after a storm." Shaw tells us that in thick hazy weather he has observed those luminous appearances which at sea skip about the masts and yards of ships, and which the sailors call *corpusanse*, which is a corruption of the Spanish *Cuerpo Santo*. *Scotish Encyclopædia*, v. *Lights*. Steevens quotes the subsequent passage from Hakluyt's Voyages, 1598: "I do remember that in the great and boysterous storme of this foule weather, in the night there came upon the top of our maine yard and maine mast a certaine little light, much like unto the light of a little candle, which the Spaniards call the *Cuerpo Santo*. This light continued aboord our ship about three houres, flying from maste to maste, and from top to top; and sometimes it would be in two or three places at once." *The British Apollo*, 1710, in reference to the vapor which by mariners is called a corpo zanto, usually accompanying a storm. informs us: "Whenever this meteor is seen, it is an argument that the tempest which it accompanied was caused by a sulphureous spirit, rarefying and violently moving the clouds. For the cause of the fire is a sulphurous and bituminous matter, driven downwards by the impetuous motion of the air and kindled by much agitation. Sometimes there are several of these seen in the same tempest, wandering about in various motions, as other ignes fatui do, tho' sometimes they appear to rest upon the sails or masts of the ship; but for the most part they leap upwards or downwards without any intermission, making a flame like the faint burning of a candle. If five of them are seen near together, they are called by the Portugese *cora de nostra Senhora*, and are looked upon as a sure sign that the storm is almost over. Burton, in his "Anatomy," 1621, says that the "spirits or fire in form of fire-drakes and blazing-stars, sit on ship masts," &c. Hence the passage in the "Tempest":

—"On the top masts,
The yards, and bowsprits, would I flame
  distinctly."

Fryer, in his "Travels," quoted by Southey, observes. "I think I am not too positive in stating them to be a meteor-like substance, exhaled in the day, and at night (for except then they shew not themselves) kindled by the violent motion of the air, fixing themselves to those parts of the ship that are most attractive; for I can witness they usually spent themselves at the spindles of the top-mast-heads or about the iron loops of the yard-arms, and if any went towards them they shifted always to some part of the like nature." So, in an account of "Fiery Impressions that appear mostly at Sea, called by mariners Castor and Pollux": "When thin clammy vapours, arising from the salt water and ugly slime, hover over the sea, they, by the motion in the winds and hot blasts, are often fired; these impressions will oftentimes cleave to the masts and ropes of ships by reason of their clamminess and glutinous substance and the mariners by experience find that when but one flame appears it is the forerunner of a storm; but when two are seen near together, they betoken fair weather and good lucke in a voyage. The naturall cause why these may foretell fair or foul weather, is, that one flame alone may forewarn a tempest, forasmuch as the matter being joyn'd and not dissolved, so it is like that the matter of the tempest, which never wanteth, as winds and clouds, is still together, and not dissipate, so it is likely a storm is engendering; but two flames appearing together, denote that the exhalation is divided, which is very thick, and so the thick matter of the tempest is dissolved and scattered abroad by the same cause that the flame is divided: therefore no violent storm can ensue, but rather a calme is promised." *History of Stormes*, 1704. p. 22.

Dickenson, in his *Greene in Conceipt*, 1598, p. 27, says :

"As when a wave-bruis'd barke, long
        tost by the windes in a tempest,
Straies on a forraine coast, in danger
        still to be swallow'd,
After a world of feares, with a winter of
        horrible objects—
The shipman's solace, faier Ledas
        twinnes at an instant
Signes of a calme are seen, and seene,
        are shrilly saluted."

Thomas Heyrick, a relative of the author of "Hesperides," writes :

"For lo ! a suddain storm did rend the
        air :
The sullen Heaven, curling in frowns
        its brow,
Did dire presaging omens show ;
Ill-boding Helena alone was there."

SubmarineVoyage, 1691, p. 2. The foregoing statements represent, for the most part, no scientific view of a subject, which was familiar to the ancients, even if they could not properly account for the phenomenon ; but is has long been reduced to an effect arising from natural causes ; and an excellent account of it may be found in the *Penny Magazine* for March, 1845. We should probably have never heard of this remarkable appearance, had our ancestors and preceding ages been acquainted with the laws of electricity and with metallic conductors.

Cat, or **Kit-Cat.**—In "The Captain," by Fletcher, written (and probably performed) before 1613, the cat-sticks, with which this game is played, are mentioned. Braithwaite, in his *Strappado for the Divell*, 1615, says :

"If mother Red-cap chance to haue an
        oxe
Rosted all whole, O how you'le flye
        to it,
Like widgeons, or like wild geese in full
        flocks,
That for his pennie each may haue
        his bitte :

*   *   *   *   *

Set out a pageant, whoo'l not thither
        runne?
As 'twere to whip the cat at Abington."

Lenton, in the "Young Gallants Whirligig," 1629, describes the young gallant (perhaps from personal experience), when he has reached the age for study, as preferring light literature to Littleton and Coke, and adds :

"———— instead of that
Perhaps hee's playing of a game at cat."

Poor Robin thus refers to it in his "Almanac" for 1709 :

"Thus harmless country lads and lasses
In mirth the time away so passes ;
Here men at foot-ball they do fall ;
There boys at cat and trap-ball.
Whilst Tom and Doll aside are slank,
Tumbling and kissing on a bank ;
Will pairs with Kate, Robin with Mary,
Andrew with Susan, Frank with Sarah.
In harmless mirth pass time away,
No wanton thoughts lead them astray,
But harmless are as birds in May."

Moor, in his *Suffolk Words*, describes it :—"A game played by boys. Three small holes are made in the ground triangularly, about twenty feet apart, to mark the positon of as many boys, who each holds a small stick, a little bigger than one's thumb, called cat, to be struck by those holding the sticks. On its being struck, the boys run from hole to hole, dipping the ends of their sticks in as they pass, and counting one, two, three, &c. as they do so, up to thirty-one, which is game. Or the greater number of holes gained in the innings may indicate the winners, as at cricket. If the cat be struck and caught, the striking party is out, and another of his sidesmen takes his place, if the set be strong enough to admit of it. If there be only six players, it may be previously agreed that three put-outs shall end the innings. Another mode of putting out is to throw the cat home, after being struck, and placing or pitching it into an unoccupied hole, while the in-party are running, A certain number of misses (not striking the cat) may be agreed on to be equivalent to a put-out. The game may be played by two, placed as at cricket, or four, or I believe more." The phrase "not big enough to whip a cat in" arose doubtless from this diversion, and not in reference to the animal so-called, although the contrary might be inferred perhaps from the well-known anecdote of Foote and his new house at Fulham.

Cat and Dog. — Jamieson tells us this is the name of an ancient sport used in Angus and Lothian. It is mentioned with other sports in the *Scotch Rogue*, 1722. "The following account," Jamieson adds, "is given of it." "Three play at this game, who are provided with clubs. They cut out two holes, each about a foot in diameter, and seven inches in depth. The distance between them is about twenty-six feet. One stands at each hole with a club. These clubs are called dogs. A piece of wood about four inches long, and one inch in diameter, called a cat, is thrown from the one hole towards the other by a third person. The object is, to prevent the cat from getting into the hole. Every time that it enters the hole, he who has the club at that hole, loses the club, and he who threw the cat gets possession both of the club and of the hole, while the former possessor is obliged to take charge of the cat. If the cat be struck, he who strikes it changes place with the person who holds the other club; and as often as these positions are changed, one is counted as won in the game, by the two who hold the clubs, and who are viewed as partners. "This is not unlike the stool-ball described by Strutt, but it more nearly resembles Club-ball, an ancient English game. It seems to be an early form of cricket."

Cat in Barrel.—"This is a sport which was common in the 18th century at Kelso on the Tweed. A large concourse of men, women, and children assembled in a field about half a mile from the town, and a cat having been put into a barrel stuffed full of soot, was suspended on a cross-beam between two high poles. A certain number of the whip-men, or husbandmen, who took part in this savage and unmanly amusement, then kept striking, as they rode to and fro on horseback, the barrel in which the unfortunate animal was confined, until at last, under the heavy blows of their clubs and mallets, it broke and allowed the cat to drop. The victim was then seized and tortured to death." *A Description of Kelso*, 1789. Steevens, on the passage in "Much Ado about Nothing":

"If I do, hang me in a bottle like a
    cat, and shoot at me";

observes that "in some counties in England, a cat was formerly closed up with a quantity of soot in a wooden bottle, (such as that in which shepherds carry their liquor), and was suspended on a line. He who beat out the bottom as he ran under it, and was nimble enough to escape its contents, was regarded as the hero of this inhuman diversion." He cites some passages that shew it was a custom formerly to shoot with arrows "at a catte in a basket." In a print entitled "Frost Fair," 1740, there is the following reference: "No. 6. Cat in the basket booth." Reed's quotations shew that a fictitious cat was sometimes used, and perhaps this booth was set apart for some sport not unlike cock-throwing (where a make-believe cock was oftener than not substituted for the real thing), or the modern Aunt Sally.

Cats.—Among omens, the movements of cats have always been regarded as important indications. The entrances and exits of strange cats are considered portentous by many even at the present time. When the cat washes its face, it was thought to be a sign of rain; so it was in Melton's time, and Herrick enumerates it among the current superstitions of his era. A modern writer maintains the same idea, and connects the practice with "the well-known disposition of that creature to the

manifestation of electric phenomena." Couch of Polperro, *Illustrations of Instinct*, 1847, p. 13. But surely the cat washes its face after meals, as we do, or some of us, independently of the weather, and its neglect to perform this operation is usually ascribed to ill-health. Willsford remarks quaintly enough: "Cats coveting the fire more than ordinary, or licking their feet and trimming the hair of their heads and mustachios, presages rainy weather." This is explained elsewhere on scientific principles: "the moisture, which is in the air before the rain, insinuating itself into the fur of this animal, moves her to smooth the same and cover her body with it, so that she may less feel the inconvenience of winter, as, on the contrary she opens her fur in summer that she may the better receive the refreshing of the moist season."— *Athenian Oracle, Suppl.* 474. The poet-earl of Westmoreland had a cat with him in confinement, from which he used apparently to draw prognostications of the weather. The cat licking or scratching its ear was regarded in the light of an omen; and hence we get the well-worn proverb, "before the cat can lick her ear." The cat sneezing was considered as a lucky omen to a bride who was to be married the next day. Southey, when he was in Spain, found a belief current that the glossy appearance of the cat's skin portended fair weather. It was a vulgar notion, observes Mason, that cats, when hungry, would eat coals. In the "Woman's Prize, or Tamer Tamed," Tranio says to Moroso:

"I would learn to eat coals with an
    angry cat"—

and, in Fletcher's "Bonduca," the first daughter says:

    "they are cowards,
Eat coals like compell'd cats—"

Trusler tells us, speaking of cats, that it has been judiciously observed that "the conceit of a cat's having nine lives hath cost at least nine lives in ten of the whole race of them. Scarce a boy in the street but has in this point outdone even Hercules himself, who was renowned for killing a monster that had but three lives," *Hogarth Moralized*, 134.

Brand seems to have thought that the prevailing antipathy to cats, which is incidental to many persons of the highest intelligence, was due to their supposed share in the sorceries of witches. The passage in Shakespear, where Lady Macbeth refers to the "poor cat in the adage," predisposes a dislike to wet, which has been generally ascribed to this animal. But the idea seems to be a popular fallacy. Even the tiger will wade some way into a river, and catch fish, General Robinson, an old Indian officer, once watched from a tree one engaged in this way, and continuing to catch and eat the fish till he was so surfeited that a buffalo, who had been tied to the tree as a bait, was left undisturbed, and the beast walked quietly off. In a *jeu-d'esprit* entitled " Les Chats," 8vo. Rotterdam, 1728, there are some very curious particulars relating to these animals, which are detailed with no common degree of learning. Compare *Witch's Cat.*

Catch-Fool. — This is named as a game, in the same sentence as Noddy, in Johnson's *Academy of Love,* 1641. It occurs under similar circumstances in a *Notable Discovery of Cosenage,* 1592; but it is there called *Catch-dolt.*

St. Catharine's or **St. Kattern's Day.** — *(November* 25). — Of St. Catherine of Alexandria, who is reputed to have suffered martyrdom on the wheel, whence we get the St. Catherine's wheel, there is an early metrical life printed in Halliwell's *Contributions to Early English Literature,* 1849. One of the ancient London Brotherhoods or Trading Gilds of Haberdashers was known as that of St. Catherine the Virgin. Hazlitt's Livery Companies, 1892, p. 115, 285. Camden says: " The very women and girls keep a fast every Wednesday and Saturday throughout the yeare, and some of them also on St. Catherine's Day; nor will they omit it though it happen on their birthday, or if they are ever so much out of order. The reason given by some for this is, that the girls may get good husbands, and the women better by the death or desertion of their present ones, or at least by an alteration in their manners." Woodes, in his *Conflict of Conscience,* 1581, tells us that we ought to pray to this Saint to cure " lawlessness of mind." St. Catharine is noticed in Naogeorgus as the favourer of learned men. The same writer adds :

" What should I tell what sophisters on Cathrins Day devise?
Or else the superstitious joyes that maisters exercise."

Miss Baker, in the appendix to her " Northamptonshire Glossary," 1854, says, in reference to the holiday on this day: " I have never been able to ascertain that it is observed at any place in this county, except at Peterborough, when, till the introduction of the new poor laws the female children belonging to the workhouse, attended by the master, went in procession round the city. They were all attired in white, and decorated with various coloured ribbons, principally scarlet; the tallest girl was selected to represent the queen, and was adorned with a crown and sceptre. The procession stopped at the houses of the principal inhabitants, and they sung the

following rude ballad, begging for money at every house, as they passed along. (Here the ballad follows). St. Catharine being the patron of spinners, as well as of spinsters, and spinning being formerly the employment of the females in the workhouse, it naturally followed that they should be selected to commemorate the anniversary of this saint; and that this commemoration is of great antiquity appears from the early entries in the Dean and Chapter's accounts of payments, on St. Catherine's Day, for wheels and reels for the children of the workhouse." But a correspondent of " Notes and Queries," October 3rd, 1868, remarks that the usage, treated by the last writer as peculiar to Peterborough, is unquestionably of general observance in Northamptonshire, and is popularly supposed to be derived from one of the Queens Katherine in the time of Henry VIII.—probably Katherine Parr, who was a Northamptonshire woman. Mr. Plummer says, that this festival " is known to have been kept, for several generations, throughout the whole of the Northamptonshire lace-making districts, as well as those in Bedfordshire. By some it is called ' candle-day,' from its forming the commencement of the season for working at lace-making by candlelight. The popular tradition is that ' Queen Katherine was a great friend to the lacemakers.' " Another correspondent, in the same number, adds, that the wheelwrights also observe this as their holiday. Brome, in his " Travels," 1700, observes: " In Lothien, two miles from Edenburgh southward, is a spring called St. Katherines Well, flowing continually with a kind of black fatness, or oil, above the water, proceeding (as it is thought) from the parret coal, which is frequent in these parts; 'tis of a marvellous nature, for as the coal, whereof it proceeds, is very apt quickly to kindle into a flame, so is the oil of a sudden operation to heal all scabs and tumours that trouble the outward skin, and the head and hands are speedily healed by virtue of this oil, which retains a very sweet smell; and at Aberdeen is another well very efficacious to dissolve the stone, to expel sand from the reins and bladder, being good for the chollick and drunk in July and August, not inferior, they report, to the spaw in Germany." M. Le Roux de Lincy, in his " Livre des Proverbes Français," 1859, t. i. p. 119, notices two French proverbs relating to St. Catherine, but not the common one: " Coiffer Sainte-Catharine," i.e., to follow celibacy, or live and die an old maid. See " Notes and Queries," Oct. 31, 1868.

Cathern Bowl.—Mr. Halliwell, in his " Popular Rhymes and Nursery Tales," 1849, furnishes a set of verses sung by

Worcestershire children on this festival, "when they go round to the farmhouses, collecting apples and beer." "The Dean of Worcester," he adds, "informs me that the Chapter have a practice of preparing a rich bowl of wine and spices, called 'the Cathern Bowl,' for the inhabitants of the college precincts upon that day."

Catherning.—In the Churchwardens' accounts of Horley, Surrey, I find: "Mem. that reste in the hands of the wyffe of John Kelyoke and John Atye, 4 merkes, the yere of ower Lorde God 1521, of Sent Kateryn mony." "Mem. that rests in the hands of the wyff of John Atthy and the wyff of Rye Mansell, 3 pounds 2s. 9d. the yere of our Lorde God 1522, of Sent Kateryn mony." *Summa totalis S'cte Katerine V[irginis] Luminis*, remanet in manibus uxoris Johannis Peers et uxoris Wyl'i Celarer, an'o d'ni 1526, tres libras et undecim solidos. Summa totalis *S'cte Katerine Luminis*, remanet in manibus uxoris Wyl'i Cowper, & uxoris Thome Leakeford, an'o d'ni 1527, quatuor marcas. Summa totalis *Katerine Luminis*, remanet in manibus uxoris Thome Leakeforth, et uxoris Henrici Huett, an'o d'ni 1528, quatuor marcas. Item remanet in manibus uxoris Joh'is Bray, *de eodem Lumine*, anno supradicto 17s."—Ibid. Mr. Brand notes, that he bought the original MS. of Mr. Waight, bookseller in Holborn, Sept. 2, 1801, for 14s. According to La Motte, "St. Catherine is esteemed in the Church of Rome as the Saint and Patroness of the spinsters; and her holiday is observed, not in Popish countries only, but even in many places in this nation [France]: young women meeting on the 25th of November, and making merry together, which they call Catherning." "Essay on Poetry and Painting," 1730, p. 126.

Catoptromancy. — See *Glass (Looking)*.

Cattle Lore and Leechdom.— Reginald Scot tells us: Against witches "hang boughs (hallowed on Midsummer Day) at the stall door where the cattle stand." "Discovery of Witchcraft," 1584, ed. 1665, p. 144. He has "A special charm to preserve all cattel from witchcraft": At Easter, you must take certain drops that lie uppermost of the holy paschal candle, and make a little wax candle thereof; and upon some Sunday morning rathe, light it and hold it so as it may drop upon and between the horns and ears of the beast, saying, In nomine Patris et Filii, &c., and burn the beast a little between the horns on the ears with the same wax, and that which is left thereof, stick it cross-wise about the stable or stall, or

upon the threshold, or over the door, where the cattle use to go in and out: and, for all that year your cattle shall never be bewitched." *Discovery*, p. 160. Browne, in his "Pastorals," 1613-14, alludes to what seems to have been a superstition in his time :

"Nor shall this helpe their sheep, whose stomacks failes,
By tying knots of wooll neere to their tailes :
But as the place next to the knot doth die,
So shall it all the bodie mortifie."

This is another form of the belief, which once actuated the farmers' wives in the Highlands, who used to tie a piece of red worsted thread round their cows' tails, to preserve them from evil influences. Coles tells us: "If asses chaunce to feed much upon hemlock, they will fall so fast asleep that they will seem to be dead: insomuch, that some thinking them to be dead indeed, have flayed off their skins, yet after the hemlock had done operating, they have stirred and wakened out of their sleep, to the griefe and amazement of the owners, and to the laughter of others. Wood nightshade, or bitter-sweet, being hung about the neck of cattell that have the staggers, helpeth them." *Introd.*, 1656, p. 69. Grose tells us that "a slunk or abortive calf, buried in the highway over which cattle frequently pass will greatly prevent that misfortune happening to cows. This is commonly practiced in Suffolk." A superstitious notion prevails in West Devonshire that, at twelve o'clock at night on Christmas Eve, the oxen in their stalls are always found on their knees, as in an attitude of devotion, and that (which is still more singular) since the alteration of the style they continue to do this only on the Eve of old Christmas Day. An honest countryman, living on the edge of St. Stephen's Down, near Launceston, Cornwall, informed Brand, October 28th, 1790, that he once, with some others, made a trial of the truth of the above, and watching several oxen in their stalls at the above time, at twelve o'clock at night, they observed the two oldest oxen only fall upon their knees, and, as he expressed it in the idiom of the country, make "a cruel moan like Christian creatures." Brand says: "I could not but with great difficulty keep my countenance: he saw, and seemed angry that I gave so little credit to his tale, and walking off in a pettish humour, seemed to marvel at my unbelief." There is an old print of the Nativity, in which the oxen in the stable, near the Virgin and Child, are represented upon their knees, as in a suppliant posture. This graphic representation has probably given rise to the above superstitious notion on this head."

"Charms," Pinkerton observes, "are the chief remedies applied for the diseases of animals. I have been myself acquainted with an Antiburgher clergyman in these parts, who pretended skill in these charms, two small pieces of wood, curiously wrought, to be kept in his father's cow-house, as a security for the health of his cows. It is common to bind into a cow's tail a small piece of mountain-ash-wood, as a charm against witchcraft. Few old women are now suspected of witchcraft: but many tales are told of the conventions of witches in the kirks in former times." *Heron's Journey through part of Scotland,* ii., 293. The minister of Logierait, Perthshire, writing in 1795, says: "Recourse is often had to charms, for the cure of diseases of horses and cows, no less than in the human species. In the case of various diseases, a pilgrimage is performed to a place called Strathfillan, forty miles distant from Logierait, where the patient bathes in a certain pool, and performs some other rites in a chapel which stands near. It is chiefly in the case of madness, however, that the pilgrimage to Strathfillan is believed to be salutary. The unfortunate person is first bathed in the pool, then left for a night bound in the chapel, and, if found loose in the morning, is expected to recover." *Stat. Acc.*, v. 84. "There is a disease," he adds, "called Glacach by the Highlanders, which, as it affects the chest and lungs, is evidently of a consumptive nature. It is called the Macdonalds' disease, 'because there are particular tribes of Macdonalds, who are believed to cure it with the charms of their touch, and the use of a certain set of words. There must be no fee given of any kind. Their faith in the touch of a Macdonald is very great.'" Similarly, the minister of Applecross, Co. Ross, describing the state of his parish about the same time, says: "There are none of the common calamities or distressful accidents incident to man or beast, but hath had its particular charm or incantation; they are generally made up of a group of unconnected words, and an irregular address to the Deity, or to some one of the saints. The desire of health, and the power of superstition reconciled many to the use of them; nor are they as yet, among the lower class, wholly fallen into disuse. Credulity and ignorance are congenial; every country hath had its vulgar errors; opinions early imbibed, and cherished for generations, are difficult to be eradicated."— *Stat. Acc. of Scotland,* iii., 379. Pennant tells us, in his " Tour in Scotland," "that the farmers carefully preserve their cattle

against witchcraft by placing boughs of mountain-ash and honey-suckle in their cow-houses on the second of May. They hope to preserve the milk of their cows, and their wives from miscarriage, by tying threads about them: they bleed the supposed witch to preserve themselves from her charms." Martin says: "It is a received opinion in these (the Western) Islands, as well as in the neighbouring part of the main land, that women, by a charm or some other secret way, are able to convey the increase of their neighbours cows' milk to their own use. and that the milk so charmed doth not produce the ordinary quantity of butter, and the curds made of that milk are so tough, that it cannot be made so firm as the other cheese, and also is much lighter in weight. The butter so taken away and joined to the charmer's butter is evidently discernible by a mark of separation, viz. the diversity of colours: that which is charmed being paler than the other. If butter, having these marks, be found on a suspected woman, she is presently said to be guilty. To recover this loss they take a little of the rennet from all the suspected persons, and put it into an eggshell full of milk: and when that from the charmer is mingled with it, it presently curdles, and not before. Some women make use of the root of groundsel as an amulet against such charms, by putting it among the cream. *Western Islands of Scotland,* p. 120.

Caul, or **Sely How.**—Cauls are little membranes found on some children, encompassing the head, when born, and which there may be some reason to ascribe to certain physical conditions between the man and the woman concerned, where unseasonable cohabitation has occurred. This is thought a good omen to the child itself, and the vulgar opinion is, that whoever obtains it by purchase will be fortunate, and escape dangers. An instance of great fortune in one born with this coif is given by Ælius Lampridius in his "History of Diadumenianus," who came afterwards to the sovereign dignity of the empire. This superstition was very prevalent in the primitive ages of the Church. St. Chrysostom inveighs against it in several of his homilies. He is particularly severe against one Prætus, a clergyman who, being desirous of being fortunate, bought such a coif of a midwife. Sir Thomas Browne thus attempts to account for this phenomenon: " To speak strictly," he says, "the effect is natural, and thus to be conceived: the infant hath three teguments or membranaceous filmes, which cover it in the womb, i.e. the corion, amnios, and allantois; the corion is the outward membrane, wherein are implanted the veins, arteries, and umbilical vessels, whereby its nourishment is conveyed; the allantois, a thin coat, seated under the corion, wherein are received the watery separations conveyed by the urachus, that the acrimony thereof should not offend the skin : the amnios is a general investment, containing the sudorous, or thin seriosity perspirable through the skin. Now about the time when the infant breaketh these coverings, it sometimes carrieth with it, about the head, a part of the amnios or neerest coat : which, saith Spigelius, either proceedeth from the toughness of the membrane or weaknesse of the infant that cannot get clear thereof and therefore herein significations are natural and concluding upon the infant, but not to be extended unto magical signalities, or any other person." Lemnius tells us, that if this caul be of a blackish colour it is an omen of ill fortune to the child; but if of a reddish one, it betokens every thing that is good. He observes "There is an old opinion, not only prevalent amongst the common and ignorant people, but also amongst men of great note, and physicians also, how that children born with a caul over their faces, are born with an omen, or sign of good or bad luck : when as they know not that this is common to all, and that the child in the womb was defended by three membranes." *Occult Miracles of Nature.* 1658, ii., 8. "In Scotland," says Ruddiman, "the women call a haly or sely How (i.e. holy or fortunate cap or hood), a film or membrane stretched over the heads of children new-born, which is nothing else but a part of that which covers the fœtus in the womb; and they give out that children so born will be very fortunate." *Glossary to Douglas's Virgil,* 1710. In the North of England, and in Scotland, a midwife is called a howdy or howdy wife. Grose says, that a person possessed of a caul may know the state of health of the party who was born with it: if alive and well, it is firm and crisp: if dead or sick, relaxed and flaccid. In Willis of Gloucester's "Mount Tabor," 1639, we are told that "There was one special remarkable thing concerning my self, who being my parents' first son, but their second child (they having a daughter before me), when I came into the world, my head, face, and foreparts of the body, were all covered over with a thin kell or skin, wrought like an artificiall veile; as also my eldest sonne, being likewise my second childe, was borne with the like extraordinary covering: our midwives and gossips holding such children as come so veiled into the world, to be very fortunate (as they call it), there being not one childe amongst many hundreds that are so borne; and this to fall out in the same

manner both to the father and the sonne being much more rare," &c. He goes on to make religious reflections thereupon, which are foreign to our present purpose. He entitles this chapter "Concerning an extraordinary veile which covered my body, at my comming into the world." Burton, in his "Anatomy," 1621, relates an odd story relevant to this part of the matter: "Guianerius speakes of a silly jealous fellowe, that seeing his child newborne included in a kell, thought sure a Franciscan that used to come to his house was the father of it, it was so like a friers cowle, and thereupon threatned the frier to kill him." A writer in the "Athenian Oracle" states that the virtues of the caul were transferred, in case it should be lost by the first owner, to the person who might find it.

This caul, thought medical in diseases, is also esteemed an infallible preservative against drowning, and, under that idea, is frequently advertised for sale in our public papers, and purchased by seamen. "To the gentlemen of the Navy, and others going long voyages to sea. To be disposed of, a child's caul. Enquire at the Bartlett Buildings Coffee House in Holborn. N.B. To avoid unnecessary trouble the price is Twenty Guineas."—*London Morning Post,* Aug. 21, 1779. I read also an advertisement, similar to the above, in the "Daily Advertiser," in July, 1790. In the "Times" for February 20, 1813, the following advertisement occurred : "A child's caul to be sold, in the highest perfection. Enquire at No. 2, Church Street, Minories. To prevent trouble, price £12." And, in the same newspaper for February 27, 1813, two advertisements of cauls together : Caul. A child's caul to be sold. Enquire at No. 2, Greystoke-Place, Fetter Lane."—"To persons going to sea. A child's caul, in a perfect state, to be sold cheap. Apply at 5, Duke Street, Manchester Square, where it may be seen." Advertisements of this nature still appear in the newspapers, and a very general belief continues to be entertained by the uneducated and more superstitious portion of the community in the virtue of child's cauls. Midwives used to sell this membrane to advocates, as an especial means of making them eloquent. They sold it also for magical use. Sir Thomas Browne says; "Thus we read in the Life of Antoninus by Spartianus, that children are sometimes born with this natural cap, which midwives were wont to sell to credulous lawyers, who held an opinion that it contributed to their promotion." Douce observes : "One is immediately struck with the affinity of the judges' coif to this practice of antiquity.

To strengthen this opinion it may be added that if ancient lawyers availed themselves of this popular superstition, or fell into it themselves, if they gave great sums to win these cauls, is it not very natural to suppose that they would feel themselves inclined to wear them?" Comp. Nares, *Glossary,* 1859, in v. " Etre né coiffé " is a proverb in the French language signifying birth under fortunate auspices, and the phenomenon occurs, when the child is born enveloped in the caul (a very rare event) so as to cover the head. In *Gil Blas* the robbers tell the hero of the story that he must have been *né coiffé* to fall into such good hands, since he had left Oviédo to seek his fortune. Livre 1, ch. iv. M. Le Roux de Lincy ("Proverbes Français," edit. 1859) has left a somewhat meagre account of this subject; but the present seemed to be hardly the proper place to supply his omissions. All the dictionaries tell us *what* a caul is; but none seems to say whence it arises, and the question may be worth putting whether it proceeds from physiological causes and from sexual relations at an advanced stage in the growth of the embryo. See *suprá.* Its virtue is purely empirical.

Cent-Foot.—A game at cards, possibly the same as *foot-saunt* mentioned by Gosson in his *School of Abuse,* 1579. Roger, second Lord North of Kyrtling, who died in 1600, and who s ems to have been an ardent and unlucky gambler, mentions in his "Household Book" for 1575-6 having lost 15s. at Saint—probably this game of cent — on May 15, 1576. But 15s. was nothing to a man who frequently parted with £20 or £30 at one sitting. One cannot help suspecting that it was owing to his extravagance that the family estate fell shortly afterward into such hopeless decay. The game is referred to also by Braithwaite: "Playes at Cent-foot purposely to discover the pregnancy of her conceit." "Barnabæ Itinerarium," 1638, sign. H 2, and "Boulster Lecture," 1640, p. 163. Comp. Davies, *Suppl. Glossary,* 1881, p. 251.

Cerealia.—Shaw, in his account of Elgin and the Shire of Murray, tells us, "that in the middle of June, farmers go round their corn with burning torches, in memory of the Cerealia."

Chadwell, or **St. Chad's Well.**—Brand says: "I found on a visit to the source of the New River between Hertford and Ware, in August, 1793, an old stone inscribed ' Chadwell,' a corruption, no doubt, of St. Chad's Well. So copious a spring could not fail of attracting the notice of the inhabitants in the earliest times, who accordingly dedicated it to St. Chad, never once dreaming, perhaps, that in succeeding ages it should be converted

to so beneficial a purpose as to supply more than half the capital of England with one of the most indispensable necessaries of human life."

Chameleon, The.—Ross asserts it to be true that this creature lives on air. (however Browne writes to the contrary), for the following reasons: "1. The testimonies both of ancient and modern writers, except a few, and the witnesses of some yet living, who have kept chameleons a long time, and never saw them feed but on air. 2. To what end hath Nature given it such large lungs beyond its proportion? Sure not for refrigeration; lesse lungs would serve for this use, seeing their heat is weak; it must be then for nutrition. 3. There is so little blood in it, that we may easily see it doth not feed on solid meat. 4. To what end should it continually gape more than other animals but that it stands more in need of air than they, for nutrition as well as generation? 5. He that kept the chameleon which I saw, never perceived it void excrements backwards: an argument it had no solid food."

Chancel. — Gilbert White says, in speaking of Selborne Church: "I have all along talked of the east and west end, as if the chancel stood exactly true to those points of the compass; but this is by no means the case, for the fabrick bears so much to the north of the east, that the four corners of the tower, and not the four sides, stand to the four cardinal points. The, best method of accounting for this deviation seems to be, that the workmen, who probably were employed in the longest days, endeavoured to set the chancels to the rising of the sun." Hutton, speaking of St. Bartholomew's Chapel, Birmingham, observes : "The chancel hath this singular difference from others, that it veres toward the north. Whether the projector committed an error I leave to the critics. It was the general practice of the pagan church to fix their altar, upon which they sacrificed, in the east, towards the rising sun, the object of worship. The Christian Church, in the time of the Romans, immediately succeeded the Pagan, and scrupulously adopted the same method; which has been strictly adhered to." *History of Birmingham,* p. 113. It may not be generally known, that the presence of the monument of Shakespear in the chancel of Stratford Church was at all events partly due to his right to interment there as owner of the great tithes. Hazlitt, *Monograph on Shakespear,* 1903, pp. 46, 49.

Changeling. — It appears from Strype's Annals, under 1567, that then mid-wives took an oath, inter alia, not to " suffer any other bodies child to be set, brought, or laid before any woman delivered of child in the place of her natural child, so far forth as I can know and understand. Also I will not use any kind of sorcery or incantation in the time of the travail of any woman." The word changeling, in its modern acceptation, implies one almost an idiot, evincing what was once the popular creed on this subject, for as all the frail children were a little backward of their tongue and seemingly idiots, therefore, stunted and idotical children were supposed changelings.

This superstition has not escaped the learned Moresin: " Papatus credit albatas Mulieres, et id genus Larvas, pueros integros auferre, aliosque suggerere monstruosos, et debiles multis partibus; aut ad Baptisterium aliis commutare; aut ad Templi introitum." Papatus, p. 139. It was thought that fairies could only change their weakly and starveling elves for the more robust offspring of men before baptism, whence the custom in the Highlands. One of the methods of discovering whether a child belongs to the fairies or not, is printed in a book entitled " A Pleasant Treatise of Witchcraft," 1673. In the highlands of Scotland, as Pennant informs us, children are watched till the christening is over, lest they should be stolen or changed by the fairies. This belief was entertained by the ancients. Something like this obtained in England. Gregory mentions ' an ordinarie superstition of the old wives, who dare not intrust a childe in a cradle by itself alone without a candle." This he attributes to their fear of nighthags. In the " Gentle Shepherd," Bauldy describing Mause as a witch, says of her:

" At midnight hours o'er the kirk-yard
    she raves,
And howks unchristen'd weans out of
    their graves."

To this notion Shakespear alludes when he makes Henry IV., speaking of Hotspur, in comparison with his own profligate son, say as follows:

        " O that it could be prov'd
That some night-tripping fairy had ex-
    chang'd,
In cradle-cloaths our children where they
    lay,
And call'd mine Percy, his Plantaganet!
Then would I have his Harry, and he
    mine."

Spenser has the like thought in the first book of the " Faery Queene ":
" From thence a fairy thee unweeting
    reft
There as thou slep'st in tender swad-
    ling band,

And her base Elfin brood there for thee
    left,
Such men do changelings call, so
    chang'd by fairy theft."
Willis relates a singular anecdote : —
' Vpon an extraordinary accident which befel me in my swadling cloaths. When we come to years, we are commonly told of what befel us in our infancie, if the same were more than ordinary. Such an accident (by relation of others) befel me within a few daies after my birth, whilst my mother lay in of me being her second child, when I was taken out of the bed by her side, and by my suddain and fierce crying recovered again, being found sticking between the beds head and the wall : and if I had not cryed in that manner as I did, our gossips had a conceit that I had been quite carried away by the fairies they know not whither, and some elfe or changeling (as they call it) laid in my room." He himself, however, discrediting the gossips' account, attributes this attempt to the devil. " Certainly, that attempt of stealing me away as soone as I was borne (whatever the midwives talk of it) came from the malice of that archenemy of mankind, who is continually going about seeking whom he may betray and devoure." He concludes, " blessed be the Lord our most gracious God, that disappointed them then, and hath ever since preserved and kept mee from his manifold plots and stratagems of destruction: so as now in the seventieth yeare of mine age, I yet live to praise and magnifie his wonderfull mercies towards me in this behalfe." Mount Tabor, 1639, p. 92. Gay, in his fable of the " Mother, Nurse, and Fairy," laughs thus at the superstitious idea of changelings. A fairy's tongue is the vehicle of his elegant ridicule:

" Whence sprung the vain conceited lye
That we the world with fools supplye?
What ! give our sprightly race away
For the dull helpless sons of clay !
Besides, by partial fondness shown,
Like you, we doat upon our own.
Where ever yet was found a mother
Who'd give her booby for another?
And should we change with human
    breed,
Well might we pass for fools indeed."

Pennant, speaking of " the Fairy Oak," of which also he exhibits a portrait, relates (1796) this curious circumstance respecting it : " In this very century, a poor cottager, who lived near the spot, had a child who grew uncommonly peevish; the parents attributed this to the fairies, and imagined that it was a changeling. They took the child, put it in a cradle, and left it all night beneath the tree, in hopes that the *tylwydd têg* or fairy family, or the fairy folk, would restore their own before morning. When morning came, they found the child perfectly quiet, so went away with it, quite confirmed in their belief." *Tour in Scotland*, 1796, p. 257.

Characts, or **Characters.**— Characts seem to have been charms in the form of inscriptions. "That he use ne hide ne charme, ne characte." Dugdale's *Orig. Jurid.*, p. 81. So Gower:

"With his carrecte would him en-
    chaunte."
"Through his carectes and figures."
"And his carecte as he was tawght
    He rad."

Confessio Amantis, Books i. and vi. In "Dives and Pauper," 1493, sign. C 2, we find censured: "Charmes in gadering of herbes, or hangynge of scrowes aboute man or woman or childe or beest for any seknesse with any scripture or figures and carectes, but if it be Pater Noster, Ave, or the Crede, or holy wordes of the Gospel, or of holy Wryt, for devocion nat for curiousite, and only with the tokene of the holy Crosse." In the "Burnynge of Paules Church," 1561, the author (Bishop Pilkington) writes: — "What wicked blindness is this than, to thinke that wearing prayers written in rolles about with theym, as S. Johns Gospell, the length of our Lord, the measure of our Ladye, or other like, thei shall die ne sodain death, nor be hanged, or yf he be hanged, he shall not die. There is to manye suche, though ye laugh, and beleve it not, and not hard to shewe them with a wet finger." Our author continues to ob-serve that our devotion ought to "stande in depe sighes and groninges, wyth a full consideration of our miserable state and Goddes majestye, in the heart, and not in ynke or paper: not in hangyng written scrolles about the necke, but lamentinge unfeignedlye our synnes from the hart."

In the Earl of Northampton's "De-fensative" we read: — "One of the Reysters which served under the Fernche Admirall, at the Siege of Poictiers, was found after he was dead, to have about his necke a purse of taffata, and within the same a piece of parchment full of characters in Hebrew; beside many cycles, semicircles, tryangles, &c. with sundrie short cuttes and shred-dings of the Psalmes. Deus misereatur nostri,' &c. 'Angelis suis mandavit de te,' &c. 'Super Aspidem et Basilis-cum,' &c., as if the prophecies which pro-perly belong to Christe, might be wrested to the safeguard and defence of every private man." *Defensative*, 1583, sign. O 4 *verso*, quoting *Histoire des Troubles*, livre viii. Lodge, speaking of curi-osity, says: — "If you long to know this slave, you shall never take him without a book of characters in his

bosome. Promise to bring him to Treasure trove, and he will sell his land for it, but he will be cousened. Bring him but a table of led, with crosses, (and Adonai or Elohim written in it), he thinks it will heal the ague." *Wits Miserie*, 1596, sign. C 2. Ramesey says: "Neither doth fan-cie only cause, but also as easily cure dis-eases; as I may justly refer all magical and jugling cures thereunto, performed, as is thought, by saints, images, relicts, holy-waters, shrines, avemarys, crucifixes, benedictions, charms, characters, sigils of the planets, and of the signs, inverted words, &c., and therefore all such cures are rather to be ascribed to the force of the imagination, than any virtue in them, or their rings, amulets, lamens," &c. *Elminthologia*, 1668, p. 289. Andrews tells us that "on all the old houses still existing in Edinburgh, there are remains of talismanic or cabalistical characters, which the superstition of ear-lier ages had caused to be engraven on their fronts. These were generally com-posed of some text of scripture, of the name of God, or, perhaps, of an emblem-atic representation of the Resurrection." *Continuation of Henry*. "To this kind," says Bingham, quoted by Bourne. "be-long all ligatures and remedies, which the Schools of Physitians reject and condemn; whether in inchantments or in certain marks, which they call characters, or in some other things which are to be hanged and bound about the body, and kept in a dancing posture. Such are ear-rings hanged upon the tip of each ear, and rings made of an ostriche's bones for the finger; or, when you are told, in a fit of convulsions or shortness of breath, to hold your left thumb with your right hand." *Antiq. Vulg.* 1725, xxv. "It is recorded in divers authors (notes Mason) that in the image of Diana, which was worshipped at Ephesus, there were certaine obscure words or sentences, not agreeing together, nor depending one upon another: much like unto riddles written upon the feete, girdle and crowne of the said Diana: the which, if a man did use, having written them out, and carrying them about him, hee should have good lucke in all his busi-nesses: and hereof sprung the proverbe *Ephesiæ Literæ*, where one useth any-thing which bringeth good successe." Our author also mentions the superstition of "Curing Diseases with certain wordes or characters." *Anotomie of Sorcerie*, 1612, 90. Compare Dr. Furnivall's *Political, Religious, and Love Poems*, 1866, p. 33, and *Love Charms*, infrà.

Charms.—A charm has been defined to be "a form of word or letters, repeated or written, whereby strange things are pretended to be done, beyond the ordinary power of Nature." Mason derived the term from the Latin *carmen* (a verse or incantation). Lodge, speaking of lying, says: "He will tell you that a league from Poitiers, neere to Crontelles, there is a familie, that by a speciall grace from the father to the sonne, can heale the byting of mad dogs: and that there is another companie and sorte of people called sauveurs, that have Saint Catherines Wheele in the pallate of their mouthes, that can heale the stinging of serpents." *Wits Miserie*, 1596, pp. 12, 35. Felix, in his Anglo-Saxon Life of St. Guthlac (A.D. 749, or circâ), describes the cure of a man, whose flesh had festered through a prick from a thorn in the foot, by putting on the saint's garment. The biographer tells us in perfect good faith, that "no sooner was he (the patient) attired in the garment of so great a man, but the wound could not abide it: and lo! this same thorn, as an arrow speeds from the bow, so did it fly from the man, and go to a distance; and immediately at the same time all the swelling and all the wound departed from him, and he presently conversed with the holy man with blythe mood." Was this a physical or moral cure? For the sake of juxtaposition, the recovery of the Saxon boatman, "whose eyes had been for twelve months overspread with the white speck and dimness," by dropping on the afflicted organs some salt which the saint had consecrated, may be cited as a fair specimen of the credulity of former ages—a credulity after all, however, scarcely more gross than that we see at present around us. Gaule enquires " Whether pericepts, amulets, præfiscinals, phylacteries nioeteries ligatures, suspensions, charms, and spels, had ever been used, applyed, or carried about, but for magick and astrologie? Their supposed efficacy (in curing diseases and preventing of perils) being taught from their fabrication, configuration, and confection, under such and such sydereal aspects, conjunctions, constellations." His preceding observations upon alchymy are too pointed and sensible not to be retained: " Whether alchymie (that enticing yet nice harlot) had made so many fooles and beggars, had she not clothed or painted herself with such astrological phrases and magical practises? But I let this kitchen magick or chimney astrology passe. The sweltering drudges and smoky scullions (if they may not bring in new fuel to the fire) are soon taught (by their past observed folly) to ominate their own late repentance. But if they will obstinately persist, in hope to sell their smoak, let others beware how they buy it too dear." *Mag-astromancer posed*, p. 192.

Take the following passage:— "Others that they may colourably and cunningly hide their grosse ignorance, when they know not the cause of the disease, referre it unto charmes, witchcrafts, magnifical incantations, and sorcerie, vainely and with a brazen forehead affirming that there is no way to help them, but by characters, circles, figure-castings, exercismes, conjurations, and other impious and godlesse meanes. Others set to sale, at a great price, certaine amulets of gold and silver, stamped under an appropriate and selected constellation of the planets, with some magical character, shamelessly boasting that they will cure all diseases, and worke I know not what other wonders." The author concludes with the very sensible observation of " a great learned Clarke in our land, who in a daungerous sicknesse, being moved by some friends to use an unlettered Empericke, ' Nay, quoth he, I have lived all my life by the Booke, and I will now (God willing) likewise dye by the Booke.''—*Beware of Pick-Purses*, 1605, p. 16 (a caveat against unskilful doctors). One of our early medical men, who turned author, favours us with some information under the present head, which may be worth preserving:—" If we cannot moderate these perturbations of the minde, by reason and perswasions, or by alluring their (the patients) mindes another way, we may politikely confirme them in their fantasies, that wee may the better fasten some cure upon them; as Constantinus Africanus (if it be his booke which is inserted among Galen's Works, de Incantatione, Adjuratione, &c.) affirmeth, and practised with good successe, upon one who was *impotens ad Venerem*, and thought himself bewitched therewith, by reading unto him a foolish medicine out of Cleopatra, made with a crowes gall and oyle: whereof the patient took so great conceit that, upon the use of it, he presently recovered his strength and abilitie againe. The like opinion is to bee helde of those superstitious remedies which have crept into our possession, of charmes, exorcismes, constellations, characters, pericepts, amulets, incense, holie-water, clouts crossed and folded superstitiously, repeating of a certaine number and forme of prayers or Ave Maries, offering to certaine saintes, * * * through the wedding ring, and a hundred such like toyes and gambols; which when they prevaile in the cure of diseases, it is not for any supernaturall vertue in them, either from God or the Divell, although perhaps the Divell may have a collaterall intent or worke therein, namely, to drawe us into superstition, but by reason of the confident perswasion which melancholike and passionate people may have in them;

according to the saying of Avicen, that the confidence of the patient in the meanes used is oftentimes more available to cure diseases then all other remedies whatsoever." Jorden's *Suffocation of the Mother*, 1603., p. 24. In Bell's MS. Discourse of Witchcraft I find the following: " 28, Guard against devilish charms for men or beasts. There are many sorceries practised in our day, against which I would on this occasion bear my testimony, and do therefore seriously ask you, what is it you mean by your observation of times and seasons as lucky or unlucky? What mean you by your many spells, verses, words, so often repeated, said fasting, or going backward? How mean you to have success by carrying about with you certain herbs, plants, and branches of trees? Why is it, that fearing certain events, you do use such superstitious means to prevent them, by laying bits of timber at doors, carrying a Bible meerly for a charm without any farther use of it? What intend ye by opposing witchcraft to witchcraft, in such sort that when ye suppose one to be bewitched, ye endeavour his relief by burnings, bottles, horse-shoes and such-like magical ceremonies? How think ye to have secrets revealed unto you, your doubts resolved, and your minds informed, by turning a sieve or a key? or to discover by basons and glasses how you shall be related before you die? Or do you think to escape the guilt of sorcery, who let your Bible fall open on purpose to determine what the state of your souls is, by the first word ye light upon?"

Gay, in his "Pastorals," mentions the superstitious sowing of hempseed:

"At eve last Midsummer no sleep I sought,
But to the field a bag of hempseed brought;
—I scatter'd round the seed on every side,
And three times in a trembling accent cried,
'This hemp-seed with my virgin hand I sow,
Who shall my true love be, the crop shall mow;
I straight look'd back, and, if my eyes speak truth,
With his keen scythe behind me came the youth.
'With my sharp heel I three times mark the ground,
And turn me thrice around, around, around.'"

Chaucer, in *Troilus and Cresseide*, writes:

"But canst thou playinraket to and fro,
Nettle in, docke out, now this, now that.
Pandare—"

It appears from a communication to "Notes and Queries," that friction with a dock-leaf was then (as it is still) held in Northumberland to be a specific for the sting of a nettle. The charm to be repeated, while the rubbing process is proceeding, is:

"Nettle in, dock out,
Dock in, nettle out,
Nettle in, dock out,
Dock rub nettle out."

First Series, 111, 133. The remedy is mentioned by Fraunce in the Third Part of the Countess of Pembroke's Yvychurch, 1592. The subsequent charms were found by Mr. Brand in his Physical MS. of 1475:

"*A Charme to staunch Blood.*

Jesus that was in Bethleem born, and baptyzed was in the flumen Jordane, as stente the water at hys comyng, so stente the blood of thys Man N. thy servvaunt, thorw the vertu of thy holy Name — Jesu — and of thy Cosyn swete St. Jon. And sey thys charme fyve tymes with fyve Pater Nosters, in the worschep of the fyve woundys."

"*For Fever.*

Wryt thys wordys on a lorell lef ✠ Ysmael ✠ Ysmael ✠ adjuro vos per Angelum ut soporetur iste Homo N. and ley thys lef under hys head that he wete not therof, and let hym ete Letuse oft and drynk Ip'e seed smal grounden in a morter and temper yt with ale."

'*A Charme to draw out Yren de Quarell.*

Longius Miles Ebreus percussit latus Domini nostri Jesu Christi; Sanguis exuit etiam latus; ad se traxit lancea ✠ tetragramaton ✠ Messyas ✠ Sother Emanuel ✠ Saboath ✠ Adonay ✠ Unde sicut verba ista fuerunt verba Christi, sic exeat ferrum istud sive quarellum ab isto Christiano. Amen. And sey thys charme five tymes in the worschip of the fyve woundys of Christ.'

See also the Charms in Harl. MS. fol. 215 *verso*. Whitford, in his *Work for Householders*, 1530, observes: "The charmer is a good mà or a good womá & taketh here a pece of whyte breed/ & sayth ouer that breed nothynge but onely yᵉ Pat. nr. & maketh a crosse vpon yᵉ breed / whiche thynges ben all good/ than doth he nothynge els but lay yᵉ pece of breed vnto ye tothe yt aketh or vnto ony other sore / turnynge yᵉ crosse vnto yᵉ sore or dysease / & so is yᵉ persone healed." The writer calls this practice "euyll & dápnable." Ed. 1533, sign. C. 2 *verso*. In Bale's "Interlude concerning Nature, Moses, and Christ," 1538, idolatry is described with the following qualities:—

Mennes fortunes she can tell;
She can by sayenge her Ave Marye,
And by other charmes of sorcerye,
Ease men of the toth ake by and bye
Yea, and fatche the Devyll from Hell.

And the same personage says:

With holy oyle and Water
I can so cloyne and clatter,
That I can at the latter
    Many sutelties contryve:

I can worke wyles in battell,
If I but ones do spattle
I can make corne and cattle
    That they shall never thryve.

* * * * * *

When ale is in the fat,
If the bruar please me nat
The cast shall fall down flat
    And never have any strength :

No man shall tonne nor bake
Nor meate in season make
If I agaynst him take
    But lose his labour at length.

* * * * * *

Theyr wells I can up drye,
Cause trees and herbes to dye
And slee all pulterye
    Whereas men doth me move :

I can make stoles to daunce
And earthen pottes to praunce,
That none shall them enhaunce,
    And I do but cast my glove.

I have charmes for the ploughe,
And also for tne cowghe
She shall gyve mylke ynowghe
    So long as I am pleased :

Apace the myll shall go
So shall the credle do
And the musterde querne also
    No man therwyth dyseased.

—Edit. 1562, sign. C 1-2. These specifics
appear to partake, like others mentioned
above under *Burlesque*, of a semi-serious
character. Lord Northampton inquires:
" What godly reason can any man alyve
alledge why Mother Joane of Stowe,
speaking these wordes, and neyther more
nor lesse,
    Our Lord was the first Man,
    That ever thorne prick'd upon :
    It never blysted nor it never belted,
    And I pray God, nor this not may.
should cure either beasts, or men and
women from diseases?" *Defensative*, 1583,
sign. OO4. Buttes, in his *Dyetts Dry
Dinner*, 1599, asserts that " If one eate
three small pomegranate flowers (they
say) for an whole yeare he shall be safe
from all maner of eye-sore." And
that " It hath bene and yet is a thing
which superstition hath beleeued, that
the body anoynted with the iuyce of cich-
ory is very availeable to obtaine the

fauour of great persons." King James
enumerates ' Such kinde of charmes
as commonly daft wives use for healing
forspoken goods" (by goods he means here
cattle) " for preserving them from evill
eyes, by knitting roun trees, or sundrie
kind of herbes, to the haire or tailes of the
goodes, by curing the worme, by stem-
ming of blood ; by healing of horse crookes,
by turning of the riddle ; or by doing of
such like innumerable things by words,
without applying anything meete to the
part offended, as mediciners doe : or else
by staying married folkes to have naturally adoe with other, by knitting so many
knots upon a point at the time of their
marriage." *Demonology*, p. 100. Camden tells us that " to prevent kites from
stealing their chicken, they hang up in
the house the shells in which the chickens
were hatched." Gough's edit. 1789, iii.,
659. Lambarde. speaking of Kemsing,
Kent, tells us that the farmers of that
neighbourhood used to offer corn to the
image of Edith, daughter of King Edgar,
and Prioress of Wilton in Wiltshire, to
protect their crops from mildew and other
mishaps, and that the priest would take
a handful of the quantity (keeping the
rest himself, says Lambarde), sprinkle it
with holy water, mumble a few words of
conjuration over it, and then deliver it to
the bringer to mingle with the whole harvest, to which it was supposed and pretended to communicate a sort of sanctity.
Perambulation of Kent, 1570, ed. 1826,
p. 457-8. Sir Thomas Browne mentions a
rural charm against dodder, tetter, and
strangling weeds, by placing a chalked
tile at the four corners, and one in the
middle of the fields, which though ridiculous in the intention, was rational in
the contrivance, and a good way to diffuse
the magic through all parts of the area
Quincunx Artificially Considered, p. 111.
I do not recollect to have seen the following mentioned among restoratives except in one of Webster's plays, Lao-
damia, in a mock-epistle to Protesi-
laus, says that when she faints ,

" Under my nose they burn a feather,
And old shoes too with other leather,

—*Ovidius Exulans*, 1673, v. 51. The following rural charms are found in Herrick :

" This I'le tell ye by the way,
Maidens, when ye leavens lay,
Crosse your dow, and your dispatch
Will be better for your batch."

" In the morning when ye rise,
Wash your hands and cleanse your eyes.
Next be sure ye have a care
To disperse the water farre

For as farre as that doth light
So farre keeps the evil spright."

"If ye feare to be affrighted,
When ye are (by chance) benighted :
In your pocket, for a trust
Carrie nothing but a crust :
For that holie piece of bread
Charmes the danger and the dread."

Some other metrical charms noticed by Pepys in his *Diary*, under Dec. 31, 1664-5, may here be introduced :

"Unto the Virgin Mary our Saviour was born,
And on his head he wore the crown of thorn ;
If you believe this true and mind it well,
This hurt will never fester, nor yet swell."

The following one is for a scald or burn :

"There came three angels out of the west,
One brought fire and two brought frost :
Out fire, and in frost,
In the name of Father, Son, and Holy Ghost."

"Christ was of a virgin born,
And he was pricked by a thorn ;
And it did neither bell nor swell,
As I trust in Jesus this never will."

In "Trinum Magicum," p. 169, it is said : "Herbam Urticani tenens in manu cum millefolio, securus est ab omni metu, et ab omni phantasmate."

Shaw gives the following account, from personal observation, of some physical charms used in his time in Moray. In hectic and consumptive diseases they pared the nails of the fingers and toes of the patient, put these parings into a rag cut from his clothes, then waved their hand with the rag thrice round his head, crying *Deas soil*, after which they buried the rag in some unknown place. Pliny, in his "Natural History," mentions it as practised by the magicians or Druids of his time. When a contagious disease entered among the cattle, the fire was extinguished in some villages round ; then they forced fire with a wheel or by rubbing a piece of dry wood upon another, and therewith burned juniper in the stalls of the cattle, that the smoke might purify the air about them : they likewise boiled juniper in water, which they sprinkled upon the cattle ; this done, the fires in the houses were rekindled from the forced fire. It was, no doubt, a Druid custom. Hist. of Moray, p. 248. Coles says : "It is said that if a handfull of arsmart be put under the saddle, upon a tired horse's back, it will make him travaile fresh and lustily : If a footman take mugwort and put into his shoes in the morning, he may goe forty miles before noon and not be weary. The seed of fleabane (says he) strewed between the sheets causeth chastity. If one that hath eaten comin doe

but breathe on a painted face, the colour will vanish away straight. The seeds of docks tyed to the left arme of a woman do helpe barrenesse. All kinde of docks have this property, that what flesh, or meat, is sod therewith, though it be never so old, hard, or tough, it will become tender and meet to be eaten. Calamint will recover stinking meat, if it be laid amongst it whilst it is raw. The often smelling to basil breedeth a scorpion in the brain. That the root of male-piony dryed, tied to the neck, doth help the incubus, which we call the mare. That if maids will take wild tansey, and lay it to soake in buttermilke nine days, and wash their faces therewith, it will make them look very faire" (—a belief, which is also held in respect to May dew, as elsewhere stated). *Intro. to the Knowledge of Plants*, 1656, p. 68. "Dew cakes with honey were given to those who entered Trophonius' Cave, to free them from any mischiefs from the phantoms which should appear. Loier's *Treatise of Spectres*, 1605, p. 136. Bulbianus says, that where Purslain is laid in the bed, those in it will not be disturbed by any vision that night. A diamond fastened to the left arm, so as to touch the skin, prevents all nocturnal fears To expel phantoms and rid people of folly, take the precious stone chrysolite, set it in gold, and let them weare it about em." Ostanes the magician prescribed the dipping of our feet in the morning in human urine as a preservative *against* charms. Warner, speaking of the old register of Christ Church, Hants, tells us that it contains some curious receipts of the seventeenth century in certain cases of indisposition, which his delicacy, however, forbad him to make public. *Hampshire*, 1795, 111, 131.

Mungo Park observes in his Travels in the interior of Africa that white chicken tied by the leg to a branch of a particular tree was thought by the people there to secure a prosperous issue to one's journey. 'Homer relates how Autolycus's sons staunched Ulysses's blood, flowing from a wound he received in hunting a wild boar, by a charm ; the same is observed by Pliny, who adds farther that 'sic Theophrastus ischidiacos sanari, Cato prodidit luxatis membris carmen auxiliari, Marcus Varro pod agris' : it was reported by Theophrastus, that the hip-gout was cured in the same manner ; by Cato, that a charm would relieve any member out of joint ; and by Marcus Varro, that it would cure the gout in the feet. Chiron in Pindar is said to use the same remedy in some distempers, but not in all."—Potter's *Greek Antiq.* i., 355. Grose observes that "Certain herbs, stones, and other substances, as also particular words written on parchment, as a charm, have the property of preserving men from wounds in the midst of a battle or engagement. This was so universally credited, that an oath was administered to persons going to fight a legal duel, 'that they had no charm, ne herb of virtue.' The power or rendering themselves invulnerable is still believed by the Germans: it is performed by divers charms and ceremonies: and so firm is their belief of its efficacy, that they will rather attribute any hurt they may receive, after its performance, to some omission in the performance, than defect in its virtue."

In the "Daily Telegraph" newspaper for December 11th, 1867, occurs this extraordinary piece of intelligence : "On the 9th inst., before the magistrates at Plymouth, a respectably dressed woman named Mary Catharine Murray, and who is about fifty years of age, was charged, under a warrant, with having 'unlawfully used certain subtle means and devices, to wit by a piece of parchment called a charm, and other subtle means to deceive and impose on one of her Majesty's subjects named Thomas Rendle.' The story told by Rendle, who is a poor farm labourer, living at Modbury is to the following effect : His wife, who is sixty-two years old, was taken ill about five months ago. He thought she was 'ill-wished,' and a nephew of his recommended him to go to the prisoner, as he was sure she, being wise, could cure the old woman. Rendle went to the prisoner's house in Plymouth on the 7th of August. She asked him what he was come for and he said, 'People tell me that my wife is ill-wished.' Prisoner asked him his age, and he told her 69. She opened a large book—her in two or three weeks, provided he him if he came for himself or any other person. He said he had come for his wife. She asked him his wife's age, and he said 62 next January. She said she could cure her in two or three weeks, provided he paid her one guinea to begin with. Prisoner said his wife had to go and see the planets, and would have to go into the churchyard and gather some herbs for twenty-one nights. She promised to send some medicine, and took down his address, and he then left. The following letter was sent to him about a week after : 'Sir and Madam—I find that it will be needful for you to have some powders to use, and a packet to wear. I have sent for the articles to make the powders. They will cost me 1s. each powder, and you will need to use two a day for three weeks. That will make 42 in the whole, and the packet, or the skin which makes the packet, will cost me 21s. That will last you as long as you live, if it should be 80 years longer.

The things I bought for you cost me 6s., and that will make £3 9s. You must have the things, and I should not send to you, but I am out of money, and the articles will be waiting at the station for me on Friday, so if you will remit me the money by the return of post, I will send it to you on Saturday, as you must put it on on Sunday, and also begin to use the powders on that day. Be sure you do not fail to send me an answer by return of post, and believe me to remain yours truly, M. C. MURRAY.' His wife had to take the medicine in a glass in the morning and evening. The packets of powder were to be burnt in the fire, one in the morning and the other in the evening. His wife took all the medicine, and she was at present worse. About two months afterwards the prisoner came to his house. She had a glass of water, and he saw some shadows in the water, and at her bidding his wife took up a poker and smashed the glass. The prisoner said she had seen a man and woman in the water, and the woman was the worst. She gave them a piece of parchment, on which were figures of the planets and extracts from foreign languages; this his wife was to wear. The prisoner then felt his wife's pulse. Altogether he paid the prisoner £4 10s. The prisoner acknowledged that what Rendle said was all true. He had thirty-one bottles of herbal mixture, at 3s. per bottle. She assured the magistrates that she believed in what they were pleased to call superstition. Rendle's niece said she had frequently seen the prisoner for the purpose of returning empty bottles, and also to get medicine. The prisoner had given her mother-in-law some powders to burn in her own room, which the prisoner said would do her good. The prisoner told her that her mother-in-law was ill-wished, and afterwards said she was bewitched. Her mother-in-law had had the parish doctor at Modbury attending her. The Mayor : Is the money paid to the prisoner the scrapings this old man has got together? Witness : Yes, sir ; he has 10s. a week. The prisoner ordered the 91st Psalm to be read when the last powder packet was sent. The person that burnt the powder was to read the Psalm. The prisoner generally sent two packets at a time with the bottles. The prisoner denied saying anything about the Psalms, or about the woman being bewitched. The powders sent were for her to smell. She had cured Mr. Rendle's niece of paralysis. A Magistrate : Was there any charm in that case?—Prisoner : No, sir. After a short deliberation, the Mayor said, that as the prisoner had only just been apprehended, the Bench thought it right not to deal with the case then, and therefore would remand her until Thursday next.

Bail was refused." Such examples of ignorance in the latter half of the nineteenth century seem to shew that the time has come for initiating a general system of lay-education among the people. The subject of charms is one on which several volumes might be written. The nine series of "Notes and Queries" already completed contain a vast assemblage of material and illustration; and every week adds to the store. Fortunately, the excellent indexes supplied to that useful periodical render it worse than superfluous to transplant hither more than occasional passages. In the "Saxon Leech-

and Nursery Tales," 1849, and from Hazlitt's *Proverbs*, 1882.

Chase.—A point at the game of tennis beyond that struck by the adversary. Halliwell in v.

Chasing the Cheese.—At Birdlip, near Cheltenham, there is an ancient anniversary observance so termed. Its origin is not known, but it may be suggested that it has some consanguinity with an episode or traditional incident narrated in the *Gothamite Tales*, attributed to Andrew Borde, where the fourth story deals with a man of Gotham, who went to Nottingham to sell cheese, and, descending

CHESS-PLAYING.
(From an ancient MS.)

doms, and Wart Cunning, and Starcraft," edited by Mr. Cockayne, is a mass of matter on this subject. There are some curious charms in the "Mountebank's Masue," edited for the Shakespear Society, 1848, and in "Lancashire Folk-Lore," 1867. See several curious charms against thieves in Scot's Discovery of Witchcraft, b. ii. c. 17, and particularly St. Aldelbert's curse against them. That celebrated curse in Tristram Shandy, which is an original one, still remaining in Rochester Cathedral, is nothing to this, which is perhaps the most complete of its kind. Some additions to this section might easily have been introduced from Halliwell's "Popular Rhymes

the hill to Nottingham-bridge, one of his cheeses fell out of the cart, and rolled down the hill. Whereupon, seeing that they could run alone, he let loose all the others, charging them to meet him in the market place. But when he found they were not there, all having strayed or been taken, he took horse, and rode toward York, whither he conceived that they might have gone. Hazlitt's *Old English Jest Books*, 1864, iii., 6-7.

Chatelaine.—An article of use and ornament originating with the mediæval *chatelaine* or lady of the chateau. "An old marchant had hanging at his girdle, a pouch, a spectacle-case, a punniard, a pen and inckhorne, and a hand-kertcher, with many other trinkets besides : which a merry companion seeing, said, it was like a haberdashers shop of small wares." — Copley's *Wits, Fits, and Fancies*, 1595. In Erondel's "French Garden," 1605, in a dialogue describing a lady's dress, the mistress thus addresses her waiting woman : "Give me my girdle, and see that all the furniture be at it : looke if my cizers, the pincers, the pen-knife, the knife to close letters, with the bodkin, the ear-picker, and the seale be in the case : where is my purse to weare upon my gowne," &c. In Field's "A Woman's a Weather-cocke" act v. sc. 1, Bellafront is introduced with a knife hanging at her girdle, with which she threatens to stab herself if her father forces her to marry any other than Scudmore. This seems to have been a forerunner of the modern chatelaines, which some years ago were so favourite an article of ornament among our country-women, and were made receptàcles for trinkets, keys, scissors, &c. Mr. Brand had an old print of a female foreigner entitled "Forma Pallii Mulieris Clevensis euntis ad forum," in which are delineated, as hanging from her girdle, her purse, her keys, and two sheathed knives.

Cheek.—Melton observes that "when the left cheek burnes, it is a signe somebody talks well of you ; but if the right cheek burnes, it is a sign of ill." *Astrologaster*, 1620, p. 45. In a later writer we read : "That you shou'd think to deceive me ! Why all the while I was last in your company, my heart beat all on that side you stood, and my cheek next you burnt and glow'd." Ravenscroft's *Canterbury Guests*, p. 20.

Cheesecake.—By the following passage in Ferne's "Glory of Generositie," p. 71, it should seem that cheesecakes composed a principal dainty at the feast of sheep-shearing. "Well vor your paines (if you come to our sheep-shearing veast) bum vaith yous taste of our cheese cake." This is put into the mouth of Columell the Ploughman.

Cherry Fair. — Cherry-fairs were often formerly, and may be still indeed, held in the cherry orchards ; they were scenes of considerable licence. There are not many allusions to them in old writers or records ; but in the story of "How the Wise Man Taught His Son," the transitory nature of man's life is not inelegantly likened to one of these scenes of temporary bustle and gaiety :

"And so, sone, thys worldys wele
Hyt fayrth but as a chery fayre."

And the same simile occurs in one of Hocclove's pieces. See Dyce's Skelton, ii., 85, and *Fairs, infrâ*.

Cherry Pit. — Cherry Pit is a play wherein they pitch cherry-stones into a little hole. It is noticed in Herrick's "Hesperides," 1648. But the earliest allusion to the sport is probably that found in the interlude of "The Worlde and the Chylde," 1522 :

"I can play at the chery pytte,
And I can wystell you a fytte,
Syres, in a whylowe ryne.'"

It is also mentioned by Skelton in "Speke Parot," written about the same time.

Chess.—This was a British or Welsh game, and is mentioned in the Triads. The board, on which it was played, was called the *tawlbwrd*, and one of these was held to be an essential feature in every gentleman's establishment. Chess-boards were made of wood, bone, or even ivory, the last being valued at three cows or sixty pence. Chess was also a favourite game in mediæval Italy and elsewhere abroad.

Chester.—King, speaking of the inhabitants of Chester, says, "touching their housekeeping, it is bountiful and comparable with any other shire in the realm : and that is to be seen at their weddings and burials, but chiefly at their wakes, which they yearly hold (although it be of late years well laid down)." *Vale Royal of England*, 20. In the same work there is an account that, at the City of Chester in the year 1533, "the offerings of ball and foot-balls were put down, and the silver bell offered to the Maior on Shrove Tuesday." *Vale Royal*, p. 94. King notes : "Anno 1575. This year Sir John Savage, maior, caused the Popish plays of Chester to be played the Sunday, Munday, Tuesday, and Wednesday after Mid-somerset Day, in contempt of an inhibition, and the Primat's Letters from York and from the Earl of Huntingdon." *Vale-Royal*, 1656, p. 88. "Anno 1563, upon the Sunday after Midsummer Day the History of Eneas and Queen Dido was play'd in the Roods Eye ; and were set out by one William Croston, gent. and one Mr. Man, on which triumph there was made two forts and shipping on the water, besides many horsemen well armed and appointed." Collier's *Annals of the Stage*, 1831, i., 168, *et seqq.* We farther learn that Henry Hardware, Esq., mayor of Chester in 1599, "for his time, altered many antient customs, as the shooting for the sheriff's breakfast : the going of the giants at Midsommer, &c., and would not suffer any playes, bear-baits, or bull-bait." *Vale Royal*, 1656, p. 208. Pennant tells us of the place without the walls called the Rood Eye, where the lusty youth in former days exercised themselves in manly sports of the age ; in archery, running, leaping, and wrestling; in mock fights and gallant and romantic triumphs. A standard was the prize of emulation, which was won in 1578 by Sheriff Montford on Shrove-Tuesday.

Childbirth.—In "A short Description of Antichrist," &c., 1554, is this passage: " I note all their Popishe traditions of confirmacion of yonge children wth oynting of oyle and creame, and with a ragge knitte aboute the necke of tho yonge babe," &c. This was the hallowed sheet. Bulwer remarks that " There is a tradition our midwives have concerning children borne open-handed, that such will prove of a bountiful disposition and frank-handed." The following occurs in the second part of Dekker's " Honest Whore," 1630: " I am the most wretched fellow: sure some left-handed priest christened me I am so unlucky." Coles says: " It hath been observed, that if a woman with childe eate quinces much, and coriander seed (the nature of both which is to represse and stay vapours that ascend to the braine) it will make the child ingenious: and, if the mother eate much onyons, or beanes, or such vapourous food, it endangereth the childe to become lunaticke, or of imperfect memory. Boemus relates, that in Darien in America the women eate an herb when they are great with childe, which makes them bring forth withoute paine." *Introduction to the Knowledge of Plants*, 69. Misson says: "The custom here is not to make great feasts at the birth of their children. They drink a glass of wine and eat a bit of a certain cake, which is seldom made but upon these occasions." *Travels*, translated by Ozell, p. 35, It was a belief in Angus that, if a child was put from the breast in the moon's wane, it would decay so long as the orb continued to decrease. These superstitions were generally diffused, and seem to have been entertained by the Scots in common with the Swedes, where the same ideas prevailed; nor can it be said that such notions are yet, or will for many a long day, be thoroughly rooted out. The following Scotish modern superstitions respecting new-born children are enumerated by Rosse in the *Fortunate Shepherdess*, 1778 :

" Gryte was the care, and tut'ry that was ha'en,
Baith night and day about the bony Weeane,
The Jizzen-bed wi' rantry leaves was sain'd,
And sik like things as the auld Grannies kend,
Jeans paps wi' sa't and water washen clean,
Reed that her milk get wrang, fan it was green.

Neist the first hippen to the green was flung,
And thereat seeful words baith said and sung.
A clear brunt coal wi' the het tongs was ta'en
Frae out the Ingle-mids fu' clear and clean,
And throw the corsy-belly letten fa,
For fear the weeane should be ta'en awa;
Dowing and growing, was the daily pray'r,
And Nory was brought up wi' unco care."

Under " Natal or Natalitious Gifts," Blount observes that " among the Grecians, the fifth day after the child's birth, the neighbours sent in gifts, or small tokens; from which custom, that among Christians of the godfathers sending gifts to the baptized infant, is thought to have flowed : and that also of the neighbours sending gifts to the mother of it, as is still used in North Wales." It is very observable here, that there was a feast at Athens, kept by private families, called Amphidromia, on the fifth day after the birth of the child, when it was the custom for the gossips to run round the fire with the infant in their arms, and then, having delivered it to the nurse, they were entertained with feasting and dancing. Several French (or foreign) customs of child-birth are noticed in the " Traitè des Superstitions" of M. Thiers, vol. i. p. 320-34.

Childermass, or **Holy Innocents' Day.**—(December 26th.) This day is of most unlucky omen. None ever marries on a Childermas Day. It appears from the " Paston Letters," that the Coronation of Edward IV. was put off till the Monday, because the preceding Sunday was Childermas Day. Forby, in his " Vocabulary," 1830, says that the day on which this festival falls was reckoned unlucky for the commencement of any work or task. In the " Spectator," No. 7, we learn that the same notion of the weekly recurrence of this unlucky day was entertained at that time. The word itself is genuine Saxon, *childe masse dag.*

Childirmas - dai, in Wicklif's time. Childery-masse in Rob. Glouc. — " Gent. Mag." Jan. 1799. In the statutes of the Collegiate Church of St. Mary Ottery, founded in 1337. is a direction, that none of the singing boys shall be suffered to proceed beyond the boundaries of the parish on Innocents' Day. It is certainly curious that in 1278 Archbishop Peckham issued an injunction to restrain the performance of service by little girls (*parvulæ*) on this festival at Godstow nunnery. Processions of children on this day were forbidden by the proclamation of July 22nd, 1540. A curious Latin play or mystery on the Slaughter of the Innocents, and the flight into Egypt of Joseph and Mary, with the Infant Jesus, is termed Interfectio Puerorum, and strangely exhibits the primitive mediæval literalism in dealing with these subjects, in common with those English productions, with which readers are more familiar. Bourne tells us, chap. xviii. that " according to the monks it was very unlucky to begin any work on Childermas Day : and whatsoever day that falls on, whether on the Monday, Tuesday, or any other, nothing must be begun on that day through the year." Gregory observes that " It hath been a custom, and yet is elsewhere, to whip the children upon Innocents Day morning, that the memory of Herod's murder of the Innocents might stick the closer, and in a moderate proportion to act over the crueltie again in kinde." Gregorii *Posthuma*, 1649. See Cotgarve's " Dict." and the " Dictionn. de Furetiere."

Strype, under 1582, mentions a riot in Finsbury, about Christmas holidays, " by some loose young men of the Inns of Chancery, one of whom, named Light, was especially indicted for singing in the church, upon Childermas Day, Fallantida dilli, &c.—an idle loose song then used." In " Sir John Oldcastle," 1600, act ii. sc. 2, Murley objects to the rendezvous of the Wickliffites on a Friday :— " Friday, quoth'a, a dismal day ; Childermas Day this year was Friday." Melton, in his " Astrologaster," 1620, p. 45, informs us it was formerly an article in the creed of popular superstition, that it was not lucky to put on a new suit, pare one's nails, or begin any thing on a Childermas Day.

Dufresne, in a note to Clement Marot's cxxxvth Epigram, observes, that on Innocents' Day there used to be a custom of slapping on the hinder parts any young folks who were surprised in bed on that morning, and occasionally it proceeded further. But this practice had even then fallen into disuse. The following is the passage in Dufresne :—" Innocentes. Allusion a un usage pratiqué lors en France, où les jeunes personnes qu'on pouvoit surprendre au lit le jour des Innocens, recevoient sur le derrière quelques claques, & quelque fois un peu plus, quand les sujet en valoient la peine. Cela ne se pratique plus aujourd'hui : nous sommes bien plus sages & plus reservés que nos pères." Douce cites a passage from *Le Voyageur à Paris*, to show that an odd species of burlesque was performed on this festival by some of the religious orders. Naogeorgus, in his Fourth Book, devotes some space to this festival. See *Boy-Bishop*.

Children.—In John Bale's " Comedye concernynge thre Lawes of Nature, Moses, and Christ," 1538, Idolatry says :

" Yea, but now ych am a she
And a good mydwyfe perdé,
Yonge chyldren can I charme,
With whysperynges and whysshynges,
With crossynges and with kyssynges,
With blasynges and with blessynges,
That spretes do them no harme."

In Scotland (Edinburgh) a piece of silver, an egg, and some bread presented to a child on entering a house for the first time, are supposed to bring luck. Hutchinson tells us that children in Northumberland, when first sent abroad in the arms of the nurse to visit a neighbour, are presented with an egg, salt, and fine bread. *Northumberland*, ii., 4 and 13. He observes that " the egg was a sacred emblem, and seems a gift well adapted to infancy." Comp. *Cakes* and *Salt.* Herrick names a crust of holy bread laid under the head of a sleeping child as a charm against hags, and a knife placed near the child's heart with the point upward as a charm against peril in general. Among superstitions relating to children, the following is cited by Bourne from Bingham, on St. Austin : — " If when two friends are talking together, a stone, or a dog, or a child, happens to come between them, they tread the stone to pieces, as the divider of their friendship, and this is tolerable in comparison of beating an innocent child that comes between them. But it is more pleasant that sometimes the child's quarrel is revenged by the dogs : for many times they are so superstitious as to dare to beat the dog that comes between them, who turning again upon him that smites him, sends him from seeking a vain remedy, to seek a real physician indeed." *Antiq. Vulg.* ch. xii. Lupton says : " a piece of a child's navell string, born in a ring, is good against the falling sickness, the pains in the head, and the collick." *Notable Things*, ed. 1660, p. 92.

There is a singular custom prevailing in the country of the Lesgins, one of the seventeen Tartarian nations. " Whenever the Usmei, or chief, has a son, he is carried round from village to village, and alternately suckled by every woman who has a child at her breast, till he is weaned. This custom by establishing a kind of brotherhood between the prince and his subjects, singularly endears them to each other." *European Magazine*, June, 1801, p. 408. See, for a singular notion about children's bread and butter, Petri Molinæi " Vates," p. 154. Compare *Bede's Well, Caul, Child-Birth*, and *Lying-In.*

Children's Games.—The essayist in the "Gentleman's Magazine" for February, 1738, says, that before the troubles, "cross-purposes was the game played at by children of all parties. Upon the death of Charles I. the ridicule of the times turned against monarchy; which during the Commonwealth was burlesqued by every child in Great Britain, who set himself up in mock majesty, and played at Questions and Commands; as for instance, King I am, says one boy; another answers, I am your man; then his Majesty demands, what service he will do him; to which the obsequious courtier replies, the best and worst, and all I can. During all Oliver's time, the chief diversion was, the Parson hath Lost his Fudling Cap: which needs no explanation. At the Restoration succeeded Love-Games, as I love my love with an A: a flower and a lady; and I am a lusty wooer—changed in the latter end of this reign, as well as all King James IId.'s, to 'I am come to torment you.' At the Revolution, when all people recovered their liberty, the children played promiscuously at what game they liked best—the most favourite one, however, was Puss in the Corner. Every body knows that in this play, four boys or girls post themselves at the four corners of a room, and a fifth in the middle, who keeps himself upon the watch to slip into one of the corner places, whilst the present possessors are endeavouring to supplant one another. This was intended to ridicule the scrambling for places — too much in fashion amongst the children of England, both spiritual and temporal."

Chin, The.—He was, says Forby, in his "Vocabulary of East Anglia, 1830," "a sort of imp which inhabits the chimneys of nurseries, and is sometimes called down to take away naughty children."

Chincough. — There is a belief in Cheshire that, if a toad is held for a moment within the mouth of the patient, it is apt to catch the disease, and so cure the person suffering from it. A correspondent of "Notes and Queries" speaks of a case, in which such a phenomenon actually occurred; but the experiment is one which would not be very willingly tried. Roasted mice were formerly held in Norfolk a sure remedy for this complaint; nor is it certain that the belief is extinct even now. A poor woman's son once found himself greatly relieved after eating three roast mice! A superstition still remains in Devonshire and Cornwall, that any person who rides on a pye-balled horse can cure the chin-cough.

Chiromancy.—Agrippa, speaking of chiromancy, says that, it "fancies seven mountains in the palm of a man's hand, according to the number of the seven planets; and by the lines which are there to be seen, judges of the complection, condition and fortune of the person; imagining the harmonious disposition of the lines to be, as it were, certain cælestial characters stamped upon us by God and Nature, and which, as Job saith, God imprinted or put in the hands of men, that so every one might know his works; though it be plain, that the divine author doth not there treat of vain chiromancy, but of the liberty of the will." He gives a great catalogue of names of such authors as have written on this science falsely so called, but observes that "none of them have been able to make any farther progress than conjecture and observation of experience. Now that there is no certainty in these conjectures and observations, is manifest from thence, upon the will; and about which the masters thereof of equal learning and authority do very much differ." *Vanity of Sciences*, p. 101. Ferrand tells us that "this art of chiromancy hath been so strangely infected with superstitions, deceit, cheating, and (if I durst say so) with magic also, that the canonists, and of late years Pope Sixtus Quintus, have been constrained utterly to condemn it. So that now no man professes publickly this cheating art, but theeves, rogues, and beggarly rascals; which are now every where knowne by the name of Bohemians, Egyptians, and Caramaras." *Erotomania*, 1640, p. 173. The lines in the palm of the hand, according to Indagine, are distinguished by formal names, such as the table line or line of fortune, the line of life or of the heart, the middle natural line, the line of the liver or stomach, &c., &c., &c., the triangle, the quadrangle. The thumb too, and fingers have their "Hills" given them, from the tops of which these manual diviners pretend that they had a prospect of futurity. The reader will smile at the name and not very delicate etymon of it, given in this work to the little finger. It is called the ear finger, because it is commonly used to make clean the ears. *Palmistry and Physiognomy*, trans. by F. Withers, 1656. Newton inquires whether the "governors of the commonwealth" "have suffered palmesters, fortune-tellers, stage-players, sawce-boxes, enterluders, puppit-players, loyterers, vagabonds, landleapers, and such like cozening makeshifts to practice their cogging tricks and rogish trades, within the circuite of their authoritie, and to deceive the simple people with their vile forgerie and palterie." *Tryall of a Man's Own Selfe*, 1602, p. 45. Mason ridicules the vanity and frivolity of palmistry, "where Men's fortunes are tolde by looking on the palmes of the hands." *Anatomie of Sorcerie*, 1612, p. 90. Gaule exposes the folly of palmistry which tells us, "that the lines spreading at the bottom joynt of the thumb, signe contentions; the line above the middle of the thumbe, if it meet round about, portends a hanging destiny; many lines transverse upon the last joynt of the fore-finger, note riches by heirdome; and right lines there, are a note of a jovial nature; lines in the points of the middle finger (like a gridiron) note a melancholy wit, and unhappy: if the signe on the little finger be conspicuous, they note a good witt and eloquent, but the contrary, if obscure. Equal lines upon the first joynt of the ring-finger, are marks of an happy wit." *Mag-Astromancer posed*, p. 188. " To strike another's palm," says Bulwer, in his Chirologia, 1644, pp 93, 105, " is the habit of expression of those who plight their troth, buy, sell, covenant, &c. He that would see the vigour of this gesture in puris naturalibus must repair to the horse-cirque or sheep-pens in Smithfield, where those crafty Olympique merchants will take you for no Chapman, unless you strike them with good lucke and smite them earnest in the palme."

Chrisome.—In Strype, it is said to be enjoined that, " to avoid contention, let the curate have the value of the chrisome, not under the value of 4d. and above as they can agree, and as the state of the parents may require." It is well known that " Chrisome (says Blount) signifies properly the white cloth, which is set by the minister of baptism upon the head of a child newly anointed with chrism (a kind of hallowed ointment used by Roman Catholics in the Sacrament of Baptism and for certain other unctions, composed of oyl and balm) after his baptism. Now it is vulgarly taken for the white cloth put about or upon a child newly christened, in token of his baptism; wherewith the women used to shroud the child, if dying within the month; otherwise it is usually brought to church at the day of purification." *Glossographia* in v. In Shipman's " Gossips," 1666, we read:

" Since friends are scarce, and neighbours many,
Who will lend mouths, but not a penny,
I (if you grant not a supply)
Must e'en provide a chrisome pye."

In Henry V., ii., 3, Shakespear makes Falstaff go away, " an' it had been any Chrisom child."

Christ-Church, Oxford.—Every evening, at five minutes past nine, the great bell Tom rings 101 times in commemoration of the number of scholars, for which the foundation was at first erected.

Christ-Cross-row.—The alphabet, from the practice of writing it in the form of a cross on the horn-book or battledore.

Christening.—The following order

for the christening of a prince or princess of England was established (or confirmed) in the reign of Henry VII.: " — ffor the cristynynge off the prince or a princese, the chirche or the chapelle dore where the cristynynge shalbe, the dore must be hangid roof and sides all w^t clothe of golde and carpets well vndyre the feet; then the font must be set on hight, y^t the pepill may see the cristenynge, and presse not to ny; and the font must be hangid withe a riche sele, and overlaid about w^t carpets on the greces (steps) and oy^r places; and the font must be hangid all about w^t clothe of gold, and laid w^{t}in withe small lyn clothe; and the chirche must be hangid all about the sides w^t arras; and the highe aucter muste be araid in the recheste wise, well carpetted afor the aucter; then in the side of the chirche be sides the font must be hangid a travers, and a feyre of coles well brynt or they come there, withe fumidory cast y^{r}in for the eyre, and a faire chauffure w^t water basyn of silver; Also yt muste be ordined that the gossepes be neghe loggid againste the Quenes delyverans; and when God sendithe tym that the prince be borne, then the gossapes to be redy to go w^t the childe to the chirche, and a duches to bere the cusyne afore it on her shulder on a kerchef of small reynes: and if it be a prince, an erle to bere his trayne; and it be a princes, a countesse to bere the trayne; and then y^r must be born afore it to the chirche ij cc torches, xxiiij of them about the child, and the oy^r dele borne w^t yomen afore it; and when yey com to the chirche, the torches to stand alle about the fonte, as ny the walles as they may: Then must the sargiant of the pantry be redy at the chirche dore w^t a towelle about his neke, w^t a faire salt sellere of gold in his hand, w^t salt y^{r}in; then the sergiant of the ewery to be there w^t basyn and ewere for the go-s sepes to wesche w^t; and the sergiant of the spicery and 2 butlers to be y^r redy w^t spice and wine, that when the prince is cristenyde, the gossepes and oy^r estats may take spice and wyne, and a bischope to crystyn the child: and when ye childe is baptizede, all the torches to be lightide, and then to be born vp the highe auctere; and there to be confermyde; and then spice and wyne to be takyne, and the void to be hade; and there the yefts to be gevyne and the yefts takene, to erles, barrons, and baronetts [bannerets]; and they have to bere them afore the child to the Quenes chambre dore. . . . And if it be a Princese, then the wefts to be borne of ladys, and they to bere yem to the Quene." *Antiq. Repert*, 1807, i., 305. A curious representation of the procession at the christening of Prince Arthur, eldest son of Henry VII., here referred to, is given from a drawing in outline there. Grindal, writing from London to Henry Bullinger, Feb. 8, 1567, says: "Her (Mary's) eldest son was baptized in December last, after the popish manner by some mitred pseudo-bishop; but two only could be found out of the whole nobility of that kingdom, who thought proper to be present at the christening. The rest only accompanied the infant, both in going and returning, as far as the door of the chapel." *Zürich Letters*, Parker Soc. 1st Series, 182. It appears to have been anciently the custom at christening entertainments, for the guests not only to eat as much as they pleased, but also for the ladies, at least, to carry away as much as they liked in their pockets. In Strype's Stow accounts are given of two great christenings, in 1561 and 1562. After the first was "a splendid banquet at home"; and the other, we read, "was concluded with a great banquet, consisting of wafers and hypocras, French, Gascoign, and Rhenish wines, with great plenty, and all their servants had a banquet in the hall with divers dishes." Wafers and hippocras wine were the customary refreshment served up after the return from a christening, as appears from the case of Alderman White's child in 1559, when the Marquis of Winchester, Lord Treasurer, stood as one of the sponsors. The same entertainment was also very usual (with other dainties) at weddings about the same period. Compare *Wafers*. In Brathwaite's "Whimzies," 1631, speaking of a yealous (jealous) neighbour, the author says: "Store of bisket, wafers, and careawayes, hee bestowes at his childs christning, yet are his cares nothing lessned; he is perswaded that he may eate his part of this babe, and never breake his fast." At the christening entertainments of many of the poorer sort of people in the North of England (who are so unfortunate as to provide more mouths than they can with convenience find meat for) great collections are oftentimes made by the guests, such as will far more than defray the expenses of the feast of which they have been partaking. Moresin informs us of a remarkable custom, which he himself was an eye-witness of in Scotland. They take, says he, on their return from church, the newly-baptized infant, and vibrate it three or four times gently over a flame, saying, and repeating it thrice, "Let the flame consume thee now or never." *Papatus*, i., p. 72. Borlase writes: "The same lustration, by carrying of fire, is performed round about women after child-bearing, and round about children before they are christened, as an effectual means to preserve both the mother and the infant from the power of evil spirits." In the "Autobiography of Sir John Bramston," Sir John relates how after the death of King Edward VI., in

1553, Rose, a daughter of Sir William Lock, in the time of her first husband, Anthony Hickman, fled ultimately to Antwerp. from the persecution of Mary's government, they being Protestants. Mr. and Mrs. Hickman took two children abroad with them, and while they remained at Antwerp, she had a third, which she caused to be baptized in the house according to the rites of the Reformed Church. "The fashion was," writes the author of these memoirs," "to hange a peece of lawne out at the window where a child was to be baptised; and her house havinge two dores into two streetes, she hunge lawne out at each doore, soe the neighbours of each side, thinckinge the child was caried out at the other dore, inquired no farther." It is customary in the North also for the midwife, &c. to provide two slices, one of bread and the other of cheese, which are presented to the first person they meet in the procession to church at a christening. The person who receives this homely present must give the child in return three different things wishing it at the same time health and beauty. The gentleman who informed Brand of this, happening once to fall in the way of such a party, and to receive the above present, was at a loss how to make the triple return, till he bethought himself of laying upon the child which was held out to him, a shilling, a halfpenny, and a pinch of snuff. When they meet more than one person together, it is usual to single out the nearest to the woman that carries the child. The same sort of practice was in vogue in Durham and Northumberland in 1886; fruit-cake and cheese were the articles there and then presented. The cake was in fact a currant loaf. *Antiquary*, February, 1886, p. 84. In the "Statistical Account of Scotland," we read that the inhabitants "would consider it as an unhappy omen, were they by any means disappointed in getting themselves married, or their children baptized, on the very day which they had previously fixed in their mind for that purpose. Again, parish of Kilsinan, Argyleshire, we read: "There is one pernicious practice that prevails much in this parish, which took its rise from this source, which is, that of carrying their children out to baptism on the first or second day after birth. Many of them, although they had it in their option to have their children baptized in their own houses, by waiting one day, prefer carrying them seven or eight miles to church in the worst weather in December or January, by which folly they too often sacrifice the lives of their infants to the phantom of superstition." Again, the minister of the parishes of South Ronaldsay and Burray, Orkney, says: "Within these last seven years, (i.e.

circâ 1790), the minister has been twice interrupted in administering baptism to a female child before the male child, who was baptized immediately after. When the service was over, he was gravely told he had done very wrong, for as the female child was first baptized, she would, on her coming to the years of discretion, most certainly have a strong beard, and the boy would have none." Lastly, the minister of Logierait, Perthshire, says : " When a child was baptized privately, it was, not long since, customary to put the child upon a clean basket, having a cloth previously spread over it, with bread and cheese put into the cloth; and thus to move the basket three times successively round the iron crook, which hangs over the fire, from the roof of the house, for the purpose of supporting the pots when water is boiled, or victuals are prepared. This might be anciently intended to counteract the malignant arts which witches and evil spirits were imagined to practice against new-born infants." Grose tells us there is a superstition that a child who does not cry when sprinkled in baptism will not live. He has added another idea equally well founded, that children prematurely wise are not long-lived, that is, rarely reach maturity ; a notion which we find quoted by Shakespear, and put into the mouth of Richard III. That an unbaptized infant cannot die, is a belief still entertained in Lancashire ; but the authors of " Lancashire Folk-Lore, " 1867, do not appear to have been aware, that the superstiton is a very ancient and wide-spread one, and that this description of spirit was known as the Latewitch. There was formerly a custom of having sermons at christenings. I (says Mr. Brand) had the honour of presenting to the Earl of Leicester one preached at the baptism of Theophilus Earl of Huntingdon.

Christmas Box.—Hutchinson observes on these gifts to servants and mechanics, for their good services in the labouring part of the year, " The Paganalia of the Romans, instituted by Servius Tullius, were celebrated in the beginning of the year : an altar was erected in each village, where all persons gave money. This was a mode originally devised for gaining the number of inhabitants." *Hist. of Northumb.*, ii., 20. " Denique in nostris Ecclesiis nocte natali Parentes varia munuscula, Crepundia, Cistellas, Vestes Vehicula, Poma, Nuces, &c. liberis suis donant, quibus plerumque Virga additur, ut metu castigationis eo facilius regantur. Dantur hæc munuscula nomine S. Christi, quem per tegulas vel fenestras illabi, vel cum Angelis domos obire fingunt. Mos iste similiter a Saturnalibus Gentilium descendere videtur, in quibus Ethnicos sportulas sive varia Munera ultro citroque mi-

sisse, antiquissimus patrum Tertullianus meminit in lib. de Persecut. Hildebrandus, *De Diebus Festis*, 1735. See Du Cange's " Glossary," v. Natali. Drechler, in his Treatise " De Larvis," p. 30, quotes the 79th Canon of the General Council held at Constantiople in 690-1, for the apparent origin of this custom : " Quando aliqui post Diem Natalem Christi Dei nostri reperiuntur coquentes similam et se hanc mutuó donantes, prætextu scil. honoris secundinarum impollutæ Virginis Matris, statuimus ut deinceps nihil tale fiat a fidelibus." These cakes, Drechler imagines, were originally given as presents in remembrance of the Virgin, and other aritcles were, in course of time, added or substituted, the original object being kept in view. We are told that the Christmas Box money is derived hence. The Romish priests had masses said for almost every thing : if a ship went out to the Indies, the priests had a box in her, under the protection of some saint : and for masses, as their cant was, to be said for them to that saint, &c. the poor people must put something into the priest's box, which was not opened till the ship's return. The mass at that time was called Christmas : the box called Christmas Box, or money gathered against that time, that masses might be made by the priests to the saints to forgive the people the debaucheries of that time : and from this, servants had the liberty to get box money, that they too might be enabled to pay the priest for his masses, knowing well the truth of the proverb : " No Penny, No Pater Noster."— *Athenian Oracle*, by Dunton, i., 360. In the illustration of the cut to Blaxton's " English Usurer," 1634, the author, speaking of the usurer and swine, says : deficient in giving; like the Christmas earthen boxes of apprentices, apt to take in money, but he restores none till hee be broken like a potters vessell into many shares." And in Mason's " Handful of Essaies," 1621, signat. c 2, we find a similar thought—" like a swine he never doth good till his death : as an apprentices box of earth, apt he is to take all, but to restore none till hee be broken." The box was evidently at one time of earthenware. Aubrey, in his " Natural History of Wiltshire," circa 1670, speaking of a pot in which some Roman Denarii were found, says : " it resembles in appearance an apprentices earthen Christmas box." " One asked a fellow, what Westminster Hall was like. Marry, quoth the other, it is like a butler's box at Christmas amongst gamesters : for whosoeuer loseth, the box will bee sure to be a winner."—Taylor's *Wit and Mirth*, 1629.

————th'are some fair gamesters use
To pay the box well, especially at In and
　In,

Innes of Court butlers would have but a Bad Christmas of it else."

—Cotgrave's *Treasury of Wit and Language*, 1655. Gay, in his "Trivia," mentions this:

"Some boys are rich by birth beyond all wants,
Belov'd by uncles, and kind, good, old aunts;
When time comes round, a Christmas box they bear,
And one day makes them rich for all the year."

In a catalogue of Presbyterian books, I find one, with the following title, "Christmas cordials fit for refreshing the souls and cheering the hearts; and more fit for Christmas-boxes than gold or silver."

"The Christmas box," (says the Connoisseur), "was formerly the bounty of well-disposed people, who were willing to contribute something towards rewarding the industrious, and supplying them with necessaries. But the gift is now almost demanded as a right, and our journeymen, apprentices, &c., are grown so polite, that instead of reserving their Christmas box for its original use, their ready cash serves them only for pocket-money; and instead of visiting their friends and relations, they commence the fine gentlemen of the week." The bestowing of Christmas boxes indeed, is one of those absurd customs of antiquity which, till within these few years had spread itself almost into a national grievance. The butcher and the baker sent their journeymen and apprentices to levy contributions on their customers, who were paid back again in fees to the servants of the different families. The tradesman had, in consequence, a pretence to lengthen out his bill, and the master and mistress to lower the wages on account of the vails. Presents were made by bakers to their customers at this time in old days: a baby of paste, or a cake with the figure of a lamb on it; but. although in the formation of cakes all sorts of fantastic shapes are still resorted to, and lambs in sugar and flour are still occasionally to be seen, the good ancient custom of giving such things away has died out. At Wrexham, in Denbighshire, the tradespeople unanimously resolved in 1867 to give no Christmas boxes and to present, instead, £35 to the local charities. Comp. Nares and Halliwell in v. Monsieur de Valois says that the Kings of France gave presents to their soldiers at this season.

Christmas Candle, the, at St. John's College, Oxford.—This candle, and the socket, which was still preserved in the Buttery, in 1813, used formerly to be burned at Christmas in an ancient stone socket, upon which was engraved a figure of the Holy Lamb. It was in use during the twelev days of Christmas, and stood on the public supper board. It was not, however, peculiar to St. John's. In the "Country Farmers' Catechism," 1703, occurs this passage: "She ne'er has no fits, nor uses no cold tea, as the 'Ladies Catechism' says, but keeps her body in health with working all the week, and goes to church on Sundays: my daughter don't look with sickly pale looks, like an unfit Christmas candle; they don't eat oatmeal, lime, or ashes, for pain at their stomachs; they don't ride on the fellows backs before they are twelve years old, nor lie on their own before they are fifteen, but look as fresh as new blown roses, with their daily exercise, and stay still they are fit for husbands before they have them."

Christmas Day.—This is observed without any real authority or probability of correctness on the 25th of December. Christmas Day, in the primitive Church, was always observed as the Sabbath Day, and, like that, preceded by an eve or vigil. Hence our present Christmas Eve. Bourne cites an oration of Gregory Nazianzen, which throws light upon the ancient rites of Christmas Day. "Let us not, says he, "celebrate the feast after an earthly, but an heavenly manner; let not our doors be crowned; let not dancing be encouraged; let not the cross-paths be adorned, the eyes fed, nor the ears delighted; let us not feast to excess, nor be drunk with wine." Certain coarse and obscene usages on Christmas Eve seem to be indicated by Barrington, where, speaking of the people, he says: "They were also, by the customs prevailing in particular districts, subject to services not only of the most servile, but the most ludicrous nature: 'Utpote die Nativitatis Domini coram eo saltare, buccas cum sonitu inflare et ventris crepitum edere." *Observ. on the Statutes*, p. 306. Upon Wednesday, December 22, 1647, the cryer of Canterbury, by the appointment of Master Mayor, openly proclaimed that Christmas Day, and all other superstitious festivals, should be put down, and that a market should be kept upon Christmas Day. See "Canterbury Christmas; or, a true Relation of the Insurrection in Canterbury on Christmas Day last," 1648. An order of Parliament, December 24, 1652, directed "that no observation shall be had of the five and twentieth day of December, commonly called Christmas Day; nor any solemnity used or exercised in churches upon that day in respect thereof." A credible person born and brought up in a village not far from Bury St. Edmunds, informed Mr. Brand that, when he was a boy, there was a rural custom there among the youths, of "hunting owls and squirrels on Christmas Day." Forby alludes to this now obsolete practice in his "Vocabulary of East Anglia," 1830. A correspondent of "Notes and Queries" for March 22 and June 21, 1862, points out that in some parts of the country (he was brought up in the West Riding of Yorkshire) a very curious superstition is connected with Christmas and New Year's mornings. It is that the first person who should enter the house on those two occasions ought, for luck, to have dark hair; and an old woman in his neighbourhood accounted for the belief by saying that Judas, the betrayer of the Saviour, had red hair, a circumstance which engendered a deep prejudice against that or any other light colour ever after. But it may be said here, as so often in relation to questions of the kind—*causa latet res ipsa notissima.* The writer observes: "All the ill-luck, that is, the untoward circumstances of the year, would be ascribed to the accident of a person of light hair having been the first to enter a dwelling on the mornings referred to. I have known instances, where such persons, innocently presenting themselves, have met with anything but a Christmas welcome. It was anciently believed that a child born on a Christmasday, when that day fell on a Sunday, would be very fortunate. A MS. in the Bodleian has this passage:

"And what chyld on that day boorn be,
Of gret worscheyp schall he be."

Mr. Thomas Wright, in his "Essays," 1846, says: "It is still an article of popular faith in Scotland, that persons born at Christmas and on Good Friday, have more power of communicating with spirits and hobgoblins than other people," and quotes Scot's "Marmion" for an illustration so far at least as Christmas is concerned.

Christmas Eve.—It is customary on this night with young people in the North of England to dive for apples, or catch at them, when stuck upon one end of a kind of hanging beam, at the other extremity of which is fixed a lighted candle, and that with their mouths only, their hands being tied behind their backs. Nuts and apples chiefly compose the entertainment, and from the custom of flinging the former into the fire, or cracking them with their teeth, it has doubtless had its vulgar name of Nutcrack Night. Little troops of boys and girls still go about at Newcastle-upon-Tyne, and other places in the North of England (and in Yorkshire), some few nights before, on Christmas-eve night, and on that of the day itself. The Hagmena is still preserved among them, and they always conclude their begging song with wishing a merry Christmas and a happy New Year. Compare *Hagmena.* In Goldsmith's time, the country folks religiously observed this nutcracking festival, as he tells us in his " Vicar of Wake-

field." Stafford says, they (certain deluded men) " make me call to mind an old Christmas gambole, contrived with a thred which being fastened to some beame, hath at the nether end of it a sticke, at the one end of which is tied a candle, and at the other end an apple; so that when a man comes to bite at the apple, the candle burnes his nose. The application is as easy as the trick common." *Niobe,* 1611, p. 107. The catching at the apple and candle may be called playing at something like the ancient English game of the quintain, which is now almost totally forgotten. Hutchinson, somewhat fancifully perhaps, identified this Christian usage with the rites anciently observed in honour of Pomona. *Hist. of North.,* vol. ii. p. 18. Polwhele describes it in his " Old English Gentleman," p. 120:

"Or catch th' elusive apple with a bound,
As with its taper it flew whizzing round."

Luther, in his " Colloquia," i. 233, tells us that " upon the eve of Christmas Day the women run about and strike a swinish hour (pulsant horam suillam): if a great hog grunts, it denotes the future husband to be an old man, if a small one, a young man." Naogeorgus describes the midnight mass on Christmas Eve, the manner in which the priests used to pilfer the offerings laid on the altar, " least other should it have," and the wooden effigy of the Son of God, which used to be placed there likewise, that the children of both sexes might dance round it, the parents looking on, and applauding. Sir Herbert Croft informs us, that the inhabitants of Hamburg were obliged by custom to give their servants carp for supper on Christmas Eve. *Letter from Germany,* 1797, p. 82.

Christmas Holidays.—"If we compare," says Prynne, " our Bacchanalian Christmasses and New Years Tides with these Saturnalia and Feasts of Janus, we shall finde such near affinitye betweene them both in regard of time (they being both in the end of December and on the first of January) and in their manner of solemnizing (both of them being spent in revelling, epicurisme, wantonesse, idlenesse, dancing, drinking, stage-plaies, masques, and carnall pompe and jollity), that we must needes conclude the one to be but the very ape or issue of the other. Hence Polydor Virgil affirmes in expresse tearmes that our Christmas Lords of Misrule (which custom, saith he, is chiefly observed in England) together with dancing, masques, mummeries, stage-playes, and such other Christmas disorders now in use with Christians, were derived from these Roman Saturnalia and Bacchanalian festivals; which (concludes he) should cause all pious Christians eternally to abominate them." Selden was of opinion that from Christmas Day to Epiphany morning no one should fast save of his own option or at the bidding of the priest. *Analecton Anglo-Britannicum*, lib. ii., p. 208.

The Christmas of 1502 appears to have been kept with some splendour, for in the "Privy Purse Expenses of Elizabeth of York," there is a payment of twenty pounds to the grooms and pages of the Queen's chamber alone "against Cristmas." According to his biographer, Sir Thos. More "was, by his father's procurement, received into the house of the right reverend, wise, and learned prelate Cardinall Mourton, where (thoughe hee was yonge of yeares, yet) would he at Christmas tyd sodenly sometymes stepp in among the players, and never studinge for the matter, make a parte of his owne there presently amonge them, which made the lookers-on more sport than all the players besid. In whose witt and towardnesse the Cardinall much delightinge, would often say of him unto the nobles that divers tymes dyned with him: 'This child here wayting at the table, who soever shall live to see it, will prove a marveilous man.'" Andrews, in his "Hist. of Great Britain," vol. i. pt. 2, 4to. 1795, p. 329, mentions "the humorous Pageant of Christmas, personified by an old man hung round with savory dainties" which, he says, in common with "dancing round the Maypole and riding the hobby-horse," suffered a severe check at the Reformation. In the East of London, about Shoreditch and Mile-End, while the district was still open country, there were periodical celebrations of sports in holiday time. In 1577 we observe a licence to print the History of the High and Mighty William, Duke of Shoreditch, a personage named William Barlow, who had obtained the favour of Henry VIII. by his skill as a bowman, and on whom his Majesty had conferred this and other jocular titles. Nothing farther is known of such a publication, and of a later one in 1583 there is only a late print at the end of Wood's *Bowman's Glory*, 1682. In 1588 Queen Elizabeth attended a grand spectacle at Mile End, called *Arthur's Show*, q.v. Braithwaite, in his " Rules for the House of an Earle" (*circâ* 1640) laments the expenditure of money which would have been better laid out in the good old substantial fare, upon confectionery. He says: "I have knowen that the finest confectionary shoppe in Bearbinder Lane and the Blacke Fryers must be sought into for all kindes of conserved, preserved, and candied fruictes, and flowers, the chardge of a banquet arrising to as great a summe of monye as woulde have kept a good house all Christe-

mas, wherin should have been great dishes filled with great peeces of beefe, veale, swanne, venison, capons, and such like English meates." The same author, in his "Whimzies," 1631, describing a good and hospitable housekeeper, has left the following picture of Christmas festivities: "Suppose Christmas now approaching, the evergreen ivie trimming and adorning the portals and partcloses of so frequented a building; the usual carolls, to observe antiquitie, cheerefully sounding: and that which is the complement of his inferior comforts, his neighbours, whom he tenders as members of his owne family, joyne with him in this consort of mirth and melody." In the second part, he calls a piper "an ill wind that begins to blow upon Christmasse Eve, and so continues, very lowd and blustring, all the twelve dayes: or an airy meteor, composed of flatuous matter, that then appeares, and vanisheth, to the great peace of the whole family, the thirteenth day." Breton, also, in his "Fantasticks," 1626, has much that is highly interesting on this subject. Under November, he says: "The cooke and the comfitmaker make ready for Christmas, and the minstrels in the Countrey beat their boyes for false fingring." Of Christmas Day itself he observes: "It is now Christmas, and not a cup of drinke must passe without a carroll, the beasts, fowle, and fish, come to a general execution, and the corne is ground to dust for the bakehouse and the pantry: Cards and dice purge many a purse, and the youths shew their agility in shooing of the wild mare." The twelve days' rejoicing and merry-making at this season of the year are mentioned in "The Praise of Christmas," a ballad about 1630:

"When Christmas-tide comes in like a bride,
　With holly and ivy clad,
Twelve days in the year, much mirth and good cheer
　In every household is had."

One of the most curious pictures in little of an old Christmas is that given (glimpselike) in Laurence Price's unique Christmas Book for 1657. He there describes the sea-faring man's Christmas dinner and the tradesman's, and admits us to the interior of an honest cobbler's house, where there was merry-making in an humble way, and music. One of the last pages is occupied with "The Cobbler's Song." In a tract of 1651, Old Christmas is introduced describing the former annual festivities of the season as follows: "After dinner we arose from the boord and sate by the fire, where the harth was embrodered all over with roasted apples, piping hot, expecting a bole of ale for a cooler, which immediately was transformed into Lamb-wool. After which we discoursed merily, without either prophaness or obscenity; some went to cards; others sang carols and pleasant songs (suitable to the times); then the poor labouring hinds and maid-servants, with the plow-boys, went nimbly to dancing; the poor toyling wretches being glad of my company, because they had little or no sport at all till I came amongst them; and therefore they skipped and leaped for joy, singing a carol to the tune of Hey,

'Let's dance and sing, and make good
    cheer,
For Christmas comes but once a year.

"Thus at active games and gambols of hot-cockles, shooing the wild mare, and the like harmless sports, some part of the tedious night was spent, and early in the morning I took my leave of them, promising they should have my presence again the next 25th of December." *Vindication of Christmas*, 4v. 1651. Stevenson, speaking of January, says, "For the recreations of this month, they are within doors, as it relates to Christmasse; it shares the chearfull carrols of the wassell cup. The Lord of Misrule is no meane man for his time; masking and mumming, and choosing king and queen." Under December are the following notices: "Now capons and hens, besides turkeys, geese, and ducks, with beef and mutton—must all die —for in twelve days a multitude of people will not be fed with a little. Now plumbes and spice, sugar and honey, square it among pies and broath. Now a journeyman cares not a rush for his master though he begs his plum-porridge all the twelve dayes. Now or never must the music be in tune, for the youth must dance and sing to get them a heat, while the aged set by the fire. The country maid leaves half her market, and must be sent againe if she forgets a pair of cards on Christmasse Even. Great is the contention of holly and ivy, whether master or dame weares the breeches. Dice and the cards benefit the butler: and, if the cook do not lack wit, he will sweetly lick his fingers."

"Christmase is come, make ready the
    good cheare:
Apollo will be frolicke once a yeare:
I speake not here of Englands twelve
    dayes madness,
But humble gratitude and hearty glad-
    nesse.
These but observed, let instruments
    speak out,
We may be merry, and we ought, no
    doubt;
Christmas, 'tis the birth-day of Christ
    our King;
Are we disputing when the angels
    sing?"
—*Twelve Moneths*, 1661, p. 4. "Poor Robin" for 1677 notes the festive doings of Christmas as follows:

"Now grocer's trade
    Is in request,
For plums and spices
    Of the best.
Good cheer doth with
    This month agree,
And dainty chaps
    Must sweetned be.
Mirth and gladness
    Doth abound,
And strong beer in
    Each house is found.
Minc'd pies, roast beef
    With other cheer
And feasting, doth
    Conclude the year."

In 1682 appeared "The Christmas Ordinary, a private show; wherein is expressed the jovial Freedom of that Festival: as it was acted at a Gentleman's House among other Revels, by W. R. Master of Arts." Another account of the Christmas gambols occurs in Speed's "Batt upon Batt," 1694, p. 5:

"Our Batt can dance, play at high
    jinks with dice,
At any primitive, orthodoxal vice.
Shooing the wild mare, tumbling the
    young wenches,
Drinking all night, and sleeping on the
    benches.
Shew me a man can shuffle fair and cut,
Yet always have three trays in hand at
    Putt:
Shew me a man can turn up Noddy still,
And deal himself three fives too when
    he will:
Conclude with one and thirty, and a
    pair,
Never fail ten in stock, and yet play
    fair,
If Batt be not that wight, I lose my
    aim."

Misson says: "From Christmas Day till after Twelfth Day is a time of Christian rejoicing; a mixture of devotion and pleasure. They give treats, and make it their whole business to drive away melancholy. Whereas little presents from one another are made only on the first day of the year in France, they begin here at Christmas; and they are not so much presents from friend to friend, or from equal to equal (which is less practis'd in England now than formerly), as from superior to inferior. In the taverns the landlord gives part of what is eaten and drank in his house that and the next two days: for instance, they reckon you for the wine, and tell you there is nothing to pay for bread, nor for your slice of Westphalia," i.e., ham. He had observed, p. 29, "The English and most other Protestant nations are utterly unacquainted with those diversions of the carnival which are so famous at Venice, and known more or less in all other Roman Catholic countries. The great festival times here are from Christmas to Twelfth Day inclusive, at Easter, and at Whitsuntide." *Travels in England*, trans. by Ozell, p. 34. The Minister of Montrose tells us: "At Christmas and the New Year, the opulent burghers begin to feast with their friends, and go a round of visits, which takes up the space of many weeks. Upon such occasions, the gravest is expected to be merry, and to join in a cheerful song." *Stat. Acc. of Scotland*, v., 48. In the "World," No. 104, the following occurs: "Our ancestors considered Christmas in the double light of a holy commemoration and a chearful festival; and accordingly distinguished it by devotion, by vacation from business, by merriment and hospitality. They seemed eagerly bent to make themselves and every body about them happy. With what punctual zeal did they wish one another a merry Christmas? and what an omission would it have been thought, to have concluded a letter without the compliments of the season? The great hall resounded with the tumultuous joys of servants and tenants, and the gambols they played served as amusement to the lord of the mansion and his family, who. by encouraging every art conducive to mirth and entertainment, endeavoured to soften the rigour of the season, and mitigate the influence of winter. What a fund of delight was the chusing King and Queen upon Twelfth Night! and how greatly ought we to regret the neglect of minced pyes, which, besides the ideas of merrymaking inseparable from them, were always considered as the test of schismatics! How zealously were they swallowed by the orthodox, to the utter confusion of all fanatical recusants! If any country gentleman should be so unfortunate in this age as to lie under a suspicion of heresy, where will he find so easy a method of acquitting himself as by the ordeal of plumb-porridge?" "In Christmas holidays," says the author of "Round about our Coal Fire," (about 1730), "the tables were all spread from the first to the last; the sirloins of beef, the minced pies, the plumb-porridge, the capons, turkeys, geese and plumb-puddings, were all brought upon the board: every one eat heartily, and was welcome, which gave rise to the proverb, 'Merry in the hall when beards wag all.'"

Sir Walter Scott, in a letter to Joanna Baillie, 1st January, 1819, says: "I wish you could have seen about a hundred children, being almost supported by their fathers' or brothers' labour, come down yesterday to dance to the pipes, and get a piece of cake and bannock, and pence apiece (no very deadly largess) in honour of Hagmanay. I declare to you, my dear friend, that when I thought the poor fellows who kept these children so neat, and well taught, and well behaved, were slaving the whole day for eighteenpence or twentypence at the most, I was ashamed of their gratitude, and of their becks and bows." In another letter (Jan. 1, 1815), Scott says: "Yesterday being Hogmanay, there was a constant succession of *Guisards* i.e., boys dressed up in fantastic caps, with their shirts over their jackets, and with wooden swords in their hands. These players acted a sort of scene before us, of which the hero was one Goloskin."

In an amusing news-letter from John Pory to a friend, dated December 13th, 1632, the writer says:— "Sir William Curtis writes from Brussells, that the French there with the Queen Mother and monsieur made account to have kept a brave Christmas here in London, and for that purpose had trussed up their trinkets half-topmast high; but it seemeth they reckoned before their host." An agreeable writer describes the busy and bright scene in the churches of Rome on this anniversary, when the people of all ranks flock thither, the peasantry in their holiday attire, and there are processions of priests everywhere. The ceremonial observances last during the whole night until the advent of Christmas Day itself. The Pope and College attend service at Santa Maria Maggiore. *Diary of an Invalid*, by H. Matthews, 1820.

Christmas Mummers.—A proclamation issued 8 Edward III., A.D. 1334, by the authorities of the City of London, concludes thus: "Also we do forbid, on the same pain of imprisonment, that any man shall go about at this feast of Christmas with companions disguised with false faces, or in any other manner, to the houses of the good folks of the City, for playing at dice there . . . ." Riley's *Memorials of London*, 1868, p. 192. At Tenby, among the Christmas mummings, was a dialogue between Father Christmas, St. George, Oliver Cromwell, and Beelzebub, where St. George is made to say:

"First, then, I fought in France;
Second, I fought in Spain;
Thirdly, I came to Tenby,
To fight the Turk again."

Where by *Turk* we are to understand the corsairs of Barbary, who at one time infested nearly every coast.

Christmas Pie.—Selden thought that the coffin of our Christmas pies, in shape long, is in imitation of the cratch, i.e., the manger wherein the infant Jesus was laid; and they were long known as *coffin pasties*. The modern survival is the covered fruit tart in an oval dish. Scogin, in the edition of his "Jests," published in 1626, is made on his death-bed to say : " Masters, I tell you all that stand about mee, if I might live to eate a Christmasse pye, I care not if I dye by and by after : for Christmasse pyes be good meat.' In Robert Fletcher's poem styled "Christmas Day," we find the ingredients and shape of the Christmas pie :

> " Christ-mass? give me my beads : the word implies
> A plot, by its ingredients, beef and pyes.
> The cloyster'd steaks with salt and pepper lye
> Like nunnes with patches in a monastrie.
> Prophaneness in a conclave? Nay, much more,
> Idolatrie in crust ! Babylon's whore
> Rak'd from the grave, and bak'd by hanches, then
> Serv'd up in coffins to unholy men ;
> Defil'd with superstition, like the Gentiles
> Of old, that worship'd onions, roots, and lentiles ! "

Ex Otio Negotium, 1656, p. 114. Misson describes the composition of a Christmas pasty as follows : " In every family they make at Christmas a famous pie, which they call a Christmas pie. The making of this is a great science ; it is a learned medley of neats' tongue, the brawn of a chicken, eggs, sugar, currants, citron and orange-peel, various sorts of spice, &c." *Travels in England*, 322. In the " Gentleman's Magazine" for December, 1733, is an essay on " Christmas Pye," in which the author tells us : "That this dish is most in vogue at this time of the year, some think is owing to the barrenness of the season, and the scarcity of fruit and milk to make tarts, custards, and other desserts ; this being a compound that furnishes a dessert itself. But I rather think it bears a religious kind of relation to the festivity from whence it takes its name. Our tables are always set out with this dish just at the time and probably for the same reason that our windows are adorned with ivy. I am the more confirmed in this opinion from the zealous opposition it meets with from Quakers, who distinguish their feasts by an heretical sort of pudding known by their name, and inveigh against Christmas pye as an invention of the scarlet whore of Babylon, an hodgepodge of superstition, popery, the devil, and all his works. Lewis, speaking of the enthusiasts in the grand rebellion, tells us, that under the censure of lewd customs they include all sorts of public sports, exercises, and recreations, how innocent soever. Nay, the poor rosemary and bays, and Christmas Pye, is made an abomination. The famous Bickerstaffe rose up against such as would cut out the clergy from having any share in it. 'The Christmas Pye,' says he 'is in its own nature a kind of consecrated cake, and a badge of distinction, and yet 'tis often forbidden to the Druid of the family. Strange ! that a sirloin of beef, whether boiled or roasted, when entire, is exposed to his utmost depredations and incisions : but if minced into small pieces, and tossed up with plums and sugar, changes its property, and forsooth is meat for his master.' Thus with a becoming zeal he defends the chaplains of noblemen in particular, and the clergy in general, who it seems were debarred, under pretence that a sweet tooth and a liqourish palate are inconsistent with the sanctity of their character."

> " Come guard this night the Christmas-pie
> That the thiefe, though ne'r so slie,
> With his flesh hooks don't come nie
>   To catch it ;
> From him, who all alone sits there,
> Having his eyes still in his eare,
> And a deale of nightly feare
>   To watch it."
>   *Herrick.*

> " Let Christmas boast her customary treat,
> A mixture strange of suet, currants, meat,
> Where various tastes combine, the greasy and the sweet."
>   *Oxford Sausage, p.* FT.

In the North of England, a goose is always the chief ingredient in the composition of a Christmas pye. Ramsay, in his "Elegy on Lucky Wood," tells us, that among other baits by which the good ale-wife drew customers to her house, she never failed to tempt them at Christmas with a goose-pye.

> " Than ay at Yule, whene'er we came,
>   A bra' goose pye,
> And was na that a good belly baum?
>   None dare deny."

Christmas Prince.—In an audit book of Trinity College, Oxford, for 1559 Warton found a disbursement " Pro prandio Principis Natalicii." A Christmas Prince, or Lord of Misrule, he adds, corresponding to the Imperator at Cambridge, was a common temporary magistrate in the Colleges at Oxford. Wood, in his *Athenæ*, speaking of the " Christmas Prince of St. John's College, whom the juniors have annually for the most part elected from the first foundation of the College, says : " The custom was not only observed in that College, but in several other houses, particularly in Merton College, where, from the first foundation, the Fellows anually elected, about St. Edmund's Day, in November, a Christmas Lord or Lord of Misrule, styled in the registers Rex Fabarum and Rex Regni

Fabarum; which custom continued till the Reformation of Religion, and then, that producing Puritanism, and Puritanism Presbytery, the profession of it looked upon such laudable and ingenious customs as popish, diabolical and antichristian." It is to be collected from the pageant known as the *Christmas Prince*, that the students of St. John's College, Oxford, met on All-Hallow Eve, 1607, and a fire was lighted in the Hall, "accordinge to the custome and status of the same place, at wᶜʰ time the whole companye, or most part of the students of the same house mette toogether to beginne their Christmas." On the next night, November 1, it seems, a second meeting was appointed, when it was proposed, for the preservation of order and peace, that a Christmas Lord or Prince of the Revels, should be chosen. We learn that no Christmas Lord had been created since 1577. In the present case, Thomas Tucker obtained a majority of suffrages, and being elected in his absence, was sought for, carried in triumph about the hall, and afterwards allowed to return to his own quarters, "to thinke of their loues and good will, and to consider of his owne charge and place." Is it worth while to inquire, if Thomas Tucker, Esq., had any conection with little Tom Tucker of the nursery rhyme?

Of this splendid and gay pageant there is the following contemporary description : — "On Christmas day in ye morning he (the Christmas lord or prince) was attended vnto prayers by yᵉ whole company of the Bacchelours, and some others of his gentlemen vshers, bare before him. At diner beinge sett downe in yᵉ Hall at yᵉ high table in yᵉ Vice Præsidents place (for yᵉ Præsident himself was then allso psent) hee was serued wth 20 dishes to a messe, all wᶜʰ were brought in by gentlemen of yᵉ howse attired in his guards coats, vshered in by yᵉ Lʳᵈ Comptroller, and other officers of yᵉ Hall. The first mess was a boar's head, wᶜʰ was carried by yᵉ tallest and lustiest of all yᵉ guard, before whom, (as attendants) wente first, one attired in a horsemans coate, wth a boars-speare in his hande, next to him an other huntsman in greene, wth a bloody falscion drawne; next to him 2 pages in tafatye sarcenet, each of yᵉᵐ wth a mess of mustard next to whome came hee yᵗ carried yᵉ boares-head, crost wth a greene silk scarfe, by wᶜʰ hunge yᵉ empty scabbard of yᵉ faulchion, wᶜʰ was carried before him." As the boar's head entered the hall, they sang a carol, and during the dinner the prince's musicians played. They had been sent for from Reading, because the town-music, it appears, had given His Highness "the slip," as they always did when any one wanted them particularly." After supper

there was an interlude, "contaynynge the order of yᵉ Saturnalls, and shewinge the first cause of Christmas-candles, and in the ende there was an application made to the Day and Natiuitie of Christ." On the 26th, it had been intended to perform the tragical show of *Philomela*, but the carpenters were behindhand, and the show had to be postponed until the 29th. It seems that the person who represented Philomela on this occasion had so sweet a voice that the audience only regretted that it should be lost, and the coeval narrator quaintly says that they "could have found in their hartes that the story should have rather been falsified then so good a voyce lost." On New Year's Day the Prince sent to the President of St. John's, by the hands of Mr. Richard Swinnerton, one of the squires of his body, a pair of gloves, with these two verses :

> "The prince and his councell in signe
> of their loves,
> Present you their Præsident with these
> paire of gloves."

For further particulars of the quasi- dramatic exhibitions, and other merry-makings during the twelve days of Christmas, see the tract itself in *Miscellanea Antiqua Anglicana*, 1816.

Warton tells us that in an original draught of the statutes of Trinity College, Cambridge, founded in 1546, one of the Chapters is entitled, "De Præfecto Ludorum qui Imperator dicitur," under whose direction and authority Latin comedies and tragedies are to be exhibited in the Hall at Christmas; as also six spectacula, or as many dialogues. With regard to the peculiar business and office of Imperator, it is ordered, that one of the masters of arts shall be placed over the juniors every Christmas, for the regulation of their games and diversions at that season of festivity. His sovereignty is to last during the twelve days of Christmas: and he is to exercise the same power on Candlemas Day. His fee is forty shillings. Fuller, in his "Good Thoughts in Worse Times," 1647, p. 139, tells us: " Some sixty yeares since, in the University of Cambridge, it was solemnly debated betwixt the heads to debarre young schollers of that liberty allowed them in Christmas, as inconsistent with the discipline of students. But some grave governors mentioned the good use thereof, because thereby, in twelve days, they more discover the dispositions of scholars than in twelve moneths before." The Lords of Misrule in colleges were preached against at Cambridge by the Puritans in the reign of James the First, as inconsistent with a place of religious education and as a relict of the Pagan ritual. An account of a splendid Christmas festival, in the Inner Temple is given by Gerard Leigh in his *Accidence of Armoury*, 1562,

The hero of the occasion was Dudley, Earl of Leicester, who assumed the designation of Palaphilos, Prince of Sophie. He was entertained by a chosen member of the Inn playing the part for the time of a sovereign prince, as at the Middle Temple, Lincoln's Inn, and Gray's Inn, and was attended by his Lord Chancellor, Privy Seal, Treasurer, Lord Chief Justice, Chief Baron of the Exchequer, besides many other dignitaries of the law, and upward of four-score guars. Dugdale, speaking of the Fooleries of the Lord of Misrule there on St. Stephen's Day, says: "Supper ended, the Constable-Marshall presented himself with drums afore him, mounted upon a scaffold born by four men, and goeth three times round about the harthe, crying out aloud, 'A Lord, a Lord,' &c. Then he descendeth, and goeth to dance, &c., and after he calleth his Court, every one by name, e.g. Sir Randle Rackabite, of Raskall-Hall, in the County of Rake-hell, &c. &c. This done, the Lord of Misrule addresseth himself to the banquet : which ended, with some minstralsye, mirth, and dancing, every man departeth to rest." A very magnificent pageant was exhibited at the Inner Temple in the Christmas which immediately succeeded the Restoration ; Charles II. and many of the nobility were present in person.

When the Societies of the Law performed these shows within their own respective refectories, at Christmas, or any other festival, a Christmas prince or revelmaster was constantly appointed. At a Christmas celebrated in the Hall of the Middle Temple in the year 1635, the jurisdiction, privileges, and parade of this mock-monarch are thus circumstantially described. He was attended by his lord-keeper, lord treasurer, with eight white staves, a captain of his band of pensioners, and of his guard ; and with two chaplains, who were so seriously impressed with an idea of his regal dignity, that when they preached before him on the preceding Sunday in the Temple Church, on ascending the pulpit they saluted him with three low bows. He dined both in the hall and in his privy chamber under a cloth of estate. The pole-axes for his gentlemen pensioners were borrowed of Lord Salisbury. Lord Holland, his temporary Justice in Eyre, supplied him with venison on demand, and the lord mayor and sheriffs of London. with wine. On twelfth-day, at going to church, he received many petitions, which he gave to his master of requests ; and, like other kings, he had a favourite, whom with others, gentlemen of high quality, he knighted at returning from church. His expences, all from his own purse, amounted to two thousand pounds. After he was deposed, the King knighted him at Whitehall. In MS. Ashmole, 826, is a copy of the Writ of Privy Seal of the Christmas Prince of the Middle Temple, signed "Ri. Pr. de l'amour," directed "To our trusty and well-beloved servant, Mr. John Garrett," during his attendance at court, 26 Dec., 1635. Garrett was the person to whom Taylor the water-poet inscribed one of his facetious publications.

These events were not always restricted to Christmas itself, for a masque, composed at very short notice by Sir William Davenant, was exhibited in the Middle Temple Hall, 24 February, 1635, in honour of the Elector Palatine under the title of *The Triumphs of the Prince D'Amour*, with music and symphonies by Henry and William Lawes. In 1660 appeared a volume of miscellaneous poems entitled *Le Prince D'Amour*, and dedicated to the authorities of the Middle Temple. Dugdale, speaking of the Christmas festivities kept in Lincoln's Inn, cites an order dated 9th Hen. VIII., "that the King of Cockneys, on Childermas Day, should sit and have due service ; and that he and all his officers should use honest manner and good order, without any waste or destruction making in wine, brawn, chely, or other vitals : as also that he, and his marshal, butler, and constable marshal, should have their lawful and honest commandments by delivery of the officers of Christmas, and that the said King of Cockneys, ne none of his officers medyl neither in the buttery, nor in the stuard of Christmas his office, upon pain of 40s. for every such medling. And lastly, that Jack Straw, and all his adherents, should be thenceforth utterly banisht and no more to be used in this house, upon pain to forfeit, for every time, five pounds, to be levied on every Fellow hapning to offend against this rule." *Orig. Juridiciales*, 247. The King of Cockneys may be concluded to be the same character as Dugdale elsewhere describes, where he states that the Inn chose a king on Christmas Day. At Gray's Inn they had their Prince of Purpool or Portypool —the Manor in which the Inn lies—and in 1594 was performed here the *Gray's Inn Masque*, by Francis Davison, in the presence of Queen Elizabeth and her Court. It was ostensibly devised by his Highness's command. This performance remained in MS. till 1688. See Hazlitt's *Manual of Old Plays*, 1892, v. *Gesta Grayorum*. The Inn had distinguished itself so early as 1566 by presenting English dramatic versions of the *Jocasta* of Euripides (through an Italian version of Seneca's paraphrase), and the *Suppositi* of Ariosto. Dugdale, in his "Origines Juridiciales," p. 286, speaking of "Orders for Government— Gray's Inne," cites an order of 4 Car. I.

(Nov. 17) that "all playing at dice, cards, or otherwise, in the hall, buttry, or butler's chamber should be thenceforth barred and forbidden at all times of the year. the twenty days in Christmas onely excepted." An entertaining account of this annual buffoonery at the Inns of Court is given in "Noctes Templariæ," 1599. I must beg leave to refer the reader to this work, as the narrative is too long for transcription, and would scarcely bear curtailment. Manning's *Mem. of Sir B. Ruddyerd*, 1841. A Christmas Prince or King, however, acquired as early as Henry the Eighth's time a contemptuous signification, for in a letter of 1537 the Curate of St. Margaret's, Lothbury, writing to a correspondent at Plymouth, says, that the people made no more of God than if he had been "a Christmas King." And indeed, at Lincoln's Inn, according to what we have heard from Dugdale, he does not appear ever to have possessed so great a prestige or so exalted a jurisdiction as elsewhere. Churchyard, in the "Lamentacion of Freyndshypp," a ballad printed about 1565, says:

"Men are so used these dayes wyth wordes,
They take them but for jestes and boordes,
That Christmas Lordes were wonte to speke."

Guilpin, in his "Skialetheia," 1598, figures a man, who has been in the service of one of these characters, assuming on that account, lofty airs, and maintaining a disdainful silence—

"Thinks scorne to speake, especially now since
H' hath beene a player to a Christmas Prince."

Langley's Translation of Polydore Vergil, fol. 102 verso, mentions "The Christemass Lordes, that be commonly made at the nativitee of our Lorde, to whom all the householde and familie, with the Master himselfe, must be obedient, began of the equabilitie that the servauntes had with their masters in Saturnus Feastes that they were called Saturnalia: wherein the servauntes have like autoritie with their masters duryng the tyme of the sayd feastes."

Christmas Song.—"Poor Robin" for 1695, has the following :

"Now thrice welcome, Christmas,
Which brings us good cheer,
Minc'd pies and plumb-porridge,
Good ale and strong beer ;
With pig, goose, and capon,
The best that may be,
So well doth the weather
And our stomachs agree.

Observe how the chimneys
Do smoak all about,
The cooks are providing
For dinner, no doubt ;
But those on whose tables
No victuals appear,
O may they keep Lent
All the rest of the year !

With holly and ivy
So green and so gay ;
We deck up our houses
As fresh as the day,
With bays and rosemary,
And lawrel compleat
And every one now
Is a king in conceit.
     *   *   *   *

But as for curmudgeons,
Who will not be free,
I wish they may die
On the three-legged tree."

Christmas Tree.—A very intelligent writer in Willis's "Current Notes" for February, 1854, observes: "The Christmas-tree has become a prevailing fashion in England at this season, and is by most persons supposed to be derived from Germany: such, however, is not the fact: the Christmas-tree is from Egypt, and its origin dates from a period long antecedent to the Christian era. The palm-tree is known to put forth a shoot every month, and a spray of this tree, with twelve shoots on it, was used in Egypt, at the time of the winter solstice, as a symbol of the year completed. Egyptian associations of a very early date still mingle with the tradition and custom of the Christmas-tree ; there are as many pyramids, as trees used in Germany, in the celebration of Christmas by those whose means do not admit of their purchasing trees and the concomitant tapers. These pyramids consist of slight erections of slips of wood, arranged like a pyramidal epergne, covered with green paper, and decorated with festoons of paper-chain work, which flutters in the wind, and constitutes, a make-believe foliage. This latter, however, is an innovation of modern days." But the Christmas-tree, notwithstanding what has gone before, no doubt came to us from Germany directly, and is still a flourishing institution among us. It is usually an evergreen decorated with lights and also with presents for the guests, the latter depending, of course, on the means or generosity of the entertainer.

Christopher, St.—His history is in his name, Χριστοφορος being said to have carried our Saviour, when a child, over an arm of the sea. This legend is in Voragine, and in most of the works on the subject. By her will made in 1495, Cecily, Duchess of York, bequeathed to her daughter-in-law, the Queen of Edward IV., among other things, "a pix with the fleshe of Saint Christofer." Wills from Doctors' Commons, Camd. Soc. 1863, p. 2. A popular account of the saint occurs in "A helpe to Discourse." The noted incident described above is a very favourite and common subject in the early paintings on glass. See Ottley's "Hist. of Printing," ch ix. and Notes and Queries, Fourth Series, ii. 313, *et seqq.* This saint occurs on the coins of Würtemberg and other continental states and towns, doubtless from his association with the child Jesus.

Chudleigh Glen, Devonshire.
This is one of the places where the early practice of propitiation by leaving something in the nature of a clout or rag, or a handkerchief, is still said to prevail, especially among holiday-makers at Whitsuntide.

Church Ales.
Payments and receipts or accounts of these various church-ales are very frequent items in all the early Churchwardens' books. Attention may be particularly directed to Mr. Ouvry's Extracts from those of Wing, Co. Bucks, in the thirty-sixth volume of "Archæologia." The entries go back as far as 1527. We here meet with several credits given in the books under each year for the May ale, the Hock-tide ale, the Whitsun ale, and the Sepulchre ale. In 1537, the first-named, after all expenses paid, realised 34s. In 1550, the May ale produced £2 0s. 2d., but the amount of this and of the other ales was liable to much fluctuation both here and elsewhere. It depended on circumstances. In 1564, the May ale was worth £3 9s. 7d., and in later years the increase seems to have been steady; but in some cases it is a little uncertain, whether the totals given are to be understood as gross or net. In 1562, at West Tarring, or Tarring Peverel, Sussex, the bill of fare included, *inter alia*, five calves, eight lambs, four sheep, five bushels of malt, two calves' heads, a leg of mutton, with pepper, saffron, and other spices. Lower's *Compendious History of Sussex*, 1870, ii. 198. In the Churchwardens' accounts of Minchinhampton under 1580, among the receipts, occur "gathered the hoglvn money, which ys xs. iiijd.; we made of oure Whiteson ale, iij. li. vs." "Archæol." vol. xxxv. p. 432. In 1588, the "clere gaine of the church ale" was £4 10s. and in 1589, £4 15s. Ibid. p. 435. It appears from Kethe's Sermon at Blandford, 1570, that it was the custom at that time for the church ales to be kept upon the sabbath day: which holy day, says our author, "the multitude call their revelyng day, which day is spent in bulbeatings, bearebeatings, bowlings, dicyng, cardyng, daunsynges, drunkennes and whoredome," "in so much as men could not keepe their servaunts

from lyinge out of theyr owne houses the same sabbath-day at night." Worsley, speaking of the parish of Whitwell, tells us, that there is a lease in the parish chest, dated 1574, "of a house called the church house, held by the inhabitants of Whitwell, parishioners of Gatcombe, of the lord of the manor, and demised by them to John Brode, in which is the following proviso: "Provided always, that, if the quarter shall need at any time to make a quarter-ale, or church-ale, for the maintenance of the chapel, that it shall be lawful for them to have the use of the said house, with all the rooms, both above and beneath, during their ale." Stubbes, in his "Anatomie of Abuses," 1585, p. 95, gives the following account of "The Maner of Church-Ales in England.": In certaine towns where dronken Bacchus beares swaie against Christmas and Easter, Whitsondaie, or some other tyme, the churchewardens of every parishe, with the consent of the whole parish, provide half a score or twenty quarters of mault, wherof some they buy of the churche stocke, and some is given them of the parishioners themselves, every one conferring somewhat, according to his abilitie; which mault being made into very strong ale or beere, is sette to sale together in the church or some other place assigned to that purpose. Then when this is set abroche, well is he that can gette the soonest to it, and spend the most at it. In this kinde of practice they continue sixe weekes, a quarter of a yeare, yea, halfe a year together. That money, they say, is to repaire their churches and chappels with, to buy bookes for service, cuppes for the celebration of the Sacrament, surplesses for sir John, and such other necessaries. And they maintaine other extraordinarie charges in their parish besides.' In his *Introduction to the Survey of North Wiltshire*, 1670, Aubrey remarks: "There were no rates for the poor in my grandfather's days; but for Kington St. Michael (no small parish) the church ale at Whitsuntide did the business. In every parish is (or was) a church-house, to which belonged spits, crocks, &c., utensils for dressing provision. Here the housekeepers met, and were merry, and gave their charity." The following document was contributed, many years ago, to *Notes and Queries*: "An agreement of the inhabitants of the towns and parishes of Elvaston, Thurlaston, and Ambaston, of the one part, and the inhabitants of the town of Okebrook, within the said parish of Elvaston, in co. Derby, on the other part, by John Abbot of the Dale, Ralph Saucheverell, Esq., John Bradshaw, and Henry Tithel, gent. Witnesseth, that the inhabitants, as well of the said parish of Elvaston as of the said town of Okebrook, shall brew four ales, and every ale of one quarter of malt—that at their own costs and charges, betwixt this and the feast of St. John Baptist next coming. And that every inhabitant of the town of Okebrook shall be at the several ales; and every husband and his wife shall pay two-pence, every cottager one penny; and all the inhabitants of Elvaston shall have and receive all the profits and advantages coming of the said ales to the use and behoof of the said church of Elvaston, &c. And the inhabitants of Okebrook shall carry all manner of tymber being in the Dale wood now felled, that the said Prestchyrch of the said towns shall occupye to the use and profit of the said church."

Church Decorations at Christmas.—Bourne observes that this custom of adorning the windows at this season with bay and laurel is but seldom used in the North; but in the South, particularly at our Universities, it is very common to deck not only the common windows of the town, but also the chapels of the colleges, with branches of laurel, which was used by the ancient Romans as the emblem of peace, joy, and victory. In the Christian sense it may be applied to the victory gained over the Powers of Darkness by the coming of Christ. "Trimmyng of the temples," says Polydore Vergil, "with hangynges, floures, boughes, and garlondes, was taken of the heathen people, whiche decked their idols and houses with suche array." Bourne cites the Council of Bracara, Canon 73, as forbidding Christians to deck their houses with bay leaves and green boughs; but this extended only to their doing it at the same time with the Pagans. *Antiq. Vulg.* 173. "Non liceat iniquas observantias agere Kalendarum et ociis vacare Gentilibus, neque lauro, neque viriditate arborum cingere domos. Omnis enim hæc observatio Paganismi est."—Bracc Can. 73, Instell. Prynne, in his *Histrio-Mastix*, 1633, p. 581, cites nearly the same words from the 73d Canon of the Concilium Antisiodorense, in France, A.D. 614. In the same work, p. 21, he cites the Councils as forbidding the early Christians to "decke up their houses with lawrell, yvie, and greene boughes (as we used to doe in the Christian season)." Adding from Ovid *Fasti*, lib. iii.:

"Hedera est gratissima Baccho."

Compare also Tertull. de Idol. cap. 15. In the Roman Calendar, I find the following observation on Christmas Eve: Templa exornantur. Among the annual disbursements of St. Mary-at-Hill, London, there is the following entry: "Holme and ivy at Christmas Eve, iiijd." In the Churchwardens' accounts of St. Laurence's parish, Reading, 1505, quoted by Coates, we read: "It. payed to Makrell for the holy

bush agayn Christmas, ijd." In the accounts of St. Martin Outwich, London, 1524, is: "Item for holy and ivy at Christmas, ijd. ob.——1525, Payd for holy and ivye at Chrystmas, ijd." In similar accounts for St. Margaret, Westminster, 1647, we read: "Item, paid for rosemarie and bayes that was stuck about the church at Christmas, 1s. 6d." Coles, in his "Art of Simpling," 1656, p. 64, tells us, "In some places setting up of holly. ivy, rosemary, bayes, yew, &c., in churches at Christmas is still in use." The use of box as well as yew, "to decke up houses in winter," is noticed in Parkinson's "Garden of Flowers," &c., 1629, p. 606.

Stow, in his "Survey," says that, "against the feast of Christmas, every man's house, as also their parish churches, were decked with holme, ivy, bayes, and whatsoever the season of the year afforded to be green. The conduits and standards in the streets were likewise garnished: among the which I read that in the year 1444, by tempest of thunder and lightning, towards the morning of Candlemas Day, at the Leadenhall. in Cornhill, a standard of tree, being set up in the midst of the pavement, fast in the ground, nailed full of holme and ivie, for disport of Christmas to the people, was torne up and caste down by the malignant spirit (as was thought), and the stones of the pavement all about were cast in the streets, and into divers houses so that the people were sore aghast at the great tempests." This illustrates the Spectator's observation, where he tells us that our forefathers looked into Nature with other eyes than we do now, and always ascribed common natural effects to supernatural causes. It should seem that this joy of the people at Christmas was death to their infernal enemy. Envying their festal pleasures, and owing them a grudge, he took this opportunity of spoiling their sport. In Herbert's "Country Parson," 1675, p. 56, the author tells us: "Our parson takes order that the church be swept and kept clean, without dust or cobwebs, and at great festivals strawed and stuck with boughs, and perfumed with incense."

"When rosemary and bays, the poet's crown,
Are brawl'd in frequent cries through all the town;
Then judge the festival of Christmas near,
Christmas, the joyous period of the year!
Now with bright holly all the temples strow
With lawrel green, and sacred mistletoe."

—Gay's *Trivia*. A writer in the "Gentleman's Magazine" for 1765, conjectures that the ancient custom of dressing churches and houses at Christmas with laurel, box, holly, or ivy was in allusion to many figurative expressions in the prophets relative to Christ, the Branch of Righteousness, &c., or that it was in remembrance of the Oratory of wrythen Wands or Boughs, which was the first Christian Church erected in Britain. Before we can admit either of these hypotheses, the question must be determined whether or not this custom did not prevail at this season prior to the introduction of the Christian faith amongst us. The custom of decking churches at Christmas is still continued in Devonshire, as it was in Brand's day." Chandler tells us, in his "Travels in Greece," that it is related where Druidism prevailed the houses were decked with evergreens in December, that the sylvan spirits might repair to them, and remain unnipped with frost and cold winds, until a milder season had renewed the foliage of their darling abodes.

Churching of Women.—In a proclamation, dated 16th November, 30 Henry VIII., among many "laudable ceremonies and rytes" enjoined to be retained is the following: "Ceremonies used at purification of women delivered of chylde, and offerynge of theyr crysomes." In "A Part of a Register" (1593), in a list of "grosse poyntes of Poperie, evident to all men," is enumerated the following: "The churching of women with this psalme, that the sunne and moone shall not burn them": as is also, "The offeringe of the woman at hir churching." In the Chichester Articles of Inquiry, 1639, occurs the passage: "Doth the woman who is to be churched use the antient accustomed habit in such cases, with a white vail or kerchiefe upon her head?" It was anciently a custom for women in England to bear lights when they were churched, as appears from the following royal bon mot (for the historical truth of which there is no sufficient authority). William the Conqueror, by reason of sickness, kept his chamber a long time, whereat the French King, scoffing, said, "The King of England lyeth long in child-bed": which, when it was reported unto King William, he answered, "When I am churched, there shall be a thousand lights in France"; "(alluding to the lights that women used to bear when they were churched): and after, wasting the French territories with that he performed within a few daies fire and sword." Compare *Carol* and *Yule*. In "The Burnynge of St. Paules Church in London, 1561," sign. I. 4 b. we read: "In Flaunders everye Saturdaye betwixt Christmas and Candlemas they eate flesh for joy. and have pardon for it, because our Ladye laye so long in childe-bedde, say they. We here may not

eat so; the Pope is not so good to us; yet surely it were as good reason that we should eat fleshe with them all that while that our Lady lay in child-bed, as that we shuld bear our candel at her churchinge at Candlemas with theym as they doe. It is seldome sene that men offer candels at womens churchinges, saving at our Ladies; but reason it is that she have some preferment if the Pope would be so good maister to us as to let us eat flesh with theym." Lupton says in his first book of "Notable Things": "If a man be the first that a woman meets after she comes out of the church, when she is newly churched, it signifies that her next child will be a boy; if she meet a woman, then a wench is likely to be her next child. This is credibly reported to me to be true." In the "Statistical Account of Scotland," it is said : "It was most unhappy for a woman, after bringing forth a child, to offer a visit, or for her neighbours to receive it, till she had been duly churched. How strongly did this enforce gratitude to the Supreme Being for a safe delivery! On the day when such a woman was churched, every family, favoured with a call, were bound to set meat and drink before her: and when they omitted to do so, they and theirs were to be loaded with her hunger. What was this, but an obligation on all who had it in their power to do the needful to prevent a feeble woman from fainting for want?" On a passage in his "History of Craven," where Master John Norton "gate leave of my old Lord to have half a stagg for his wife's churching." Whitaker observes in a note: "Hence it appears that thanksgivings after child-birth were anciently celebrated with feasting. He adds: "For this custom I have a still older authority: 'In ii^{bur} hosheveds vini albi empt' apud Ebor. erga purificationem Dominæ, tam post partum Mag'ri mei nuper de Clifford, quam post partum Mag'ri mei nunc de Clifford. . .lxvis. viijd.'" *Compotus Tho. Dom Clifford*, 15. *Henry VI.* Harrison, in his "Description of Britain," complains of the excessive feasting, as well at other festive meetings, as at "Purifications of women." It appears anciently to have been customary to give a large entertainment at the churching. In Deloney's "Thomas of Reading," 1632, signa. H iii. we read: "Sutton's Wife of Salisbury, which had lately bin delivered of a sonne, against her going to church prepared great cheare: at what time Simons wife of Southampton came thither, and so did divers others of the clothiers wives, onely to make merry at this churching-feast." In "The Batchellor's Banquet," 1603, attributed to Dekker. the lady (A 3) is introduced telling her husband: "You willed me (I was sent for) to go to Mistress M. Churching, and when I came thither I found great cheer and no small company of wives." And at c 2, the lady is asked : " If I had ever a new gown to be churched in." Among Shipman's Poems. is one dated 1667, and entitled, "The Churching Feast to Sr Clifford for a fat doe." Herrick, however, where he speaks of the churching ceremony omits reference to this entertainment. The ceremony of churching women in general sprang, no doubt, from the development of Candlemas into a festival of purification for the Virgin.

Church Steeples.—The custom of rustics in marking the outlines of their shoes on the tops of their church steeples, and engraving their names in the areas has been by Smart, in his "Hop-Garden," very sensibly referred to motives of vanity. As is the following, in the subsequent lines, to the pride of office :

" With pride of heart the Churchwarden surveys
High o'er the belfry, girt with birds and flow'rs,
His story wrote in capitals : ' 'Twas I
That bought the font ; and I repair'd the pews.' "

Churchyards.—It having been a current opinion in the times of heathenism, that places of burial were frequently haunted by spectres and apparitions, it is easy to imagine that the opinion has been transmitted from them, among the ignorant and unlearned, throughout all the ages of Christianity to this present day. The ancients believed that the ghosts of departed persons came out of their tombs and sepulchres, and wandered about the place where their remains lay buried. Thus Virgil tells us, that Mœris could call the ghosts out of their sepulchres and Ovid, that ghosts came out of their sepulchres and wandered about : and Clemens Alexandrinus upbraids them with the gods they worshipped ; which, says he, are wont to appear at tombs and sepulchres, and which are nothing but fading spectres and airy forms. *Admonit. Ad. Gent*, p. 37. Mede observes from a passage of this same ancient father, that the heathens supposed the presence and power of Dæmons (for so the Greeks call the souls of men departed) at their coffins and sepulchres, as tho' there always remained some natural tie between the deceased and their relicts. Churchyards are certainly as little frequented by apparitions and ghosts as other places, and therefore it is a weakness to be afraid of passing through them. Superstition, however, will always attend ignorance ; and the night, as she continues to be the mother of dews, will also never fail of being the fruitful parent of chimerical fears. Even Shakespear says :

" Now it is the time of night,
That the graves all gaping wide,
Ev'ry one lets forth his sprite
In the church-way path to glide."

And Dryden :
" When the sun sets, shadows that shew'd at noon
But small, appear most long and terrible."

A more modern author follows on the same side :
" Oft in the lone church yard at night I've seen
By glimpse of moon-shine, checqu'ring thro' the trees,
The school-boy, with his satchel in his hand,
Whistling aloud to bear his courage up,
And, lightly tripping o'er the long flat stones
(With nettles skirted, and with moss o'ergrown),
That tell in homely phrase who lie below.
Sudden he starts ! and hears, or thinks he hears,
The sound of something purring at his heels :
Full fast he flies, and dares not look behind him,
Till, out of breath, he overtakes his fellows ;
Who gather round, and wonder at the tale
Of horrid apparition, tall and ghastly,
That walks at dead of night, or takes his stand,
O'er some new open'd grave ; and (strange to tell !)
Evanishes at crowing of the cock."

—*Blair's Grave.* We learn from Moresin, that churchyards were used for the purposes of interment in order to remove superstition.

Burial was in ancient times without the walls of cities and towns. Lycurgus, he tells us, first introduced grave stones within the walls, and as it were brought home the ghosts to the very doors. Thus we compel horses, that are apt to startle, to make the nearest approaches we can to the objects at which they have taken the alarm. "Christians," says Laurence, " distinguished their oratories into an atrium, a church yard ; a sanctum, a church ; a sanctum sanctorum, a chancell. They did conceive a greater degree of sanctitie in one of them, than in another, and on one place of them than another ; churchyards they thought profaned by sports ; the whole circuit both before and after Christ was privileged for refuge, none out of the communion of the kirke permitted to lie there, any consecrate ground preferred for interment before that which was not consecrat, and that in an higher esteem which was in an higher degree of consecration, and that in the highest which was neerest the altar." "Sermon preached before the King, &c.," p. 9, cited in "The Canterburian's Self-conviction, &c.," 1640, p. 83, note. Bailey tells us that, in ancient times amongst Christians, upon any extraordinary solemnity, particularly the anniversary dedication of a church, tradesmen used to bring and sell their wares even in the churchyards, especially upon the festival of the dedication; as at Westminster on St. Peter's Day; at London on St. Bartholomew's; at Durham on St. Cuthbert's Day, &c.; but riots and disturbances often happening, by reason of the numbers assembled together, privileges were by royal charter granted, for various causes, to particular places, towns, and places of strength, where magistrates presided to keep the people in order. In the Suffolk Articles of Enquiry, 1638, we read: "Have any playes, feasts, banquets, suppers, church ales, drinkings, temporal courts or leets, lay juries, musters, exercise of dauncing, stoole ball, foot ball, or the like, or any other prophane usage been suffered to be kept in your church, chappell, or church yard?" At Barnes, Surrey, among other ordinary benefactions, there was the Rose Acre, at present commuted for a sum in consols. The ground was left by a person so named, on condition that over his grave in the churchyard against the south wall of the church a rose-tree should be always kept growing and so it is unto this day. In "Magna Carta," 1556, I find the statute, "Ne Rector prosternet Arbores in Cemiterio."

Churn Supper.—There was a churn or kern supper (so they pronounce it vulgarly in Northumberland), and a shouting the church or kern. This, Aram informs us, was different from that of the Mell Supper: the former being always provided when all was shorn, the latter after all was got in. I should have thought that most certainly kern supper was no more than corn supper, had not Aram asserted that it was called the Churn Supper, because from immemorial times it was customary to produce in a churn a great quantity of cream, and to circulate it in cups to each of the rustic company, to be eaten with bread. This custom, in Aram's time, survived about Whitby and Scarborough, in the Eastern parts of Yorkshire, and round about Gisburne, &c., in the West. In other places cream has been commuted for ale, and the tankard politely preferred to the churn.

Cinque. — The famous Cornelius Scriblerus writes: "The play which the Italians call Cinque and the French Mourre is extremely antient. It was played by Hymen and Cupid at the marriage of Psyche, and was termed by the Latins *digitis micare*." The French game of Mourre is thus explained by Littrè: "un jeu qui consiste à montrer rapidement une partie des doigts leveé et l'autre fermée, afin de donner à deviner le nombre de ceux qui sont levès." Cornelius was apparently justified in dissuading Martin from bestowing his time on this recreation.

Cinque Ports.—Mr. Miall Green, of Streatham Hill, owner of the yachts Thalatta, Yolande, and Figaro, was on the 2nd December, 1901, elected deputy-mayor of Brightlingsea, an apanage of the Cinque Ports, in succession to Capt. Sycamore, of the Shamrock. The ceremony is a curious one, the council chamber being the tower of the parish church, while the vicar acts as recorder. Each elected freeman pays 11 pennies to the civic exchequer. Comp. *Brightlingsea*.

Clameur de Haro. — I presume that the Ara mentioned in Walford's *Fairs, Past and Present*, 1883, p. 9, is another form of Haro, being the cry when the settling time arrived at a certain stage in the operations. The following remarks appeared in the *Daily News* for June 1, 1882: "Several learned members of the French Académie des Sciences have come to the conclusion that the old fashioned 'Clameur de Haro' might be revived to advantage in civil procedure, as a means of enabling small landed proprietors and other humble owners of house property to fight their more wealthy opponents on better terms than they can under the existing laws. It is scarcely probable that the French Parliament will legislate in the sense suggested, but in the course of the discussion which has been going on, M. Glasson, who read a long essay on the subject, gave some very interesting information as to the origin of the word. According to M. Glasson the 'Clameur de Haro' is identical with the 'Legatro of the Bavarians and the Thuringians, and the first trace of it in France is to be found in the 'Grand Coutumier de Normandie.' The 'Clameur de Haro,' or cry for justice, only resorted to in criminal cases at first, is referred to under the name of 'Clamor Violentiæ' in the Saxon laws. It may be assumed, therefore, that when William the Conqueror came to England, he found the equivalent of the 'Clameur de Haro' in existence, and the changes which he made in the application of it tended to bring the English mode of procedure into closer conformity of detail with that which prevailed in Normandy. In course of time the 'Clameur de Haro' was made applicable to civil as well as to criminal affairs, and long after it had fallen into disuse for the latter—its utility becoming less and less as the organization of society grew more and more perfect— it was retained in use throughout the north-west provinces of France for cases of disputed possession, and was not actually repealed until the close of the 18th century. It still exists in the neighbouring Channel Islands, and the owners of property attach great value to it. A very striking instance of this was afforded in Jersey the other day, the owner of some property through which a railway was to be cut raising the 'Clameur de Haro.' He was so stout that he had great difficulty in fulfilling the indispensable formality of falling on his knees and getting up again with the cry in old French — ' Haro ! Haro ! A l'aide, mon Prince, on me fait tort.' It is not stated whether he gained his point ; but there can be no doubt as to the attachment of the Channel Islanders to this survival of the Middle Ages." In the *Encyclopædia* of Chambers, 1874, v., 699 *back*, there is an implied suggestion, which is probably of no weight whatever, that *Haro* is a corruption or abbreviated form of Ha ! Rollo ! the appeal of the party having been originally to Duke Rollo.

Clavie.—Under the heading of " Relics of Fire-Worship in Scotland," the *Daily News* of January 4, 1878, has the following communication :—" On the last day of the year, old style, which falls on the 12th January, the festival of " The Clavie " takes place at Burghead, a fishing village near Forres. On a headland in that vilage still stands an old Roman altar, locally called the " Douro." On the evening of January 12 a large tar barrel is set on fire and carried by one of the fishermen round the town, while the assembled folks shout and holloa. If the man who carries the barrel falls, it is an evil omen. The man with the lighted barrel having gone with it round the town carries it up to the top of the hill, and places it on the Douro. More fuel is immediately added. The sparks as they fly upwards are supposed to be witches and evil spirits leaving the town ; the people therefore shout at and curse them as they disappear in vacancy. When the burning tar barrel falls in pieces, the fisherwives rush in and endeavour to get a lighted bit of wood from its remains ; with this light the fire on the cottage hearth is at once kindled, and it is considered lucky to keep in this flame all the rest of the year. The charcoal of the Clavie is collected and put in bits up the chimney, to prevent the witches and evil spirits coming into the house. The Duoro (i.e., the Roman altar) is covered with a thick layer of tar from the fires that are annually lighted upon it. Close to the Douro is a very ancient Roman well, and, close to the well, several

rude but curious Roman sculptures can be seen let into a garden wall.

Clay-Daubing. — Brockett notices the Cumberland usage by which the friends of a newly-married couple met together, and erected them a cottage, before separating. This (he says) was called clay-daubing.

Cleaver.—A school-boy's toy. See Halliwell in v.

Cleke.—See *Gleek*.

Clement's Day, St.—(November 23). Plot, describing a Clog Almanack, (which is now in the Bodleian library), says, " a pot is marked against the 23rd of November, for the Feast of St. Clement, from the ancient custom of going about that night to beg drink to make merry with." In the Privy Purse Expenses of the Princess Mary, under November, 1537, is this entry : " Itm. geuen to the bakers of the Prince house on saynt Clementes Even comyng wt theyr Bolle. . . .vs." ; upon which the Editor (Sir F. Madden), referring to Hone's " Every Day Book," observes : " In more modern times, the blacksmiths seem to have usurped the privilege of the bakers." In a proclamation, July 22, 1540, it is ordered : " Neither that children should be decked, ne go about upon S. Nicholas, S. Katherine, S. Clement, the Holy Innocents, and such likes dayes." In some almanacks, this day is marked at Old Martinmass, because it is still here and there retained as one of the quarterly divisions of the year, on which payments fall due. At Tenby, on St. Clement's Day, the effigy of a carpenter was carried round the town, and subsequently cut to pieces. In Staffordshire, on this day, the children go about begging for apples, and singing these rude verses :

" Clemeny, Clemeny, God be wi' you,
Christmas comes but once a ye-ar ;
When it comes, it will soon be gone,
Give me an apple, and I'll be gone."

Closh.—A form of ninepins, noticed by Minsheu as forbidden by Statute 17 Edw. IV., cap. 3, and again in 18-20-23, Henry VIII. The ninepins were either of wood or of the shank-bones of a horse or ox. This sport was sometimes called closh-cayles. From a statement by Strutt it may be perhaps inferred that there were two varieties of closh or closh-cayles, that played with a ball, and that played with a club or stick, the latter resembling the French *jeu de quilles à baston*. The French word quille, however, —our cayles —was applied to the stick employed in other sports. Among our ancestors, as is still largely the case, all this family of recreations was popular rather than fashionable. Sir Thomas Elyot, in his *Governor*, 1531, classes *claishe pynnes* with bowls and quoits.

Coal.—Thomas Hill, in his *Natural and Artificial Conclusions*, 1581, describes " The vertue of a rare cole, that is to be found but one hour in the day, and one day in the yeare." " Divers authors," he adds, " affirm concerning the verity and vertue of this cole, viz., that it is onely to be found upon Midsummer Eve, just at noon, under every root of plantine and of mugwort ; the effects whereof are wonderful : for whosoever weareth or beareth the same about with them, shall be freed from the plague, fever, ague, and sundry other diseases. And one author especially writeth, and constantly averreth, that he never knew any that used to carry of this marvellous cole about them, who ever were to his knowledge sick of the plague, or (indeed) complained of any other maladie." Lupton observes, " It is certainly and constantly affirmed that on Midsummer Eve there is found, under the root of mugwort, a coal which saves or keeps them safe from the plague, carbuncle, lightning, the quartan ague, and from burning, that bear the same about them: and Mizaldus, the writer hereof, saith, that he doth hear that it is to be found the same day under the root of plantane, which I know to be of truth, for I have found them the same day under the root of plantane, which is especially and chiefly to be found at noon." *Notable Things*, first printed in 1579, ed. 1660, book ii. p. 59. " The last summer," says Aubrey, " on the day of St. John Baptist, 1694, I accidentally was walking in the pasture behind Montague House, (Bloomsbury) ; it was 12 o'clock,I saw there about two or three and twenty young women, most of them well habited, on their knees, very busy, as if they had been weeding. A young man told me that they were looking for a coal under the root of a plantain, to put under their heads that night, and they should dream who would be their husbands. It was to be that day and hour."

Coat-Money. — See Davis, *Suppl. Glossary*, 1881, in v.

Cob or **Cobbing.**—A punishment used by seamen for petty offences or irregularities among themselves: it consists in bastanadoing the offender on the posteriors with a cobbing stick, or pipe staff ; the number usually inflicted is a dozen. At the first stroke the executioner repeats the word watch, on which all persons present are to take off their hats, on pain of like punishment : the last stroke is always given as hard as possible, and is called the purse. Ashore, among soldiers, where this punishment is sometimes adopted, watch and the purse are not included in the number, but given over and above, or, in the vulgar phrase, free, gratis, for nothing. This piece of discipline is also inflicted in Ireland by the schoolboys on persons coming into the school without taking off their hats ; it is there called school-butter."

Cob Loaf Stealing. — Compare *Aston*.

Cob-Nút.—A game which consists in pitching at a row of nuts piled up in heaps of four, three at the bottom and one at the top of each heap. Halliwell in v.

Cock. — A mode of evading the law against profane expressions, used both in conversation and literature in James I.'s time. It is common in the old plays. Compare Nares, 1859, in v. The modern equivalent is *Scott*. Our youths say *Great Scott* for *Great God*.

Cockal.—The game played with the huckle or pastern bone of the sheep, instead of dice, corresponding with the ancient *ludus talaris* or *astralagus*. Compare Nares, *Gloss.* 1859, in v. In Levinus Lemnius, we read : " The antients used to play at cokall or casting of huckle bones, which is done with smooth sheeps bones. The Dutch call them pickelen, wherewith our young maids that are not yet ripe use to play for a husband, and young married folks despise these as soon as they are married. But young men used to contend one with another with a kind of bone taken forth of oxe-feet. The Dutch call them Coten, and they play with these at a set time of the year. Moreover cockles which the Dutch call Teelings are different from dice, for they are square with four sides, and dice have six. Cockals are used by maids amongst us, and do no wayes waste any ones estate. For either they passe away the time with them, or if they have time to be idle, they play for some small matter, as for chesnuts, filberds, pins, buttons, and some such Juncats."— *Occult Miracles of Nature*, 1658, p. 768. In Kinder's translation from the same author of *A Sanctuarie of Salvation*, p. 144, these bones are called " Huckle-bones or coytes." In Polydore Vergil we have another description of this game : "There is a game also that is played with the posterne bone in the hynder foote of a sheepe, oxe, gote, fallowe or redde dere, whiche in Latin is called Talus. It hath foure chaunces, the ace point, that is named Canis, or Caniculas, was one of the sides ; he that cast it leyed doune a peny or so muche as the gamers were agreed on ; the other side was called Venus, that signifieth seven. He that cast the chaunce wan sixe and all that was layd doune for the castyng of Canis. The two other sides were called Chius and Senio. He that did throwe Chius wan three. And he that cast Senio gained foure. This game (as I take it) is used of children in Northfolke, and they call it the chaunce bone ; they play with three or foure of those bones together ; it is either the same or very lyke to it." Langley's Abridg., fol. 1. Herrick seems to speak of cockall as a children's sport, played with points and pins. For farther information relating to this game, as played by the ancients, the reader may consult Joannis Meursii Ludibunda, sivi de Ludis Græcorum, 1625, p. 7, πάσσαλος and Dan. Souterii "Palimedes," p. 81, but more particularly " I Tali ed altri Strumenti lusori degli antichi Romani discritti " da Fransecso de' Ficoroni, 1734. And for the Greek analogue St. John's *Manners and Customs of Ancient Greece*, 1842, i., 160-1.

Cockatrice or **Basilisk.** — Sir Thomas Browne informs us that the generation of a basilisk is supposed to proceed from a cock's egg hatched under a toad or serpent. A conceit which he observes is as monstrous as the brood itself. This writer endeavours to account for its killing at a distance. "It killeth at a distance — it poisoneth by the eye, and by priority of vision. Now that deleterious it may be at some distance, and destructive without corporal contaction, what uncertainty soever there be in the effect, there is no high improbability in the relation. For if plagues or pestilential atomes have been conveyed in the air from different regions : if men at a distance have infected each other : if the shadowes of some trees be noxious : if torpedoes deliver their opium at a distance, and stupifie beyond themselves : we cannot reasonably deny that there may proceed from subtiller seeds more agile emanations, which contemn those laws, and invade at distance unexpected. Thus it is not impossible what is affirmed of this animal ; the visible rayes of their eyes carrying forth the subtilest portion of their poison which, received by the eye of man or beast, infecteth first the brain and is from thence communicated unto the heart." He adds : " Our basilisk is generally described with legs, wings, a serpentine and winding taile, and a crist or comb somewhat like a cock. But the basilisk of elder times was a proper kind of serpent, not above three palmes long, as some account, and differenced from other serpents by advancing his head and some white marks or coronary spots upon the crown, as all authentic writers have delivered." A cockatrice hatched from a cock's egg is described by a foreign author as one of the terrors of the superstitious man, and as an omen of the most pernicious sort. Werenfel's " Dissertation on Superstition," transl. into Engl. p. 7. This reminds us of Dryden's lines :

" Mischiefs are like the cockatrice's eye ;
If they see first, they kill ; if seen, they die."

Compare Nares, *Glossary*, 1859, in v.

Cockchafer.—I conclude that we must not allow the German children's invocation to the cockchafer or lady-bird (lady-bug or lady-cow) to rank among modes of predestination ; but it may be perhaps, in its present form, the relic of an older and more serious superstition :

" May-bug, May-bug, tell this to me,
How many years my life is to be?
One year, two years," &c.

Or, as the Swiss couplet runs (translated) :
" O chafer, O chafer, fly off and awa',
For milk, and for bread, and a silver spoon bra'."

For which notices I am indebted to Mr. Atkinson. But there are variant versions. Comp. Halliwell's *Nursery Rhymes*, 6th ed. pp. 263, 272.

Cock-Crow.—The ancients, because the cock gives notice of the approach and break of day, have, with a propriety equal to any thing in their mythology, dedicated this bird to Apollo. They have also made him the emblem of watchfulness, from the circumstance of his summoning men to their business by his crowing, and have therefore dedicated him also to Mercury. With the lark he may be poetically styled the " Herald of the Morn." Philostratus, giving an account of the Apparition of Achilles' Shade to Apollonius Tyaneus, says, that it vanished with a little glimmer as soon as the cock crowed. " Vit. Apol." vol. iv. p. 16. Reed's " Shakespear," vol. vol. iv. p. 16. Bourne very seriously examines the fact whether spirits roam about in the night, or are obliged to go away at cock-crow. The traditions of all ages appropriate the appearance of spirits to the night. The Jews had an opinion that hurtful spirits walked about in the night. The same opinion obtained among the ancient Christians, who divided the night into four watches called the evening, midnight, cock-crowing, and the morning. The opinion that spirits fly away at cock-crow is certainly very ancient, for we find it mentioned by the Christian poet Prudentius, who flourished in the beginning of the fourth century, as a tradition of common belief :

" They say the wandering powers, that love
The silent darkness of the night,
At cock-crowing give o'er to rove,
And all in fear do take their flight.
The approaching salutary morn,
Th' approach divine of hated day,
Makes darkness to its place return,
And drives the midnight ghosts away.
They know that this an emblem is,
Of what precedes our lasting bliss,
That morn when graves give up their dead
In certain hope to meet their God."

Bourne tells us he never met with any reasons assigned for the departure of spirits at the cock-crowing : " but," he adds, " there have been produced at that time of night, things of very memorable worth, which might perhaps raise the pious credulity of some men to imagine that there was something more in it than in other times. It was about the time of cock-crowing when our Saviour was born, and the angels sang the first Christmas carol to the poor shepherds in the fields of Bethlehem. Now it may be presumed, as the Saviour of the world was then born, and the heavenly Host had then descended to proclaim the news, that the Angel of Darkness would be terrified and confounded, and immediately fly away: and perhaps this consideration has partly been the foundation of this opinion." It was also about this time when our Saviour rose from the dead. "A third reason is, that passage in the Book of Genesis, where Jacob wrestled with the angel for a blessing, where the angels say unto him 'Let me go, for the day breaketh.'" Bourne, however, thinks this tradition seems more especially to have arisen from some particular circumstances attending the time of cockcrowing; and which, as Prudentius, before cited, seems to say, "are an emblem of the approach of the Day of Resurrection." "The circumstances, therefore, of the time of cock-crowing," he adds, "being so natural a figure and representation of the morning of the Resurrection; the night so shadowing out the night of the grave: the third watch, being, as some suppose, the time our Saviour will come to judgement at: the noise of the cock awakening sleepy man and telling him, as it were, the night is far spent, the day is at hand: representing so naturally the voice of the Arch-angel awakening the dead, and calling up the righteous to everlasting day: so naturally does the time of cock-crowing shadow out these things, that probably some good well-meaning men might have been brought to believe that the very devils themselves, when the cock crew and reminded them of them, did fear and tremble, and shun the light."

In the prose Life of St. Guthlac, Hermit of Crowland, by one Felix, *circâ* 749, there is the following passage: "It happened one night, when it was the time of cock-crowing, and the blessed man Guthlac fell to his morning prayers, he was suddenly entranced in light slumber—." I quote from Mr. Goodwin's translation of the Anglo-Saxon original. The following is from Chaucer's "Assemble of Foules," f. 235 :

"The tame ruddocke and the coward kite,
The cocke, that horologe is of Thropes lite."

Spenser writes :
—— "The morning cocke crew loud ;
And at the sound it shrunk in haste away ,
And vanish'd from our sight."

Allot, in "England's Parnassus," 1600, printed the two following lines from Drayton's "Endimion and Phœbe, (1593)."
"And now the cocke, the morning's trumpeter,
Plaid hunts up for the day-starre to appeare."—

Where Gray has followed our poet :
"The cock's shrill clarion, or the echoing horn,
No more shall rouse them from their lowly bed."
"But soft, methinks I scent the morning air—
Brief let me be."

And again,
"The glow-worm shows the matin to be near."

In the "Merry Devil of Edmonton," 1608 :
"More watchfull than the day-proclayming cocke."

It appears from a passage in "Romeo and Juliet," that Shakespear means that they were carousing till three o'clock :
"—— The second cock has crow'd,
The curfew-bell has toll'd ; 'tis three o'clock."

Perhaps Tusser makes this point clear :
"Cocke croweth at midnight times few above six,
With pause to his neighbour to answer betwix :
At three aclocke thicker, and then as ye knowe,
Like all in to mattens neere day they doo crowe ;
At midnight, at three, and an hour yer day,
They utter their language as well as they may."

By a passage in "Macbeth," "we were carousing till the second cock," it should seem to appear as if there were two separate times of cock-crowing. The commentators, however, say nothing of this. They explain the passage as follows: "Till the second cock :—Cock-crowing." So in "King Lear": "He begins at curfew, and walks till the first cock." Which is illustrated by a passage in the "Twelve Merry Jestes of the Widow Edith," 1525 :
"The time they pas merely til ten of the clok,
Yea, and I shall not lye, till after the first cok."
"The cock crows and the morn grows on,
When 'tis decreed I must be gone."
—*Hudibras*, Canto i. p. iii.

In Blair's *Grave* is a passage which seems to form an exception from the general time of cock-crowing:

" Some say, that ever 'gainst that season comes,
Wherein our Saviour's birth is celebrated,
This bird of dawning singeth all night
long.
And then, they say, no spirit dares stir
abroad;
The nights are wholesome; then no
planets strike,
No fairy takes, nor witch hath power to
charm,
So hallow'd and so gracious is the time."

Bourne tells us, there is a tradition among the common people that at the time of cock-crowing the midnight spirits forsake these lower regions, and go to their pro-per places. Hence it is that in the coun-try villages, where the way of life requires more early labour, the inhabitants always go cheerfully to work at that time: where-as if they are called abroad sooner, they are apt to imagine everything they see or hear to be a wandering ghost. Shakespeare has given us an excellent account of this vulgar notion in his " Hamlet." The pre-sent writer suggested long since that the " early village cock " of Shakespear should be *early village clock*, as the word chanti-cleer has been given, and *cock* in the pass-age is a pleonasm. See my edition of W. Browne, 1868, i., 197. Peter Suavenius, who visited Scotland about 1535, relates in his MS. Diary that there is a place there, eight miles in circuit, where the cocks never crow.

Cock-Fighting.—Bailey tells us that the origin of this sport was derived from the Athenians on the following occa-sion: when Themistocles was marching his army against the Persians, he, by the way, espying two cocks fighting, caused his army to behold them, and addressed them as follows: " Behold, these do not fight for their household gods, for the monuments of their ancestors, nor for glory, nor for liberty, nor for the safety of their chil-dren, but only because the one will not give way unto the other." This so en-couraged the Grecians that they fought strenuously and obtained the victory over the Persians; upon which cock-fighting was by a particular law ordained to be annually practised by the Athenians. Cock-fighting was an institution partly re-ligious and partly political at Athens, and was continued there for the purpose of im-proving the seeds of valour in the minds of the Athenian youth. But it was after-wards abused and perverted, both there and in other parts of Greece, to a common pastime and amusement, without any moral, political, or religious intention,

and as it is now followed and practiced amongst us. Men have long availed them-selves of the antipathy which one cock shows to another, and have encouraged that natural hatred with arts that may be said to disgrace human reason. Pegge has proved that though the ancient Greeks piqued themselves on their politeness, call-ing all other nations barbarous, yet they were the authors of this cruel and inhuman mode of diversion. The inhabitants of Delos were great lovers of this sport; and Tanagra, a city of Bœotia, the Isle of Rhodes, Chalcis in Euboea and the country of Media, were famous for their generous and magnanimous race of chickens. It appears that the Greeks had some method of preparing the birds for battle. An ac-count of the origin of this custom amongst the Athenians may be seen in Ælian," lib. ii. cap. xxviii. It may be worth noting that George Wilson, in his " Commenda-tion of cocks and cock-fighting," 1607, en-deavours to show that cock-fighting was before the coming of Christ. Lord North-ampton says: " The Romaines tooke the crowing of a cocke for an abode of victory, though no philosopher be ignorant that this procedeth of a gallant lustinesse upon the first digestion." *Defensative*, 1583, sign. T. 2 *verso*. It is probable that cock-fighting was first introduced into this island by the Romans; the bird itself was here before Cæsar's arrival. *Bell-Gall.* v. sect. 12.

Fitzstephen is the first of our writers that mentions cock-fighting, describ-ing it as the sport of school boys on Shrove-Tuesday. The cock-pit, it seems, was the school, and the master was the comptroller and director of the sport. Fitzstephen writes: " — that we may be-gin with the pastimes of the boys (as we have all been boys), annually on the day which is called Shrove-Tuesday, the boys of the respective schools bring to the masters each one his fighting-cock, and they are indulged all the morning with seeing their cocks fight in the school-room." Ed. 1772, p. 45. In the statutes of St. Paul's School, A.D. 1518, the following clause occurs: " I will they use no cock-fighting nor ridinge about of victorye, nor disputing at St. Bartilemewe, which is but foolish babling and losse of time." Knight's *Life of Dean Colet*, p. 362. From this time, at least, the diversion, however absurd and even impious, was continued among us. It was followed, though disapproved and pro-hibited in the 39 Edw. III.: also in the reign of Henry VIII. and in 1569. It has been called by some a royal diversion, and, as every one knows, the cock-pit at White-hall was erected by Henry VIII. for the more magnificent celebration of the sport. It was prohibited, however, by an Act of March 31, 1654. Moresin informs us that the Papists derived this custom of exhibiting cockfights on one day every year from the Athenians, and from an institution of Themistocles. "Cæl. Rhod." lib. ix. variar lect. cap. xlvi. idem Pargami fiebat. Alex. ab. Alex. lib. v. cap. 8., *Papatus*, p. 66.

The Fathers of the Church inveigh with great warmth against the spectacles of the arena, the wanton shedding of human blood in sport; one would have thought that with that of the gladiators, cock-fighting would also have been discarded under the mild and human Genius of Christianity. But, as Pegge observes, it was reserved for this enlightened æra to practice it with new and aggravated circumstances of cruelty. In the *Privy Purse Expences of Henry VII.*, under 1493, there is the entry: "March 2. To Master Bray, for rewardes to them that brought cokkes at Shrovetide at Westmr., £1." In the middle of the 16th century we find the gentlemen of Yorkshire keenly interested in this sport, and there is a letter from Sir Henry Savile to William Plumpton, Esq., announcing "a meeting of cocks" at Sheffield, to which their common acquaintance were expected to come, save from more or less considerable distances. It was a match between Lancashire, Derbyshire, and Hallamshire. *Plumpton Correspondence*, 1839, pp. 250-1. Stubbes, in his "Anatomie of Abuses," 1583, inveighs against cock-fighting, which in his day seems to have been practiced on the Sabbath in England:

" Cock Fightyng in Ailgna [Anglia].

"Besides these exercises, they flock thicke and threefolde to the cockfightes, an exercise nothing inferiour to the rest, where nothing is vsed, but swearing, forswearing, deceit, fraud, collusion, cosenage, skoldyng, railyng, conuitious talkyng, fightyng, brawlyng, quarrelyng, drinkyng, and whoryng, and whiche is worst of all, robbing of one an other of their goodes, and that not by direct, but indirecte meanes and attempts. And yet to blaunche and set out these mischeefs withall, (as though they were vertues), they haue their appointed waies and set houres when these deuilries must be exercised. They haue houses erected to that purpose flagges and ensignes hanged out, to giue notice of it to others, and proclamation goes out, to proclame the same, to the ende that many maie come to the dedication of this solemne feast of mischeefe." It is odd enough, that the poverty of Roger Ascham, who was preceptor to Queen Elizabeth, and one of the most learned persons of his time, was attributed by the no less learned Camden to dicing and cock-fighting! It appears that James I. was remarkably fond of cock-fighting. Breton,

in his *Fantasticks*, 1626, says under Aug.: "I had a touch at your recreations before, and that your cock may not kick your coyn out of your pocket, I shall give you some marks to choose a good one by; Know, then, that the best characters desirable in a fighting cock, are his shape, colour, courage, and sharp heel; for his shape, the middle size is ever accounted best, because they be now most matchable strong, nimble, and ready for your pleasure in his batel; and so the exceeding little cock is as hard to match, and is commonly weak and tedious in his maner of fighting; he would be of a proud and upright shape, with a small head, like a spar-hawk, quick large eye, and a strong back crooked, and big at the setting on, and in colour suitable to the plume of his feathers, as black, yellow, or reddish; the beam of his legs would be very strong, and according to his plume, blew, gray, or yellow; his spurs long, rough and sharp, and a little bending, and looking inward; for his colour, the gray pyle, the yellow pyle, or the red with the blanck breast, is esteemed the best, the pyde is not so good, and the white and dun are the worst; if it be red about the head like scarlet, it is a sign of lust, strength, and courage; but if it be pale, it is a signe of sickness and faintness; for his courage, you shall observe it in his walk, by his treading, and in the pride of his going, and in his pen by his oft-crowing; for the sharpness of his heel, it is only seen in his fighting; for what cock is said to be sharp or narrow heel'd, which every time he risketh, he hitteth and draws blood of his adversary, gilding his spurs in blood, and threatening at every blow an end of the battel. I wish you such a Cock." I have quoted this interesting passage from Stevenson's *Twelve Months*, 1661, but it is the same work as Breton's under a different title.

Of this sport, as it was conducted in London in 1669, an Italian resident has left a graphic account. "The places made for the cock-fights are a sort of little theatre, where the spectators sit all round on steps under cover. At the bottom of these is a round table six *braccia* in diameter, or thereabouts, and raised about two *braccia* from the ground: it is covered with matting all stained with the blood of cocks. The days on which they are going to have the contests are always advertised by large printed bills, stuck up at all the corners of the streets, and distributed through the city. When a large crowd of people has been got together, two cocks are brought out in sacks by two of those men whose business it is to breed them and look after them. One of these men goes in at one side of the theatre, and the other at the opposite entrance, and having taken their cocks out of the bags, they hold them in their hands, whilst the first betting is going on, which everyone does without any rule or regulation whatever, being solely actuated by his own judgment, which makes him fancy one cock more than another. The cocks have their wings cut and their crests removed. They are not generally finely-grown birds, but are very strong, and of extraordinary pluck. Half-way up their legs they are armed with a kind of spur of very sharp steel, with which, when they flutter up into the air, and come to close quarters with their beaks, they wound each other severely. As soon as they are set at liberty, the combatants glare at each other for a little while, and fix each other with their eyes. They then proceed to the contest with their necks stretched out, and all their feathers ruffled. At first they approach one another slowly, step by step; then all of a sudden they dart at one another, flapping their wings to raise themselves from the ground so as to attack each other in mid-air, and wound one another with their beaks with such fury that at the commencement you would think that a very keen contest was going to ensue. However, the truth is that they tire themselves by degrees, and the end becomes very tedious, simply reducing itself to this: that one sets to work to kill the other by the sheer fury of its pecking on the head and eyes of its enemy, which part of the scene will last over a quarter of an hour, and sometimes nearly half an hour. During the time that the contest lasts, you hear a perpetual buzz amongst those who are betting, who are doubling, trebling— nay, even quadrupling—their original bets; and there are those who make new ones, according as they see how the cocks are getting on. It often happens that when one of the birds appears to be conquered, and on the point of death, it will become restored to such wonderful vigour that it vanquishes the stronger and kills him, and when it happens, as in the last case, that the beaten cock seems roused up to courage again, then are the wildest bets made—twenty, thirty or a hundred to one. Sometimes it happens that both birds are left dead on the field of battle; sometimes when the first is dead, the other will drag itself on to the body of its enemy, and with the little breath that remains to it, will flap its wings and crow for victory. After this he will lay himself down to die. When one duel is finished, other cocks are brought on as long as there are people left to ask for them. You pay a shilling to enter, which goes into the purse of those who for this end breed the cocks. So that six or eight couples of cocks, which do not always die on the same day, are paid for with the sum of from forty to fifty crowns. This race of animal is not so plucky, when

once it is taken out of the island, it having been proved that in Normandy they do not do as well as in England. The hatred between them is natural, so that immediately they cease to be chickens they have to be fed separately, otherwise they would quickly kill one another." *Antiquary,* August 1884.

In the "Statistical Account of Scotland," vol. iii., p. 378, the minister of Applecross, co. Ross, speaking of the Schoolmaster's perquisites, says: "he has the cock-fight dues, which are equal to one quarter's payment for each scholar." In "Lluellin's Poems," 1646, is a song, in which the author seems ironically to satirize this cruel sport. In a copy of verses upon two cocks fighting, by Dr. R. Wild, the spirited qualities of the combatants are given in the following most brilliant couplet:

"They scorn the dunghill; 'tis their only prize
To dig for pearls within each other's eyes."

Our Poet makes his conquered or dying cock dictate a will, some of the quaint items of which follow:

"Imp. first of all, let never be forgot,
My body freely I bequeath to th' pot,
Decently to be boil'd, and for it's tomb,
Let me be buried in some hungry womb.
Item, executors I will have none
But he that on my side laid seven to one,
And like a gentleman that he may live,
To him and to his heirs my comb I give."

Misson, in his "Travels in England," about 1698, p. 39, says: "Cockfighting is one of the great English diversions. They build amphitheatres for this purpose, and persons of quality sometimes appear at them. Great wagers are laid; but I am told that a man may be damnably bubbled, if he is not very sharp." At p. 304 he tells us: "Cock fighting is a royal pleasure in England. The combats between bulls and dogs, bears and dogs, and sometimes bulls and bears, are not battels to death, as those of cocks." It appears that in 1763 there was no such diversion as public cock-fighting at Edinburgh. In 1783, there were many public cock-fighting matches, or mains, as they were technically termed; and a regular cock-pit was built for the accommodation of this school of gambling and cruelty, where every distinction of rank and character is levelled. In 1790, the cock-pit continued to be frequented." Gunning, in his "Reminiscences of Cambridge," under 1796, observes in a note: "Cock-fighting was much in fashion at this time, and as the races of the country towns approached, matches between the gentlemen of Cambridge and Suffolk were frequently announced." It seems that the defaulters at a cock-pit, like welchers at a horse-race, were roughly treated; for Gunning, speaking of a noted hand at the game, adds: "The last account that reached the University was that he (the defaulter) was seen in the basket, at a cock-pit, the usual punishment for men who made bets which they were unable to pay—." In Brand's time cock-fighting still continued to be a favourite sport of the colliers in the North of England. The clamorous wants of their families solicited them to go to work in vain, when a match was heard of. Brand relates that in performing the service appropriated to the visitation of the sick with a collier, who died a few days afterwards, "to my great astonishment I was interrupted by the crowing of a game cock hung in a bag over his head. To this exultation an immediate answer was given by another cock concealed in a closet, to which the first replied, and instantly the last rejoined. I never remember to have met with an incident so truly of the tragicomical cast as this, and could not proceed in the execution of that very solemn office, till one of the disputants was removed. It had been industriously hung beside him, it should seem for the sake of company. He had thus an opportunity of casting at an object he had dearly loved in the days of his health and strength, what Gray has well called "a long lingering look behind." The authors of "Lancashire Folk Lore," 1867, say: "About thirty years ago, cock-fighting formed a common pastime about Mellor and Blackburn. A blacksmith, named Miller, used to keep a large number of cocks for fighting purposes. He was said to have sold himself to the devil, in order to have money enough for betting, and it was remarked that he rarely won." They also notice that the Denton estates were held in 1780 under leases, the terms of which required the tenants to provide the landlord with a dog and a cock, or the equivalent in money. The late Mr. Thomas Miles, land-agent of Keyham, near Leicester, who probably knew more of the concerns of the families for miles round than any individual of his time, used to mention that Jones, the parson at Ashby, would have a cloth laid over the drawing-room carpet on Sundays between services, and have a couple of cocks in "to give them wind." This was about 1830. Cockfighting is much in vogue even now among the vulgar of all ranks in this country; but it is no longer countenanced either legally or socially. "On Thursday, at the Birmingham Police-court, John Brown, a publican, was summoned to answer the complaint of the police for unlawfully keeping open his house, and acting in the management of a room, for the purpose of fighting of cocks, on the 27th of July last. A detective deposed to having obtained entrance to the defendant's house and to witnessing all the preparations for a cock-fight—the pit, birds, &c. In the evening he again went to the house and found traces of a fight having taken place, as well as cocks which had evidently been engaged in combat. For the defence it was alleged that there had neither been fighting nor intention to fight, and that the birds found trimmed as if for battle had merely been trimmed for the purpose of being painted on canvas. The defendant was ordered to pay a fine of £5 and costs."—*Daily News* for Saturday, Sept. 26, 1868.

Carpentier's *Glossary* calls "Gallorum pugna":—Ludi genus inter pueros scholares, non uno in loco usitati. Lit. remis. An. 1383, in Reg. 134. Chartoph. Reg. ch. 37. "En ce Karesme entrant. . . . à une feste ou dance que l'en faisoit lors d'Enfans pour la jouste des coqs, ainsi qu'il est accoustume (en Dauphiné)." In the same work under the words "Gallorum pugna," A.D. 1458, some differences are mentioned as subsisting between the Mayor and Aldermen of Abbeville, and the Dean and Chapter of the Church of St. Ulfra, which are made up on the following condition: "C'est assavoir que lesdiz Doyen et Cappitre, accordent que doresenavant ilz souffreront et consentiront, que cellui qui demourra Roy d' l'escolle la nuit des Quaresmiaulx apporte ou fache apporter devers le Maieur de laditte Ville ou Camp. S. George, le Cocq, qui demourra ledit jour ou autre jour victorieux, ou autre Cocq; et que ledit Roy presente au dit Maieur *pour d'icellui faire le cholle en la maniere* accoutumée. Du Cange, in his "Glossary," tom. ii. col. 1679, says, that although this practice was confined to school-boys in several provinces of France, it was nevertheless forbidden in the Council of Copria (supposed to be Cognac) in the year 1260. The Decree recites "that although it was then become obsolete, as well in Grammar Schools as in other places, yet mischiefs had arisen, &c." Du Cange *in verbo*, and see Carpentier v. *Jasia*. In a MS. Book of Prayers, executed in the Netherlands at the end of the fifteenth century, one of the representations intended as ornamental designs for the volume, is a cock-fight.

Cock Lorel.—The name of a famous thief, said to have lived in the time of Henry VIII., and by one old writer described as a tinker by trade. The phrase seems to have become generic. Compare Nares, *Glossary*, 1859, in v., and Hazlitt's *Handbook*, 1867, p. 113. The true period of this celebrity is doubtful. Wynkyn de Worde printed a tract, entitled *Cock Lorels Bote*.

Cockney.—The term Cock applied to a man familiarly as a mark of affection is not known to be of any antiquity; but Cockney would otherwise seem to be a colloquial corruption of that monosyllable, and to signify an effeminate person, one who has been over-petted, or as we should say, a milk-sop. I am not so sanguine as Mr. Way ("Prompt. Parv." art. "Cockney,") that the word is to be traced to "Cockayne," an opinion which is apparently shared by Mr. Halliwell, "Archaic Dictionary," 1847, art. "Cockney," but rather think it is the other way. That, having originally signified a spoiled boy or man, it should have acquired the secondary meaning of a Londoner, is by no means strange, when it is considered that Londoners are even now, in the very extended sense of the phrase, looked upon by all the rest of the world as people good for very little beyond sedentary pursuits. In Nash's "Pierce Peniles," 1592, there is the following passage, leaving no doubt as to the writer's interpretation of the term at that period :—"A young heyre, or cockney, that is his mother's darling, if hee have playde the waste-good at the Innes of the Court, or about London, and that neither his students pension, nor his unthrifts credite, will serve to maintaine, &c.," and the citation from a MS. ascribed to the 14th century, in Pegge's *Anecdotes of the English Language*, 1844, p.v. exactly confirms this view: "Puer in deliciis matris nutritus, Anglice a cockney."

Cock Penny. — The scholars at Clitheroe Free Grammar-School had to pay at Shrovetide what is called a cockpenny, which the authors of "Lancashire Folk-Lore," 1867, supposed to be a substitute for bringing the animal itself to school, which formerly was very common. This cock-penny used to be paid also at Burnley Grammar School, but has been long discontinued.

Cockpit. — This term was not only applied to a place where cock-fights were held, and to the theatres in Drury Lane and Whitehall originally devoted to the same purpose, but to the part of a vessel of war, where courts of inquiry were held. There is a tract in verse on this last acceptation by Charles Fletcher, M.D., 1787.

Cock's-Odin. — Cock's-Odin was, from its name, probably a traditionary game handed down from Danish times; for of the Danes there are many memorials scattered all over the Border. The play itself, however, throws no light upon any recognisable circumstance of their cruel invasions. It consisted merely of one boy sent forth to conceal himself within a certain range, and, after due law, the rest set out like so many hounds to discover and catch him if they could. What Odin could have to do with the fugitive I cannot conjecture; and whether the cock's victorious crow can be emblematical of triumph, is only a speculation worthy of a most inveterate Dryasdust.

Cock's-Spur.—Pliny mentions the spur, and calls it Telum, but the gafle is a mere modern invention, as likewise is the great, and, I suppose, necessary exactness in matching them. The Asiatics, however, use spurs that act on each side like a lancet, and which almost immediately decide the battle. Hence they are never permitted by the modern cock-fighters.

Cock-Throwing and **Thrashing.**—The writer of a pamphlet entitled "Clemency to Brutes, &c." 1761, has the following observation : "Whence it had its rise among us I could never yet learn to my satisfaction : but the common account of it is, that the crowing of a cock prevented our Saxon ancestors from massacring their conquerors, another part of our ancestors, the Danes, on the morning of a Shrove Tuesday, whilst asleep in their beds." "Battering with missive weapons a cock tied to a stake, is an annual diversion," says an essayist in the "Gentleman's Magazine," for Jan., 1737, "that for time immemorial has prevailed in this island." A cock has the misfortune to be called in Latin by the same word which signifies a Frenchman. "In our wars with France, in former ages, our ingenious forefathers," says he, "invented this emblematical way of expressing their derision of, and resentment towards that nation ; and poor Monsieur at the stake was pelted by men and boys in a very rough and hostile manner." He instances the same thought at Blenheim House, where over the portals is finely carved in stone the figure of a monstrous lion tearing to pieces a harmless cock, which may be justly called a pun in architecture. Among the games represented in the margin of the "Roman d'Alexandre," in the Bodleian, is a drawing of two boys carrying a third on a stick thrust between his legs, who holds a cock in his hands. They are followed by another boy, with a flag or standard emblazoned with a cudgel. Strutt has engraved the group in pl. xxxv. of his "Sports and Pastimes." He supposes, p. 293, that it represents a boyish triumph : the hero of the party having either won the cock, or his bird escaped unhurt from the dangers to which he had been exposed. The date of the illumination is 1343. Another early example of this custom may be adduced from the fifteenth century poem, "How the Goode Wif Thought hir Daughter." It is where the good wife admonishes her child to avoid certain unbecoming pastimes; she says :

"Goe thou noght to wrastelynge ne she-
        tynge at the cokke,
As it were a strumpet or a gegelotte."

Hence it appears that women and girls were fond of attending these diversions. In common with football, cockthrashing is mentioned, in 1409, as a sport then in vogue, on which certain persons used to levy money under pretence of applying it to the purposes of the players. In Smith's Life of the Fourth Lord Berkeley, who died in 1417, speaking of his recreations and delights, he tells the reader, " Hee also would to the threshing of the cocke, pucke with hens blindfolde and the like." Vol. ii. fol. 459. At Pinner, near Harrow, the cruel custom of throwing at cocks was formerly made a matter of public celebrity, as appears by an ancient account of receipts and expenditures. The money collected at this sport was applied in aid of the poor rates. "1682. Received for cocks at Shrovetide, 12s. 0d. 1628. Received for cocks in towne, 19s. 10d. Out of towne, 6d." This custom appears to have continued as late as the year 1680. Lysons' Environs, vol. ii. p. 588. Quarles, in his Preface to *Argalus and Parthenia*, 1629, allusively to the fate of that work, observes : " I have suffered him to live, that he might stand like a *Jack-a-Lent*, or a *Shroving Cake* for every one to spend a cudgel at." Grose tells us that, " To whip the cock is a piece of sport practised at wakes, horse-races, and fairs, in Leicestershire : a cock being tied or fastened into a hat or basket, half-a-dozen carters, blindfolded, and armed with their cart-whips, are placed round it, who, after being turned thrice about, begin to whip the cock, which if any one strikes so as to make it cry out, it becomes his property ; the joke is that, instead of whipping the cock, they flog each other heartily." Hogarth has satirized this barbarity in the first of the prints called " The Four Stages of Cruelty." Trusler's description is as follows : " We have several groupes of boys at their different barbarous diversions ; one is throwing at a cock, the universal Shrove-tide amusement, beating the harmless feathered animal to jelly." There is a passage in the " Newcastle Courant " for March, 15th, 1783. " Leeds, March 11th, 1783 : Tuesday se'nnight, being Shrovetide, as a person was amusing himself along with several others, with the barbarous custom of throwing at a cock, at Howden Clough, near Birstal, the stick pitched upon the head of Jonathan Speight, a youth about thirteen years of age, and killed him on the spot. The man was committed to York Castle on Friday." In " Witt's Recreations," 1640, it is thus referred to :—

" Cock a-doodle-do, 'tis the bravest
        game,
    Take a cock from his dame,
    And bind him to a stake.

How he strutts, how he throwes,
How he swaggers, how he crowes,
As if the day newly brake.
How his mistris cackles ,
Thus to find him in shackles,
And ty'd to a pack-threed garter ;
    Oh the bears and the bulls
    Are but corpulent gulls
To the valiant Shrove-tide martyr."

The custom of throwing at cocks at Shrove Tuesday was still retained in Mr. Brand's time (1794) at Heston in Middlesex, in a field near the church. Constables (says B.) have been often directed to attend on the occasion, in order to put a stop to so barbarous a custom, but hitherto they have attended in vain. I gathered the following particulars from a person who regretted that in his younger years he had often been a partaker of the sport. The owner of the cock trains his bird for some time before Shrove Tuesday, and throws a stick at him himself, in order to prepare him for the fatal day, by accustoming him to watch the threatened danger, and, by springing aside, avoid the fatal blow. He holds the poor victim on the spot marked out by a cord fixed to his leg, at the distance of nine or ten yards, so as to be out of the way of the stick himself. Another spot is marked, at the distance of twenty-two yards, for the person who throws to stand upon. He has three shys, or throws, for twopence, and wins the cock if he can knock him down and run up and catch him before the bird recovers his legs. The inhuman pastime does not end with the cock's life, for when killed it is put into a hat, and won a second time by the person who can strike it out. Broomsticks are generally used to shy with. The cock, if well trained, eludes the blows of his cruel persecutors for a long time, and thereby clears to his master a considerable sum of money. But I fear lest, by describing the mode of throwing at cocks, I should deserve the censure of Boerhaave on another occasion : " To teach the arts of cruelty is equivalent to committing them." This custom was retained in many schools in Scotland within the 18th century. The schoolmasters were said to preside at the battle, and claimed the run-away cocks, called fugees, as their perquisites. Akerman (" Wiltshire Glossary," 1842, *in voce*) notices this pastime under its local designation of " Cock-Sqwoilin." In " Newmarket : or an Esay on the Turf," 1771, vol. ii. p. 174, we read : " In the Northern part of England it is no unusual diversion to tie a rope across a street and let it swing about the distance of ten yards from the ground. To the middle of this a living cock is tied by the legs. As he swings in the air, a set of young people ride one after another, full speed, under the rope, and rising in their stirrups, catch at the animal's head, which is close clipped and well soaped in order to elude the grasp. Now he who is able to keepe his seat in the saddle and his hold of the bird's head, so as to carry it off in his hand, bears away the palm, and becomes the noble hero of the day." A print of this barbarous custom may be seen in the "Trionfi, &c. della Venetia"; see also Menestrier, "Traité des Tournois," p. 346. The Shrove-Tuesday's massacre of this useful and spirited creature is now virtually at an end, as are also those monstrous barbarities, the battle royal and Welsh main. Compare *Pancakes* and *Shrove-Tuesday.*

Cock Watt, mentioned by Decker in "Jests to make you Merrie," 1607, as "the walking Spirit of Newgate."

Cockle-Bread.—See *Hot Cockles.*

Cockle and Mussel Feast.— At the commencement of November, in accordance with a custom of very ancient origin, members of the Clitheroe Corporation assemble at the annual "cockle and mussel feast" for the purpose of choosing a Mayor for the ensuing year. Although this singular title is still retained, cockles and mussels form only an insignificant portion of the entertainment.

Coffee-Farthings. — See Shrovetide.

Coffin.—We have the very coffin of the present age described in Durandus. "Corpus lotum et sindone obvolutum, ac Luculo conditum, Veteres in cœnaculis, seu Tricliniis exponebant," *Rationale*, p. 225. Loculus is a box or chest. Thus in old registers I find coffins called kists, i.q. chests. Gough's *Sep. Mon.*, ii., *Introd.* In the *Squyr of Low Degrè*, the King's daughter encloses the hero, her lover, as she supposes, in a *maser tre*, i.e., a hollow trunk, with three locks. See *Embalming*, infrâ. "Uncovered coffins of wainscot," observes Mr. Atkinson, in the "Cleveland Glossary," 1868, "were common some years ago, with the initials and figures of the name and age studded on the lid in brass-headed nails; but coffins covered with black are now commonly seen. The coffin is almost never borne on the shoulders, but either suspended by means of towels passed under it, or on short staves provide for the purpose by the undertakers, and which were customarily, in past days, cast into the grave before beginning to fill it up. The author saw one of these bearing staves dug out when re-digging an old grave in August, 1863. Men are usually borne by men, women by women, and children by boys and girls according to sex. Women who have died in childbirth have white sheets thrown over their coffins." Compare *Funeral Customs.*

Colchester Trump.—See *Ruff.*

Coldharbour. — A name found in many parts of England, and under the local appellation elsewhere, and most reasonably explained to signify the shelters once existing in different parts of a country, where a disused residence, Roman or otherwise, had been fitted up for the accommodation of travellers content with temporary protection from the weather; and these places usually consisted of apartments with bare walls. The German equivalent is *Kalten-harberg.* Wright's *Domestic Manners and Sentiments*, 1862, p. 76.

Collop or **Shrove Monday.**— In the North of England, and elsewhere, the Monday preceding Shrove Tuesday or Pancake Tuesday, is called Collop Monday; eggs and collops composed an usual dish at dinner on this day, as pancakes do on the following, from which customs they have plainly derived their names. *Gentleman's Magazine,* 1790, p. 719. It should seem that on Collop Monday they took their leave of flesh in the papal times, which was anciently prepared to last during the winter by salting, drying, and being hung up. Slices of this kind of meat are to this day termed collops in the North, whereas they are called steaks when cut off from fresh or unsalted flesh; a kind of food which I am inclined to think our ancestors seldom tasted in the depth of winter. A collop is a slice of meat or cutlet from an animal, metaphorically a child, in which sense Shakespear and Lyly use it. The etymology is doubtful, unless it is from the old Latin *colponer*, to cut.

Colt-Pixy.—In Hampshire they give the name of colt-pixy to a supposed spirit or fairy, which, in the shape of a horse, wickers, i.e., neighs, and misleads horses into bogs, &c.

Columbaria. — Pigeon-houses, an inheritance, in common with so many others, from the ancient Hellenic farm-yard, formerly maintained on a very large scale both in England and abroad. There was one at Hawthornden, the seat of Drummond the poet. These monastic and seigniorial adjuncts became very obnoxious by reason of the devastations of the pigeons among the crops and orchards, and their prolific increase. Occasionally the buildings were of an ornamental character; see Otto Jahn, *Die Wandgemälde des Columbariums in der Villa Pamfili,* München, 1857, with engravings.

Columbine.—Steevens, commenting on the mention of columbine in "Hamlet," says: "From Cutwode's 'Caltha Poetarum,' 1599, it should seem as if this flower was the emblem of cuckoldom:

'The blue cornuted columbine, Like to the crooked horns of Acheloy.'"

"Columbine," says another of the commentators, S.W. "was an emblem of cuckoldom, on account of the horns of its nectaria which are remarkable in this plant." A third commentator, Holt White, says: "The columbine was emblematical of forsaken lovers:

'The columbine, in tawny often taken,
Is then ascrib'd to such as are forsaken.'"

Browne's *Britannia's Pastorals*, Book ii.

Combination-Room.—The apartment at Cambridge where the fellows retire after dinner for conversation and wine.

Comet.—(i.) In the Earl of Northampton's "Defensative," 1583, sign. v. 4, we read: "When dyvers, upon greater scrupulosity than cause, went about to disswade her Majestye, lying then at Richmonde, from looking on the comet which appeared last; with a courage aunswerable to the greatnesse of her State, shee caused the windowe to be sette open, and cast out thys worde, *jacta est alea*, the dyce are throwne, affirming that her stedfast hope and confidence was too firmly planted in the Providence of God, to be blasted or affrighted with those beames, which either had a ground in Nature whereupon to rise, or at least no warrant out of Scripture to portend the mishappes of Princes." He adds: "I can affirm thus much, as a present witnesse, by mine owne experience." The writer is referring to the comet, or blazing star, which appeared on the 10th October, 1580, some months after the earthquake in April. The latter is supposed to be referred to in *Romeo and Juliet*. Francis Shakleton published an account of the comet of October. (ii.) A game at cards. See Davis, *Suppl. Glossary*, 1881, in v.

Commerce.—See *I am a Spanish Merchant*.

Communion Table.—See *Bowing*.

Communion Tokens.—Pieces of pewter formerly given to those who applied to receive the sacrament, after satisfying the minister that they were fit for such a ceremony.

Conduits.—Speaking of the different conduits in or about London, Strype, in his additions to Stow, says: "These conduits used to be in former times visited. And particularly, on the 18th of Sept., 1562, the Lord Mayor (Harper), Aldermen, and many Worshipful Persons, and divers of the Masters and Wardens of the Twelve Companies, rid to the conduit heads for to see them after the old custom; and afore dinner they hunted the hare, and killed her, and thence to dinner at the Head of the Conduit. There was a good number, entertained with good cheer by the Chamberlain. And after dinner they went to hunting the fox. There was a great cry for a mile; and at length the hounds killed him at the end of S. Giles's. Great hallowing at his death, and blowing of horns." *Survey*, 1720, i., 25.

Confarreation.—The following extract is from an old grant, cited in Du Cange, v. Confarreatio: "Miciacum concedimus et quicquid est Fisci nostri intra Fluminum alveos et *per sanctam Confarreationem et Annulum* inexceptionaliter tradimus." The ceremony used at the solemnnization of a marriage was called confarreation, in token of a most firm conjunction between the man and the wife, with a cake of wheat or barley. This, Blount tells us, is still retained in part with us by that which is called the bride-cake used at weddings. Moffet informs us that "the English, when the bride comes from church, are wont to cast wheat upon her head; and when the bride and bridegroom return home, one presents them with a pot of butter, as presaging plenty, and abundance of all good things." "Health's Improvement," p. 218. This ceremony of confarreation has not been omitted by Moresin ("Papatus," p. 165.) Nor has it been overlooked by Herrick ("Hesperides," p. 128). See also Langley's Polydore Vergil, fol. 9, verso. It was also a Hebrew custom. See Selden's "Uxor Hebraica" (Opera tom. iii. pp. 633, 668). Comp. *Bride-Cake* and *Wedding Cake*.

Conjuration.—There is a curious letter from the Abbot of Abingdon to Secretary Cromwell, about 1536, in which the writer gives an account of a priest who had been captured for practising conjuration. There is the following description of this person: "It shall please your Maistership to be advertised that my officers have taken here a Preyste, a suspecte person, and with hym certeyn bokes of conjuracions, in the whyche ys conteyned many conclusions of that worke; as fyndyng out of tresure hydde, consecratyng of ryngs with stones in theym, and consecratyng of a cristal stone wheryn a chylde shall looke, and se many thyngs. Ther ys also many fygors in hyt whiche haue dyvers thyngs in theym, and amongs all, one the whiche hath a swerde crossed ouer with a septor." King James, in his "Dæmonologie," says: "The art of sorcery consists in divers forms of circles and conjurations rightly joined together, few or more in number according to the number of persons conjurers (always passing the singular number), according to the qualitie of the circle and form of the apparition. Two principal things cannot well in that errand be wanted: holy water (whereby the Devil mocks the papists), and some present of a living thing unto him. There are likewise certain daies and houres that they observe in this purpose. These things being all ready and prepared, circles are made, triangular, quadrangular, round, double, or single, according to the form of the apparition they crave. But to speak of the diverse formes of the circles, of the innumerable characters and crosses that are within and without, and out-through the same; of the diverse forms of apparitions that the craftie spirit illudes them with, and of all such particulars in that action, I remit it over to many that have busied their heads in describing of the same. as being but curious and altogether unprofitable. And this farre only I touch, that, when the conjured spirit appeares, which will not be while after many circumstances long prayers, and much mutterings, and murmurings of the conjurers, like a papiste prieste dispatching a hunting mass—how soon, I say, he appears, if they have missed one jote of all their rites: or if any of their feete once slyd over the circle, through terror of this fearful apparition, he paies himself at that time, in his owne hand, of that due debt which they ought him and otherwise would have delaied longer to have paied him: I meane, he carries them with him, body and soul. If this be not now a just cause to make them weary of these formes of conjuration, I leave it to you to judge upon; considering the longsomeness of the labour, the precise keeping of daies and houres (as I have said), the terribleness of the apparition and the present peril that they stand in, in missing the least circumstance or freite that they ought to observe: and, on the other part, the devill is glad to moove them to a plaine and square dealing with them as I said before." "This," Grose observes, "is a pretty accurate description of this mode of conjuration, styled the circular method; but, with all due respect to his Majesty's learning, square and triangular circles are figures not to be found in Euclid or any of the common writers on geometry. But perhaps King James learnt his mathematics from the same system as Doctor Sacheverell, who, in one of his speeches or sermons, made use of the following simile: 'They concur like parallel lines, meeting in one common center.'"

Conjuror.—Scot tells us that with regard to conjurors, " The circles by which they defend themselves are commonly nine foot in breadth, but the Eastern magicians must give seven." *Discovery*, ed. 1665, 72. Melton, speaking of conjurors, says, "They always observe the time of the moone before they set their figure, and when they set their figure and spread their circle, first exorcise the wine and water, which they sprinkle on their circle, then mumble in an unknown language. Doe they not crosse and exorcise their surplus, their silver wand, gowne, cap, and every instrument they use about their blacke and damnable art? Nay, they crosse the place whereon they stand, because they think the Devill hath no power to come to it, when they have blest it." *Astrologaster*, 1620, p. 16. The following passage occurs in Dekker's " Strange Horse Race," 1613, sign. D 3, " He darting an eye upon them, able to counfound a thousand conjurors in their own circles (though with a wet finger they could fetch up a little devill)." Allusions to this character are not uncommon in our old plays. In " Albumazar," a comedy, 1615:

" He tels of lost plate, horses, and straye cattell
Directly, as he had stolne them all himselfe."

Again, in " Ram Alley," 1611:
— " Fortune-teller, a petty rogue
That never saw five shillings in a heape,
Will take upon him to divine Men's fate,
Yet never knows himselfe shall dy a beggar,
Or be hanged up for pilfering table-cloaths,
Shirts, and smocks, hanged out to dry on hedges."

In Osborne's " Advice to his Son," 1656, p. 100, speaking of the soldiery, that author says, " they, like the spirits of conjurors, do oftentimes teare their masters and raisers in pieces, for want of other imployment." Butler says of his conjuror that he could
" Chase evil spirits away by dint
Of cickle, horse-shoes, hollow flint."

Addison, in his " Drummer, or the Haunted House," has introduced a rather apposite scene:
"Gardn. Prithee, John, what sort of a creature is a conjuror?
Butl. Why he's made much as other men are, if it was not for his long grey beard. His beard is at least half a yard long: he's dressed in a strange dark cloke, as black as a cole. He has a long white wand in his hand.
Coachm. I fancy 'tis made out of witch-elm.
Gard. I warrant you if the ghost appears he'll whisk ye that wand before his eyes, and strike you the drum-stick out of his hand.
Butl. No; the wand, look ye, is to make a circle; and if he once gets the ghost in a circle, then he has him. A circle, you must know, is a conjuror's trap.

Coach. But what will he do with him, when he has him there?

Butl. Why then he'll overpower him with his learning.

Gard. If he can once compass him and get him in Lob's pound, he'll make nothing of him, but speak a few hard words to him, and perhaps bind him over to his good behaviour for a thousand years.

Coachm. Ay, ay he'll send him packing to his grave again with a flea in his ear, I warrant him.

Butl. But if the conjuror be but well paid, he'll take pains upon the ghost and lay him, look ye, in the Red Sea—and then he's laid for ever.

Gardn. Why, John, there must be a power of spirits in that same Red Sea. I warrant ye they are as plenty as fish. I wish the spirit may not carry off a corner of the house with him.

Butl. As for that, Peter, you may be sure that the steward has made his bargain with the cunning man before-hand, that he shall stand to all costs and damages."

Conquering. — This is a game in which schoolboys fit snail-shells together, point to point, and whichever succeeds in breaking the other, is said to be the conqueror. One shell is occasionally the hero, in this way, of a hundred battles, the strength of the shells being very unequal.

Consummation.—In the time of Montaigne, at least, it grew to be a belief in France that when any ill-will or jealousy existed against the husband, the latter might counteract the malignant influence by repeating a certain charm three times, tying at each turn a ribbon, with a medal attached to it, round his middle, the said medal or plate being inscribed with cabalistic characters. The plate was to be placed exactly upon the reins, and the third and last time was to be securely fastened, that it could not slip off, care being also taken to spread a gown on the bed, so as to cover both the man and the woman. We do not hear of any English analogue; yet it is a class of usage which might easily pass into desuetude and oblivion. The same writer has in his graphic and candid fashion adduced many other illustrations of nuptial practices in his country during the sixteenth century; but they fall outside our immediate range. *Essays*, by Hazlitt, 1902, i., 99. Compare *Amulets*, suprâ.

Coral. — The well-known toy, which is generally suspended from the necks of infants to assist them in cutting their teeth, is with the greatest probability supposed to have had its origin in an ancient superstition, which considered coral as an amulet or defensative against fascination: for this we have the authority of Pliny. "Aruspices religiosum Coralli gestamen amoliendis periculis arbitrantur: et Surculi Lnfantiæ alligati tutelam habere creduntur." It was thought too to preserve and fasten the teeth in men. In Bartholomeus "de Proprietatibus Rerum," we read: "Wytches tell, that this stone (*coral*) withstondeth lyghtenynge.—It putteth of lyghtnyng, whirlwynde, tempeste and stormes fro shyppes and houses that it is in. The red coral helpeth ayenst the fendes gyle and scorne, and ayenst divers wonderous doyng and multiplieth fruite and spedeth begynnyng and ending of causes and of nedes." Coles, in his "Adam in Eden," speaking of coral, says: "It helpeth children to breed their teeth, their gums being rubbed therewith; and to that purpose they have it fastened at the ends of their mantles." And Plat, in his "Jewel-House of Art and Nature," 1594, says, "Coral is good to be hanged about children's necks, as well to rub their gums, as to preserve them from the falling sickness: it hath also some special sympathy with nature, for the best coral being worn about the neck, will turn pale and wan, if the party that wears it be sick, and comes to its former colour again, as they recover health." Scot, in his "Discovery of Witchcraft," 1584, says: "The coral preserveth such as bear it from fascination or bewitching, and in this respect they are hanged about children's necks. But from whence that superstition is derived, or who invented the lye I know not: but I see how ready the people are to give credit thereunto by the multitude of corrals that were employed." Steevens informs us that there appears to have been an old superstition that coral would change its colour and look pale when the wearer of it was sick. Reed's *Shakespear*, vii., 308. So in the play of "The Three Ladies of London," 1584:

"You must say jet will take up a straw, amber will make one fat,
Coral will look pale when you be sick, and chrystal will stanch blood."

In Erondel's "French Garden," 1605, edit. 1621, signat. H 2, in a dialogue relative to the dress of a child, we have another proof of the long continuance of this custom: "You need not give him his corall with the small golden chayne, for I beleeve it is better to let him sleepe untill the afternoone."

Corby Pole Fair.—See *Fairs*.

Cork. — *Throwing the Dart by the Mayor of Cork*, an annual usage. See *Illustrated London News*, June 2, 1855.

Cornichon-va-devant.—A kind of game played in France in the sixteenth century, of which the precise nature is uncertain, and therefore whether there is or was any English analogue. Montaigne's *Essays*, by W. C. Hazlitt, 1902, iv., 275.

Corning.—Brand's servant, B. Jelks, informed him that there was a custom in Warwickshire for the poor on St. Thomas's Day, to go with a bag to beg corn of the farmers, which they called going a-corning.

Cornish Leechdoms.—Communicated by the late T. Q. Couch. There are numerous disjointed fragments of superstition which have been so sadly misshapen by time as to defy all attempts to classify them, and yet are worthy of being preserved against the period when the progress of education shall have rendered them obsolete. These are the superstitions connected with animals, plants, and things inanimate, and the medical or other virtues attributed to them. The domestic treatment of disease among our poor consists chiefly of charms and ceremonies, and even when recourse is had to material remedies, as much importance is attached to the rites which attend their employment as to the agents used. In many cases we may notice remnants of the old doctrine of signatures, and the idea of sympathies and antipathies between separate and dissimilar bodies. The brightest coloured decoctions, as saffron-water, are given to "throw out" exanthematous eruptions; whilst the nettle rash is treated by copious draughts of nettle tea. The fisherman, whose hand is wounded by a hook, is very careful to preserve the hook from rust during the healing of the wound.

The following instances will illustrate the household medicine of the poorer of our country people: If the infant is suffering from the thrush, it is taken, fasting, on three following mornings, to have its mouth blown into by a posthumous child. If afflicted with the hooping cough, it is fed with the bread and butter of a family, the heads of which bear respectively the names John and Joan. In the time of an epidemic, so numerous are the applications, that the poor couple have little reason to be grateful to their godfathers and godmothers for their gift of these particular names. Or, if a piebald horse is to be found in the neighbourhood, the child is taken to it, and passed thrice under the belly of the animal; the mere possession of such a beast confers the power of curing the disease. The owner of a piebald horse states that he has frequently been stopped on the road by anxious mothers, who inquired of him, in a casual way, what was good for the hooping cough? and the thing he mentioned, however inappropriate or absurd, was held to be a certain remedy in that particular case. The passing of children through holes in the earth, rocks, or trees,

was once an established rite, and the old Saxon penitentiaries record strict and protracted fasts against "the woman who useth any witchcraft to her child, or who draws it through the earth at the meeting of roads, because that is great heathenness." Remnants of this Pagan usage are still to be observed among the peasantry. Boils are said to be cured by creeping on the hands and knees beneath a bramble which has grown into the earth at both ends. Children afflicted with hernia are still passed through a slit made in an ash sapling, before sunrise, fasting, after which the slit portions are bound up, in the hope that, as they unite, the malady will be cured. The ash is a tree of many virtues: venomous reptiles are never known to rest under its shadow, and a single blow from an ash-stick is instant death to an adder; struck by any other wand, it is said to retain marks of life, till the sun goes down. The mountain ash, or care, has a still greater reputation in the curing of ills arising from supernatural as well as ordinary causes: it is the dread of evil spirits, and renders null the spells of the witch. The countryman will carry for years a small piece of it in his pocket, as a protection against the ill-wish, or as a remedy for the rheumatism. If his cow is out of health, and he suspects that she is overlooked, away he runs to the nearest wood and brings home branches of care, which he suspends over her stall, or wreathes round her horns, after which he considers her safe. The cure for warts are many and various. A piece of flesh is taken secretly, rubbed over the warts, and buried in the earth, and as the flesh decays the warts vanish. Or some mysterious vagrant desires to have them carefully counted, and, marking the number on the inside of his hat, leaves the neighbourhood, and takes the warts with him.

There are a few animals the subject of superstitious veneration, and a much greater number whose actions are supposed to convey intimations of the future. We are too little acquainted with the details of the practice of augury among the Druids, and the differences between it and its observance by our Saxon and Danish forefathers, to be able to mark the origin of each particular superstition; at all events the belief is too general to have been the result of local or individual observation, and has all the appearance of being a system once entire, but long since exploded. The desire to look into the future belongs to all times and all conditions; but the persistency and generality with which the faculty of foreshadowing coming events has been attached to particular animals is very remarkable. In some instances it would almost seem as if they were considered more in the light of causes than prognostics; yet as the doctrine of fatalism, in a restricted sense, runs through all our popular beliefs, we may consider, for instance, the conduct of the inhospitable housewife who drives off the cock that crows upon the door-step, warning her of the approach of strangers, as only a fresh illustration of a very old fallacy, which consists in the belief that when the prophet is silenced, his predictions are averted. Here are some of our superstitions connected with certain animals. The howling of dogs, the continued croaking of ravens over a house, and the ticking of the death-watch, portend death. The magpie is a bird of good or ill omen, according to the number seen at one time. A crowing hen is a bird of ill-luck. A country lad informed me that if, on first hearing the cuckoo, the sounds proceed from the right, it signifies "that you will go vore in the world"; if from the left, "that the ensuing year will be one of ill-fortune." Particular honour is paid to the robin and the wren. It is a very prevalent belief that a pillow stuffed with the feathers of wild birds delays the departure of the dying. Death is also thought to be prolonged until the ebb of the tide. The killing of the first adder seen for the season is a sign that the person is to triumph over his enemies. The slough of an adder hung to the rafters preserves the house against fire. The wonderful polity of bees could scarcely have escaped observation in the earliest ages, and they were accordingly supposed to be endued with a portion "divinæ mentis." Our forefathers appear to have been among those who considered bees as possessing something higher than ordinary instinct, for there is yet a degree of deference paid to them that would scarcely be offered to beings endowed with only the usual kind of animal intelligence. On the death of any relative, the husbandman takes care to acquaint the bees of it, by moving the hive, or putting it in mourning by attaching to it pieces of black cloth or crape; which neglected, they are said to leave the hive. The sale of bees is a very unlucky proceeding, so they are always given, and a bushel of wheat (the constant value of a swarm) is expected in return. In some house where death has occurred, the indoor plants are also hung with black, for if this be neglected they are said to droop and die. The cricket is a bringer of good luck, and its departure from a house is a sign of coming misfortune. Among the omens believed in, or existing in proverbs, we may further mention that the breaking of a looking-glass entails seven years' trouble, but no want. The dirgeful singing of children portends

a funeral. There is scarcely a sensation but has its meaning. If you shudder, it implies that some one is walking over the spot that is to be your grave. If the left palm itches, you will soon have to pay; if the right, to receive money. If the knee itches, you will kneel in a strange church. If the sole of the foot tingles, you will walk over strange ground. If the ear tingles, you will hear of "hastis" news. If the cheek burns, some one is talking scandal of you. I have frequently heard the following lines spoken:

> "Right cheek! left cheek! why do you burn?
> Cursed be she that doth me any harm.
> If it be a maid, let her be staid:
> If it be a widow; long let her mourn:
> But if it be my own true love,
> Burn, cheek, burn!"

Even the white patches at the roots of the nails, called *gifts*, are not without their significance.

Cornish Pixies, The.—The legends which follow are taken from a manuscript collection, all careful copies of oral traditions still extant; the first was communicated to the *Athenæum*, many years ago, by the late Jonathan Couch of Polperro; the remainder were furnished to the present writer by his son, the late Mr. Couch of Bodmin: A farmer, who formerly lived on an estate in this neighbourhood called Langreek, was returning one evening from a distant part of the farm, and in crossing a particular field, saw, to his surprise, sitting on a stone in the middle of it, a miserable looking creature, human in appearance, though dwarfish in size, and apparently starving with cold and hunger. Pitying its condition, and perhaps aware that it was of elfish origin, and that good luck would amply repay him for his kind treatment of it, he took it home, placed it by the warm hearth on a stool, fed it with milk, and shewed it great kindness. Though at first lumpish, and only half sensible, the poor bantling soon revived, and though it never spoke, became lively and playful. From the amusement it gave by its strange tricks, it soon became a general favourite in the family. After the lapse of three or four days, whilst it was at play, a shrill voice in the farm yard or "town place," was heard to call three times,—"Colman Grey!" at which the little fellow sprang up, and gaining voice, cried, "Ho! ho! ho! my daddy is come!" flew through the key-hole, and was never afterwards heard of. A field on the Langreek estate retains the name of "Colman Grey" to this day. The pixies seem to have delighted in mischief for its own sake. Old Robin Hicks, a fisherman of Polperro who, many years ago, lived in a house on the cliffs near the quay, has more than once, on stormy winter nights, been alarmed at his supper by a voice sharp and shrill, coming apparently through the key-hole—"Robin! Robin! your boat's adrift!" He has risen and hastened down on the quay to find his boat riding safely at her moorings. The piskies would testify their joy at the success of their deceit by laughing and "tacking their hands." Another story is told by our fishermen but many of its particulars are forgotten. John Taprail, long since dead, had moored his boat in the evening beside a barge of much larger size belonging to John Rendle, who traded in her between this place and Plymouth. In the middle of the night he was awoke by a voice requesting him to get up and "shift his rope over Rendle." He accordingly rose, but found to his chagrin that he had been called unnecessarily, for both the boat and the barge were riding quietly at their ropes. On his way back again, when very near his home, he observed a number of the little people arranged in a circle under shelter of a boat that was lying high and dry on the beach. Each was holding his little cap in his hand, except one, who, sitting in the centre, was engaged in distributing a heap of money, throwing it into the caps after the manner in which cards are dealt. John Taprail crept slily towards them sheltered by the boat, and reaching round his own cap managed to introduce it into the circle. When it had received a good portion of the money, he slowly and cautiously withdrew it, and made off with the booty : the interloper, however, was discovered, and the whole circle joined in pursuing him. Having got a good start of the piskies, he managed to reach his house, and to close the door on his pursuers; but his escape was a narrow one, for he had left the skirts of his sea coat in their hands. The next tradition well shows their caprice, and that they are easily offended by an offer of reward, however delicately tendered. A farmer, residing at a particular farmhouse in this neighbourhood, was surprised at the extraordinary quantity of corn which was threshed during the night, as well as puzzled to discover the mysterious agency by which it was effected. His curiosity led him to enquire closely into the matter. One moonlight night he crept stealthily to the barn-door, looked through a chink and, to his astonishment, saw a little fellow, clad in a ragged green suit, wielding the flail with great skill and rapidity. The farmer crept away unperceived, feeling very grateful to the pisky for his services. All night he lay awake, thinking in what way he could best show his gratitude. He settled, at length, that as the little fellow's clothes were somewhat the worse for wear, the gift of a new suit would be the proper way to lessen the obligation ; so he had a suit of green made of what he judged to be the proper size, and this he carried early in the evening to the barn, and left there for the pisky's acceptance. At night he stole to the barn-door, to see how the gift was taken. He was just in time to see the elf put on the suit, with which he was very well pleased, for, looking down on himself, admiringly, he sang—

"Pisky fine, and pisky gay,
Now will pisky fly away."

From thenceforth the farmer received no assistance from the fairy flail. Another version of the pisky's song, equally common with the above, is—

"Pisky new coat, and pisky new hood,
Pisky now will do no more good."

It is said of another farmer that he discovered two piskies threshing lustily in his barn, now and then interrupting their work, and enquiring of each other, in the smallest falsetto voice, "I tweat! you tweat?" After a while the flails ceased, and they surveyed their work. "We've threshed enough," observed one. "Quite enough! and thank ye!" said the incautious farmer. The elves instantly vanished, and never more visited that barn. It will scarcely be necessary to remind the reader of the similarity of these tales and those which Milton speaks of as told by a country hearth. A farmer's boy, living at Portallow, was sent, one dark night, to procure some little household necessaries from a shop at Polperro. He was trudging backwards, having executed his business at the grocer's, and had reached Talland-sand hill, when he heard some one say, "I'm for Portallow green!" "As you are going my way," thought the lad, "I may as well have your company." Accordingly he listened for a repetition of the voice, intending to hail it. "I'm for Portallow green!" was repeated after a short interval. "I'm for Portallow green!" shouted the boy. Quick as thought he found himself on the green, surrounded by a throng of little laughing pixies. They were, however, scarcely settled before the cry was heard from several tiny voices, "I'm for Seaton beach!" (a fine expanse of sand on the coast between Looe and Plymouth, and about seven miles distant from Portallow). Whether he was charmed by this brief taste of pisky society, or was taken with their pleasant mode of travelling, is not stated, but he immediately rejoined, "I'm for Seaton beach!" Off he was whisked, and in a moment found himself on Seaton beach, engaged in a dance of the most lively and fantastic kind, for the nimble manner in which his feet were flung about, in measure with the fairy tune which was played by one of the elves, was a perfect wonder to himself. After they had for a while danced "their ringlets to the whistling wind," the cry was changed to "I'm for the King of France's cellar!" Strange to say, he offered no objection even to so long a journey. "I'm for the King of France's cellar!" shouted the adventurous youth, as he threw his parcel on the edge of the beach, near the tide. Immediately he found himself in a spacious cellar engaged with his mysterious companions in tasting the richest of wines, after which they passed through grand rooms, fitted up with a splendour which quite dazzled him. The tables were covered with fine plate and rich viands, as if in expectation of a feast. Thinking it would be as well to take away with him some small memorial of his travels, he pocketed a rich silver goblet. After a short stay, the piskies said, "I'm for Seaton beach," which was repeated by the boy, and he was taken back as quickly as he went, reaching the beach in time to recover his parcel from the flowing tide. Their next destination was Portallow Green, where they left our wondering traveller, who soon reached his home, delivered his message, and received a compliment from the good wife for his dispatch. "You'd say so, if you only know'd where I've been," said he. "I've been with the piskies to Seaton beach, and I've been to the King of France's cellar, and all in five minutes." "The boy is mazed," said the farmer. "I thought you'd say I was mazed, if I didn't bring something with me to show vor't," he replied, at the same time producing the goblet. The farmer and his family examined it, wondered at it, and finished by giving a full belief to the boy's strange story. The goblet is unfortunately not now to be produced in proof to those who may still doubt, but we are told that it remained the property of the boy's family for generations after. Our legend of the pisky midwife is so well related by Mrs. Bray, in her book on the "Tamar and Tavy," that it need not be again told, the only material difference being, that it was the accidental application to her right eye of the soap with which she was washing the baby that opened to her the secrets of fairy-land. I have been unable to discover any traces of a belief in water spirits. An old man, just deceased, was accustomed to relate that he saw on a stormy day a woman, her face buried in her long dank locks, sitting on the rocks at Talland sand, and weeping. On his approach, she slid into the sea, and disappeared. The story is easily accounted for by supposing that he saw a seal (an animal that has been noticed in that locality on more than one occasion), the long hair being an allowable embellishment. Our fishermen talk of "môrmaids," and the egg-cases of the rays and sharks are popularly called "môrmaids' purses." It is extremely doubtful whether they formed a part of the old mythology.

Besides the piskies, but of a widely different character and origin, are the spectre huntsman and his pack, known as the "Devil and his dandy dogs." The genius of this tradition is essentially Scandinavian, and reminds us of the "Wirtend heer," and the grim sights and terrible sounds which affright the peasant at night in the forests of the north. Though at first the frightful spectres were the ghosts of slain warriors speeding from Valhalla, and pursuing their prey through the murky air, the tradition has become variously altered in different countries, but in all retaining enough of the terrible to mark its derivation. The "Devil and his dandy dogs" frequent our bleak and dismal moors on tempestuous nights, and are also occasionally heard in the more cultivated districts by the coasts, where they are less frightful in their character. They are most commonly seen by those who are out at nights on wicked errands, and woe betide the poor wretch who crosses their path. An interesting legend will illustrate the little we have heard of this superstition in its wilder forms. A poor herdsman was journeying homeward across the moors one windy night, when he heard, at a distance among the tors, the baying of hounds which, time and circumstances considered, he immediately recognised as the dismal chorus of the dandy dogs. Very much alarmed, he hurried onwards as fast as the treacherous nature of the soil and the uncertainty of the path would allow; but the melancholy yelping of the hounds, and the holloa of the huntsman as it sounded across the waste, became every moment nearer and nearer. After a considerable run, they had so gained upon him, that on looking back he could distinctly see hunter and dogs. The former was terrible to look at, and had the usual complement of "saucer" eyes, horns, and tail, accorded by the common consent of story-tellers to the legendary devil. He was, of course, black, and carried a long hunting-pole. The dogs, too, were black, many in number, each of them snorting fire, and uttering a yelp of peculiarly frightful character. With no cottage, rock, or tree to give him shelter, in despair he was about to abandon himself to their fury, when at once a happy thought suggested a resource. Just as they were about to rush upon him he fell on his knees in prayer, earnest no doubt. Immediately, as if resistance had been offered, the whole pack stood at bay, howling loudly and dismally. The hunter shouted " bo shrove !" "which," says my informant, " means in the old language, ' the boy prays ! ' " and at the words they all drew off and disappeared. The dandy dogs are not unfrequently seen on the sea-coast, and the stories told are so well attested, that there is reason to conclude the narrators have really seen a pack of weasels, of which it is well known that they hunt gregariously at night, and when so engaged do not scruple to attack man.

It is certainly surprising to find those stories which we have been taught to associate with a particular house or family told of persons and places very remote. There is, however, only space here to point to certain instances of this community of fable. There is a great similarity, for instance, between the story of Colman Grey, and that of Gilpin Homer, as given in the notes to the " Lay of the Last Minstrel," and we are reminded of the same story when reading of the " Killcrops," in Luther's " Colloquia Mensalia." Our story of the pisky thresher has its counterpart in the fairy lore of almost all the countries in Europe, and so close is the resemblance, that the pisky song would seem almost a verbatim translation from one language to another. In England, at Hilton Hall, the fairy sang—

" Here's a cloak, and here's a hood !
The cauld lad of Hilton will do no more good."

The brownie of Scotland is offended in like manner at a present of clothes, and cries :

" A new mantle and a new hood !
Poor Brownie ! ye'll ne'er do mair gude."

The tale of the midwife is also of very wide distribution, and may be found, with slight variation, in Gervase of Tilbury. The legend of " I'm for Portallow green " resembles, in many points, that told of Lord Duffus, in the " Minstrelsy of the Scottish Border "; and that related of a butler in the noble house of Monteith. The reader will also be reminded of the story of the "Haunted Cellar," by Crofton Croker. These curious superstitions have received many modifications in the course of ages. The promulgators of later creeds appear to have despaired at the task of rooting out old and stubborn prejudices, and to have preferred grafting their new doctrines on the old. As instances of these modifications may be mentioned, the widely spread belief that piskies are the souls of unbaptized children ; the modern name of the spectre huntsman and his hounds ; and the efficacy of prayer in driving off the latter. From the little I know of the fairy superstitions of Cornwall (which little has been gleaned entirely from oral tradition), it would not be easy to classify the beings of the popular creed : still there are characteristics which, when more is known of them, may serve to distribute them into classes resembling those of the continental nations, whose mythology has kept its distinctions more definitely than our own. Our domestic spirit, who rewards the thrifty servant, and punishes the slattern, and who, in the old manor house at Killigarth, when the family was at church, was wont to watch the joint as it roasted on the spit, and to admonish the servant to remove it when sufficiently drest, agrees with the gobelin of Normandy, the kobold of Germany, the nisse of Norway, the Tomte gubbe of Sweden, and the brownie of Scotland, and may be found distinct from our little pastoral fairy, whose chief amusement is music and dancing, laughter and mischief, and who makes those rings in our meadows " of which the ewe not bites."

In Cornwall we might expect to find the " swart fairy of the mine " occupying a prominent place in our mythology. It would therefore be interesting to know whether this is the case from those who are acquainted with the " folk lore " of our mining districts, especially as it has been a disputed point whether the Duegars or dwarf tribe dwelling in hills and caverns, and distinguished for their skill in metallurgy really formed a portion of the old belief, or were, as Sir Walter Scott thought them, the diminutive natives of the Lappish and Finnish nations, driven to the mountains by their invaders. The general belief seems to be " that they are personifications of the subterraneous powers of nature "; for. as Keightley observes, " all parts of every ancient mythology are but personified powers, attributes, and moral qualities."

There is " An account of Anne Jefferies, now living in the county of Cornwall, who was fed for six months by a small sort of airy people called fairies ; and of the strange and wonderful cures she performed, with salves and medicines she received from them, for which she never took one penny of her patients : In a letter from Moses Pitt to the right reverend Father in God, Dr. Edward Fowler, Lord Bishop of Gloucester : 1696." This tract states that Anne Jefferies (for that was her maiden name) was born in the parish of St. Teath in the county of Cornwall, in December, 1626, and is still living, 1696, aged 70. She is married to one William

Warren, formerly hind to the late eminent physician Dr. Richard Lower, deceased, and now to S^r. Andrew Slanning of Devon, Bart.—That A.D. 1645, as she was one day sitting knitting in an arbour in the garden there came over the hedge of a sudden, six persons of a small stature all clothed in green, which frighted her so much as to throw her into a great sickness. They continued their appearance to her, never less than two at a time, nor never more than eight, always in even numbers, 2, 4, 6, 8. "She forsook eating our victuals" (continues the narrator in whose family she lived as a servant) "and was fed by these fairies from the harvest time to the next Christmas Day; upon which day she came to our table and said, because it was that day she would eat some roast beef with us, which she did, I myself being then at table. One day," he adds, "she gave me a piece of her fairy bread, which I did eat, and think it was the most delicious bread that ever I did eat, either before or since. One day," the credulous narrator goes on, "these fairies gave my sister Mary a silver cup which held about a quart, bidding her give it my mother; but my mother would not accept it. I presume this was the time my sister owns she saw the fairies. I confess to your lordship I never did see them. I have seen Anne in the orchard dancing among the trees; and she told me she was then dancing with the fairies." Morgan's "Phœnix Britannicus," p. 545. Morgan tells us that the copy from which he reprinted it had at the bottom of its title-page this N.B in MS.: "Recommended by the Right Rev. to his friend Mrs. Eliz. Rye." He means, no doubt, the above Bishop of Gloucester, who it should seem had tacked to his creed this article of belief in fairies. It is with great diffidence that I shall venture to consider Anne's case *en Medicin*; yet I presume some very obvious physical reasons might be given why a wench of nineteen should fall into sickness and see objects that were green without the smallest necessity of calling in the aid of the marvellous. It appears that Anne was afterwards thrown into gaol, as an impostor, nor does even the friendly narrator of her singular story, Moses Pitt, give us any plausible account why the fairies, like false earthly friends, forsook her in the time of her distress.

Cornlaiters.—Hutchinson, speaking of the parish of Whitbeck, says: "Newly married peasants beg corn to sow their first crop with, and are called cornlaiters." *Cumberland*, i., 553.

Corporal Oath is supposed to have been derived—"not from the touching of the New Testament, or the bodily act of kissing it, but from the ancient use of touching the *Corporale*, or cloth which covered the consecrated elements."

Corpus Christi Day. — Corpus Christi Day, a moveable feast, is in all Roman Catholic countries celebrated with music, lights, flowers strewed all along the streets, their richest tapestries hung out upon the walls, &c. In the Municipal Records of York, there are vestiges of the performance of the Corpus Christi Play in that city as far back as 1388, and from a fragment of the Chamberlain's Account for 1397, which is extant, we learn that in the latter year the King was present at the spectacle; but from the general tenor of later entries among the archives, there can be no question, that the practice was of far higher antiquity than the reign of Richard II. Mr. Davies, who enters into long details on this subject, says: "The Corporation took great pains to render the exhibition acceptable to their royal visitor. Barriers were erected for the King's accommodation; the pageant was repaired and newly painted; four new scenes and a new banner were provided; the players and the city minstrels were paid additional rewards; and the minstrels of the king and his suite, which probably took part in the performances, received a liberal gratuity." In the Extracts, 18 Edward IV., are two entries relative to the performance of the Corpus Christi play at York in that year: "And paid for a banner of Thomas Gaunt, for the Corpus Christi play, at the inn of Henry Watson, 4d. And paid Margaret the sempstress for the repair of the banners of the Corpus Christi play, 3d." Mr. Davies observes: "We possess no authentic information of the time, when the observance of the festival was first introduced into England."

The Chronicle of Sprott, which notices its institution by Pope Urban IV., whose pontificate commenced in 1261, records 'the confirmation of the festival of Corpus Christi' in the year 1318; and perhaps, during this interval, it was transplanted from Italy into other parts of the Christian world. . . In the year 1313, Philip the Fair gave in Paris one of the most sumptuous fêtes that had been seen for a long time in France. The King of England, Edward II., was invited expressly, and crossed the sea with his Queen Isabella, and a splendid train of nobility. . . In the reign of Edward II. was written the miracle play of the 'Harrowing of Hell,' the earliest dramatic composition hitherto discovered in the English language. It seems therefore not improbable that the celebration of the Corpus Christi festival on its first introduction into this country was accompanied by the exhibition of pageant plays produced by the several companies, into which the tradesmen and artizans of cities and towns were then incorporated." Extracts from the Records of York, 1843, "Appendix," p. 228-9; York Plays, edited by Miss Toulmin Smith, 1885, Introduction.

The following is an account of the expenses incurred on the occasion: "And in expenses incurred this year by the Mayor, aldermen, and many others of the Council of the Chamber at the Feast of Corpus Christi, seeing and directing the play in the house of Nicholas Bewick, according to custom, together with 40s. 4d. paid for red and white wine, given and sent to knights, ladies, gentlemen, and nobles then being within the city; and also 9s. paid for the rent of the chamber, and 3s. 4d. paid to one preaching and delivering a sermon on the morrow of the said feast, in the Cathedral Church of St. Peter of York, after the celebration of the procession, according to the like custom. . . . £4 18s. 11d." In the churchwardens' and chamberlain's accounts at Kingston occur these entries: "21 Hen. VII. Mem. That we, Adam Backhous and Harry Nycol, amountyd of a Play. . . . £4 0s. 0d. 27 Hen. VII. Paid for pack-thred on Corpus Christi day, 1d." "This," Lysons observes, "was probably used for hanging the pageants, containing the History of our Saviour, which were exhibited on this day, and explained by the Mendicant Friars." In the same accounts for St. Mary at Hill, London, 17 and 19 Edw. IV., the following entry occurs: "Garlands on Corpus Christi Day, xd." I find also among the Church disbursements: "For four (six, or eight) men bearing torches about the parish" on this day, payments of 1d. each. Among the same accounts, for the 19 and 20 Edward IV., we have: "For flaggs and garlondis, and pak-thredde for the torches, upon Corpus Christi Day, and for six men to bere the said torches, iiijs. vijd." And in 1845, "For the hire of the garments for pageants, is. viijd." In the Wax-Chandlers' account, 1512, a charge of 2s. 8d. is made for garnishing eight torches on Corpus Christi Day. Rose-garlands on Corpus Christi Day are also mentioned under 1524 and 1525, in the accounts of St. Martin Outwich. In "John Bon and Mast Person" (1548), by Luke Shepherd, the parson commends John for leaving his work early in order to attend the celebration of Corpus Christi, for, says he:—

"— Surely some ther be wyl go to ploughe an carte,
And set not by thys holy Corpus Christi even.
   John. They are more to blame, I swere by saynt Steuen,

But tell me, mast person, one thing, and you can;
What Saynt is Copsi Curtsy, a man or a woman?"

At the celebration of the Feast of Corpus Christi, at Aix in Provence, there is a procession of saints, among whom St. Simeon is represented with a mitre and cap, carrying in his left hand a basket of eggs. *Hist. de la Fête Dieu,* p. 100. Douce. Naogeorgus ("Popish Kingd." transl. by Googe, 1570, fol. 53 verso) describes at some length the customs prevalent in his day in Germany on Corpus Christi Day.

Corpus Christi Eve.—In North Wales, at Llanasaph, there is a custom of strewing green herbs and flowers at the doors of houses on Corpus Christi Eve.— *Pennant.*

Corvina Stone.—A sort of amulet named in the work of John Florio, 1625, as having been given by Ferdinando, Grand Duke of Tuscany, to Anne of Denmark, and as having passed into the possession of the testator who bequeathed it to William Earl of Pembroke. Florio describes it in his *Italian Dictionary,* 1611, as a stone of many virtues, which they say is found in a raven's nest, fetcht thither by the raven, if in her absence a man have sodden bad eggs, and laid them in the nest again, to make them new again. *Corvina* readily suggests the etymology *corvo.*

Coscinomantia.—Of *coscinomantia* it is said, that this method of divination is assisted by spirits, and that it was considered a surer one than any other by the people on the continent. The process was accomplished by two persons holding the sieve with a forceps or pair of pincers by their middle fingers, and repeating six unintelligible words over it; whereupon, the names of all those who are suspected of the theft, act of violence, or whatever it may be that they seek to discover, being called, at the mention of the culprit the utensil moves, trembles, or turns round under the influence of the presiding (though invisible) spirit, and the divination is completed. Delrio's account is similar, *Disquis. Magicæ,* 245; and it has been merely translated (as it were) by Grose. Holiday, an English author, who repeats the same description, adds, that the ceremony was also employed for the purpose of ascertaining whom such an one was to have in marriage. *Marriage of the Arts,* 1618, ed. 1630, 92. The charm is not overlooked by Mason and Melton. *Anotomie of Sorcerie,* 1612, 9; *Astrologaster,* 1620, 45. Lodge seems to intimate that it was sometimes performed by a sieve and key, *Wits Miserie,* 1596, p. 12, which was no doubt the case, as this other form of the operation is explained in a later work thus : " A Bible having a key fastened in the middle, and being held between the two forefingers of two persons, will turn round after some words said ; as, if one desires to find out a thief, a certain verse taken out of a Psalm is to be repeated, and those who are suspected nominated, and if they are guilty, the book and key will turn, else not." *Athenian Oracle*, i., 425. Scot tells us that " Popish Priests, as the Chaldeans used the divination by sive and sheers for the detection of theft, do practice with a Psalter and key fastened upon the forty-ninth (fiftieth) Psalm to discover a thief ; and when the names of the suspected persons are orderly put into the pipe of the key at the reading of these words of the Psalm ' If thou sawest a thief thou did'st consent unto him,' the Book will wagg, and fall out of the fingers of them that hold it, and he whose name remaineth in the key must be the thief." *Discovery*, ed. 1665, p. 286. This is called in the *Athenian Oracle* (ii., 309) " The trick of the sieve and Scizzars, the coskiniomancy of the Antients, as old as Theocritus : "

> " To Agrio too I made the same demand,
> A cunning woman she, I cross'd her hand :
> She turn'd the sieve and sheers, and told me true,
> That I should love, but not be lov'd by you."

The original words are : —

Εἶπε καὶ ᾿Αγροιὼ ταλαθέα, κοσκινόμαντις,
῍Α πρὰν ποιωλογεῖσα, παραιβάτις, οὖνεκ᾽ ἐγὼ μεν
Τὶν ὅλος ἔγκειμαι· τὺ δὲ μεῦ λόγον οὐδένα ποιῇ.

Agrippa devotes the 21st chapter of his *Occult Philosophy* to this subject, and furnishes a representation from an iron plate of the mode of performing this species of divination. He says : " Huc enim Coscinomantia scribenda venit, quæ Dæmone urgente, per Cribrum Divinationem suscitari docet, quis rei patratæ author sit, quis hoc commiserit furtum, quis hoc dederit vulnus, aut quicquid tale fuerit. Cribrum enim inter duorum astantium medios digitos, per forcipem suspendunt, ac dejuratione facta per sex Verba, nec sibi ipsis, nec aliis intellecta, quæ sunt : *Dies Mies Jeschet Benedoftet, Dovvina Enitemaus*, Dæmonem in hoc compellunt ut reo nominato (nam omnes suspectos nominare oportet) confestim circum agatur sed per obliquum instrumentum è forcipe pendens, ut reum prodat : Iconem hic ponimus. Annis abactis plus minus triginta, ter hujus divinationis genere sum ipse usus—ubi semper pro voto aleam cecidisse comperi. Hanc Divinationem cæteris arbitrabantur veri-

orem, sicut etiam Erasmus scribit in proverbio, ' Cribro divinare.' "
Butler mentions this :—

> " Th' oracle of sieve and shears,
> That turns as certain as the spheres."

Hudibras, Part 2, iii., 559. But, after all, it may remain a matter of legitimate doubt, whether this superstition was ever widely prevalent in England. Scot is the earliest writer of our nation who refers to it, and his testimony does not seem to disturb an impression that all the English accounts (which implicitly follow each other) are borrowed from the continental writers, and do not establish the existence of this mode of detection as a genuine English practice or belief, except as a marriage charm.

Cotswold Games.—These were athletic sports annually held in those parts, especially about Willersley and Chipping-Campden. They seem to have been established by Robert Dover, an attorney of Barton on the Heath, in Warwickshire, son of John Dover, a Norfolk man ; and James I. allowed him to appropriate for the temporary purpose a certain open space, while Endimion Porter, a gentleman whose name is agreeably associated with those of many of the literary celebrities of the time, procured him some of the King's wardrobe, including a hat and feather, and ruff. Dover entered with great spirit into this entertainment, which seems to have spread over two days ; a large concourse of people assembled to witness the proceedings ; and in 1636 an account of the custom, with encomiastic verses by poets of the day, appeared, embellished with a frontispiece illustrative of some of the features of the programme. The usage was interrupted by the Civil War, but subsequently revived and still remained in vogue in the time of Rudder the Gloucestershire historian. The anniversary was then celebrated at a point called Dover's Hill, on Thursday in Whitsun week. *Poetical Works of William Basse* (1602-53), 1893, pp. 105-6.

Coxcomb.—Originally the fool's cap, from the comb with which it was decorated. Comp. Nares, 1859, in v. In a secondary and now more usual sense the word now denotes a vain, conceited, meddling fellow. *Reed's Shakespear*, 1803, vol. xvii. p. 358. In " The First Part of Antonio and Mellida," 1602, we read : " Good faith, Ile accept of the cockescombe so you will not refuse the bable."

Crack-Nut Sunday.—The Sunday next before Michaelmas Eve. The practice was carried on in Church by all ages, so as to disturb the service. See Brayley and Britton's *Surrey*, iii., 41, referring particularly to Kingston.

Cramp.—In "Ovid Travestie," 1673, Epistle of Hero to Leander, the following charms are facetiously mentioned as specifics against cramp:

"——Wear bone ring on thumb, or tye
Strong pack-thread below your thigh."

In the North of England, the children run round the tree, repeating these verses:

"Cramp, be thou painless,
As our Lady was sinless,
When she bare Jesus."

Mr. Brand remembered that is was a custom in the North of England for boys that swam, to wear an eel skin about their naked leg to prevent the cramp. Rings made from coffin-hinges are supposed to do so. See Grose's "Dictionary of the Vulgar Tongue," v. Scower.

Cramp-Rings.—Borde, in his "Introduction to Knowledge," 1542, speaking of England, says: "The Kynges of Englande doth halowe every yere crampe rynges, ye which rynges worne on ones fynger doth helpe them whych hath the crampe." The same author, in his "Breviary of Health," 1557, fol. 166, speaking of the cramp, adopts the following superstition among the remedies thereof: "The Kynges Majestie hath a great helpe in this matter in halowyng crampe ringes, and so geven without money or petition." The ceremonies of blessing cramp rings on Good Friday will be found in Waldron's "Literary Museum," 1789.—*Douce.* In Cartwright's *Ordinary.* apparently written in 1634, Moth the Antiquary betrothes the widow Potluck with "his biggest cramp-ring." In the *Life of Benvenuto Cellini,* by himself, (1500-71), it is stated that these rings were imported from England into Italy in the sixteenth century, and cost tenpence. They were then known as *anelli del granchio;* but they now term them *anelli di salute.* Note in the Engl. transl. by J. A. Symonds, 3rd ed. p. 301.

Creeling.—In the "Statistical Account of Scotland," 1792, the minister of Galston, in Ayrshire, informs us of a singular custom there: "When a young man wishes to pay his addresses to his sweetheart, instead of going to her father's and professing his passion, he goes to a publichouse; and having let the landlady into the secret of his attachment, the object of his wishes is immediately sent for, who never almost refuses to come. She is entertained with ale and whiskey, or brandy; and the marriage is concluded on. The second day after the marriage a creeling, as it is called, takes place. The young wedding pair, with their friends, assemble in a convenient spot. A small creel or basket is prepared for the occasion, into which they put some stones: the young men carry it alternately, and allow themselves to be caught by the maidens, who have a kiss when they succeed. After a great deal of innocent mirth and pleasantry, the creel falls at length to the young husband's share, who is obliged to carry it generally for a long time, none of the young women having compassion upon him. At last, his fair mate kindly relieves him from his burden; and her complaisance in this particular is considered as a proof of her satisfaction with the choice she has made. The creel goes round again; more merriment succeeds; and all the company dine together and talk over the feats of the field." Ramsay, in his "Poems," 1721, refers to the creeling usage, and adds in a note: "'Tis a custom for the friends to endeavour the next day after the wedding to make the new-married man as drunk as possible." Perhaps the French phrase, 'Adieu, panniers, vendages sont faites,' may allude to a similar custom."

Creeping to the Cross.—The Catholic ceremony of "creeping to the cross" on Good Friday is given, from an ancient book of the "Ceremonial of the Kings of England," in the Notes to the Northumberland Household Book. The Usher was to lay a carpet for the Kinge to "creepe to the Crosse upon." The Queen and her ladies were also to "creepe to the Crosse." In a proclamation, dated 26th February, 30 Henry VIII., we read: "On Good Friday it shall be declared howe creepyng to the Crosse signifyeth an humblynge of ourselfe to Christe before the Crosse, and the kyssynge of it a memorie of our redemption made upon the Crosse." This usage was retained for some time after the restoration of the Protestant religion under Elizabeth. In a letter written about 1566 by the Bishop of London to Sir W. Cecil, the Bishop speaks of some who, "att Dunbarre, on Good Frydaye sawe certeyn persons goo barefooted and bare-legged to the churche, to creepe to the crosse." See also Bonner's "Injunctions," A.D. 1555, signat. A. 2. In "A short Description of Antichrist," &c. the author notes the Popish custom of "creeping to the Crosse with egges and apples."

Cremation. — The ancient Christians, to testify the abhorrence of heathen rites, rejected the Pagan custom of burning the dead, depositing the inanimate body entire in the ground. Thus I found at Rutchester, one of the stations upon the Roman Wall in Northumberland, a sepulchre hewn out of the living rock, wherein Leland says Paulinus who converted the Northumbrians to Christianity was interred. The whole subject of cremation is ably taken up and treated in the thirty-seventh volume of the Archæologia by William Michael Wylie, Esq. Mr. Wylie shews that the burning of the dead was commonly put in practice in this country in early times; and he observes: "The recent researches of Mr. Akerman, in a Keltic cemetery at Brighthampton in Oxfordshire, disclosed a great number of examples of cremation, unmixed with inhumation.

It may not be generally known that there is an Earth-to-Earth Society, established to resist and discountenance this method of dissolution. Its published reasons against cremation are mainly legal or clerical. Perhaps this matter ought not to be dismissed without a passing reference to the rather revolting practice of destroying the remains of executed convicts by means of quick lime, partly no doubt in consequence of the law, which directs that such persons shall be buried within the precincts of the gaol at which the execution occurred. It is well-known that the body of Ritson the antiquary, by his own express desire, underwent this barbarous form of combustion, which all the ingenuity of the author of "Urn-Burial" could not reconcile with Christian ideas.

Cresset.—See Nares and Halliwell in v., and Hazlitt's *Livery Companies*, 1892, p. 310.

Cricket.—This sport, now so common and popular, has only of recent years attracted archæological notice, and been found in some form or other to go back to the fourteenth, if not thirteenth, century. By some it is supposed to be an evolution from club-ball, and it is cognate with rounders and hockey. A Bodleian MS. of 1344 represents a female figure bowling to a man, who holds in his hand a bat prepared to strike; and in 1350 John Parish, of Guildford, enclosed a plot of ground there for the purpose of playing at cricket. Whether the allusion in 1305, cited in the *Antiquary*, intends cricket under the designation of *creag*, seems uncertain. During the seventeenth century references to the game are not numerous, which may possibly arise from its familiarity at that time, as it is one of the pastimes enumerated in a news-letter of May 6, 1670, from the chaplain of the ship Assistance, lying off Antioch, when he speaks of the sailors occupying their leisure in this sort of way, the curious feature being that they should have found the means of doing so in such a locality without having taken the implements with them. The fact appears to be that what we at present recognise as cricket was simply club or bat-and-ball at the outset, and that wicket, wicket-keeper, scouts and other accessories came afterward—long afterward.

In the ancient romance of *Merlin*, where the King's messengers are in search for a particular object of a

child born without a mortal father, they meet with a party of children, who are said in the popular summary by Dunlop to be playing at cricket, Merlin being of the number. Of course this is no authority for the game; but the occupation of the miraculous boy and his comrades may very well have been club-ball—a pastime of the highest antiquity. In Chamberlain's *Angliæ Notitia*, 1694, the game is thus explicitly named:—"The natives will endure long and hard labour; inasmuch that after 12 hours' hard work, they will go in the evening to football, stool ball, cricket, prison-base, wrestling, cudgel-playing, or some such like vehement exercise for their recreation." It is said, in the *World Bewitch'd*, 1699, p. 22, that, on the approach of summer, "Quoits, cricket, nine-pins, and trap-ball will be very much in fashion, and more tradesmen may be seen playing in the fields than working in their shops." But Lillywhite does not seem to trace back farther than 1746, at all events for any events of importance. *Cricket Scores and Biographies of Celebrated Cricketers*, 1862-3. The print published by Bowles and Carver in 1784 of this game, as it was then played by the Gentlemen's Club, White Conduit House, exhibits the usual accessories of wickets, stumps, fielders, batsman, and bowler. The party wears knee-breeches, shoes or high-lows, and all, except two, who are seated on the ground, and may be umpires, are in shirt-sleeves. The seated figures, and one or two of the others have pigtails, and the former cloaks and sombrero hats. The length of the course in the engraving seems less than would suit modern experts. The wicket is in the form of two forked stumps; the bat resembles a club. A few years earlier (1779), a match was played at Sevenoaks in Kent, between the Countess of Derby and other noble ladies, all represented in a contemporary print as attired in ordinary outdoor dress and elaborate head-gear. The bowler is stooping to serve the ball, and the wicket has only two stumps. The cricket grounds at Darnall, near Sheffield, appear to have been celebrated in the earlier part of the last century (1820), and there is a coloured engraving by Robert Cruikshank, shewing the North East view of the place. It is not many years since this sport was played by men and boys wearing their tall hats, nor indeed is the practice yet entirely discontinued. A friend has seen a print of the boys at Tonbridge School in the earlier part of the century in which they are so represented.

As far back as 1800, in the Court Rolls of the Manor of Wimbledon, complaints were registered of the annoyance and danger arising from cricket balls to passengers and vehicles near the gate leading from Windsor-street to Barnes on Lower Putney Common. The Wimbledon Cricket Club has periodically printed for the use of its members an account of the matches and scores since the establishment of the institution in 1871. Lord's Cricket Ground, still so celebrated, owed its name to Thos. Lord, one of the attendants at the White Conduit Club at the end of the 18th century. Lord subsequently established the Marylebone Club, now Lord's.

Smith, in his *Book for a Rainy Day*, 1861, tells us that in 1803 the Duke of Dorset, Lord Winchelsea, Lord Talbot, and others, played at this game in an open field near White Conduit House. The Marylebone Club appears to have been one of the more prominent institutions of this character in old days. In 1823 Henry Bentley printed "A correct Account of all the Cricket Matches which have been played by the Mary-le-Bone Club and all the other principal Matches from 1786 to 1822," and in 1825 appeared at Basingstoke a small duodecimo volume entitled "Laws of the game of Cricket as revised by the Cricket Club at St. Marylebone." The encouragement of the game in Kent was largely due to Sir Horace Mann, the correspondent of Horace Walpole. Mann, with the Duke of Dorset and Lord Tankerville, presidents of the Surrey and Hants Elevens, Sir William Draper and others, formed a committee, which met at the Star and Garter, in Pall Mall, and drew up rules for the game, about 1770. In the *Kentish Gazette* for April, 1794, is an advertisement of a game of cricket to be played under the auspices of Sir Horace Mann at Harrietsham on ponies. Some incidental particulars about the game and those who were distinguished as players under George II. and George III., may be gathered from the Notes by Scriblerus Maximus to an heroic poem entitled *Cricket*, published without date, and dedicated to John Earl of Sandwich (1729-92). The Kentish men appear at this time to have held high rank as cricketers. But the game had evidently been long ere this well established. The men of Wareham in Sussex, also acquired in the eighteenth century a great name for their proficiency in the sport. Lower's *Compend. Hist. of Sussex*, 1870, ii., 231. Dr. Furnivall informs me that he met, in a 17th century book, with the term yorker in the use of a ball, which is so pitched by the bowler as to strike the ground between the batsman's feet, and make it impossible for him to hit it. Comp. *Cat and Dog*, &c., and see Halliwell in v.

Cricket, The.—Pliny mentions the cricket as much esteemed by the ancient magicians: there is no doubt that our superstitions concerning these little domestics have been transmitted to us from his times. *Nat. Hist.*, book xxix. It is a lucky sign to have crickets in the house:

> "*Ad Grillum.*
> O qui meæ culinæ,
> Argutulus choraules,
> Et hospes es canorus
> *Quacunque commoreris*
> *Felicitatis Omen.*"

—Bourne's *Poematia*, edit. 1764, p. 133. Grose says it is held extremely unlucky to kill a cricket, perhaps from the idea of its being a breach of hospitality, this insect taking refuge in houses. Several old writers mention this superstition as strong and general. Melton, in his *Astrologaster*, 1620, p. 45, tells us that the abandonment of a chimney by crickets is a fatal sign, and Gay in his *Pastoral Dirge*, and an early dramatist seem to say that the shrieking of the insect in the oven or chimney was to be viewed in the same unfavourable light. Dodsley's *Old Plays*, 1780, vi. 357. In the Spectator's day the voice of the cricket was held to be potent for good or evil. In Dryden and Lee's "Œdipus," it is even ranked with the owl and the raven, birds of the worst omen. To come to a more modern and intelligent writer, White of Selborne observes to us : "they" (crickets) "are the housewife's barometer, foretelling her when it will rain, and are prognostic sometimes, she thinks, of ill or good luck, of the death of a near relation, or the approach of an absent lover. By being the constant companions of her solitary hours, they naturally become the objects of her superstition. Tender insects, that live abroad, either enjoy only the short period of one summer, or else doze away the cold, uncomfortable months in profound slumbers; but these residing, as it were, in a torrid zone, are always alert and merry; a good Christmas fire is to them like the heats of the dog-days. Though they are frequently heard by day, yet it is their natural time of motion in the night."

Croquet. — A game probably of French origin, as it is depicted in an engraving, dated 1624, by Callot, representing the players at Nancy in Lorraine at that time. It is said in some verses accompanying the series of prints, of which this forms one, to be a diversion of the spring of the year. A Wimbledon correspondent of *Notes and Queries* (Jan. 4, 1873), thus describes the illustration :—"The scene of the pastime is a broad, straight walk, running between parterres, and apparently 100 feet in length. At either end is erected a single hoop, of width and height seemingly 2¼ feet. Several balls are grouped close to one of these hoops, round which stand some players, mallet in hand; while, a few feet in front of the other hoop, another player is about to deliver a stroke, and is evidently aiming to send his ball up among its companions near the goal opposite him. Mallets, balls, hoops, and players, though on a minute scale, are all so distinctly drawn, that no mistake can occur in perceiving at a glance the action of performers and the instruments of performance. All the players are males; and in this respect most certainly the croquet which was going on before Callot's eyes at Nancy, in the Year of Grace, 1624, is sadly at a disadvantage, when compared with the modern reproduction.

Cross.—Hall, in his "Characters," 1608, speaking of the superstitious man, says: "Some wayes he will not go, and some he dares not; either there are bugs, or he faineth them. Every lanterne is a ghost, and every noise is of chaines. He knows not why, but his custom is to go a little about, and to leave the Cross still on the right hand." In Articles to be enquired of within the Archdeaconry of Yorke, 1640, I find the following:—"Whether at the death of any there be praying for the dead at crosses, or places where crosses have been, in the way to the church." In "The Canterburian's Self-Conviction," 1640, chap. 6. is this passage: "They avow that signing with the signe of the Crosse at rysing or lying downe, at going out or ccming in, at lighting of candles, closing of windowes, or any such action, is not only a pious and profitable ceremonie, but a very apostolick tradition." The following very curious "Old Wives' Prayer" is found in Herrick's "Hesperides," p. 205:

"Holy-rood, come forth and shield
Us ith' citie, and the field:
Safely guard us, now and aye,
From the blast that burns by day;
And those sounds that us affright
In the dead of dampish night.
Drive all hurtful Feinds us fro,
By the time the cocks first crow."

Pennant, in his "Tours in Wales," says: "At the delivery of the bread and wine at the Sacrament, several, before they receive the bread or cup, though held out to them, will flourish a little with their thumb, something like making the figure of the Cross. They do it (the women mostly) when they say their prayers on their first coming to church." In Boswell's "Life of Johnson," it is observed: "In days of superstition they thought that holding the poker before the fire would drive away the witch, who hindered the fire from burning, as it made the sign of the Cross."

Cross and Pile.—See *Heads and Tails.*

Cross Days.—These are the Monday, Tuesday, and Wednesday preceding Holy Thursday in Rogation Week. They are referred to under this name in the *Plumpton Correspondence*, under date of May 18, 1501. It appears that in North Wales, among the slate quarrymen of Penrhyn, there is a superstition still prevalent that, if any work is done on Ascension Day, some accidents will follow, and the *Daily News* of June 10, 1878, reports that "during last week thousands of men employed at the Welsh slate quarries here refused to work on Ascension Thursday." It adds: "A few years ago the agents persuaded the men to break through the superstitious observance, and there were accidents each year, a not unlikely occurrence, seeing the extent of the works carried on and the dangerous occupation of the men. This year, however, the men one and all refused to work."

Cross in Writing.—I have no doubt but that this is a remain of Popery. Thus persons, who cannot write, are directed to make their marks, instead of signing their names, which is generally done in the form of a cross. From the form of a cross at the beginning of a horn-book, the alphabet is called the Christ-Cross row. The cross used in shop books Butler seems to derive from the same origin:

"And some against all idolizing
The cross in shop-books or baptizing."

Hudibras, p. 3, c. 2, l. 313. The round O of a milk-score is, if I mistake not, also marked with a cross for a shilling, though unnoted by Lluellin in a passage where he speaks of the barmaid writing—

"For a tester half a moone,
And a great round O for a shilling."

A not unusual superscription to early letters was a cross with or without the word Jesus. Dalrymple, in his "Travels in Spain," says, that there "not a woman gets into a coach to go a hundred yards, nor a postillion on his horse, without crossing themselves. Even the tops of tavern-bills and the directions of letters are marked with crosses."

Cross - Legged. — Sir Thomas Browne cites Pliny for the opinion of the ancients that to sit cross-legged was unlucky and improper, and Athenæus for the fact, that it was regarded as a practice which had power to hinder childbirth. Park, on the contrary, noted in his copy of Bourne and Brand: "To sit cross-legged, I have always understood, was intended to produce good or fortunate consequences. Hence it was employed as a charm at school by one boy who wished well for another, in order to deprecate some punishment which both might tremble to have incurred the expectation of. At a card-table, I have also caught some superstitious players sitting cross-legged with a view of bringing good luck." It was a point of belief that a witch, by sitting cross-legged, could prevent a woman's delivery, and Heywood, in his "Silver Age," 1613, has bestowed on Juno this power, where the goddess hinders the labour of Alcmena. The dramatist followed the classical legend to a certain extent, while he made it conform to the superstitious creed of his own country. Flecknoe, speaking of "your fanatick reformers," says: "Had they their will, a bird should not fly in the air with its wings across, a ship with its cross-yard sail upon the sea, nor prophane taylor sit cross-legged on his shop-board, or have cross-bottoms to winde his thread upon." This whimsical detestation of the cross-form, no doubt, took its rise from the odium at that time against everything derived from Popery.

Cross Monday.—In Bridges "History of Northamptonshire" are recorded various instances of having processions on Cross Monday.

Cross Point.—See *Horse-Trick.*

Cross-Questions.—Said to be a game by Nares, *Glossary,* in v. Perhaps allied to *Questions and Commands,* and to *Cross-Questions and Cross-Answers.* Compare Hazlitt's *Handbook* and *Bibl. Coll.* v. *Breton,* and *Children's Games* suprâ.

Cross Ruff.—This is a species of ruff, a game at cards. There was ruff (q.v.), double-ruff, and cross-ruff. In *A Notable Discovery of Cosenage,* 1591, the preface states, among other matters, how the author, going into the West of England, found at a country ale-house half-a-dozen farmers playing at cross-ruff, and hoped to win all their money, when he found to his disappointment that they had read Greene's exposure of *conycatchers,* and were on their guard. This, with others, is quoted in "Poor Robin's Almanac" for 1693:

"Christmas to hungry stomachs gives relief,
With mutton, pork, pies, pasties, and roast beef;
And men at cards spend many idle hours,
At loadum, whisk, cross-ruff, put, and all-fours."

Crowdie.—In Scotland, Eden says, they used to eat crowdie on Shrove Tuesday, as in England they did pancakes. He adds: "On this day there is always put into the bason or porringer, out of which the unmarried folks are to eat, a ring, the finding of which, by fair means, is supposed to be ominous of the finder's being first married." Crowdie is made by pouring boiling water over oat-meal and stirring it a little. It is eaten with milk or butter. The more modern manner of preparing is described in the *Musæ Anglicanæ,* 1689, ii., 86.

Crow-Keeper.—See Nares, *Glossary,* in v., and Hazlitt's *Proverbs,* 1882, p. 181.

Cry.—See *Auctions,* where the employment of the *Preco* or *Crier* is recorded. But the cry was used on a multifarious diversity of occasions: 1, for the announcement of the issue of new money; 2, for the publication of the decrees of Councils; 3, for the advertisement of plays to be performed; 4, for the recovery of lost property; 5, for proclaiming the approach of royal or high personages to their seats; 6, for the notification of any local event, not only prior to typography and journalism, but down to the present time in some rural districts. In ancient times the crier or usher carried, not a bell, but a trumpet. Lacroix, *Mœurs et Usages,* 1872, p. 337; Hazlitt's *Venetian Republic,* 1900, ii., 355, 457; Hazlitt's Monograph on Shakespear, 1902, p. 103. The heraldic *Oyez* and the legal *Oyer and Terminer* are evolutions from the ancient use of the cry in manifold cases; and *Oyentia* is a feudal term for the public indication of the time for paying a periodical tribute. Maigne D'Arnis *Lexicon Mediæ et Infimæ Latinitatis,* 1856, in v.

Cry Coke.—To cry *Coke* is in vulgar language synonymous with crying Peccavi. Coke, says Ruddiman, in his Glossary to Douglas's "Virgil," is the sound which Cocks utter, especially when they are beaten, from which Skinner is of opinion they have the name of Cock.

Crying the Mare.—There is a harvest sport in Hertfordshire, called "Crying the Mare" (it is the same in Shropshire), when the reapers tie together the tops of the last blades of corn, which is Mare, and standing at some distance, throw their sickles at it, and he who cuts the knot, has the prize, with acclamations and good cheer. I was informed of the following custom on this occasion at Hitchin in the same county where each farmer drives furiously home with the last load of his corn, while the people run after him with bowls full of water in order to throw on it: this is also accompanied with great shouting. Blount tells us farther that "after the knot is cut, then they cry with a loud voice three times, 'I have her.' Others answer, as many times, 'What have you?'—'A mare, a mare, a mare.'

—'Whose is she?' thrice also.— J. B. (naming the owner three times).— 'Whither will you send her?'—'To J. à Nicks,' (naming some neighbour who has not all his corn reaped); then they all shout three times, and so the ceremony ends with good cheer. "In Yorkshire upon the like occasion they have a Harvest Dame, in Bedfordshire a Jack and a Gill."

Crying the Nack.—A harvest custom in Dorsetshire and Devonshire. A correspondent of *Notes and Queries* writes:—"I was present last year at a farm in North Devon where the curious old custom of "calling the nack" was observed. The reapers were gathered round a pond, where they sang three times, first in low tones, gradually increasing in loudness, the words:—

"Arnack, arnack, arnack,
We haven, we haven, we haven,
God send the nack."

After which they all laughed and shouted. They then retired to the house—not to supper, for the ceremony was not yet over. One of the party had the "nack" secreted on his person. A member of the farmer's family tried to discover the possessor, before he entered the kitchen in order to drench him, or, as they said, "wet the nack," with a bucket of water. Failing to do this, the farmer was obliged to supply a larger quantity of beer than would otherwise have been given to each individual after supper. The "nack" is preserved in the farmer's kitchen for the year."

Cucking, or Goging Stool.— Called also a tumbrel, tribuch, and trebuchet; also a thewe. In the "Promptorium Parvulorum," "Esyn, or Cukkyn," is interpreted by *stercoriso*: and in the "Domesday Survey," in the account of the City of Chester," we read: "Vir sive mulier falsam mensuram in civitate faciens deprehensus, iiii. solid. emendab'. Similiter malam servisiam faciens, aut in Cathedrâ, ponebatur Stercoris, aut iiii. solid. dab' prepositis." See Cowel in v. ex Carta Joh. regis, dat. 11 Jun. anno regni 1. It is called *thewe* in Lambarde's "Eirenarcha," lib. i. c. 12. The following extract from Cowel, in v. Thew, (with the extract just quoted from Lysons) seems to prove this: "Georgius Grey Comes Cantii clamat in maner. de Bushton & Ayton punire delinquentes contra Assisam Panis et Corvisiæ, per tres vices per amerciamenta, & quarta vice Pistores per Pilloriam, Braciatores per Tumbrellam, & Rixatrices per Thewe, hoc est, ponere eas super scabellum vocat. a Cucking Stool. Pl. in Itin. apud Cestr. 14 Hen. VII." But comp. *Stool of Repentance*, infrâ. The

cucking-stool was an engine invented for the punishment of scolds and unquiet women, by ducking them in the water, after having placed them in a stool or chair fixed at the end of a long pole, by which they were immerged in some muddy or stinking pond. Blount tells us that some think it a corruption from ducking stool, but that others derive it from Choaking Stool. Though of the most remote antiquity, it is now, it should seem, totally disused. An essayist in the "Gentleman's Magazine," for May, 1732, observes that "The stools of infamy are the ducking stool, and the stool of repentance. The first was invented for taming female shrews. Lysons gives us a curious extract from the churchwardens' and chamberlain's accounts at Kingston-upon-Thames in 1572, which contains a bill of expenses for making one of these cucking stools, which, he says, must have been much in use formerly, as there are frequent entries of money paid for its repair. *Environs*, i., 233. Blakeway, in his *History of Shrewsbury*, 1779, p. 172, furnishes the subjoined entries:—"1572. The making of the cucking stool, 8s.; iron work for the same, 3s.; timber for the same, 7s. 6d.; 3 brasses for the same and three wheels, 4s. 10d." There is an order of the Corporation of Shrewsbury, 1669, that "A ducking stool be erected, for the punishment of all scolds." Borlase tells us that: "Among the punishments inflicted in Cornwall, of old time, was that of the cocking-stool, a seat of infamy where strumpets and scolds, with bare foot and head, were condemned to abide the derision of those that passed by, for such time as the bailiffs of manors, which had the privilege of such jurisdiction, did appoint. *Nat. Hist. of Cornwall*, p. 303. A certificate of the punishment of an incorrigible scold by ducking, dated 1673, and addressed by the churchwardens of Waddington, co. York, to Thomas Parker, Esq., of Browsholme, hereditary bowbearer of Bolland Forest under the Duke of Buccleuch, is to be seen in "Current Notes" for December, 1855.

In Skene's "Regiam Majestatem, ch. 69, this punishment occurs as having been used anciently in Scotland: speaking of Browsters, i.e., "Wemen quha brewes aill to be sauld" it is said, "gif she makes gude ail, that is sufficient. Bot gif she makes evill ail, contrair to the use and consuetude of the burgh, and is convict thereof, she sall pay ane unlaw of aucht shillinges, or sal suffer the justice of the burgh, that is, she sall be put upon the cock-stule, and the aill sall be distributed to the pure folke." Braithwaite, speaking of a Xantippean, says: "He (her husband) vowes therefore to bring her in all disgrace to the cucking-stoole ; and shee vowes againe to bring him with all contempt, to the stoole of repent-ance." *Whimzies*, 1631, p. 182. In one of the jest-books, there is the following anecdote : "Some gentlemen travelling, and coming near to a town, saw an old woman spinning near the ducking stool : one, to make the company merry, asked the good woman what that chair was made for? Said she, you know what it is. In-deed, said he, not I, unless it be the chair you use to spin in. No, no, said she, you know it to be otherwise : have you not heard that it is the cradle your good mother hath often layn in?" *New Help to Discourse*, 1684, p. 216. These stools seem to have been in common use when Misson, the French traveller, visited this country, and when Gay wrote his Pasto-rals : they are thus described by the latter :

"I'll speed me to the pond, where the high stool
On the long plank hangs o'er the muddy pool,
That stool, the dread of every scolding queen," &c.

Misson says : "La maniere de punir les femmes querelleuses et debauchées est assez plaisante en Angleterre. On attache une chaise à bras à l'extremité de deux Especes de Solives, longues de douze ou quinze pieds et dans un eloignement paral-lele, en sorte que ces deux pieces de bois embrassent par leur deux bouts voisins la chaise qui est entre deux, & qui y est at-tachée par la côte comme avec un essieu, de telle maniere, qu'elle a du Jeu, et qu'elle demeure toujours dans l'etat na-turel & horisontal auquel une Chaise doit être afin qu'on puisse s'asseoir dessus, soit qu'on l'éleve, soit qu'on l'abaisse. On dresse un pôteau sur le bord d'un Etang ou d'une Riviere, & sur ce poteau on pose presque en equilibre, la double piece de bois à une des extremitez de laquelle la Chaise se trouve au dessus de l'eau. On met la Femme dans cette Chaise et on la plonge ainsi autant de fois qu'il a été ordonné, pour raffraichir un peu sa chaleur immoderée." See Ozell's Translation, p. 65. In "Miscellaneous Poems," &c., by Benjamin West, of Wee-don-Beck, Northamptonshire, 8vo. 1780, is preserved a copy of verses, said to have been written near sixty years ago, entitled "The Ducking Stool." A note informs us, "To the honour of the fair sex in the neighbourhood of R***y. this machine has been taken down (as useless) several years." The stool is represented in a cut annexed to the "Dumps," designed and engraved by Louis du Guernier, and also in the frontispiece of "The old Woman of Ratcliff Highway." A specimen was to be seen within a few years on the banks of the Stour at Fordwich in Kent. Some ad-ditional particulars, illustrating this obso-lete usage, but to the same purport, were printed in Willis's "Current Notes" for February and April, 1854. See Wright and Fairholt's *Archæological Album*, 1845, p. 49-54, and Halliwell's *Dict.*, 1860, in v. Morant, speaking of Canuden, in the hun-dred of Rochford, mentions "Cuckingstole Croft, as given for the maintenance of a light in this church, as appears by inquisi-tion, 10 Eliz." *Essex*, i., 317.

CUCKING STOOL.

Cuckold.—I know not how this word, which is generally derived from cuculus, a cuckoo, has happened to be given to the injured husband, for it seems more pro-perly to belong to the adulterer, the cuckoo being well known to be a bird that deposits its eggs in other bird's nests. The Romans seemed to have used this cu-culus in its proper sense as the adulterer, calling with equal propriety the cuckold himself Carruca or hedge-sparrow, which bird is well known to adopt the other's spurious offspring. Richardson and Worcester, in their Dictionaries, en-dorse Tooke's etymology of cuckold, which seems, after all, to be the correct one, namely, cucol, from the Italian cucolo, a cuckoo ; the word should be cucol, as in some of our old writers, and not cucold (or cuckold), and we get the word from the past participle of the English verb formed from the Italian substantive : cucolo, cucol, cucol'd. Douce says : "That the word cuculus was a term of reproach amongst the antients there is not the least doubt, and that it was used in the sense of our cuckold is equally clear. Plautus has so introduced it on more than one occasion. In his *Asinaria* he makes a woman thus speak of her husband :

" Ac etiam cubat Cuculus, surge, Amator, i domum " :

and again :

" Cano capite te Cuculum Uxor domum ex lustris rapit."

And yet in another place, where Pseudolus says to Callidorus " Quid fles, Cucule?" the above sense is out of the question, and it is to be taken merely as a term of reproach. Horace certainly uses the word as it is explained by Pliny in the passage already given, and the conclusion there drawn appears to be that which best reconciles the more modern sense of the term, being likewise supported by a note in the Variorum Horace, from " Historia Mirabilium," by Carystius. The application of the above passage to our use of the word cuckold, as connected with the cuckoo, is that the husband, timid, and incapable of protecting his honour, like that bird, is called by its name, and thus converted into an object of contempt and derision. In the " Athenian Oracle " it is remarked of cuckoldry : " The Romans were honourable, and yet Pompey, Cæsar, Augustus, Lucullus, Cato and others had this fate, but not its infamy and scandal." In " Paradoxical Assertions," by Robert Heath, 1664, it is said : " Since Plautus wittily, and with more reason calls the adulterer, and not him whose wife is adulterated, Cuculum, the cuckold, because he begets children on others wives, which the credulous father believes his own : why should not he then that corrupts another man's wife be rather called the Cuckow, for he sits and sings merrily whilst his eggs are hatched by his neighbour's hens?" Chaucer, in his " Prosopopeia of Jealousie," brings her in with a garland of gold yellow, and a cuckoo sitting on her fist. Two items in *A. C. Mery Talys*, 1526, turn on this somewhat unconventional topic : the story of the wife whose pigs died in farrowing, and who being told that she should get a cuckold's hat, and farrow them therein, applied to a female neighbour, whereupon the latter angrily retorted that her husband was no cuckold, and so had no hat, and the woman, after inquiring all round, declared that if she lived another year, she would get one of her own ; the second, the account of the miller's rejoinder to the merchant, who observed that he had heard say every true miller had a golden thumb. " Truth it is," quoth he, " that my thumb is gilt, how be it ye have no power to see it, for there is a property incident thereto, that he that is a cuckold shall never have power to see it." Comp. Hazlitt's *Pro-*

verbs, 1882, p. 56, where the converse is suggested, in which case we should conclude that the reason was because his jaundiced eye would take the thumb to be yellow or golden.

There is a song in Ritson's collection in which a jealous wife is represented as putting on her yellow hose.

" Here is Maryone Marchauntes at Allgate,
Her husbòde dwells at yᵉ signe of yᵉ Cokoldes Pate."

—*Cock Lorels Bote.* In the *Boke of Mayd Emlyn* (about 1540), it is stated that the lady had five husbands, all cuckolds, and that she *made their beards*, whether they liked or not, and gave them a pretty hoodful of bells to wear. Hazlitt's *Popular Poetry*, iv., 83. Dickenson, in " Greene in Conceipt," 1598, uses this expression of a cornute : " but certainely, beleeved, that Giraldo his master was as soundly armde for the heade, as either Capricorne, or the stoutest horned signe in the Zodiacke." " It is said,—Many a man knows no end of his goods : right : many a man has good horns, and knows no end of them. Well, that is the dowry of his wife ; 'tis none of his own getting. Horns? Even so :— Poor men alone?—No, no ; the noblest deer hath them as huge as the rascal."— *As You Like It*, act iii., sc. 3. Among the witticisms on cuckolds that occur in our old plays, must not be omitted the following in " Ram Alley," 1611 :

" Why, my good father, what should you do with a wife?
Would you be crested? Will you needs thrust your head
In one of Vulcan's helmets? Will you perforce
Weare a city cap and a Court feather?"[1]

The following passage is in "Plaine Percevall, the peacemaker of England " : — You say true, Sal sapit omnia ; and service without salt, by the rite of England, is a cuckold's fee if he claim it."

" On Dr. Cuckold.
" Who so famóus was of late,
He was with finger pointed at :
What cannot learning do, and single state?
" Being married, he so famous grew,
As he was pointed at with two :
What cannot learning and a wife now do? "

Flecknoe's *Diarium*, 1656. Butler, in his " Hudibras," informs us for what a singular purpose carvers used formerly to invoke the names of cuckolds. This allusion arose, according to a passage in the 59th No. of the " British Apollo," from the dexterity of one Thomas Web, carver to the Lord Mayor in Charles the First's time, and his fame in a less favourable respect, whence came the proverb, "Think of a cuckold," addressed to one who cannot carve the joint before him. In Hazlitt's *Early Popular Poetry,* 1864 - 6, vol. i., will be found the curious Arthurian piece, called the *Cuckold's Dance,* with a body of notices illustrative at the present subject, including the dance of *Cuckolds all a-row.* The latter became at the Restoration a favourite dance-tune. Compare the same writer's *Proverbs,* 1882. In the background of Hogarth's signboard of "The Man Loaded with Mischief," is an inn called "The Cuckold's fortune." Cuckold's Point, below Rotherhithe or Redriff, was anciently known as Cuckold's Haven. In "Tarlton's Jests," first publshed probably about 1590, we are told, "How Tarlton landed at Cuckold's Hauen," "whereupon one gaue him this theame next day:

'Tarlton, tell mee, for fayne would I know,
If thou wert landed at Cuckold's hauen, or no?

Tarlton answered thus:
'Yes, sir, I take 't in no scorne,
For many land there, yet misse of the horne.'"

The following is an extract from Hentzner's "Travels in England," 1598: "Upon taking the air down the river (from London), on the left hand lies Ratcliffe, a considerable suburb. On the opposite shore is fixed a long pole, with ram's horns upon it, the intention of which was vulgarly said to be a reflection upon wilful and contented cuckolds." Pennant, in his "Zoology," 1776, speaking of the cuckoo, says: "His note is so uniform, that his name in all languages seems to have been derived from it, and in all other countries it is used in the same reproachful sense. The reproach seems to arise from this bird making use of the bed or nest of another to deposit its eggs in; leaving the care of its young to a wrong parent; but Juvenal, in his 6th Satire, with more justice, gives the infamy to the bird in whose nest the supposititious eggs were layed,

'Tu tibi tunc Curruca places—'"

A case lately occurred in which a cuckoo was found to have deposited its eggs in the nest of a wagtail, which was sitting upon them. *Daily News,* Sept. 4, 1879. Johnson, in his Dictionary, says: "The cuckow is said to suck the eggs of other birds, and lay her own to be hatched in their place; from which practice it was usual to alarm a husband at the approach of an adulterer by calling 'cuckoo,' which by mistake was in time applied to the husband." He was vulgarly supposed to suck other birds' eggs to make his voice clear as in the old rhyme:

"He sucks little birds' eggs,
To make his voice clear;
And when he sings cuckoo,
The summer is near."

The following item is from the *Morning Post* of May 17, 1821: "A singular custom prevails in Shropshire at this period of the year, which is peculiar to that county. As soon as the first cuckoo has been heard, all the labouring classes leave work, if in the middle of the day, and the time is devoted to mirth and jollity over what is called the cuckoo ale." The annexed communication was made by a writer, signing himself G., to the *Daily News* of Sept. 5, 1879: "In July last, at a small road-side crossing on the London and South Western Railway on the banks of the Axe, in Dorsetshire, and at a place well known to anglers, called Tythorleigh-bridge, I had in my hands a full-fledged young cuckoo which had just dropped from the nest of a small finch that haunts the river side and goes by some local name I am not at this moment prepared to spell. The man at the station, who rejoices equally in the name of Joe, a wooden leg, and an unblemished reputation, is in his way a bit of a naturalist, and took almost as much interest in the young cuckoo as in the flowers which cover and surround his cottage. He had watched the bird for some time, and seemed from other instances to have no doubt as to the truth of the tradition. The young cuckoo, when once removed from the nest and before it can use its wings, will not remain there, but scrambles down and gets into the hedges at the roadside. In that case it generally dies; but the foster parents, which in this instance we saw in a painful state of agitation on the telegraph wires and neighbouring trees, will in the meantime follow it and feed it. The young cuckoo just fledged was certainly larger than a full-grown thrush or black-bird, and was as savage as a young eagle. From the size of the nest it must have very much inconvenienced the foster parents. One can easily understand that the old hen cuckoo before depositing its own egg would clear out the eggs of the finch, as tradition relates."

In the March number of the "Gentleman's Magazine" for 1895, among the general articles, G. W. Murdoch has one ridiculing the popular myth that the cuckoo arrives in March. It is, he says, a fiction of the imagination, and he only admits one probable authentication of so early an arrival of the cuckoo in half-a-century—all personal testimonies to the contrary notwithstanding. He also goes as far as to say that the myth of the March cuckoo can be disproved beyond the shadow of a scientific doubt, and, pursuing the scientific branch of the subject, goes on to say that for reasons which branch off and take root in several departments of human cult in relation to the phenomena of pyschological and pure animistic evolution, the cuckoo holds quite an unique position in avi-fauna life. It holds, too, no inconsiderable place in the dim, and now almost intangible, relics of Totemistic worship, and fills a very large space in the traditional records and literature of folk-lore. In ornithic science it has been the subject of the most profound study, has stimulated the liveliest controversies— not settled yet—and inspired many delightful prose treatises and imperishable poems. Even at the present day the cuckoo is regarded as a sacred bird by the peasantry of some parts of Ireland, and in Connaught and Connemara it is believed to be unlucky to kill it, even by accidentally mistaking it for the sparrow-hawk, with which it is habitually confounded by superficial observers. In that respect the cuckoo holds a position analogous to the robin, and the universality of the superstition among primitive folks is an established canon of the literature of Totemistic cult. But the article is not all scientific argument. Mr. Murdoch has some stories to tell.

At Hefful or Heathfield Fair in Sussex, on April 14, the first cuckoo is said to be let out of a basket by an old woman, or, in other words, the note of the bird is popularly supposed to be first heard on that occasion. The following is a childish game (if it may be so described) :

"Cuckoo in cherry tree,
Come down and tell me
How many years I have to live."

The cuckoo has been long considered as a bird of omen. Gay, in his "Shepherd's Week," in the fourth Pastoral, describes the popular dread of hearing the first song of the cuckoo in the spring, and the usage of taking off the shoe of the left foot. Greene, in "A quip for an upstart Courtier," 1592, calls a cuckoo the cuckold's quirister : "It was just at that time when the cuckolds quirrister began to bewray Aprill gentlemen, with his never chaunged notes." In the play of "Timon," edited by Mr. Dyce, act i. sc. 2, Eutrapelus says to Abyssus : "Di'st euer heare a cuckowe of a note more inauspicious?" In the same drama, act ii. sc. 5, Timon himself is made to say, in allusion to horns :

"A common badge to men of eache degree,
How many hange their heades downe, leaste they splitte
The signe posts with their hornes—"

Guilpin, in his "Skialetheia," 1598, says :

"For let Severus heare
A cuckow sing in June, he sweats for feare—"

Why the writer chooses June, I do not know ; the proverbial lines run :

"In April,
The cuckoo shews his bill ;
In May,
He sings all day ;
In June,
He alters his tune ;
In July,
Away he'll fly ;
Come August,
Away he must."

In Clarke's "Polimanteia," 1595, we read : "the nightingall and the cuckow both grow hoarse at the rising of Syrius, the dogge-starre."

In the introduction to a reprint of the *Gothamite Tales*, 1630, inserted in *Old English Jest Books*, 1864, the present writer drew attention to the familiar myth of the Wise Men of Gotham hedging in the cuckoo ; and on the title of the old edition is a woodcut representing this profitable occupation. I am not at present in a positon to say whether the emblem of the Belgian lion-rampant enclosed in a hedge, and grasping in one claw a staff surmounted by the Stadtholder's bonnet, which occurs on some of the copper money of the Netherlands in the early part of the seventeenth century, is connected with the same tradition. The type of *Le lion à la haie* occurs on a piece of William IV., Count of Hainault (1404-17). struck at Valenciennes, and on money of Jacqueline of Bavaria, Countess of Hainault, from 1427 to 1433.

Among the many human and animistic transformation - records to be found in the Slavonic folk tales translated by Mr. A. H. Wratislaw, M.A., is a charming one of a young damsel who fell in love with a snake and bore it two children, one of whom was turned into a nightingale, and the other into a cuckoo. Among the Danes and Norwegians the early note of the bird is welcomed in divers but very human ways. Young girls, on hearing it, kiss their hands "in the direction from which the music comes and cry out. 'When shall I be married?' while the aged ask, 'When shall I be relieved from pain and affliction?'" *Globe*, March 2, 1895.

Cuckoo-Spit.—The larvæ of the cicada.

Cuerpo Santo. — See *Castor and Pollux*.

Curcuddoch, Curcuddie.—"To dance Curcuddie or Curcuddoch," (says Jamieson, in his Dictionary) "is a phrase used in Scotland to denote a play among children in which they sit on their houghs, and hop round in a circular form. Many of these old terms," Dr. Jamieson adds, "which now are almost entirely confined to the mouths of children, may be overlooked as nonsensical or merely arbitrary. But the most of them, we are persuaded, are as regularly formed as any other in the language. The first syllable of this word is undoubtedly the verb *curr*, to sit on the houghs or hams. The second may be from Teut. *kudde*, a flock; *kudd-en*, coire, convenire, congregari, aggregari; *kudde-wijs*, gregatim, catervatim, q. 'to curr together.' The same game is called Harry Hurcheon in the north of Scotland, either from the resemblance of one in this position to a hurcheon or hedge-hog, squatting under a bush; or from the Belg. *hurken*, to squat, to hurkle." This seems to be a form of *Cockle-Bread* or *Hot Cockles*.

Curfew.—Peshall says: "The custom of ringing the Curfew Bell at Carfax every night at eight o'clock. was by order of King Alfred, the restorer of our University, who ordained that all the inhabitants of Oxford should, at the ringing of that bell, cover up their fires and go to bed, which custom is observed to this day, and the bell as constantly rings at eight as Great Tom tolls at nine. It is also a custom, added to the former, after the ringing and tolling this bell, to let the inhabitants know the day of the month by so many tolls." *History of Oxford*, p. 177. A similar practice prevailed in parts of North Wales till very recently. The curfew is commonly believed to have been of Norman origin. A law was made by William the Conqueror that all people should put out their fires and lights at the eight o'clock bell, and go to bed. *Stow's Survey*, 1754, v. i., c. 15. The practice of this custom, we are told, to its full extent, was observed during that and the following reign only. Thomson has inimitably described its tyranny. In the second mayoralty of Sir Henry Colet, Knt. (father of Dean Colet), A.D. 1495, and under his direction, the solemn charge was given to the quest of wardmote in every ward, as it stands printed in the Custumary of London: "Also yf ther be anye paryshe clerke that ryngeth curfewe after the curfewe be ronge at Bowe Chyrche, or Saint Brydes Churche, or Saint Gyles without Cripplegat, all suche to be presented." From "A C. Mery Talys," 1526, we see that, in the time of Henry VIII. it was the duty of the sexton to ring the curfew-bell. In the Faversham Articles, 22 Hen. VIII., we read: "Imprimis, the sexton, or his sufficient deputy, shall lye in the churchsteeple; and at eight o'clock every night shall ring the curfewe by the space of a

quarter of an hour, with such bell as of old time hath been accustomed." I find, however, in "The Merry Devil of Edmonton," 1608, the sexton says:

"Well, 'tis nine a'clocke, 'tis time to ring curfew."

Shakespear, in "King Lear," act iii. sc. 4, writes:

Edgar: "This is the foul fiend Flibbertigibbet: He begins at curfew, and walks to the first cock." The following is an extract from the Churchwardens' and Chamberlain's Accounts of Kingston - upon Thames: "1651. For ringing the curfew bell for one year, £1 10s. 0d." Bridges, speaking of Byfield Church, tells us: "A bell is rung here at four in the morning, and at eight in the evening, for which the clerk hath 20s. yearly, paid him by the Rector." *Northamptonshire*, i., 110. Hutchins, speaking of Mappouder Church, mentions land given "to find a man to ring the morning and Curfeu Bell throughout the year." Also, under Ibberton, is mentioned one acre given for ringing the eight o'clock bell, and £4 for ringing the morning bell. *Dorsetshire*, ii., 267. Macaulay says: "The custom of ringing Curfew, which is still kept up at Claybrook, has probably obtained without intermission since the days of the Norman Conqueror." *Hist. of Claybrook*, 1791, p. 128. In 1848 the curfew was still rung at Hastings from Michaelmas till Lady-day, and the same was the case at Wrexham in North Wales, and elsewhere, till even a later date. Barrington, *Observations on the Statutes*, p. 153, tells us that "Curfew is written Curphour in a Scotish poem written before 1568. It is observed in the annotations on these poems, that by Act 144, Parl. 13, Jam. I., this bell was to be rung in boroughs at nine in the evening: and that the hour was afterwards changed to ten, at the solicitation of the wife of James Stewart, the favourite of James the sixth. There was a narrow street in Perth in the last century still called Couvre-Feu-Row, leading west to the Black Friars, where the Couvre Feu Bell gave warning to the inhabitants to cover their fires and go to rest when the clock struck ten.

We find the Couvre feu mentioned as a common and approved regulation on the Continent. It was used in most of the monasteries and towns of the North of Europe, the intent being merely to prevent the accidents of fires. All the common houses consisted at this time of timber. Moscow, therefore, being built with this material, generally suffered once in 20 years, and it was much the same at Stockholm, where in comparatively recent days persons were not allowed to smoke in the streets, and it was obligatory on all to co-operate at call in extinguishing fires. In mediæval Venice there was an analogous regulation, from which only the Barber's Quarter was exempt, because the members of that Gild probably united the surgical faculty, as with us, and their aid might be required during the night..

Curling.—See "Curling, an Ancient Scottish Game." By James Taylor, M.A., with illustrations by C. A. Doyle, 8vo., 1884.

Cushion-Dance.—A riotous sort of dance, formerly usual at weddings. It is thus mentioned in the "Apothegms of King James," 1658, p. 60. A wedding entertainment is spoken of. "At last when the masque was ended, and time had brought in the supper, the cushion led the dance out of the parlour into the hall," &c. In "The Dancing Master," 1698, p. 7, is an account of "Joan Sanderson, or the Cushion Dance, an old Round Dance. This dance is begun by a single person (either man or woman), who taking a cushion in his hand, dances about the room, and at the end of the tune he stops and sings, ' This dance it will no further go.' The musician answers, 'I pray you good Sir, why say you so? Man. ' Because Joan Sanderson will not come to.' Musick. 'She must come to, and she shall come to, and she must come whether she will or no.' Then he lays down the cushion before a woman, on which she kneels and he kisses her, singing, 'Welcom, Joan Sanderson, welcom, welcom.' Then she rises, takes up the cushion, and both dance, singing, ' Prinkum-prank'um is a fine dance, and shall we go dance it once again, and once again, and shall we go dance it once again?' Then making a stop, the woman sings as before, ' This dance it will no farther go.' Musick. 'I pray you. Madam, why say you so?' Woman. ' Because John Sanderson will not come to.' Musick. 'He must come to,' &c., (as before). And so she lays down the cushion before a man who, kneeling upon it, salutes her, she singing, 'Welcome John Sanderson,' &c. Then he taking up the cushion, they take both hands and dance round, singing as before, and thus they do till the whole company are taken into the ring. Then the cushion is laid before the first man, the woman singing, 'This dance,' &c. (as before), only instead of 'Come to,' they sing 'Go fro,' and instead of 'Welcome,' John Sanderson,' &c., they sing 'Farewell John Sanderson, farewell, farewell,' and so they go out, one by one, as they came in. Note, the woman is kiss'd by all the men in the ring, at her coming in, and going out, and likewise the man by the women." A correspondent of *Notes and Queries* thus de-

scribes the cushion-dance, as it was performed in Derbyshire, about sixty years since:—" The company were seated round presently, one carrying a large square cushion, the other an ordinary drinking-horn, china bowl, or silver tankard, according to the possessions of the family. The one carrying the cushion locked the door, putting the key in his pocket. Both gentlemen then went to the fiddler's corner, and after the cushion-bearer had put a coin in the vessel carried by the other, the fiddler struck up a lively tune, to which the young men began to dance round the room, singing or reciting to the music:—

> " Frinkum, frankum is a fine song,
> An' we will dance it all along;
> All along and round about,
> Till we find the pretty maid out."

After making the circuit of the room, they halted on reaching the fiddler's corner, and the cushion-bearer, still to the music of the fiddle, sang or recited:

> " Our song it will no further go ! "

The fiddler :—

> " Pray, kind sir, why say you so—"

The cushion-bearer :—

> " Because Jane Sanders won't come to."

The fiddler :—

> " She must come to, she shall come to,
> An' I'll make her whether she will or no ! "

The cushion-bearer and vessel-holder then proceeded with the dance, going as before round the room, singing " Frinkum, frankum," &c., till the cushion-bearer came to the lady of his choice, before whom he paused, placed the cushion on the floor at her feet, and knelt upon it. The vessel-bearer then offered the cup to the lady, who put money in it and knelt on the cushion in front of the kneeling gentleman. The pair kissed, arose, and the gentleman, first giving the cushion to the lady with a bow, placed herself behind her, taking hold of some portion of her dress. The cup-bearer fell in also, and they danced on to the fiddler's corner, and the ceremony was again gone through as at first with the substitution of the name of " John " for " Jane," thus :—

The lady :—

> " Our song it will no further go ! "

The fiddler :—

> " Pray, kind miss, why say you so ? "

The lady :—

> " Because John Sandars won't come to."

The fiddler:—

" He must come to, he shall come to,
An' I'll make him whether he will or
     no."

The dancing then proceeded, and the lady, on reaching her choice (a gentleman, of necessity), placed the cushion at his feet. He put money in the horn and knelt. They kissed and rose, he taking the cushion and his place in front of the lady, heading the next dance round, the lady taking him by the coat-tails, the first gentleman behind the lady, with the horn-bearer in the rear. In this way the dance went on till all present, alternately a lady and gentleman, had taken part in the ceremony. The dance concluded with a romp in file round the room to the quickening music of the fiddler, who at the close received the whole of the money collected by the horn-bearer." Compare, for farther particulars Nares, *Glossary*, 1859, in v., and Halliwell's *Dict.*, 1860, in v.

Cuthbert, St., Bishop of Durham.—The anniversary of the death of this holy and eminent personage, March 20, 687, in voluntary retirement, is one of the festivals of the church. An unusually long and complete account of his life and work may be seen in Chambers's *Encyclopædia*. Comp. *Bromfield* and *Luck of Eden Hall*. In Kensington Church, Middlesex, there is a painted window, in which St. Cuthbert is said to be represented playing at golf. He was by birth, one understands, an Irishman, but by original employment a North-country shepherd.

Cutting Off the Fiddler's Head.—See *Manx*.

Cuzship. — They had formerly in printing offices an usage called *cuzship*, which is described by Gent, the York printer of the last century, in his *Autobiography*, where he speaks of his attachment to the staff of Mr. Mears, the stationer and printer. He tells us that, in addition to *Beer-money*, he was obliged to submit to the immemorial custom of being sworn a cuz, the origin of which he could not learn. He proceeds:—"It commenced by walking round the chapel (printing rooms being called such, because first begun to be practised in Westminster Abbey) singing an alphabetical anthem, tuned literally to the vowels; striking me, kneeling, with a broadsword, and pouring ale upon my head; my title was exhibited, and to this effect: 'Thomas Gent, Baron of College Green, Earl of Fingall, with power to the limits of Dublin bar, captain-general of the Teagues, near the Lake of Allen, and lord high admiral over all the bogs in Ireland.'" He adds that they even gave

him godfathers, which his Presbyterian training had not previously accorded.

Cymmortha, or Cymmorth Gwan.—Pughe remarks: " The wearing of the leek on St. David's Day probably originated from the custom of *Cymhortha*, or the neighbourly aid practised among farmers, which is of various kinds. In some districts of South Wales, all the neighbours of a small farmer without means appoint a day when they all attend to plough his land, and the like; and at such a time it is a custom for each individual to bring his portion of leeks, to be used in making pottage for the whole company : and they bring nothing else but the leeks in particular for the occasion." Anciently it was a custom in Wales, to institute associations among neighbours and friends for the performance of any work or undertaking, and this usage, which appears to have had its rise in motives of industrial expediency, was gradually turned both to political and social account. These Cymmortha formed the pretext, as early as the reign of Henry IV. for insurrectionary gatherings, and by 4 Hen. iv. c. 27, it was ordained, " that no westrye, rhymer, minstrel, nor vagabond be in any wise sustained in the land of Wales to make Cymmorthas or gatherings upon the common people there." Sir H. Ellis, to whom I am indebted for this information, (" Orig. Letters," 2nd Series, 1827), adds, that " Wood, speaking of Bala, says, ' It is a small town at the bottom of the lake of that name, and is celebrated for its vast trade in woollen stockings, in the knitting of which men, women, and children are incessantly employed. They assemble in the winter at each other's houses, listening to some ancient song, or provincial tale, and this meeting is called *Cymmorth Gwan*, or Knitting Assembly.'" The Cymmortha (or Comortha) was, in fact, a sort of Primitive Trades' Union, and part of the system was the relief of those members of it, who, by some unavoidable cause, happened to fall into distress. That such was the case is pretty evident from a letter addressed to Lord Burghley by Richard Price of Brecknock, January 31, 1575-6. The Cymmortha was more than once forbidden by statute; but the Bishop of Coventry and Lichfield, in a letter to Thomas Cromwell, describes an odd privilege granted by the King to a gentleman in pecuniary straits, one George Mathew, Esquire, in the twenty-seventh year of his reign; it was the right of holding a Commortha for his personal benefit, " any statute, ordinaunce, or other thing to the contrary hereof notwithstanding." The Bishop estimates the value of the Royal license to Mathew at not less than 1,000 marks. Owen's *Welsh Dictionary*, v.v. *Cawa,* and

Cymborth, may be consulted; but there is nothing of importance which is not noticed above.

Cypress.—It is doubtful whether the cypress was meant by the ancients to be an emblem of an immortal state, or of annihilation after death; since the properties of the tree apply, happily enough, to each. The cypress was used on funeral occasions, say the commentators on Virgil, "vel quia cariem non sentit, ad gloriæ immortalitatem significandam; vel quia semel excisa, non renascitur, ad mortem exprimendam"; Servius' Com. on Œneid. iii., p. 64, and the Delphin edit.; but, instead of that, the ancient Christians used the things before mentioned, and deposited them under the corpse in the grave to signify that they who die in Christ, do not cease to live; for though, as to the body, they die to the world, yet, as to their souls, they live and revive to God. And as the carrying of these evergreens is an emblem of the soul's immortality, so it is also of the resurrection of the body: for as these herbs are not entirely plucked up, but only cut down, and will, at the returning season, revive and spring up again; so the body, like them, is but cut down for a while, and will rise and shoot up again at the resurrection. For, in the language of the evangelical prophet, our bones shall flourish like an herb. The reader conversant with the classics will call to mind here the beautiful thought in the Idyllium on Bion by Moschus: though the fine spirit of it will evaporate when we apply it to the Christian doctrine of the resurrection. The antithesis will be destroyed. Moschi *Idyll*, iii., l. 100. The cypress, however, appears to have been retained to later times. Coles says: "Cypresse garlands are of great account at funeralls amongst the gentiler sort, but rosemary and bayes are used by the commons both at funeralls and weddings. They are all plants which fade not a good while after they are gathered, and used (as I conceive) to intimate unto us that the remembrance of the present solemnity might not dye presently, but be kept in minde for many yeares." *Introduction to the Knowledge of Plants*, 64. The line,

"And cypress which doth biers adorn,"

is cited in Poole's "English Parnassus," 1657. Spenser mentions

"The aspin, good for staves, the cypress funerall."

Dekker, in his "Wonderfull Yeare," 1603, signat. c 3 verso, describes a charnell-house pavement, "instead of greene rushes, strewde with blasted rosemary, wither'd hyacinthes, fatalle cypresse, and ewe, thickly mingled with heapes of dead men's

bones." He says, signat. D 2 verso, "Rosemary, which had wont to be sold for twelve pence an armefull, went now" (on account of the Plague), "at six shillings a handfull." In "The Exequies," by Stanley, we read:

"Yet strew
Upon my dismall grave,
Such offerings as you have,
Bind with cypresse and sad ewe,
For kinder flowers can take no birth
Or growth from such unhappy earth."

Poems, 1651, p. 54. In "The Marrow of Complements," &c., 1655, is "A Mayden's Song for her dead Lover," in which cypress and yew are particularly mentioned as funeral plants:

"Come you whose loves are dead,
And, whilst I sing,
Weepe and wring
Every hand, and every head
Bind with cypresse and sad ewe,
Ribbands black, and candles blue;
For him that was of men most true.
"Come with heavy moaning,
And on his grave
Let him have
Sacrifice of sighes and groaning,
Let him have faire flowers enough,
White, and purple, green, and yellow,
For him that was of men most true."

In "Round about our Coal Fire," circâ 1730, I find the following passage on this subject:—"The rooms were embowered with holly, ivy, cyprus, bays, laurel, and Miseltoe, and a bouncing Christmas log in the chimney." In this acount the cypress is quite a new article. Indeed, I should as soon have expected to have seen the yew as the cyprus used on this joyful occasion.

Dab.—Pegge, in the "Gentleman's Magazine" for September, 1767, derives the word *Dab*, in the phrase of "a dab at such or such a thing," as a vulgar corruption of the Latin *adeptus*.

Daffodil.—Herrick describes a
"*Divination by a Daffodil.*
When a Daffadil I see,
Hanging down her head t'wards me;
Guesse I may, what I must be:
First, I shall decline my head;
Secondly, I shall be dead,
Lastly, safely buried."
Hesperides, 1648, p. 40.

Dagger-Money.—See *Newcastle-on-Tyne*.

Dancing at Weddings.—Among the Anglo-Saxons, after the nuptial feast, "the remaining part of the day was spent by the youth of both sexes in mirth and dancing, while the graver sort sat down to their drinking bout, in which they highly delighted." Among the higher ranks there was, in later times, a wedding sermon, an epithalamium, and at night a masque. It was a general custom between the wedding dinner and supper to have dancing. In "The Christian State of Matrimony," 1543, fol. 49, we read : " After the bancket and feast, there begynnethe a vayne, madde, and unmanerlye fashion, for the bryde must be brought into an open dauncynge place. Then is there such a rennynge, leapynge, and flyngyng amonge them, then is there suche a lyftynge up and discoverynge of the damselles clothes and other womennes apparell, that a man might thynke they were sworne to the Devels Daunce. Then muste the poore bryde kepe foote with al dauncers and refuse none, how scabbed, foule, droncken, rude, and shameles soever he be. Then must she oft tymes heare and se much wyckednesse and many an uncomely word; and that noyse and romblyng endureth even tyll supper." So, in the "Summe of the Holy Scripture," 1547, signat. H 3 verso : " Suffer not your children to go to weddings or banckettes; for nowe a daies one can learne nothing there but ribaudry and foule wordes." In Selden's " Table Talk," first printed in 1689, under the head " Excommunication," is an allusion to the custom of dancing at weddings: " Like the wench that was to be married : she asked her mother, when 'twas done, if she should go to bed presently? No, says her mother, you must dine first. And then to bed, mother? No, you must dance after dinner. And then to bed, mother? No, you must go to supper," &c. " Quas epulas omnes Tripudia atque Saltationes comitantur. Postremo Sponsa adrepta ex Saltatione subito atque Sponsus in Thalamum deducuntur." " Antiq. Convivial.," fol. 68. This requisite has not been omitted in the " Collier's Wedding." :

" The pipers wind and take their post,
And go before to clear the coast."

I do not know to what particular revel-day Browne refers in the second song of his First Book, where he speaks of the shepherd, who wears the trophies of his manly skill or strength :

" Piping he sate, as merry as his looke,
And by him lay his bottle and his hooke.
His buskins (edg'd with siluer) were of silke,
Which held a legge more white then mornings milk.
Those buskins he had got and brought away
For dancing best vpon the reuell day."

Works, by Hazlitt, 1868, i., 68. In Heywood's " Fayre Mayd of the Exchange," 1607, Bernard enters with news of a wedding in Gracechurch Street, where dancing is going on :—

" Bernard. By Jesu ! the rarest dancing in Christendom.
Bowdler. Sweet rascal, where? Oh, do not kill my soul
With such delays. . . .
Ber. At a wedding in Gracious Street.
Bowd. Come, come away; I long to see the man
In dancing art that does more than I can.
Ber. Than you, sir? he lives not.
Bowd. Why, I did understand thee so.
Ber. You only excepted, the world besides
Cannot afford more exquisite dancers
Than are now cap'ring at that bride-ale house."

The following passage is curious, from its enumeration of several old dances, which were usual at weddings :

" J. Slime. I come to dance, not to quarrel. Come, what shall it be? Rogero?
Jem. Rogero ! no ! we will dance the beginning of the world.
Sisly. I love no dance so well as John come kiss me now.
Nich. I that have ere now deserv'd a cushion, call for the cushion-dance.
R. Brick. For my part, I like nothing so well as Tom Tyler.
Jem. No; we'll have the Hunting of the Fox.
J. Slime. The hay; the hay ! there's nothing like the hay—
Nich. I have said, do say, and will say again—
Jem. Every man agree to have it as Nick says.
All. Content.
Nich. It hath been, it now is, and it shall be—
Sisly. What, Master Nicholas? What?
Nich. Put on your smock o' Monday.
Jem. So the dance will come cleanly off. Come, for God's sake agree of something: if you like not that, put it to the musicians, or let me speak for all, and we'll have Sellengers round."

Elsewhere we read : " The custom of dancing in the church-yard at their feasts and revels is universal in Radnorshire, and very common in other parts of the Principality. Indeed this solemn abode is rendered a kind of circus for every sport and exercise. The young men play at fives and tennis against the wall of the church. It is not, however, to be understood that they literally dance over the graves of their progenitors. This amusement takes place on the north side of the Church-yard, where it is the custom not to bury. It is rather singular, however, that the association of the place, surrounded by memorials of mortality, should not deaden the impulses of joy in minds, in other respects not insensible to the suggestions of vulgar superstition." Malkin's *S. Wales*, 1804, p. 261. Again, under Aberedwy, "In this church yard are two uncommonly large yew trees, evidently of great age, but in unimpaired luxuriance and preservation, under the shade of which an intelligent clergyman of the neighbourhood informed me that he had frequently seen sixty ccuple dancing at Aberedwy Feast on the 14th of June. The boughs of the two trees intertwine, and afford ample space for the evolutions of so numerous a company within their ample covering." Every Englishman has heard of the "Dance round our coal fire," ridiculed by the Duke of Buckingham in the *Rehearsal*; which receives illustration from the probably ancient practice of dancing round the fires in our Inns of Court (and perhaps other halls in great men's houses). This practice was still in 1733 observed at an entertainment at the Inner Temple Hall, on Lord Chancellor Talbot taking leave of the house, when the Master of the Revels took the Chancellor by the hand, and he, Mr. Page; who, with the judges, serjeants, and benchers, danced round the coal fire, according to the old ceremony, three times, and all the times the antient song, with music, was sung by a man in a Bar gown."

Dandies.—See *Cockal*.

Dark Lantern.—Barrington, speaking of the Curfew, observes "that there is a general vulgar error, that it is not lawful to go about with a dark lantern. All popular errors," he adds, "have some foundation : and the regulation of the curfew may possibly have been the occasion of this." But he derives this notion from Guy Fawkes' dark lantern. *Observations on the Statutes*, 154 *note*.

Darvel Gathern, Worship of. — 5th April. — It appears that one of the objects of pilgrimage in the Principality of Wales before the Reformation, was the Image of Darvell Gathern in the diocese of St. Asaph; who or what Darvell Gathern was, does not appear ; but the superstition is mentioned by Hall the Chronicler and others. In a letter from Ellis Price to Secretary Cromwell, dated 6th April, 1538, there is the following account of it :— "There ys an Image of Darvellgadarn, within the said diocese, in whome the people have so greate confidence, hope, and truste, that they cumme dayly a pillgramage unto hym, somme withe kyne, other with oxen or horsis, and the reste withe money : in so muche that there was fyve or syxe hundrethe pilgrimes to a mans estimacion, that offered to the saide image the fifte daie of this presente monethe of Aprill. The innocente people hath ben sore aluryd and entised to worship the saide image, in so muche that there is a commyn sayinge as yet amongst them that who so ever will offer anie thinge to the saide Image of Darvellgadern, he hathe power to fatche hym or them that so offers oute of Hell when they be dampned." Besides this "commyn sayinge," there appears from Hall to have been a prophecy current "that the image should set a whole forest on fire" ; and this was supposed to be fulfilled, when the idol was burnt in Smithfield with a friar so named, in May, 1538. For a few farther particulars, the reader may turn to Ellis's "Original Letters," First Series, pages 83-4 of the second volume. There is a second letter from Ellis Price to Cromwell, at a somewhat later date ; but we do not get any nearer to a solution of the mystery as to Darvel Gadern, beyond the patent fact that he was held in great veneration by the Welsh. Sir H. Ellis in a note indeed quotes the following passage from Michael Woodde's "Dialogue between two Neighbours," 1554 : "If the Welshman would have a purse, he praied to Darvel Gatherne." Pennant calls him St. Derfel Gatherne.

Date-Stone.—The following legend, intended to honour the Virgin Mother, was considered by Brand worth inserting, and I have retained it : "Eating some dates with an old man, but a credulous Christian, he said : that the letter O remained upon the stone of a date for a remembrance that our blessed Lady, the Virgin, with her divine Babe in her arms, resting herself at the foot of a palm-tree (which inclined her branches and offered a cluster of dates to her Creator), our lady plucked some of the dates, and eating, satisfied with the taste and flavour, cryed out in amazement, 'O how sweet they are!' This exclamation engraved the letter O, the first word of her speech, upon the date stone, which being very hard, better preserved it.' "

Daubing.—See *Bride-Wain*.

David's Day (March 1).—St. David, Archbishop of Menevy, now from him called St. David's, in Pembrokeshire, flourished, according to Pits, in the fifth and sixth centuries of the Christian era, and died at the age of a hundred and forty years. In the "Episcopal Almanack for 1677," he is described as uncle to King Arthur. There is a Welsh pedigree which shows him to have been the son of Caradog, Lord of Cardiganshire, by Non, daughter of Ynyr, of Caer Gawch. "The Britons on this day constantly wear a leek, in memory of a famous and notable victory obtained by them over the Saxons, they, during the battle, having leeks in their hats for their military colours and distinction of themselves, by the persuasion of the said prelate, St. David." Another account adds, that they were fighting, under their king Cadwallo, near a field that was replenished with that vegetable. But the battle is recorded by Jeffrey of Monmouth in the 8th and 9th chapters of his twelfth book. In the " Chronicles of Englonde," edit. 1500, signat. C 3, we have, in allusion to the Welsh :

> " They haue gruell to potage,
> And lekes kynde to companage— "

And again—

> " Atte mete and after eke,
> Her solace is salte and leke."

The " Salisbury Primer " contains the following :

> " Davyd of Wales loveth well lekes.
> That wyll make Gregory lene chekes ;
> Yf Edwarde do eate some with them,
> Mary sende hym to Bedlem."

Sir John Harington, in his " Brief View of the State of the Church," 1653, speaks of an indulgence of Pope Calixtus II., by which one pilgrimage to St. David's was made equivalent to two to Rome, whence came the distich :

> " Roma semel quantum,
> Bis dat Menevia tantum."

Henry VII., having Welsh blood in his veins, was supposed to be under rather peculiar obligations, possibly, as regarded the observance of St. David's festival ; on the anniversary of 1494-5, under the date of March 6, we find in that prince's "Privy Purse Expenses " ; " To the Walshemen towards ther feste, £2,"—meaning the Welshmen who happened to be about the *Dance*, with a body of notices illustrative of the present subject, including Court. The feast given to the Welshmen on this festival remained in force during the reign of Henry VIII. On two or three occasions, the yeomen of the guard presented the Princess Mary with a leek, for which they received 15s. in reward.

Dr. Owen Pughe says : " In consequence of the romances of the middle ages which created the Seven Champions of Christendom, St. David has been dignified with the title of patron Saint of Wales : but this rank, however, is hardly known among the people of the Principality, being a title diffused among them from England in modern times. The writer of this account never heard of such a patron saint, nor of the leek as his symbol, until he became acquainted therewith in London." *Cambrian Biography*, 1803, p. 86. The following lines occur in Harl. MS., 1977, fol. 9 :

> "I like the leeke above all herbes and flowers.
> When first we wore the same the feild was ours.
> The leeke is white and green, whereby is ment
> That Britaines are both stout and eminent ;
> Next to the lion and the unicorn,
> The leeke the fairest emblyn that is worne."

In Shakespear's " Henry the Fifth," act v. sc. i., Gower asks Fluellen, " But why wear your leek to-day ? Saint Davy's Day is past." From Fluellen's reply we gather that he wore his leek in consequence of an affront he had received but the day before from Pistol whom he afterwards compels to eat the leek, skin and all, in revenge for the insult, quaintly observing to him " When you take occasions to see leeks hereafter, I pray you, mock at them, that is all." Gower too upbraids Pistol for mocking "at an ancient tradition—begun upon an honourable respect, and worn as a memorable trophy of pre-deceased valour." In " The Bishop's last Goodnight," 1642, the 14th stanza runs thus :

> " Landaff, provide for St. David's Day,
> Lest the leeke and red-herring run away :
> Are you resolved to go or stay?
> You are called for, Landaff :
> Come in, Landaff."

There is a poetical broadside in double columns, entitled : " The Welsh-mens Glory, or the famous Victories of the Ancient Britons obtained upon St. David's Day." It begins :

> " The honor, glory, and the grace,
> Of valiant Brute's tryumphant race,
> Shewing the reasons wherefore they
> Wear leeks upon St. David's Day.

Ursula is introduced in "The Vow-breaker, or, the fayre Maid of Clifton," 1636, act i. sc. i. as telling Anne—"Thou marry German ! His head's like a Welchman's crest on St. Davy's Day ! He looks like a hoary frost in December ! Now, Venus blesse me ! I'd rather ly by a statue." From a notice in the " Flying Post " for 1699, it appears that it was then usual for the Court to wear a leek on this day :— " Yesterday, being St. David's Day, the King, according to custom, wore a leek in honour of the ancient Britons, the same being presented to him by the Serjeant-porter, whose place it is, and for which he claims the cloaths which his Majesty wore that day. The courtiers, in imitation of his Majesty, wore leeks likewise." Misson, in his " Travels in England," translated by Ozell, p. 334, says, speaking of the Welsh custom of wearing leeks, "The King himself is so complaisant as to bear them company." Coles, in his "Adam in Eden" says, concerning leeks, "The gentlemen in Wales have them in great regard, both for their feeding, and to wear in their hats upon St. David's Day." To a querist in "The British Apollo," the following answer is given : "The ceremony is observed on the first of March, in commemoration of a signal victory obtained by the Britons, under the command of a famous general, known vulgarly by the name of St. David. The Britons wore a leek in their hats to distinguish their friends from their enemies in the heat of the battle." There is the following proverb on this day :

"Upon St. David's Day, put oats and barley in the clay."

It is a custom still kept up on this festival, for each of the scholars at Westminster, being Welshmen, to receive a guinea from some ancient endowment made for the purpose. About twenty received it in 1879. See *Eton School.*

Dawzin.—The faculty of divination is believed in the west to be confined to certain favoured persons, and is termed Dawzin.

Days.—See *Lucky and Unlucky,* and *Perilous Days,* infrâ.

Dead Body, Seizure of a, for Debt.—The earliest instance on record occurs, perhaps, in the Romance of Sir Amadace. The security was retained till the claim was satisfied. It is difficult, Daines Barrington observes, to account for many of the prevailing vulgar errors with regard to what is supposed to be law. Such are that the body of a debtor may be taken in execution after his death : which, however, was practised in Prussia before Frederic II. abolished it by the Code Frederique. A singular case occurred at Venice in 1763, where the attempt was made to seize the remains of a Doge on this account. See Hazlitt's *Venetian Republic,* 1900, ii., 308 and *Errors,* infra. In Massinger's "Fatall Dowry," 1632, act ii. sc. 1, are some curious thoughts on this subject, spoken at the funeral of a marshal in the army, who died in debt, on account of which the corpse was arrested :

"What ! weepe ye, souldiers? . . .
The jaylors and the creditors do
weepe ; . . . .
Be these thy bodies balme : these and
thy vertue
Keepe thy fame ever odoriferous—
Whilst the great, proud, rich, undeserving man. . . .
Shall quickly, both in bone and name consume,
Though wrapt in lead, spice, seare-cloth, and perfume.

—This is a sacrifice : our Showre shall crowne
His sepulcher with olive, myrrh, and bayes,
The plants of peace, of sorrow, victorie."

Death-Howl.—Howling at funerals appears to have been of general use in the Papal times from the following passage in Veron, in his *Hunting of Purgatory,* 1561, where, speaking of St. Chrysostom, he says : "No mention at al doth he make of that manner of singinge or rather unsemely howling that your Papists use for the salvation of theyr dead, therby, under a pretence of godlinesse, picking the purses of the pore simple and ignorant people." Stafford observes : "It is a wonder to see the childish whining we nowadayes use at the funeralls of our friends. If we could houl them back againe, our lamentations were to some purpose ; but as they are, they are vaine, and in vain." *Meditations and Resolutions,* 1612, p. 16. The minister of Nig, co. Kincardine, reported in 1793, of the people thereabout : "On the sudden death of their relations, or fear of it, by the sea turning dangerous, the fisher people, especially the females, express their sorrow by exclamation of voice and gesture of body, like the Eastern nations, and those in an early state of civilization." Mungo Park, in his "Travels," relates that among the Moors, a child died in one of the tents, "and the mother and the relations immediately began the death-howl. They were joined by a number of female visitors, who came on purpose to assist at this melancholy concert. I had no opportunity of seeing the burial, which is generally performed secretly in the dusk of the evening, and frequently at only a few yards distance from the tent. Over the grave they plant one particular shrub ; and no stranger is allowed to pluck a leaf, or even to touch it." Speaking elsewhere of the negroes, he says : "When a person of consequence dies, the relations and neighbours meet together and manifest their sorrow by loud howlings." Compare *Ireland.*

Death-Omens. — Nearly all the death-omens then credited are set forth by Deloney in his romance of "Thomas of Reading," probably published anterior to 1600. Lupton, in his *Third Book,* says : "If the forehead of the sick wax red, and his brows fall down, and his nose wax sharp and cold, and his left eye becomes little, and the corner of his eye run, if he turn to the wall, if his ears be cold, or if he may suffer no brightness, and if his womb fall, if he pulls straws or the cloaths of his bed, or if he pick often his nostrils with his fingers, and if he wake much, these are almost certain tokens of death." The sharpness of the nose and the pulling of the bed-clothes were adopted by Shakespear in the deathbed scene of Falstaff in Henry V. By the flying and crying of ravens over their houses, especially in the dusk evening, and where one is sick, they conclude death: the same they conclude by the much crying of owles in the night, neer their houses at such a time," according to the author of *Demonology*, 1597. Werenfels says, p. 7, "The superstitious person could wish indeed that his estate might go to his next and best friends after his death, but he had rather leave it to any body than make his will, for fear lest he should presently die after it." The subsequent lines, from Dryden and Lee's *Œdipus*,iv., 1, need no apology for their introduction:

"For when we think Fate hovers o'er our heads,
Our apprehensions shoot beyond all bounds,
Owls, ravens, crickets seem the Watch of Death;
Nature's worst vermin scare her godlike sons;
Echoes, the very leavings of a voice,
Grow babling ghosts and call us to our graves:
Each mole-hill thought swells to a huge Olympus,
While we, fantastic dreamers, heave and puff,
And sweat with an imagination's weight;
As if, like Atlas, with these mortal shoulders
We could sustain the burden of the world."

Hear Molinæus:—"Si visitans Ægrum, lapidem inventum per viam attollat et sub lapide inveniatur Vermis se movens, aut formica vivens, faustum Omen est, et indicium fore ut æger convalescat; si nihil invenitur, res est conclamata, et certa mors, ut docet Burchardus, Decretorum, lib. xix." "Vates," p. 154. Lupton, in his third book of *Notable Things*, says : "If a firr tree be touched, withered, or burned with lightening, it signifies that the master or mistresse thereof shall shortly die." Comp. *Bay-Tree*. In Heylin's "Life of Laud," it is stated, that "the Bishop, going into his study, which nobody could get into but himself, found his own picture lying all along on its face, which extremely perplexed him, he looking upon it as ominous." Grose tells us that, besides general notices of death, many families have particular warnings or notices; some of the appearance of a bird, and others by the figure of a tall woman dressed all in white, who goes shrieking about the house. This apparition is common in Ireland, where it is called Benshea and the Shrieking Woman. Pennant says, that many of the great families in Scotland had their dæmon or genius, who gave them monitions of future events. Thus the family of Rothmurchas had the bodack au dun, or the ghost of the hill: Kinchardines the spectre of the bloody hand. Gartinbeg House was haunted by Bodach Gartin, and Tulloch Germs by Maug Monlack or the girl with the hairy left hand. The Synod gave frequent orders that inquiry should be made into the truth of this apparition; and one or two declared that they had seen one that answered the description.

Camerarius writes: "There bee some Princes of Germanie that have particular and apparent presages and tokens, full of noise, before or about the day of their death, as extraordinairie roaring of lions and barking of dogs, fearful noises and bustlings by night in castles, striking of clocks, and tolling of bels at undue times and howres, and other warnings whereof none could give any reason." *Living Librarie*, 1621, p. 284. Delrio adds, that in Bohemia a female spectre in mourning is accustomed to appear in a certain castle of an illustrious family, before one of the wives of its seigneurs dies. *Disquisitiones Magicœ*, p. 592. Compare *Luck of Eden Hall*, infrâ, and Hazlitt's *Proverbs*, 1882, p. 763.

Death-Rattle.—The dead or death rattle, a particular kind of noise made in respiring by a person in the extremity of sickness, is still considered in the North, as well as in other parts, of England, as an omen of death. Levinus Lemnius, in his "Occult Miracles of Nature," lib. ii. ch. 15, is very learned concerning it: "In Belgica regione, totoque Septentrionalis plagæ tractu, morituri certa argumenta proferunt emigrandi, edito sonitu murmuloso, nec est, qui absque hujusmodi indicio vitam non finiat. Siquidem imminente morte sonum edunt, tanquam aquæ labentis per salebras, locaque anfractuosa atque incurva, murmur, aut qualem Siphunculi ac Fistulæ in aquæ ductibus sonitum excitant. Cùm enim vocalem arteriam occludi contingat, spiritus qui confertim erumpere gestit, nactus angustum meatum, collapsamque fistulam, gargarismo quodam prodit, ac raucum per lævia murmur efficit, scatebrisque arentes deserit artus. Conglomeratus itaque spiritus, spumaque turgida commixtus, sonitum excitat, reciprocanti maris æstui assimilem. Quod ipsum in nonnullis etiam fit ob panniculos ac membranas in rugas contractas, sic ut spiritus obliquè ac sinuoso volumine decurrat. Hi, autem, qui valido sunt vastoque corpore, et qui violenta morte periunt, gravius resonant, diutiusque cum morte luctantur, ob humoris copiam ac densos crassosque spiritus. Iis vero qui extenuato sunt corpore, ac lenta morte contabescunt, minus impetuose lenique sonitu fertur Spiritus, ac sensim placideque extinguuntur, ac quodammodo obdormiscunt."

Death - Watch. — "How many people have I seen, says Defoe, "in the most terrible palpitations for months together, expecting every hour the approach of some calamity, only by a little worm, which breeds in old wainscot, and, endeavouring to eat its way out, makes a noise like the movement of a watch." *Duncan Campbell*, 1732, p. 61. Wallis gives the following account of the insect so called, whose ticking has been thought by ancient superstition to forbode death in a family. "The small scarab called the Death-Watch (Scarabæus galeatus pulsator) is frequent among dust and in decayed rotten wood, lonely and retired. It is one of the smallest of the Vagipennia, of a dark brown, with irregular light brown spots, the belly plicated, and the wings under the cases pellucid; like other beetles, the helmet turned up, as is supposed for hearing; the upper lip hard and shining. By its regular pulsations, like the ticking of a watch, it sometimes surprises those that are strangers to its nature and properties, who fancy its beating portends a family change, and the shortening of the thread of life. Put into a box, it may be heard and seen in the act of pulsation, with a small proboscis against the side of it, for food more probably than for hymenæal pleasure as some have fancied." *History of Northumberland*, i., 367. Baxter observes that "There are many things that ignorance causeth multitudes to take for prodigies. I have had many discreet friends that have been affrighted with the noise called a death-watch, whereas I have since, near three years ago, oft found by trial, that it is a noise made upon paper, by a little, nimble, running worm, just like a louse, but whiter, and quicker; and it is most usually behind a paper pasted to a wall, especially to wainscot: and it is rarely, if ever heard, but in the heat of summer." Then immediately after he adds : "But he who can deny it to be a prodigy, which is recorded by Melchior Adamus, of a great and good man, who had a clock-watch that had layen in a chest many years unused; and when he lay dying, at eleven o'clock, of itself, in that chest, it struck eleven in the hearing of many." *World of Spirits*, 1691, 203.

Deaths.—The custom, formerly only too much diffused, of removing the pillow from the head of a dying person in order to accelerate the end, is sometimes ascribed to the superstitious notion, that the presence of a pigeon's feather among the rest prevents the fatal catastrophe.

But there was also a belief that this practice afforded relief to the individual *articulo mortis*.

Dedication of Churches.—As in the times of Paganism annual festivals were celebrated in honour and memory of their gods, goddesses, and heroes, when the people resorted together at their temples and tombs; and as the Jews constantly kept their anniversary feast of Dedication in remembrance of Judas Maccabæus their deliverer; so it hath been an ancient custom among the Christians of this island to keep a feast every year upon a certain week or day, in remembrance of the finishing of the building of their parish church, and of the first solemn dedicating of it to the service of God, and committing it to the protection of some guardian saint or angel. At the conversion of the Saxons, says Bourne, by Austin the monk, the heathen Paganalia were continued among the converts, with some regulations, by an order of Gregory I., to Melitus the Abbot, who accompanied Austin in his mission to this island. His words are to this effect : On the day of dedication, or the birth-day of Holy Martyrs, whose relics are there placed, let the people make to themselves booths of the boughs of trees, round about those very churches which had been the temples of idols, and in a religious way to observe a feast : that beasts may no longer be slaughtered by way of sacrifice to the devil but for their own eating and the glory of God : and that when they are satisfied they may return thanks to him who is the giver of all good things. Silas Taylor says, that "in the days of yore, when a Church was to be built, they watched and prayed on the Vigil of the Dedication, and took that point of the horizon where the sun arose for the east, which makes that variation, so that few stand true except those built between the two equinoxes. I have experimented some churches, and have found the line to point to that part of the horizon where the sun rises, on the day of that Saint to whom the church is dedicated." But it being observed that the number of holidays was excessively increased, to the detriment of civil government and secular affairs, and also that the great irregularities and licentiousness which had crept into these festivities by degrees, especially in the churches, chapels, and churchyards, were found highly injurious to piety, virtue, and good manners, statutes and canons were made to regulate them : and by an Act of Convocation passed by Henry the Eighth in 1536, their number was in some measure lessened. The Feast of the Dedication of every Church was ordered to be kept upon one and the same day everywhere; that is, on the first Sunday in October : and the saint's day to which the church was dedicated entirely laid aside. This act is now disregarded ; but probably it arose thence that the Feast of Wakes was first put off till the Sunday following the proper day, that the people might not have too many avocations from their necessary and domestic business. "Ut die Dedicationis, vel Natalitiis Sanctorum Martyrum, quorum illic Reliquiæ ponuntur, tabernacula sibi circa easdem Ecclesias, quæ ex fanis commutatæ sunt de ramis arborum faciant," &c.—*Bed.* lib. . . . . cap. 30. Borlase says, the Parish Feasts instituted in commemoration of the dedication of parochial churches were highly esteemed among the primitive Christians, and originally kept on the saint's day to whose memory the church was dedicated. The generosity of the founder and endower thereof was at the same time celebrated, and a service composed suitable to the occasion. This is still done in the colleges of Oxford, to the memory of the respective founders. On the eve of this day prayers were said and hymns were sung all night in the church ; and from these watchings the festivals were styled Wakes ; which name still continues in many parts of England, though the vigils have been long abolished. Dugdale's *Warwickshire*, p. 575 ; and compare *May-Day.* The following entries occur in the accounts of St.-Mary-at-Hill, 1495 : " For bred and wyn and ale to Bowear (a singer) and his co., and to the Quere on Dedication Even, and on the morrow, i.s. vjd." 1555. "Of the Sumcyon of our Ladys Day, which is our church holyday, for drinkyng over-night at Mr. Haywards, at the King's Head, with certen of the parish and certen of the chapel and other singing men, in wyne, pears, and sugar, and other chargis, viiis. jd. For a dynner for our Ladys Day, for all the syngyng men and syngyng children, il. For a pounde and halfe of sugar at dinner, is. vijd. ob. 1557. For garlands for our Ladys Day & for strawenge yerbes, ijs. ijd. For bryngyng down the images to Rome Land and other things to be burnt." In these accounts, "To singing men and children from the King's Chapel, and elsewhere," on some of the grand festivals, particularly the parish feast (our Lady's Assumption), a reward in money and a feast are charged in several years. Carew, who wrote about 1585, tells us that "The Saints Feast is kept upon the Dedication Day by every householder of the parish, within his own dores, each entertaining such forrayne acquaintance, as will not fayle ,when their like turne cometh about, to requite them with the like kindness." *Survey of Cornwall*, 1602, p. 69. But Borlase informs us that, in his time, it being very inconvenient, especially in harvest

time, to observe the parish feast on the saint's day, they were by the bishop's special authority transferred to the following Sunday. Charles I. in his "Book of Sports," 1633, removed the prohibition which had been exercised against these dedication-feasts. This tract is little more than a re-issue of James the First's Book, 1618. In Aubrey's "Natural History of Wiltshire," first printed in 1847, we read : "The night before the Day of Dedication of the Church, certain officers were chosen for gathering the money for charitable uses. Old John Wastfield of Langley was Peter man at St. Peter's Chapel there," and from the same source it appears that it was customary to spend the eve of the Dedication-day in fasting and prayer. In the southern parts of this nation, says Bourne, most country villages are wont to observe some Sunday in a more particular manner than the rest, i.e., the Sunday after the day of dedication, or day of the saint to whom the church was dedicated. Then the inhabitants deck themselves in their gaudiest clothes, and have open doors and splendid entertainments for the reception and treating of their relations and friends, who visit them on that occasion from each neighbouring town. The morning is spent for the most part at church, though not as that morning was wont to be spent, in commemorating the saint or martyr, or in gratefully remembering the builder and endower. The remaining part of the day is spent in eating and drinking. Thus they also spend a day or two afterwards in all sorts of rural pastimes and exercises : such as dancing on the green, wrestling, cudgelling &c. *Antiq. Vulg.*, ch. 30. "In the Northern Counties," says Hutchinson, "these holy feasts are not yet abolished ; and in the county of Durham many are yet celebrated. They were originally feasts of dedication in commemoration of the consecration of the church, in imitation of Solomon's great convocation at the consecrating the Temple of Jerusalem. The religious tenor is totally forgotten, and the Sabbath is made a day of every dissipation and vice which it is possible to conceive could crowd upon a villager's manners and rural life. The manner of holding these festivals in former times was under tents and booths erected in the church-yard, where all kinds of diversions were introduced. Interludes were there performed, being a species of threatrical performance consisting of a rehearsal of some passages in Holy Writ personated by actors. This kind of exhibition is spoken of by travellers, who have visited Jerusalem, where the religious even presume to exhibit the Crucifixion and Ascension with all their tremendous circumstances. On these celebrations in this country, great feasts were displayed, and vast abundance of meat and drink." *History of Northumberland,* ii., 26. In Bridges' "Northamptonshire" are very many instances recorded of the wake being still kept on or near to the day of the saint to whom the church was dedicated. In the "Spectator," No. 161, for Sept. 4, 1711, the writer, speaking of this anniversary, tells us, that "the squire of the parish treats the whole company every year with a hogshead of ale ; and proposes a beaver hat as a recompense to him who gives most falls." In this country an element of licentiousness undoubtedly crept into this description of festival, and we find a clergyman, one Rosewell, in a sermon which he published in 1711, earnestly opposed to the continuance of the wake on the eve before the dedication. But when an order had been made in 1627 and in 1631, at Exeter and in Somersetshire, for the suppression of the wakes, both the ministers and the people desired their continuance, not only for preserving the memorial of the dedication of their several churches, but for civilizing their parishioners, composing differences by the mediation and meeting of friends, increasing of love and unity by these feasts of charity, and for the relief and comfort of the poor.

Kirchmaier, or Naogeorgus, in his *Popish Kingdom,* translated by Googe, 1570, draws a curious and edifying picture of the enthusiasm and licentiousness attendant by degrees in this festival abroad :

" The dedication of the Church is yerely
    had in minde,
With worship passing Catholicke, and
    in a wondrous kinde :
From out the steeple hie is hangde a
    crosse and banner fayre,
The pavement of the temple strowde
    with hearbes of pleasant ayre,
The pulpits and the aulters all that in
    the Church are seene,
And every pewe and piller great, are
    deckt with boughes of greene :
The tabernacles opened are, and images
    are drest,
But chiefly he that patron is, doth shine
    above the rest :
A borde there standes, whereon their
    bulles and pardons thick they lay,
That given are to every one that keepes
    this holyday :
The Idoll of the Patron eke, without the
    doore doth stande,
And beggeth fast of every man, with
    pardons in his hande :
Who for bicause he lackes his tongue,
    and hath not yet the skill
In common peoples languages when
    they speak well or ill :

He hath his own interpretor, that alwayes standeth by,
And vnto every man that commeth in or
    out doth cry :
Desiring them the Patrone there, with
    giftes to have in minde,
And Popishe pardons for to buie, release
    of sinnes to finde.

    *   *   *   *   *

On every side the neighbours come, and
    such as dwell not nere,
Come of their owne good willes, and
    some required to be there.
And every man his weapon hath, their
    swords and launces long,
Their axes, curriars, pystolets, with
    pikes and darts among.
The yong men in their best array, and
    trimmest maydes appeare,
Both jeasters, roges, and minstrels with
    their instruments are heare.
The pedlar doth his pack untrusse, the
    host his pots doth fill,
And on the table breade and drinke doth
    set for all that will :
Nor eyther of them their heape deceyves,
    for of the others all,
To them th' advauntage of this feaste,
    and gaine, doth chiefly fall.
The service done, they eyther to the
    taverne fast doe flie,
Or to their neighbours house, whereas
    they feede unreasonablie :
For sixe or seven courses they vnto the
    table bring,
And for their suppers may compare with
    any heathen king.
The table taken up, they rise, and all
    the youth apace,
The minstrell with them called go to
    some convenient place :
Where when with bagpipe hoarce, he
    hath begon his musicke fine,
And vnto such as are preparde to daunce
    hath given signe,
Comes thither streight both boys and
    girls, and men that aged bee,
And maryed folkes of middle age, there
    also comes to see,
Old wrinckled hagges, and youthfull
    dames, that minde to daunce aloft,
Then sundrie pastimes do begin, and
    filthie daunces oft :
When drunkards they do lead the
    daunce with fray and bloody fight,
That handes, and eares, and head, and
    face, are torne in wofull plight.
The streames of bloud run downe the
    armes, and oftentimes is seene.
The carkasse of some ruffian slaine, is
    left upon the greene.
Here many, for their lovers sweete, some
    daintie thing do buie,
And many to the taverne goe, and drink
    for companie,
Whereas they foolish songs do sing, and
    noyses great do make :

Some in the meane while play at cardes,
  and some the dice do shake.
Their custome also is, the priest into the
  house to pull :
Whom when they have, they thinke their
  game accomplished at full :
He farre in noise exceedes them all, and
  eke in drinking drie
The cuppes, a prince he is, and holdes
  their heades that speewing lie."

Compare *Wake.*

Demoniac.—The very curious and
extraordinary "Saxon Leechdoms," edited
by Mr. Cockayne, contain a receipt for
" a fiend-sick man, or *demoniac.*" It was
" a spew-drink, or emetic : lupin, bishopwort, henbane, cropleek ; pound these together, add ale for a liquid, let it stand
for a night, add fifty libcorns, or cathartic
grains, and holy water. A drink for a
fiend-sick man, to be drunk out of a church
bell : githrife, cynoglossum, yarrow, &c.,
work up the drink off clear ale, sing seven
masses over the worts, add garlic and holy
water, and drip the drink into every
drink which he will subsequently drink,
and let him sing the psalms, Beati Immac-
ulati, and Exsurgat, and Salvum me fac,
deus, and then let him drink out of a
church bell, and let the mass priest after
the drink sing this over him, Domine,
sancte pater omnipotens." Following
these two specifics for fiend-sick men, is a
third, equally repugnant to modern ideas
of common sense, for a lunatic.

Denier à Dieu.—See *God's Penny.*

Denier de Foi.—Douce, in a paper
read before the Society of Antiquaries in
January, 1810, observes : " The small piece
of silver, that accompanies this paper is
inscribed *Denier de Foy* or *pour Épouser,*
having on one side a heart between two
hands, and on the other two fleurs de lis.
It is not in reality a current piece of
money, but only a local or a particular
token or symbol of property. It is, as the
inscription imports, a French betrothing
penny, given before the marriage ceremony." I do not think that Douce proves
more than the delivery of a token in earnest of dower, and of his betrothing penny
there are, to the best of my knowledge, no
Anglo-Saxon or English examples in existence. There is another sort inscribed
Denier Tournois pour Epouser. These
pieces occur both in gold and silver ; see
supplement to Hazlitt's *Coins of Europe,*
1897, p. 33. But, after all, the token exhibited by Douce appears to have been
nothing more than an example of the festing-penny, familiar enough in the northern counties of England, and no doubt properly identified with the Danish custom of
hiring or binding apprentices with some
such token. Festing is, of course, a form
of fasting or fastening. The fœsteninge-

ring was similarly the betrothing-ring or,
as it is now called, the engaged-ring. To
fest, in the North of England, is to bind
as an apprentice. Mr. Atkinson, in his
Cleveland Glossary, 1868, after observing
that the festing-penny of the North of
England is analogous to the Scandinavian
betrothing penny (shown by Douce to have
been also known in France), adds : " if a
servant who has been duly hired and received her hiring or festing-penny, wishes
to cancel her bargain. . . she always sends
back the festing penny. . . Two instances
of this kind have occurred in this (Danby)
parish in the course of the spring hiring-
time of the present year, 1865."

Dequoy or **Decoy.**—See *Cards.*

Dessil.—Martin says : " In this Island
of Lewis there was an antient custom to
make a fiery circle about the houses, corn,
cattle, &c., belonging to each particular
family. A man carried fire in his right
hand, and went round, and it was called
Dessil, from the right hand, which, in the
antient language, is called Dess. There is
another way of the dessil, or carrying fire
round about women before they are
churched, and about children until they
be christened, both of which are performed
in the morning and at night. They told
me this fire round was an effectual means
to preserve both the mother and the infant from the power of evil spirits, who
are ready at such times to do mischief,
and sometimes carry away the infants, and
return them poor meagre skeletons, and
these infants are said to have voracious
appetites, constantly craving for meat.
In this case it was usual for those who believed that their children were thus taken
away, to dig a grave in the fields upon
Quarter Day, and there to lay the fairy
skeleton till next morning : at which time
the parents went to the place, where they
doubted not to find their own child instead
of the skeleton." *Hist. of W. Islands,* p.
116. He elsewhere observes, " Loch-siant
Well in Skie is much frequented by strangers as well as by the inhabitants of the
Isle, who generally believe it to be a specifick for several diseases ; such as stitches,
headaches, stone, consumption, megrim.
Several of the common people oblige themselves by a vow to come to this well and
make the ordinary tour about it, called
Dessil, which is performed thus : They
move thrice round the well, proceeding
sun-ways, from east to west, and so on.
This is done after drinking of the water ;
and when one goes away from the well, it
is a never-failing custom to leave some
small offering on the stone which covers
the well. There is a small coppice near it,
of which none of the natives dare venture
to cut the least branch, for fear of some
signal judgement to follow upon it." *Description of W. Islands of Scotland,* 140.

He also speak of a well of similar quality, at which, after drinking, they make a tour and then leave an offering of some small token, such as a pin, needle, farthing, or the like, on the stone cover which is above the well.

Deuce.—Deuce may be said to be another popular name for the Devil. Few, perhaps, who make use of the expression "Deuce take you," particularly those of the softer sex, who accompanying it with the gentle pat of a fan, cannot be supposed to mean any ill by it, are aware that it is synonymous with "sending you to the Devil." Dusius was the ancient popular name for a kind of demon or devil among the Gauls, so that this saying, the meaning of which so few understand, has at least its antiquity to recommend it. It is mentioned by St. Augustine (*De Civitate Dei*, c. 23) as a libidinous demon, who used to violate the chastity of women, and, with the incubus of old, was charged with doing a great deal of mischief of so subtle a nature, that, as none saw it, it did not seem possible to be prevented. Later times have done both these devils justice, candidly supposing them to have been much traduced by a certain set of delinquents, who used to father upon invisible and imaginary agents the crimes of real men.

Devil.—In some of the early Mysteries Satan is introduced as *Saint Mahown*. The Glossary to Burns mentions Hornie as one of his Majesty's names. And another is *Old Boots*, whence the saying, "It rains like Old Boots."

There is a story in one of the Chronicles, under the year 1165, that the Devil was seen riding like a great black horse, before a storm which happened in Yorkshire in that year, and that the marks of his feet were visible in several places, particularly on the cliff at Scarborough, where he sprang into the sea. Not many years ago, an extraordinary sensation was produced in the South of England, by the discovery of marks in various parts of the country, which could not be identified with the prints of any known beast or bird, unless it was that there was some similitude to a donkey's shoe. The people in those parts did not like to say it was the Devil, perhaps; but it is not unlikely that some of them thought so. At the same time, no explanation of the mystery has, I believe, been offered to this day. Perhaps this extraordinary presence may have been nothing more than the cloven hoof which, in the deep snows of winter, is said to haunt the Dewerstone, a rocky elevation on the borders of Dartmoor. But this latter phenomenon is reported to be accompanied by a naked human foot, of which a case occurred in Devonshire, and created a wide and long sensation, many years since. Several instances of mysterious footprints are collected in "Lancashire Folk-Lore," 1867. There is no vulgar story of the Devil having appeared anywhere without a cloven foot. It is observable also that this infernal enemy, in graphic representations of him, is seldom or never pictured without one. Othello says:

"I look down towards his feet; but
  that's a fable;
If that thou be'st a devil, I cannot kill
  thee";

which Johnson explains: "I look towards his feet, to see, if, according to the common opinion, his feet be cloven." Grose says:—"Although the devil can partly transform himself into a variety of shapes, he cannot change his cloven foot, which will always mark him under every appearance." Scott has the following curious passage on this subject: "In our childhood, our mother's maids have so terrified us with an ugly devil, having horns on his head, fire in his mouth, and a tail in his breech, eyes like a basin, fangs like a dog, claws like a bear, a skin like a Niger, and a voyce roaring like a lyon, whereby we start and are afraid when we hear one cry Bough!" He adds: "and they have so frayed us with bul-beggars, spirits, witches, urchens, elves, hags, fairies, satyrs, pans, faunes, sylens, Kit with the canstick, Tritons, centaures, dwarfes, gyants, imps, calcars, conjurers, nymphes, changelings, incubus, Robin Good-fellow, the spoorn, the mare, the man in the oak, the Hell-wain, the fire-drake, the puckle, Tom-thombe, hob-goblin, Tom-tumbler, Boneless, and such other bugs, that we are afraid of our own shadowes; insomuch that some never feare the devil but in a darke night, &c. *Discovery*, ed. 1665. p. 65. Philip Stubbes, in his "Two wonderful and rare examples" (1581), describes a remarkable case which happened to Mistress Bowcer, at Donnington, in Leicestershire: "And nowe," says Stubbs, I will proceede to shewe one other as straunge a judgement happening in Leicestershire, in a towne called Donnington, where dwelled a poore man named Iohn Twell, who deceased, owing unto one Oswald Bowcer the summe of fiue shilling, which the sayde Oswalde did forgiue the sayde man before named, as he lay vpon his death bedde; but the sayde Oswaldes wife, called Ioane, would in no way forgive the said Twell, as long (she sayde) as she had to live. Whereupon, not long after, the Deuill appeared vnto her in the form of the sayd Twell deceased, expressing all the lyneamentes of the body of the dead man : which might well be, for we reade in the Bible, in the like order did Satan counterfeit the body of Samuell. But to proceede to the matter : this euill spirit uttered vnto her these speeches, and said he had brought her money from Íohn Twell deceased, and willed her incontinent to disburse the sayd money vnto her husband for his paines. Which she, with as covetous a desire, receyved, saying, God thanke you. She had no sooner named God, but the money consumed away from betweene her handes, as it were a vapour of smoake, tyll it was all consumed : wherewith the Deuill, giving her a most fearfull and sore stroke, vanished out of her sight. Wherewith her whole body became as blacke as pitche, replenished all over with a moste filthy scurfe and other things."

The Rev. George Gordon, who drew up the old statistical account of Sorn, co. Ayr, in 1798, observes : "There is a tradition well authenticated that King James the fifth honoured his treasurer Sir William Hamilton with a visit at Sorn Castle, on occasion of the marriage of his daughter to Lord Seton. The King's visit at Sorn Castle took place in winter ; and being heartily tired of his journey through so long a track of moor, moss, and miry clay, where there was neither road nor bridge, he is reported to have said with that good-humoured pleasantry which was a characteristic of so many of his family, that ' were he to play the Deil a trick, he would send him from Glascow to Sorn in winter.' " "The trick now-a-days," continues the writer, "would not prove a very serious one; for Satan, old as he is, might travel very comfortably one half of the way in a mail-coach, and the other half in a post-chaise. Neither would he be forced, like King James, for want of better accommodation, to sit down about mid-way, by the side of a well (hence called King's Well), and there take a cold refreshment in a cold day. At the very same place he might now find a tolerable inn and a warm dinner." *S.A.*, xx. 170. An early writer, speaking of a man who desired an interview with the Prince of Darkness, says that he was recommended to go in quest of him to wild Scotland, his favourite sojourn, but that when the traveller proceeded to act on this advice, he failed to discover his majesty, and merely met with an old woman, who pretended to have some knowledge of him. Michel, *Les Ecossais en France*, 1862, p. 2. At this time, no doubt, the farther extremities of the country, at least, were practically a *terra incognita*, about which any legends might be set afloat. Winslow, in his *Good News from New England*, 1624, speaking of the sacrifices of the Indians to the Devil, says : "They have told me I should see the Devil at those times come to the vestry ; but I assured myself and them of the con-

trary : which so proved. Yea, themselves have confessed, they never saw him, when any of us were present." In a tract in the Huth library, printed about 1645, among other " Signs and Wonders from Heaven," is an account how the Evil One came to a farmer's house at Swaffham in West Norfolk under the form of a gentlewoman on horseback. In Massinger's " Virgin Martyr," 1622, act iii. sc. 1, Harpax, an evil spirit, following Theophilus in the shape of a secretary, speaks thus of the superstitious Christian's description of his infernal master :

" I'll tell you what now of the Devil :
He's no such horrid creature ; cloven-footed,
Black, saucer-ey'd, his nostrils breathing fire,
As these lying Christians make him."

In a contemporary description of the appearance of the Devil at St. Alban's, Herts, in 1648, it is said that he then assumed the likeness of a ram, and that a butcher cut his throat, sold a portion of the flesh, and cooked the remainder for himself and a select party of friends, all of which was " attested by divers letters of persons of very good credit," and the tract itself purported to have been published " for confutation of those that believe there are no such things as spirits or devils." Hone's *Ancient Mysteries*, 1823, p. 89. This infernal visitant appears in no instance to have been treated with more *sang froid* on his appearing, or rather perhaps his imagined appearance, than by one Mr. White of Dorchester, assessor to the Westminster Assembly at Lambeth, as recorded by Mr. Samuel Clarke : " The Devil, in a light night, stood by his bedside : he looked awhile whether he would say or do anything, and then said, ' If thou hast nothing else to do, I have ' : and so turned himself to sleep." Baxter's *Certainty of the World of Spirits*, 1691, p. 63. He adds, that " Many say it from Mr. White himself." One has only to wonder, on this occasion, that a person who could so effectually lay the Devil, could have been induced to think, or rather dream, of raising him. Sir Thomas Browne is full on this subject of popular superstition in his " Vulgar Errors " : " The ground of this opinion at first," says he, " might be his frequent appearing in the shape of a goat," (this accounts also for his horns and tail), " which answers the description. This was the opinion of the antient Christians, concerning the Apparition of Panites, Fauns, and Satyrs ; and of this form we read of one that appeared to Anthony in the Wilderness. The same is also confirmed from expositions of Holy Scripture. For whereas it is said, Thou shalt not offer unto Devils: the original word is Seghui-rim, that is, rough and hairy goats, because in that shape the Devil most often appeared, as is expounded by the Rabins, as Tremellius hath also explained, and as the word Ashimah, the God of Emath, is by some conceived." He observes, also, that the goat was the emblem of the sin-offering, and is the emblem of sinful men at the Day of Judgment. It is observed in the "Connoisseur," No. 109, that "the famous Sir Thomas Browne refuted the generally-received opinion, that the Devil is black, has horns upon his head, wears a long curling tail and a cloven stump : nay has even denied that, wheresoever he goes, he always leaves a smell of brimstone behind him." Baxter tells us that "Devils have a greater game to play invisibly than by apparitions. O happy world, if they did not do a hundred thousand times more hurt by the baits of pleasure, lust, and honour, and by pride, and love of money, and sensuality, than they do by witches." *World of Spirits*, 1691, p. 223. In "Sphinx and Œdipus," (part of "A Helpe to Discourse," 1627), I read that "the Devil never appears in the shape of a dove, or a lamb, but in those of goats, dogs, and cats, or such like : and that to the Witch of Edmonton he appeared in the shape of a dog, and called his name Dom." An essayist in the "Gentleman's Magazine" for October, 1732, observes that, "As for the great Evil Spirit, 'tis for his interest to be masked and invisible. Amongst his sworn vassals and subjects he may allow himself to appear in disguise at a public paw-wawing, (which is attested by a cloud of travellers), but there is no instance of his appearing among us, except that produced by Mr. Echard, to a man in so close confederacy with him, that 'twas reasonable to suppose they should now and then contrive a personal meeting."

The old ceremonies used in raising the devil, such as making a circle with chalk, setting an old hat in the centre of it, repeating the Lord's Prayer backward, and so forth, even when Brand wrote about 1795, had become, he says, "altogether obsolete, and seem to be forgotten even amongst our boys." Obsession of the devil is distinguished from possession in this. In possession the evil one was said to enter into the body of the man. In obsession, without entering into the body of the person, he was thought to besiege and torment him without. To be lifted up into the air, and afterwards to be thrown down violently, without receiving any hurt; to speak strange languages that the person had never learned; not to be able to come near holy things or the sacraments, but to have an aversion to them; to know and foretell secret things; to perform things that ex-

ceed the person's strength; to say or do things that the person would not or durst not say, if he were not externally moved to it, were the ancient marks and criterions of possessions. Jorden observes : "I doe not deny but that there may be both possessions, and obsessions, and witchcraft, &c., and dispossession also through the prayers and supplications of God's servants, which is the only means left unto us for our reliefe in that case. But such examples being verye rare now-a-dayes, I would in the feare of God advise men to be very circumspect in pronouncing of a possession : both because the impostures be many, and the effects of naturall diseases be strange to such as have not looked thoroughly into them." *Suffocation of the Mother*, 1603, Dedic. The semi-mythical legend of Faustus, of which the most authentic version, so to speak, is in the Editor's *National Tales and Legends*, 1892, introduces us to a plurality of demons, having Lucifer as their chief and Mephistopheles as an agent on earth; and there is a scene in the story where a parliament of devils assembles, under the eyes of Faustus. In the *History of Friar Rush*, a romance of the 16th century, the Evil One is represented as holding occasional receptions, or levees of his emissaries, and listening to their reports of the most recent achievements performed by them in his behalf. One of them was Rush himself. Another bore the unusual name of Norpell. The more atrocious their exploits, the warmer of course was his Satanic majesty's commendation. There was an early metrical tract under the title of the *Parliament of Devils*, two or three times printed about 1520, and possibly responsible for the suggestion of the *Rush* piece just mentioned. Cassian, mentioning a host of devils who had been abroad in the night, says, that as soon as the morn approached, they all vanished and fled away : which farther evinces that this was the current opinion of the time. Vallancey *Coll*. viii., c. 16.

Devil on Two Sticks.—A correspondent of *Notes and Queries* (about 1880) writes as follows :—"I possess the means of playing the game, but not the art. Sometimes, when I see the stick and hour-glass shaped 'devil,' I wish I could handle them, for I have seen an old friend display great skill with the sticks in his garden, sending the 'devil' humming on high, and catching it with great accuracy. My old uncles used to talk of it; they knew and played the game early in this century. It may be of interest to know that such games have been found very useful *faute de mieux*. I remember one day, more than thirty years ago, paying a visit to one of the dearest old ladies I ever knew, named

Lady Scovell, the wife of Sir George Scovell, whom she had accompanied in his Peninsular campaigns when he was one of the most useful and most trusted of the Duke's staff. I found her disentangling a number of cups and balls, the strings of which had been all mixed by a carpet-crawling urchin, who had upset the basket containing them. I was surprised at the variety of shapes and sizes. The balls had to be caught on common average cups, cups flattened almost to a table, cups cut away on both sides till only a crescent was left, and, of course, the usual spike. On my asking her how she came by such a collection she told me that during the war she came home one winter to see her friends whilst the army was in quarters, and whilst at home she got a letter from Sir Rowland (Lord) Hill, saying the weather was so bad they very often could not get out, and he begged her to bring with her on her return any indoor games for himself and staff. Lady Scovell said she at once got these varieties of cups and balls and devils on two sticks made, and (having taken them to Spain) she added that they answered the purpose admirably, but it was rather funny to see the general and staff in the afternoon, when the day's work was finished, moving about the rooms hard at work at these games, and one backing himself against another." And this was seventy years ago.

Devil's Bit.—Coles tells us that "there is one herb, flat at the bottome, and seemeth as if the nether part of its root were bit off, and is called Devil's-bit, whereof it is reported that the devill, knowing that that part of the root would cure all diseases, out of his inveterate malice to mankind, bites it off." *Knowledge of Plants*, 1656, p. 37.

Devil-Worship.—Dr Paul Carus, in his *History of the Devil*, makes the Spirit of Evil the primary object of propitiatory homage on the part of archaic communities more disposed to dread the apparent source of what they suffered than that of what they enjoyed. On the principal of Dualism, in a more enlightened age, it still remains in a way a salutary inducement to rectitude to suppose the existence of a Power not merely able, but anxious, to punish the evil-doer. The modern popular theories of the Devil are the converse of that of universal original subjection to such a creation as the Thibetan All-Devourer, and depict man as originally pure and sinless, and the Evil One as a rebellious and degraded minister of God.

Dew.—Willsford tells us: "Mettals in general, against much wet or rainy weather, will seem to have a dew hang upon them, and be much apter to sully or foul any thing that is rubbed with the metal; as you may see in pewter dishes against rain, as if they did sweat, leaving a smutch upon the table cloaths: with this Pliny concludes as a signe of tempests approaching. . . . Stones against rain will have a dew hang upon them; but the sweating of stones is from several causes, and sometimes is a sign of much drought. Glasses of all sorts will have a dew upon them in moist weather: Glasse windows will also shew a frost, by turning the air that touches them into water, and then congealing of it." *Nature's Secrets*, p. 138. This depends, of course, on the difference between the internal and external temperature. At Hertford Assizes, 4 Car. I., the following testimony, which of course, merely reflects the popular view of the subject, was taken by Sir John Maynard, Serjeant at Law, from the deposition of the minister of the parish where a murder was committed: "That the body being taken out of the grave thirty days after the party's death, and lying on the grass, and the four defendants (suspected of murdering her) being required, each of them touched the dead body, whereupon the brow of the dead, which before was of a livid and carrion colour, began to have a dew, or gentle sweat, arise on it, which encreased by degrees, till the sweat ran down in drops on the face, the brow turned to a fresh and lively colour; and the deceased opened one of her eyes, and shut again three several times: she likewise thrust out the ring or marriage finger three times, and pulled it in again, and the finger dropt blood on the grass." The minister of the next parish, who also was present, being sworn, gave evidence exactly as above. *Gentleman's Magazine*, 1731. Compare *May-Day*.

Dice.—In the Municipal Records of the City of London we first become aware of the employment of dice by reason of abuses in connection with the introduction of them under 1311 for the purpose of cheating. Unsuspecting persons were even then enticed into taverns by well-dressed sharpers, and robbed in this way. Other notices, where false dice occur, may be found under 1334 and 1376, where tables or backgammon is mentioned as a second amusement and medium of deceit. Riley's *Memorials*, 1868, pp. 86, 193, 395. In the account of the entertainment given to Richard, son of the Black Prince, in 1337, the mummers shewed by a pair of dice their desire to play with the young Prince. Hazlitt's *Warton*, 1871, iii., 161. Sir T. Elyot, in his "Governor," 1531, has some remarks on this subject, which, as illustrating the state of feeling in Henry VIII.'s time, may be worth a place here: "I suppose there is not a more playne figure of idlenesse, then playing at dice. For besides, that therin is no maner of exercise of the body or minde, they which play thereat, must seeme to haue no portion of witte or cunnyng, if they will be called fayre players, or in some company auoyde the stabbe of a dagger, if they bee taken with any craftie conueyance." In "The Common Cries of London," an early Elizabethan ballad by W. Turner, there is a curious passage seeming to shew that the street-hawkers used sometimes to carry dice in their pockets either for amusement, or for the purpose of practising on some inexperienced customer :

> "Ripe, cherry ripe!
>   The costermonger cries;
> Pippins fine or pears!
>   Another after hies,
> With a basket on his head,
>   His living to advance,
> And in his purse a pair of dice,
>   For to play at mumchance."

Comp. *London.* Dr. Wilde left a sum of money by will, the interest of which was to be invested in the purchase of Bibles, which were to be tossed for every year at the Communion-table at the parish church at St. Ives, in Huntingdonshire, by six boys and six girls, being parishioners. The operation now takes place in the vestry. Jonson seems to have informed Drummond of Hawthornden in 1619. that at Christmas Eve, when Queen Elizabeth would play at dice, there were special ones provided for her, so that her highness might always win. Masson's Drummond, 1873, p. 94. Compare *Cards.*

Dick o' Tuesday.—See *Will o' the Wisp.*

Diet or **Debates (The).**—A social game at cards, played with a pack of 24. Twelve of the cards have costume figures. The inscriptions are in French, German, and English. The set before me appears to belong to 1830 or thereabouts.

Dish Fair.—Drake tells us that " A Fair is always kept in Mickle Gate (York) on St. Luke's Day, for all sorts of small wares. It is commonly called Dish Fair, from the great quantity of wooden dishes, ladles, &c., brought to it. There is an old custom used at this fair of bearing a wooden ladle in a sling on two stangs about it, carried by four sturdy labourers, and each labourer was formerly supported by another. This, without doubt, is a ridicule on the meanness of the wares brought to this fair, small benefit accruing to the labourers at it. Held by Charter Jan. 25, an. Reg. Regis, Hen. vii. 17." *Eboracum*, p. 219.

Distaff's (St.) or **Rock Day.**—(January 7). So this day is jocularly termed by Herrick in his *Hesperides*,

1648, and by Henry Bold, in his *Wit a Sporting*, 1657, in some lines copied from the earlier writer.

Divinations. — Divinations differ from omens in this, that the omen is an indication of something that is to come to pass, which happens to a person, as it were by accident, without his seeking for it : whereas divination is the obtaining of the knowledge of something future by some endeavour of his own, or means which he himself designedly makes use of for that end. There were among the ancients divinations by water, fire, earth, air ; by the flight of birds, by lots, by dreams, by the wind, &c. Gaule enumerates as follows the several species of divination : "Stareomancy, or divining by the elements; äeromancy, or divining by the ayr ; pyromancy, by fire ; hydromancy, by water ; geomancy, by earth ; theomancy, pretending to divine by the revelation of the spirit, and by the Scriptures or word of God ; dæmonomancy, by the suggestions of evill dæmons, or devils ; idolomancy, by idolls, images, figures ; psychomancy, by men's souls, affections, wills, religious or morall dispositions ; antinopomancy, by the entrails of men, women, and children ; theriomancy, by beasts ; ornithomancy, by birds ; ichtyomancy, by fishes ; botanomancy, by herbs ; lithomancy, by stones ; cleromancy, by lotts ; orniromancy, by dreams ; onomatomancy, by names ; arithmancy, by numbers ; logarithmancy, by logarithmes ; sternomancy, from the breast to the belly ; gastromancy, by the sound of or signs upon the belly ; omphalomancy, by the navel ; chiromancy, by the hands ; pedomancy, by the feet ; onychomancy, by the nayles ; cephalonomancy, by brayling of an asses head ; tuphramancy, by ashes ; capnomancy, by smoak ; livanomancy, by burning of frankincence ; carromancy, by melting of wax ; lecanomancy, by a basin of water ; catoxtromancy, by looking glasses ; chartomancy, by writing in papers " (this is retained in chusing valentines, &c.); "macharomancy, by knives or swords ; christallomancy, by glasses ; dactylomancy, by rings ; coseinomancy, by sieves ; axinomancy, by sawes ; cattabomancy, by vessels of brasse or other metall ; roadomancy, by starres ; spatalomancy, by skins, bones, excrements ; sciomancy, by shadows ; astragalomancy, by dice ; oinomancy, by wine ; sycomancy, by figgs ; typomancy, by the coagulation of cheese ; alphitomancy, by meal, flower, or branne ; critomancy, by grain or corn ; alectomancy, by cocks or pullen ; gyromancy, by rounds or circles ; lampadomancy, by candles and lamps ; and in one word for all, nagomancy or necromancy, by inspecting, consulting, and divining by, with or from the dead.

Borlase says that the Druids "besides the ominous appearance of the entrails, had several ways of divining. They divined by augury, that is, from the observations they made on the voices, flying, eating, mirth or sadness, health or sickness of birds." *Antiq. of Cornwall,* p. 133. A later writer tells us that Boadicea or Bonduca is said to have taken an omen with a hare, and that on that account this animal was eschewed as an article of food—a fact mentioned by Cæsar in his *Commentaries.* But he proceeds to mention that the hare was not eaten by the Cymry in the tenth century. and was regarded as worthless, insomuch, that in the laws of Hoel Dda it was not protected as the goose was, by any fine; and there was a notion indeed that it changed its sex from year to year, becoming alternately a male and a female. *Notes on Ancient Britain,* by W. Barnes, 1858, p. 5. In Caxton's "Description of England," we read: "It semeth of these men a grete wonder that in a boon of a wethers ryght sholder whan the fleshe is soden awaye and not rosted, they knowe what have be done, is done, and shall be done, as it were by spyryte of prophecye and a wonderful crafte. They telle what is done in ferre countres, tokenes of peas or of warre, the state of the royame, sleynge of men, and spousebreche, such thynges theye declare certayne of tokenes and sygnes that is in suche a sholder bone." Drayton mentions:

" A diuination strange the Dutch-made-
    English haue
Appropriate to that place (as though
    some power it gaue)
By th' shoulder of a ram from off the
    right side par'd
Which vsuallie they boile, the spade-
    boane being bar'd,
Which when the wizard takes, and
    gazes there-vpon,
Things long to come fore showes, as
    things done long agon."

He alludes to a colony of Flemings in Pembrokeshire. *Polyolbion,* Song v., p. 81, 84-5. We are referred to Giraldus Cambrensis, i., cap. 11. Selden writes hereupon: "Under Hen. II., one William Mangunel, a gentleman of those parts, finding, by his skill of prediction, that his wife had played false with him, and conceiued by his own nephew, formally dresses the shoulder-bone of one of his own rammes; and, sitting at dinner, (pretending it to be taken out of his neighbours' flocke), requests his wife (equalling him in these divinations) to giue her judgment: she curiously observes, and at last with great laughter casts it from her; the gentleman importun-

ing her reason of so vehement an affection, receiues answer of her, that his wife, out of whose flocke that ram was taken, had by incestuous copulation with her husband's nephew fraughted herself with a yong one. Lay all together, and iuge, gentlewomen, the sequele of this cross accident. But why she could not as well diuine of whose flocke it was, as the other secret, when I haue more skill in osteomantie, I will tell you." Pennant gives an account of this sort of divination as used in Scotland and there called sleina-nachd, or reading the speal bone, or the blade-bone of a shoulder of mutton, well scraped (Mr. Shaw says picked; no iron must touch it). When Lord Loudon, he says, was obliged to retreat before the rebels to the Isle of Skie, a common soldier, on the very moment the battle of Culloden was decided, proclaimed the victory at that distance, pretending to have discovered the event by looking through the bone. "Tour in Scotland," 1769, p. 155. See also his "Tour to the Hebrides," p. 282, for another instance of the use of the speal bone. The word speal is evidently derived from the French *espaule,* humerus. Hanway gives us to understand, that in Persia, too, they have a kind of divination by the bone of a sheep. *Travels,* i., 177. Owen, in his "Welch Dictionary," voce Cyniver, mentions " A play in which the youth of both sexes seek for an even-leaved sprig of the ash: and the first of either sex that finds one, calls out Cyniver, and is answered by the first of the other that succeeds; and these two, if the omen fails not, are to be joined in wedlock." Divination by arrows is ancient, according to Gibbon, and famous in the East. *D. and F.,* 4°, ed. x., 345. Brooke, in his "Ghost of Richard the Third," 1614, figures the king in his youth endeavouring by one of the ancient forms of divination to ascertain his destiny. The poem is, in imitation of the "Mirror for Magistrates," written in the first person:

" —— Then at the slaughter-house, with
    hungry sight,
Vpon slaine beasts my sensuall part did
    feede;
And (that which gentler natures might
    affright)
I search'd their entrayles, as in them to
    reade
(Like th' ancient bards) what fate
    should thence betide."

Lilly the astrologer made, it should seem by the desire of Charles I. an experiment, to know in what quarter of the nation the King might be most safe, after he should have effected his escape, and not be discovered until he himself pleased. Madame Whorewood was deputed to receive Lilly's judgment. He seems to have had high fees, for he owns he got on this occasion twenty pieces of gold. It seems to have been believed that there was some divination, or other supernatural medium, by which the robbers of orchards might be detected, for in " Cataplus, a Mock Poem," 1672, the writer says of the Sibyl :

" Thou canst in orchard lay a charm
To catch base felon by the arm."

Randolph, in his " Amyntas," 1638, makes fairies declare a partiality for apples stolen from orchards in the night :

"*Jocastus.* What divine noise fraught with immortal harmony
Salutes my ears?
Bromius. Why this immortal harmony
Rather salutes your orchard : these young rascals,
These pescod shellers do so cheat my master,
We cannot have an apple in the orchard,
But straight some fairy longs for 't."

Of course, however, in this particular case, the fairies are counterfeit, like those in the " Merry Wives of Windsor " ; while in the story in *A C. Mery Talys,* 1526, folio v. the depredators are mistaken for evil spirits. Charms or spells for divining purposes are, or not very long ago at least were, made by our peasantry in various districts from the blades of the oat, wheat, and even, according to Miss Baker, of the reed. Clare describes the special uses of these in his *Shepherd's Calendar.* It is still a common amusement with girls to ascertain, as they pretend, whom they are going to marry, to take some description of grass, and to count the spiral fronds, saying :

Tinker,
Tailor,
Soldier,
Sailor,
Rich man,
Poor man,
Beggar man,
Thief,

till they come to the end of them, and it is supposed to be the last frond, which decides it.

" Tu ne quæsieris scire nefas quem mihi, quem tibi
Finem Di dederint, Leuconoë : nec Babylonios
Tentaris numeros."
Hor. *Carm.* lib. i. Od. ii.

Diviner.—John of Salisbury enumerates no fewer than thirteen different kinds of diviners or fortune tellers, who (in his time) pretended to foretell future events, some by one means and some by another. *De Nugis Curialium,* lib. i., c. 12. Henry tells us that, "after the

Anglo-Saxons and Danes embraced the Christian religion, the clergy were commanded by the canons to preach very frequently against diviners, sorcerers, auguries, omens, charms, incantations, and all the filth of the wicked and dotages of the Gentiles." *Hist. of Gr. Britain,* ii., 550, 4°, ed. He cites Johnson's *Eccl. Canons,* A.D. 747, c. 3.

Divining Rod.—Not only the Chaldeans used rods for divination, but almost every nation, which has pretended to that science, has practised the same method. Herodotus mentions it as a custom of the Scythians, Ammianus Marcellinus, of a tribe of that nation, the Alani, and Tacitus of the old Germans. *Bartholinus,* p. 676. Divination by the rod or wand is mentioned in the prophecy of Ezekiel. Hosea, too, reproaches the Jews as being infected with the like superstition : " My people ask counsel at their stocks, and their staff declareth unto them." We read in the *Gentleman's Magazine* for November, 1751 : " So early as Agricola the divining rod was in much request, and has obtained great credit for its discovering where to dig for metals and springs of water ; for some years past its reputation has been on the decline, but lately it has been revived with great success by an ingenious gentleman who from numerous experiments hath good reason to believe its effects to be more than imagination. He says that hazel and willow rods, he has by experience found, will actually answer with all persons in a good state of health, if they are used with moderation and at some distance of time, and after meals, when the operator is in good spirits. The hazel, willow, and elm are all attracted by springs of water : some persons have the virtue intermittently ; the rod in their hands will attract one half hour, and repel the next. The rod is attracted by all metals, coals, amber, and lime stone, but with different degrees of strength. The best rods are those from the hazel or nut tree, as they are pliant and tough, and cut in the winter months. A shoot that terminates equally forked is to be preferred, about two feet and a half long ; but as such a forked rod is rarely to be met with, two single ones, of a length and size, may be tied together with thread, and will answer as well as the other." It has been alleged that " the experiment of a hazel's tendency to a vein of lead ore is limited to St. John Baptist's Eve, and that with an hazel of that same year's growth." *Athenian Oracle,* Suppl., 234. Gay describes some other rustic methods of divination with hazel nuts, and he mentions two other kinds by the lady-fly and by apple-parings. Pennant mentions that this was still employed and credited within his memory, and was supposed, by having a sympathy with the hidden ore, to supersede the necessity for ordinary methods of searching. The instrument used by a foreign adventurer in the writer's neighbourhood is described by him as being no more than a rod forked at one end, which had been cut in a planetary hour, on Saturn's day and hour, because Saturn was the significator of lead. Jupiter, Venus, Sol, and Mercury, also participated in the operation according to their reputed several attributes and powers. *Tours in Wales*, 1810, i., 75.

" Virgula divina.

Some sorcerers do boast they have a rod,
  Gather'd with vows and sacrifice,
And (borne about) will strangely nod
  To hidden treasure where it lies;
Mankind is (sure) that rod divine,
  For to the wealthiest (ever) they incline.*"*

Sheppard's *Epigr.* 1651, p. 141. I find the following account from Theophylact on the subject of *rabdomanteia* or rod divination : " They set up two staffs ; and having whispered some verses and incantations, the staffs fell by the operation of dæmons. Then they considered which way each of them fell, forward, backward, to the right or left hand, and agreeably gave responses, having made use of the fall of their staffs for their signs." *Bell's MS. Discourse on Witchcraft*, 1705, p. 41. In Camerarius we read : "No man can tell why forked sticks of hazill (rather than sticks of other trees growing upon the very same places) are fit to shew the places where the veines of gold and silver are, the sticke bending itselfe in the places, at the bottome, where the same veines are." *Living Librarie*, 1621, p. 283. In the " Gentleman's Magazine " for February, 1752, it is observed : "M. Linnæus, when he was upon his voyage to Scania, hearing his secretary highly extol the virtues of his divining wand, and willing to convince him of its insufficiency, and for that purpose concealed a purse of one hundred ducats under a ranunculus, which grew by itself in a meadow, and bid the Secretary find it if he could. The wand discovered nothing, and M. Linnæus' mark was soon trampled down by the company who were present ; so that when M. Linnæus went to finish the experiment by fetching the gold himself, he was utterly at a loss where to seek it. The man with the wand assisted him, and he pronounced that it could not lie the way they were going, but quite the contrary : so pursued the direction of his wand, and actually dug out the gold. M. Linnæus adds, that such another experiment would be sufficient to make a proselyte of him." The notion, still prevalent in the North and other mining districts of England, of the

hazel's tendency to a vein of lead ore, seam or stratum of coal, &c., seems to be a vestige of this rod divination. The *virgula divina*, or *baculus divinatorius*, is a forked branch in the form of a Y, cut off an hazel or apple-stick of twelve months' growth by means whereof people have pretended to discover mines or springs, &c., under ground. The method of using it is this : the person who bears it, walking very slowly over the places where he suspects mines or spring may be, the effluvia exhaling from the metals, or vapour from the water impregnating the wood, makes it dip or incline, which is the sign of a discovery. The manner was, to hold the rod with both hands horizontally, and to go along the tract of land where the lode was supposed to lie, until the rod bent of itself, which at once indicated the presence of the desired metal. Such an experiment is known to have been made, in perfect good faith, not many years since. Mr. Baring-Gould stated in 1866 that it was still employed in Wiltshire (and on the Continent) for this purpose. See Vallemont " Physique Occulte, ou Traité de la Baguette Divinatoire ; et de son utilité pour la decouverte des sources de l'eau de rivières, de Trésors cachez, &c." 1693. Also Lilly's " History of his Life and Times," p. 32, for a curious experiment (which he confesses however to have failed in) to discover hidden treasure by the hazel rod. As regards the discovery of springs underground by this process, the belief in it is said still to have survived in Normandy in 1874. *Vaux de Vire*, of Jean le Houx, by Muirhead, 1875, p. xvi.

With the divining rod seems connected a *lusus naturæ* of ash tree bough, resembling the *litui* of the Roman augurs and the Christian pastoral staff, which still obtains a place, if not on this account I know not why, in the catalogue of popular superstitions. In the last century Brand himself saw one of these, which he thought extremely beautiful and curious, in the house of an old woman at Beer Alston, in Devonshire, of whom he would most gladly have purchased it ; but she declined parting with it on any account, thinking it would be unlucky to do so. Gostling has some observations on this subject. He thinks the *lituus* or staff with the crook at one end, which the augurs of old carried as badges of their profession and instruments in the superstitious exercise of it, was not made of metal, but of the substance above mentioned. Whether, says he, to call it a work of art or nature may be doubted : some were probably of the former kind : others Hogarth, in his " Analysis of Beauty," calls *lusus naturæ*, found in plants of different sorts, and in one of the plates to that work gives a specimen of a very elegant one, a branch of ash. I should rather, continues he, style it a distemper or distortion of nature; for it seems the effect of a wound by some insect which, piercing to the heart of the plant with its proboscis, poisons that, while the bark remains uninjured, and proceeds in its growth, but formed into various stripes, flatness and curves, for want of the support which Nature designed it. The beauty some of these arrive at might well consecrate them to the mysterious fopperies of heathenism, and their rarity occasion imitation of them by art. The pastoral staff of the Church of Rome seems to have been formed from the vegetable litui, though the general idea is, I know, that it is an imitation of the shepherd's crook. The engravings given in the "Antiquarian Repertory" are of carved branches of the ash. *Antiq. Repert.*, 1807, ii., 164. Moresin, in his "Papatus," p. 126, says: "Pedum Episcopale est Litui Augurum, de quo Livius, i."

Divisions of Time.—The day, civil and political, has been divided into thirteen parts. The after-midnight and the dead of the night are the most solemn of them all, and have therefore, it should seem, been appropriated by ancient superstition to the walking of spirits. 1. After midnight. 2. Cock-crow. 3. The space between the first cock-crow and break of day. 4. The dawn of the morning. 5. Morning. 6. Noon. 7. Afternoon. 8. Sunset. 9. Twilight. 10. Evening. 11. Candle-time. 12. Bed-time. 13. The dead of the night. The Church of Rome, according to Durandus *De Nocturnis*, made four nocturnal vigils: the conticinium, gallicinium or cock-crow, intempestum, and antelucinum. There is a curious discourse on this subject in Peck's "Desiderata Curiosa," vol. i. p. 223, *et seq.* The distribution of the day into two equal terms of twelve hours *ante* and *post meridiem* was in early times only partially observed. Hazlitt's *Venetian Republic*, 1900, ii., 607.

Dog.—An opinion prevails that the howling of a dog by night in a neighbourhood is a presage of death to any that are sick in it. Keuchenii Crepundia, 113. Dogs have been known to stand and howl over the bodies of their masters, when they have been murdered, or died an accidental or sudden death: taking such note of what is past, is an instance of great sensibility in this faithful animal, without supposing that it has in the smallest degree any prescience of the future. Keuchenius adds, that when dogs rolled themselves in the dust, it was a sign of wind; which is also mentioned by Gaule and Willsford in their often-quoted works. The latter observes: "Dogs tumbling and wal-

lowing themselves much and often upon the earth, if their guts rumble and stink very much, are signs of rain or wind for certain." Shakespear, in Henry VI., part iii., act v. sc. 6, ranks this among omens:

"The owl shriek'd at thy birth—an evil sign!
The night-crow cry'd, aboding luckless time;
Dogs howl'd, and hideous tempest shook down trees."

Home speaks of this portent as a sign of death; which, adds Alexander Ross, is "plaine by historie and experience." *Demonologie*, 1650, p. 60. Grose substantiates this view, and indeed the superstition is still a common one among all classes of people. The following passage is cited in Poole's *English Parnassus*, 1657, v. *Omens*:

"The air that night was fill'd with dismal groans,
And people oft awaked with the howls Of wolves and fatal dogs."

"Julius Obsequens sheweth" (says Alexander Ross) that there was an "extraordinary howling of dogs before the sedition in Rome, about the dictatorship of Pompey: he sheweth also, (c. 127) that before the civil wars between Augustus and Antonius, among many other prodigies, there was great howling of dogs near the house of Lepidus the Pontifice. Camerarius tells us that some German princes have certain tokens and peculiar presages of their deaths, amongst others are the howling of dogs. Capitolinus tells us that the dogs by their howling presaged the death of Maximinus. Pausanias (in Messe) relates that before the destruction of the Messenians, the dogs brake out into a more fierce howling than ordinary; and we read in Fincelius that in the year 1553, some weeks before the overthrow of the Saxons, the dogs in Mysina flocked together, and used strange howlings in the woods and fields. The like howling is observed by Virgil, presaging the Roman calamities in the Pharsalick War. So Statius and Lucan to the same purpose." Defoe clearly leant to this belief, "unaccountable as it might seem," in cases, of course, where the howling was spontaneous. *Mem. of Duncan Campbel*, 1732, p. 76. Homer, in the "Odyssey," makes the dogs of Eumæus recognize Minerva, while the goddess remains invisible to Telemachus. I scarcely know if Douce thought that this was an evidence that the ancients credited the animal with the faculty of seeing ghosts: but the heathen divinities were endowed with the power of manifesting themselves to any particular person in a company, without being seen by the others. In the

Treasury of St. Denis they are said to preserve the silver keys of the saint, which by being laid on the face of the patient, cure the bite of a mad dog. *Les Raretez qui se voyent dans l'Eglise Royale de S. Denis,* 1749, p. 4.

Dog-Whipper. — See *St. Luke's Day.*

Dole.—The giving of a dole, and the inviting of the poor on this occasion, are synonymous terms. There are some strong figurative expressions on this subject in St. Ambrose's Funeral Oration on Satyrus, cited by Durandus. Speaking of those who mourned on the occasion, he says:— "The poor also shed their tears; precious and fruitful tears, that washed away the sins of the deceased. They let fall floods of redeeming tears." From such passages as the above in the first Christian writers, literally understood, the Romanists may have derived their superstitious doctrine of praying for the dead. "Preterea convocabantur et invitabantur necdum Sacerdotes et Religiosi, sed et egeni pauperes." *Durandus.* Had Pope an eye to this in ordering by will poor men to support his pall? Doles were used at funerals, as we learn from St. Chrysostom, to procure rest to the soul of the deceased, that he might find his judge propitious. *Homilia in Matthei* cap. 9.

In "Dives and Pauper," 1493, we read: "*Dives.* What seyst thou of them that wole no solemnyté have in their buryinge, but be putt in erthe anon, and that that shulde be spent aboute the buriyng they bydde that it shulde be yoven to the pore folke blynde and lame?—*Pauper.* Comonly in such prive buriynges bene ful smalle doles and lytel almes yoven, and in solemne buriynges been grete doles and moche almesse yoven, for moche pore people come thanne to seke almesse. But whanne it is done prively, fewe wytte therof, and fewe come to axe almesse! for they wote nat whanne ne where, ne whom they shulde axe it. And therefore I leve sikerly that summe fals executoures that wolde kepe all to themself biganne firste this errour and this foyle, that wolden make themself riche with ded mennys godes, and nat dele to the pore after dedes wylle, as nowe all false executoures use by custome." By the will of William de Montacute, Earl of Salisbury (1397), he directs "that twenty-five shillings should be daily distributed among three hundred poor people from the time of his death to the arrival of his body at the Conventual Church of Bustleham [Bustleton] in which it was to be deposited." Warner's *Hampshire,* 11, 73. Strutt tells us that Sir Robert Knolles, in the eighth year of Henry IV. died at his Manor in Norfolk, and his dead body was brought in a litter to London with great pomp, and much

torch-light, and it was buried in the White Friars Church, "where was done for him a solemn obsequie, with a great feaste and lyberal dole to the poore." This custom, says Strutt, of giving a funeral feast to the chief mourners, was universally practised all over the kingdom, as well as giving alms to the poor, in proportion to the quality and finances of the deceased. *Manners and Customs,* ii., 109. Nichols, speaking of Stathern in Framland Hundred, says: "In 1790, there were 432 inhabitants; the number taken by the last person who carried about bread, which was given for dole at a funeral; a custom formerly common throughout this part of England, though now fallen much into disuse. The practice was sometimes to bequeath it by will; but, whether so specified or not, the ceremony was seldom omitted. On such occasions a small loaf was sent to every person, without any distinction of age or circumstances, and not to receive it was a mark of particular disrespect." *Leicestershire,* vol. ii., part 1., p. 357. Lysons's *Env.,* iii., 341. Pennant says:— "Offerings at funerals are kept up here (Whiteford), and I believe, in all the Welsh Churches." *Hist. of Whiteford,* p. 99. The same writer observes: "In North Wales, pence and half-pence (in lieu of little rolls of bread) which were heretofore, and by some still are, given on these occasions, are now distributed to the poor, who flock in great numbers to the house of the dead before the corpse is brought out. When the corpse is brought out of the house, layd upon the bier and covered, before it be taken up, the next of kin to the deceased, widow, mother, daughter, or cousin (never done by a man), gives over the corps to one of the poorest neighbours three 2d. or four 3d. white loaves of bread, or a cheese with a piece of money stuck in it, and then a new wooden cup of drink, which some will require the poor person who receives it immediately to drink a little of. When this is done, the minister, if present, says the Lord's Prayer, and then they set forward for church. The things mentioned above as given to a poor body, are brought upon a large dish, over the corpse, and the poor body returns thanks for them, and blesses God for the happiness of his friend and neighbour deceased." Compare *Sin-Eater* and Ditchfield, chap. 18. In the 18th century, it appears that at Glasgow large donations at funerals were made to the poor, "which are never less than £5, and never exceeded ten guineas, in which case the bells of the city are tolled." *Stat. Acc. of Scotland,* v. 523. It was formerly customary for a sum of money to be given to certain persons or institutions, with whom or which the deceased had been connected. This usage is illustrated by a document inserted among the "Egerton Papers," being the memoranda relating to the will of one of the Rokeby family, who died in 1600. Among the items are gifts of sums of money to the principals of Lincoln's Inn, Furnival's Inn, and Thavis' Inn, for drink to be supplied to the members of those societies in honour of the occasion. This custom of funeral libations is still not uncommon in the country. By his will made in 1639, Francis Pynner, of Bury St. Edmunds, directed that out of certain rents and revenues accruing from his property, from and after the Michaelmas following his decease, forty poor parishioners of St. Mary's, Bury, should, on coming to the church, be entitled to a twopenny wheaten loaf on the last Friday in every month throughout the year, for ever. See a curious account of doles in Ducarel's *Tour through Normandy*.

Dolemoors.—Collinson says: "In the parishes of Congresbury and Puxton, are two large pieces of common land called East and West Dolemoors, (from the Saxon dal, which signifies a share or portion), which are divided into single acres, each bearing a peculiar and different mark cut in the turf, such as a horn, four oxen and a mare, two oxen and a mare, a pole-axe, cross, dung-fork, oven, duck's-nest, hand-reel, and hare's-tail. On the Saturday before Old-Midsummer, several proprietors of estates in the parishes of Congresbury, Puxton, and Week St. Lawrence, or their tenants, assemble on the commons. A number of apples are previously prepared, marked in the same manner with the before-mentioned acres, which are distributed by a young lad to each of the commoners from a bag or hat. At the close of the distribution each person repairs to his allotment, as his apple directs him, and takes posession for the ensuing year. An adjournment then takes place to the house of the overseer of Dolemoors (an officer annually elected from the tenants) where four acres, reserved for the purposes of paying expenses, are let by inch of candle, and the remainder of the day is spent in that sociability and hearty mirth so congenial to the soul of a Somersetshire yeoman." *Somersetshire*, iii., 586.

Door-Drink.—See *Bridling Cast and Stirrup Cup*.

Dore, Mary.—Warner, mentioning Mary Dore, the "parochial witch of Beaulieu," who died about 1750, says, "her spells were chiefly used for purposes of self-extrication in situations of danger; and I have conversed with a rustic whose father had seen the old lady convert herself more than once into the form of a hare or cat, when likely to be apprehended in wood-stealing, to which she was somewhat addicted. *Hampshire*, 1793, ii., 241.

Doree.—Pennant informs us that "Superstition hath made the Dorée rival to the Hadock for the honour of having been the fish out of whose mouth St. Peter took the tribute-money, leaving on its sides those incontestible proofs of the identity of the fish, the marks of his finger and thumb." *Zoology*, 1776, iii., 221. It is rather difficult at this time to determine on which part to decide the dispute; for the doree likewise asserts an origin of its spots of a similar nature, but of a much earlier date than the former. St. Christopher, in wading through an arm of the sea, having caught a fish of this kind *en passant*, as an eternal memorial of the fact, left the impression on its sides to be transmitted to all posterity.

Dorrish.—The story of the Squire of Dorrish, an ancient Devonshire family, is related as follows: "Returning home late on a winter night after a considerable consumption of brandy punch at the house of a neighbouring squire, he fell from his horse where a brook, running at the foot of a hill on which stands the house of Dorrish, is crossed by a narrow bridge, and was killed. This was early in the 18th century. From that time to this his spirit has been gradually advancing up the hill toward the house, at the rate of a "cockstride" in every moon. A bridge as narrow and as sharp as the edge of a sword is provided for the unfortunate squire. Whenever he falls off (and it is supposed that this must occasionally happen), he is obliged to return to the stream where his life was ended, and to begin again. His present position is therefore quite uncertain, but there is no doubt that he will one day reach his own front door, and what may then happen no one can possibly foresee. The sharp sword here unquestionably represents the "brig of dread" of the northern Lykewake:—

'This ae night, this ae night,
    Everie night and alle
  To brig of dread thou comes at last—
    And Christ receive thy sawle.'"

Double Hand.—Taylor the Water-poet, in his "Great Eater of Kent," 1630, says: "I have known a great man very expert on the Jewe-harpe, a rich merchants wife a quicke gamester at Irish (especially when she came to bearing of men) that she wolde seldome misse entring. Monsieur le Ferr, a Frenchman, was the first inventor of the admirable game of double-hand, hot-cockles; and Gregorie Dawson, an Englishman, devised the unmatchable mystery of blindman buffe."

Doublets or **Dublets.**—See *Tick-Tack*.

Dough.—*Dough* or *Dow* is vulgarly used in the North for a little cake, though it properly signifies a mass of flour tempered with water, salt and yeast, and kneaded fit for baking. It is derived, as Junius tells us, from the Dutch *Deeg*, which comes from the Theostican *thihen*, to grow bigger, or rise, as the bakers term it. The sailors call pudding dough, but pronounce it duff. Du Cange says: "*Panis Natalitius, cujusmodi fieri solet in die Natalis Domini, et præberi Dominis a prædiorum conductoribus, in quibusdam Provinciis, qui ex farina delicatiori, ovis et lacti confici solent: Cuignets appellant Picardi, quod in cuneorum varias species efformentur.*" Gloss. v. *Panis Natalitius.* See also Ihre *Gloss. Suio-Goth*, i., 1009.

Dough-Nut Day.—A name formerly given to Shrove-Tuesday by the children at Baldock, Herts, from small cakes fried in brass skillets over the fire with hog's lard.

Douro.—See *Clavie*.

Dove.—A correspondent of "Notes and Queries" sent the following account in 1857 to that miscellany. "A month or two back, a family, on leaving one of the Channel Islands, presented to a gardener (it is uncertain whether an inhabitant of the island or no) some pet doves, the conveyance of them to England being likely to prove troublesome. A few days afterwards the man brought them back, stating that he was engaged to be married, and the possession of the birds might be (as he had been informed) an obstacle to the course of true love running smooth." This was put in the shape of a query, but no answer appeared. 2nd S., iv., 25. Doves were formerly threshed in some places at Shrove-tide.

Dovercourt, Rood of.—"In the same year of our Lord, 1532, there was an Idoll named the Roode of Dovercourt, whereunto was much and great resort of people. For at that time there was a great rumour blown abroad amongst the ignorant sort, that the power of the *Idoll of Dovercourt* was so great that no man had power to shut the church doore where he stood, and therefore they let the church dore, both night and day, continually stand open, for the more credit unto the blinde rumour." Fox's *Book of Martyrs*, ii. 302. He adds that four men, determining to destroy it, travelled ten miles from Dedham, where they resided, took away the rood, and burnt it, for which act three of them afterwards suffered death. In *Grim the Collier of Croydon* (Hazlitt's Dodsley, viii., 398) Miles Forest says:

"Have you not heard, my lords, the wondrous feats
Of Holy Dunstan, Abbot of Canterbury?
What miracles he hath achieved of late;
And how the rood of Dovercourt did speak,
Confirming his opinion to be true?—"

Dovercourt was the mother-church of Harwich.

Dover's Games.—Sports held from time immemorial on the hill in the Cotswolds, still known as Dover's Hill. Robert Dover, called Captain Dover, promoted their revival, when they had grown more or less obsolete, about 1596. In 1636, a collection of poems by various writers appeared with a frontispiece representing Dover in a suit, which had been given to him by James I. Among the writers is Randolph, who contributes *An Eclogue on the noble Assemblies revived on Cotswold Hills by Master Robert Dover*.

Down Plat.—See *St. Luke's Day*.

Draco Volans.—See *Aërolites*.

Dragon.—In the old romances the dragons are frequently denominated worms, a phrase employed by our forefathers with considerable latitude, as I think will be allowed when I mention that, in the "Towneley Mysteries," the plague of locusts in Egypt is described as a visitation of "wyld wormes." The modern Greeks seem to have classed what we now are sufficiently familiar with under the denomination of the water-spout among dragons. Mr. Wright, in his "Essays," 1846, quotes a curious extract from the chronicle of John of Bromton in confirmation of this theory. The spout is described by the chronicler as a great black dragon descending from the clouds, and hiding its head in the water, while its tail reached to the sky; and he tells us that any ships which were passing at the time, he swallowed up with all their contents. The theatre of this reputed monster's depredations was the Gulf of Satalia. It was supposed that a serpent, to become a dragon, must eat a serpent. This partly realizes the ophiophagous genus of serpents, which does not thereby suffer such a metamorphosis. I found the following note in "The Muses' Threnodie," by Henry Adamson, 1638, repr. 1774: "We read of a cave called 'The Dragon Hole,' in a steep rock on the face of Kinnoul Hill, of very difficult and dangerous access. On the first day of May, during the era of Popery, a great concourse of people assembled at that place to celebrate superstitious games, now," adds the writer, "unknown to us, which the Reformers prohibited under heavy censures and severe penalties, of which we are informed from the ancient records of the Kirk Session of Perth." It may, perhaps, be mentioned that the Chinese to this day believe in the existence of dragons, and attribute natural phenomena, such as eclipses, to their malignant agency. They shout at the dragon when there is an eclipse, and as soon as the solar or lunar orb has recovered its usual splendour, it is the dragon which has been discomfited and put to flight.

Dragon's Blood.—A resinous compound, which is still employed by young girls, chiefly in the rural districts, as a charm for restoring to the person, who burns it, and repeats over the flame certain cabalistic words, the object of affection. But it is also employed by married women who have become estranged from their husbands, and desire reconciliation. *Antiquary*, June and July, 1891.

Draw Gloves.—There was a sport entitled "Draw Gloves," of which, however, I find no description. The following *jeu d'esprit* is found in Herrick:

Draw Gloves.

" At Draw-gloves we'l play,
And prethee let's lay
A wager, and let it be this;
Who first to the summe
Of twenty shall come,
Shall have for his winning a kisse."

And in another poem by him, "To the Maides to Walk Abroad" there is the following:

" Come sit we under yonder tree,
Where merry as the maids we'l be,
And as on primroses we sit,
We'l venter (if we can) at wit:
If not, at draw-gloves we will play:
So spend some minutes of the day;
Or else spin out the threed of sands,
Playing at questions and commands."

See Davis, *Suppl. Glossary*, 1881, p. 202.

Draw Straws, To.—In the *Vaux de Vire* of Jean le Houx, Muirhead's translation, 1875, p. 103, we find:

"If after mirth our wine
Run short, in pleasant way
We draw straws, to divine
Who for some more shall pay."

I have not met with any English parallel of this, no doubt, at one time common Norman usage.

Dreams.—Dreams, as the sacred writings inform us, have on certain occasions, been used as the divine mediums of revelation. As connected with our present design, they may either come under the head of omens or that of divination. Homer has told us that dreams come from Jupiter, and in all ages and every kingdom the idea that some knowledge of the future is to be derived from them, has always composed a very striking article in the creed of popular superstitions. Bartholinus, *De Causis contemptæ a Danis Mortis*, p. 678. Henry tells us: "We find Peter of Blois, who was one of the most learned men of the age in which he flourished, writing an account of his dreams to his friend the Bishop of Bath, and telling him how anxious he had been about the interpretation of them; and that he had employed for that purpose divination by the Psalter. The English, it seems probable, had still more superstitious curiosity, and paid greater attention to dreams and omens than the Normans; for when William Rufus was dissuaded from going abroad on the morning of that day on which he was killed, because the Abbot of Gloucester had dreamed something which portended danger, he is said to have made this reply: 'Do you imagine that I am an Englishman, to be frighted by a dream, or the sneezing of an old woman?'" *Hist. of Gr. Britain*, 111, 572. Cornelius Agrippa, speaking of "Interpretation of Dreams," says: "To this delusion not a few great philosophers have given not a little credit, especially Democritus, Aristotle, and his follower Themistius, Sinesius also the Platonick, so far building upon examples of dreams, which some accident hath made to be true; and thence they endeavour to persuade men that there are no dreams but what are real. But as to the causes of dreams, both external and internal, they do not all agree in one judgment. For the Platonicks reckon them among the specifick and concrete notions of the soul. Avicen makes the cause of dreams to be an ultimate intelligence moving the moon in the middle of that light with which the fancies of men are illuminate while they sleep. Aristotle refers the cause thereof to common sense, but placed in the fancy. Averroes places the cause in the imagination. Democritus ascribes it to little images or representatives separated from the things themselves. Albertus, to the superior influences which continually flow from the skie through many specifick mediums. The physicians impute the cause thereof to vapours and humours : others to the affections and cares predominant in persons when awake. Others joyn the powers of the soul, celestial influences and images together, all making but one cause. Artemidorus and Daldianus have written of the interpretation of dreams : and certain books go about under Abraham's name, whom Philo, in his Book of the Gyants and of Civil Life, asserts to have been the first practiser thereof. Other treatises there are falsified under the names of David and Solomon, wherein are to be read nothing but meer dreams concerning dreams. But Marcus Cicero, in his Book of Divination, hath given sufficient reasons against the vanity and folly of those that give credit to dreams, which I purposely here omit." *Vanity of Sciences*, p. 105. Every dream, according to Wolfius, takes its rise from some sensation, and is continued by the succession of phantasms in the mind. His reasons are that when we dream we imagine something, or the mind produces phantasms;

but no phantasms can arise in the mind without a previous sensation. Hence neither can a dream arise without some previous sensation. Here it may be stated, says Douce, that if our author meant a previous sensation of the thing dreamt of, it is certainly not so.

"Dreams are but the rais'd
Impressions of premeditated things,
Our serious apprehension left upon
Our minds, or else th' imaginary shapes
Of objects proper to the complexion,
Or disposition of our bodies."

Cotgrave's *English Treasury of Wit and Language*, 1655. Physicians seem to be the only persons at present who interpret dreams. Frightful dreams are perhaps always indications of some violent oppression of Nature, especially of dyspepsia. Hippocrates has many curious observations on dreams. Ennius made that very sensible remark, that what men studied and pondered in the day-time the same they dreamed on at night. Scot informs us of "The art and order to be used in digging for money, revealed by dreams." "There must be made," says he, "upon a hazel wand three crosses, and certain words must be said over it, and hereunto must be added certain characters and barbarous names. And whilst the treasure is a digging, there must be read the Psalms De Profundis, &c., and then a certain prayer: and if the time of digging be neglected, the Devil will carry all the treasure away." *Discovery*, ed. 1665, 102. Some verses on this occasion are preserved by Aubrey. *Miscellanies*, 1696, ed. 1857, 132. A writer in the "Gentleman's Magazine" for September, 1751, wittily observes that "Dreams have for many ages been esteemed as the noblest resources at a dead lift: the dreams of Homer were held in such esteem that they were styled golden dreams: and among the Grecians we find a whole country using no other way for information, but going to sleep. The Oropians, and all the votaries of Amphiaraus are proofs of this assertion, as may be seen in Pausan. Attic." In the "Gentleman's Magazine" for January, 1799, are some curious rhymes on the subject of dreams, from Harl. MS. 541, fol. 228 verso:

"Vpon my ryght syde y maie leye, blesid lady to the y F y
For the teres that ye lete vpon your swete sonnys feete,
Sende me grace for to slepe, & good dremys for to mete
Slepyng wakyng til morowe daye bee.
Owr lorde is the frevte, oure lady is the tree
Blessid be the blossom that sprange lady of the.
In nôie patris & filii & sp's sā amen."

In "Mery Tales and Quicke Answeres" (circâ 1540) is a not very delicate story "of him that dreamed he founde gold." See "Old English Jest-Books," i. In "A C. Mery Talvs," 1525, is the story of Sir Richard Whittington's Dream (ibid.) In the "Opticke Glasse of Hvmors," by T. W. 1607, there is a curious section on this subject (ed. 1639, p. 141). In Lyly's "Sapho and Phao," 1584, are some pleasant observations on dreams, act iv. sc. 3: "And can there be no trueth in dreams? Yea, dreams have their trueth.—Dreames are but dotings, which come either by things we see in the day, or meates that we eate, and so the common sense preferring it to be the imaginative. 'I dreamed,' says Ismena, 'mine eye tooth was loose, and that I thrust it out with my tongue.' 'It fortelleth,' replies Mileta, 'the losse of a friend: and I ever thought thee so ful of prattle, that thou wouldest thrust out the best friend with the tatling.'" In Overbury's "Character of a Milkmaid" is the passage: "Her dreams are so chaste that shee dare tell them: only a Fridaies dream is all her superstition: that she concealles for feare of Anger." There is a nursery adage:

"Friday night's dream
On the Saturday told,
Is sure to come true,
Be it never so old."

Various are the popular superstitions, or at least the faint traces of them that still are made use of to procure dreams of divination: such as fasting St. Agnes' Fast; laying a piece of the first cut of the groaning cheese under the pillow, to cause young persons to dream of their lovers, and putting a Bible in the like situation, with a sixpence clapped in the Book of Ruth, and so on. Strutt says: "Writing their name on a paper at twelve o'clock, burning the same, then carefully gathering up the ashes, and laying them close wrapp'd in a paper upon a looking-glass. marked with a cross, under their pillows: this should make them dream of their loves." *Manners and Customs*, 111, 180. Mr. Brand observed that in his day, except amongst the most ignorant and vulgar, the whole imaginary structure had fallen to the ground; but surely this assertion was a little premature, looking at the still extensive belief, even among intelligent people, in this class of revelation, one that will never, perhaps, wholly be extinguished under any circumstances.

Dreams, Interpretation of.—The following may in some measure supply what Agrippa thought proper to omit in a passage above-cited: "Cicero, among others, relates this. A certain man dreamed that there was an egg hid under his bed; the soothsayer to whom he applied himself for the interpretation of the dream told him that in the same place where he imagined to see the egg there was treasure hid; whereupon he caused the place to be digged up, and there accordingly he found silver, and in the midst of it a good quantity of gold, and, to give the interpreter some testimony of his acknowledgment he brought him some pieces of the silver which he had found; but the soothsayer, hoping also to have some of the gold, said: 'And will you not give me some of the yolk too?'" Amyraldus, translated by Lowde, 1676. Bacon observes that the interpretation of natural dreams has been much laboured, but mixed with numerous extravagancies, and adds, that at present it stands not upon its best foundation. Shylock, in the "Merchant of Venice," says:

"There is some ill a brewing towards my rest,
For I did dream of money-bags to-night."

Hall, in his "Characters of Vertues and Vices," 1608, speaking of the superstitious man, observes: "But, if his troubled fancie shall second his thoughts with the dreame of a fair garden, or greene rushes, or the salutation of a dead friend, he takes leave of the world, and sayes he cannot live."—"There is no dream of his without an interpretation, without a prediction, and if the event answer not his exposition, he expounds it according to the event." Melton says: "That if a man dreame of egs or fire, he shall heare of anger." "That to dreame of the Devil is good lucke." "That to dreame of gold good lucke, but of silver ill." *Astrologaster*, 1620, No. 13. In another old work, it is said: "To dreame of eagles flying over our heads, to dreame of marriages, dancing and banquetting, foretells some of our kinsfolkes are departed: to dream of silver, if thou hast it given to thyselfe, sorrow: of gold, good fortune: to lose an axle toth or an eye, the death of some friend: to dream of bloody teeth, the death of the dreamer: to weepe in sleepe, joy: to see one's face in the water, or to see the dead, long life: to handle lead, to see a hare, death: to dream of chickens and birds, ill-luck," &c. *Help to Discourse*, 1633, p. 330. In a "Strange Metamorphosis of Man," &c., 1634, it is observed: "Nor is he (the bay-tree) altogether free from superstition; for he wil make you beleeve that if you put his leaves under your pillow, you shall be sure to have true dreames." In Sampson's "Vow-Breaker," 1636, act iii. sc. 1, Ursula speaks: "I have heard you say that dreames and visions were fabulous; and, yet one time I dreamt fowle water ran through the floore, and the next day the house was on fire. You us'd to say hobgoblins, fairies and the like, were nothing

but our owne affrightments, and yet o' my troth, cuz, I once dream'd of a young batchelour, and was ridd with a night-mare." "He that dreams he hath lost a tooth, shall lose a friend, (he has lost one), and he that dreams that a rib is taken out of his side, shall ere long see the death of his wife." See Lowde's Amyraldus, p. 22, and the passage from Lyly already cited. Gaule gives us "the snorting in sleep," the dreaming of gold, silver, eggs, gardens, weddings, dead men, dung," &c. *Mag-Astromancer posed*, p. 181. Some extracts from *A Treatise of the Interpretation of Sundry Dreames*, 1601 (licensed for the press in 1566) may not be unacceptable:

"1. First, to see the ayre faire and cleere, promiseth good vnto all persons: especially vnto such, which seeke after things lost, and would iourney into strange places: for all things be made apparent to a cleare ayre. 2. To see the ayre darkned, mysty, or cloudy, doth then portend the hinderance of actions, or heauinesse. 3. To see rayne fall without a tempest or with wind, signifieth good (in a manner) vnto all persons. 4. To see showres, haile, thick cloude, and tempests, doe pronounce troubles, harmes, and perills vnto all persons, except to seruants and such in present troubles. 5. To see fire in the ayre, cleere, pure, and little, doth foreshow threatnings of some noble estates: but vnto many, this dreame portendeth the incursion of enemies, pouerty and hunger. 6. To see lightning passe neere by him, without a tempest, and not to touch the body, doth after threaten banishment out of the place, in which he dwelleth. 7. To think himselfe striken with lightning, promise vnto him which lacketh a wife, to marry one, whether hee bee poore or rich. And married, the separation of his wife from him: and the like to be vnderstood of brethren, friends, kinsfolke and acquaintance, to become enemies vnto him. 8. A certaine person dreamed that hee saw the outward pillar or bed-post smitten and burnt with lightning, and not long after dyed his wife. 9. To thinke thy selfe drawne by force of a dead person knowne to thee, vnto a place vnknowne, doth after signifie, that he shall be taken with a grieuous sicknes, of which he shall dye: but if hee escape, it shall be very hardly. 10. Hee which thinketh hee seeth a dead person sleeping, such a person shall dye quietly. 11. To see either father or mother that be dead, is lesser euill, then to see any other dead person. 12. He which seeth a dead person, looking sad, deformed and in torne clothes, doth after signifie a misfortune to ensue vnto the dreamer. 13. The sick person to dreame that he maried a maiden, signifieth death to ensue. But good it is vnto him which beginneth a new businesse, for that it shall come into a good purpose. 14. To marie a widow, signifieth the compassng of old matters or businesses, but contrarie in the new. 15. To see the sun rising out of the east, cleere and fair, and setting the like in the west, signifieth good vnto all persons. 16. And a sicke person to see the sun rising out of the west, signifieth amendment vnto health. 17. And the sonne seeming darke or bloody, or for the great heat making a noyse, is dangerous & euill vnto all persons, for that it declareth vnto some, the hindrance of actions, and vnto others sicknesse, and perill vnto their children, or disease and paine of their eyes. 18. Hee which seeth his image in the moone, not hauing children, doth foreshew the birth of a sonne to ensue ; but to the woman like dreaming, to haue a daughter. 19. To see the starres fall from heauen, doth signifie vnto the rich much pouerty and care to ensue. 20. He which seeth a great starre fall from heauen on his head doth after promise great good luck to ensue. 21. To see thy house faire swept with a broome, signifieth the consumption of thy money. 22. To see another man's faire swept, signifieth that the dreamer shall possesse the money of that house. 23. To seeme to open a new doore, shall after mary a wife profitable vnto him. 24. To dreame, to cut downe a tree, or plucke it vp by the rootes, doth after signifie that hee shall slay a man or a beast. 25. To dreame to see a hoy or crayer, or other small vessel to enter into a house & after to go out againe : signifieth that the principall of the same house shal after die, and the rather, if water appeareth there, for that the same signifieth teares, and the vessel the coffin, in which dead bodies be caried. 26. And beeing in a ship, whosoeuer dreameth to see fire in any part of the ship, from that side or part of the ship shal the wind arise the next morrow. 27. Whatsoeuer seemeth to happen to the ship, whiles thou thinkest thy selfe in her, the same shall hapen vnto thy wife : or being a widower, vnto thy children. 28. Whosoeuer dreameth to see any lanterne light in a ship or other barke, it doth after signifie a great calme, or quietnesse of the wind to ensue. 29. Whosoeuer beeing on the sea, dreameth to see sea-gulles, sea-pies, or any other like sea-birds, it doth signifie vnto saylers or mariners to bee after in very great perill, but no losse altogether. 30. He that dreameth to haue a mill, & doth grind in the same, promiseth good vnto the dreamer, and a prosperous life. 31. He that thinketh to eate fresh fish, shall talke euilly of men. 32. To eat salt fish, signifieth the losse of his money, either by fraud, or by a wile. 33. To dreame to ride on a blacke horse, signifieth losse & sorrow to ensue. 34. To see red oxen in the dream declares the mightier & sharper sicknesses. 35. To see oxen lying or sleeping, declareth euill or harme to happen vnto the dreamer."

"Somniandi modus Franciscanorum hinc duxit originem. Antiqui moris fuit Oracula et futurorum præscientiam quibusdam adhibitis sacris per insomnia dari : qui mos talis erat, ut Victimas cæderent, mox Sacrificio peracto sub pellibus cæsarum Ovium incubantes, somnia, captarent, eaque lymphatica insomnia verissimos exitus sortiri. Alex. ab Alex. lib. iii. c. 26. Et Monachi super storea cubant in qua alius Frater ecstaticus fuerat somniatus, sacrificat missam, preces et jejunia adhibet, inde ut communiter fit de amoribus per somnia consulit. redditque responsa pro occurrentibus spectris," &c. Moresini *Papatus*, 1594, p. 162. Compare *Dumb-cake*.

Drinking, A.—In the "Statistical Account of Scotland" the minister of Kirmichael tells us : "In extraordinary cases of distress, we have a custom which deserves to be taken notice of ; and that is, when any of the lower people happen to be reduced by sicknesses, losses or misfortunes of any kind, a friend is sent to as many of their neighbours as they think needful, to invite them to what they call a drinking. This drinking consists in a little small beer, with a bit of bread and cheese, and sometimes a small glass of brandy or whiskey, previously provided by the needy persons or their friends. The guests convene at the time appointed, and after collecting a shilling a-piece, and sometimes more, they divert themselves for about a couple of hours with music and dancing, and then go home. Such as cannot attend themselves, usually send their charitable contribution by any neighbour that chooses to go. These meetings sometimes produce five, six and seven pounds to the needy person or family." *Stat. Acc.*, i., 59. In the same work, it is said, under the parish of Gargunnock, co. Stirling : "There is one prevailing custom among our country people, which is sometimes productive of much evil. Everything is bought and sold over a bottle. The people who go to the fair in the full possession of their faculties, do not always transact their business, or return to their homes, in the same state." *Stat. Acc.*, xviii., 123. This, however, was in the eighteenth century.

Drinking Usages. — In Nash's "Pierce Pennilesse," 1592, occurs : "Nowe he is nobody that cannot drinke Supernagulum, carouse the hunters hoope, quaffe upse freze crosse, with healths, gloves, mumpes, polockes, and a thousand such domineering inventions." In Young's "England's Bane," 1617, are some curious passages (partly taken direct from other authors) concerning the then customs of drinking: "I myselfe have seen and (to my grief of conscience) may now say have in presence, yea, and amongst others been an actor in the businesse, when upon our knees, after healthes to many private punkes, a health have been drunke to all the whoores in the world." Again: "He is a man of no fashion that cannot drinkee supernaculum, carouse the hunters hoop, quaffe upseyfreese crosse, bowse in Permoysant, in Pimlico, in crambo, with healthes, gloves, numpes, frolicks, and a thousand such domineering inventions, as by the bell, by the cards, by the dye, by the dozen, by the yard, and so by measure we drink out of measure. There are in London drinking schooles: so that drunkennesse is professed with us a liberal arte and science." Again: "I have seene a company among the very woods and forests," (he speaks of the New Forest and Windsor Forest), "drinking for a muggle. Sixe determined to try their strengths who could drink most glasses for the muggle. The first drinkes a glasse of a pint, the second two, the next three, and so on every one multiplieth till the last taketh sixe. Then the first beginneth againe and taketh seven, and in this manner they drink thrice a peece round, every man taking a glasse more then his fellow, so that hee that dranke least, which was the first, drank one and twentie pints, and the sixth man thirty-six." Our author observes: "Before we were acquainted with the lingering wars of the Low Countries, drunkennes was held in the highest degree of hatred that might be amongst us." "Ebrius experiens, or the Drunkard's Humor," signat. M 3. Some remarkable anecdotes of this class are given also by Ward of Ipswich, in his "Woe to Drunkards," 1622. The term *Upsey freeze*, so often employed by the writers of the times of James I. and Charles I., is a corrupt form of *op zyn Vriesch*, in the Friesland fashion, and was introduced when the English became better acquainted with the Low Countries under Elizabeth. Robert Harris speaks, in the dedication to his *Drunkard's Cup*, of drinking as a sort of profession at this time: "There is (they say) an art of drinking now, and in the world it is become a great profession. There are degrees and titles, given under the names of roaring boyes, damned crew, &c. There are lawes and ceremonies to be observed both by the firsts and seconds, &c. There is a drinking by the foot, by the yard, &c., a drinking by the douzens, by the scoures, &c., for the wager, for the victory, man against man, house against house, town against town, and how not? There are also terms of art, fetched from Hell, (for the better distinguishing of the practitioners); one is coloured, another is

foxt, a third is gone to the dogs, a fourth is well to live," &c. In the body of the sermon, he mentions "the strange saucinesse of base vermine, in tossing the name of his most excellent Majesty in their foaming mouthes, and in dareing to make that a shooing horne to draw on drink, by drinking healths to him." He adds elsewhere explanatorily: "I doe not speak of those beasts that must be answered and have right done them in the same measure, gesture, course, &c., but of such onely as leave you to your measure (You will keepe a turne and your time in pledging); is it any hurt to pledge such? How pledge them? You mistake if you think that we speak against any true civility If thou lust to pledge the lords prophets in woes, pledge good fellowes in their measures and challenges: if not so, learne still to shape a peremptory answer to an unreasonable demand. Say —I will pray for the King's health, and drinke for mine owne." He uses "somewhat whitled," and "buckt with drink" as terms expressing the different degrees of drunkenness. In another (well-known) work, I find a singular passage. which I confess I do not thoroughly understand, concerning the then modes of drinking. The writer is describing a drinking bout of female gossips: "Dispatching a lusty rummer of Rhenish to little Periwig, who passed it instantly to Steephen Malten, and she conveigh'd with much agility to Daplusee, who made bold to stretch the Countesses gowne into a pledge, and cover and come, which was the only plausible mode of drinking they delighted in: This was precisely observ'd by the other three, that their moistned braines gave leave for their glibb'd tongues to chat liberally." Gayton's *Notes on Don Quixote*, 1654, p. 234. In Shakespear's "Timon of Athens," act i. sc. 5, is the following passage:

> "If I
> Were a huge man, I should fear to drink at meals,
> Lest they should spy my wind pipe's dangerous notes;
> Great men should drink with harness on their throats":

Upon which Strutt observes: "The old manner of pledging each other when they drank, was thus: the person who was going to drink, asked any one of the company who sat next him, whether he would pledge him, on which he answering that he would, held up his knife or sword, to guard him whilst he drank; for while a man is drinking he necessarily is in an unguarded posture, exposed to the treacherous stroke of some hidden or secret enemy." Strutt's authority was William of Malmesbury, and he observes from the delineation he gives us (and it must be noted that his plates, being copies of ancient illuminated manuscripts, are of unquestionable authority), that it seems perfectly well to agree with the reported custom; the middle figure is addressing himself to his companion, who seems to tell him that he pledges him, holding up his knife in token of his readiness to assist and protect him. After all, I cannot help hazarding an opinion that the expression meant no more than that if you took your cup or glass I pledged myself to you that I would follow your example. The common ellipsis, "to" is wanting. Thus we say, "I'll give you," instead of "I'll give to you"; "I'll pledge you," and "I'll pledge to you." But I offer this with great deference to the established opinions on the subject. But the custom is said to have first taken its rise from the death of Edward the Martyr, who was by the contrivance of Elfrida, his stepmother, treacherously stabbed in the back as he was drinking. Daines Barrington illustrates the former danger to which life was subject: He says, "The *Speculum Regale* advises the courtier, when he is in the King's presence, to pull off his cloak; and one of the reasons given is, that he shews by this means that he hath no concealed weapons to make an attempt upon the King's life." *Observ. on the Statutes,* 1775, p. 206. In 1553, during Wyatt's rebellion the seven serjeants and other lawyers in Westminster Hall pleaded in harness. Compare *Healths, Supernaculum, &c.*

Drinking Vessels. — Heywood says : "Of drinking cups divers and sundry sorts we have; some of elme, some of box, some of maple, some of holly, &c. Mazers, broad-mouth'd dishes, noggins, whiskins, piggins, crinzes, ale-bowls, wassell-bowls, court-dishes, tankards, kannes, from a pottle to a pint, from a pint to a gill. Other bottles we have of leather, but they are most used among the shepheards and harvest people of the countrey : small jacks wee have in many ale-houses of the Citie and suburbs, tip't with silver, besides the great black jacks and bombards at Court, which when the Frenchmen first saw, they reported, at their returne into their countrey, that the Englishmen used to drink out of their bootes: we have, besides, cups made of hornes of beasts, of cocker-nuts, of goords, of the eggs of estriches, others made of the shells of divers fishes brought from the Indies and other places and shining like mother of pearl. Come to plate, every taverne can afford you flat bowles, French bowles, prounet cups, beare bowles, beakers; and private householders in the Citie, when they make a feast to entertain their friends, can furnish their cupbords with flagons, tankards, beere-cups, wine-bowles, some white, some percell guilt, some guilt all over, some with covers, others without,

of sundry shapes and qualities. . . There is now profest an eighth liberal art or science, call'd *Ars Bibendi*, i.e., the art of drinking. The students or professors thereof call a greene garland, or painted hcope hang'd out, a colledge : a signe where there is a lodging, mansmeate, and horse-meate, an inne of court, an hall, or an hostle : where nothing is sold but ale and tobacco, a grammar schoole : a red or blew lattice, that they terme a free schoole for all commers. . . . The bookes which they study, and whose leaves they so often turne over, are, for the most part, three of the old translations and three of the new. Those of the old translation : 1. The Tankard. 2. The black Jack. 3. The quart-pot rib'd, or thorondell. Those of the new be these : 1. The jugge. 2. The beaker. 3. The double or single can, or black pot." Among the proper phrases belonging to the library occur, " to drink upse-phreese, supernaculum, to swallow a flap-dragon, or a rawe egge—to see that no lesse than three at once be bare to a health. . . Many of our nation have used the Lowe-countrey-warres so long, that though they have left their money and clothes behind, yet they have brought home their habit of drinking." At p. 60, he gives the following phrases then in use for being drunk." He is foxt, hee is flawed, he is flustered, hee is suttle, cupshot, cut in the leg or backe, hee hath seene the French king, he hath swallowed an haire or a taverne-token, hee hath whipt the cat, he hath been at the scriveners and learn'd to make indentures, hee hath bit his grannam, or is bit by a barne-weesell, with an hundred such-like adages and sentences." *Philocothonista,* 1635, p. 45.

Drive Knaves out of Town.— See *Troule-in-Madame.*

Drowned Bodies.—Several correspondents of *Notes and Queries* writing from Peterborough and elsewhere, refer to the notion, a very foolish one, that, where a person has been drowned, a button from his waistcoat, mounted on a piece of wood, will indicate the spot, where the body lies, by ceasing to float on its arrival thither. The annexed extract is from the *Echo,* 1874 : " Students of folk-lore will bear us out in the assertion that the recovery of drowned bodies was formerly made the occasion of a variety of superstitious practice, ranging from the horrible to the grotesque. Had any enthusiastic collector of such waifs from the ebbing flood of past folly been standing on the bridge of Namur a few days since, he might have witnessed a spectacle, doubtless common enough in the middle ages, but extremely rare in our own. Four individuals, sitting on a trough, drifted down the Sambre between the bridge and the lock. Three of them held boat-hooks, the fourth read aloud some formula out of a book, and a lighted candle, stuck in a washerwoman's tub, floated by the side of the trough. These persons were looking for a drowned man ; the reader was evoking the deceased by means of sacred words, while the candle was expected to stop and go out as soon as it stood over the spot where the corpse lay. The party did not, indeed, trust wholly to their mediæval recipe, but supplemented it by sounding the bed of the river with their poles, yet there was, it must be owned, enough in their conduct to suggest to the *Organ de Namur* the indignant query, ' Is it possible that in the year of grace, 1874, adult and vaccinated citizens know no better than this?' "

Druid's Eggs, or Ova Anguina.
—The ancient Britons, says Pennant, *Zoology*, iii. 31, had a strange superstition in respect of the viper, and of which there still remained in his time (if it is even yet extinct) in Wales a strong tradition. The account Pliny (*Nat. Hist.* lib. xxix., c. 12) gives of it we find thus translated by Mason in his " Caractacus." The person speaking is a Druid :

" —— The potent adder stone
Gender'd 'fore th' autumnal moon :
When in undulating twine
The foaming snakes prolific join ;
When they hiss, and when they bear
Their wondrous egg aloof in air ;
Thence, before to earth it fall
The Druid, in his hallow'd pall,
 Receives the prize,
 And instant flies,
Follow'd by th' envenom'd brood
Till he cross the crystal flood."

This wondrous egg seems to be nothing more than a bead of glass, used by the Druids as a charm to impose on the vulgar, whom they taught to believe that the possessor would be fortunate in all his attempts, and that it would give him the favour of the great. Our modern Druidesses, he adds, give much the same account of the ovum Anguinum, *Glain Neidr*, as the Welsh call it, or the adder gem, as the Roman philosopher does, but seem not to have so exalted an opinion of its powers, using it only to assist children in cutting their teeth, or to cure the Chin-cough, or to drive away an ague. He gives a plate of these bands, made of glass of a very rich blue colour : some of which are plain and others streaked.

" Near Aberfraw," in the Isle of Anglesey," says Gough, " are frequently found the Glain Naidr or Druid glass rings. Of these the vulgar opinion in Cornwall and most part of Wales is, that they are produced through all Cornwall by snakes joining their heads together and hissing, which forms a kind of bubble like a ring about

the head of one of them, which the rest by continual hissing blow on till it comes off at the tail, when it immediately hardens and resembles a glass ring. Whoever found it was to prosper in all his undertakings. These rings are called Glain Nadroedh, or Gemmæ Anguinæ. Glûne in Irish signifies glass. In Monmouthshire they are called Maen magl, and corruptly Glaim for Glain. They are small glass annulets, commonly about half as wide as our finger rings, but much thicker, usually of a green colour, though some are blue, and others curiously waved with blue, red, and white. Mr. Lluyd had seen two or three earthen rings of this kind, but glazed with blue, and adorned with transverse strokes or furrows on the outside. The smallest of them might be supposed to have been glass beads worn for ornaments by the Romans, because some quantities of them, with several amber beads, had been lately discovered in a stone pit near Garford in Berkshire, where they also dug up Roman coins, skeletons, and pieces of arms and armour. But it may be objected, that a battle being fought there between the Romans and Britons, as appears by the bones and arms, these glass beads might as probaly belong to the latter. And indeed it seems very likely that these snake stones, as we call them, were used as charms or amulets among our Druids of Britain on the same occasion as the snake-eggs among the Gaulish Druids. Thus, continues Mr. Lluyd, we find it very evident that the opinion of the vulgar concerning the generation of these adder-beads, or snake-stones, is no other than a relic of the superstition or perhaps imposture of the Druids ; but whether what we call snake stones be the very same amulets that the British Druids made use of, or whether this fabulous origin was ascribed formerly to the same thing, and in aftertimes applied to these glass beads, I shall not undertake to determine. As for Pliny's Ovum Anguinum it can be no other than a shell (marine or fossil) of the kind we call *Echinus marinus*, whereof one sort, though not the same he describes, is found at this day in most parts of Wales. Dr. Borlase, who had penetrated more deeply into the Druidical monuments in this Kingdom than any writer before or since, observes that instead of the natural anguinum which must have been very rare, artificial rings of stone, glass, and sometimes baked clay, were substituted as of equal validity." The Doctor adds, from Mr. Lluyd's Letter, March 10th, 1701, that " the Cornish retain variety of charms, and have still, towards the Land's End, the amulets of Maen Magal and Glainneider, which latter they call a Melprev (or Milprev, i.e., a thousand worms), and have a charm for the snake to make it, when they have found one asleep, and stuck a hazel wand in the centre of her spiræ." Gough's *Camden*, 1789, ii., 571; Rowlands, *Mona Antiqua*, 342. "The opinion of the Cornish," Borlase continues, "is somewhat differently given by Carew. The country-people have a persuasion that the snakes here breathing upon a hazel wand, produce a stone ring of blue colour, in which there appears the yellow figure of a snake, and that beasts bit and envenom'd being given some water to drink, wherein this stone has been infus'd, will perfectly recover of the poison." *Antiq. of Cornwall*, p. 137. These beads are not unfrequently found in barrows, or occasionally with skeletons whose nation and age are not ascertained. Stukeley's *Abury*, p. 44. Bishop Gibson engraved three: one of earth enamelled blue, found near Dolgelly, in Merionethshire; a second of green glass, found at Aberfraw; and a third, found near Maes y Pandy, co. Merioneth.

Subjoined is the original passage from Pliny: — "Præterea est ovorum genus in magna Galliarum fama, omissum Græcis. Angues innumeri æstate convoluti, salivis faucium corporumque spumis artifici complexu glomerantur anguinum appellatur. Druidæ sibilis id dicunt in sublime jactari, sagoque oportere intercipi, ne tellurem attingat. Profugere raptorem equo: serpentes enim insequi, donec arceantur amnis alicujus interventu. Experimentum ejus esse, si contra aquas fluitet vel auro vinctum. Atque, ut est Magorum solertia occultandis fraudibus sagax, certa Luna capiendum censent, tanquam, congruere operationem eam serpentium, humani sit arbitrii. Vidi equidem id ovum mali orbiculati modici magnitudine, crusta cartilaginis, velut acetabulis brachiorum polypi crebris, insigne Druidis. Ad victorias litium, ac regum aditus, mire laudatur: tantæ vanitatis, ut habentem id in lite in sinu equitem Romanum e Vocontiis, a Divo Claudio Principe interemptum non ob aliud sciam."— *Plinii Hist. Nat.*, edit. *Harduin*, lib. xxix. 12.

Drumming-Well. — Baxter gives the following anecdote of himself: "When I was a school-boy at Oundle, in Northamptonshire, about the Scots coming into England, I heard a well, in one Dob's Yard, drum like any drum beating a march. I heard it at a distance: then I went and put my head into the mouth of the well, and heard it distinctly, and nobody in the well. It lasted several days and nights so as all the country people came to hear it. And so it drummed on several changes of times. When King Charles the Second died, I went to the Church carrier at the Ram Inn in Smithfield, who told me their well had drumm'd, and many people came to hear it, and I heard it drumm'd once since." *World of Spirits*, 1691, 157. Dodsley refers to the same phenomenon: "In Northamptonshire I observed, as in most other places, the superstition of the country people with regard to their local wonders. The well at Oundle is said to drum against any important event; yet nobody in the place could give me a rational account of their having heard it, though almost every one believes the truth of the tradition." Dodsley's *Travels of Tom Thumb*, 17.

Drunkard's Cloak. — According to Gardiner's *England's Grievance*, 1656, in the time of the Commonwealth, the magistrates of Newcastle punished scolds with the branks, and drunkards by making them carry a tub, with holes in the sides for the arms to pass through, called the drunkard's cloak, through the streets of that town.

Drunken Groat.---It appears from Allan Ramsay, that in Scotland, of those "wha had been fow yestreen," i.e., drunk the night before, "payment of the drunken groat is very peremptorily demanded by the common people, next morning: but if they frankly confess the debt due, they are passed for two-pence."

Drunkenness.—That it is good to be drunk once a month, says the author of the "Vulgar Errors," is a common flattery of sensuality, supporting itself upon physic and the healthful effects of inebriation. It is a striking instance of "the doing ill," as we say, "that good may come out of it." It may happen that inebriation, by causing vomiting, may cleanse the stomach, &c., but it seems a very dangerous kind of dose, and of which the "repetatur haustus," too quickly repeated, will prove that men may pervert that which Nature intended for a cordial into the most baneful of all poisons. It has been vulgarly called "giving a fillip to Nature." But it is at the present time a not uncommon maxim among physicians that occasional indulgence is rather beneficial to the system than the reverse.

Duck and Drake.—A game played by throwing shells or stones along the surface of the water. See Halliwell in v. It appears from the *Nomenclator* of Junius, 1585, quoted by Nares, that the full original name was *A duck and a drake and a halfpenny cake*. It was an amusement known to the Greeks. St. John's *Manners and Customs of Ancient Greece*, 1842, i., 153. Butler makes it one of the important qualifications of his conjurer to tell:

"What figur'd slates are best to make,
On watry surface duck or drake."
Hudibras, part 2, c. iii.

Duckstone.—A game played by trying to knock a small stone off a larger one which supports it. Halliwell in v.

Duke Humphrey.—The common expression "to dine with Duke Humphrey" was applied to persons who, being unable to procure a dinner, walked about and loitered during the dinner time in the open spaces about St. Paul's, to which, in the earlier part of the day, many persons used to resort for exercise, to hear news, &c. One of the aisles was called Duke Humphreys Walk, not that there ever was in reality a cenotaph there to the Duke's memory who, every one knows, was buried at St. Albans, but because, says Stowe, ignorant people mistook the monument of Sir John Beauchamp, who died in 1358, for that of Humphrey Duke of Gloucester. Stow's *Survey*, 1720, iii., 165, The error is also pointed out by Fuller. See Hazlitt's *Proverbs*, 1882, p. 428. On this mistake the following dialogue is founded :

"What ancient monument is this?
It is, as some say, of Duke Humphrie of
　　Gloucester,
Who is buried here.
They say that he hath commonly his
　　Lieftenant
Here in Paules, to know if there be
Any newes from Fraunce or other
　　strange Countries,
'Tis true my friend, and also he hath
His steward, who inviteth the bring-
　　ers of
These newes to take the paines to dine
　　with His Grace."

Elyot's *Fruits for the French*, 1593, part 2, 165. Now, it appears from one of Anthony Munday's Additions to Stow, that it was the fashion in the time of James I. for certain persons, under the false impression that the monument of Sir John Beauchamp was that of the Duke to make annually " a solemn meeting at his tomb, on St. Andrew's Day, in the morning, (before Christmas), and to conclude on a breakfast or dinner——." It therefore seems, that there was a good foundation for the phrase in absolute fact and the probability is, that the ridicule attached (even in Stow's time) to the practice of paying homage to the wrong man, or to the right man in the wrong place, led eventually to the adoption of the idea and saying in derision of such unfortunates as paced the open spaces about St. Paul's during the dinner hour for want of something better to do, " in idle and frivolous opinion of whom," farther observes Munday, "some men, of late times, have assured themselves to be servants, and to hold diversity of offices under the good Duke Humphrey." Munday notices a curious ceremony performed by the tankard bearers, watermen, and others, on May-day, also in honour of the Duke, " by strewing herbs, and sprinkling fair water" on the tomb. An abundance of passages in the works of our old writers tend to confirm this explanation. Thus in " A Health to the gentlemanly profession of servingmen," 1598, the writer says : " I meete a gentleman that may dispende yeerely by his reuenues. 2000 pounds of good and lawfull English money, with onely one boy at his heeles, walking up Ludgate hill, and by that tyme I come to Paules middle walke, I shall see Dauie Debet, with vi. or viii. tall fellowes attending him, whetting their kniues readie to dine with Duke Humfrie." Harvey, in his " Fovre Letters and Certaine Sonnets," &c., 1592, speaks of a poverty-stricken person who has left home " to seek his dinner in Poules with Duke Humfrey ——." In "The Return of the Knight of the Post from Hell," 1606, we have : " In the end comming into Poules to behold the old Duke and his guests." In Nash's satirical "Prognostication" for 1591, we read : " Sundry fellows in their silkes shall be appointed to keepe Duke Humfrye company in Poules, because they know not where to get their dinners abroad."

" 'Tis Ruffio : trow'st thou where he
　　din'd to day?
In sooth I saw him sit with Duke Hum-
　　fray :
Many good welcoms and much gratis
　　cheere
Keepes hee for everie stragling cava-
　　liere ;
An open house, haunted with great re-
　　sort."

Hall's *Virgidemiæ*, 1597. "To the ninth of this month, it will be as good dining well in a matted chamber, as dialoguing with Duke Humphrey in Paules." *Vox Graculi*, 1623, p. 54. Speaking of the monument in St. Paul's of Owen the Epigrammatist, Gayton says :

" He was set up with such a peaking
　　face,
As if to the Humphreyans h'had been
　　saying grace."

The same writer elsewhere inquires :

" Wherefore we do amand Duke Hum-
　　phrey's guest,
For their provision truly is o'th'least :
A dog doth fare much better with his
　　bones,
Than those whose table, meat, and drink
　　are stones."

—*Art of Longevity*, 1659, p. 1. Compare Nares. *Glossary*, 1859 in v.

Dulce Domum.—At St. Mary's College, Winton, the Dulce Domum is sung on the evening preceding the Whitsun holidays; the masters, scholars, and choristers, attended by a band of music, walk in procession round the courts of the college, singing it. It is, no doubt, of very remote antiquity, and its origin must be traced not to any ridiculous tradition, but to the tenderest feelings of human nature :

" Concinamus, O Sodales !
Eja ! quid silemus?
Nobile canticum !
Dulce melos, domum !
Dulce domum resonemus !

Chorus.—Domum, domum, dulce domum !
Domum, domum, dulce domum !
Dulce, dulce, dulce domum !
Dulce domum resonemus," &c.

But the Dulce Domum is one of those usages which are fast wearing out; it was not confined to Winchester School, but was general. In my time, it was regularly sung every Christmas, before the breaking up, at Merchant Taylors' School, and I remember that the whole school, in the presence of the masters, suddenly, as if by previous concert, burst into a full chorus.

Dumb Borsholder of Chart.—There was, till of late years, says Hasted, a singular, though a very ancient custom, kept up, of electing a deputy to the Dumb Borsholder of Chart, near Wateringbury, in Kent, claiming liberty over fifteen houses in the precinct of the hamlet of Sizein - Well, every householder of which was formerly obliged to pay the keeper of this borsholder one penny yearly. The Dumb Borsholder was always first called at the Court-Leet holden for the hundred of Twyford, when its keeper, who was yearly appointed by that Court, held it up to his call, with a neckcloth or handkerchief put through the iron ring fixed at the top, and answered for it. The Borsholder and the Court Leet have been discontinued for about fifty years : and the Borsholder, who is put in by the Quarter Sessions for Wateringbury, claims over the whole parish. This Dumb Borsholder is made of wood, about three feet and a half an inch long, with an iron ring at the top, and four more by the sides, near the bottom, where it has a square iron spike fixed, four inches and a half long, to fix it in the ground, or, on occasion, to break open doors, &c. which used to be done, without a warrant of any Justice, on suspicion of goods having been unlawfully come by and concealed in any of these fifteen houses. It is not easy, at this distance of time, to ascertain the origin of this dumb officer. Perhaps it might have been made use of as a badge or ensign by the office of the market here. The last person who acted as deputy to it was one Thomas Clampard, a blacksmith, who died in 1748, whose heirs have it now in their possession. *History of Kent,* folio ed., ii., 284.

Dumb-Cake.—The dumb-cake is a species of dreaming bread, prepared by unmarried females, with ingredients traditionally suggested in witching doggerel. When baked, it is cut into three divisions : a part of each to be eaten, and the remainder to be put under the pillow. When the clock strikes twelve, each votary must go to bed backwards, and keep a profound silence, whatever may appear. Indeed, should a word be uttered, either during the process or before falling asleep, the spell is broken, and some direful calamity may be dreaded. Those who are to be married, or are full of hope, fancy they see visions of their future partners hurrying after them; while they who are to live and die old maids are not very sanguine of obtaining their errand, seeing nothing at all.

Dun's in the Mire.—We find this game noticed at least as early as Chaucer's time, in the " Manciples Prologue" :

" Then gan our hoste to jape and to play
And sayd; sires, what? Dun is in the mire."

In Rowlands' " Humors Ordinarie," 1600, I see it enumerated among other pastimes :

" At shoue-groat, venter-poynt, or crosse and pile. . . .
At leaping ore a Midsommer bone-fier,
Or at the drawing dunne out of the myer."

But in Drue's " Dutchess of Suffolke," 1631, signat. E 3, the expression is used in a different way :

" Well done, my masters, lend 's your hands,
Draw dun out of the ditch,
Draw, pull, helpe all, so, so, well done."
" They pull him out."

They had shoved Bishop Bonner into a well and were pulling him out. " Dun is in the mire," says Gifford, " is a Christmas gambol, at which I have often played. A log of wood is brought into the midst of the room : this is Dun (the cart-horse), and a cry is raised that he is stuck in the mire. Two of the company advance either with or without ropes, to draw him out. After repeated attempts, they find themselves unable to do it, and call for more assistance. The game continues, till all the company take part in it, when Dun is extricated of course; and the merriment arises from the awkward and affected efforts of the rustics to lift the log, and from sundry arch contrivances to let the ends of it fall on one another's toes." Dun's in the mire hence, no doubt, became a proverbial expression. Dyce's *Beaumont and Fletcher*, vol. i. p. 71, note; Hazlitt's *Proverbs*, 1882, p. 123.

Dunmow Flitch.—A custom formerly prevailed. and is still observed, at Dunmow, in Essex, of giving a flitch of bacon to any married man or woman, who would swear that neither of them, in a year and a day, either sleeping or waking, repented of their marriage. Blount attributes the origin of this ceremony to an institution of the Lord Fitzwalter, in the reign of Henry III. who ordered that "whatever married man did not repent of his marriage, or quarrel with his wife in a year and a day after it, should go to his Priory, and demand the bacon, on his swearing to the truth, kneeling on two stones in the church-yard." The form and ceremony of the claim, as made in 1701 by William Parsley, of Much Easton, in the County of Essex, butcher, and Jane his wife, are detailed in the same work. Dugdale, "Mon. Angl." vol. ii. p. 79; Morant's "Essex," vol. ii., p. 429; and "Antiq. Repert." edit. 1807, vol. iii., p. 341-4. The author of "Piers Ploughman" (1362) and Chaucer in his "Wife of Bath's Prologue," refer to the Dunmow flitch:—

"I sette hem so on werke, by my fay,
That many a night they songen weylaway.
The bacoun was nought set for hem, I trowe,
That som men fecche in Essex at Donmowe."

We also find a reference to the usage in a MS. which is supposed to have been written not much more than half a century after the death of Chaucer:

"I can fynd no man now that wille enquere,
The parfyte wais unto Dunmowe;
For they repent hem within a yere,
And many within a weke, and sonner, men trow;
That cawsith the weis to be rowgh and over grow,
That no man may find path or gap,
The world is turnyd to another shap."

The usage is mentioned in the Chartulary of Dunmow Priory, under 1445, 1467, and 1510. It is to be collected from a MS. in the College of Arms, written by Sir Richard St. George, Garter, about 1640, that this notable usage originated either in Robert Fitzwater, a favourite of Henry II., or in one of his successors in the lordship of Dunmow and its Priory. It is said of this Fitzwater, by the writer of the MS., that "he betooke himself in his latter dayes to prayers and deeds of charity. . . and reedified the decayed priorie of Dunmow. . . . in which priorie arose a custome begune and instituted either by him or some other of his successors . . . .

I have enquired of the manner of yt, and can learne no more but that yt continued untill the Dissolution of that house as also the Abbey." St. George proceeds to say, that in his time two hard-pointed stones were to be seen in the churchyard, on which the claimant was required to take the oath kneeling humbly in the presence of the prior, convent, and people; which process, together with the length and elaborate character of the declaration exacted, "with solemn singing" into the bargain, seems to have brought St. George to the conclusion that the "partie or pilgrim for bacon," as he terms him, had rather a "painful pilgrimage." We are to infer, from Garter's account, that it was at that time considered sufficient for the husband to attend; and he acquaints us that, after the endurance of the solemn ordeal, he was, if his claim were admitted, carried in triumph through the town, with his flitch before him. The quantity given does not seem to have been strictly uniform, for Garter says, "I find that some had a gammon and others a fleeke, or a flitch." The earliest record of the presentation of the flitch appears to be in 7 Edw. IV., when Stephen Samuel, of Ayrton, in Essex, claimed and obtained his gammon, on satisfying the usual conditions. In 23 Hen. VI., Richard Wright, of Badborough, near Norwich, was similarly awarded the palm of conjugal harmony; but in his case it was only a flitch. Again, in 1510, 2 Hen. VIII., Thomas Lefuller, of Cogshall, Essex, was allowed the full gammon. But on what ground this variation was made, we do not learn. The singular oath administered to them ran thus, according to Dugdale:

"You shall swear by the Custom of our Confession,
That you never made any nuptial transgression,
Since you were married to your wife,
By household brawles, or contentious strife;
Or otherwise, in bed or board
Offended each other in deed or word;
Or since the Parish Clerk said Amen,
Wished yourselves unmarried agen.
Or in a twelvemonth and a day
Repented not in thought any way.
But continued true and in desire,
As when you joined hands in the Holy Quire.
If to these conditions without all feare
Of your own accord you will freely swear,
A Gammon of Bacon you shall receive,
And beare it hence with love and good leave;
For this is our custom in Dunmow well known,
Though the sport be ours, the Bacon's your own."

It is scarcely necessary to observe, that the preceding lines have every mark of being a modern local version of the more ancient formula, now apparently not preserved. Dugdale, however, thought them worth printing in his "Monasticon." In Playford's *Catch that Catch Can*, 1685, is a copy of the oath set to music. See a letter from Horace Walpole to Lady Aylesbury, August 23rd, 1760. The parties were to take this oath before the prior and convent and the whole town, humbly kneeling in the churchyard upon the two hard pointed stones, as has just been noticed. They were afterwards taken upon men's shoulders, and carried, first, about the priory churchyard, and after through the town, with all the friars and brethren, and all the townsfolk, young and old, followed them with shouts and acclamations, with their bacon before them. Brand describes a large print, entitled "An exact perspective view of Dunmow, late the Priory in the County of Essex, with a representation of the ceremony and procession in that Mannor, on Thursday the 20th of June, 1751, when Thomas Shapeshaft of the parish of Weathersfield in the county aforesaid, weaver, and Anne his wife, came to demand, and did actually receive a gammon of bacon, having first kneeled down upon two bare stones within the church doore and taken the oath, &c. N.B. Before the dissolution of monasteries it does not appear, by searching the most antient records, to have been demanded above three times, and, including this, just as often since. Taken on the spot and engraved by David Ogborne." The *Gentleman's Magazine*, xxi., 282, calls the individual John Shakeshanks, woolcomber.

It seems that no religious distinctions were observed, but that the flitch was open to all comers, who had lived in a state of absolute content and felicity a year and a day from the date of their union. It was also stipulated that it was to hang up in the hall of the Manor-house, "redy arrayde all times of the yere, bott in Lent." Instead of one claimant, namely, the husband, it became customary, it appears, at a later date, for both the man and the woman to attend, and a large oak chair was preserved in Dunmow Church in the present century, in which the fortunate couple were installed, so soon as the decision in their favour was made known. It is probably still to be seen; at any rate an engraved view of it is given in the "Antiquarian Repertory." It is there described as "undoubtedly of great antiquity, probably the official chair of the prior, or that of the lord of the manor." In 1902 fourteen couples

entered for the prize, but were reduced to two, Mr. and Mrs. Wallis of Derby, and Mr. and Mrs. Brook of Bromley, Kent. Both parties were successful before the judge in the case, Mr. J. V. Mackenzie, in establishing their claims, and duly received their flitches. The claimants had their own counsel, and the donors of the bacon theirs; and a composite jury of six maidens and six bachelors had been, as usual, empanelled to consider the evidence. It is said that down to 1772 only eight claims were preferred or allowed, and that the custom was falling into disuse, until it revived about 1850 under the auspices of Mr. Harrison Ainsworth.

According to the "Contes d'Eutrapel," cited by Tyrwhitt, it was a Breton usage, prevailing at St. Helaine, near Rennes. But Dr. Bell, in his researches into Shakespear's "Puck" has shown that the usage has also a German counterpart; and I am inclined certainly to acquiesce in the line of argument, which seems to secure for the idea in its origin a Teutonic source. Comp. *Whichenovre*.

Dwarf.—It appears that the Saxons treated the malady which is now well known under the name of convulsions, as the visitation of a dwarf. It was a belief which they brought with them from the north of Europe, and which was common to the whole Gothic family. The Saxon Leechdoms furnish a receipt for this disease or affliction, which was said to be "doing away a dwarf." Unlike the night-mare, which was exclusively a nocturnal visitor, the dwarf came to his victim, as may be supposed from the character of the complaint which the superstition thus personifies, at any time during the four-and-twenty hours. Mr. Cockayne has some remarks on this matter in his preface.

Dyzemas Day. — In Northamptonshire, or some parts of it, Titheday is known as Dyzemas Day. Miss Baker observes: "A sexagenarian, on the southern side of the county, to whom I was indebted for the name, informed me that within his remembrance this day was kept as sacred as the sabbath, and it was considered very unlucky to commence any undertaking, or even to wash on the same day of the week throughout the year, on which the anniversary of this day last fell." *Northamptonshire Glossary*, 1854, in v. But the latter notion is not peculiar to the county in question. It is also current in the North of England and elsewhere. According to some authorities, the day is also called Dyzeman's Day in the North.

Earnest.—See *God's Penny*.

Ear-Omens. — Itching in the ear, or on the lobes of it, is still received as a symptom that one is being talked of behind one's back; but we may perhaps collect from one of John Heywood's Epigrams, 1562, that in his day it bore another signification, and portended that the party, whose ear itched, had been guilty of an untruth; and the same sense is evidently from the context to be given to a passage in the interlude of *Jack Juggler* (about 1550) : —

"But I promise you, I do curstlie feare,
For I feel a vengeable burning in my left ere "—

The speaker has been inventing a falsehood. Browne, in his "Vulgar Errors," adds : " He (Pliny) supposes it to have proceeded from the notion of a signifying genius, or universal Mercury, that conducted sounds to their distant subjects, and taught to hear by touch." Delrio and Keuchenius seem to have been of opinion that a tingling in the right ear portended good, and in the left the reverse, in which they are supported by the old Scotish saying, cited by Douce in his MSS. notes on Brand: "Right lug, left lug, whilk lug lows. If the left ear, they talk harm ; if the right, good." Delrio, "Disquis. Magic." p. 473; Keuchenius "Crepundia," 1662, p. 113. In "Much Ado About Nothing," 1600, act iii. sc. 2, Beatrice says : "What fire is in mine ears?" which Warburton explains as alluding to a proverbial saying of the common people, that their ears burn when others are talking of them. On which Reed observes that the opinion is mentioned by Pliny. Moreover is not this an opinion generally received, that when our ears do glow and tingle, some there be that in our absence doe talke of us? "—Holland's "Translation," b. xxviii. p. 297. Pliny's own words are : " Absentes tinnitu Aurium præsentire sermones de se receptum est." Gaule has not omitted in his list of " Vain Observations and Superstitious Ominations thereupon," the tingling of the ear, the itching of the eye, &c." *Mag-Astromancer posed*, 181, and Home tells us: " If their ears tingle, they say it is a signe they have some enemies abroad, that doe or are about to speake evill of them : so, if their right eye itcheth, then it betokens joyfull laughter : and so, from the itching of the nose, and elbow, and severall affectings of severall parts, they make severall predictions too silly to be mentioned, though regarded by them." *Demonology*, 1650, p. 61.

Herrick refers to this belief :

" *On himselfe.*
" One eare tingles ; some there be,
That are snarling now at me ;
Be they those that Homer bit,
I will give them thanks for it."

Easter. — Turner, in his " History of the Anglo-Saxons," derives Easter from the Saxon Goddess Eostre, and probably this etymology is the true one. In Lysons' " Environs," vol. i. p. 230, among his curious extracts from the Churchwardens' and Chamberlain's Books at Kingston-upon-Thames, are the following entries concerning some of the ancient doings on Easter Day:—" 5 Hen. VIII. For thred for the Resurrection, 1d.; for three yerds of dornek for a pleyers cote, and the makyng, 1s. 3d. 12 Hen. VIII. Paid for a skin of parchment and gunpowder, for the play on Easter Day, 8d. For brede and ale for them that made the stage and other things belonging to the play, 1s. 2d." By the subsequent entry these pageantries should seem to have been continued during the reign of Queen Elizabeth, 1565. " Rec^d of the players of the stage at Easter, £1 2s. 1½d." Among the ancient annual disbursements of the Church of St. Mary-at-Hill, I find the following entry against Easter : " Three great garlands for the crosses, of roses and lavender : three dozen other garlands for the quire : 3s." The same also occurs in the Churchwardens' Accounts, ibid. 1512. Also among the Church disbursements, ibid. in the Waxchandler's Accompt, " for making the Pascal at Ester, 2s. 8d." Ibid. 1486. " At Ester, for the howllyn people for the pascal, 11s. 5d." In the Churchwardens' Accompts of St. Martin Outwich, London, under the year 1525, is the following item: " Paid for brome ageynst Ester, 1^d." It seems from the " Privy Purse Expenses of Elizabeth of York," 1502, that it was then customary to present gratuities to the officers of the kitchen, saucery, and scullery, and to the gate-porters; and in the " Northumberland Household Book," 1512, there is a long enumeration of the bounty which the Earl and his family were accustomed to distribute on this festival. A pair of gloves was a present at Easter, as well as at Christmas. Whitelocke's *Liber Famelicus*, 1858, under 1615. " To houl over the paschal," is mentioned among the customs of the Roman Catholics censured by John Bale in his " Declaration of Bonner's Articles," 1554. There is a proverb :

"If Easter falls in Lady Day's lap,
Beware, Old England, of a clap."

Easter, Pasch, or **Paste Eggs.**—Gebelin informs us that this custom of giving eggs at Easter is to be traced up to the theology and philosophy of the Egyptians, Persians, Gauls, Greeks, Romans, &c., among all of whom an egg was an emblem of the universe, the work of the supreme Divinity; and Hutchinson indeed remarks that "Eggs were held by the Egyptians as a sacred emblem of the renovation of mankind after the Deluge. The Jews adopted it to suit the circumstances of their history, as a type of their departure from the land of Egypt; and it was used in the feast of the Passover as part of the furniture of the table, with the paschal lamb. The Christians have certainly used it on this day, as retaining the elements of future life, for an emblem of the Resurrection. It seems as if the egg was thus decorated for a religious trophy after the days of mortification and abstinence were over, and festivity had taken their place; and as an emblem of the resurrection of life, certified to us by the Resurrection, from the regions of death and the grave." The ancient Egyptians, if the resurrection of the body had been a tenet of their faith, would perhaps have thought an egg no improper hieroglyphical representation of it. The extraction of a living creature by incubation, after the vital principle has lain a long while dormant, or seemingly extinct, is a process so truly marvellous, that, if it could be disbelieved, would be thought by some as a thing incredible to the full, as that the Author of Life should be able to reanimate the dead. Easter, says Gebelin, and the New Year, have been marked by similar distinctions: among the Persians, the New Year is looked upon as the renewal of all things, and is noted for the triumph of the Sun of Nature, as Easter is with Christians for that of the Sun of Justice, the Saviour of the World, over death by his Resurrection. The Feast of the New Year, he adds, was celebrated at the Vernal Equinox, that is, at a time when the Christians removing their New Year to the Winter Solstice, kept only the Festival of Easter. Hence, with the latter, the feast of eggs has been attached to Easter, so that eggs are no longer made presents of at the New Year. Bryant says, "An egg, containing in it the elements of life, was thought no improper emblem of the ark, in which were preserved the rudiments of the future world: hence in the Dionusiaca and in other mysteries, one part of the nocturnal ceremony consisted in the consecration of an egg. By this, as we are informed by Porphyry, was signified the world. It seems to have been a favourite symbol, and very antient, and we find it adopted among many nations. It was said by the Persians of Orosmasdes, that he formed mankind and inclosed them in an egg. A writer in the "Gentleman's Magazine," for July, 1783, supposes the egg at Easter "an emblem of the rising up out of the grave, in the same manner as the chick entombed, as it were, in the egg, is in due time brought to life." He takes the flowers which are used to decorate the churches at this time to bear the same import. A correspondent of "Notes and Queries," traces to pagan times and to the Mahometan feast of nooroose, or the waters, an anniversary celebration of the Creation and Deluge, the Christian practice of offering eggs at Easter. He cites Sir R. Ker Porter's "Travels in Georgia, Persia, &c.," 1821, in confirmation of this theory. Le Brun, in his "Voyages," tells us that the Persians, on the 20th of March, 1704, kept the festival of the Solar New Year, which he says lasted several days, when they mutually presented each other, among other things, with coloured eggs. They were sometimes tinted yellow, sometimes red, sometimes sky-blue. In Italy, Spain, and in Provence, says Father Carmeli, where almost every ancient superstition is retained. there are in the public places certain sports with eggs. This custom he derives from the Jews or the Pagans, for he observes it is common to both. This custom still prevails in the Greek Church. Chandler, in his "Travels in Asia Minor," gives the following account of the manner of celebrating Easter among the modern Greeks: "The Greeks now celebrated Easter. A small bier, prettily deckt with orange and citron buds, jasmine, flowers, and boughs, was placed in the church, with a Christ crucified, rudely painted on board, for the body. We saw it in the evening, and, before day-break, were suddenly awakened by the blaze and crackling of a large bonfire, with singing and shouting in honour of the Resurrection. They made us presents of coloured eggs and cakes of Easter bread." "They (the Russians) have an order at Easter, which they alwaies observe, and that is this: every yeere, against Easter, to die or colour red, with Brazzel (Brazil wood), a great number of egges, of which every man and woman giveth one unto the priest of the parish upon Easter Day in the morning. And, moreover, the common people use to carrie in their hands one of these red egges, not only upon Easter Day, but also three or foure days after, and gentlemen and gentlewomen have egges gilded, which they carry in like maner. They use it, as they say, for a great love, and in token of the Resurrection, whereof they rejoice. For when two friends meete during the Easter holydayes they come and take one another by the hand, the one of them saith, 'The Lord, or Christ, is risen'; the other answereth, 'It is so, of a trueth'; and they then kiss, and exchange their egges, both men and women, continuing in kissing four dayes together." Our ancient voyage-writer means no more here, it should seem, than that the ceremony was kept up for four days. Le Brun, in his "Travels," 1702, noticed the same custom, when he visited Russia, and, after him, the Abbé d'Auteroche describes in his journey to Siberia, this ceremonial as still kept up with unabated enthusiasm. Le Brun says that it lasted fifteen days, and among people of all ranks. The author of "Le Voyageur à Paris," tom. ii. p. 112, "supposes that the practice of painting and decorating eggs at Easter, amongst the Catholics, arose from the joy which was occasioned by their returning to this favourite food after so long an abstinence from it during Lent. 'Dans plusieurs villes,' he adds, 'les clercs des Eglises, les etudians des Ecoles et les autres jeunes Gens, s'assemblaient sur une place au bruit des Sonnettes et des Tambours, portant des etandarts burlesques pour se rendre a l'Eglise principale, ou ils chantoient laudes avant de commencer leur quête d'œufs.'" — Douce. Ihre, in his "Glossarium Suio-gothicum," 1769, v. egg, explains a Paskegg to mean one that at Easter time is sent by persons to each other, variously ornamented and coloured, and in token of rejoicing at the termination of the Lenten fast. Among the Russians it was not thought too great a freedom, he says, according to travellers, to offer such eggs to the Emperor.

Hyde, in his "Oriental Sports," tells us of one with eggs among the Christians of Mesopotamia on Easter Day and forty days afterwards, during which time their children buy themselves as many eggs as they can, and stain them with a red colour in memory of the blood of Christ shed as at that time of his Crucifixion. Some tinge them with green and yellow. Stained eggs are sold all the while in the market. The sport consists in striking their eggs one against another, and the egg that first breaks is won by the owner of the egg that struck it. Immediately another egg is pitted against the winning egg, and so they go on, till the last remaining egg wins all the others, which their respective owners shall before have won. This sport, he observes, is not retained in the Midland parts of England, but seems to be alluded to in the old proverb, "An egg at Easter," because the liberty to eat eggs begins again at that festival, and thence must have arisen this festive egg-game. For neither the Romanists nor those of the Eastern Church begin to eat eggs till Easter.

That the Church of Rome has considered eggs as emblematical of the Resurrection, may be gathered from the subsequent prayer which the reader will find in an extract from the Ritual of Pope Paul the Fifth, for the use of England, Ireland, and Scotland. It contains various other forms of benediction. "Bless, O Lord! we beseech thee, this thy creature of eggs, that it may become a wholesome sustenance to thy faithful servants, eating it in thankfulness to thee, on account of the Resurrection of our Lord," &c. In the Roman Calendar I find the following: "Ova annunciatæ, ut aiunt, reponuntur." Le Brun plausibly suggests that these eggs were kept for luck (as we say) from Good Friday to Good Friday, like our cross-buns. In Bale's "Yet a Course at the Romishe Foxe," 1542, signat. D 4, the author enumerates some "auncyent rytes and lawdable ceremonyes of holy churche" then it should seem laid aside, in the following censure of the Bishop: "Than ought my Lorde also to suffre the same selfe ponnyshment for not rostyng egges in the Palme ashes fyre," &c. In the Beehive of the Romish Church, 1579, they are termed Holy Pace Eggs. Coles, in his "Latin Dictionary," renders the Pasch, or Easter egg, by "Ovum Paschale croccum, seu luteum." In the Household of Edward the First, in his eighteenth year ("Archæol." 1805) is the following item in the Accounts of Easter Sunday:—"For four hundred and a half of eggs, eighteen pence." The original item runs thus: "Pro iiijᶜ. di' ov' xviijᵈ." In the North of England, observes Hyde, in Cumberland and Westmoreland, boys beg, on Easter Eve, eggs to play with, and beggars ask for them to eat. These eggs are hardened by boiling, and tinged with the juice of herbs, broom-flowers, &c. The eggs being thus prepared, the boys go out and play with them in the fields: rolling them up and down, like bowls, upon the ground, or throwing them up, like balls, into the air. Eggs, stained with various colours in boiling, and sometimes covered with leaf-gold, are at Easter presented to children, at Newcastle-upon-Tyne, and other places in the North, where these young gentry ask for their "paste eggs," as for a fairing, at this season. In the neighbourhood of Newcastle, they are tinged yellow with the blossoms of furze, called there whin-bloom. The title of a tract, printed in 1644, "To Sion's Lovers, being a golden Egge, to avoid Infection, &c." undoubtedly refers to this superstition. "On y fit aussi des deffences de vendre des œufs de couleur apres Pasques, parce que les enfans s'en joüoyent auparavant, qui estoit de mauvais exemple."—*Satyre Menippée de la Vertu du Catholicon d'Espagne*, 8vo., 1595, fol. 94. The English version of this work renders *œufs de couleur* speckled eggs.

Easter Eve.—Various superstitions crept in by degrees among the rites of this day: such as putting out all the fires in churches and kindling them anew from flint, blessing the Easter wax, &c. According to Naogeorgus, the ceremony of extinguishing the fires in order to rekindle them, was common on the Continent among the Catholics. The paschal taper, which Naogeorgus describes as typical of "Christ that conquered hell," and which on the Continent and among us used to be hallowed, and perfumed with frankincense, was an important item in the ceremonies and also in the expenses of this feast. It appears that, in 1557, the taper used in the Abbey Church at Westminster was of 300 lbs. weight. In the ancient annual Church Disbursements of St. Mary-at-Hill, in the City of London, I find the following article: "For a quarter of coles for the hallowed fire on Easter Eve, 6d." Also the subsequent: "To the Clerk and Sexton (for two men) for watching the Sepulchre from Good Friday to Easter Eve, and for their meate and drink, 14d." I find also in the Churchwardens' Accounts, ibid. 5th Hen. VI. the following entries: "For the Sepulchre, for divers naylis and wyres and glu, 9d. ob. Also payd to Thomas Joynor for makyng of the same Sepulchre, 4s. Also payd for bokeram for penons, and for the makynge, 22d." In Coates's "Hist. of Reading," p. 130, under Churchwardens' Accounts for the year 1558, &c., there are several quotations of money laid out for this purpose. Part of the cost consisted in hiring men, who should watch the sepulchre in imitation of the soldiers, who actually performed the duty. It appears too, that with true parochial instinct the materials were sold when the time was up, and the next year took care of itself. Two of the entries are: "Paide to Roger Brock for watching of the Sepulchre, 8d." "Paide more to the saide Roger for fyres and colles, 8d." In "A Short Description of Antichrist, &c.," the author censures, among other popish customs, "the halowyng of fiere." They had a custom in Dorsetshire formerly of forming a procession of boys on Easter Eve, with torches and a small black flag. The procession chanted these lines:

"We fasted in the light,
For this is the night."

Easter Eve is, in some places, known as Holy Saturday. It is a great day among the Irish Catholics, who hold high festival at midnight for a few hours, and then retire till sunrise, when they get up to see that luminary dance in honour of the Resurrection. Nor is this usage confined to the lower classes.

Easter Holidays.—Easter has ever been considered by the Church as a season of great festivity. By the law concerning holidays, made in the time of King Alfred the Great, it was appointed that the week after Easter should be kept holy. It seems from Fitzstephen, cited by Stowe, that the water-quintain was a popular diversion at this season. Belithus, a ritualist of ancient times, tells us that it was customary in some churches for the bishops and archbishops themselves to play with the inferior clergy at hand-ball, and this, as Durandus asserts, even on Easter-day itself. Why they should play at hand-ball at this time, rather than any other game, Bourne tells us he has not been able to discover; certain it is, however, that the present custom of playing at that game on Easter holidays for a tanzy-cake has been derived from thence. Erasmus, speaking of the proverb, "Mea est pila," that is "I've got the ball," tells us, that it signifies "I have obtained the victory. I am master of my wishes." The Romanists certainly erected a standard on Easterday in token of our Lord's victory; but it would perhaps be indulging fancy too far to suppose that the Bishops and governors of churches, who used to play at hand-ball at this season, did it in a mystical way, and with reference to the triumphal joy of the season. Certain it is, however, that many of their customs and superstitions are founded on still more trivial circumstances, even according to their own explanations of them, than this imaginary analogy. In the Privy Purse Expenses of Henry VII. Mr. Brand found the following article: "From 16 to 18 Nov. 9 Hen. VII. Item, to Walter Alwyn for the revells at Estermess xiijli. vjs. viijd." Durandus tells us, that on Easter Tuesday, wives used to beat their husbands, on the day following the husbands their wives. The custom is still retained at the City of Durham in the Easter holidays. On Easter Sunday, in Yorkshire, the young men in the villages of that county had a custom of taking off the young girls' buckles. On Easter Monday, the young men's shoes and buckles were taken off by the young women. On the Wednesday they were redeemed by little pecuniary forfeits, out of which an entertainment, called a tansey-cake, was made, with dancing. Naogeorgus writes:

"At midnight then with carefull minde,
    they up to mattens ries,
The Clarke doth come, and, after him,
    the priest with staring eies."

"At midnight strait, not tarying till
    the daylight doe appeere,
Some getes in flesh and glutton lyke,
    they feede upon their cheere.
They rost their flesh, and custardes
    great, and egges and radish store,
And trifles, clouted creame, and cheese,
    and whatsoeuer more
At first they list to eate, they bring into
    the Temple straight,
That so the Priest may halow them with
    wordes of wond'rous waight.
The Friers besides, and pelting Priestes
    from house to house do roame,
Receyving gaine of every man that this
    will have at home.
Some raddish rootes this day doe take
    before all other meate,
Against the quartan ague, and such
    other sicknesse great."
"Straight after this, into the fieldes
    they walke to take the viewe,
And to their woonted life they fall, and
    bid the reast adewe."

In *Wit and Drollery*, 1682, there is a graphic account of the sort of company, which flocked to Westminster Abbey at this time:—"You must suppose it to be Easter Holy Days: at what time Sisly and Dol, Kate and Peggy, Moll and Nan are marching to Westminster, with a Leash of Prentices before 'em; who go rowing themselves along with their right arms to make more hast, and now and then with a greasy hanckercher wipe away the dripping that bathes their forehead. At the Door they meet crow'd of Wapping Seamen, Southwark Broom-men, the Inhabitants of the Bank-Side, with a Butcher or two prick't in among them. There awhile they stand gaping for the Master of the Show, staring upon the suburbs of their dearest delight, just as they stand gaping upon the painted Cloath before they go into the Puppet Play. By and by they hear the Bunch of Keys which rejoyces their hearts like the sound of the Pancake-Bell. For now the Man of Comfort peeps over the spikes, and beholding such a learned Auditory, opens the Gate of Paradise, and by that time they are half got into the first Chappel, for time is very pretious, he lifts up his Voice among the Toombs, and begins his Lurrey in manner and form following." Then we get a metrical rehearsal of the inmates of the several monuments, which at this time of day we regard with qualified credulity.

It is related in Aubanus's descrip-tion of ancient rites in Germany, that there were at this season foot-courses in the meadows, in which the victors carried off each a cake, given to be run for, as we say, by some better sort of person in the neighbourhood. Sometimes two cakes were proposed, one for the young men, another for the girls; and there was a great concourse of people on the occasion. This is a custom by no means unlike the playing at hand-ball for a tanzy-cake, the winning of which depends chiefly upon swiftness of foot. It is a trial too of fleetness and speed, as well as the foot-race.

Easter King.—Charles the Fifth, whilst he was in possession of his regal dignity, thought so slightingly of it, that when, one day, in passing through a village in Spain, he met a peasant who was dressed with a tin crown upon his head, and a spit in his hand for a truncheon, as the Easter King (according to the custom of that great festival in Spain), who told the Emperor that he should take off his hat to him: "My good friend," replied the Prince, "I wish you joy of your new office: you will find it a very troublesome one, I can assure you."

Easter Monday.—They have an ancient custom at Coleshill, in the county of Warwick, that if the young men of the town can catch a hare, and bring it to the parson of the parish before ten o'clock on Easter Monday, the parson is bound to give them a calf's head and a hundred of eggs for their breakfast, and a groat in money. Hazlitt's Blount, 1874, p. 78.

Easter Offering.—Originally a halfpenny, then a penny, later on raised to half a silver groat or twopence, payable by each parishioner waiting on the incumbent of the parish, who was expected to return it in entertainment. Subsequently the charge became a groat, and the minister offered no equivalent. These payments continue customary; but it is believed that there is no obligation beyond fourpence a head, to be collected by the clergyman or his sufficient deputy. In *Doctor Double Ale*, a poem written about 1550 (Hazlitt's *P. P.*, iii., 311) we are told:

"This man, to sum mens thinking,
Doth stay hym much vpon the Kyng,
As in the due demaunding,
Of that he calleth an head peny,
And of the paskall halfpenny."

Comp. Machyn's *Diary*, Camd. Soc., p. 62.

Easter Sunday or **Easter Day.**—Eggs and green sauce, the latter composed of herbs, were a very usual repast on the Continent and here on Easter Day. It is mentioned in the "Doctrine of the Masse Book" as an authorised dish for this occasion. At Gray's Inn, and perhaps at the other Inns of Court, there is the testimony of Dugdale that the commons used to consist on this day of the same sort of viands (so to speak), and until the 23 Eliz. the charge of providing the repast for the students devolved on the chief cook; after that, it was defrayed by the Society. A superstitious practice appears to have prevailed upon the Continent, of abstaining from flesh on Easter Sunday, to escape a fever for the whole year. I know not whether it ever reached this Island. It was condemned by the Provisional Council of Rheims in 1583, and by that of Toulouse in 1590. See "Traite des Superstitions," vol. i., p. 319, 320. The first dish that was brought up to the table on Easter Day, was a red herring riding away on horseback; i.e., a herring ordered by the cook something after the likeness of a man on horseback, set in a corn-salad. The custom of eating a gammon of bacon at Easter, which is still kept up in many parts of England was founded on this, viz., "to shew their abhorrence to Judaism at that solemn commemoration of our Lord's Resurrection." Aubrey (1679). It was the practice in Germany (during the sixteenth century at least) for the preachers to intermix their sermons with facetious stories on Easter Day. This may be gathered from the "Convivialium Sermonum Liber." Bas. 1542, sig. K8. Douce's *MSS. Notes.* It is still a common usage, of which the origin is assuredly not held in remembrance by many of those who observe it, of wearing something new on Easter Sunday. Poor Robin says:—

" At Easter let your clothes be new,
Or else be sure you will it rue."

Lamb is very usually eaten for the first time on this festival. An old-established usage at Northmore, near Witney, in Oxfordshire, was for the men and women, after evening service, to throw apples in the churchyard, those that had been married within the year throwing thrice as many as the rest; and all subsequently adjourned to the minister's house, where they were entertained on bread and cheese. Hearne's *Diary,* Jan. 19, 1725, and Note. Comp. *Sun.*

Eating.—If, says Grose, in eating, you miss your mouth, and the victuals fall, it is very unlucky, and denotes approaching sickness.

Eden Hall.—See *Luck of Eden Hall.*

Edgeware.—Sir William Blackstone says, that it was usual for the lord of this manor to provide a minstrel or piper for the diversion of the tenants, while they were employed in his service. He refers to the manor-rolls which are among the Archives of All-Souls' College.—Lysons' *Environs,* 1st ed., ii., p. 244. Lysons searched the rolls without success, but accepts the statement on Blackstone's authority; and he adds that a piece of ground in the parish still (1795) goes by the name of Piper's Green.

At a Court of the manor of Edgeware, anno 1552, the inhabitants were presented for not having a tumbrel and cuckingstool. This looks as if the punishments were different. Lysons' *Environs,* ii., 244. At a court of the same Manor, in 1555, " it was presented that the butts at Edgeware were very ruinous, and that the inhabitants ought to repair them; which was ordered to be done before the ensuing Whitsontide."

Edgewell Tree.—Allan Ramsay, speaking of Edge-well Tree, describes it to be " an oak tree which grows on the side of a fine spring, nigh the Castle of Dalhousie, very much observed by the country people, who gave out, that before any of the family died, a branch fell from the Edge-well Tree. The old tree some few years ago fell altogether, but another sprung from the same root, which is now tall and flourishing, and lang be't sae."

Egg and Spoon.—An amusement which consists in a certain number running a race, each carrying an egg on a flat spoon, and the one, who arrives at the goal without disaster, wins. We seem here to have an evolution from the Venetian egg-game, described in Zompini's *Cries of Venice,* 1785.

Egg Feast.—The Egg Feast, mentioned in the Oxford Almanack, and formerly held there on Egg Saturday, that immediately preceding Shrove Tuesday, was held when the scholars took leave of that kind of food. Comp. Halliwell, v. *Egg-Feast.* Novelties in Easter eggs are constantly introduced from year to year in the English market. For 1903 they advertised natural eggs, chocolate eggs, plover's eggs, wooden eggs with snakes, globes, skipping ropes, and other toys inside.

Egg Saturday.—The Saturday before Shrove Tuesday. See *Easter Eggs.*

Egg Service.—One, where eggs are contributed for some special purpose, as when at Biggar, Lanarkshire, eighty dozen were quite recently collected, and sent to the children's hospitals in Glasgow and Edinburgh.

Egg Shell.—To break the egg-shell after the meat is out, is a relic of superstition mentioned in Pliny. Sir Thomas Browne tells us that the intent of this was to prevent witchcraft; for lest witches should draw or prick their names therein, and veneficiously mischief their persons, they broke the shell, as Delecampius has observed. Delrio, in his " Disquisitiones

Magicæ," has a passage on this subject. Scot says : " Men are preserved from witchcraft by sprinkling of Holy Water, receiving consecrated salt ; by candles hallowed on Candlemas Day, and by green leaves consecrated on Palm Sunday." Coles tells us that " Matthiolus saith that Herba paris takes away evill done by witchcraft, and affirms that he knew it to be true by experience." In Fletcher's *Women Pleased* occurs :

" The Devil should think of purchasing that egg-shell
To victual out a witch for the Burmoothes."

Eggs.—Stocker, on the line in Persius, Sat. v., 1, 185 :

" Tunc nigri Lemures *ovoque pericula rupto,*"

observes : " If an egg broke when put on the fire, it portended jeopardy to the person or property of the individual." The Rev. James Layton informed Mr. Roach Smith that the East Anglian rustics had a general custom when an egg was eaten, of thrusting the spoon through the bottom of the shell, so that the witches might not sail in it. But the Romans, according to Pliny, observed a similar usage. C. R. Smith's *Richborough*, 1850, p. 206.

Elder. — Gerarde, " Herball," ed. 1633, p. 1428, says : " The Arbor Judæ is thought to be that whereon Judas hanged himself, and not upon the elder tree as it is vulgarly said." I am clear (says Brand) that the mushrooms or excrescences of the elder tree, called Auricula Judæ in Latin, and commonly rendered " Jews' Eares," ought to be translated " Judas' Eares from the popular superstition above - mentioned. Coles says : " It " (Jewes' Eares) "is called in Latine Fungus Sambucinus and Auricula Judæ : some having supposed the elder tree to be that whereon Judas hanged himself, and that, ever since, these mushrooms, like unto eares, have grown thereon, which I will not persuade you to believe." There was an early Italian belief that the tree was the carob or St. John's Bread-tree, which is mentioned in St. Luke, chap. xv. v. 16, and by Pulci in his *Morgante Maggiore*. The late Mr. Dyce was acquainted with a gentleman, a great travellor, who had seen the tree, whether the ordinary elder or the *Arbor Judæ*, is not clear. Mitford's *Notes* on *Beaumont and Fletcher* and *Shakespeare*, 1856, p. 41.

Lupton, in his fifth book of " Notable Things," edit. 1660, p. 132, says : " Make powder of the flowers of elder, gathered on Midsummer Day, being before well dried, and use a spoonfull

thereof in a good draught of borage-water, morning and evening, first and last, for the space of a month : and it will make you seem young a great while." Blagrave writes : " It is reported that if you gently strike a horse that cannot stale, with a stick of this elder, and bind some of the leaves to his belly, it will make him stale presently. It is also said, and some persons of good credit have told me, (but I never made any experiment of it), that if one ride with two little sticks of elder in his pockets, he shall not fret nor gaul, let the horse go never so hard." *Supplement to Culpeper's English Physician*, 1674, p. 62. The first of these superstitions is again mentioned in Coles's " Adam in Eden." In the " Athenian Oracle " is the following relation : " A friend of mine being lately upon the road a horseback, was extremely incommoded by loss of leather ; which coming to the knowledge of one of his fellow travellers, he over-persuaded him to put two elder sticks in his pocket, which not only eased him of his pain, but secured the remaining portion of his posteriours, not yet excoriated, throughout the rest of his journey," 111, 545. Coles says : " It hath beene credibly reported to me from severall hands, that if a man take an elder stick, and cut it on both sides so that he preserve the joynt, and put in his pocket when he rides a journey, he shall never gall." *Introduction to the Knowledge of Plants*, 1656, p. 63. Fleeknoe also mentions, in his *Diarium*, 1656, p. 65 :—

" How alder-stick in pocket carried,
By horseman who on high-way feared
His breech should nere be gall'd or wearied,
Although he rid on trotting horse,
Or cow, or cowl-staff which was worse,
It had, he said, such vertuous force,
Where Vertue oft, from Judas came
(Who hang'd himself upon the same,
For which, in sooth, he was to blame,)
Or't had some other magick force,
To harden breech, or soften horse,
I leave't to th' learned to discourse."

In the *Anatomy of the Elder*, 1653, are some particulars in connexion with this part of the subject. "The common people keep as a great secret in curing wounds, the leaves of the elder which they have gathered the last day of April ; which, to disappoint the charms of witches, they had affixed to their dores and windows." There is mentioned an amulet against the erysipelas, " made of the elder on which the sunn never shined. If the piece betwixt the two knots be hung about the patient's neck, it is much commended. Some cut it in little pieces, and sew it in a knot in a piece of a man's shirt, which seems superstitious." Two instances of its success are recorded. "There is likewise set down," against the epilepsia, "a singular amulet made of the elder growing on a sallow. If in the month of October, a little before the full moon, you pluck a twig of the elder, and cut the cane that is betwixt two of its knees, or knots, in nine pieces, and these pieces being bound in a piece of linnen, be in a thread, so hung about the neck, that they touch the spoon of the heart, or the sword-formed cartilage; and that they may stay more firmly in that place they are to be bound thereon with a linnen or silken roller wrapt about the body, till the thred break of itself. The thred being broken and the roller removed, the amulet is not at all to be touched with bare hands, but it ought to be taken hold on by some instrument and buried in a place that nobody may touch it." We are told, "Some hang a cross, made of the elder and sallow, mutually inwrapping one another about the children's neck," pp. 54, 207, 211. Among other rustic charms may be mentioned : Curing a lame pig by boring a little hole in his ear, and putting a small peg of elder into it. In the epilogue to Lyly's "Campaspe," 1584, a passage is found which implies that elder was given at that time as a token of disgrace : "Laurell for a garland and ealder for a disgrace." So again, in "An Hue and Crie after Cromwell," 1649, p. 4, we read :

"Cooke, the Recorder, have an elder tree,
And steel a slip to reward treacherie."

There is a vulgar prejudice that "if boys be beaten with an elder-stick, it hinders their growth."

Elephants. — There is a belief founded on observation, that this quadruped will not only start at the grunt of the wild pig, but at a lizard or other small object, from which he may feel a difficulty in protecting himself. This is constantly noticed in respect to the specimens which are brought to Europe, and are disconcerted by a mouse in the den among the straw. Charles Gibbon, in his *Order of Equality*, 1604, merely mentions that elephants are terrified by the grunting of pigs. He should have explained that the pig in question was the tenant of Indian jungles.

Elf.—The elf was also called urchin or goblin. The "Urchins' Daunce" is preserved in one of Ravenscroft's musical volumes, and has been republished in Dr. Rimbault's book of "Songs and Ballads," 1851.

Elf-Disease. There appear to have been two kinds of elf-disease, land-elf disease, and water-elf disease. The symptoms and treatment were different. The nostrums which were prescribed by our Saxon doctors in each case are described at length in Mr. Cockayne's "Saxon Leechdoms." Mr. Cockayne includes a "salve against the elfin race and nocturnal goblin visitors, and for the women with whom the devil hath carnal commerce." The specific is as follows : "Take the ewe hop plant, wormwood, bishopwort, lupin, ashthroat, harewort, vipers bugloss, heathberry plants, cropleek, garlic, grains of hedgerise, githrise, fennel ; put these worts into a vessel, set them under the altar, sing over them nine masses, boil them in butter and sheep's grease, add much holy salt, strain through a cloth, throw the worts into running water." If any one was troubled by night elves, his forehead was to be smeared with this salve, and also his eyes, and any sore parts of his body, and he was to be "censed with incense," and signed frequently with the cross, and then his condition would soon be better. A disease, consisting of a hardness of the side, was. called in the dark ages of superstition the elf-cake. In the seventh book of Lupton's "Thousand Notable Things," No. 55, is the following prescription which, it is said, will help the hardness of the side called the elf-cake. "Take the root of gladen, and make powder thereof, and give the diseased party half a spoon-ful thereof to drink in white wine, and let him eat thereof so much in his pottage at one time, and it will help him within a while." A cure for the above disorder is in Harl. MS. 2378, f. 47 and 57 : "For the elf-cake." This is of the time of Henry VI., and the same as that from Lupton. Camden says : "When any one in Ireland happens to fall, he springs up again, and turning round three times to the right, digs the earth with a sword or knife, and takes up a turf, because they say the earth reflects his shadow to him : (quod illi terram umbram reddere dicunt : they imagine there is a spirit in the earth) ; and if he falls sick within two or three days after, a woman skilled in those matters is sent to the spot, and there says, ' I call thee P. from the east, west, south, and north, from the groves, woods, rivers, marshes, fairies white, red, black, &c.' and, after uttering certain short prayers, she returns home to the sick person, to see whether it be the distemper which they call esane, which they suppose inflicted by the fairies, and whispering in his ear another short prayer, with the Pater-noster, puts some burning coals into a cup of clear water, and forms a better judgment of the disorder than most physicians." *Britannia*, 1789, iii., 668.

Elf-Fire or the *ignis fatuus*.—"Wrededeld vocatur Ignis qui ex attritu duorum

Lignorum elicitur, & quia superstitiosis varie usurpari dicitur." Ihre, "Glossar. Suio-Goth." 1769. Comp. *Will o' the Wisp.*

Elf-Locks.—A matted lock of hair in the neck. See the glossary to Kennet's "Parochial Antiquities." v. Lokys. "His haires are curl'd and full of elves-locks, and nitty for want of kembing." He is speaking of a "Ruffian, a swash buckler, and a braggart." Lodge's "Wits Miserie," 1596, p. 62. So Shakespear, in "Romeo and Juliet," 1597:

——"This is that very Mab,
That plats the manes of horses in the night,
And brakes the elf-locks in foul sluttish hairs,
Which once untangled, much misfortune bodes."

Warburton thought this superstition had its origin in the "Plica Polonica." Again, in "King Lear," Edgar says, "Elf all my hair in knots." Drayton, in his "Poems," 1637, says:

"O, that I were but a witch but for her sake!
Yfaith her Queenship little rest should take;
Id scratch that face, that may not feel the aire,
And knit whole ropes of witch-knots in her haire.'

Mr. Halliwell, who cites the above passage in illustration of the word witch-knot, in his "Archaic Dictionary," 1847, adds, under Elf: "To Elf—To entangle in knots." In Holland's "Don Zara del Fogo, a mock romance," 1656, "My guts, quoth Soto, are contorted like a dragons tayle, in elf-knots, as if some tripe-wife had tack't them together for chitterlings."

Elf - Shot. — Fairies were sometimes thought to be mischievously inclined by shooting at cattle with arrows headed with flint-stones. These were often found, and called elf-shots. They were simply the stone arrow-heads used by the aboriginal Irish and by the early Scots. They are still occasionally found in different parts of the world, having been in universal use, before weapons were made of metal. It was thought that if the part of the animal affected by the elf-shot was rubbed with the arrow-head, and was then put into the water which it drank, there was no danger of fever or other ill-effect. Plot, speaking of elf-arrows, says: "These they find in Scotland in much greater plenty, especially in the præfectuary of Aberdeen, which, as the learned Sir Robert Sibbald informs us, they there called elf-arrows, lamiarum sagittas, imagining they drop from the clouds, not being to be found upon a dili-

gent search, but now and then by chance in the high beaten roads. The animal affected was, in order to a cure, to be touched with one of these, or made to drink the water in which one of them had been dipped." *Staffordshire*, p. 369. Allan Ramsay, in his "Poems," 1721, p. 224, explains elf-shot thus: "Bewitch'd, shot by fairies. Country people tell odd tales of this distemper amongst cows. When elf-shot, the cow falls down suddenly dead; no part of the skin is pierced, but often a little triangular flat stone is found near the beast, as they report, which is called the elf's arrow." In an authoritative Scotish publication of the 18th century, we are told that stone or flint arrow heads, called elf, or fairy-stones, used not uncommonly to be found in various districts, as at Lauder, at Wick (Caithness), and Fordice (co. Banff). About 1793, the minister of Wick reported: "Some small stones have been found which seem to be a species of flint, about an inch long and half an inch broad, of a triangular shape, and barbed on each side. The common people confidently assert that they are fairies' arrows, which they shoot at cattle, when they instantly fall down dead, though the hide of the animal remains quite entire. Some of these arrows have been found buried a foot under ground, and are supposed to have been in ancient times fixed in shafts, and shot from bows." Again: "Elves, by their arrows, destroyed, and not seldom unmercifully, cows and oxen." But now, it is added: "the elf has withdrawn his arrow." *Stat. Acc. of Scotland*, i., 78, x. 15; xxi., 148. The subsequent lines are found in Collins:

"There ev'ry herd by sad experience knows
How, wing'd with fate, their elf-shot arrows fly,
When the sick ewe her summer food foregoes,
Or stretch'd on earth the heart-smit heifers lie."

Odes, p. 10. The author of the "Whitby Glossary," quoted by Atkinson, tells us that, "to cure an awf- (or elf-) shotten animal it must be touched with one of the shots, and the water administered in which one of them has been dipped." Mr. Atkinson adds: "In one district of Jutland it is believed that cattle, when elf-shot, become stiff, and surely die, unless speedy help is at hand. The quickest and surest remedy consists in driving the beast up out of the moss, and firing a shot over it; only care must be taken to fire from the head in the direction of the tail." *Cleveland Glossary*, 1868, v. *Elf*. The naturalists of the dark ages owed many obligations to our fairies, for whatever they found wonderful and could not account for, they easily got rid of by charging to their account.

Eligius, St., Eloy, or **Loy.**—(December 1). This saint was Bishop of Noyon, and flourished in the sixth century. The late Mr. Robert Bell, in a note to Chaucer's "Freres Tale," observes: "The 'Book of Homilies,' in enumerating the different forms of invoking the Saints, gives as an example, 'to the horse, God and Saint Loy save thee.'" In Chaucer it is a carter is addressing his horse:

"'Hayt now,' quod he, 'ther Jhesu
  Crist yow blesse,
And al his hondwerk, bothe more and
  lesse !
That was wel twight, myn oughne lyard
  boy,
I pray God save thy body and Saint
  Loy.'"

Chaucer makes his Prioress swear by St. Eloy :

"Hire gretest othe was but by seint
  Eloy."

Lyndsay, in his "Monarke," 1554, says:
"Sum makis offrande to sanct Eloye,
That he thare hors may weill conuoye."

And again Woodes, in the *Conflict of Conscience*, 1581, says:
"Sent Loy saue your horse, Sent Anthony your swyne."

Taylor the Water-poet has an anecdote of a countryman who was saying his devotions before an old image of the saint, when it fell down, and hurt him severely. It is in "Wit and Mirth," 1629. In the "Booke in Meeter of Robin Conscience" (circa 1585), one of the interlocutors swears by St. Loy. We read in the account of Tottenham High Cross in "The Ambulator," 1790: "In a brick field, on the west side of the great road, belonging to Mr. Charles Saunders, is St. Loy's Well, which is said to be always full, and never to run over: and in a field, opposite the Vicarage House, rises a spring called 'Bishop's Well,' of which the common people report many strange cures."

Eligius in his lifetime was moneyer to Dagobert I. and II., Kings of Paris, and became after death and canonization patron of the Goldsmiths and Farriers. See Hazlitt's supplement to his *Coins of Europe*, 1897, v. *Paris*, and Idem, *Remains of the Early Popular Poetry of England*, 1864-6, iii., 236.

Elizabeth's Day, St.—This was the 19th November, and had no original reference to English customs, but to the natal day of Elizabeth, daughter of Alexander, King of Hungary, who was canonized, and of whom there is a life in English. See Hazlitt's *Bibl. Coll.*, i., 285. The anniversary was subsequently adopted as a festival in honour of the accession of Elizabeth of England on the 17th of the month.

Elizabeth's, Queen, Accession.—(*St. Hugh's Day*, Nov. 17). From a variety of notices scattered in different publications, the anniversary of Queen Elizabeth's Accession appears to have been constantly observed even within the 18th century ; and in many of the almanacks was noted, certainly as late as 1684, and probably considerably later. In "The Pleasant Conceits of Old Hobson," 1607, inserted in "Old English Jest-Books," there is the following reference to St. Hugh's Day and its observances : "Vpon Saint Hewes day being the seventeenth of November, upon which day the tryumph was holden for Queene Elizabeths hapy government, as bonefiers, ringing of bells, and such like ; but in the parish where Maister Hobson dwelled, he being Churchwarden, was no ringing at all, by reason the steeple was a-mending and the bells downe." It appears from the "Status Scholæ Etonensis," 1560, that the scholars at Eton elected their Boy on this day, as the members of the college were accustomed to do on the feast of St. Nicholas. The author of "A Protestant Memorial for the Seventeenth of November, being the Inauguration Day of Queen Elizabeth," 1713, mentions this as still in observance, and adds : "I say we have now a new motive to this zeal, the preservation of our most gracious queen Anne being to be added to the vindication of the most gracious queen Elizabeth."

Elmo's, St., Fire.—See *Castor and Pollux*. We hear of the phenomenon occurring to Helen of Troy and to Servius Tullius, when the future King of Rome was a boy in the household of Tarquinius Priscus. Donaldson's *Miscellanea Virgiliana*, 1825, pp. 176-7, where other examples or allusions are cited from Virgil and Horace.

Elvish-Marked.—Shakespear has the expression elvish-marked, on which Steevens observes : "The common people in Scotland (as I learn from Kelly's 'Proverbs') have still an aversion to those who have any natural defect or redundancy, as thinking them marked out for mischief." In Ady's *Candle in the Dark*, 1659, p. 120, we read : "There be also often found in women with childe, and in women that do nurse children with their breasts," and on other occasions, "certain spots, black and blue, as if they were pinched or beaten, which some common ignorant people call fairy-nips, which, notwithstanding do come from the causes aforesaid : and yet for these have many ignorant searchers given evidence against poor innocent people (that is, accused them of being witches).''

Embalming.—This was a very common practice in this country in Catholic times, and remains so abroad to this day. In one of the most interesting of our early romances, "The Squyr of Low Degre," there is a description of the manner in which the daughter of the King of Hungary buried and embalmed the body (as she supposed) of her lover the squire, but in reality that of the false steward :

"Into the chamber she dyd him bere ;
His bowels soone she dyd out drawe,
And buryed them in goddes lawe.
She sered that body with specery,
With wyrgin waxe and commendry ;
And closed hym in a maser tre,
And set on hym lockes thre.
She put him in a marble stone,
With quaynt gynnes many one,
And set hym at hir beddeshead,
And euery day she kyst that dead.''

Hazlitt's *Popular Poetry*, ii., 49. Some embalmed remains were discovered at Bury St. Edmunds in 1772, which, on examination, were found to be in as perfectly sound a condition as an Egyptian mummy. Even the brain, the colour of the eyes and hair, the shape of the features, every thing, had remained through hundreds of years inaccessible to decomposing influences. *Antiq. Repertory*, 1808, iii., 331-2. The remains of Napoleon I., embalmed in 1821, were found to be in perfect state in 1840, when the tomb was opened preparatory to their removal to France. The Egyptians embalmed even their cats, and vast numbers of these mummies have been in modern times converted to common use.

Ember or **Imber Days.** — The "Festyvall," speaking of the Quatuor Tempora, or Ymbre Days, now called Ember Days, fol. 41, b., says they were so called, "bycause that our elder fathers wolde on these dayes ete no brede but cakes made under ashes." But in Tarlton's "Newes out of Purgatorie," 1590, the anonymous author perhaps semi-seriously ascribes the term to a different cause, "one pope," says he, "sat with a smocke about his necke, and that was he that made the imbering weekes, in honor of his faire and beautifull curtizan, Imbra."

Englewood, or **Inglewood, Cumberland.**—"At Hesket (in Cumberland) yearly on St. Barnabas's Day, by the highway-side, under a thorn tree, (according to the very ancient manner of holding assemblies in the open air), is kept the court for the whole Forest of Englewood "—the "Englyssh-wood " of the ballad of *Adam Bel*.

Ensham, Oxfordshire. — See *Whitsuntide*.

Ephialtes.—The ephialtes, or nightmare, is called by the common people witch-riding, and Wytche is the old English name for the complaint. This is, in fact an old Gothic or Scandinavian superstition. The term Ephialtes may be accounted scarcely correct, as it is merely the traditional name of one of the giants, who made war against the gods, and was slain by Apollo. Marca, whence our nightmare is derived, was in the Runic theology a spectre of the night, which seized men in their sleep, and suddenly deprived them of speech and motion. A great deal of curious learning upon the night-mare, or nacht-mare, as it is called in German, may be seen in Keysler and in Ihre. *Antiquitates Selectæ Septentrionales*, p. 497, *et seqq; Glossarium Suio-Gothicum*, ii., 135. According to Pliny's "Natural History," the antients believed that a nail drawn out of a sepulchre, and placed on the threshold of the bedchamber-door, would drive away phantoms and visions which terrified people in the night. The night-mare is, of course, now almost universally referred to its true origin, dyspepsia or indigestion, but even now it is easy to account for the prevalence of the superstition among a credulous and uneducated people, when the frightfully painful nature of the struggle during its continuance, and the astonishingly vivid phantoms conjured up before us, are considered. In Scot there is the following spell against this incubus :

"S. George, S. George, our Ladies Knight,
He walkt by day, so did he by night,
Until such time as he her found :
He her beat, and he her bound,
Until her troth she to him plight,
He would not come to her that night."

Dyce's *Beaumont and Fletcher*, vii., 388, *Note*.

"*Black Jesting Pawn*. So make him my white jennet, while I prance it. After the Black Knight's litter.
White Pawn. And you'd look then
Just like the Devil striding o'er a nightmare,
Made of a miller's daughter."

A Game at Chesse, by Thomas Middleton, 1624 (" Works," 1840, vol. iv. p. 368). Comp. Halliwell v. *Night-Mare*.

There is an account of Johannes Cuntius of Pertsch, in Silesia, inserted in the "Antiquarian Repertory," from Henry More's Philosophical Writings. This person was suspected of having sold one of his sons, and of having made a contract with the Devil; he died suddenly under painful circumstances: and the narrative informs us (ii. 321), "He had not been dead a day or two, but several rumours were spread in the town, of a spiritus incubus or ephialtes, in the shape of Cuntius, that would have forced a woman. But this ephialtes seems to be different from our conception of the night-mare.

Epiphany.—See *Twelfth Day.*

Epping Forest Stag-Hunt.— The "Chelmsford Chronicle" of April 15, 1805, contained a notice to the following effect: "On Monday last Epping Forest was enlivened, according to ancient custom, with the celebrated stag hunt. The road from Whitechapel to the 'Bald-faced Stag,' on the Forest, was covered with Cockney sportsmen, chiefly dressed in the costume of the chace, viz. scarlet frock, black jockey cap, new boots, and buckskin breeches. By ten o'clock the assemblage of civic hunters, mounted on all sorts and shapes, could not fall short of 1,200. There were numberless Dianas also of the chace, from Rotherhithe, the Minories, &c., some in riding habits, mounted on titups, and others by the sides of their mothers, in gigs, tax-carts, and other vehicles appropriate to the sports of the field. The Saffron Walden stag-hounds made their joyful appearance about half after ten, but without any of the Mellishes or Bosanquets, who were more knowing sportsmen than to risque either themselves, or their horses, in so desperate a burst! The huntsman having capped their half-crowns, the horn blew just before twelve, as a signal for the old fat one-eyed stag (kept for the day) being enlarged from the cart. He made a bound of several yards, over the heads of some pedestrians, at first starting—when such a clatter commenced, as the days of Nimrod never knew. Some of the scarlet jackets were sprawling in the high road a few minutes after starting—so that a lamentable return of maimed! missing! thrown! and thrown-out! may naturally be supposed." In the *Standard* newspaper of April 24, 1870, occurs the subjoined paragraph: "Lieut. Colonel Palmer, the verderer of the Forest and judge of the Forest Courts, attended the King's Oak, High Beach, to receive any of the Royal Princes, the Lord Mayor and aldermen of London, and such of the citizens of London and others from the vicinity who might see fit to attend for the sake of exercising their ancient privilege of hunting a stag in Epping Forest on Easter Monday. The Hon. Frederick Petre lent his pack of stag hounds for the purpose, and a fine deer was turned out about three o'clock in the afternoon, in the presence of a very large assemblage of sporting and peaceable holiday folks of all ranks, trades, and ages. The stag showed much sport, and after a run of 45 minutes was taken upon the border of Sir Thomas Fowell Buxton's Park, at Warlies. A strong body of the Metropolitan Police were upon the ground at the request of some of the parties who have made illegal inclosures of portions of the Forest, in the expectation that the fences would be thrown down; but nothing of the kind was attempted, or ever intended, as such encroachments as have been made in this forest, and which it may be necessary to throw out, will be removed in a strictly legal manner by the forest officers, when the freeholders of the County of Essex and her Majesty's ministers fulfil the engagements they recently entered into by the desire of the majority of the House of Commons, and which have received the sanction and cordial approbation of her Most Gracious Majesty the Queen." And it is also noticed in the journals for 1875. But in 1883, an announcement appeared that it was to be at last discontinued.

Erasmus, St.—There were two saints of this name. St. Eline, one of the martyrs of the fourth century, was also called St. Erasmus; his day is Nov. 25. The life of the bishop and martyr, whose day is June 2, was printed by Julian Notary in 1520. He was supposed to exercise a beneficial influence in certain diseases, especially the colic. There is a letter from Henry Lord Stafford to Cromwell, then Lord Privy Seal, about 1539, in which the writer speaks of the destruction of an image of St. Erasmus. He describes it as "an idoll, callid of ignorant persons Sainct Erasmus."

Eringo.—See a notice of its supposed aphrodisiac qualities in Nares *Glossary,* 1859, in v.

Erra Pater.—See a good account in Nares, *Glossary,* 1859, in v.

Errors, Vulgar or Popular.— The *Schola Salernitana* records some curious fallacies: that rue sprinkled in a house kills all the fleas; that, when the young swallows are blind, the mother, by applying the plant celendine, can make them see: that watercresses taken as a beverage, or as an ointment, are specifics against baldness and the itch; that willow-juice poured into the corn-ear will kill the blight; and that the rind of the tree boiled in vinegar will remove warts; and the present catalogue of absurdities might be enlarged with great ease. Vaughan informs us, "That the mole hath no eyes, nor the elephant knees, are two well known vulgar errors: both which notwithstanding, by daily and manifest experience are found to be untrue." *Brief Natural History*, p. 89, Comp. Hazlitt's *Proverbs*, 1882, p. 228, where deafness is falsely ascribed to the adder in a popular saying. There is a vulgar error that the hare is one year a male and the other a female. That a wolf if he see a man first, suddenly strikes him dumb. To the relators this Scaliger wishes as many blows as at different times he has seen wolves without losing his voice. That there is a nation of pigmies, not above two or three feet high, and that they solemnly set themselves in battle array to fight against the cranes. Strabo thought this a fiction; but in our age geographical research has made us acquainted with nations of warlike dwarfs. A writer in the "Gentleman's Magazine" for June, 1771, refutes the following errors; asserting "that the Scorpion does not sting itself when surrounded by fire, and that its sting is not even venomous." "That the tarantula is not poisonous, and that music has no particular effects on persons bitten by it, more than on those stung by a wasp." "That the lizard is not friendly to man in particular, much less does it awaken him on the approach of a serpent." "That the stroke of the cramp fish is not occasioned by a muscle." "That the bite of the spider is not venomous,, that it is found in Ireland too plentifully, that it has no dislike to fixing its web on Irish oak, and that it has no antipathy to the toad." "That the porcupine does not shoot out its quills for annoying his enemy; he only sheds them annually, as other feathered animals do." "That the jackall, commonly called the lion's provider, has no connection at all with the lion," &c. Barrington says, it is supposed to be penal to open a coal mine, or to kill a crow, within five miles of London: as also to shoot with a wind-gun: as to the wind-gun, he takes that to arise from a statute of Henry VII. prohibiting the use of a cross-bow without a licence; but this, I apprehend, refers to statute 6 Hen. VIII. It is also a vulgar error to suppose that there is a statute which obliges the owners of asses to crop their ears, lest the length of them should frighten the horses which they meet on the road.

In the "Gentleman's Magazine" for September, 1734, we have the following from Bayle: "There is nothing strange in errors becoming universal, considering how little men consult their reason. What multitudes believe, one after another, that a man weighs more fasting than full; that a sheepskin drum bursts at the beat of a wolfskin drum; that young vipers destroy the old females when they come to the birth, (of which

Scaliger from his own experience asserted the falsehood) and strike the male dead at the instant of their conception, with many other truths of equal validity?" To these vulgar errors, adds Barrington, *Observations on the Statutes*, p. 474, may be added perhaps the notion, that a woman's marrying a man under the gallows, will save him from the execution. This probably arose from a wife having brought an appeal against the murderer of her husband; who afterwards, repenting the prosecution of her lover, not only forgave the offence, but was willing to marry the appellee. In the case of Margaret Clark, executed for firing her master's house in Southwark, 1680, it is said, at her execution, "there was a fellow who designed to marry her under the gallows (according to the antient laudable custome) but she being in hopes of a reprieve, seemed unwilling, but when the rope was about her neck, she cryed she was willing, and then the fellow's friends dissuaded him from marrying her; and so she lost her husband and her life together." But among some savage tribes a woman may save a person of the other sex, who has been taken prisoner, from a cruel death by demanding him in marriage. Captain Marryat has introduced this incident into one of his novels.

I may likewise add to these that any one may be put into the Crown office for no cause whatsoever, or the most trifling injury. It is a legal fiction rather than an error to describe those born or drowned at sea as parishioners of Stepney. Other vulgar errors are, that the old statutes have prohibited the planting of vineyards or the use of sawing mills, relating to which I cannot find any statute: they are however established in Scotland, to the very great advantage both of the proprietor and the country. One of Mr. Brand's correspondents sent him a notice of two other vulgar errors, viz.: When a man designs to marry a woman who is in debt, if he take her from the hands of the priest, clothed only in her shift, it is supposed that he will not be liable to her engagements. The second is that there was no land tax before the reign of William the Third. Barrington supposes that an exemption granted to surgeons from serving on juries is the foundation of the vulgar error that a surgeon or butcher (from the barbarity of their business) may be challenged as jurors. *Observations on the Statutes*, 475. This is still a prevailing notion; and it may perhaps hardly be out of place to add that it is no vulgar error, but a matter of established and recognised usage, that no butcher, attorney, or (I think) brewer shall be placed on the commission of the peace.

The Lord Chancellor sends a notice to this effect to any new borough, which has to forward for his approval the list of candidates.

Ethelberg, St., or Alburg's Day.—(October 11). Fosbrooke mentions, amidst the annual store of provision at Barking Nunnery, "wheat and milk for Frimitè upon St. Alburg's Day."

Ethelreda, St., otherwise *St. Audrey,* or *Auldrey,* whence it is alleged that we get the word tawdry, because at the Saint's Fair held at various places, Ely included, on the 17th October, a great deal of cheap finery was offered for sale. This holy lady is said to have died from a swelling in her throat occasioned by the divine anger at her vanity, when young, in wearing fine necklaces; but the story also goes, that she was on religious grounds peculiarly abstemious in her use of water for washing purposes.

Eton School. — At Eton College, in place of a boy-bishop and his crozier, they introduced a captain and an ensign, replacing the religious by a sort of military element, and the chieftain of the band conducted his followers to a scene of action in the open air, where no consecrated walls were in danger of being profaned, and where the gay striplings could at least exhibit their wonted pleasantries with more propriety of character. The exacting of money from the spectators and passengers, for the use of the principal, remained much the same, but, it seems, no evidence has been transmitted whether the deacons then, as the salt-bearers did afterwards, made an offer of a little salt in return when they demanded the annual subsidy. I have been so fortunate, however, as to discover, that in some degree, a similar use of salt, that is, an emblematical one; among the scholars of a foreign university, at the well-known ceremony of Deposition, in a publication dated at Strasburg in Alsace, so late as A.D. 1666. The consideration of every other emblem used on the above occasion, and explained in that work, being foreign to my purpose, I shall confine myself to that of the salt alone, which one of the heads of the college explains thus to the young academicians: "With regard to the ceremony of salt," says the writer of the account of the Strasburg "Depositio," "the sentiments and opinions both of divines and phliosophers concur in making salt the emblem of wisdom or learning; and that, not only on account of what it is composed of, but also with respect to the several uses to which it is applied. As to its component parts, as it consists of the purest matter, so ought

wisdom to be pure, sound, immaculate, and incorruptible: and similar to the effects which salt produces upon bodies, ought to be those of wisdom and learning upon the mind." There are twenty plates illustrating the several stages of the Depositio. The last represents the giving of the salt, which a person is holding on a plate in his left hand, and with his right hand about to put a pinch of it upon the tongue of each Beanus or Freshman. A glass holding wine (I suppose), is standing near him. Underneath is the following couplet, which is much to our purpose; for even the use of wine was not altogether unknown in our Montem procession at Eton:

"Sal Sophiæ gustate, bibatis vinaque læta,
Augeat immensus vos in utrisque Deus!"

In another part of the oration he tells them, "This rite of salt is a pledge or earnest which you give that you will most strenuously apply yourselves to the study of good arts, and as earnestly devote yourselves to the several duties of your vocation." How obvious is it then to make the same application of the use of salt in the old ceremony at Eton! Here, too, is said to have been formerly one of the pleasantries of the salt-bearers to fill any boorish looking countryman's mouth with it, if, after he has given them a trifle, he asked for anything in return, to the no small entertainment of the spectators.

I should conjecture that Salt Hill was the central place where anciently all the festivities used on this occasion were annually displayed, and here only, it should seem, the salt was originally distributed, from which circumstance it has undoubtedly had its name. See the "Status Scholæ Etonensis," 1560, Mense Januarii. I have heard it asserted, but find no foundation of the fact, that in the papal times there was an exclusive grant to Eton College, from the Pope, to sell consecrated salt for making holy water. In a letter from John Byrom to John Aubrey, 1693, the writer informs his correspondent that he had heard of the college holding certain lands by the custom of salting. He thought that the practice was to be traced to the Scriptural quotation: "Ye are the salt of the earth," and to the idea of purification. Aubrey's Letters, &c., 1813, ii., 168. The custom of having a procession of the scholars can be clearly proved as far back as the reign of Elizabeth, who, when she visited this College, desired to see an account of all the antient ceremonies observed there from its foundation to that period, in the number of which it appears that an annual procession of the scholars was one, and that at such times verses were repeated, and sums of money were gathered from the public for a dinner, &c., to which fund was added the small pittances extorted from the boys who were recently admitted, by those of a longer standing." Mr. Cambridge, an old Etonian, informed Mr. Brand, August 9th, 1794, that, in his time, the salt-bearers and scouts carried, each of them, salt in a handkerchief, and made every person take a pinch out of it before they gave their contributions.

In Huggett's MSS. Collections for the History of Windsor and Eton College is the following account of "Ad Montem": "The present manner is widely different from the simplicity of its first institution. Now the Sales Epigrammatum are changed into the Sal purum; and it is a play-day without exercise. Here is a procession of the school quite in the military way. The scholars of the superior classes dress in the proper regimentals of captain, lieutenant, &c., which they borrow or hire from London on the occasion. The procession is likewise in the military order, with drums, trumpets, &c. They then march three times round the school-yard, and from thence to Salt Hill, on which one of the scholars, dress'd in black and with a band, as chaplain, reads certain prayers: after which a dinner dressed in the College kitchen is provided by the captain for his guests at the inn there; the rest getting a dinner for themselves at the other houses for entertainment. But long before the procession begins, two of the scholars called salt-bearers, dressed in white, with a handkerchief of salt in their hands, and attended each with some sturdy young fellow hired for the occasion, go round the College, and through the town, and from thence up into the high road, and offering salt to all, but scarce leaving it to their choice whether they will give or not: for money they will have, if possible, and that even from servants. The fifth and sixth forms dine with the captain. The noblemen usually do, and many other scholars whose friends are willing to be at the expence. The price of the dinner to each is 10s. 6d. and 2s. 6d. more for salt-money. Every scholar gives a shilling for salt, the noblemen more. At this time also they gather the recent money, which is . . . . from every scholar that has been entered within the year. Dinner being over, they march back in the order as before into the school yard, and with the third round the ceremony is concluded. The motto on the ensign

colours is, "Pro More et Monte.' Every scholar, who is no officer, marches with a long pole, focii or two and two. At the same time and place the head-master of the school makes a dinner at his own expence for his acquaintance, assistants, &c. Of late years the captain has cleared, after all expences are paid, upwards of £100. The Montem day used to be fixed for the first Tuesday in Hilary Term, which begins January 23rd. In the year 1759, the day was altered to Tuesday in the Whitsun week (which was then June 5th); the Whitsun holidays having a few years before been altered from five weeks holiday at election. This procession to Montem is every third year, and sometimes oftener." In one of the "Public Advertisers," in 1778, is the oldest printed account of the ceremony I have been able to find. It was then biennial: On Tuesday, being Whit Tuesday, the gentlemen of Eton School went, as usual, in military procession to Salt Hill. This custom of walking to the Hill returns every second year, and generally collects together a great deal of company of all ranks. The King and Queen, in their phæton, met the procession at Arbor-hill, in Slough-road. When they halted, the flag was flourished by the ensign. The boys went, according to custom, round the mill, &c. The parson and clark were then called, and there these temporary ecclesiasticks went through the usual Latin service, which was not interrupted, though delayed for some time by the laughter that was excited by the antiquated appearance of the clerk, who had dressed himself according to the *ton* of 1745, and acted his part with as minute a consistency as he had dressed the character. The procession began at half-past twelve from Eton. The collection was an extraordinary good one, as their Majesties gave, each of them, fifty guineas." Warton has preserved the form of the acquittance given by a Boy-bishop to the receiver of his subsidy, then amounting to the considerable sum of £3 15s. 1d. ob. The sum collected at the Montem on Whit-Tuesday, 1790, was full £500. This sum went to the captain, who was the senior of the collegers at the time of the ceremony. The motto for that year was "Pro More et Monte." Their majesties presented each a purse of fifty guineas. The fancy dresses of the salt bearers and their deputies, who were called scouts, were usually of different coloured silks, and very expensive. Formerly the dresses used in this procession were obtained from the theatres. In the "Gentleman's Magazine" for June, 1793, is the following account of the Montem procession for that year:—"On Whit-

Tuesday, according to triennial custom, the procession of the young gentlemen educated at Eton-School to Salt Hill took place. About eleven, the gentlemen assembled in the school-yard, and were soon after properly arranged in the procession, according to their rank in the school. Their Majesties, with the Prince of Wales, Princesses Royal, Augusta, Elizabeth, and Amelia, the Duchess of York, and Prince William of Gloucester, arrived at the College about twelve, and took their station in the stable-yard. The young gentlemen marched twice round the school yard, and then went, in true military parade, with music playing, drums beating, and colours flying, into the stable yard, where they passed the royal family, the ensign having first flourished the flag, by way of salute to their Majesties. The procession then moved on, through the playing fields, to Salt Hill, where they were again received by the royal family; when, after again marching by, and saluting them, the young gentlemen paraded to dinner. To the honour of Eton, the number of gentlemen who marched in the procession amounted to 500. The collection for the benefit of the captain far exceeded all former ones; the sum spoken of amounts to near £1,000. The motto on the flag, and on the tickets distributed on the occasion, was "Mos pro Lege." Their Majesties, the Prince of Wales, Princesses and Duchess of York, made their donations to the salt-bearers. In the evening the gentlemen returned, in proper military uniform, to Eton; and afterwards the salt-bearers and scouts appeared on the terrace in their dresses, and were particularly noticed by their Majesties."

"When boys at Eton, once a year
In military pomp appear;
He who just trembled at the rod,
Treads it a hero, talks a god,
And in an instant can create
A dozen officers of state.
His little legion all assail,
Arrest without release or bail;
Each passing traveller must halt,
Must pay the tax, and eat the salt.
You don't love salt, you say; and storm—
Look o' these staves, sir—and conform."

—*The Tunbridge Miscellany*, 1712. A long article on the Montem at Eton will be found in "Notes and Queries" for November 9, 1867. The custom was abolished in 1876. It appears from the "Status Scholæ Etonensis," 1560, that the Eton Scholars used to act plays in the Christmas holidays. St. Nicholas Day continued in Mr. Brand's time to be a gaudy-day in Eton College; and

though the Montem was then generally kept on Whit Tuesday, yet it is certain that it was formerly kept in the winter time, a little before the Christmas holidays, as a person of high rank, who had been a scholar there, told Brand; or, as others informed him, in February. Dr. Davies, one of the provosts, remembered when they used to cut a passage through the snow from Eton to the hill called Salt Hill, upon which, after the procession had arrived there, the chaplain with his clerk used to read prayers; upon the conclusion of which it was customary for the chaplain to kick his clerk down the hill. It is said that the first time Queen Charlotte was present at this ceremony, she thought this sort of sport so very irreligious, and expressed her royal dissatisfaction at it so much, that the kicking part of the service was very properly laid aside. It is observable that in Latin verses in the "Musæ Etonenses," 1755, pp. 62 and 113, to both of which "Pro More et Monte" is the motto, the season is described to be winter.

It is also a practice at Eton School which, unlike the Montem, is still kept up, to present each new head master by the hand of the captain, upon his entry into office, that is, at the first eleven o'clock school, over which he presides, with a birch tied up with blue ribbons. On this occasion the captain makes a short address, and the master is expected to reply, deprecating the necessity of chastisement, and hoping the present state of mutual confidence may remain unaltered. The Barring-out ceremony, already described at length under *Bromfield*, was long used here. The boys used on the day of the Circumcision, in former times, to play for little New Year's gifts before and after supper: and they had a custom that day, for good luck's sake, of making verses, and sending them to the Provost, Masters, &c., as also of presenting them to each other. "Status Scholæ Etonensis," A.D. 1560, MS. Brit. Mus. Donat. 4843, fol. 423. It was the custom on Shrove Monday for the scholars to write verses either in praise or dispraise of Father Bacchus: poets being considered as immediately under his protection. He was therefore sung on this occasion in all kinds of metres, and the verses of the boys of the seventh and sixth and some of the fifth forms, were affixed to the inner doors of the College. Verses are still written and put up on this day; but I believe the young poets are no longer confined to the subject of writing eulogiums on the god of wine. It still however retains the name of the *Bacchus*. "Status Scholæ Etonensis," fol. 423. On Shrove Tuesday the boys were allowed to play from eight o'clock for the whole day; and mention occurs in the work so often cited of the cook coming and fastening a pancake to a crow, which the young crows are calling upon, near it, at the school-door. The crows generally have hatched their young at this season.

In 1560, on Ash Wednesday, it was the custom of the scholars to choose themselves confessors out of the masters or chaplains, to whom they were to confess their sins. *Status Scholæ Etonensis*, fol. 425. It is stated that, on the day of St. Philip and St. James, if it be fair weather, and the Master grants leave, those boys who choose it may rise at four o'clock to gather May branches, if they can do it without wetting their feet: and that on that day they adorn the windows of the bed-chamber with green leaves, and the houses are perfumed with fragrant herbs. The boys of the School had anciently their bonfires on the east side of the Church, on St. Peter's Day, and at midsummer on St. John's Day. After morning prayers, also, they used to sing three antiphones in the church, and their beds they decorated with prints and verses descriptive of events in the life of the saint and his predecessors. *Status Scholæ Etonensis*, 1560. It seems from the same authority that in September, "on a certain day," most probably the fourteenth, the boys were to have a play-day, in order to go out and gather nuts, with a portion of which, when they returned, they were to make presents to the different masters. It is ordered, however, that before this leave be granted them, they should write verses on the fruitfulness of autumn, the deadly colds, &c., of advancing winter. There is on St. David's Day (March 1) an annual procession of boats. This year (1903) the day falling on a Sunday, the ceremony was observed on the 28th February. There were nine 8-oars and one 10-oars, and each had its own colours.

"It was an ancient custom," says Huggett, "for the butcher of the College to give on the election Saturday a ram to be hunted by the scholars; but by reason (as I have heard) of the ram crossing the Thames, and running through Windsor market-place with the scholars after it, where some mischief was done, as also by long courses in that hot season, the health of some of the scholars being thereby thought endangered, about thirty years ago the ram was ham-strung, and, after the speech, was with clubs knocked on the head in the stable-yard. But, this carrying a show of barbarity in it, the custom was entirely left off in the election of 1747; but the ram, as usual, is served up in pasties at the high table. "Browne Willis would derive this custom from what is (or was) used in the manor of East Wrotham, Norfolk (the rectory and, I believe, the manor of which belongs to this College) where the lord of the manor after the harvest gave half an acre of barley and a ram to the tenants thereof. The which ram, if they caught it, was their own, if not, it was for the lord again." Hazlitt's *Blount*, 1874, p. 382. In the "Gentleman's Magazine" for August, 1731, is the following: "Monday, August 2, was the election at Eton College, when the scholars, according to custom, hunted a ram, by which the Provost and Fellows hold a manor." Even in Beckwith's time, however, this usage had been given up. Edit. of *Blount*, 1815, p. 495; Carlisle's *Endowed Grammar Schools*, 1818.

Even or Odd? i.q., *Odd or Even?* a game of chance mentioned in the dedication by the anonymous writer to Mr. William Lilly, of "Pantagruel's Prognostication," about 1645. He classed it with Handy-dandy. It was played by the boys in ancient Greece.

Evil Eye.—The following passage is cited from one of Bacon's works. It seems some have been so curious as to note that the times when the stroke, or percussion of an envious eye does most hurt, are particularly when the party envied is beheld in glory and triumph." *Minor Morals*, i., 124. Lupton says: "The eyes be not only instruments of enchantment, but also the voice and evil tongues of certain persons; for there are found in Africk, as Gellius saith, families of men, that, if they chance exceedingly to praise fair trees, pure seeds, goodly children, excellent horses, fair and well-liking cattle, soon after they will wither and pine away, and so dye. No cause or hurt known of their withering or death. Thereupon the custome came, that, when any do praise any thing, that we should say, God blesse it or keepe it. Arist. in Prob. by the report of Mizaldus." *Notable Things*, ed. 1660, p. 201. In the 18th century, if not now, the evil eye was an article of general faith in Scotland. In 1795, however, the minister of Monzie, co. Perth, reported: "The power of an evil eye is still believed, although the faith of the people in witchcraft is much enfeebled." It appears that the people of Stirlingshire then still clang to some of their old prejudices. A writer says: "The dregs of superstition are still to be found. The less informed suspect something like witchcraft about poor old women, and are afraid of their evil eye among the cattle. If a cow is suddenly taken ill, it is ascribed to some extraordinary cause. If a person when called to see one does not say 'I wish her luck,' there would be a suspicion he had some bad design." *Stat. Acc. of Scotland*, xiv., 526. Pinkerton acquaints us that "Cattle are subject to be injured by what is called an evil eye, for some persons are supposed to have naturally a blasting power in their eyes with which they injure whatever offends, or is hopelessly desired by them. Witches and warlocks are also much disposed to wreak their malignity on cattle." *Heron's Journey*, ii., 223. Martin says: — "All these (Western) Islanders, and several thousands of the neighbouring Continent, are of opinion that some particular persons have an evil eye, which affects children and cattle. This, they say, occasions frequent mischances, and sometimes death." *Description of the Western Islands of Scotland.* p. 123. The same author, speaking in the last century of the Isle of Harris, says: "There is a variety of nuts, called molluska beans, some of which are used as amulets against witchcraft or an evil eye, particularly the white one: and upon this account they are wore about children's necks, and if any evil is intended to them. they say the nut changes into a black colour. That they did change colour I found true by my own observation. but cannot be positive as to the cause of it. Malcolm Campbell, steward of Harris, told me that some weeks before my arrival there, all his cows gave blood instead of milk for several days together: one of the neighbours told his wife that this must be witchcraft, and it would be easy to remove it, if she would but take the white nut, called the Virgin Mary's nut, and lay it in the pail into which she was to milk the cows. This advice she presently followed, and having milked one cow into the pail with the nut in it, the milk was all blood, and the nut changed its colour into dark brown. She used the nut again, and all the cows gave pure good milk, which they ascribe to the virtue of the nut. This very nut Mr. Campbell presented me with, and I still keep it by me." In going once to visit the remains of Brinkburne Abbey in Northumberland, Brand himself found a reputed witch in a lonely cottage by the side of a wood, where the parish had placed her to save expenses, and keep her out of the way. On enquiry at a neighbouring farm house, he was told, though he was a long while before he could elicit anything from the inhabitants in it concerning her, that every body was afraid of her cat, and that she herself was thought to have an evil eye, and that it was accounted dangerous to meet her in a morning "black-fasting."

Volney, in his "Travels in Egypt and Syria," vol. i. p. 246, says: "The ignorant mothers of many of the modern Egyptians, whose hollow eyes, pale faces, swoln bellies, and meagre extremities make them seem as if they had not long to live, believe this to be the effect of the evil eye of some envious person, who has bewitched them; and this ancient prejudice is still general in Turkey." "Nothing," says Mr. Dallaway, in his "Account of Constantinople," 1797, p. 391, "can exceed the superstition of the Turks respecting the evil eye of an enemy or infidel. Passages from the Koran are painted on the outside of the houses, globes of glass are suspended from the ceilings, and a part of the superfluous caparison of their horses is designed to attract attention, and divert a sinister influence." That this superstition was known to the Romans we have the authority of Virgil:

"Nescio quis teneros oculus mihi fascinat agnos."

Ecl. iii. Comp. *Spitting.*

Evil May Day.—What is known as Evil May-day was an insurrection of the apprentices of London in 1517. It is described sufficiently at large in the chronicles. Johnson, in his "Crowne-Garland of Goulden Roses," 1659, has the "Story of Ill May-day in the time of King Henry VIII., and why it was so called, and how Queen Katherine begged the lives of two thousand London 'prentices. To the tune of 'Essex's Last Good night.'" But the Queen does not seem to have been present on the occasion, and it was Wolsey, who interceded, not for 2,000, but for 400, apprentices brought before the King barefoot, with halters round their necks. A sedition of a very similar character occurred in 1586, and is referred to in a letter from Fleetwood, Recorder of London, to the Lord Treasurer Burleigh. But in one from the Venetian Resident in London, Sebastian Giustinian, to his Government, dated from Westminster, Sept. 26, 1517, it appears that a second conspiracy had been arranged for Michaelmas Eve, to murder all strangers, and sack their houses, while the King and Wolsey were out of town. Three of the ringleaders were arrested, and 3,000 householders and public functionaries were under arms for the protection of life and property. Nothing farther seems to have occurred.—*Four Years at the Court of Henry VIII.*, edited by R. Brown, ii., 130. These movements indicate the growth of the foreign or alien element in the commercial life of London.

Exequies.—See *Funeral Customs.*

Exhibition.—A term now limited to academical instruction and to men studying at the Universities. But it was formerly understood of fees payable for the education of children at home or otherwise. In a letter, 26th November, 1501, to Sir Robert Plumpton, the writer states in reference to a payment made by her: "What parte, or how much thereof, my sayd nevue, Germayne, hath sent to your mastership, I am ignorant, saving that he shewed me that he sendeth you but xli. towards the exhibicions of my nese, his wyfe." The latter, though described as married, was probably betrothed only, and resident under the paternal roof. *Plumpton Correspondence*, 1839, p. 163.

Exorcism. — The following spell is from Herrick:

"Holy Water come and bring;
Cast in salt, for seasoning;
Set the brush for sprinkling:

Sacred spittle bring ye hither;
Meale and it now mix together;
And a little oyle to either:

Give the tapers here their light;
Ring the saints-bell to affright
Far from hence the evill sprite."

Adamson, in his "Muses' Threnodie," 1638, (repr. 1774, p. 213) observes: "Many are the instances, even to this day, of charms practised among the vulgar, especially in the Highlands, attended with forms of prayer. In the Miscellaneous MS., written by Baillie Dundee, among several medicinal receipts, I find an exorcism against all kinds of worms in the body, in the name of the Father, Son, and Holy Ghost, to be repeated three mornings, as a certain remedy. The poor women who were prosecuted for witchcraft, administered herbs and exorcized their patients." Upon the subject of exorcising, the following books may be consulted with advantage: "Fustis Dæmonum, cui adjicitur Flagellum Dæmonum," 1608, (a prohibited book among the Roman Catholics); and Polidorus "Practica Exorcistarum ad Dæmones expellendum," 1606. From this last Bourne's form has been taken. Comp. *Charms and Sorcery.*

Eye.—In the third idyll of Theocritus, paraphrased by Thomas Bradshawe under the title of the "Shepherd's Starre," 1591, Corydon says: "But my right eye watreth, 'tis a signe of somewhat, do I see her yet?" In Creech's later version the same passage runs:

"My right eye itches, and shall I see
My love?"

The watering or itching was sometimes treated as a lucky omen, sometimes the reverse. Compare *Ear Omens.*

Eye, Black's your. — There is a vulgar saying in the North, and probably in many other parts of England, "No one can say black is your eye." In Wanley's "Vox Dei," 1658, p. 85, the author, speaking of St. Paul having said that he was teaching the righteousness which is in the law blameless, observes upon it. "No man could say (as the proverb hath it) black was his eye"; meaning that nobody can justly speak ill of you. In his "Discovery," 1584, says Reginald Scot: "Many writers agree with Virgil and Theocritus in the effect of bewitching eyes, affirming that in Scythia there are women called Bithiæ, having two balls, or rather blacks, in the apples of their eyes. These, forsooth, with their angry looks do bewitch and hurt, not only young lambs, but young children." The phrase occurs, however, in Parrot's "Mastive or Young Whelpe of the old Dog," 1615. One of the epigrams is as follows:

"Doll, in disdaine, doth from her heeles defie;
The best that breathes shall tell her black's her eye:
And that it's true she speaks, who can say nay?
When none that lookes on't but will sweare 'tis gray."

Fabulous Creatures of the Middle Ages.—In the *Archæological Album*, 1845, pp. 174-86, will be found a valuable description of many of these fanciful objects of dread to our ancestors, some doubtless realities under written descriptions or pictorial forms, which do not enable us to identify them. Such was the attercop, a poisonous spider, perhaps a sort of tarantula concerning which is an anecdote of the fourteenth century, connected with Shrewsbury and the magical properties of St. Winifred's Well, and which collaterally illustrates the evolution from reptiles into birds, as the accompanying cut from a Saxon herbal may shew; the white bird, called *caladrius*,

ATTERCOP.

which haunted the halls of kings and princes, and if any sick person was going to die, averted its head from him, but if he was about to recover, looked him in the face; the *serra* or *serre*, with the head of a lion and the tail of a fish, with wings, which could stay a ship, so long as it could remain in the air; and the mediæval syren, which followed the type of the ancient myth. Some of these early superstitions have been extinguished by the progress of scientific knowledge, even the belief in the disastrous consequences attendant on the slaughter of the albatross, which forms the plot of Coleridge's crude *Rime of the Ancient Mariner.* Comp. *Remora* and *Unicorn.*

Face - Cloth. — The face-cloth is of great antiquity. Strutt tells us that " after the closing of the eyes, &c., a linen cloth was put over the face of the deceased. Thus we are told that Henry the Fourth, in his last illness, seeming to be dead, his Chamberlain covered his face with a linen cloth." Stafford says : " I am so great an enemie to ceremonies, as that I would onelie wish to have that one ceremonie at my buriall, which I had at my birth ; I mean, swadling : and yet I am indifferent for that too."

Facer. — Allan Ramsay mentions a set of drinkers called Facers, who, he says, " were a club of fair drinkers who inclined rather to spend a shilling on ale than twopence for meat. They had their name from a rule they observed of obliging themselves to throw all they left in the cup in their own faces : Wherefore, to save their face and their cloaths, they prudently sucked the liquor clean out."

Fain Play.—See *St. Nicholas's Day.* and *Touch.*

Fairies.—In the " British Apollo," 1708, No. I. supernumerary for April, we are told : " The opinion of fairies has been asserted by Pliny and several historians, and Aristotle himself gave some countenance to it, whose words are these : Εσι δε ὁ τοπος &c., i.e. Hic Locus est quem incolunt Pygmei, non est Fabula, sed pusillum Genus ut aiunt : wherein Aristotle plays the sophist. For though by ' non est Fabula ' he seems at first to confirm it, yet coming in at last with his ' ut aiunt,' he shakes the belief he had before put upon it. Our Society, therefore, are of opinion, that Homer was the first author of this conceit, who often used similies, as well to delight the ear as to illustrate his matter : and in his third Iliad compares the Trojane to manes, when they descend against fairies. So that, that which was only a pleasant fiction in the fountain, became a solemn story in the stream, and current still among us." Bishop Percy tells us that, on the assurance of a learned friend in Wales, the existence of fairies is alluded to by the most ancient British bards, among whom their commonest name was that of the spirits of the mountains. *Reliques,* iii., 207. " It will afford entertainment," says he, " to a contemplative mind to trace these whimsical opinions up to their origin. Whoever considers how early, how extensively, and how uniformly they have prevailed in these nations, will not readily assent to the hypothesis of those who fetch them from the East so late as the time of the Croisades. Whereas it is well known that our Saxon ancestors, long before they left their German forests, believed the existence of a kind of diminutive Demons, or middle species between men and spirits, whom they called Duergar or dwarfs, and to whom they attributed many wonderful performances far exceeding human art." " I made strict inquiries" (Brand says) " after the fairies in the uncultivated wilds of Northumberland, but even there I could only meet with a man who said that he had seen one that had seen fairies. Truth is hard to come at in most cases. None, I believe, ever came nearer to it in this than I have done." Chaucer is very facetious concerning them in his " Canterbury Tales," where he puts his creed of fairy mythology into the mouth of the Wife of Bath :

" In olde dayes of the kyng Arthour
Of which that Britouns speken gret honour,
All was this lond fulfilled of fayrie ;
The elf-queen with hir joly compaignie,
Daunced ful oft in many a grene mede,
This was the old oppynyoun as I rede.
I speke of many hundrid yeres ago,
But now can no man see noon elves mo.
For now the grete charite and prayeres
Of lymytours and other holy freres,
That sechen every lond and every streme,
As thick as motis in the sonne-beme.

*   *   *   *   *   *   *

That makith that there ben no fayeries
For ther as wont was to walken an elf,
Ther walkith noon but the lymytour himself,
As he goth in his lymytatioun,
Wommen may now go safely up and doun,
In every bussch, and under every tre,

There is none other incubus but he," &c. The genius of Shakespear converting whatever it handled into gold, has been singularly happy in its display of the fairy mythology. I know not whether anything can be imagined to go beyond the flights of his imagination on the subject ; and it seems to realize all that has been fabled of magic, when he exerts his creative fancy in giving to

" These airy nothings,
A local habitation and a name."

That accomplished antiquary, the Rev. Joseph Hunter, long since drew attention to the work of Leo Allatius on certain Greek superstitions of modern times, printed in 1645, as illustrating the fairy mythology of *A Midsummer Night's Dream*, and he remarks that at that date at all events the Greeks were as familiar as ourselves with all these legends and fancies, and that Robin Goodfellow or Puck was invested with the same attributes as he is held to possess here. *New Illustrations of Shakespear*, 1845, i., 286. An amusing scene is introduced into the "Merry Wives of Windsor," 1602, where Falstaff is pinched black and blue by the pretended fairies, Mistress Quickly and her confederates. Selden observes that there was never a merry world since the fairies left dancing and the parson left conjuring. The opinion of the latter kept thieves in awe, and did as much good in a country as a Justice of Peace. In the superstitions and customs concerning children, I have before noticed their practice of stealing unbaptized infants and leaving their own progeny in their stead. Puttenham mentions this as an opinion of the nurses. *Arte of English Poesie*, 1589, p. 144. It is also noticed in the "Irish Hudibras," 1689 :—

"Drink dairies dry, and stroke the Cattle:
Steal sucklings, and through key-holes fling,
Topeing and dancing in a ring."

—P. 122. It was an article in the popular creed concerning fairies, that they were a kind of intermediate beings, partaking of the nature both of men and spirits : that they had material bodies and yet the power of making themselves invisible and of passing them through any sort of enclosures. They were thought to be remarkably small in stature, with fair complexions, from which last circumstance they have derived their English name. The habits of both sexes of fairies are represented to have been generally green. With all the passions and wants of human beings, they are represented as great lovers and patrons of cleanliness and propriety, for the observance of which they were said frequently to reward good servants by dropping money into their shoes in the night; and on the other hand they were reported to punish most severely the sluts and slovens by pinching them black and blue. This tradition is illustrated by "Robin Good-Fellow, his Mad Prankes and Merry Jests," 1628, where the tricks of the fairies are related. But Jonson, in his song, "The Pranks of Puck," has deviated from the old prose narrative, which, though not now known in any impression earlier than in 1628, was clearly in existence before Jonson began to write, and also from the metrical tale founded on it, entitled "The Merry

Puck." Jonson attributes to Robin, on what appears to be insufficient authority what the "Mad Prankes" and the poem give to the fairies Pinch and Pach. Hazlitt's *Fairy Tales*, &c., 1875. Thus Lluellin :

— "We nere pity girles, that doe
Find no treasure in their shoe,
But are nip't by the tyrannous fairy.
List the noice of the chaires,
Wakes the wench to her pray'rs
Queen Mab comes worse than a witch in,
Back and sides she entailes
To the print of her nailes,
She'l teach her to snort in the kitchin."

And in Browne's "Pastorals," 1614 :

"Where oft the Fairy Queen
At twy-light sate and did command her Elues
To pinch those maids that had not swept their shelues :
And further, if by maidens ouer-sight
Within doores water were not brought at night :
Or if they spread no table, set no bread,
They shall haue nips from toe vnto the head :
And for the maid that had perform'd each thing
She in the water-paile bade leaue a ring."

Roxb. Lib., ed. i., 66. Lilly, in his "Life and Times," tells us that fairies love neatness and cleanness of apparel, a strict diet, and upright life: "fervent prayers unto God," he adds, "conduce much to the assistance of those who are curious these ways." He means, it should seem, those who wish to cultivate an acquaintance with them. Concerning fairies, King James has the following passages: "That there was a king and queene of Phairie, that they had a jolly court and traine—they had a teynd and dutie, as it were of all goods—they naturally rode and went, eate and dranke, and did all other actions like natural men and women. Witches have been transported with the phairie to a hill, which opening, they went in and there saw a faire Queen, who being now lighter, gave them a stone that had sundrie vertues." *Demonology*, p. 132. In Poole's "Parnassus," 1657, are given the names of the fairy court: "Oberon the Emperor, Mab the Empress. Perriwiggin, Perriwinckle, Puck, Hob-goblin, Tomalin, Tom Thumb, Courtiers. Hop, Mop, Drop, Pip, Trip, Skip, Tub, Tib, Tick, Pink, Pin, Quick, Gill, Im, Tit, Wap, Win, Nit, the maids of honour. Nymphidia, the mother of the Maids." An old writer undertakes to explain why Englishmen creep to the chimney in winter and summer also: — "Doth not the warm zeal of an Englishman's devotion (who was ever observed to contend most stifly pro aris et focis) make them maintain and defend the sacred hearth, as the sanctuary and chief place of residence of the tutelary lares and household gods, and the only court where the lady fairies convene to dance and revel?" *Paradoxical Assertions* by R. H., 1664, part 2, p. 14. Randolph, in his "Amyntas," 1638, describes the Queen's palace: "A curious park paled round about with pick-teeth— a house made all with mother of pearle— an ivory tennis court—a nutmeg parlour —a saphyre dairy room—a ginger hall— chambers of agate—kitchens all of crystal —the jacks are gold—the spits are all of Spanish needles." "Grant that the sweet fairies may nightly put money in your shoes, and sweepe your house cleane," occurs as one of the good wishes introduced by Holiday in his "Marriage of the Arts," 1618, signat. E verso.

Gertrude. Good lord, that there are no fairies nowadays, Syn.

Syndefy. Why, Madam?

Gertrude. To do miracles, and bring ladies money."—*Eastward Hoe*, 1605, v. i. "My grandmother," says the author of "Round about our Coal Fire," (circa 1730), "has often told me of fairies dancing upon our greene, and that they were little little creatures clothed in green." The author has these farther particulars of the popular notions concerning them. "The moment anyone saw them and took notice of them, they were struck blind of an eye. They lived under ground, and generally came out of a molehill." The same writer has the subsequent passage: "When the master and mistress were laid on their pillows, the men and maids, if they had a game at romps and blundered up stairs, or jumbled a chair, the next morning every one would swear 'twas the fairies, and that they heard them stamping up and down stairs all night, crying Water's lock'd, Water's lock'd, when there was not water in every pail in the kitchen." P. 42. I know not why, but they are reported to have been particularly fond of making cakes, and to have been very noisy during the operation. It was a common superstition that, if the gifts or favours of a fairy were revealed by the recipient, they vanished or were discontinued. Of this we have an example in the injunction given by the fairy to Sir Launfal, and elsewhere. Field, in "A Woman's a Weathercock," 1612, makes Nevill say to Scudamore:

"I see you labour with some serious thing,
And think (like fairy's treasure) to reveal it
Will cause it vanish."

A charm against fairies was turning the coat. Thus Bishop Corbet in his "Iter Boreale":

—"William found
A meanes for our deliv'rance; turn your cloakes,
Quoth hee, for Pucke is busy in these oakes:
If ever we at Bosworth will be found
Then turne your cloakes, for this is fairy ground."

From another passage, it should seem that there was a popular belief that if you struck a fairy or walking spirit, that it would dissolve into air. Our prelate was just mentioning the turning of the cloak above:

"But, ere the witchcraft was perform'd, we meete
A very man, who had not cloven feete,
Tho' William, still of little faith, doth doubt,
'Tis Robin or some spirit walkes about.

Strike him, quoth he, and it will turne to aire,
Crosse yourselves thrice, and strike him —strike him that dare
Thought I, for sure this massie Forester
In blows will prove the better conjurer."

The Bishop was right, for it proved to be the keeper of the forest, who showed them their way which they had lost. The following on the same subject is from the ode by Collins on *The Superstitions of the Highlands*, 1788:

—'Still 'tis said, the Fairy people meet
Beneath each birken shade on mead or hill.
There each trim lass, that skims the milky store,
To the swart tribes their creamy bowls allots;
By night they sip it round the cottage door,
While airy minstrels warble jocund notes."

I have printed in my *Fairy Mythology of Shakespear*, 1875, some "Conjurations for Fairies," from two MSS. In the three old madrigals from Ravenscroft and Weelkes, inserted in the same volume, there seems to be no sufficient distinction made between two things very broadly distinct, I apprehend — the fairies or nymphs of Grecian mythology and the fairies or elves or modern European folk-lore.

Compare *Knockers*. The historian Wace informs us, in "Le Roman de Rou," that he went expressly to the forest of Brecheliant, in Bretagne, on a report which had reached him that there fairies were to be veritably seen; but he hunted every corner of the forest, and returned from his sleeveless errand, not a little vexed at his disappointment. "A fool," says he, "I went, and a fool I returned." Alfred Maury, *Les Forêts de la Gaule*, 1867, p. 331.

Fairies in Scotland.—It appears that in Scotland formerly "Fairies held from time immemorial certain fields which could not be taken away without gratifying those merry sprites by a piece of money" : but that at a later period (the 18th century) "Fairies, without requiring compensation, have renounced their possessions." From the same source we derive the following details respecting a remarkably romantic linn formed by the water of the Crichup, co. Dumfries, inaccessible in a great measure to real beings. *Stat. Acc. of Scotland*, xxi., 148. "This linn was considered as the habitation of imaginary ones; and at the entrance into it there was a curious cell or cave, called the Elf's Kirk, where, according to the superstition of the times, the imaginary inhabitants of the Linn were supposed to hold their meetings. This cave, proving a good free stone quarry, has lately (1794) been demolished for the purpose of building houses, and from being the abodes of elves, has been converted into habitations for men." Ibid., xiii., 245. "The Queen of Fairie, mentioned in Jean Weir's Indictment, is probably the same Sovereign with the Queen of Elf-land, who makes a figure in the case of Alison Pearson, 15th May, 1588; which I believe is the first of the kind in the Record." *Additions and Notes to Maclaurin's Arguments and Decisions in remarkable Cases.* Law Courts, Scotland, 1774, p. 726. In 1795, the statistical report on Stronsay and Eday, two parishes in Orkney, supplied the annexed items of information : "The common people of this district remain to this day so credulous, as to think that fairies do exist; that an inferior species of witchcraft is still practiced, and that houses have been haunted, not only in former ages, but that they are haunted, at least noises are heard which cannot be accounted for on rational principles, even in our days. An instance of the latter happened only three years ago, in the house of John Spence, boat-carpenter." xv., 430. Under another head (Parish of Kirkmichael) the report states: "Not more firmly established in this country is the belief in ghosts than that in fairies. The legendary records of fancy, transmitted from age to age, have assigned their mansions to that class of genii, in detached hillocks covered with verdure, situated on the banks of purling brooks, or surrounded by thickets of wood.

These hillocks are called sioth-dhunan, abbreviated sioth-anan, from sioth, peace, and dun, a mound. They derive this name from the practice of the Druids, who were wont occasionally to retire to green eminences to administer justice, establish peace, and compose differences between contending parties. As that venerable order taught a Saoghl hal, or World beyond the present, their followers, when they were no more, fondly imagined, that seats where they exercised a virtue so beneficial to mankind, were still inhabited by them in their disembodied state. In the autumnal season, when the moon shines from a serene sky, often is the wayfaring traveller arrested by the musick of the hills, more melodious than the straine of Orpheus. Often struck with a more solemn scene, he beholds the visionary hunters engaged in the chace, and pursuing the deer of the clouds, while the hollow rocks, in long-sounding echoes, reverberate their cries. "There are several now living, who assert that they have seen and heard this aërial hunting, and that they have been suddenly surrounded by visionary forms, and assailed by a multitude of voices. About fifty years ago (this was written about 1793), a clergyman in the neighbourhood, whose faith was more regulated by the scepticism of philosophy than the credulity of superstition, could not be prevailed upon to yield his assent to the opinion of the times. At length, however, he felt from experience that he doubted what he ought to have believed. One night as he was returning home, at a late hour, from a presbytery, he was seized by the fairies, and carried aloft into the air. Through fields of æther and fleecy-clouds he journied many a mile, descrying, like Sancho Panza on his Clavileno, the earth far distant below him, and no bigger than a nut-shell. Being thus sufficiently convinced of the reality of their existence, they let him down at the door of his own house, where he afterward often recited to the wondering circle the marvellous tale of his adventure," xii., 461. A note adds : "Notwithstanding the progressive increase of knowledge and proportional decay of superstition in the Highlands, these genii are still supposed by many of the people to exist in the woods and sequestered valleys of the mountains, where they frequently appear to the lonely traveller, clothed in green, with dishevelled hair floating over their shoulders, and with faces more blooming than the vermil blush of a summer morning. At night in particular, when fancy assimilates to its own preconceived ideas every appearance and every sound, the wandering enthusiast is frequently entertained by their musick, more melodious than he ever before heard. It is curious to observe, how much this agreeable delusion corresponds with the superstitious opinion of the Romans, concerning the same class of genii, represented under different names. The Epicurean Lucretius describes the credulity in the following beautiful verses :

"Hæc loca capripedes satyros, nymphasque tenere
Finitimi pingunt, et faunos esse loquuntur;
Quorum noctivago strepitu, ludoque jocanti
Adfirmant volgo taciturna silentia rumpi
Chordarumque sonos fieri, dulcesque querelas
Tibia quas fundit digitas pulsata canentum" :

A farther note by Brand himself in reference to the above incident says :
"In plain English, I should suspect that spirits of a different sort from fairies had taken the honest clergyman by the head, and though he has omitted the circumstance in his marvellous narration, I have no doubt but that the good man saw double on the occasion, and that his own mare, not fairies, landed him safe at his own door."

In a statistical report of the condition of Strachur and Stralachlan, co. Argyle, in the 18th century, occurs the subjoined passage: "About eight miles to the eastward of Cailleachvear, a small conical hill rises considerably above the neighbouring hills. It is seen from Inverary, and from many parts at a great distance. It is called Sien-Sluia, the fairy habitation of a multitude" : adding in a note, "A belief in fairies prevailed very much in the Highlands of old : nor at this day is it quite obliterated. A small conical hill, called Sien, was assigned them for a dwelling, from which melodious music was frequently heard, and gleams of light seen in dark nights." *Stat. Acc.*, iv., 560. Pinkerton, writing in 1799, informs us that "The fairies are little beings of doubtful character, sometimes benevolent, sometimes mischievous. On Hallowe'en and on some other evenings, they and the Gyar-Carlins are sure to be abroad and to stap those they meet and are displeased with, full of butter and heare-awns. In winter nights they are heard curling on every sheet of ice. Having a septennial sacrifice of a human being to make to the Devil, they sometimes carry away children, leaving little vixens of their own in the cradle. The diseases of cattle are very commonly attributed to their mischievous operation. Cows are often elf-shot." *Heron's Journey*, ii., 227. A writer describing the superstitions current in the vicinity of

St. Andrew's, Scotland, says : "In private breweries, to prevent the interference of the fairies, a live coal is thrown into the vat. A cow's milk no fairy can take away, if a burning coal is conducted across her back and under her belly immediately after her delivery. The same mischievous elves cannot enter into a house at night if, before bedtime, the lower end of the crook or iron chain, by which a vessel is suspended over the fire, be raised up a few links." *Letter from Professor Playfair to Mr. Brand*, January 26, 1804.

Fairy Butter.—A species of gelatine. See Forby's *Vocabulary of East Anglia*, 1830, p. 108.

Fairy Poetry.—In the "Maydes Metamorphosis," 1601, occurs the following fairy song :—

"Round about, round about, in a fine ring-a :
Thus we dance, thus we dance, and thus we sing-a :
Trip and go, to and fro, over this green-a,
All about, in and out, for our brave queen-a.

Round about, round about, in a fine ring-a :
Thus we dance, thus we dance, and thus we sing-a :
Trip and go, to and fro, over this green-a,
All about, in and out, for our brave queen-a.

We've danc'd round about in a fine ring-a :
We have danc'd lustily, and thus we sing-a :
All about, in and out, over this green-a,
To and fro, trip and go, to our brave queen-a."

So, again, Drayton :
"*Doron.* Come, frolick youth, and follow me,
My frantique boy, and I'le show thee
The countrey of the fayries."

—*Muses Elizium*, 1630, p. 24. Randolph describes fairy hunting :
"*Dor.* I hope King Oberon and his royal Mab are well?
Joe. They are. I never saw their Graces eat such a meal before.
Joe. They are rid a hunting.
Dor. Hare, or deer, my lord?
Joe. Neither : a brace of snails of the first head."

I find the following in Herrick's "Hesperides :

"*The Fairies.*"
If ye will with Mab finde grace,
Set each platter in its place;
Rake the fier up and get
Water in ere sun be set:

Wash your pailes and clense your
    dairies,
Sluts are loathsome to the fairies:
Sweep your house, who doth not so,
Mab will pinch her by the toe."

There are some allusions in Corbet's
ballad entitled "The Fairies Farewell."

"Farewell rewards and fairies,
    Good house wives now may say;
For now fowle sluts in dairies
    Do fare as well as they:
And, though they sweepe their hearths
    no lesse
Then maides were wont to doe,
Yet who of late for cleanlinesse
    Findes six pence in her shooe?

Lament, lament. old Abbies,
    The fairies lost command,
They did but change priest's babies,
    And now grown puritanes,
Who live as changelings ever since
    For love of your demaines.

At morning and at evening both
    You merry were and glad,
So little care of sleepe and sloath
    These pretty ladies had:
When Tom came home from labour,
    Or Cisse to milking rose,
Then merrily went their tabor,
    And nimbly went their toes.
Witnesse those rings and roundelayes
    Of theirs which yet remaine,
Were footed in Queene Maries dayes
    On many a grassy plaine.

A tell-tale in their company
    They never could endure,
And who so kept not secretly
    Their mirth was punisht sure.
It was a iust and Christian deed
    To pinch such black and blew:
O how the Common-wealth doth need
    Such Iustices as you!"

The following is in Poole's *Parnassus*,
1657, p. 333:

"There is Mab, the mistress fairy,
That doth nightly rob the dairy,
And can help or hurt the churning
As she please, without discerning.
She that pinches country wenches
If they rub not clean their benches:
And with sharper nails remembers,
When they rake not up the embers.
But if so they chance to feast her,
In their shooe she drops a tester.
This is she that empties cradles,
Takes out children, puts in ladles.
Trains forth midwives in their slum-
    ber
With a sive, the holes to number;
And then leads them from their
    boroughs
Thorough ponds and water-furrows."

Here is Dr. King's description of "Orpheus' Fairy Entertainment":—

"A roasted ant that's nicely done
By one small atom of the sun;
These are flies eggs in moon-shine
    poach'd;
This is a flea's thigh in collops scotch'd,
'Twas hunted yesterday i' th' Park,
And like t' have scap'd us in the dark.
This is a dish entirely new,
Butterflies brains dissolv'd in dew;
These lovers' vows, these courtiers'
    hopes,
Things to be eat by microscopes:
These sucking mites, a glow-worm's
    heart,
This is a delicious rainbow-tart."

King's Works, 1776, 111, 112. And Pope
says:

"Of airy elves by moon-light shadows
    seen,
The silver token and the circled green."
—*Rape of the Lock.*

Fairs. — A fair is a greater kind of
market, granted to any town by privilege,
for the more speedy and commodious providing of such things as the place stands
in need of. Fairs are generally kept once
or twice in a year. Proclamation is to be
made how long they are to continue, and
no person is allowed to sell any goods after
the time of the fair is ended, on forfeiture
of double their value. The term appears
to be derived from Latin *foris*, outside the
town, whence the French *foire*, because
fairs, as distinguished from markets, were
held beyond the urban precincts. Warton tells us, that before flourishing towns
were established, and the necessaries of
life, from the convenience of communication and the increase of provincial civility,
could be procured in various places, goods
and commodities of every kind were
chiefly sold at fairs; to these, as to one
universal mart, the people resorted periodically, and supplied most of their wants
for the ensuing year. The display of
merchandise and the conflux of customers,
at these principal and almost only em-
poria of domestic commerce, were prodigious: and they were often held on open
and extensive plains on that account as
well as to prevent infection. Robert of
Brunne, in 1303, notices that fairs disappeared in a night. He likens to their
short existence ill-gotten wealth:

"Here mayst thou se, euyl wunne
    thyng,
With eyre shal neuer make gode endyng;
Namly with thyng of holy cherche
Shalt thou neuer spede wel to werche,
That mayst thou se by parsones eyres:
Hyt fareth wyth hem as doth with these
    feyres;

Now ys the feyre byggede weyl,
And on the morne ys ther neuer a deyl.
Ryche tresoure now furthe men leye,
And on the touther day hyt ys all
  aweye."

Handlyng Synne, i. ed. Furnivall, p.
292. A constant incidence of the grant
of manors in ancient times was the leave
to establish local fairs and markets, to
the tolls of which the lord might be entitled, and which would gradually tend to
develope his property. Of attendance at fairs on the Sabbath, Humphrey
Roberts of King's Langley speaks in his
"Complaint for Reformation," 1572:
"Leaue therefore," he says, "your carefull toyle and labours vpon the Saboth
day : as cartyng, carying of sackes and
packes, byinge and sellyng: yea keping
of faiers and markets—." Sometimes,
when the day fell on the Sabbath, the fair
was held on the Monday, as Hearne says
of Wantage Fair in 1723, where among
other sports introduced were backsword or
cudgel-play between the hill-country and
the vale-country, Berkshire being celebrated for this amusement. Wantage at
this time enjoyed three fairs, one on July
7 (Translation of St. Thomas á Becket), a
second on October 6 (St. Faith's Day),
and a third, then of recent origin, called
the Constable's Fair, granted by the high
constable after being chosen for Wantage.
Hearne's *Diary,* July 10, 1723. In 1872
the fairs at Charlton, near Woolwich, and
Blackheath, were held for the last time.
The former was known as Horn Fair, and
from the disorderly character of the proceedings arose the proverb, "All is fair
at Horn Fair." Hazlitt's *Proverbs,* 1882,
p. 49. Greenwich Fair was still kept within
living memory,one of the attractions being
that of rolling down the hill. There
is a small broadside account in doggerel verse of the humours of Bow Fair.
Among the attendants at fairs in the
olden time, the sharpers and pickpockets
mustered pretty strongly. In the ballad
of "Ragged and Torn and True," it is
said :

  "The pick-pockets in a throng,
    At a market or a faire,
  Will try whose purse is strong,
    That they may the money share."

In the *Life and Adventures of
Bamfylde Moore Carew,* 1745, we read
how at Bridgewater Fair the deaf,
blind, dumb, lame, and other sham-
mers were present in great force,
and how on one occasion the mayor
having let it be known that he intended
to cure them of their complaints, caused
them to be taken to the Darkhouse, where
a medical man examined them, but (per-

haps intentionally) leaving the door unlocked, they all decamped.

There are two old English proverbs that
relate to fairs : "Men speak of the fair
as things went with them there "; as also,
"To come a day after the fair." The
first seems intended to rhyme. The second
is still perfectly common.

Mr. Cornelius Walford has collected
in his volume on the subject, 1883,
a large body of information on Fairs
in England, their origin, antiquity,
development, and disappearance. Some
of those still held date from Anglo-
Saxon times, and were established by virtue of royal grants ; they necessarily occasioned a body of statutory enactments
peculiarly bearing on their incidence, of
which not the least remarkable and
troublesome was the complication arising
from the strong alien element in these
institutions. C. Walford, *Fairs, Past
and Present,* 1883, p. 19, et seqq. ; Wheatley, *Round about Piccadilly and Pall
Mall,* 1870, pp. 200-02. In his valuable
paper on the *King's Peace,* Mr. Hubert
Hall has explained the meaning and
origin of the "Peace of the Fair," or in
other words the official regulations for the
maintenance of order and justice in view
of the large body of foreigners whom these
institutions gradually attracted. *Antiquary,* November 1888, p. 189.

At the Lammas Fair at Exeter
and at Barnstaple the opening of
the proceedings was denoted by the
hoisting of a large glove on a pole,
and at the latter place, in more
recent times, the pole was dressed
with dahlias. By the Statute of 2 Edw.
III. c. 13, it was ordered that "A cry
shalbe made at the begynnyng of euery
feyre how longe it shall indure & that
none shall sell after vpon payne to be gre-
uously punyshed agaynst the Kynge."
The authority of the proprietor or lord
of the fair was only co-existent in duration with the fair itself ; merchants continuing to trade after the legal conclusion
of the fair were amerced in double the
value of the goods so sold ; nothing but
the necessaries of life were to be on sale
on feast-days and Sundays ; except only
"fore sonday in the heruyst"; the Londoners were permitted to attend all fairs
under pain of ten pounds' fine to the hin-
derer or hinderers. The articles are
"Wine, wax, beiffes, muttons, wheite, &
malt." This proves that fairs still continued to be the principal marts for purchasing necessaries in large quantities,
which now are supplied by frequent trading towns : and the mention of beiffes and
muttons (which are salted oxen or sheep)
shews that at so late a period they knew
little of breeding cattle. It may seem
surprising that their own neighbourhood,

including the cities of Oxford and Coventry, could not supply them with commodities neither rare nor costly : which they thus fetched at a considerable expense of carriage. It is a rubric in some of the monastic rules, " De Euntibus ad Nundinas " ; i.e., concerning those who go to fairs. Warton's *H. E. P.* by Hazlitt, ii., 260.

Prior to 1406, at Oswestry in Shropshire, the Welsh tenants of the lord were accustomed to keep watch and ward for three days and nights at the four gates of the town during the fairs of St. Andrew and St. Oswald ; but owing to the irregularities committed by their men the service was commuted for a payment, which went to hire Englishmen to perform the same duty. Pennant's *Tours in Wales*, 1810, i., 345-6. Minstrels and balladsingers, it seems, attended fairs in the time of Elizabeth, and we hear of two men, Outroaring Dick and Wat Wimbers, gaining twenty shillings a day at Braintree fair in Essex. They were noted trebles. Hazlitt's Warton, 1871, iv., 428. Great complaint was made in the reign of Henry VI. of the irregularities and disorderly proceedings at our English fairs, especially on festivals, such as Sunday, Good Friday, Ascension Day, and so forth, and in 23 Hen. VI. we find a petition submitted to that monarch for the suppression of fairs throughout the country on holy days set apart for the service of the Church, including the Sabbath itself. The petitioners required the fulfilment of their prayer from after the next Michaelmas then ensuing in perpetuity ; but the king declined, in his response, to make more than a partial and temporary concession. *Antiq. Repert.*, 1807, iii., 444-5. It appears from the " Northumberland Household Book," 1512, that the stores of his lordship's house at Wresill, for the whole year, were laid in from fairs. From the ancient fabliau of the " Merchant turned Monk," and from other sources, we gather that the same was the case in France, if not in other continental countries, at this early period. Braithwaite, in describing what ought to be the qualifications of the chief officers of an earl, writes : " They must be able to iudge, not onely of the prices, but of the goodnes of all kindes of corne, cattell, and other household provisions ; and the better to enable themselves therto, are oftentimes to ride to fayres and great markets, and ther to have conference with graziers and purveiors, being men of witt and experience—" Some Rules and Orders for the government of the house of an Earle. (circâ 1640), *apud Miscell. Antiq. Angl.*, 1821. Hearne furnishes an interesting account of St. Frideswide's Fair at Oxford, originally granted by

Henry I. to be held for twelve days together within the precincts of the priory, beginning with the feast of St. Benedict, but removed by Henry III. to St. Frideswide's Day, October 19. It was kept in St. Frideswide's meadow, and during its continuance the prior exercised supreme jurisdiction over the village of Oxford, and subsequently over the city, of which the keys were delivered to him for the time being. Abuses, however, gradually led to the discontinuance of this custom in the reign of Richard II., when the Chancellor of the University interdicted the farther visits of the traders, and so abolished the fair. Hearne's *Diary*, June 8, 1730. In *Canidia, or the Witches*, by R. D., 1683, is furnished a not very flattering account of the proceedings at Sturbridge Fair, vulgarly called Stirbitch Fair. It is curious to find, however, that in 1686 the library of James Chamberlaine was sold there.

The ceremonial of proclaiming Bridge Fair was duly observed at Peterborough in 1898. At noon on the 4th of October the Mayor and Corporation walked in procession to the bridge spanning the river, where the Town Crier declared the fair open, to be held as well in Northamptonshire as in Huntingdonshire. The original charter dates back to the time of Henry VIII. According to custom, the Mayor afterwards entertained the members of the Corporation to a sausage and champagne luncheon at an hotel adjacent to the fair field. In the Churchwardens' Accounts of St. Laurence Parish, Reading, A.D. 1499, is the following article : — " Receypt. It. Rec. at the Fayer for a stonding in the Church porch, iiijd." Coates' *History of Reading*, p. 214. By " Advertisements partly for due order in the publique administration of Common Prayers," &c., 25 Jan. 7 Eliz., it was enjoined, "that in all faires and common markets, falling uppon the Sunday, there be no shewing of any wares before the service be done." Machyn in his Diary mentions that on St. Peter's Day (June 29), 1557, a small fair, for the sale of wool and other like commodities, was held in the churchyard of St. Margaret's, in the City of London.

A conspicuous feature in the management of these institutions was the system of tolls exacted from the frequenters, especially in the case of foreigners. It used to be said that in some of the principal French fairs the dues absorbed half the profits of alien vendors. At the same time, it seems to have been often customary to allow goods imported from other countries to enter, and the unsold portion to leave, ports on a reduced scale of harbour and excise dues. But at Corby, co. of North-ampton, between Kettering and King's Cliff, they still hold, once in twenty years, under a charter of Elizabeth, confirmed by Charles II., what is termed Pole Fair on May 19. By the said charter the men and tenants of the ancient demesne of Corby, once belonging to the St. Johns, subsequently to the Willoughby D'Eres-bys and Latimers, and now to Lady Car-digan, were freed from town and bridge tolls throughout the kingdom, and from serving on juries and in the Militia. The charter is read at four o'clock in the morn-ing at each entrance to the village; the stocks are brought out; bars or poles are laid across all the approaches; and all, who do not pay the toll, are carried—the men on poles, and the women on chairs, round the streets, and placed in durance, till the demand is met. In 1902 the fair was very numerously attended, and on the 21st May the President of the National Record Association visited the village, and was pleased to find that the ancient usage had not been relinquished. The president was himself chaired, and borne through the streets, preceded by a band, placed in the stocks with the oldest inhabitant, and duly released on compliance with the re-quisition.

At Barnet Fair, they at all events, when we were last there, sold a varied assortment of gilt gingerbread, re-presenting soldiers, animals, and other figures. The four Cambridge fairs were: Reach Fair, held in Rogation Week; Barnwell or Midsummer Fair; the Nuns' or Garlic Fair; and Stourbridge Fair. The best account of the last is in Gunning's *Reminiscences* (1789-1854). Compare *Sturbridge Fair*, infrâ. A picture of Harlow Bush Fair, Essex, was formerly on the wall of the first-floor room at the old Elephant Tavern in Fenchurch Street, and was attributed to Hogarth. Timbs, *Clubs and Club-Life*, 1872, p. 401. It was at the Fair of Abingdon in Berkshire, that the servants of the house were ab-sent when Amy Robsart was murdered at Cumnor. A fair is usually held at Read-ing on Candlemas Day for cattle and horses; but of late the day for holding it has not always been rigidly observed. Mr. Brand gathered from a newspaper that an annual fair was then held in the Broad Gate at Lincoln on the 14th September, called Fool's Fair, for the sale of cattle, so called, on that authority, as follows: "King William and his Queen having visited Lincoln, while on their tour through the Kingdom, made the citizens an offer to serve them in any manner they liked best. They asked for a fair, though it was harvest, when few people can attend it, and though the town had no trade nor any manufacture. The King smiled, and granted their request; observ-ing, that it was a humble one indeed." In the eighteenth century Thomas Day, author of *Sandford and Merton*, 1786, in-stituted what was known as Fairlop Fair, which used to be opened in Epping Forest by drawing a ship made of one fir tree on a trunk with six horses round a cer-tain area in the Forest three times.

Among the Hardwicke Papers, re-cently sold to the British Museum, were grants by the Crown of fairs to Hawarden, co. Flint, Woburn, co. Bedford (on the 1st of January yearly, &c., from 1762), and to Westcot, near Dorking (1726). In the last century, Ly-sons, speaking of the numerous fairs at Okehampton, Devon, says that the holi-day fair held on the Saturday after Christ-mas was called the Giglet. *Magna Britan-nia, Devonshire*, p. 370. At Faversham, in Kent, two fairs were formerly allowed, each lasting ten days. One, called St. Valentine's Fair, commenced on Febru-ary 14, the other on August 1st. In the 18th century, in the parish of Wamphray, in Scotland, it seems that hiring fairs used to be much frequented. "Those," it is said "who are to hire, wear a green sprig in their hat: and it is very seldom that servants will hire in any other place." *Stat. Acc.*, xxi., 457. Whit-stable Fair was held on Good Friday. In two poetical writings of the earlier half of the 18th century are descriptions of the old-fashioned fair worth reproducing:

"Now pedlars' stalls with glitt'ring
    toys are laid,
The various fairings of the country
    maid;
Long silken laces hang upon the twine,
And rows of pins and amber bracelets
    shine.
Here the tight lass, knives, combs and
    scissars spies,
And looks on thimbles with desiring
    eyes.
The mountebank now treads the stage,
    and sells
His pills, his balsams, and his ague-
    spells;
Now o'er and o'er the nimble tumbler
    springs,
And on the rope the ventrous maiden
    swings;
Jack Pudding in his party-colour'd
    jacket
Tosses the gloves, and jokes at every
    packet;
Here raree-shows are seen, and Punch's
    feats,
And pockets pick'd in crouds, and vari-
    ous cheats."
—*Gay's Sixth Pastoral.*

"Next morn, I ween, the village char-
ter'd fair,
A day that's ne'er forgot throughout
the year:
Soon as the lark expands her auburn
fan,
Foretelling day, before the day began,
Then 'Jehu Ball' re-echoes down the
lane,
Crack goes the whip, and rattling
sounds the chain.
With tinkling bells the stately beast
grown proud.
Champs on the bit, and neighing roars
aloud.
The bridles dotted o'er with many a
flow'r,
The six-team'd waggon forms a leafy
bow'r.
Young Damon whistled to Dorinda's
song,
The fiddle tuneful play'd the time along.
At length arriv'd, the statute fills the
fair,
Dorcas and Lydia, Bella too was there:
Favours and gauzes, variegated gay,
Punch loudly squeaks, the drum pro-
claims the play.
The pole high rear'd, the dance, the
gambol shew'd
Mirth and diversion to the gaping
crowd:
Sam with broad smile, and Poll with
dimpled face,
Revers'd the apron, shews she wants a
place.
The race in sacks, the quoit, the cir-
cling reel,
While Prue more thoughtful buys a
spinning wheel.
The grinning Andrew perch'd on Folly's
stool.
Proves th' artificial, not the natural
fool:
For Hodge declares he thinks, devoid of
art,
He must be wise, who acts so well his
part !"
—H. Rowe's *Poems*, 1796.

One of the constant attractions in fairs
both in London and in the provinces was
the theatrical show, usually in a booth,
and limited to a brief representation, to
suit a succession of spectators. Favourite subjects were the *Creation, Noah's
Flood,* the *Nine Worthies,* and *Punchinello,* or *Punch and Judy.* Hazlitt's
Manual of Old Plays, 1892, pp. 34, 167,
187. The Towneley series of Mysteries is
described as having been periodically exhibited at Woodkirk Fair, as well
as at Wakefield, and it is sometimes referred to as the Woodkirk series.

We are told that in the 18th century a
practice still continued at Dundonald, in
Ayrshire, "of kindling a large fire, or
tawnle as it is usually termed, of wood,

upon some eminence, and making merry
around it, upon the eve of the Wednesday
of Marymass Fair in Irvine (which begins
on the third Monday of August and continues the whole week). As most fair
days in the country were formerly popish
holidays, and their eves were usually
spent in religious ceremonies and in diversions, it has been supposed that tawnles
were first lighted up by our Catholic
fathers, though some derive their origin
from the Druidical Times." From the
same source we learn that Christ's Kirk
May Fair, Kenethmont, Aberdeenshire,
"was kept on the Green, and in the
night; hence it was by the people called
Sleepy-market. About a century ago,
the proprietor changed it from night
to day; but so strong was the pre-
possession of the people in favour of the
old custom, that, rather than comply with
the alteration, they chose to neglect it
altogether." The same account, speaking of Marykirk, co. Kincardine, says:
"On the outside of the church, strongly
fixed to the wall, are the Joggs. These
were made use of, where the weekly market and annual fair stood, to confine and
punish those who had broken the peace,
or used too much freedom with the property of others. The stocks were used for
the feet, and the joggs for the neck of the
offender, in which he was confined, at
least, during the time of the fair."
Though the worthy minister who drew up
this account has omitted the etymology of
joggs, I should think it a very obvious
one—from *Jugum,* a yoke. *Stat. Account
of Scotland,* vii., 622; xiii., 77: xviii., 612.

In Mr. G. L. Gomme's *Presidential Address* to the Folk-Lore Society, 1894, occurs an account of an early usage at a
place in Lanarkshire, about the time of
St. Luke's Fair, and the President points
out that the Kourds have a precisely similar cult. The narrative is rather long;
but it is too curious to omit or abridge,
and so I crave leave to reproduce it:—

"An ancient custom, for the observance
of which Rutherglen has long been famous, is the baking of sour cakes. Some
peculiar circumstances attending the operation render an account of the manner
in which it is done not altogether unnecessary. About eight or ten days before St.
Luke's Fair (for they are baked at no
other time of the year), a certain quantity
of oatmeal is made into dough with warm
water, and laid up in a vessel to ferment.
Being brought to a proper degree of fer-
mentation and consistency, it is rolled up
into balls, proportionable to the intended
largeness of the cakes. With the dough
is commonly mixed a small quantity of
sugar, and a little aniseed or cinnamon.
The baking is executed by women only,

and they seldom begin their work till after sunset, and a night or two before the fair. A large space of the house, chosen for the purpose, is marked out by a line drawn upon it. The area within is considered as consecrated ground, and is not, by any of the bystanders, to be touched with impunity. A transgression incurs a small fine, which is always laid out on drinks for the use of the company. This hallowed spot is occupied by six or eight women, all of whom, except the toaster, seat themselves on the ground in a circular figure, having their feet turned towards the fire. Each of them is provided with a bake-board about two feet square, which they hold on their knees. The woman who toasts the cakes, which is done on a girdle suspended over the fire, is called the queen or bride, and the rest are called her maidens. These are distinguished from one another by names given them for the occasion. She who sits next the fire towards the east is called the Todler; her companion on the left hand is called the Hodler, and the rest have arbitrary names given them by the bride —as Mrs. Baker, best and worst maids, etc. The operation is begun by the Todler, who takes a ball of the dough, forms it into a small cake, and then casts it on the bake-board of the Hodler, who beats it out a little thinner. This being done, she in her turn throws it on the board of her neighbour, and thus it goes round from east to west in the direction of the course of the sun, until it comes to the toaster, by which time it is as thin and smooth as a sheet of paper. The first cake that is cast on the girdle is usually named as a gift to some well-known cuckold, from a superstitious opinion that thereby the rest will be preserved from mischance. Sometimes the cake is too thin as to be carried by the current of air up into the chimney. As the baking is wholly performed by the hand, a great deal of noise is the consequence. The beats, however, are not irregular, nor destitute of an agreeable harmony, especially when they are accompanied with vocal music, which is frequently the case. Great dexterity is necessary, not only to beat out the cakes with no other instrument than the hand, so that no part of them shall be thicker than another, but especially to cast them from one board on another without ruffling or breaking them. The toasting requires considerable skill, for which reason the most experienced person in the company is chosen for that part of the work. One cake is sent round in quick succession to another, so that none of the company is suffered to be idle. The whole is a scene of activity, mirth, and diversion, and might afford an excellent subject for a picture. As there is no account, even by

tradition itself, concerning the origin of this custom, it must be very ancient. The bread thus baked was, doubtless, never intended for common use. It is not easy to conceive why mankind, especially in a rude age, would strictly observe so many ceremonies, and be at so great pains in making a cake which, when folded together, makes but a scanty mouthful. Besides, it is always given away in presents to strangers who frequent the Fair. The custom seems to have been originally derived from paganism, and to contain not a few of the sacred rites peculiar to that impure religion—as the leavened dough, and the mixing it with sugar and spices, the consecrated ground, etc., etc. But the particular deity for whose honour these cakes were at first made is not, perhaps, easy to determine."

In his *Jolly Beggars*, Burns makes the girl, who is enamoured of "Soldier laddie," meet him at Cunningham Fair, dressed out in all his military finery.

Fosbrooke tells us, "Much quarrelling and fighting sometimes attended the monastic fairs, held in the churchyard; and Henry observes from Muratori, that, "When a fair was held in Italy within the precincts of a cathedral or monastery, it was not uncommon to oblige every man to take an oath at the gate, before he was admitted, that he would neither lie, nor steal, nor cheat, while he continued in the fair." *British Monachism*, ii., 217. According to Olaus Magnus, the ancient Northern nations held annual ice fairs. Frost fairs and blanket fairs have been known on the Thames. The last great frost fair among us was in 1814. See "Old Ballads illustrating the Great Frost of 1683-4" (Percy Soc.); and Handbook of Early English Lit. Art. Frosts. Down to our own time, the great fair at Nijni Novgorod in Russia formed the source of supply and exchange on a scale of unparalleled magnitude and variety. C. Walford's *Fairs Past and Present*, 1883. Compare *Ascension Day, Cherry Fairs, Cuckoo, Greenwich Fair, Bartholomew Fair, Honey Fair, Horn Fair, Sturbridge Fair*, &c.

Fairing.—It was customary at all fairs to present fairings, which are gifts, bought at these annual markets. The custom prevailed in the days of Chaucer, as appears by the subsequent passage in the "Wife of Bathes Prologue," where she boasts of having managed her several husbands so well:

"I governed hem so well after my lawe
That eche of hem ful blisful was, and
    fawe
To bringe me gay thinges fro the faire
They were ful glad," &c.

And in "Rusticæ Nundinæ," 1730:

> "Ad sua quisque redit; festivis Daph-
> nen Amyntas
> Exonerat Xeniis, dandoque astringit
> Amores."

When these institutions were more general and more important, considerable sums were laid out by wealthier persons in this way. The first Earl of Bristol, in his *Diary*, 1735-6-8, notes sums of £6 15s. 0d., £3 12s. 0d., and £7 7s. 0d., bestowed on members of his family for the purchase of fairings at Bury St. Edmunds. But of course, the more usual, and at least equally interesting and characteristic, home-bringings were of a humbler description, like that mentioned in the old song:—

> "O dear! what can the matter be?
> Johnny's so long at the fair:
> He promis'd to buy me a bunch of
> blue ribbons
> To tie up my bonnie brown hair."

Fairy Rings.—The haunts of fairies were thought to have been groves, mountains, the southern sides of hills, and verdant meadows, where their diversion was dancing hand in hand in a circle, as alluded to by Shakespear in his "Midsummer Night's Dream." The traces of their tiny feet are supposed to remain visible on the grass long afterward, and are called fairy-rings or circles. Shakespear's words are:

> "To dance on ringlets to the whistling
> wind."

"Ringlets of Grass," Dr. Grey observes, "are very common in meadows, which are higher, sowrer, and of a deeper green than the grass that grows round them: and by the common people are usually called fairy circles." Again, in "The Tempest," act v. sc. 1, Prospero says:

> "Ye elves ————you demy puppets,
> that
> By moon-shine do the green-sour ring-
> lets make,
> Whereof the ewe not bites."

So again,

> "To dew her orbs upon the green."

And Drayton:

> "They in their courses make that
> round,
> In meadows and in marshes found,
> Of them so call'd the fairy ground."

They are again alluded to in Randolph's "Amyntas":

> "They do request you now
> To give them leave to dance a fairy
> ring."

Browne, the Devonshire poet, describes:

> ―"a pleasant mead
> Where fairies often did their measures
> tread,
> Which in the meadows made such circles
> greene,
> As if with garlands it had crowned
> beene.
> Within one of these rounds was to be
> seene
> A hillocke rise, where oft the fairy
> queene
> At twy-light sate."

—*Pastorals* (Roxb. Lib. ed. i., 66). "They had fine musicke always among themselves," says an author already cited, "and danced in a moon-shiny night, around, or in a ring, as one may see at this day upon every common in England where mushroomes grow." *Round about our Coal Fire*, p. 41. The author of "Mons Catherinæ" has not forgotten to notice these ringlets in his poem:

> "Sive illic Lemurum populus sub nocte
> choreas
> Plauserit exiguas, viridesque attriverit
> herbas."

They are also mentioned in George Smith's "Pastorals," 1770, p. 24.

Olaus Magnus, "De Gentibus Septentrionalibus," writes: "Similes illis spectris, quæ in multis locis, præsertim nocturno tempore, suum saltatorium Orbem cum omnium Musarum concentu versare solent." It appears from the same author (ibid. p. 410) that these dancers always parched up the grass, and therefore it is properly made the office of Puck to refresh it. See Steevens's Note on Reed's edit. of Shakespear, 1803, vol. iv. p. 343. The most clear and satisfactory remarks by earlier writers on the origin of fairy rings are probably those of Dr. Wollaston, made during a few years' residence in the country. The cause of their appearance he ascribes to the growth of certain species of agaric, which so entirely absorb all nutriment from the soil beneath that the herbage is for a while destroyed. Mr. Herbert Spencer, following in the same track, shews that fairy rings are nothing more than the seeds shed by a particular kind of fungus, which, as Wollaston had previously observed, impoverishes the ground in which it grows to such an extent as to prevent the procreation of a new root in the second year. Thus the old fungus sheds its seed in a circular form, and perishes, leaving only the ring formed round it. But the same sort of process is observable of other species of vegetation, and in particular of the iris, which exhausts the soil in which it immediately grows, and throws out new roots beyond in search of fresh nourishment. A learned German, Baron von Reichenbach, reducing this superstition to that level of scientific commonplace which has already degraded the nightmare into indigestion, and the dwarf into convulsions, is inclined to recognise in these fancied fairy-rings or dances nothing more than " the operation of the phenomenon termed 'the odylic light' emitted from magnetic substances." But it seems proper to mention that in the " British Apollo," 1710, a physical cause was suspected, the rings being there assigned to the direct agency of lightning. In support of this hypothesis the reader may consult Priestley's " Present State of Electricity." See also No. cxvii. p. 391, of the " Philosophical Transactions," where it is stated that Mr. Walker, walking abroad after a storm of thunder and lightning, observed a round circle of about four or five yards diameter, whose rim was about a foot broad, newly burnt bare, as appeared from the colour and brittleness of the grass roots. See " Gent. Mag." for Dec. 1790. But in fact, Brand himself says : Some ascribe the phænomenon of the circle or ring, supposed by the vulgar to be traced by the fairies in their dances, to the effects of lightning, as being frequently produced after storms of that kind, and by the colour and brittleness of the grass-roots when first observed. The " Athenian Oracle," mentions a popular belief that " if a house be built upon the ground where fairy rings are, whoever shall inhabit therein does wonderfully prosper."

Fairy Sparks, &c.—Certain luminous appearances, often seen on clothes in the night, are called in Kent fairy sparks or shell-fire, as Ray informs us in his " East and South Country Words." I was (says Brand) told by Mr. Pennant, that there is a substance found at great depths in crevices of lime-stone rocks, in sinking for lead ore, near Holywell, in Flintshire, which is called Menyn Tylna Teg, or fairies' butter. So also in Northumberland the common people call a certain fungous excrescence, sometimes found about the roots of old trees, fairy butter. After great rains, and in a certain degree of putrefaction, it is reduced to a consistency which, together with its colour, makes it not unlike butter, and hence the name.

Faith's, St., Day.—(October 6). See *Love Charms.*

Falling Stars.—See *Aërolites.*

Falstaff, Shakespear's.—See *Death-Omens.*

Faring.—This is mentioned as a popular game at cards, or dice, or both,

in the " English Courtier and the Countrey Gentleman," 1586.

Faro.—Sometimes called *Pharaoh.* See Davis, *Suppl. Glossary,* 1881, p. 488.

Fast and Loose.—This game, played with a skewer and a leathern belt or girdle placed in folds edgewise on a table, is also known as Pricking at the Belt. A description of it by Sir John Hawkins occurs in a note to Davenport's *City Night-Cap* in Hazlitt's edition of Dodsley. It was a game at which vagrants (so-called gypsies) cheated common people out of their money. Comp. Nares, 1859, in v.

Fast-E'en Tuesday.—See *Shrove Tuesday.*

Faustus or **Faust.** — See my *National Tales and Legends,* 1892, for the earliest attempt to place this story on its true footing.

Favours. — In the " Defence of Conny-Catching," 1592, Signat, C 3, verso, is the following passage : " Is there not heere resident about London, a crew of terryble hacksters in the habite of gentlemen wel appareled, and yet some weare bootes for want of stockings, with a locke worne at theyr lefte eare for their mistrisse favour." The subsequent is taken from Lodge's " Wit's Miserie," 1596, p. 47 : " When he rides, you shall know him by his fan : and, if he walke abroad, and misse his mistres favour about his neck, arme, or thigh, he hangs the maid like the soldier in the field that is disarmed." In Marston's " Dutch Courtezan," a pair of lovers are introduced plighting their troth as follows :

" *Enter Freeville.* Pages with torches. Enter Beatrice above." After some very impassioned conversation, Beatrice says : " I give you faith; and prethee, since, poore soule ! I am so easie to beleeve thee, make it much more pitty to deceive me. Weare this slight favour in my remembrance " (throweth down a ring to him).

" *Freev.* Which, when I part from,
Hope, the best of life, ever part from me !
——Graceful mistresse, our nuptiall day holds.
" *Beatrice.* With happy Constancye a wished day."

Of gentlemen's presents on similar occasions, a lady, in Beaumont and Fletcher's " Cupid's Revenge," 1615, Dyce's B. and F., 11, 390, says :

" Given earings we will wear;
Bracelets of our lovers' hair,
Which they on our arms shall twist
With their names carv'd, on our wrist."

In England these knots of ribbons were

distributed in great abundance formerly, even at the marriages of persons of the first distinction. They were worn at the hat, (the gentlemens', I suppose), and consisted of ribbons of various colours. If I mistake not, white ribbons are the only ones used at present.

"What posies for our wedding-rings,
What gloves we'll give, and ribban-
    ings."
—*Herrick*.

Bride favours appear to have been worn by the peasantry of France on similar occasions on the arm. Favours are still assumed on a variety of occasions.

Faw.—See *Gypsies*.

Fawkes, Guy.—(Nov. 5). The ignorant processions of boys, who carry about the effigy of the unfortunate York-shire gentleman, sing the following verses, which are, perhaps, scarcely worth inser-tion on any other ground than the gradual evanescence of all our old vulgar usages :

Remember, remember
The fifth of November,
    Gunpowder treason and plot :
I see no reason,
Why gunpowder treason
    Should ever be forgot.
Guy Fawkes Guy,
Hit him in the eye, etc.

The late Mr. Robert Davies, the scholarly Town Clerk of York, devoted a pamphlet to the family history of the Fawkes's of York, small 8vo., 1850. Good and sen-sible Bishop Sanderson exclaims : "God grant that we nor ours ever live to see November the fifth forgotten or the solem-nity of it silenced." The figures of the Pope and the Devil were formerly burnt on this occasion. There is an account of the remarkable cavalcade on the even-ing of this day in the year 1679, at the time the Exclusion Bill was in agitation. The Pope, it should seem, was carried in a pageant representing a chair of state covered with scarlet, richly embroidered and fringed; and at his back, not an effigy, but a person representing the Devil, acting as his holiness's privy-coun-cillor; and "frequently caressing, hug-ging, and whispering him, and oftentimes instructing him aloud." The procession was set forth at Moorgate, and passed first to Aldgate, thence through Leadenhall Street, by the Royal Exchange and Cheap-side to Temple Bar. The statue of the Queen on the inner or eastern side of Temple Bar having been conspicuously ornamented, the figure of the Pope was brought before it, when, after a song, partly alluding to the protection afforded by Elizabeth to Protestants, and partly to the existing circumstances of the times, a vast bonfire having been prepared "over

against the Inner Temple Gate, his holi-ness, after some compliments and reluc-tances, was decently toppled from all his grandeur into the impartial flames; the crafty Devil leaving his infallibilityship in the lurch, and laughing as heartily at his deserved ignominious end as subtle Jesuits do at the ruin of bigoted lay Catho-lics, whom themselves have drawn in." This enlightened demonstration was found so attractive, that, in 1680 it was repeated with additions. In 1715, the effigy of the old Pretender was burnt by the people, as well as those of the Pope and the Devil, on this anniversary, and the additional feature in the demonstration does not seem to have been given up, even when the Jacobite cause was finally abandoned.

This is one of the grand days with the Societies of the Temple, when an extra bottle of wine is allowed to each mess in hall; it used to be observed as a holiday at some of the public schools and offices. Before the custom declined in popularity every-where, it was the practice of the boys to dress up an image of Guy Fawkes, hold-ing in one hand a dark lanthorn, and in the other a bundle of matches, and to carry it about the streets begging money in these words, "Pray remember Guy Fawkes !" In the evening there are bon-fires, and these frightful figures are burnt in the midst of them. In "Poor Robin" for 1677 are the following observations :

"Now boys with
Squibs and crackers play,
And bonfires' blaze
Turns night to day."

This old usage finds no favour with the High Church party at present so para-mount, or with the community at large, and is in fact happily dying out.

Feathers. — There is a well-known article of popular belief in some districts, particularly in the eastern counties, that the presence of game-feathers in a feather bed will prolong the agonies of death. There is a curious paper on this subject by Mr. Albert Way, in the fourth volume of "Notes and Queries." 1st series. The same idea is entertained in some parts of Yorkshire with regard to pigeon's feathers, and in Cumberland respecting those of the turkey. The objection to game feathers is widely prevalent, occurring in Derby-shire and in several parts of Wales; and I hardly think that the superstition can be explained on the utilitarian theory pro-pounded by the writer in the "Athen-æum," "that none of these feathers are fit for use, being too hard and sharp in the barrel." It is impossible, according to Grose, for a person to die, while resting on a pillow stuffed with the feathers of a dove; but he will struggle with death in the most exquisite torture. The pillows of dying persons are therefore taken away, says he, when they appear in great agonies, lest they may have pigeons' feathers in them. A more ridiculous or degrading superstition can scarcely be imagined, and as to the removal of the pillow from under the head of a dying person, it is almost always followed by suffocation. Nurses, when they are not carefully watched, will snatch this support away suddenly, to accelerate the result, and save trouble. The " British Apollo " very properly characterizes this as an " old woman's story," and adds : " But the scent of pigeon's feathers is so strong, that they are not fit to make beds with, insomuch that the offence of their smell may be said (like other strong smells) to revive any body dying, and if troubled with hysteric fits. But as common practice, by reason of the nauseousness of the smell, has introduced a disuse of pigeons' feathers to make beds, so no experience doth or hath ever given us any example of the reality of the fact."

Fernseed. — The ancients, who often paid more attention to received opinions than to the evidence of their senses, believed that fern bore no seed (Pliny's " Nat. Hist.," by Holland, lib. xxvii. ch. 9). Our ancestors imagined that this plant produced seed which was invisible. Hence, from an extraordinary mode of reasoning, founded on the fantastic doctrine of signatures, they concluded that they who possessed the secret of wearing this seed about them would become invisible. This superstition Shakespear's good sense taught him to ridicule. It was also supposed to seed in a single night, and is called in Browne's Pastorals, 1614 :

" The wond'rous one-night seeding ferne."

Johnson the Botanist, in his edition of Gerarde, 1633, says : " Fern is one of those plants which have their seed on the back of the leaf, so small as to escape the sight. Those who perceived that fern was propagated by semination, and yet could never see the seed, were much at a loss for a solution of the difficulty ; and, as wonder always endeavours to augment itself, they ascribed to fernseed many strange properties, some of which the rustick virgins have not yet forgotten or exploded." In a MS. of the time of Queen Elizabeth there is the following receipt : " Gather fearne-seed on Midsomer Eve betweene 11 and 12 noone and weare it about thee continually." It is said to be also gatherable at night. Fernseed, according to a passage quoted by Grose, was looked upon as having great magical powers, and must be gathered on

Midsummer Eve. A person who once went to gather it reported that the spirits whisked by his ears, and sometimes struck his hat and other parts of his body, and at length, when he thought he had got a good quantity of it, and secured it in papers and a box, when he came home, he found both empty. A respectable countryman at Heston, in Middlesex, informed Brand in June, 1793, that when he was a young man, he was often present at the ceremony of catching the fern-seed at midnight, on the eve of St. John Baptist. The attempt, he said, was often unsuccessful, for the seed was to fall into the plate of its own accord, and that too without shaking the plant. Dr. Rowe, of Launceston, apprised him, October 17th, 1790, of some rites with fern-seed which were still performed at that place. Mr. Couch of Bodmin observes : " Midsummer-day, the feast of the Summer Solstice, is marked only (among the Cornish tinners) by the elevation of a bush or a tall pole, on the highest eminence of the stream work."

Torreblanca, in his " Demonologia," suspects those persons of witchcraft who gather fern - seed on this night. Lemnius tells us : " They prepare fern gathered in a tempestuous night, rue, trifoly, vervain, against magical impostures." In " The Pylgremage of Pure Devotyon, newly translatyd into Englishe," is this passage : " Peraventure they ymagyne the symylytude of a tode to be there, evyn as we suppose when we cutte the fearne-stalke there to be an egel, and evyn as chyldren (whiche they se nat indede) in the clowdes, thynke they see dragones spyttynge fyre, and hylles flammynge with fyre, and armyd men encounterynge." Of course this notion about fernseed is perfectly fanciful and equally groundless. Shakespear justly ridicules it in *Henry IV.*, i., 2 :

" *Gadshill.* We steal as in a castle, cocksure ; we have the receipt of fern-seed, we walk invisible.

Chamberlain. Nay, I think rather you are more beholden to the night than to the fern-seed, for your walking invisible."

Steevens remarks : " This circumstance [its gift of invisibility] relative to the fern-seed is alluded to in Beaumont and Fletcher's ' Fair Maid of the Inn' :—

' Had you Gyges' ring?
Or the herb that gives invisibility?'

" Again, in Ben Jonson's ' New Inn ' :
' I had
No medicine, Sir, to go invisible,
No fern-seed in my pocket.' "

In " Flaine Percevall the Peace-maker of England," sign. C 3, the author remarks : " I thinke the mad slave hath tasted on a fern-stalke, that he walkes so invisible." Butler alludes to this superstitious notion :

"That spring like fern, that infect weed Equivocally, without seed."

Addison laughs at a doctor who was arrived at the knowledge of the green and red dragon, and had discovered the female fern-seed.—*Tatler*, No. 240.

Festing Penny.—See *Denier de Foi.*

Fetch or **Fetich.**.—There are, says Grose, the exact figures and resemblances of persons then living, often seen not only by their friends at a distance, but many times by themselves : of which there are several instances in Aubrey's "Miscellanies." These apparitions are called fetches, and in Cumberland swarths : they most commonly appear to distant friends and relations, at the very instant preceding the death of the person whose figure they put on. Sometimes there is a greater interval between the appearance and death. For a particular relation of the appearance of a fetch-light or deadman's candle, to a gentleman in Carmarthenshire, see the "Athenian Oracle," vol. i. pp. 76, 77, and ibid., vol. iii. p. 150 ; also, Aubrey's "Miscellanies," p. 176 ; and Baxter's "World of Spirits," 1691, pp. 131-137.

Field-Ale or **Filkdale.**—Refreshment furnished in the field or open air to bailiffs of hundreds, and supplied from funds contributed by the inhabitants of the particular hundred. It has long fallen into disuse. Tomlins, *Law Dict.*, 1835, in v.

Field Mice.—The following illustration of the barbarous practice of enclosing field-mice was received by Mr. Brand in a letter, dated May 9, 1806, from Robt. Studley Vidal, Esq., of Cornborough near Bideford, a gentleman to whom he was much indebted for incidental information on the local customs of Devonshire :

"An usage of the superstitious kind has just come under my notice, and which, as the pen is in my hand, I will shortly describe, though I rather think it is not peculiar to these parts. A neighbour of mine, on examining his sheep the other day, found that one of them had entirely lost the use of its hinder parts. On seeing it I expressed an opinion that the animal must have received a blow across the back or some other sort of violence which had injured the spinal marrow, and thus rendered it paralytic : but I was soon given to understand that my remarks only served to prove how little I knew of country affairs, for that the affection of the sheep was nothing uncommon, and that the cause of it was well known,

namely a mouse having crept over its back. I could not but smile at the idea ; which my instructor considering as a mark of incredulity, he proceeded very gravely to inform me that I should be convinced of the truth of what he said by the means which he would use to restore the animal ; and which were never known to fail. He accordingly dispatched his people here and there in quest of a field mouse ; and having procured one, he told me that he should carry it to a particular tree at some distance and, inclosing it within a hollow in the trunk, leave it there to perish. He further informed me that he should bring back some of the branches of the tree with him for the purpose of their being drawn now and then across the sheep's back, and concluded by assuring me, with a very scientific look, that I should soon be convinced of the efficacy of this process, for that, as soon as the poor devoted mouse had yielded up his life a prey to famine, the sheep would be restored to its former strength and vigour. I can, however, state with certainty, that the sheep was not at all benefited by this mysterious sacrifice of the mouse. The tree, I find, is of the sort called witchelm or witch-hazel." It is more properly described as the wych elm or hazel.

Fifollets or **Feux Follets.**—See *Will o' the Wisp.*

Fifteen or Eleven.—Some old trick (? at cards). See Thynne's *Debate between Pride and Lowliness* (1570), p. 51 of repr.

Fifth of November. — See *Fawkes (Guy)* and *St. Hugh's Day.*

Fig Sunday.—A popular name for the Sunday before Easter, in allusion to Jesus Christ's alleged desire to eat that fruit on his way from Bethany. Brand says that it is known under this name in Northamptonshire and Hertfordshire. Miss Baker, writing in 1854, says : "It is the universal custom with both rich and poor to eat figs on this day. On the Saturday preceding this day, the market at Northampton is abundantly supplied with figs, and there are more purchased at this time than throughout the rest of the year : even the charity children in some places are regaled with them. . ." *Northampt. Gloss.*, 1854. A correspondent of Hone, in the "Year Book," col. 1593, remarks : "At Kempton in Hertfordshire, five miles from Hertford, it hath long been, and, for aught the writer knoweth, still is a custom for the inhabitants, 'rich and poor, great and small,' to eat figs on the Sunday before Easter, there termed 'Fig Sunday.' A dealer in 'groceries,' resident at Kempton, affirmed to me from his own lengthy observations, that more figs are sold in the village the few days previous than in all the year beside." This was written in 1832.

Figging Craft.—A term applied in a tract elsewhere mentioned (See *Mumchance*) to cheaters at dice.

Figgy Pudding.—Plum pudding, so called in some parts. The Editor's father always used this form.

Finding or Losing Things.—Melton says : "That if a man, walking in the fields, finde any foure-leaved grasse, he shall in a small while after find some good thing. That it is nought for a man or woman to lose their hose garter. That it is a sign of ill lucke to find money." *Astrologaster*, 1620, p. 46. Greene in "The Groundworke of Conny-catching," 1592, (an alteration of Harman's "Caveat," 1567), sign. B, tells us, "'Tis ill lucke to keepe found money. Therefore it must be spent." Mason mentions as an omen of good luck, "If drinke be spilled upon a man ; or if he find old iron." Hence it is accounted a lucky omen to find a horse shoe. *Anatomie of Sorcerie*, 1612, 90, and *Horseshoe*, infrâ. Homes remarks : "How frequent is it with people (especially of the more ignorant sort, which makes the things more suspected), to think and say, (as Master Perkins relates), if they finde some pieces of iron, it is a prediction of good luck to the finders. If they find a piece of silver, it is a foretoken of ill luck to them. *Demonologie*, 1650, p. 60. Even the learned Boyle admits that he once stooped to pick up a horse-shoe, but it was only, he tells us, "to make merry with this fond conceit of the superstitious vulgar." *Occasional Reflections*, 1665, p. 217. It was considered unlucky to let a pin lie on the floor. So the common nursery rhyme instructs us :

"See a pin and pick it up,
All the day you'll have good luck ;
See a pin and let it lay,
Bad luck you'll have all the day."

Fire.—There is some curious matter bearing on this prolific subject in Mr. Wright's "Essays on the Superstitions of the Middle Ages," 1846, in the chapter devoted to mythology. One of the magical devices, against which there is a general protest in a Saxon homily, quoted by this learned writer, was directed against any one "who places his child on the roof, or in a furnace, for the recovery of his health. . . ." That a belief in the power of resuscitation by fire had at one time some hold on the popular mind in our country, we have evidence in the strange production called "The Treatyse of the Smyth whych that forged hym a new dame," printed about the middle of the sixteenth century, but a great deal

older than the date of publication in its structure and doctrine. The piece may be seen in Hazlitt's *Popular Poetry*, 1864-6.

Fire-Balls.—See *Aërolites*.

Fire-Drake.—(*Draco volans*). White calls the fiery dragon "a weaker kind of lightning. Its livid colour, and its falling without noise and slowly, demonstrate a great mixture of watry exhalation in it. 'Tis sufficient for its shape that it has some resemblance of a dragon, not the expresse figure." *Institutions*, 1656, p. 156. By the subsequent description, copied by Blount from Bullokar's "Expositor," 1616, the fire-drake should seem to be a distinct appearance from the ignis fatuus : "There is a fire sometimes seen flying in the night, like a dragon : it is called a fire-drake. Common people think it a spirit that keeps some treasure hid ; but philosophers affirm it to be a great unequal exhalation inflamed between two clouds, the one hot, the other cold (which is the reason that it also smokes), the middle part whereof, according to the proportion of the hot cloud, being greater than the rest, makes it seem like a belly, and both ends like a head and tail." I suppose our author, when he says the above is like a dragon, refers to the common graphic description of that imaginary creature. The name is used in 1663 as characteristic of a ruffianly knight-adventurer. Hazlitt's *Handbook*, 1867, p. 198. In the "Life of Anthony a Wood," under date of May 16, 1668, is the following : "Between 9 and 10 of the clock at night, there was seen by them, Matthew Hutton and Anthony Wood and those of the family of Borstall near Brill, in Bucks, a draco volans fall from the sky. It made the place so light for a time, that a man might see to read. It seemed to A. W. to be as long as All Saints' steeple in Oxon, being long and narrow ; and when it came to the lower region, it vanished into sparkles, and as some say, gave a report. Great raines and inundations followed, &c." *Lives of Leland, Hearne and Wood*, 1772, ii., 212.

"A Fire-Drake," says Steevens, "is both a serpent, antiently called a brenning-drake or dipsas, and a name formerly given to a Will o' the Wisp, or ignus fatuus. So in Drayton's 'Nymphidia' ;

'By the hissing of the snake,
The rustling of the fire-drake.'"

Again, in the anonymous play of "Cæsar and Pompey," 1607 :

"So have I seene a fire-drake glide along
Before a dying man, to point his grave,
And in it stick and hide."

Aubanus, p. 270, speaking of his German experiences or observations, tells us: "Ignis fit, cui Orbiculi quidam lignei perforati imponuntur, qui quum inflammantur, flexilibus virgis præfixi, arte et vi in aërem supra Moganum amnem excutiuntur : Draconem igneum volare putant, qui prius non viderunt."

Plot, in his "Oxfordshire," fol. 203, mentions "that, about the year 750, a battle was fought near Burford, perhaps on the place still called Battle-Edge, west of the town towards Upton, between Cuthred or Cuthbert, a tributary king of the West Saxons, and Ethelbald king of Mercia, whose insupportable exactions the former king not being able to endure, he came into the field against Ethelbald, met, and overthrew him there, winning his banner, whereon was depicted a golden dragon; but this was an ordinary device or cognizance, and not an artificial *draco volans*, like that of Aubanus. Comp. *Excerpta Historica*, 1833, p. 404.

Fire Omens.—Willsford tells us: "When our common fires do burn with a pale flame, they presage foul weather. If the fire do make a huzzing noise, it is a sign of tempests near at hand. When the fire sparkleth very much, it is a sign of rain. If the ashes on the herth do clodder together of themselves, it is a sign of rain. When pots are newly taken off the fire, if they sparkle (the soot upon them being incensed), it presages rain. When the fire scorcheth, and burneth more vehemently than it useth to do, it is a sign of frosty weather; but if the living coals do shine brighter than commonly at other times, expect then rain. If wood or any other fuel do crackle and break forth wind more than ordinary, it is an evident sign of some tempestuous weather neer at hand; the much and suddain falling of soot presages rain." *Nature's Secrets*, 1658, p. 120. Defoe seems to say that in his time superstitious persons imagined every variety of shape in the fire: swords, and other weapons, buildings of all kinds, wedding-rings, bags of money, and, in fact, whatever they wished. *Mem. of Duncan Campbel*, 1732, p. 61. In the "Vicar of Wakefield," among the omens of the Doctor's daughters, are "Purses bounded from the fire." In the North of England, the cinders that bound from the fire are carefully examined by old women and children, and according to their respective forms are called either coffins or purses, and consequently thought to be the presages of death or wealth. A coal, says Grose, in the shape of a coffin, flying out of the fire to any particular person, betokens their death not far off. But, on the other hand, according to Moulin,

the flame suddenly bursting from the ashes was a good sign. *Vates*, p. 219.

"So when a child, as playful children use,
Has burnt to tinder a stale last year's News,
The flame extinct, he views the roving fire—
There goes my lady, and there goes the squire,
There goes the parson, oh! illustrious spark,
And there, scarce less illustrious, goes the clerk!"

—Cowper's *Poems*, 1798, vol. i., p. 272. A flake of soot hanging at the bars of the grate, says Grose, also denotes the visit of a stranger. Some clap their hands when they see the latter, and by the number of times they do this, they judge the number of days that will elapse before the person comes. Many fantastic shapes are discerned in the fire, in the candle, and in the tea-cup by some people. I have had the figure of a dog carrying a parcel shown to me in the last-mentioned; but I hardly know whether this was supposed to be indicative of good or the reverse. I do not know whether this has anything to do with Cowper's idea, in his "Winter Evening," that the fungus in the candle "implies the arrival of a parcel."

Fires.—That fires were very frequent in London, Fitzstephen proves. The Saxon Chronicle also makes frequent mention of towns being burned, which might be expected for the same reason, the Saxon term for building being ꝣᴇꞇꞁᵬᵯbꝑꞁᵬᵫn. "Solæ pestes Londoniæ sunt Stultorum immodica potatio, et frequens Incendium."

Firing at the Apple Trees.—In Devonshire, on Twelfth Day Eve, the farmers used to rally out with guns and blunderbusses, and fire with powder only at the apple-trees in the orchards, pronouncing an invocation in doggerel, praying for a bountiful harvest of fruit. A representation of this ceremony was given in the *Illustrated London News* of January 11, 1851, and is reproduced on a smaller scale in the *Antiquary* for March, 1895, where the verses are given, with an account by a correspondent at Exeter. The origin of this custom is said to be unknown; the harmless fusillade may have been intended either as a salute to the good genius of the orchard or as a conjuration against evil spirits. The ancients attributed to their sylvan deities the prosperity of their fruit-seasons or otherwise.

First Foot or **Qual-tagh.** — In the North of England the first person who enters the house on Christmas or New Year's Eve is called, says Brockett, the First Foot.

Fives.—See *Tennis.*

Flapdragon.—See Halliwell in v.

Fleas.—I find the following in Hill's "Natural and Artificial Conclusions," 1581 : "A very easie and merry conceit to keep off fleas from your beds or chambers. Plinie reporteth that if, when you first hear the cuckow, you mark well where your right foot standeth, and take up of that earth, the fleas will by no means breed either in your house or chamber, where any of the same earth is thrown or scattered." So M. Thiers, "La première fois qu'on entend le Coucou, cerner la terre qui est sous le pied droit de celuy qui l'entend, & la répandre dans les maisons afin d'enchasser les puces." Among the jests of Scogin is "How Scogin sold Powder to Kill Fleas." He broke up some wood from a rotten post, and went about among the old wives, pretending that it was a famous receipt. Comp. *Old English Jest Books,* 1864, ii., 84.

Flibbertigibbet. — See Nares, *Gloss.,* 1859, in v.

Flies.—Willsford says : "Flies in the spring or summer season, if they grow busier or blinder than at other times, or that they are observed to shroud themselves in warm places, expect then quickly for to follow, either hail, cold storms of rain, or very much wet weather ; and if those little creatures are noted early in autumn to repare unto their winter quarters, it presages frosty mornings, cold storms, with the approach of hoary winter. Atomes or flies, swarming together and sporting themselves in the sunbeams, is a good omen of fair weather." *Nature's Secrets,* 1658, p. 135. "Amongst our deep sea fishermen at Greenock there is a most comical idea, that if a fly falls into the glass from which any one has been drinking, or is about to drink, it is considered a sure and true omen of good luck to the drinker, and is always noticed as such by the company."—*Notes and Queries,* Dec. 22, 1855. An anecdote in an early jest book possibly alludes to this idea. A traveller being at a banquet, where a fly chanced to fall into his glass, he took it out before he drank, but afterwards put it in again. Being asked his reason, he answered, that for his own part he did not like flies, but others might.

Flouncing.—The custom of flouncing is said to be peculiar to Guernsey. It is an entertainment given by the parents of a young couple, when they are engaged, and the match has received approval. The girl is introduced to her husband's family and friends by her future father-in-law, and the man similarly by hers : after this, they must keep aloof from all flirtation, however lengthy the courtship may prove. The belief is, that if either party break faith, the other side can lay claim to a moiety of his or her effects.

Flowers, Herbs, &c., on Days of Humiliation and Thanksgiving.—In the Parish Accounts of St. Margaret, Westminster, under 1650-1, are the following items, the interest of two of which is more than archæological :

"Item, paid for herbs that were strewed in the windows of the church, and about the same, att two severall daies of Humiliation, 3s. 10d. Item, paid for herbs that were strewed in the church upon a daie of thanksgiving, 2s. 6d. Item, paid for herbs that were strewed in the church on the 24th day of May, 1651, being a day of humiliation, 3s. Item, paid to the ringers, for ringing on the 24th of October, being a day of thanksgiving for the victorie over the Scotts at Worcester, 7s. Item, paid for hearbes and lawrell that were strewed in the church the same day, 8s." Mrs. Joyce Jeffries, of Hereford and other places, in the time of Charles I. used, as her account-books shew, to have her pew in All Saints' Church, Hereford, dressed with flowers at Christmas by the clerk's wife. It is still the universal practice to deck churches and private dwellings with holly at Christmas, and the evergreen is usually left to the end of February, or till Good Friday. In towns the custom is rather a mechanical habit, it is to be feared, than any genuine homage to a time-honoured observance. *Archæologia,* xxxvii., 200

Flowers, &c., at Marriages.—There was anciently a custom at marriages of strewing herbs and flowers, as also rushes, from the house or houses where persons betrothed resided, to the church. Herrick and Braithwaite refer to this usage. The former writes :

"All haile to Hymen and his marriage day,
Strew rushes and quickly come away ;
Strew Rushes, maides, and ever as you strew,
Think one day, maydes, like will be done for you."

Hesp., 1648, p. 129. *Strappado for the Divell,* 1615, p. 74. Browne, who wrote his Pastorals before 1614, evidently in the following lines describes some village wedding in his native Devon :

"As I haue seene vpon a Bridall day
Full many maids clad in their best array,
In honour of the Bride come with their flaskets
Fill'd full with flowers : others in wicker baskets

Bring from the marish rushes, to o'er-
spread
The ground, whereon to church the
louers tread:
Whilst that the quaintest youth of all
the plaine
Vshers their way with many a piping
straine."

Every one will call to mind the passage
in Shakespear to this purpose:

" Our bridal flowers serve for a buried
corse."

Armin's " History of the Two Maids of
Moreclacke," 1609, opens thus, preparatory to a wedding: " Enter a maid strewing flowers, and a serving-man perfuming
the door. The maid says ' strew, strew,'
—the man, ' the muscadine stays for the
bride at Church.' " So in Brooke's "Epithalamium " :—

" Now busie maydens strew sweet
flowres."

Engl. Hel., ed. 1614, R 1 v°. The strewing herbs and flowers on this occasion, as
mentioned in a note upon Barrey's play
of "Ram Alley," 1611, to have been practised formerly, is still kept up in Kent
and many other parts of England. Dodsley's *O. P.*, by Hazlitt, x., 366. In the
drama just cited, we read: " Enter Adri-
ana, and another strawing hearbes."

"*Adr.* Come straw apace. Lord! shall
I never live,
To walke to church on flowers? O, 'tis
fine,
To see a bride trip it to church so
lightly,
As if her new choppines would scorne
to bruze
A silly flower !"

In " Oxford Drollery," 1671, p. 118, is a
poem styled " A Supposition," in which
the custom of strewing herbs is thus alluded to:

" Suppose the way with fragrant herbs
were strowing,
All things were ready, we to church
were going:
And now suppose the priest had joyn'd
our hands," &c.

Flowers, &c., on Graves.—
Gough says: " The Greeks used the ama-
ranth and the polianthus, one species of
which resembles the hyacinth, parsley,
myrtle. The Romans added fillets or
bandeaux of wool. The primitive Christians reprobated these as impertinent
practices; but in Prudentius's time they
had adopted them, and they obtain in a
degree in some parts of our own country,
as the garland hung up in some village
churches in Cambridgeshire, and other

counties, after the funeral of a young
woman, and the inclosure of roses round
graves in the Welsh church yards, testify." He adds: " Aubrey takes notice
of a custom of planting rose trees on the
graves of lovers by the survivors, at Oak-
ley, Surrey, which may be a remain of
Roman manners among us; it being in
practice among them and the Greeks to
have roses yearly strewed on their graves,
as Bishop Gibson remarks from two inscriptions at Ravenna and Milan. The
practice in Propertius of burying the
dead in roses is common among our country people; and to it Anacreon seems to
allude, in his 53rd Ode. *Sep. Mon. Introd.
ii., xvii.* and cciv. Bishop Gibson is also
cited as an authority for this practice by
Strutt. " Mann. and Customs, Anglo-
Saxon Era," vol. i. p. 69. See also Bray's
" Surrey," vol. ii. p. 165. I do not find
that the custom is at present retained.—
Ellis.

Moresin observes, at p. 61: "Flores
et Serta, educto Cadavere, certatim
injiciebant Athenienses." Sir Thomas
Browne, in his " Urneburiall," tells us
that among the antients "the funerall
pyre consisted of sweet fuell, cypresse,
firre, larix, yewe, and trees perpetually
verdant." And he observes, " Whether
the planting of yewe in church yards
holds its original from antient funerall
rites, or as an embleme of Resurrection
from its perpetual verdure, may also admit conjecture." Virgil, in Dryden's
version, describing Anchises grieving for
Marcellus, makes him say:

" Full canisters of fragrant lilies bring,
Mix'd with the purple roses of the
spring:
Let me with fun'ral flow'rs his body
strow,
This gift which parents to their children owe,
This unavailing gift, at least I may
bestow."

The custom of strewing flowers upon the
graves of departed friends, which has
been already incidentally noticed, is also
derived from a custom of the ancient
Church. St. Ambrose has these words:
" I will not sprinkle his grave with flowers, but pour on his spirit the odour of
Christ. Let others scatter baskets of
flowers: Christ is our Lily, and with this
I will consecrate his relicks." And St.
Jerome tells us : " Whilst other husbands
strewed violets, roses, lilies, and purple
flowers upon the graves of their wives,
and comforted themselves with such like
offices, Pammachius bedewed her ashes
and venerable bones with the balm of
alms." *Epistola ad Pammachium de
obitu Uxoris.* Durandus tells us that the

ancient Christians, after the funeral, used to scatter flowers on the tomb. P. 237. There is a great deal of learning in Moresin upon this subject. *Papatus*, 157. It appears from Pliny's "Natural History," from Cicero in his "Oration on Lucius Plancus," and from Virgil's sixth Æneid, that this was a funeral rite among the Romans. They used also to scatter them on the unburied corpse. Gough has the following passage: "The ancients used to crown the deceased with flowers, in token of the shortness of life, and the practice is still retained in some places in regard to young women and children. The Romish Ritual recommends it in regard of those who die soon after baptism, in token of purity and virginity. It still obtains in Holland and parts of Germany. The primitive Christians buried young women with flowers, and martyrs with the instruments of their martyrdom. I have seen fresh flowers put into the coffins of children and young girls." "Sep. Mon." vol. ii. introd. p. 5. "Cum igitur infans vel Puer baptizatus defunctus fuerit ante usum Rationis, induitur juxta ætatem, et imponitur ei Corona de floribus, seu de herbis aromaticis et odoriferis, in signum integritatis Carnis et Virginitatis." "Ordo Baptizandi, &c., pro Anglia, Hibernia, et Scotia," 1626, p. 97.

Bourne further remarks that, as the form of procession is an emblem of our dying shortly after our friend, so the carrying in our hands of ivy, sprigs of laurel, rosemary, or other evergreens, is an emblem of the soul's immortality. In the account of the funeral expenses of Sir John Rudstone, Mayor of London, 1531, I find the following article: "For yerbys at the bewryal, £0 1s. 0d." So, in a song in "Wit's Interpreter," 1655, we read:

"Shrouded she is from top to toe
With lillies which all o'er her grow,
Instead of bays and rosemary."

In a book by Dr. Case, the author says: "I wil end with death, the end of all mortality, which though it be the dissolution of Nature and parting of the soul from the body, terrible in itself to flesh and blood, and amplified with a number of displeasant and uncomfortable accidents, as the shaving of the head, howling, mourning apparel, funeral boughs of yeu, box, cipresse, and the like, yet we shall find by resorting to antiquities, that musick hath had a share amongst them, as being unseasonable at no time." *Praise of Musicke*, 1586, F 8 v°. Friar Laurence in "Romeo and Juliet" says:

"Dry up your tears, and stick your Rosemary
On this fair corse."

Of Paris, the intended husband of Juliet, who, to all appearance, died on their wedding day, it is said, in the language of Shakespear,

"He came with flowers to strew his ladies grave,"

when he provoked and met his fate by the hand of Romeo. Overbury, in his "Characters," describing the "faire and happy milkmaid," says: "Thus lives she, and all her care is that she may die in the Spring time, to have store of flowers stucke upon her winding-sheet;" which has a complete parallel in the Breton usage commemorated in the traditional ballad or song, *The Flowers of May* (Bleuniou Mae), of which the concluding lines are:

"Heureuses les jeunes personnes, qui meurent au printemps!
Heureuses les jeunes personnes que l'on couvre de fleurs nouvelles."

Chants Populaires de la Bretagne, par Villemarqué, 1846, ii., 265. Gay describes thus the strewing of flowers upon the graves:

"Upon her grave the rosemary they threw,
The daisy, butter'd-flow'r, and endive blue."

He adds the custom is still used in the South of England, of fencing the graves with osiers, &c.; and glances at clerical economy, for which there is oftentimes too much occasion, in the last two lines:

"With wicker rods we fenced her tomb around,
To ward from man and beast the hallow'd ground.
Lest her new grave the parson's cattle raze,
For both his horse and cow the church yard graze."

Gough says: "It is the custom at this day all over Wales to strew the graves both within and without the church, with green herbs, branches of box, flowers, rushes and flags, for one year; after which, such as can afford it lay down a stone. *Sep. Mon.* ii., Introd. 294. The common Welsh graves are curiously matted round with single or double matting, and stuck with flowers, box, or laurel, which are frequently renewed." Pepys in his *Diary*, April 26, 1662, mentions a churchyard near Southampton, where the graves were "accustomed to be all sowed with sage." In Lancashire, it is still usual in some districts for each mourner to carry with him to the place of interment a sprig of box prepared for the purpose, and cast it, before leaving, into the grave of the departed. *Notes and Queries*, Dec. 26, 1868.

Flowers, &c., on Graves in South Wales.

Mr. Brand borrowed some notes from Malkin's *South Wales*, which, though perhaps of no great authority, I scarcely like to disturb: "The bed on which the corpse lies is always strewed with flowers, and the same custom is observed after it is laid in the coffin. They bury much earlier than we do in England; seldom later than the third day, and very frequently on the second. The habit of filling the bed, the coffin, and the room, with sweet-scented flowers, though originating probably in delicacy as well as affection, must of course have a strong tendency to expedite the progress of decay. It is an invariable practice, both by day and night, to watch a corpse; and so firm a hold has this supposed duty gained on their imaginations, that probably there is no instance upon record of a family so unfeeling and abandoned as to leave a dead body in the room by itself, for a single minute, in the interval between the death and burial. Such a violation of decency would be remembered for generations. The hospitality of the country is not less remarkable on melancholy than on joyful occasions. The invitations to a funeral are very general and extensive, and the refreshments are not light and taken standing, but substantial and prolonged. Any deficiency in the supply of ale would be as severely censured on this occasion as at a festival. The grave of the deceased is constantly overspread with plucked flowers for a week or two after the funeral. The planting of graves with flowers is confined to the villages and the poorer people. It is perhaps a prettier custom. It is very common to dress the graves on Whitsunday and other festivals, when flowers are to be procured: and the frequency of this observance is a good deal affected by the respect in which the deceased was held. My father-in-law's grave in Cowbridge Church has been strewed by his surviving servants every Sunday morning for these twenty years. It is usual for a family not to appear at church till what is called the month's end, when they go in a body, and then are considered as having returned to the common offices of life. It is a very antient and general practice in Glamorgan to plant flowers on the grave; so that many church yards have something like the splendour of a rich and various parterre. Besides this, it is usual to strew the graves with flowers and evergreens, within the church as well as out of it, thrice at least every year, on the same principle of delicate respect as the stones are whitened. No flowers or evergreens are permitted to be planted on graves but such as are sweet-scented: the pink and polyanthus, sweet Williams, gilliflowers, and carnations, mignonette, thyme, hyssop, camomile, and rosemary, make up the pious decoration of this consecrated garden. Turnsoles, pionies, the African marigold, the anemone, and many others I could mention, though beautiful, are never planted on graves, because they are not sweet-scented. It is to be observed, however, that this tender custom is sometimes converted into an instrument of satire; so that where persons have been distinguished for their pride, vanity, or any other unpopular quality, the neighbours whom they may have offended plant these also by stealth upon their graves. In the Easter week most generally the graves are newly dressed, and manured with fresh earth, when such flowers or ever-greens as may be wanted or wished for are planted. In the Whitsuntide holidays, or rather the preceding week, the graves are again looked after, weeded, and otherwise dressed, or if necessary, planted again. It is a very common saying of such persons as employ themselves in thus planting and dressing the graves of their friends, that they are cultivating their own freeholds. This work the nearest relations of the deceased always do with their own hands, and never by servants or hired persons. Should a neighbour assist, he or she never takes, never expects, and indeed is never insulted by the offer of any reward, by those who are acquainted with the ancient customs.

The vulgar practice and illiberal prejudice against old maids and old bachelors subsists among the Welsh in a very disgraceful degree, so that their graves have not unfrequently been planted by some satirical neighbours, not only with rue, but with thistles, nettles, henbane, and other noxious weeds. When a young unmarried person dies, his or her ways to the grave are also strewed with sweet flowers and ever-greens; and on such occasions it is the usual phrase, that those persons are going to their nuptial beds, not to their graves. There seems to be a remarkable coincidence between these people and the ancient Greeks, with respect to the avoiding of ill-omened words. None ever molest the flowers that grow on graves; for it is deemed a kind of sacrilege to do so. A relation or friend will occasionally take a pink, if it can be spared, or a sprig of thyme, from the grave of a beloved or respected person, to wear it in remembrance; but they never take much, lest they should deface the growth on the grave. This custom prevails principally in the most retired villages; and I have been assured, that in such villages where the right of grazing the church yard has been enforced, the practice has alienated the affections of very great numbers from the clergymen and their churches; so that many have become Dissenters for the singularly uncommon reason that they may bury their friends in Dissenting burying-grounds, plant their graves with flowers, and keep them clean and neat, without any danger of their being cropt. The white rose is always planted on a virgin's tomb. The red rose is appropriated to the grave of any person distinguished for goodness, and especially benevolence of character. The natives of the principality pride themselves much on these antient ornaments (the yews) of their church yards; and it is nearly as general a custom in Brecknockshire to decorate the graves of the deceased with slips either of bay or yew, stuck in the green turf, for an emblem of pious remembrance, as it is in Glamorganshire to pay a tribute of similar import, in the cultivation of sweet-scented flowers on the same spot. The graves of Glamorganshire, decorated with flowers and herbs, at once gratify the relations of the departed and please the observer.''

Flying Coaches.—The older name of the merry-go-round at fairs. They are mentioned in *Poor Robin* for 1733. See the passage quoted in Nares, *Gloss., in v.*

Flying Machine.—The name bestowed on the mail-coaches, which left London to convey passengers along all the great roads in the eighteenth century. It is found described in *Coaching Days and Coaching Ways*, 1903.

Font.—The font was usually covered, and the cover was made fast with a lock, in order to guard against malignant influences. There was more reason in the practice which formerly prevailed of securing the poor-boxes in the churches with locks and keys, and even iron plates, not *propter sortilegia*, but to guard the donations of the charitable against commonplace depredators. "Archæologia," vol. x. p. 207-8, where "Gent. Mag." vol. xliv. p. 500 and vol. xlv. p. 13 are cited. The passage requiring this protection to fonts is curious :" Fontes baptismales sub sera clausi teneantur propter sortilegia.''

Fool (Christmas).—In representations of the Fool, who took part in dramatic performances and in sports at festivals, he appears with all the badges of his office; the bauble in his hand, and a coxcomb hood, with asses' ears, on his head. The top of the hood rises into the form of a cock's neck and head, with a bell at the latter : and "Minshew's Dictionary," 1617, under the word *Coxcomb*, observes, that "natural idiots and fools have accustomed and still do accustome themselves to weare in their capes cockes feathers, or a hat with the necke

and head of a cock on the top, and a bell thereon.'' His hood is blue, guarded or edged with yellow at its scalloped bottom, his doublet is red, striped across, or rayed with a deeper red, and edged with yellow, his girdle yellow, his left-side hose yellow, with a red shoe, and his right-side hose blue, soled with red leather. In Gibson's "Memoranda," 1510-11, a charge of a halfpenny is made for "a turnyd ladyll spent for the foole," in connection with the Court Revel of the 15th November in that year. It seems from the prologue to "Henry the Eighth," that Shakespear's Fools should be dressed "in a long motley coat, guarded with yellow," which is illustrated by a passage in Rowlands :

> "My sleeves are like some Morris-daun-
> cing fellow,
> My stockings, ideot-like, red, greene,
> and yeallow :—"

Comp. Nares, *Glossary*, 1859, in v., for an excellent note on this subject.

Fool (Court). — In the " Privy Purse Expenses of Henry VII." numerous entries occur of money given to fools "in reward." Under date of Jan. 12, 1492-3, there is, "To Peche the fole in reward, 6s. 8d." Two other fools present themselves in this record : the *Duke of Lancas-*

A COURT FOOL (15*th Cent.*).

ter and Diego the Spanish fool. Steevens notices that the calf - skin coats, worn formerly by the professional fools in great houses, were designed to mark their calling, and to protect them from chastisement by those indisposed to tolerate their extravagances; and this custom, in his time, was still retained in Ireland, in the Christmas mummings. He observes of the later jesters: "Sometimes these gentlemen over-passed the appointed limits, and they were therefore corrected or discharged. The latter misfortune happened to Archibald Armstrong, jester to King Charles the First." Rushworth says: "It so happened that, on the 11th of the said March (1637-8), that Archibald, the King's Fool, said to his Grace the Archbishop of Canterbury, as he was going to the Council-table, 'Whea's feule now? doth not your Grace hear the news from Striveling about the Liturgy?' with other words of reflection: this was presently complained of to the Council, which produced the order for his expulsion from Court." There is in Olaus Magnus a delineation of a fool, or jester, with several bells upon his habit, with a bauble in his hand, and he has on his head a hood with asses' ears, a feather, and the resemblance of the comb of a cock. The Lord Mayor of London had his fool.

Fool (Domestic).—The following passage occurs in Lodge's "Wit's Miserie," 1596, p. 73: "He is like Captain Cloux, Foole of Lyons, that would needs die of the sullens, because his master would entertaine a new foole besides himself." Comp. *Newcastle*. A character of this kind was the unfortunate person, who might in the good old days be "begged" for a fool, if he was heir to an estate, and had no friends. These abuses were once frequent. See Thoms' *Anecdotes and Traditions*, 1839, p. 7, and Lyly's *Midas* (Works, 1858, ii., 74).

Fool Plough.—In the North of England there is a custom used at or about Shrovetide which, as will be seen, was anciently observed also in the beginning of Lent. The Fool Plough goes about, a pageant that consists of a number of sword dancers dragging a plough, with music, and one, sometimes two, in very strange attire; the Bessy, in the grotesque habit of an old woman, and the fool, almost covered with skins, a hairy cap on, and the tail of some animal hanging from his back. The office of one of these characters, in which he is very assiduous, is to go about rattling a box amongst the spectators of the dance, in which he receives their little donations. It is also called the fond plough, aliter the white plough, so denominated because the gallant young men that compose it appear to be dressed in their shirts (without coat or waistcoat) upon which great numbers of ribbands folded into roses are loosely stitched on. It appears to be a very airy habit at this cold season, but they have on warm waistcoats under it. Hutchinson, speaking of the dress of the sword-dancers at Christmas, adds: "Others, in the same kind of gay attire, draw about a plough, called the Stot Plough, and, when they receive the gift, make the exclamation *Largess!*

but if not requited at any house for their appearance, they draw the plough through the pavement, and raise the ground of the front in furrows. I have seen twenty men in the yoke of one plough." He concludes thus: "The stot-plough has been conceived by some to have no other derivation than a mere rural triumph, the plough having ceased from its labour." *History of Northumberland*, ii., 18. The Fool Plough upon the Continent appears to have been used after the solemn service of Ash Wednesday was over. Hospinian gives a very particular account of it from Naogeorgus, and explains the origin of its name.

Fools (Feast of).—See Du Cange, v. Kalendæ, and Du Tilliott, "Memoires pour servir à l'Histoire de la Fête des Foux," 1751 (as well as the present work under April Fools' Day). Du Cange, v. Cervula, Carpentier Supplem. ad Du Cange, ibid. and under *Abbas Lætitiæ*, and Delrio "Disquisit. Magis.", L. iii. P. ii. Quœst. 4. Sect. 5, p. 477. See also Hospinian "de Orig. Fest. Christ." fol. 32 b. where the practice is mentioned nearly in the same words.

Foot-Ale.—Grose says, "There is a kind of beverage called 'Foot-Ale' required from one entering on a new occupation." A person in this position is even now, in many businesses, expected to pay his footing, as it is called, in kind. Auctioneers, when they hold their first sale, are sometimes expected to treat the company all round.

Football or **Camp.**—The sport named by Fitzstephen was almost certainly hand-ball. But football was one of the most popular games in the city in the middle ages, and regulations relating to it are found at intervals in the Corporation archives. It was prohibited in the fields near the City as early as 1314. But in 1409 a proclamation of Henry IV. forbad anyone to levy money on pretence of it being for the games of football or cock-fighting. Riley's *Memorials*, 1868, p. 571. In the early part of the fifteenth century there was a gild of the Football Players, and they held their meetings at Brewers' Hall. Mr. Stahlschmidt found it recorded in an old MS. book belonging to the Brewers' Company. It is alluded to in a deed of 30 Henry VI. The ballad of *Sir Hugh, or, The Jew's Daughter*, opens with a scene in which Sir Hugh is playing at the game on Hallowday, when school boys are let out to engage in their amusements:—

"Yesterday was brave Hallowday,
And, above all days in the year,
The schoolboys all got leave to play,
And little Sir Hugh was there.

" He kicked the ball with his foot,
And kepped it with his knee,
And even in at the Jew's window
He gart the bonnie ba' flee— "

As to its antiquity two passages in the *Sussex Archæological Collections*, cited in *Notes and Queries*, may be acceptable here :—" In the proof of age of William Selwyne (baptized in 1403), a witness, John Hendyman, aged fifty-four, deposed that he knew the date, because after the baptism, he played football and broke his leg (Inq. post mort., 3 Henry VI., No. 51, cit. xv. S.A.C., 213). Again, as to the age of Robert Tank (baptized 1404), John Coumbes remembers it because he was playing football afterwards and broke his leg (Inq. p. m., 4 Hen. VI., No. 42, cit. xii. S.A.C., 43). Hence it is inferable that the game was not unusually played after christenings. Sir T. Elyot, in his *Governor*, 1531, decries the sport : "Some men wolde say that in the mediocritie, which I have soo moche praysed in shootynge, why shuld not bouling, claishe pynnes, and koytynge, be as moche commended? Veryly as for the two laste, they be to be vtterly abiected of all noble men, in lyke wyse foote balle, wherein is nothynge but beastely fury, and extreme violence, whereof procedeth hurte, and consequently rancour and malice do remayn with them that be wounded, wherefore it is to be put in perpetual sylence." King Lear having chastised Goneril's steward, the latter replies, " I'll not be struck, my Lord,"— " Nor tripped neither, you base football player," replied the Earl of Kent, tripping up his heels. (I. iv.). Ray says that in his time it prevailed most in Norfolk, Suffolk, and Essex. To Sir Thomas Browne, who came among us from another kingdom of the Octarchy, it was new; and he puts the word camp (or as he spells it, kamp) into his small collection of Norfolk words." The following description is from Forby's " Vocabulary," 1830. The writer says, that in his time two kinds of camp were recognised: rough-play and civil-play. " In the latter there is no boxing. But the following is a general description of it as it was of old, and in some places still continues. Two goals are pitched at the distance of 120 yards from each other. In a line with each are ranged the combatants : for such they truly are. The number on each side is equal; not always the same, but very commonly twelve. They ought to be uniformly dressed in light flannel jackets, distinguished by colours. The ball is deposited exactly in the mid-way. The sign or word is given by an umpire. The two sides, as they are called, rush forward. The sturdiest and most active of each encounter

those of the other. The contest for the ball begins, and never ends without black eyes and bloody noses, broken heads or shins, and some serious mischiefs. If the ball can be carried, kicked, or thrown to one of the goals, in spite of all the resistance of the other party, it is reckoned for one towards the game; which has sometimes been known to last two or three hours. But the exertion and fatigue of this is excessive . . . The prizes are commonly hats, gloves, shoes, or small sums of money."

I shall transcribe hither what I find in a quarter where it might scarcely be looked for : " This rough and, it must be confessed, somewhat dangerous sport, originally in all probability introduced into this country by the Romans, may still on Shrove Tuesday be witnessed in certain towns of South Wales. The balls consist of bulls' bladders protected by a thick covering of leather, and blown tight. Six or eight are made ready for the occasion. Every window in the town is shut by break of day, at which time all the youths of the neighbourhood assemble in the streets. The ball is then thrown up in front of the town-hall; and the multitude, dividing into two parts, strive with incredible eagerness and enthusiasm to kick the football to the other extremity of the town. In the struggle several kicks and wounds are given, and many fierce battles take place. The ball sometimes ascends thirty or forty feet above the tops of the highest houses, and falls far beyond, or goes right over into the gardens, whither it is immediately followed by a crowd of young men. The sport is kept up all day, the hungry combatants recruiting their strength from time to time by copious horns of ale and an abundant supply of the nice pancakes which the women sell in baskets at the corner of every street. To view this sport thousand of persons assemble from all the country round, so that to the secluded population of those districts it is in some sort what the battle in the Platanistas was to the Spartans, or even what the Isthmian and Nemean games were to the whole of Greece." St. John's *Manners and Customs of Ancient Greece*, 1842, i., 157. The same thing is still kept up at Dorking, Epsom, and Kingston, in Surrey; but there has been a movement so far unsuccessful (1903) at Dorking for its discontinuance. "At the Surrey Quarter Sessions at Kingston yesterday the ancient custom of playing football in the principal streets of Dorking on Shrove Tuesday was referred to in the report of the Standing Joint Committee to the Justices. The committee stated that a petition signed by upwards of one hundred inhabitants of Dorking had been received, urging the committee to adopt necessary measures to put a stop to the practice. The reasons given were that it caused a complete cessation of business on the afternoon of that day; that it caused great danger to vehicular and pedestrian traffic; that the ancient custom has now entirely lost its significance in consequence of the totally different conditions now prevailing; and that it had become an intolerable nuisance. The petitioners stated that they had decided to discontinue closing their shops and barricading against an unlawful proceeding.—The Committee reported that they were making exhaustive inquiries on the subject with a view to the suppression of the custom, and would shortly make some definite announcement."—*Daily Graphic*, 1897. A very curious practice prevails at Sedgwick in Durham, where a match is periodically played between the tradespeople and the country-folk at Chester-le-Street, and probably elsewhere, and the ball on each occasion becomes public property, and returns to its custodian, the town-clerk, by the latter putting it thrice through the bull-ring prior to proceedings and at the close. *Antiquary* for April, 1896. In the volume for 1898, there is a very animated description of the Shrovetide celebration there in that year. At Pocklington, in the East Riding of Yorkshire, there is a narrow strip of ground, where, after the races, they play at football, and it sometimes happens that one of the players throws the ball to a man attending on horseback, who rides off with it, and unless he is overtaken by one belonging to the opposite side, carries it into his own parish, where he is secure. This is also the case in Morbihan, Brittany, as described in Mr. Weld's interesting work, 1856, but the sport seems to have been there carried to almost brutal extremities. Mr. Brand was informed that, at Alnwick Castle, in Northumberland, the waits belonging to the town come playing to the castle every year on Shrove-Tuesday, at two o'clock p.m., when a football was thrown over the castle walls to the populace. He saw this done Feb. 5th, 1788.

Football in Scotland.—In Sinclair's "Statistical Account of Scotland," the minister of Kirkmichael, in Perthshire, speaking of the manners and customs of the inhabitants, says, "Foot-ball is a common amusement with the schoolboys, who also preserve the custom of cock-fighting on Shrove Tuesday." On Shrove-Tuesday at Inverness there is a standing match at football between married and unmarried women, in which the former are always victors. Every year on Shrove-Tuesday the bachelors and married men drew themselves up at the Cross of Scone, on opposite sides. A ball was then thrown up, and they played from two o'clock till sun-set. The game was this. He who at any time got the ball into his hands, ran with it till overtaken by one of the opposite party, and then, if he could shake himself loose from those on the opposite side who seized him, he ran on: if not, he threw the ball from him, unless it was wrested from him by the other party; but no person was allowed to kick it. The object of the married men was to hang it; i.e., to put it three times into a small hole in the moor, the dool or limit on the one hand: that of the bachelors was to drown it: i.e., to dip it three times into a deep place in the river, the limit on the other. The party who could effect either of these objects won the game. But, if neither party won, the ball was cut into equal parts at sunset. In the course of the play one might always see some scene of violence between the parties; but, as the proverb of this part of the country expresses, 'All was fair at the Ball of Scone.' *Stat. Acc. of Scotland*, xviii., 82. "This custom is supposed to have had its origin in the days of chivalry. An Italian (it is said) came into this part of the country, challenging all the parishes, under a certain penalty in case of declining his challenge. All the parishes declined the challenge except Scone, which beat the foreigner, and in commemoration of this gallant action the game was instituted. Whilst the custom continued, every man in the parish, the gentry not excepted, was obliged to turn out and support the side to which he belonged; and the person who neglected to do his part on that occasion was fined: but the custom being attended with certain inconveniences, was abolished a few years ago."

The allusions to the game in early writings are very numerous. Tusser says:

"In meadow or pasture (to grow the more fine)
Let campers be camping in any of thine;
Which if ye do suffer when low is the spring,
You gain to yourself a commodious thing."

Chamberlain, in a letter to Carleton, March 5, 1600-1, says: "You may do well, if you have any idle time, to play the good fellow and come and see our matches at football, for that and bowling wilbe our best entertainment." Henry Spelman, in his *Relation of Virginia*, 1609, says: "They vse beside football play, wch women and young boyes doe much play at, the men neuer. They make ther gooles as ours, only they neuer fight nor pull one another doone. The men play wth a litell balle lettinge it falle out of ther hand and striketh wth the tope of his foot, and he that can strike the balle farthest, winnes that they play for." This is the earliest American reference to the game which I remember to have seen. I quote from a modern edition of the original MS., possibly not a very accurate text. But the sense is sufficiently clear, except that the writer seems to say in one place that the men in Virginia did not play, only the women and boys, and presently he alludes to the way in which his own sex did play.

" Football with us may be with them balloon :
As they at tilt, so we at quintain, run."

Randolph, *Eclogue on the Cotswold Games* (Works, 1875, 621-3). Day in the *Blind Beggar of Bednal Green*, 1659, makes Tom Strowd say : " I'll play a gole at Campball or wrassell a fall of the hip or the hin turn with ere a Courtnoll of ye all for 20 quarters of malt, and match me height for height." Strowd's was probably the rough play, like the modern Rugby. Under date of January, 1664-5, Pepys notes : " The street full of footballs, it being a great frost." Misson, writing about 1690, says : " In winter foot-ball is a useful and charming exercise. It is a leather ball about as big as one's head, fill'd with wind. This is kick'd about from one to t'other in the streets, by him that can get at it, and that is all the art of it." There is a proverb : " All fellows at football," which means that it is a case where every man must take his chance. It is a game which levels artificial distinctions. " We are hale fellows, well met, not onely at foot-ball, but at every thing else." *Ludus Ludi Literarius*, 1672, p. 73. Comp. *Liber Albus*, Rolls ed., p. 440; Halliwell's *Dictionary* in v.; and Antiquary, xxxii., 99-100. It appears that this sport was known to the Mexicans prior to the Spanish conquest.

Football Money.—In the North of England, among the colliers, &c., it is customary for a party to watch the bridegroom's coming out of church after the ceremony, in order to demand money for a football, a claim that admits of no refusal. Thiers refers to an analogous abuse in France, and describes such practices as " insolences proscrites." " Traité des Superstitions," 1794, tom. iii., p. 477.

Foot-Saunt.—See *Cent-Foot.*

Forespoken Water.—See *Orkneys.*

Forester of the Fee.—A person who had for some service to the crown a perpetual right of hunting in a forest on payment of a certain rent. Halliwell in v. From Forester as an employment we get the proper names, *Forrester*, *Forester*, *Forster*, and *Foster.*

Forfeits in a Barber's Shop.—In " Measure for Measure," the author has written :—

—" the strong Statutes
Stand like the forfeits in a barber's shop,
As much in mock as mark ;"

On which Warburton observes, " Barbers' shops were, at all times, the resort of idle people :

' Tronstrina erat quædam : hic solebamus ferè
Plerumque eam opperiri.'———

Donatus calls it *apta sedes otiosis.* Formerly with us the better sort of people went to the barber's shop to be trimmed ; who then practised the under parts of surgery ; so that he had occasion for numerous instruments which lay there ready for use ; and the idle people, with whom his shop was generally crouded, would be perpetually handling and misusing them. To remedy which, I suppose, there was placed up against the wall a table of forfeitures, adapted to every offence of this kind ; which it was not likely would long preserve its authority." Dr. Henley adds : " I perfectly remember to have seen them " (the list of forfeits) "in Devonshire, printed like King Charles's Rules. See Nares, 1859, in v.

Fortune-Telling.—The following passage is from Lodge's *Wit's Miserie*, 1596, p. 17 : " There are many in London now adaies that are besotted with this sinne, one of whom I saw on a white horse in Fleet Street, a tanner knave I never lookt on, who with one figure (cast out of a schollers studie for a necessary servant at Bocordo) promised to find any man's oxen were they lost, restore any man's goods if they were stolne, and win any man love, where or howsoever he settled it, but his jugling knacks were quickly discovered." Baxter speaks of those men that tell men of things stolen and lost, and that show men the face of a thief in a glass, and cause the goods to be brought back, who are commonly called white witches. " When I lived," he says, " at Dudley, Hodges at Sedgley two miles off, was long and commonly counted such a one. And when I lived at Kedderminster one of my neighbours affirmed, that having his yarn stolen, he went to Hodges (ten miles off) and he told him that at such an hour he should have it brought home again, and put in at the window, and so it was ; and as I remember he shewed him the person's face in a glass.

Yet I do not think that Hodges made any known contract with the Devil, but thought it an effect of art." *World of Spirits*, 1691, p. 184. Comp. *Witches*.

In the *Daily Telegraph* newspaper for December 11, 1867, appeared the annexed paragraph : "At Leamington yesterday, a woman named Hannah Maria Moore was charged with fortune-telling. The defendant resided at a lonely cottage in the outskirts of Leamington, and has long been celebrated for her knowledge of the occult arts, and her skill in divining the future. If report be true, the rich were as credulous as the poor, and even carriages might be seen waiting after nightfall in the vicinity of her dwelling. At last, so notorious did the scandal become, that the police took steps to obtain a conviction. Accordingly, on Monday night, the wives of two of the constables paid her a visit. If her powers of divination are to be judged by what she revealed to them, they certainly were not great, for she not only failed to discover the true object of their visit, but showed great consideration for them, and, out of compassion for their indigence, only charged threepence for all her glowing promises of sweethearts, weddings, and a long line of descendants. It would appear, however, from a letter found in her possession when apprehended, that she occasionally engaged to exercise her arts so as to send sweethearts to young women, as in the communication alluded to her correspondent upbraided her for not having fulfilled her promises, and exhorted her to redouble her efforts. The bench committed her to gaol for a month with hard labour."

Fox and Geese.—On the 4th March, 1587-8, John Wolfe the printer entered at Stationers' Hall the Gynnye game, Cheste game, and Foxe and Geese."

Fox in the Hole.—A boys' game as far back as the reign of Elizabeth. See Halliwell in v. It is mentioned by Herrick in his "New Yeares Gift sent Sir Simeon Steward," preserved among the Hesperides," 1648.

Foy.—A bad husband is described at the end of *England's Jests*, 1687, as "a passionate lover of morning-draughts, which he generally continues till dinnertime ; a rigid exacter of Num-Groats, and Collector General of Foys and Biberidge. He admires the produce of that apothegm, Lets drink first : and would rather sell 20 per cent. to loss than make a dry-bargain." Eden, in his "State of the Poor," 1797, vol. i., p. 560, gives us the following passage from Fergusson's "Farmer's Ingle" :

"On some feast day, the wee-things busk it braw,
  Shall heeze her heart up wi' a silent joy,
Fu' cadgie that her head was up, and saw
  Her ain spun cleething on a darling Oy,
Careless tho' death should make the feast her foy."

After explaining Oy in a note to signify grand-child, from the Gaelic *Ogha*, he tells us "A Foy is the feast a person, who is about to leave a place, gives to his friends before his departure."

Freemen of Highgate.—See *Horns.*

Free Warren.—As far back as the reign of Henry II., the citizens of London had the right of free warren in Middlesex, Hertfordshire, the Chiltern country, and in Kent, as far as the Cray. This right was probably renewed in 1226, in which year Stow erroneously places its original concession. A limitation on the primitive liberty of hunting, fowling, &c., seems to have been made in the reign of Henry VI., when the parks, from which the venison was to be taken, were specified by the lords of the Council. In the time of Elizabeth, the right had been formally commuted for a yearly warrant from the government upon the keepers of certain parks within the county of Middlesex, for the delivery of bucks to the mayor and aldermen. Comp. Hazlitt's *Bibl. Coll.*, 2nd Series, 118 v. *Charter Warren.*

St. Frethmund, Fredysmund, or Fremund.—Son of Offa, King of Mercia, and his queen Botilda, murdered by a servant of the king his father, and canonised about 790 A.D. A long account of him from various early authorities is printed in the *Antiquary* for May, 1893, where it is stated that he is supposed to have been buried at Cropedy Church, Lincolnshire. In 1488, St. Frethmund had a chapel in the cathedral at Lincoln, as we learn from the will of Richard Danvers of Prescott, co. Oxford, made in that year, where he leaves 20s. to the chaplain to pray for his soul, and a shrine in Cropedy Church, to the repairs of which a similar amount is dedicated by the testator. It may be added that Nicolas, in his *Chronology of History*, calls him hermit and martyr, and states that his anniversary was May 11. The son of this Danvers, Sir John Danvers, died in 1514, and also left benefactions to Cropedy Church and St. Fremund's Church ; and above his tomb in Dauntsey Church, Wilts, was formerly a window stained with glass, illustrating the legend.

Friar Rush, mentioned in Harsnet's *Declaration of Popish Impostures*, 1603, as a Christmas game; but its nature is not explained.

Friar Tuck.—Tollett describes this character upon his window as in the full clerical tonsure, with a chaplet of white and red beads in his right hand: and, expressive of his professed humility, his eyes are cast upon the ground. His corded girdle and his russet habit denote him to be of the Franciscan Order, or one of the Grey Friars (the only one exempt from episcopal jurisdiction, as Tollett himself pointed out). His stockings are red, his red girdle is ornamented with a golden twist, and with a golden tassel. At his girdle hangs a wallet for the reception of provision, the only revenue of the mendicant orders of religion, who were named Walleteers or budget-bearers. Steevens supposes this Morris Friar designed for Friar Tuck, of Fountain's Dale, chaplain to Robin Hood, as King of May. The Friar's coat, as appears from some of the extracts of Churchwardens' and Chamberlain's Accounts of Kingston, was generally of russet. The original character was one of the heroes of the Robin Hood epic. Hazlitt's *National Tales and Legends*, 1892, p. 273.

Friday (Good).—See *Good Friday*.

Friday in Lide.—The first Friday in March is so called from Llyd, Anglo-Saxon for *tumult* or *loud*. "This day," says Mr. Couch, "is marked by a serio-comic custom of sending a young lad on the highest bound or hillock of the work, and allowing him to sleep there as long as he can; the length of his siesta being the measure of the afternoon nap for the tinners throughout the ensuing twelvemonth. The weather which commonly characterizes Friday in Lide is, it need scarcely be said, scarcely conducive to prolong sleep. In Saxon times the labourers were usually allowed their mid-day sleep; and I have observed that it is even now permitted to husbandmen in some parts of East Cornwall, during a stated portion of the year. Tusser speaks of it in his ' Five Hundred Points of Good Husbandry',:

'From May to mid August an hour or two,
Let Patch sleep a snatch, howsoeuer ye do:
Though sleeping one hour refresheth his song,
Yet trust not Hob Grouthead for sleeping too long.' "

Browne, in the third eclogue of the "Shepheard's Pipe," 1614, clearly alludes to this usage, where he makes Thomalin say:

" Where is euery piping lad
That the fields are not yclad
With their milk-white sheep?
Tell me: Is it Holy-day,
Or if in the month of May
Use they long to sleepe? "

The same author has the practice in view, where he says in the third song of his first Book of *Pastorals*, in reference to the song-birds in the woodland:

" Whose pleasing noates the tyred swaine have made
To steale a nap at noone-tide in the shade."

Frindsbury, Kent.—Ireland, in his " Views of the Medway," speaks of a singular custom which used to be annually observed on May Day by the boys of Frindsbury and the neighbouring town of Stroud. " They met on Rochester Bridge, where a skirmish ensued between them. This combat probably derived its origin from a drubbing received by the monks of Rochester in the reign of Edward I. These monks, on occasion of a long drought, set out on a procession for Frindsbury to pray for rain; but the day proving windy, they apprehended the lights would be blown out, the banners tossed about, and their order much discomposed. They, therefore, requested of the Master of Stroud Hospital leave to pass through the orchard of his house, which he granted without the permission of his brethren; who, when they had heard what the master had done, instantly hired a company of ribalds, armed with clubs and bats, who way-laid the poor monks in the orchard, and gave them a severe beating. The monks desisted from proceeding that way, but soon after found out a pious mode of revenge, by obliging the men of Frindsbury, with due humility, to come yearly on Whit Monday, with their clubs in procession to Rochester, as a penance for their sins. Hence probably came the by-word of Frindsbury clubs."

Fritters or **Frutters Thursday.**—In Leeds and the neighbourhood, they eat a sort of pancake on the Thursday, which in that part they call frutters (fritters) Thursday. The Leeds fritter, it is said in the " Dialect of Leeds," 1862, p. 307, is " about one-fourth the size of a pancake, thicker, and has an abundance of currants in it."

Frog in the Middle.—A game played by both sexes, and consisting of a party of four or more, of whom one sat in the middle (the frog), and was playfully buffeted by the others, till he or she could catch one of them, who had then to take the place. A representation of the mode of playing this game occurs in Wright's

Domestic Manners, 1862, p. 233. *Frog in the Middle* seems to date back to an early period.

Fullam.—Compare a note in Nares, *Gloss.* in v. where there is a cross-reference to *Gourds*, and *High-Men* ibid., and see *Huth Cat*, p. 1005.

Funeral Customs.—"All funerals," says Adam, in his "Roman Antiquities," p. 476, "used antiently to be solemnized in the night time with torches, that they might not fall in the way of magistrates and priests, who were supposed to be violated by seeing a corpse, so that they could not perform sacred rites, till they were purified by an expiatory sacrifice. Serv. in Virg. xi. 143; Donat. Ter. And. i. I, 81. And hence we get the term itself, as the primitive lights were formed of small ropes or cords (funes) dipped in wax or tallow. But in after ages public funerals (funera indictiva) were celebrated in the daytime, at an early hour in the forenoon, as it is thought from Plutarch, in Syll. with torches also. Serv. in Virg. Æn. vi. 224. Tacit. Ann. iii. 4. Private or ordinary funerals (tacita) were always at night. *Fest. in Vespilones.* Sir Thomas Browne, speaking of the ancients, observes, that "they poured oyle upon the pyre, while the intention rested in facilitating the accension: but to place good omens in the quick and speedy burning, to sacrifice unto the windes for a dispatch in this office, was a low form of superstition." *Hydriotaphia*, p. 59. But when the remains were calcined, wine was poured over them, and when they were intended for preservation, they were then collected in a vase or urn, the which in the Homeric age was finally deposited with honours in the ground or in a barrow. Such or similar rites are described as attendant on the sepulture of Beowulf.

The Greek, Roman, and Anglo-Saxon methods of interment appear to have presented close analogies, and even domestic utensils, weapons and jewelry were favourite accompaniments of the departed; and instances are recorded, where, for some unknown reason, but probably because the persons had died abroad, the barrow was a cenotaph, containing only the complimentary accessories or the affectionate homage—in one case (at Bourne Park, Kent), a shield, a horse's bit, and other similar articles at home, perhaps by a soldier on foreign service or a crusader. "Their last valediction thrice uttered by the attendants was also very solemn; 'Vale, Vale, Vale, nos te ordine quo Natura permittet sequemur': and somewhat answered by Christians, who thought it too little, if they threw not the earth thrice upon the enterred body." Gough says: "The women of Picardy have a custom of calling the deceased by his name, as he is carried to the grave. So do the Indians, and expostulate with him for dying, which reminds us of the Irish: "Och! why did ye die?" Χαιρε was among the Greeks a common parting exclamation.

Bourne tells us, that they followed the corpse to the grave, because it presented to them what would shortly follow, how they themselves should be so carried out. *Antiq. Vulg.* ch. iii. In Langley's abridgement of Polydore Vergil, 1546, we read: "In burials the old rite was that the ded corps was borne afore, and the people folowed after, as one should saie we shall dye and folowe after hym, as their laste woordes to the coarse did pretende. For thei used to say, when it was buried, on this wise, farewell, wee come after thee, and of the folowyng of the multitude thei were called exequies." It appears that among the primitive Christians the corpse was sometimes kept four days. Pelagia, in Gregory of Tours, requests of her son, that he would not bury her before the fourth day. In the will of John Hales, of Eton, "the ever-memorable," proved in March, 1666, there is a passage, in which he says that he desires to be buried "the next evening-song after he shall die," in a plain simple manner, "without sermon or ringing of bells, commensations, compotations, or such like solemnities."

Misson, speaking of funerals, says: "They let the body lie three or four days, as well to give the dead person an opportunity of coming to life again, if his soul has not quite left his body, as to prepare mourning and the ceremonies of the funeral. They send the beadle with a list of such friends and relations as they have a mind to invite; and sometimes they have printed tickets which they leave at their houses. A little before the company is together for the march," he continues, "they lay the body into the coffin upon two stools, in a room, where all that please may go and see it; then they take off the top of the coffin, and remove from off the face a little square piece of flannel, made on purpose to cover it, and not fastened to any thing. Being ready to move, one or more beadles march first, each carrying a long staff, at the end of which is a great apple, or knob of silver. The body comes just after the minister or ministers attended by the Clerk. The relations in close mourning, and all the guests, two and two, make up the rest of the procession." *Travels in England*, transl. by Ozell, 90.

It was customary, in the Christian burials of the Anglo - Saxons, to leave the head and shoulders of the corpse uncovered till the time of the burial, that relations, &c., might take a last view of their deceased friend. To this day we yet retain (in our way) this old custom, leaving the coffin of the deceased unscrewed till the time of the burial. They were wont, says Bourne, to sit by the corpse from the time of death till its exportation to the grave, either in the house it died in, or in the church itself. To prove this he cites St. Austin, concerning the watching the dead body of his mother Monica ; and Gregory of Tours, concerning that of St. Ambrose, whose body was carried into the church the same hour he died. In the monumental effigy of Berengaria, queen of Richard Cœur de Lion, at Le Mans, the figure holds a book, on the covers of which is embossed a representation of the departed, lying on a bier, with waxen torches burning in candlesticks by her side. Fairholt's *Costume in England*, 1860, p. 82. This practice was general, and is still in vogue among the Romanists. Pope refers to the practice of setting candles upon the bier during the wake or watching time :

" Ah hopeless lasting flames ! like those that burn
To light the dead, and warm th' unfruitful urn."
—*Eloïsa to Abelard.*

Some of the earliest notices of funeral observances in England, dating back to Anglo-Norman times, are connected with the Gilds of the City of London, and particularly with that of the Saddlers. A convention made between the latter and the monastery of St. Martin's-le-Grand, immediately contiguous to their ancient quarters, in 1154, shews that the brethren of the Company enjoyed the privileges of sepulture in the burial ground of the holy fraternity on payment for the ringing of the bell and the reception of the body, the sum of eightpence. Many of the London gilds still preserve the rich palls, which used to be thrown over the coffin on its passage to the place of interment within the civic precincts. Hazlitt's *Livery Companies of London*, 1892, pp. 602, 608, *et passim*. A reference to the same authority will shew the former universality of lights maintained in churches and chapels for the souls of the departed, out of funds bequeathed by testators and others. Misson mentions, under the head of funerals, "the washing the body thoroughly clean, and shaving it, if it be a man, and his beard be grown during his sickness." Pennant, in his "Tours in Wales," informs us that, " at these words 'we commit the body

to the ground,' the minister holds the spade and throws in the first spadeful of earth." He adds : " At Skiv-'og from the Park to the Church I have seen the bier carried by the next of kin, husband, brothers, and father in law. All along from the house to the church yard at every cross-way, the bier is laid down, and the Lord's Prayer rehearsed, and so when they first come into the church yard, before any of the verses appointed in the service be said. There is a custom of ringing a little bell before the corps, from the house to the church yard (Dymerchion.) Some particular places are called resting-places." " Skyvi'og. When a corpse is carried to church from any part of the town, the bearers take care to carry it so that the corps may be on their right hand, though the way be nearer and it be less trouble to go on the other side ; nor will they bring the corps through any other way than the south gate. If it should happen to rain while the corps is carried to church, it is reckoned to bode well to the deceased, whose bier is wet with the dew of Heaven. At church the evening service is read, with the Office of Burial. The minister goes to the altar, and there says the Lord's Prayer, with one of the prayers appointed to be read at the grave : after which the congregation offer upon the altar, or on a little board for that purpose fixed to the rails of the altar, their benevolence to the officiating minister. A friend of the deceased is appointed to stand at the altar, observing who gives, and how much. When all have given, he counts the money with the minister, and signifies the sum to the congregation, thanking them all for their good will." The same writer informs us that the Scotish and Irish practice of howling or shrieking at burials was equally prevalent in Wales. *Tours in Wales*, 1810, ii., 175. Not improbably it was a Celtic usage. We learn from the inscription in a copy of the *Bowman's Glory*, 1682, by W. Wood, that he was buried at Clerkenwell, attended by the Company of Archers, who shouted three times over his grave. *Gent. Mag. Lib.*, (*Bibl. Coll.*, 222). In Thomas Hill's Book on Dreams, signat. M i., is the following passage : " To a sicke person to have or weare on white garments doothe promyse death, for that dead bodyes bee caryed foorth in white clothes. And to weare on a blacke garmente, it doothe promyse, for the more parte, healthe to a sicke person, for that not dead personnes, but suche as mourne for the deade, do use to be clothed in blacke." At the funerals of unmarried persons of both sexes, as well as infants, the scarves, hatbands, and gloves given as mourning are white. Pepys saw in Westminster Hall Mistress Lane and the rest of the maids, who had been at the funeral service over a young bookseller in the Hall, and who all wore their white scarves. This was in January, 1659-60. Laying out the corpse is an office always performed by women, who claim the linen, &c., about the person of the deceased at the time of performing the ceremony. It would be thought very unlucky to the friends of the person departed, were they to keep back any portion of what is thus found. These women give this away in their turn by small divisions; and they who can obtain any part of it, think it an omen or presage of future good fortune to them or theirs.

The following is an extract from the old Register-book of Christ Church, Hants: — "April 14, 1604. Christian Steevens, the wife of Thomas Steevens, was buried in child-birth, and buried by women, for she was a Papishe." *Warner*, ii., 130. Pennant states: "The people kneel, and say the Lord's Prayer on the graves of their dead friends for some Sundays after their interment: and this is done generally upon their first coming to Church, and, after that, they dress the grave with flowers. Llanvechan." Gough adds that in Flintshire they say the prayer as the body leaves the house. *Sep. Mon.*, ii., cciv. In the time of Durandus coals, holy water, and frankincense were, in some places, put into the grave. The holy water was to drive away the devils; the frankincense to counteract the ill smells of the body." *Rationale*, vii., 35, 38. Sir Thomas Browne, in his "Urne-burial" observes, that "the custom of carrying the corpse as it were out of the world with its feet forward, is not inconsonant to reason, as contrary to the native posture of man, and his production first into it." Macaulay observes: "At the funeral of a yeoman, or farmer, the clergyman generally leads the van in the procession, in his canonical habiliments; and the relations follow the corpse, two and two, of each sex, in the order of proximity, linked in each other's arms. At the funeral of a young man it is customary to have six young women, clad in white, as pall-bearers; and the same number of young men, with white gloves and hatbands, at the funeral of a young woman. But these usages are not so universally prevalent as they were in the days of our fathers." *Hist. of Claybrook*, 1791, 131.

Judging from an illustration in an early Breviary in the British Museum, the body was at first consigned to the ground in the funeral cerements, but without any coffin, and the latter was not introduced down to a comparatively late period. *Archæol. Album*, 1845, p. 90. A similar practice is followed by the Mohammedans, and ap-

pears to have prevailed on the European continent, which doubtless derived it from the East, as England may have done from her immediate neighbours across the Channel. There is a story laid in Picardy, in fact, where a woman taken to be dead, but only in a lethargy, was followed to the grave, wrapped in a sheet, and the bearers, going too near a hedge, the thorns penetrated the covering, and restored vitality. Hazlitt's Studies in Jocular Literature, 1890, p. 120. It is this tale, to which Tallemant des Reaux seems to refer; but he gives it a various reading. *Historiettes*, ed. 1854,

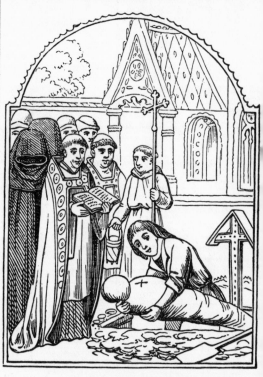

BURIAL WITHOUT A COFFIN.

i., 437. Speaking of the peculiarities in the conduct of a Cleveland funeral, Mr. Atkinson says (1868): "Till lately, when the corpse of an unmarried female was carried to the churchyard, the bearers were all single, and usually young women dressed in a kind of uniform, in some places all in white, in other in black dresses with white shawls and white straw bonnets trimmed with white. The servers (the young women who wait at the arval-supper) also always preceded the coffin, as it approached the churchyard, sometimes in white, more usually in black with a broad white ribbon worn scarf-wise over one shoulder, and crossing over the black shawl; or else with knots or rosettes of white on the breast." In Cornwall, the manner among the lower orders is to bear the coffin almost level with the ground, slung on trestle boards, the members of the procession taking turns; and the dead body occupies the centre of the group. There is no hearse or vehicle of any kind (1875). In the Cotswolds there appears to be a pretty and appropriate custom at the burials of little children, by which the coffin is borne in the case of a boy by four children of that sex in black dresses and white hats, and in that of a girl by as many young females of the village similarly attired. This probably ancient usage will doubtless grow obsolete, as the neighbourhood becomes more cenventional. *Graphic,* Oct. 25, 1902. At the recent interment of a bailiff, belonging to a farmhouse among the hills on the borders of Devonshire and West Dorsetshire, the body was borne to the churchyard in a waggon decorated with heather, the coffin being hidden under bunches of oats. Three cart-horses, whose manes were embellished with black rosettes, drew the vehicle; the lord of the manor headed the procession on a black hunter, and a hundred labourers from the farm and the neighbourhood followed the remains. *Daily Mail,* Sept. 5, 1903.

In the heart of London, in the neighbourhood of the Seven Dials, among the costermongers who are of superior standing and means, the last tribute to the defunct often costs a considerable sum, and involves a good deal of ceremony. The body is duly prepared, and laid upon a truck—the one used by the departed—with a pall over it, and the friends having assembled, a procession threads all the adjoining thoroughfares, preparatory to the departure for the place of interment. Where the deceased person was popular, as many as 400 or 500 will attend the committal to the earth, and the funeral cortége will consist of a dozen well-appointed carriages. It yet (1903) remains a characteristic trait of the English poorer class to expend a disproportionate amount on burials.

Grose says: — "If you meet a funeral procession, or one passes by you, always take off your hat: this keeps all evil spirits attending the body in good humour, but this, though very usual abroad, is very rarely practised here, at least in large towns."

In relation to the stage of the burial service where the minister says, *Earth to Earth,* and casts a handful over the coffin after deposition, there is the passage in Herrick's *Hesperides,* 1648, where, in speaking of

his youthful years, the poet says, that he shall never again visit Westminster or Cheapside :

> " Where the earth
> Of Julian Herrick gave to me my birth."

It is observed that in sandy, wet soils twenty years suffice to obliterate every vestige of a coffin and its contents except perhaps the brass plate and a few nails, where no artificial precautions have been taken. This point may be collated with a familiar passage in *Hamlet.*

In some excavations undertaken in 1576, according to Stow, in Spitalfields, certain Roman cinerary urns were brought to light, which in company with the ashes, contained a small coin of the contemporary emperor, and in the tomb of Canute, opened at Winchester in modern times, one of the hands held a silver penny of that ruler. The precise object of this practice has not been determined, although it has been suggested that it might have been a tradition from later Hellenic folklore and the ferryman Charon who, however, only accepted fares in the shape of persons canonically buried. A different class of association between coins and the dead was the deposit of money in tombs commemorative of the reign of a sovereign, as in the case of Napoleon at St. Helena in 1821.

Funerals, Ceremonial Usages at. — When the tomb of King John in Worcester Cathedral was opened in 1797, the remains were found to have been deposited in the earth, habited in the same manner as the monumental effigy outside. The King wore a supertunic of crimson embroidered with gold, with red hose and black shoes; his gilt spurs were fastened to his feet by straps of light blue, striped with green and yellow. The beard was closely trimmed. But the most remarkable variation was that on the head was a monk's cowl, corroborating the statement of the chroniclers, that John had assumed that article of dress in his last moments as a protection from the Devil. Fairholt's *Costume in England,* 1860, p. 83-4. The identical notion recurs elsewhere, as the subjoined extract shews :— "On the 13th May, 1220, (4 Hen. iii.) died Robert the second Lord Berkelye, ætis. 55 or thereabouts, and was buried in the North Isle of the Church of the Monastery of St. Augustines (Bristol) over against the high altar, in a monck's cowle, an usual fashion for great peeres in those tymes, esteemed as an amulet or defensative to the soule, and as a Scala Cœli, a ladder of life eternal." Smyth's *Berkeley MSS.,* i., 117. This was Robert de **Ber-**

keley, second baron by tenure under a charter of Queen Eleanor. In Ceremonies and Services at Court in the reign of Henry VII. there is a reference to the manner in which the body of Henry V. was brought over to England from France in 1422: "In conveynge over of King Henry V[th]. out of France into Englond," the narrative informs us, "his coursers were trappid w[t] trappers of party coloures : one sid was blewe velwet embrodured w[t] antilopes drawenge iij. iuillis; the toy[r] sid was grene velwet embrowdered withe antelopes sittinge on stires w[t] long flours springinge betwene the hornes; the trappers aftur, by the comandment of kinge Henry the VIth, were sent to the Vestry of Westminst[r] ; and of every coloure was mad a cope, a chesabille, and ij tenacles; and the gefereys of one coloure was of the clothe of oy[r] coloure." Many other curious and important particulars relative to funeral ceremonies may be gathered from the same paper ("Antiq. Repert." ed. 1807, vol. i. p. 311.). Somewhat later we find a high authority deprecating unbecoming expenditure on these occasions. Archbishop Warham in his will, 1530, says :— "Non convenit enim eum quem humiliter vivere decet, pomposé sepeliri, nisi velit, et id frustrâ, cadaveri mortuo majores honores deberi quam corpori vivo." Extravagant outlay on burials was forbidden by the ancient Greek law, which does not appear to have been uniformly respected any more than such enactments in modern times.

In the first funeral which he seems to have witnessed after the accession of Queen Elizabeth, and the return to Protestantism, Machyn is rather minute in his description. He says: "Ther was a gret compene of pepull, ij and ij together, and nodur (neither) prest nor clarke, the nuw (new) prychers in ther gowne lyke leymen, nodur nor sayhyng tyll they cam to the grave, and a-for she was put into the grayff a collect in Englys, and then put in-to the grayff, and after took some heythe (earth) and caste yt on the corse, and red a thynge . . . for the same, and contenent (incontinently) cast the heth in-to the grave, and contenent red the pystyll of sant Poll to the Stesselonians (Thessalonians) the . . chapter, and after that they song paternoster in Englys, boyth prychers and odur, and (. . .) of a nuw fassyon, and after on of them whent in-to the pulpytt and mad a sermon." This narrative, in spite of its uncouth phraseology and orthography, seemed worth transcribing, as being the earliest account we have of a funeral rite subsequently to the re-establishment of the reformed faith. At the funeral of Lady Cicily Mansfield, in 1558, Lady Petre was chief mourner.

During two centuries and a half the Dyotts of Lichfield buried their dead in the family vault in the north aisle of St. Mary's-in-the-Market by torchlight; and the usage survived down to recent times. In the *Antiquary* for 1891, there is an account of the disorderly scenes on two of these occasions; and in his monograph, *The Curiosities of the Church*, Mr. Andrews, without citing this case, has a section on torchlight burial, which, as I have noted, was habitual among the ancients. An interesting paper on Traditions and Customs Relating to Death and Burial in Lincolnshire, from the pen of Miss Florence Peacock of Bottesford Manor, appeared in the *Antiquary* for November, 1895. Monsieur Jorevin, in his *Travels in England*, 1672, describing a lord's burial near Shrewbury, tells us : "The relations and friends being assembled in the house of the defunct, the minister advanced into the middle of the chamber, where, before the company, he made a funeral oration, representing the great actions of the deceased, his virtues, his qualities, his titles of nobility, and those of the whole family, &c. It is to be remarked that during his oration, there stood upon the coffin a large pot of wine, out of which every one drank to the health of the deceased. This being finished, six men took up the corps, and carried it on their shoulders to the church." "The coffin," he adds, "was covered with a large cloth, which the four nearest relations held each by a corner with one hand, and in the other carried a bough"; (this must have been a branch of rosemary:) "the other relations and friends had in one hand a flambeau, and in the other a bough, marching thus through the street, without singing or saying any prayer, till they came to the church." After the burial service, he adds, the clergyman, "having his bough in his hand like the rest of the congregation, threw it on the dead body when it was put into the grave, as did all the relations, extinguishing their flambeaux in the earth with which the corps was to be covered. This finished, every one retired to his home without farther ceremony." *Antiq. Repert.* iv., 549, 585. Braithwaite mentions that it was the function of the gentleman of the horse to lead the earl's charger caparisoned in black velvet after the body, and that these trappings remained the official's perquisites. *Rules for the Government of the House of an Earle,* (about 1640), apud *Miscellanea Antiq. Anglicana,* 1821, p. 16. The infant son of Sir Simonds D'Ewes, who died in

March, 1629-30, was carried to the burial-place in his father's private carriage.

Funeral Customs in Scotland.—In the Minute Book of the Society of Antiquaries of London, July 21, 1725, we read: "Mr. Anderson gave the Society an account of the manner of a Highland lord's funeral. The body is put into a litter between two horses, and, attended by the whole clan, is brought to the place of burial in the churchyard. The nearest relations dig the grave, the neighbours having set out the ground, so that it may not encroach on the graves of others. While this is performing, some hired women, for that purpose, lament the dead, setting forth his genealogy and noble exploits. After the body is interred, a hundred black cattle, and two or three hundred sheep, are killed for the entertainment of the company." The minister of Borrowstones, Linlithgow, reported in 1796: "At the burials of the poor people, a custom, almost obsolete in other parts of Scotland, is continued here. The beadle perambulates the streets with a bell, and intimates the death of the individual in the following language: 'All brethren and sisters, I let ye to wit, there is a brother (or sister) departed at the pleasure of the Almighty, (here he lifts his hat), called —— All those that come to the burial, come at —— of clock. The corpse is at ——.' He also walks before the corpse to the church-yard, ringing his bell." Pennant, in his "Tour in Scotland," tells us, that on the death of a highlander, the corpse being stretched on a board, and covered with a coarse linen wrapper, the friends lay on the breast of the deceased a wooden platter, containing a small quantity of salt and earth, separate and unmixed. The earth an emblem of the corruptible body; the salt an emblem of the immortal spirit. All fire is extinguished where a corpse is kept: and it is reckoned so ominous for a dog or cat to pass over it, that the poor animal is killed without mercy. A common funeral at Avoch, in Rosshire, in the 18th century, is thus described: "The corpse is preceded by the parish officer tolling a hand-bell. The pall or mort cloth is of plain black velvet, without any decoration, except a fringe. An immense crowd of both sexes attend; and the lamentations of the women, in some cases, on seeing a beloved relative put into the grave, would almost pierce a heart of stone." *Stat. Acc. of Scotland*, xv., 636. The Scots used to believe that "It disturbed the ghost of the dead, and was fatal to the living, if a tear was allowed to fall on a winding sheet. What was the intention of this, but to prevent the effects of a wild or frantic sorrow? If a cat was permitted to leap over a corpse, it portended misfortune.

The meaning of this was to prevent that carnivorous animal from coming near the body of the deceased, lest, when the watchers were asleep, it should endeavour to prey upon it" &c. These notions appear to have been called in Scotland "frets." *Stat. Acc.*, xxi., 147. "In Scotland," observes the Rev. John Black, "it is the custom of the relations of the deceased themselves to let down the corpse into the grave, by mourning cords, fastened to the handles of the coffin: the chief mourner standing at the head, and the rest of the relations arranged according to their propinquity. When the coffin is let down and adjusted in the grave, the mourners first, and then all the surrounding multitude, uncover their heads: there is no funeral service read: no oration delivered: but that solemn pause, for about the space of ten minutes, when every one is supposed to be meditating on death and immortality, always struck my heart in the most awful manner: never more than on the occasion here alluded to. The sound of the cord, when it fell on the coffin, still seems to vibrate on my ear." *Poems*, 1799, p. 10. Speaking of Scotish manners in the 18th century, it is said: The desire of what is called a decent funeral, i.e., one to which all the inhabitants of the district are invited, and at which every part of the usual entertainment is given, is one of the strongest in the poor. The expence of it amounts to nearly two pounds. This sum, therefore, every person in mean circumstances is anxious to lay up, and he will not spare it, unless reduced to the greatest extremity." Again: "Complaints occur against the expensive mode of conducting burials in the parish of Dunlop, in Ayrshire. It is pointed out as an object of taxation." In the same publication, parish of Lochbroom, co. Ross, "At their burials and marriages," we are told, the inhabitants "too much adhere to the folly of their ancestors. On these occasions they have a custom of feasting a great number of their friends and neighbours, and this often at an expence which proves greatly to the prejudice of poor orphans and young people: although these feasts are seldom productive of any quarrels or irregularities among them." And, under parish of Campsie, co. Stirling, we read: "It was customary, till within these few years, when any head of a family died, to invite the whole parish: they were served on boards in the barn, where a prayer was pronounced before and after the service, which duty was most religiously observed. The entertainment consisted of the following parts: first, there was a drink of ale, then a dram, then a piece of short-bread, then another dram of some other species of liquor, then a piece of currant-bread, and a third dram, either of spirits or wine, which was followed by loaves and cheese, pipes and tobacco. This was the old funeral entertainment in the parish of Campsie, and was stiled their service: and sometimes this was repeated, and was then stiled a double service; and it was sure of being repeated at the Dredgy. A funeral cost, at least, a hundred pounds Scots, to any family who followed the old course. The most active young man was pointed out to the office of server; and, in those days, while the manners were simple, and at the same time serious, it was no small honour to be a server at a burial. However distant any part of the parish was from the place of the interment, it was customary for the attendants to carry the corpse on hand spokes. The mode of invitation to the entertainment was, by some special messenger; which was stiled bidding to the burial, the form being nearly in the following words:— ' You are desired to come to such-a-one's burial to-morrow, against ten hours.' No person was invited by letter; and, though invited against ten of the clock, the corpse never was interred till the evening: time not being so much valued in those days." The minister of Gargunnock, co. Stirling, reported, (1796): " The manner of conducting funerals in the country needs much amendment. From the death to the interment, the house is thronged by night and day, and the conversation is often very unsuitable to the occasion. The whole parish is invited at ten o'clock in the forenoon of the day of the funeral, but it is soon enough to attend at 3 o'clock in the afternoon. Everyone is entertained with a variety of meats and drinks. Not a few return to the dirge, and sometimes forget what they have been doing, and where they are. Attempts have been lately made to provide a remedy for this evil; but old customs are not easily abolished." The minister of Carmunnock, co. Lanark, tells us: " We must mention a custom, which still prevails, and which certainly ought to be abolished. It is usual, in this parish, as in many other parts of Scotland, when a death has taken place, to invite on such occasions the greater part of the country round, and though called to attend at an early hour in the forenoon, yet it is generally towards evening, before they think of carrying forth the corpse to the churchyard for interment. While, on these occasions, the good folks are assembled, though they never run into excess, yet no small expense is incurred by the family: who often vie with those around them, in giving, as they call it, an honourable burial to their deceased friend. Such a custom is attended with many evils, and frequently involves in

debt, or reduces to poverty many families otherwise frugal and industrious, by this piece of useless parade and ill-judged expence." *Stat. Acc.*, vi., 487; ix., 543; xv., 372; xxiii., 123, 174.

In 1612, appended to the *Abridgement of the Scots Chronicles*, in "The Description of the Isles of Scotland," by J. Monipenny, under the Island of Rona, is the following passage: " There is in this island a chapel dedicated to St. Ronan: wherein (as aged men report) there is alwayes a spade wherewith when as any is dead, they find the place of his grave marked." See Gough's *Topography*. In Sutherlandshire, in the 18th century, a contemporary says: " The friends of the deceased, and neighbors of the village, who came to witness the interment, are drawn up in rank and file, by an old sergeant, or some veteran who has been in the Army, and who attends to maintain order, and give as they term it here, the word of relief. Upon his crying Relief! the four under the bier prepare to leave their stations, and make room for other four, that instantly succeed. This progression is observed at the interval of every five minutes, till the whole attendants come in regularly, and, if the distance requires it, there is a second, a third, or a fourth round of such evolutions gone through. When the persons present are not inflamed with liquor, there is a profound silence generally observed, from the time the corpse has been taken up till the interment is over." In another part of the same description we read: " Country burials are not well regulated. The company are invited at 11 o'clock forenoon, but they are probably not all arrived at 2. Till of late a pipe and tobacco was provided for every one of the company; but this custom is entirely laid aside. *Stat. Acct. of Scotland*, iii., 525; vii., 622. The minister of Kilsinichen and Kilviceven, co. Argyll, writing in the 18th century, says: The inhabitants " are by no means superstitious, yet they still retain some opinions handed down by their ancestors, perhaps from the time of the Druids. It is believed by them that the spirit of the last person that was buried watches round the churchyard till another is buried, to whom he delivers his charge." *Stat. Acc. of Scotland*, iv., 210. In the same work, it is said, " in one division of this county, where it was believed that the ghost of the person last buried kept the gate of the church yard till relieved by the next victim of death, a singular scene occurred, when two burials were to take place in one church yard on the same day. Both parties staggered forward as fast as possible to consign their respective friend in the first place to the dust. If they met at the gate, the dead were thrown down till the living decided by blows whose ghost should be condemned to porter it. *Stat. Acc.*, xxi., 144.

Funeral Customs in Ireland. —See *Irish Funeral Customs, Wakes,* and two papers in the *Penny Magazine* for July, 1844.

Funeral Customs Abroad.— In foreign countries, no less than among ourselves, it was a peremptory regulation and usage to bury instantaneously all victims to epidemics; and it is to the lasting honour of the Venetians that in 1576, Titian dying of the plague, his remains were specially allowed to lie in state. In some places abroad, it is customary to set out the departed person's toilette, and go through many of the same forms which he or she observed in life. In the Island of Madeira, they are in the habit of closing the chamber of death during a twelve-month after the event. Armstrong says: "I have seen an old woman placed on a bier, dressed like a Franciscan monk, and so conducted by the good brothers of that order, with singing and the tinckling of the hand-bell, to their church." *History of Minorca*, p. 212. This superstition, which, as I have just noticed, was not wholly unknown in England, was observed by Milton; for when describing the Paradise of Fools, he does not forget to mention those—

'—— Who to be sure of Paradise, Dying, put on the weeds of Dominick, Or in Franciscan think to pass disguis'd.' " —*Paradise Lost*, p. 111.

The accompanying elaborate account of the funeral ceremony at the obsequies of Alfonso XII., of Spain, is taken from the *Daily News* of November 30, 1885: "The funeral of the late King took place to-day. Early in the morning the Royal Family heard mass near the body. Then, after leaving flowers, they retired. The Queen, looking heartbroken, was the last to leave the hall. At 10 o'clock the coffin was carried downstairs by the grandees. A procession was formed of the Royal household, the equerries, the King's Body Guard, the Halberdiers, and priests. The roads were lined with troops. The crowd was extremely dense. All heads were uncovered as the coffin passed. The Ministers and the Bishop of Madrid received the body at the station, the bands playing the Royal March. The train left amidst the firing of cannon and the tolling of bells. The ceremony at the Escurial was imposing. The procession from the station slowly wound up the hill to the Monastery. When the funeral car reached the principal door it was closed. The Lord Chamberlain knocked for admittance. A voice inside asked, 'Who wishes to enter?' The answer given was 'Alfonso XII.' The doors were then thrown open. The Prior of the Monastery appeared. The body was carried into the church and placed on a raised bier before the grand altar. The coffin was then covered with the four cloaks of the noble orders. A thousand tapers were lighted, and the church assumed a magnificent appearance. Black hangings embossed with the arms of Spain covered the stone walls. A mass was said and the Miserere sung. The coffin was raised once more and carried to the entrance of the stairs leading down to the vaults. No one descended there except the Prior, the Minister of Grace and Justice, and the Lord Chamberlain. The coffin was placed on a table in a magnificent black marble vault, in which the Kings of Spain lie in huge marble tombs all around. Now came the most thrilling part of the ceremony. The Lord Chamberlain unlocked the coffin, which was covered with cloth of gold, raised the glass covering from the King's face, then after requesting perfect silence, knelt down and shouted three times in the dead monarch's ear, 'Señor, Señor, Señor.' Those waiting in the church upstairs heard the call, which was like a cry of despair, for it came from the lips of the Duke of Sexto, the King's favourite companion. The Duke then rose, saying, according to the ritual, 'His Majesty does not answer. Then it is true the King is dead.' He locked the coffin, handed the keys to the Prior, and taking up his wand of office, broke it in his hand, and flung the pieces at the foot of the table. Then every one left the monastery, as the bells tolled, and the guns announced to the people that Alfonso XII. had been laid with his ancestors in the gloomy pile of Philip II." This was on the Sunday at the Escurial.

The *Times* of December 3, 1889, describes the last tribute to Luis I. of Portugal: "A singular traditional usage was carried out at Lisbon some days after the funeral of the late King. At three principal places in the city platforms were erected covered with black cloth. A procession passed from one place to the other. The chief municipal officers of the city and the chief personages of the late Royal household, all clad in deep mourning, formed the procession, which was preceded and followed by cavalry in mourning, the colours draped with black. Military bands accompanied the march, playing sad strains. Four shields, on which were painted the Royal arms, were borne aloft on long staves. A multitude of people, all suitably dressed, were present, several walking with the procession. Arrived at the platform all the principal persons took up their places upon it, and one of the shield-bearers, advancing to the front, cried out in a chanting tone, 'Weep, O Portuguese, for your King Dom Luis I. is dead.' He then dashed the shield to the ground with such violence that it was shattered. This ceremony was repeated at the other platforms. Then the procession moved to the church of Santo Antonio da Sé, where a solemn requiem service was held. During the whole ceremony all the bells of the city tolled."

Funeral Psalmody.—Various are the proofs of the ancient custom of carrying out the dead with psalmody in the primitive church : in imitation of which it is still customary in many parts of this nation, to carry out the dead with singing of psalms and hymns of triumph ; to show that they have ended their spiritual warfare, that they have finished their course with joy, and are become conquerors. This exultation, as it were, for the conquest of their deceased friend over hell, sin, and death, was the great ceremony used in all funeral processions among the ancient Christians. Bourne cites Socrates Scholasticus telling us "that when the body of Babylas the Martyr was removed by the order of Julian the Apostate, the Christians, with their women and children, rejoiced and sung psalms all the way as they bore the corpse from Daphne to Antioch. Thus was Paula buried at Bethlehem, and thus did St. Anthony bury Paul the Hermite." The following passage is curious on the subject of singing psalms before the corpse : "Cantilena feralis per Antiphonas in pompa funebri et Fano debacchata hinc est. Inter Græcos demortui cadavere deposito in inferiori domus aula ad portam, et peractis cæteris Ceremoniis, Cantores funerales accedunt et threnon canunt, quibus per intervalla respondebant domesticæ servæ, cum assistentium corona, neque solum domi, sed usque ad Sepulchrum præcedebant feretrum ita canentes." Guichard. lib. ii. cap. 2. "Funeral," apud Moresini "Papatus," &c., p. 32. Durandus cites one of the ancient councils, in which it is observed the psalms were wont to be sung, not only when the corpse was conducted to church, but that the ancients watched on the night before the burial, and spent the vigil in singing psalms. Gough tells us that music and singing made a part of the funerals. Macrobius assigns as a reason that it implied the soul's return to the origin of harmony or heaven. Hyginus understands it to mean a signal of a decent disposal

of the dead, and that they came fairly by their death, as the tolling bell among Christians." *Sep. Mon.*, ii., introd. vii. Stopford says : "The heathens sang their dead to their graves or places of burial." *Pagano-papismus*, p. 282, citing Alex. ab Alexandro, "Gen. Dier." lib. iii., cap. 7, And Macrobius, *In Somnium Scipionis*, ii., 37, affirms,. that this custom was according to the institutions of several nations, and grounded upon this reason, because they believed that souls after death returned to the original of musical sweetness, that is Heaven : and therefore in this life every soul is taken with musicall sounds, &c." Other reasons are assigned by Kirkman, and several authorities urged for this custom. *De Funeribus Romanorum*, ii., 4. In "The Burnynge of Paules Church," 1561, we read : "In burials we do not assemble a number of priestes to swepe purgatorye, or bye forgivenes of synnes, of them whiche have no authoritye to sell, but accordinge to Saint Jeroms example we followe. At the death of Fabiola, sais he, the people of Ro. were gathered to the solemnite of the buriall. Psalmes were songe, and Alleluia sounding oute on height, did shake the gildet celinges of the Temple. Here was one companye of yonge menne and there another which did singe the prayses and worthy dedes of the woman. And no mervaile if men rejoyce of her salvation, of whose conversion th' angells in heaven be glad. Thus Jerom used burialls." Ed. 1563, sign. G 6 v°. I find the following passage in Dickenson's "Greene in Conceipt," 1598, p. 43 : "It is a custome still in use with Christians, to attend the funerall of their deceased friendes, with whole chantries of choyce quire-men, singing solemnly before them : but behinde follows a troope all clad in blacke, which argues mourning : much have I marveled at this ceremony, deeming it some hidden paradox, confounding thus in one things so opposite as these signes of joy and sorrowe."

Aubrey has preserved for our advantage a song, which he had from Mr. Meautis, and which could be traced back to 1626. It is connected with a Yorkshire superstition that the souls of the departed went over Whinny Moor. Some portions of the production seem to bespeak a far greater antiquity. Thoms has printed the verses entire, and very pertinently points out that Sir Walter Scott, in quoting them in the *Minstrelsy*, omits to give a portion of one line in a stanza, where the approach to purgatory is described. The missing words are here given in italics; they occur in Aubrey's MS. in the margin, but clearly belong to the text :—

" From Brig o' Dread, *na brader than a thread*,
    Every night   and awle,
To Purgatory fire thou comest at last,
    And Christ receive thy sawle."

The bridge no broader than a thread is a fine imaginative touch, and is such an object as many of us have encountered in nightmares. The song used in Aubrey's time to be sung at funerals in Yorkshire, and is substantially identical with Scott's *Lykewake Dirge*. Atkinson, in his *Cleveland Glossary*, 1868, furnishes a different version and other similar compositions; and Pennant tells us that in his day (about 1775) a custom prevailed in North Wales of singing psalms all the way to the church.

Funeral Rings.—The practice of offering rings at funerals is introduced in the early romance of *Sir Amadas*. Anne of Cleves, who survived Henry VIII. several years, left by her will very numerous bequests, and among them we meet with several mourning-rings of various value to be distributed among her friends and dependents. By the will of Lady Anne Drury, of Hardwicke, Suffolk, who died in 1621, in the possession of considerable property, rings were to be given to all her brother's wives, to her brothers themselves, to her two brothers-in-law, and to such of her friends as the executors thought fit. This lady was the sister of Sir Edmund Bacon, Knt., of the Suffolk family of that name. Mr. Wright, in " Miscellanea Graphica," 1857, describes a gold enamelled mourning ring, "formed of two skeletons, who support a small sarcophagus. The skeletons are covered with white enamel, and the lid of the sarcophagus is also enamelled, and has a Maltese cross in red on a black ground studded with gilt hearts, and when removed displays another skeleton. Under his will in 1616 Shakespear bequeathed 26s. 8d. apiece to five of his friends to buy them memorial rings. Halliwell-Phillipps, *Outlines*, 6th ed. ii., 170-1.

Funeral Sermons.—Funeral sermons are of great antiquity. Durandus, *Rationale*, 236. This custom used to be very general in England. But the earliest funeral sermon in English, at all events in print, seems to be that preached by Bishop Fisher for the Countess of Richmond and Derby, 1509. Mr. Brand says: " I know no where that it is retained at present, except upon Portland Island, Dorsetshire, where the minister has half-a-guinea for every sermon he preaches, by which he raises annually a very considerable sum. This species of luxury in grief is very common there, and indeed, as it conveys the idea of posthumous honour, all are desirous of procuring it even for the youngest of their children as well as their deceased friends. The fee is nearly the same as that mentioned by Gay in his dirge :

" Twenty good shillings in a rag I laid,
  Be ten the parson for his sermon paid."

Gough says : " From funeral orations over Christian martyrs have followed funeral sermons for eminent Christians of all denominations, whether founded in esteem or sanctioned by fashion, or secured by reward. Our ancestors, before the Reformation, took especial care to secure the repose and well-being of their souls, by masses and other deeds of piety and charity. After that event was supposed to have dispelled the gloom of superstition, and done away the painful doctrine of Purgatory, they became more solicitous to have their memories embalmed, and the example of their good works held forth to posterity. Texts were left to be preached from, and sometimes money to pay for such preaching. Gratitude founded commemorative sermons as well as commemorative dinners for benefactors." *Sepulchral Monuments*, ii., Introd. xi. In the Genevan "Forme of prayers," 1561, occurs " the maner of buriall," in which there is the following direction : " The corps is reverentlie brought to the grave, accompanied with the congregation, without any further ceremonies : which being buried, the Minister, if he be present, and required, goeth to the Church, if it be not farr off, and maketh some comfortable exhortation to the people, touching death and resurrection." Even the " comfortable exhortation " is struck out in the Middleborough Book, 1587. In " The Burnynge of Paules Church," 1561, we read : " Gregory Nazanzene hais his funerall sermons and orations in the commendacion of the party departed ; so hais Ambrose for Theodosius and Valentinian the Emperours, for his brother Statirus," &c.

In the Public Library at Cambridge, Dd. xii., 19, is the funeral oration pronounced at Leiden by John Dinley over Sir Albert Morton. Misson says : " The common practice is to carry the corpse into the body of the church, where they set it down upon two tressels, while either a funeral sermon is preached, containing an eulogium upon the deceased, or certain prayers said, adapted to the occasion. If the body is not buried in the church, they carry it to the church yard, where it is interred, (after the minister has performed the service which may be seen in the book of common prayer), in the presence of the guests, who are round the grave, and do not leave it till the earth is thrown in upon it. Then they return home in the same order that they came." *Travels in England*, p. 93. It was till lately a custom for the Ordinary of Newgate to preach a funeral sermon before each execution. In Cotgrave's "Treasury of Wit and Language," p. 35, we read :

    " In all this sermon I have heard little commendations
    Of our dear brother departed : rich men doe not go
    To the Pit-hole without complement of Christian buriall."

Granger quotes Fuller (*Appeal of Injured Innocence*, iii., 75) for this : " When one was to preach the funeral sermon of a most vicious and generally hated person. all wondered what he would say in his praise ; the preacher's friends fearing, his foes hoping, that, for his fee, he would force his conscience to flattery. For one thing, said the minister, this man is to be spoken well of by all ; and, for another, he is to be spoken ill of by none. The first is, because God made him ; the second, because he is dead." Even such an infamous character as Madame Cresswell had her funeral sermon. She desired by will to have a sermon preached at her funeral, for which the preacher was to have ten pounds ; but upon this express condition, that he was to say nothing but what was well of her. A preacher was, with some difficulty, found, who undertook the task. He, after a sermon preached on the general subject of mortality, and the good uses to be made of it, concluded with saying, " By the will of the deceased it is expected that I should mention her, and say nothing but what was well of her. All that I shall say of her, therefore, is this : she was born well, she lived well and she died well ; for she was born with the name of Cresswell, she lived in Clerkenwell, and she died in Bridewell."

Bishop White Kennet, under *Orationes Funerales*, acquaints us that : " At the burial of the dead it was a custom for the surviving friends to offer liberally at the altar for the pious use of the priest, and the good estate of the soul of the deceased. This pious custom does still obtain in North Wales, where at the rails which decently defend the Communion Table, I have seen a small tablet or flat-board, conveniently fixt, to receive the money, which at every funeral is offered by the surviving friends, according to their own ability, and the quality of the party deceased. Which seems a providential augmentation to some of those poor churches." *Par. Antiq. Gloss.* in v.

Funeral Suppers.—The ancients had several kinds of suppers made in honour of the deceased. First, that which was laid upon the funeral pile, such as we find in the 23rd Book of Homer and the 6th Æneis of Virgil, in Catullus (Ep. lv.) and Ovid (Fasti ii.) Secondly, the supper given to the friends and relations at their return from the funeral ; as in the 24th Book of Homer's Ilias, in honour of Hector. This kind of supper is mentioned in Lucian's Treatise of Grief, and Cicero's third Book of Laws. Thirdly, the Silicernium, a supper laid at the sepulchre, called Ἑκάτης δεῖπνον. Others will have it to be a meeting of the very old relations, who went in a very solemn manner after the funeral, and took their leaves one of the other, as if they were never to meet again. The fourth was called Epulum Novendiale. Juvenal, in his fifth Satire, mentions the *cœna feralis*, which was intended to appease the ghosts of the dead, and consisted of milk, honey, water, wine, olives, and strewed flowers. The modern arvals, however, are intended to appease the appetites of the living, who have upon these occasions superseded the manes of the dead. Gough says : " An entertainment or supper, which the Greeks called Περίδειπον, and Cicero *Circompotatio*, made a part of a funeral, whence our practice of giving wine and cake among the rich, and ale among the poor." *Sep. Mon.*, ii., Introd. vi. Among Smith's Extracts from the Berkeley MSS. (printed in 1821), the following occurs : " From the time of the death of Maurice the fourth Lord Berkeley, which happened June 8, 1368, untill his interment, the reeve of his Manor of Hinton spent three quarters and seaven bushells of beanes in fatting one hundred geese towards his funerall, and divers other reeves of other Manors the like, in geese, duckes, and other pultry." In Strype's edition of Stow we read : " Margaret Atkinson, widow, by her will, October 18, 1544, orders that the next Sunday after her burial there be provided two dozen of bread, a kilderken of ale, two gammons of bacon, three shoulders of mutton, and two couple of rabbits. Desiring all the parish, as well rich as poor, to take part thereof ; and a table to be set in the midst of the church, with every thing necessary thereto." Ed. 1720, i., 259. At the funeral of Sir John Gresham, Knight, Mercer (1556), the church and streets were all hung with black and arms great store. A sermon was preached by the Archdeacon of Canterbury, " and after, all the company came home to as great a dinner as had been seen for a fish day, for all that came. For nothing was lacking." Again : At the funeral of Thomas Percy, 1561, late skinner to Queen Mary, he was "attended to his burial in Saint Mary Aldermary Church with twenty black gowns and coats, twenty clerks singing, &c. The floor strewed with rushes for the chief mourners. Mr. Crowley preached. Afterwards was a great dole of money; and then all went home to a dinner. The company of Skinners, to their Hall, to dine together. At this funeral, all the mourners offered : and so did the said company." A.D. 1562, at the funeral of Sir Humphrey Brown, Knight, Lord Chief Justice, Dec. 15, Mr. Reneger made the sermon, "and after, they went home to a great dinner. The church was hung with black and arms. The helmet and crest were offered (on the altar), and after that his target; after that his sword; then his coat-armour; then his standard was offered, and his penon : and after all, the mourners, and judges, and serjeants of the law, and servants offered." In connection with the subject of "funeral baked meats," Henry Machyn notes in his Diary, under 1552-3, March 22: "The same day, wyche was the xxij day of Marche, was bered master John Heth, dwellynge in Fanchyrche Strett, and ther whent a-ffor hym a C. Childeryn of Grey freres, boys and gyrlles, ij and iij together, and he gayff (left) them shurts and smokes, and gyrdulls, and moketors, and after they had wyne and fygs and good alle, and ther wher a grett dener; and ther wher the cumpene of Panters, and the Clarkes, and ys cumpony had xxs. to make mere with-alle at the tavarne." Machyn relates that after the interment of Sir John Rainford, Kt. on the 20th September, 1559, there was a grand dinner proposed for the mourners, at which the widow, however, did not show herself. When the party had left, her ladyship came down, and had her dinner—four eggs and a dish of butter. At the obsequies of Francis, Earl of Shrewsbury, in 1560, the funeral banquet consisted of 320 messes, each mess containing eight dishes.

Misson, under the head of funerals, says : "Before they set out, and after they return, it is usual to present the guests with some thing to drink, either red or white wine, boiled with sugar and cinnamon, or some other such liquor. Every one drinks two or three cups." Butler, the keeper of a tavern, (the Crown and Sceptre in St. Martin's Street), told Mr. Brand that there was a tun of red port wine drunk at his wife's burial, besides mull'd white wine. Note, no men ever go to womens burials, nor the women to mens, so that there were none but women at the drinking of Butler's wine.

The expressions "Forth bringing" and "bringing home" are very interesting memorials of old notions in connection with the last act of our humanity. A correspondent of *Notes and Queries* has collected examples from a variety of sources extending over 120 years (1523-1645) :—

1523. Will of Isabel Chetham, of Manchester : "The residue of all my goods not beqwethed, after my furth bryngyng made," &c.

1543. Will of Hugh Habergam, of Bradlegh in Hapton, co. Lanc., husbandman : "To be bestowed on a drynkyng at my forth bryngyng, a noble," &c.

1556. Will of John Davenport, of Henbury, co. Chester, Esq. : "Also I will that Kateryn my wife shall have, after my forthe bryngyng, my funeral expencys discharged, the rest and residue of all my hole goodes, &c.

1571. Will of John Booth, of Barton-upon-Irwell, co. Lanc., Esq. : "Shall after my death bestowe upon my funeralls and bringinge furthe," &c.

1572. Will of Philip Mainwaring, of Peover, co. Chester, Esq. : "I will that my debts, funeralls,, and bringing home shall be discharged," &c.

1584. Will of Richard Hall, Fellow of the College of Manchester : "And after my forth bringinge, the rest of my goodes to be divided," &c.

1597. Will of Alice Garsyde, of Oldham : "The charge of my forth bringing being taken out of the whole of my goods," &c.

1630. Will of Andrew Gartside, of Denshaw, in the parish of Saddleworth: "I will that my forthbringinge, funerall expenses," &c., be paid.

1633. Will of Richard Buckley, of Grottonhead, in the parish of Saddleworth: "My will is that my forthbringinge, funerall expenses be discharged," &c.

1645. Will of Thomas Leadbeater, of Cranage, co. Chester : "My desire is ..... that my children shall bring me home with bread and cheese and drink."

A writer in the "Gentleman's Magazine" for March, 1780, says : "Our ancient funerals, as well as some modern ones, were closed with merry makings, at least equal to the preceding sorrow, most of the testators directing, among other things, victuals and drink to be distributed at their exequies; one in particular, I remember, orders a sum of money for a drinking for his soul." Another writer, apparently describing the manners of Yorkshire, in the volume for July, 1798, says : "At funerals, on which occasions a large party is generally invited, the attendant who serves the company with ale or wine has upon the handle of the tankard a piece of lemon-peel, and also upoñ her left arm a clean white napkin. I believe these customs are invariably observed. From what cause they originated, some ingenious correspondent may be able to inform me." Hutchinson, speaking of Eskdale chapelry, says: "Wakes and doles are customary; and weddings, christenings, and funerals are always attended by the neighbours, sometimes to the amount of a hundred people. The popular diversions are hunting and cock-fighting." *Cumberland*, i., 579. "At the funerals of the rich in former days," says the compiler of the "Whitby Glossary," (quoted by Atkinson, in his "Cleveland Glossary," 1868), "it was here a custom to hand burnt wine to the company in a silver flagon, out of which every one drank. This cordial seems to have been a heated preparation of port wine with spices and sugar. And if any remained, it was sent round in the flagon to the houses of friends for distribution."

An allusion to these entertainments occurs in the Romance of Sir Degore (about 1500) :

> "A great feaste would he holde
> Upon his quenes mornynge day,
> That was buryed in an abay."

So Dickenson, in "Greene in Conceipt," 1598 : "His corpes was with funerall pompe conveyed to the church and there solemnly entered, nothing omitted which necessitie or custom could claime : a sermon, a banquet, and like observations." We are all familiar with the passage in *Hamlet*, 1603-4, where, speaking of his mother's marriage, Hamlet says:

> ————"The funeral bak'd meats
> Did coldly furnish forth the marriage-
> tables."

Upon which Steevens noted : "It was anciently the general custom to give a cold entertainment to mourners at a funeral. In distant counties this practice is continued among the yeomanry." In Lord North's "Forest of Varieties," 1645, is the following: "Nor are all banquets (no more than musick) ordained for merry humors, some being used even at funeralls." In his "Whimsies," 1631, p. 89, speaking of a launderer, Braithwaite says: "So much she hath reserv'd out of all the labours of her life, as will buy some small portion of diet bread, comfits, and burnt claret, to welcome in her neighbours now at her departing, of whose cost they never so freely tasted while she was living." Again, in describing a jealous neighbour, he concludes with observing: "Meate for his funerall pye is shred, some few ceremonial teares on his funerall pile are shed; but the worms are scarce entered his shroud, his corpse flowers not fully dead, till this jealous earth-worme is forgot, and another more amorous, but lesse jealous mounted his bed." Flecknoe, speaking of a "curious glutton," observes: "In fine, he thinks of nothing else, as long as he lives, and when he dyes, onely regrets that funeral feasts are quite left off, else he should have the pleasure of one feast more, (in imagination at least), even after death; which he can't endure to hear of, onely because they say there is no eating nor drinking in the other world." *Characters*, 1658, ed. 1665, p. 14.

> "In Northern customs duty was exprest
> To friends departed by their fun'ral feast.
> Tho' I've consulted Hollingshead and Stow,
> I find it very difficult to know
> Who to refresh th' attendants to the grave,
> Burnt claret first, or Naples-bisket gave."

King's Art of Cookery, p. 65. The writer of "Pleasant Remarks on the Humours of Mankind" observes: "How like epicurists do some persons drink at a funeral, as if they were met there to be merry, and make it a matter of rejoycing that they have got rid of ther friends and relations."

Funerals, References in the Poets to.

—A writer in the "Gorgious Gallery of Gallant Inventions," 1578, describing the death of Pyramus and Thisbe, says :

> "And mulberries in signe of woe, from white to blacke turnde were."

So in "Romeo and Juliet," 1597 :

> "All things, that we ordained festival,
> Turn from their office to black funeral;
> Our instruments, to melancholy bells;
> Our wedding cheer, to a sad burial feast;
> Our solemn hymns to sullen dirges change;
> Our bridal flowers serve for a buried corse,
> And all things change them to their contraries."

In "Cymbeline," act iv. sc. 2, Arviragus, speaking of the apparently dead body of Imogen, disguised in men's clothes, says :

> "And let us, Polydore, sing him to the ground,
> As once our mother; use like note and words,
> Save that Euriphile must be Fidele."

"Let my bier
Be borne by virgins, that shall sing by
course
The truth of maids and perjuries of
men."

—Beaum. and Fl. *Maids Tragedy*, 1619.
Compare *Arval, Bidding, Burial, Death,
Dole, Flowers, Graves, Lichway*, &c.

Furmety.—Furmety is made of
what is called, in a certain town
in Yorkshire, "kneed wheat," or whole
grains first boiled plump and soft,
and then put into and boiled in
milk sweetened and spiced." In Ray's
"North Country Words," "to cree wheat
or barley, is to boil it soft." Gower tells
us: "I cannot avoid reminding you upon
the present occasion that furmety makes
the principal entertainment of all our
country wakes: our common people call
it 'Firmitry.' It is an agreeable composition of boiled wheat, milk, spice, and
sugar." *Sketch of the Materials for a
History of Cheshire.* Beckwith, in the
"Gentleman's Magazine" for February,
1784, tells us that, in the country about
Rotherham, in Yorkshire, furmety used,
in his remembrance, to be always the
breakfast and supper on Christmas Eve.
In his epistle before Greene's *Arcadia*,
1589, Thomas Nash takes occasion to observe that "a tale of Ioane of Brain-
fords will, and the vnlucky frumenty, will
be as soone entertained into their Libra-
ries as the best Poëme that euer Tasso
eternis'ht." He refers to a fugitive piece
of verse by G. Kyttes, called *The Vnlucky firmentie*, of which there seems to be
a MS. copy under the title of *Panche* in
Bishop Percy's Folio MS.

Furmety Sunday.—See *Mother-
ing.*

Furry Day.—A writer in a periodical for 1790 says: "At Helstone, a gen-
teel and populous borough town in
Cornwall, it is customary to dedicate the
eighth of May to revelry (festive mirth,
not loose jollity). It is called the Furry
Day, supposed Flora's Day; not, I imagine, as many have thought, in remembrance of some festival instituted in
honour of that goddess, but rather from
the garlands commonly worn on that day.
In the morning, very early, some troublesome rogues go round the streets with
drums, or rather noisy instruments, and singing parts of a song, the whole of which
nobody now recollects, and of which I know
no more than that there is mention in
it of 'the grey goose quill,' and of going
to the green wood to bring home 'the
Summer and the May-o.' And, accordingly, hawthorn flowering branches are
worn in hats. The commonalty make it

a general holiday; and if they find any
person at work, make him ride on a pole,
carried on men's shoulders, to the river,
over which he is to leap in a wide place,
if he can; if he cannot, he must leap in,
for leap he must, or pay money. About
9 o'clock they appear before the school,
and demand holiday for the Latin boys,
which is invariably granted; after which
they collect money from house to house.
About the middle of the day they collect
together, to dance hand-in-hand round
the streets, to the sound of the fiddle, playing a particular tune, which they continue to do till it is dark. This they call
a 'Faddy.' In the afternoon, the gen-
tility go to some farmhouse in the neighbourhood, to drink tea, syllabub, etc.,
and return in a Morrice dance to the
town, where they form a faddy, and dance
through the streets till it is dark, claiming a right of going through any person's
house, in at one door, and out at the
other. And here it formerly used to end,
and the company of all kinds to disperse
quietly to their several habitations; but
latterly corruptions have in this as in
other matters crept in by degrees. The
ladies — all elegantly dressed in white
muslins, are now conducted by their
partners to the ball-room, where they
continue their dance till supper time;
after which they all faddy it out of the
house, breaking off by degrees to their
respective houses. The mobility imitate
their superiors, and also adjourn to the
several public houses, where they continue
their dance till midnight. It is, upon
the whole, a very festive, jovial, and
withall sober, and I believe singular
custom." The song, which follows from
another source, seems to betray a faint
reminiscence of the Spanish Armada:

THE FURRY-DAY SONG.
"Robin Hood and Little John,
  They both are gone to the fair,
And we'll go to the merry green wood,
  And see what they do there.
For we were up as soon as any day
  For to fetch the summer home,
The summer and the May, O,
  For the summer now has come!
Where are those Spaniards
  That make so great a boast?
They shall eat the grey goose feather,
  And we will eat the roast.
As for the brave St. George,
  St. George he was a knight:
Of all the knights in Christendom.
  St. Georgy is the right.
God bless Aunt Mary Moses,
  And all her powers and might,
And send us peace in merry England,
  Both day and night!"
The Furry Day was duly observed in 1903.

Fye.—In Scotland a ghost seems to have been known as a fye. Witness the following anecdote : " Some observing to an old woman, when in the 99th year of her age, that in the course of Nature she could not long survive—'Ay,' said the good old woman, with pointed indignation, 'what fye-token do you see about me?'" *Stat. Acc.*, xxi., 148; *Parish of Menghittes*.

Gabriel, the Archangel. — (March 26 and April 13).—The Salutation of the Virgin by this personage was supposed to be commemorated by the chapel of Our Lady at Nazareth, on the model of which that at Walsingham is reported to have been built by a lady named Richold, A.D. 1061. See *Foundation of the Chapel of Walsingham*, printed about 1495, in Hazlitt's *Fugitive Tracts*, 1875, 1st Series. In the *Vertue of the Masse* (circâ 1500), by Lydgate, St. Gabriel is named as the patron of " good rydynge "; but the whole passage seems worth copying, especially as it mentions one or two points not generally known :

" Herynge of masse dooth passynge grete auayle,
At nede at myschefe folke it doth releue,
Causeth saynt Nicholas to gyue good counsayle,
And saynt Iulyan good hostel at eue ;
To beholde saynt Crystofer none enemy shall hym greue,
And saynt Loy your Iourney shall preserue,
Horse ne caryage that daye shall not myscheue,
Masse herde before who dooth these sayntes serue.
Partynge fro masse begynnynge your Iourney,
Call saynt Myghell you to fortefye,
For sodayne haste and good prosperyte,
And for good rydynge saynt Gabryell shall you gye."

Gabriel-Rachet, The. — This, says Mr. Atkinson, in his " Cleveland Glossary," 1868, is a name for a yelping sound heard at night, more or less resembling the cry of hounds or yelping of dogs, probably due to flocks of wild geese (*anser segetum*) which chance to be flying by night, and is taken as an omen or warning of approaching death to the hearer or some one connected with him or her." Mr. Atkinson speaks of a Cleveland tradition about the local origin of the Gabriel-rachet; but probably very slight credit is due to the legend narrated by him. It seems to be nothing more or less than a form of the belief current all over the world from the remotest times in spectral

apparitions and sounds seen or heard in the deadness of night. Compare Lucas, *Studies in Nidderdale*, pp. 156-7.

Gambling.—A very curious sketch of the early passion for speculation, even of the wildest character, in playing at games both of skill and chance, is given by Mr. Wright. *Domestic Manners and Sentiments in England during the Middle Ages*, 1862, ch. x. Comp. *Games* below.

Game.—" Formerly," says Mr. Tanswell, " Lambeth was celebrated for game of all sorts, but principally in the neighbourhood of Brixton. In the 5th of Elizabeth a licence was granted to Andrew Perne, D.D., Dean of Ely (who resided at Stockwell), 'to appoint one of his servants, by special name, to shoot with any cross-bow, hand-gonne, hacquebut, or demy-hack, at all manner of dead-marks, at all manner of crows, rooks, cormorants, kytes, puttocks, and such-like, bustards, wyld swans, barnacles, and all manner of sea-fowls, and fen-fowls, wild doves, small birds, teals, coots, ducks, and all manner of deare, red, fallow, and roo.' In the reign of James I., Alexander Glover received, as 'Keeper of the game about Lambeth and Clapham, 12d. per diem, and 26s. 8d. per annum for his livery'; in all £36 10s." *History of Lambeth*, 1858, p. 15. And at the same period Putney Park was a royal demesne with deer and a keeper under the Crown. The site is still remembered in Putney Park Lane.

Game at the Hole.—So named in an entry at Stationers' Hall in 1587. The full title is : " The game at the hole, otherwise, if you be not pleased, you shall be eased."

Games.—Dr. Arbuthnot used to say, that notwithstanding all the boasts of the safe conveyance of tradition, it was no where preserved pure and uncorrupt but amongst school-boys, whose games and plays are delivered down invariably the same from one generation to another. Benedictus Abbas has preserved a very curious edict, which shews the state of gaming in the Christian army commanded by Richard the First King of England, and Philip of France, during the Crusade in the year 1190. No person in the army is permitted to play at any sort of game for money, except knights and clergymen ; who in one whole day and night shall not, each, lose more than twenty shillings, on pain of losing one hundred shillings to the archbishops of the army. The two Kings may play for what they please, but their attendants not for more than twenty shillings. Otherwise, they are to be whipped naked through the army for three days. The monarchs probably played at *Quatuor Reges* or chess, and their followers at dice. Many of the early romances comprise notices of amusements enjoyed by the characters introduced; but it is sometimes, of course, difficult to judge how much is exaggeration; and in the *Books of Hours* we often meet with interesting illustrations of this class, intended as ornamental accessories. In the 13th. c. fabliau of *Blonde of Oxford and Jean de Dammartin*, the hero and heroine play at chess, tables, and dice; and in a MS. of the romance of *Meliadus de Lyonnois*, of the fourteenth century, there are representations of parties engaged in games at chess and cards—the latter perhaps the earliest graphic view of that amusement, and apparently prior to anything known to Chatto. *Archæol. Album*, 1845, p. 75. In a fine MS. in the Bodleian, cited by Strutt, and after him by Brand, there is a series of representations of the more popular games then (1343) in favour. It is remarkable that among them are to be found many of the amusements still in fashion among the old or young, such as top-spinning, cock-fighting, chess, bowls, dice, &c., while others have completely disappeared. In a volume of Homilies of the 14th century, there is a strong illustration of the ungovernable propensity among our countrymen and countrywomen for enjoying themselves in ways, which were not in all cases highly proper. The Homily says: "*þer* is an o*þer* lepre of yonge folk: *þat þ*ei ben moche smyttid with now a daies/ and *þ*is is veyn laughtre, and idul wordis, and many o*þer* vayn iapis; *þat* seelden or neuer *þ*ei kunnen stynte from hem/ *þ*ei taken noon heede of goddis word. *þ*ei rennen to enterludes with gret delijt; yhe, *þ*at is more reu*þ*e, to strumpetis daunce / *þ*e preest for hem mai stonde alone in *þ*e chirche, but *þ*e harlot in *þ*e clepyng shal be hirid for good money: to tellen hem fablis of losengerie/ but to such maner folk: christ sei*þ* ful sharplei *þ*ese wordis./ wo to you *þ*at now lawen: for ye shuln wepe ful fore her-aftir/" This notice concurs with what a later writer observes respecting the desertion of the churches and the devotion of the people to frivolous and wicked sports. Harl. MS. 2276, fol. 37. I am indebted to my friend Mr. F. J. Furnivall for this extract.

Du Cange informs us, that the Council of Salzburg, in 1274, prohibited certain *ludi noxii* on account of the licence used at them. Wright supplies from one of the Royal MSS. in the British Museum a short list of fourteenth century games, of which the exact character is not known. *Domestic Manners*, 1862, p. 210. A farther list occurs at p. 229, and is liable to the same objection.

Some of these forgotten pastimes are of French or foreign origin; but since at the period, to which they appertain, relations between France at all events and ourselves were so constant and intimate, it may be useful to annex the names, by which they were once currently known:

Propre confusion.	Tessera.
Qui perd, se sauve.	Calculus.
Qui est large, est sage.	Urio vel Dardana pugna.
Meschief fait homme penser.	Tricolus.
	Senio.
La chasse de ferce (queen) et de chevalier.	Monarchus. Orbiculi. Taliorhicus.
Dames et demoiselles.	Vulpes. Tabula.
La Bataille de rokes.	

Some of these are recognizable as still surviving institutions, while others are obsolete variations of the game of chess. The subjoined literary notices are interesting:

"Herlotes walkes thurghe many tounes
Wyth speckede mantels and bordouns;
And ate ilke mannes house ga *þ*ai inne,
*þ*are *þ*ai hope oght for to wynne.
Bote 'herlotes' mene calles comonlye
Alle *þ*at hauntes herlottrye:
Herlotes falles to stande on *þ*e flore,
And play some tyme ate *þ*e spore,
Atte *þ*e beyne, and ate *þ*e cate,—
A foule play holde I *þ*ate,—
And *þ*are agayne may *þ*ai noght be
Whene mene byddes *þ*aim for *þ*aire fe,
ffor *þ*e rewele of *þ*aire relygyoune
Es swylke, thurgh *þ*aire professyoune;
*þ*is es a poynte of *þ*aire reule ilke tyme,
To lykene mene *þ*are *þ*ai come, in ryme.
zhyte haunte *þ*ai oft other Iapes;
Some ledes beres, and some ledes apes
*þ*at mus sautes and solace *þ*at sees:
All *þ*ise are bote foly and nycetees."

William of Nassyngton, *Myrrour of Lyfe* (14th century).

"Also use not to pley at the dice ne at the tablis,
Ne none maner gamys upon the holidais;
Use no tavernys where be jestis and fablis,
Syngyng of lewde balettes, rondelettes, or virolais;
Nor erly in mornyng to fecche home fresch mais,
For yt makyth maydins to stomble and falle in the breirs,
And afterward they telle her councele to the freirs."

MS. Laud 416, (circâ 1460) apud *Rel. Antiq.* vol. ii., p. 27. By the Statute 6 Hen. iv. c 4, labourers and servants playing at unlawful games were made liable to imprisonment for six days, and any magistrate or other officer neglecting to take cognizance of such offences was subject to a penalty. By the statute 17 Edw. IV. c. 3, this earlier enactment was confirmed as follows: "Laborers and seruauntys that vse dyse and other sych games shall haue imprisonment of .vi. dayes," and it was also provided, that "noo gouerner of howse, tenement or gardeyn suffer wyllyngly any person to occupy to playe at the classe keyles [ninepins,] halfe bowle, handyn handout or quekbourd vpon payn or inprisonment by .iii. yerys," &c. By 11 Hen. VII. c. 2, and 19 Hen. VII. c. 12, it was laid down that "no apprentyce nor seruant of husbandry, laborer, nor seruant artificer play at the tablys, tenyse, dyse, cardys, bowlys, nor at none other vnlawfull game owt of the tyme of Crystmas but for mete and drynke, and in crystmas to playe onely in the dwellyng howse of his mayster or in the presence of hys mayster."

In an account of the visit of Louis of Bruges and his suite to England in 1472 there are references to the amusements of the Court at Windsor. The Queen and her ladies played at the *morteaulx*, a game supposed to be allied to bowls, and others at *closkeys*, or ninepins, which are described as being of ivory, but were more probably of bone. *England as seen by Foreigners*, by W. B. Rye, 1865, p. xli. In the contemporary narrative of the marriage of Catherine of Arragon to Prince Arthur of England, in 1501, mention occurs of galleries and other buildings fitted up in the royal gardens:—"In the lougher ende of this gardeyn both pleasaunt gallerys, and housis of pleasure to disporte inn, at chesse, tables, dise, cardes, bylys; bowling aleys, butts for archers, and goodly tenes play." *Antiq. Repert.*, ii., 316. The statutes of Wadham College, Oxford, drawn up in 1613, prescribe that gaming with cards or dice was not permissible except on All Saints' Day, Christmas Day, and the Purification of the Blessed Virgin, when cards might be used, provided the stakes were small, and suitable hours were observed. "Thei hauke, thei hunt, they card, thei dice, they pastyme in theyr prelacies with gallaunte gentlemen, with theyr daunsinge minyons, and with theyr freshe companions, so that ploughinge is set a syde."—Latimer's *Sermon of the Plough*, 1548. Humphrey Roberts, in his "Complaint for Reformation," 1572, represents that his countrymen "vpon the Saboath Day resorte rather to bearebayting, bulbayting, dauncing, fenceplaying and suche lyke vayn exercises then to the Church."

Roberts adds: "— in London, other cyties, and in the countrey townes also, there are many other places of concourse of people: As dycing houses, bowling aleys, fencyng scooles, yea tauerns and ale-houses: wherin are such a nomber of ruffians and cutters (as they call them): that those places are become yonge helles, suche is their wickednesse. So that the tender yonglyngs, beynge come of good houses: and all others (once vsynge suche places), are, as it were, translated, or chaunged, into monsters." The resort to amusements on Sundays was evidently not unusual. In *A Devonshire Yeoman's Diary*, under 1602, we find the following entry: "August 22. I went to Trusham Church. After evening prayers went to bowles." *Antiquary*, 1892, p. 259. In the dedication to "Mihil Mumchance, his discoverie of the Art of Cheating in false Dice play," 1597, we read, "making the divel to daunce in the bottome of your purses, and to turne your angels out of their houses like bad tenants." In the same tract, "Novum, Hassard, and Swiftfoot-passage" occur as games. Some of the undermentioned games, quoted here from Rowlands' "Letting of Hvmors Blood," &c., 1611, are overlooked not only by Brand, but by Strutt and Hone:

"Man, I dare challenge thee to throw the sledge,
To iumpe, or leape ouer ditch or hedge;
To wrastle, play at stoole-ball, or to runne;
To pich the bar, or to shoote off a gunne:
To play at loggets, nine holes, or tenpinnes;
To try it out at foot-ball by the shinnes,
At ticktacke, Irish, noddy, maw, and ruffe:
At hot-cockles, leap-frog, or blindman-buffe:
To drinke halfe pots, or deale at the whole can:
To play at base, or pen and Inck-horne sir Ihan:
To daunce the Mirris, play at barly-breake:
At all exployts a man may thinke or speake,
At shoue-groat, venter-poynt, or crosse & pile,
At beshrow him thats last at yonder stile:
At leaping ore a Midsommer bone-fier:
Or at the drawing dunne out of the myer."

In Erondel's "French Garden," 1605, the titles of the following games occur:—"Trompe — Dice — Tables — Lurch—Draughts — Perforce — Pleasant—Blowing—Queen's Game—Chesse." There is added: "The maydens did play at Purposes—at Sales—To Thinke—at Wonders—at Stakes—at Vertues—at Answers, so that we could come no sooner," &c. A list of games, to which the keys seem to have been lost, is printed in *Notes and Queries*, being transcribed from three sources as under:

"We went to a sport called selling a horse for a dish of eggs and herrings."—Pepys, *Diary*, Feb. 2, 1659-60.

"The merry game of The parson has lost his cloak."—*Spectator*, N. 268.

"'What say you, Harry; have you any play to show them?'' 'Yes, sir,' said Harry, 'I have a many of them; there's first leap-frog and thrush-a-thrush."—H. Brooke, *Fool of Quality*, i. 25 (ed. 1859).

"One fault brought me into another after it, like *Water my chickens come clock*."—Ib., i. 272.

"Can you play at draughts, polish, or chess?"—Ib., i. 267.

"Some reminded him of his having beaten them at boxing, others at wrestling and all of his having played with them at prison-bars, leap-frog, shut the gate, and so forth."—Ib., ii. 168.

Several games of the middle of the 17th century are enumerated in "Wit Restor'd," 1658:

"Here's children's bawbles and mens too,
  To play with for delight.
Here's round-heads when turn'd every way
  At length will stand upright.
Here's dice, and boxes if you please
  To play at in and inn,
Here is a sett of kettle pinns
  With bowle at them to rowle:
And if you like such trundling sport
  Here is my ladyes hole.
Here's shaddow ribbon'd of all sorts,
  As various as your mind,
And here's a windmill like your selfe
  Will turne with every wind.
And heer's a church of the same stuff
  Cutt out in the new fashion."

In Cotgrave's *Wit's Interpreter*, third edition, 1671, we meet with directions for playing the courtly games of L'Ombre, Piquit, Gleek, and Cribbage; and in Cotton's *Compleat Gamester*, 1674 he adduces the usual and most gentile games on cards, dice, billiards, trucks, bowls, or chess. In a later impression, 1709, the amusements enumerated are more varied: Piquet, gleek, l'ombre, a Spanish game, cribbage, all-fours, English ruff, and honours *alias* slam, whist, French ruff, five cards, a game called costly colours, bone-ale, put, the high game, wit and reason, the art of memory, plain dealing, Queen Nazareene, lanterloo, penneech, bankafalet, beast or la béte, and basset.

Edward Chamberlayne, in his "Angliæ Notitia," 1676, enumerates what were at that time the principal recreations and exercises both of the upper and lower classes of society in this country:

"For variety of divertisements, sports, and recreations, no nation doth excel the English. The King hath abroad, his forests, chases, and parks, full of variety of game; for hunting red and fallow deer, foxes, otters; hawking, his paddock courses, horse-races, &c., and at home, tennis, pelmel, billiard, enterludes, balls, ballets, masks, &c. The Nobility and gentry have their parks, warrens, decoys, paddock-courses, horse-races, huntings, coursing, fishing, fowling, hawking, setting dogs, tumblers, lurchers, duck-hunting, cock-fighting, guns for birding, lowbells, bat-fowling; angling, nets, tennis, bowling, billiard tables, chess, draughts, cards, dice, catches, questions, purposes, stage-plays, masks, balls, dancing, singing, all sorts of musical instruments, &c. The citizens and peasants have hand-ball, foot-ball, skittles or nine-pins, shovel-board, stow-ball, goffe, trol-madame, cudgels, bear-baiting, bull-baiting, bow and arrow, throwing at cocks, shuttlecock, bowling, quoits, leaping, wrestling, pitching the bar, and ringing of bells, a recreation used in no other countrey of the world. Amongst these, cock-fighting seems to all foreigners too childish and unsuitable for the gentry, and for the common people; bull-baiting and bear-baiting seem too cruel; and for the citizens, foot-ball and throwing at cocks, very uncivil, rude, and barbarous within the City." In the "Life of the Scotch Rogue," 1722, p. 7, the following sports occur: "I was but a sorry proficient in learning: being readier at cat and dog, cappy hole, riding the hurley hacket, playing at kyles and dams, spang-bodle, wrestling, and foot-ball, and (such other sports as we use in our country), than at my book."

"Julius Pollux," (observes Cornelius Scriblerus) "describes the Omilla or chuck-farthing; tho' some will have our modern chuck-farthing to be nearer the aphetinda of the ancients. He also mentions the basilinda or King I am; and myinda, or hoopers-hide. But the chytindra described by the same author is certainly not our hot-cockle; for that was by pinching, and not by striking; tho' there are good authors who affirm the rathapygismus to be yet nearer the modern hot cockles. My son Martin may use either of them indifferently, they being equally antique. Building of houses and riding upon sticks, have been used by children in all ages; *Ædificare casas, equitare in arundine longa*. Yet I much doubt whether the riding upon sticks did not come into use after the age of the Centaurs. There is one play which shews the gravity of ancient education, called the Acinetinda, in which children contended who could longest stand still. This we have suffered to perish entirely; and if I might be allowed to guess, it was certainly first lost among the French. I will permit my son to play at Apodidascinda, which can be no other than our Puss in a corner. Julius Pollux, in his ninth Book, speaks of the melolonthe, or the kite; but I question whether the kite of antiquity was the same with ours, and though the Ορντονοπία, or quail-fighting, is what is most taken notice of, they had doubtless cock-matches also, as is evident from certain antient gems and relievos. In a word, let my son Martin disport himself at any game truly antique, except one which was invented by a people among the Thracians, who hung up one of their companions in a rope, and gave him a knife to cut himself down; which if he failed in, he was suffered to hang till he was dead; and this was only reckoned a sort of joke. I am utterly against this as barbarous and cruel." Misson says: "Besides the sports and diversions common to most other European nations, as tennis, billiards, chess, tick-tack, dancing, plays, &c., the English have some which are particular to them, or at least which they love and use more than any other people." *Travels in England*, p. 304. See a little volume entitled: "Games most in use in England, France, and Spain, viz., Basset, Piquet, Primero, L'Ombre, Chess, Billiards, Grand-trick-track, Verquere, &c., some of which were never before printed in any language. All regulated by the most experienced Masters." Published by J. Morphew about 1710. The editions of Charles Cotton's *Compleat Gamester*, and the earlier issues of Hoyle's *Games* may also be consulted. Hollar published in 1647 "Paidopœgnion, sive puerorum ludentium schemata varia, pictorum usui aptata."

The Gantelupe or **Gauntlet, To Run.**—See *Penny Magazine* for 1837, p. 339, where it is described as a military and naval punishment; but it was not confined to this country or to civilized nations. It occurs in accounts of travels among savage communities, and in works of fiction founded on them.

Garden-House.—The older *summer-house*. See Nares, *Glossary*, 1859, in v.

Garlands.—Nuptial garlands are of the most remote antiquity. They appear to have been equally used by the Jews and the Greeks and Romans. Selden's *Uxor*

Hebraica in *Opera*, iii., 655. "Among the Romans, when the marriage-day was come, the bride was bound to have a chaplet of flowers or hearbes upon her head, and to weare a girdle of sheeps wool about her middle, fastned with a true-loves-knot, the which her husband must loose. Hence rose the proverb: He hath undone her virgin's girdle: that is, of a mayde he hath made her a woman." Vaughan's *Golden Grove*, 1600, ed. 1608, sign O 2. In Ihre's "Glossarium," 1769, v. Krona, we read: "Sponsarum ornatus erat coronæ gestamen, qui mos hodieque pleno usu apud Ruricolas viget."

Among the Anglo-Saxons, after the benediction in the church, both the bride and bridegroom were crowned with crowns of flowers, kept in the church for that purpose. In the Eastern Church the chaplets used on these occasions appear to have been blessed. Selden, *ubi suprâ*, p. 661. "Coronas tenent a tergo paranymphi, quæ Capitibus Sponsorum iterum a Sacerdote non sine benedictione solenni aptantur." The form is given, p. 667. "Benedic, Domine, Annulum istum et Coronam istam, ut sicut Annulus circumdat digitum hominis et Corona Caput, ita Gratia Spiritus Sancti circumdet Sponsum et Sponsam, ut videant Filius et Filias usque ad tertiam aut quartam Generationem, &c." We ought not to overlook the miraculous garland given by the father in the Wright's Chast Wife on her nuptials to her spouse, in the tale of that name from the "Gesta Romanorum." He says to the wright, on presenting it as the only gift it is in his power to make:

"Haue here thys garlonde of roses ryche,
In alle thys lond ys none yt lyche,
For ytt wylle euer be newe.
Wete thou wele withowtyn fable,
Alle the whyle thy wyfe ys stable,
The chaplett wolle hold hewe."

In "Dives and Pauper, 1493, "The fixte Precepte," chap. 2, is the following curious passage: "Thre ornamentys longe pryncypaly to a wyfe. A rynge on hir fynger, a broch on hir brest, and a garlond on hir hede. The ringe betokenethe true love, as I have seyd, the broch betokennethe clennesse in herte and chastitye that she oweth to have, the garlande bytokeneth gladnesse and the dignitye of the sacrament of wedlok." At the marriage of Blonde of Oxford to Jean de Dammartin, in the 13th century, the bride is made to wear a gold chaplet. Compare *Nuptial Usages, infrâ*. In dressing out Grisild for her marriage in the "Clerk of Oxenford's Tale" in Chaucer, the chaplet is noted: "A corune on hire hed they han ydressed." The nuptial garlands were sometimes made of myrtle. In England, in the time of Henry VIII., the bride wore a garland of corn ears, sometimes one of flowers. Wax appears to have been used in the formation of these garlands from the subsequent passage in Hyll's book on Dreams: "A garlande of waxe (to dream of) signifyeth evill to all personnes, but especiallye to the sicke, for as much as it is commonlye occupyed aboute burialls." Gosson, in his "Ephemerides of Phialo," 1579, remarks: "In som countries the bride is crowned by the matrons with a garland of prickles, and so delivered unto her husband that hee might know he hath tied himself to a thorny plesure." Among the wares on sale or supply by Newbery in his *Dives Pragmaticus*, 1563 (Hazlitt's *Fugitive Tracts*, 1875, vol. i.), figure:

"Fyne gay and straunge garlands, for Bryde & Brydegrome."

In the Churchwardens' Accounts of St. Margaret's, Westminster, under 1540, is the following item: "Paid to Alice Lewis, a goldsmith's wife of London; for a serclett to marry maydens in, the 26th day of September, £3 10s." The following occurs in Marston's "Dutch Courtezan":

"I was afraid, I'faith, that I should ha seene a garland on this beauties herse."

In Field's "Amends for Ladies," 1618, scene the last, when the marriages are agreed upon, there is a stage direction to set garlands upon the heads of the maid and widow that are to be married. These garlands are thus described by Gay:

"To her sweet mem'ry flow'ry garlands strung,
On her now empty seat aloft were hung."

These emblems were apparently hung up in churches, and where they were composed of fresh flowers withered. Newton, under Breaches of the second Commandment, censures "the adorning with garlands, or presenting unto any image of any Saint, whom thou hast made speciall choise of to be thy patron and advocate, the firstlings of thy increase, as Corne and Graine, and other oblations." *Tryall of a Man's Own Selfe*, 1586, 54. Coles, probably speaking of the metropolis only, says: "It is not very long since the custome of setting up garlands in churches hath been left off with us." *Intro. to the Knowledge of Plants*, 64, But in the Ely Articles of Enquiry, 1662,

p. 7, I read as follows: "Are any garlands and other ordinary funeral ensigns suffred to hang where they hinder the prospect, or until they grow foul and dusty, withered and rotten?" Aubanus, in his Description of the Rites at Marriages in his country and time, has not omitted garlands. Dallaway tells us that "Marriage is by them (of the Greek Church) called the Matrimonial Coronation, from the crowns or garlands with which the parties are decorated, and which they solemnly dissolve on the eighth day following." Brand likewise refers to a French work, where it is mentioned that, at the weddings of the poorer sort, a chaplet or wreath of roses was customary in France; but these illustrations, even when they are very apt, which is not often, it must be owned, the case, are only interesting parallel examples.

The Masters and Wardens of some of the Gilds of London formerly used Election Garlands, which were often made of sumptuous materials. See particularly the fine large illustrations in Black's *History of the Leathersellers*, 1871, where the examples date from 1539.

Garrett.—For a notice of this place, otherwise known as Garvett, and its mock mayor, &c., see Additions to Hazlitt's *Blount*, 1874, in *Antiquary* for September, 1885. Its evolution from a single house to a hamlet has had many analogues, such as Vauxhall, and Schaffhausen, Mühlhausen, &c., abroad. During a considerable number of years, Sir Jeffrey Dunstan, a dealer in wigs, and Sir Henry Dimsdale, a muffin-seller, subsequently a hardware man, were successively returned as mayors of Garrett. The former was nicknamed *Old Wigs*, and the latter *Honeyjuice* or *Sir Harry*.

Garters at Weddings.—There was formerly a custom in the North of England, which will be thought to have bordered very closely upon indecency, and strongly marks the grossness of manners that prevailed among our ancestors: it was for the young men present at a wedding to strive immediately after the ceremony, who could first pluck off the bride's garters from her legs. This was done before the very altar. The bride was generally gartered with ribbons for the occasion. Whoever were so fortunate as to be victors in this singular species of contest, during which the bride was often obliged to scream out, and was very frequently thrown down, bore them about the church in triumph. Brand says: "A clergyman in Yorkshire told me, that to prevent this very indecent assault, it is usual for the bride to give garters out of her bosom. I have sometimes thought this a fragment of the ancient ceremony of loosening the virgin zone, or girdle, a custom that needs no explanation." From passages in different works, it should seem that the striving for garters was originally after the bride had been put to bed. Among the lots in the lottery presented in 1601, there occurs:

"*A Payre of Garters.*
"Though you have fortunes garters, you must be
More staid and constant in your steps than she."

Sir Abraham Ninny, in Field's "A Woman's a Weather-Cocke," 1612, act i. sc. 1, declares:

"Well, since I am disdain'd; off garters blew;
Which signifies Sir Abram's love was true.
Off cypresse blacke, for thou befits not me;
Thou art not cypresse of the cypresse tree,
Befitting Lovers: out green shoe-strings, out,
Wither in pocket, since my Luce doth pout."

In Brooke's "Epithalamium," 1614, we read:

"Youths; take his poynts; your wonted right:
And maydens, take your due, her garters."

In Aylet's Poems, 1654, is a copy of verses "on a sight of a most honorable Lady's Wedding Garter." A note to George Stuart's "Discourse between a Northumberland Gentleman and his Tenant," 1686, p. 24, tells us: "The piper at a wedding has always a piece of the bride's garter ty'd about his pipes." These garters, it should seem, were anciently worn as trophies in the hats. Misson says: "When bed-time is come, the bride-men pull of the bride's garters, which she had before unty'd, that they might hang down and so prevent a curious hand from coming too near her knee. This done, and the garters being fasten'd to the hats of the gallants, the bride maids carry the bride into the bride-chamber, where they undress her and lay her in bed." I am of opinion that the origin of the *Order of the Garter* is to be traced to this nuptial custom, anciently common to both court and country. It is the custom in Normandy for the bride to bestow her garter on some young man as a favour, or sometimes it is taken from her.

Gate Penny.—A customary tribute from tenants to their landlords. See Halliwell in v.

Gawby Day.—(December 28). This day at Wrexham is called Gawby Day, perhaps from *Gauby*, a Northern term for a countryman or a bumpkin; and the town is filled with servants, both men and women. Formerly and originally they came up from the country to be hired; but now it has become a mere holiday. See Atkinson's *Cleveland Glossary*, 1868, in v.

George's Day, St.—(April 23rd). Among the ordinances made by Henry V. for his army abroad, printed in "Excerpta Historica," 1833, is one "For theim that bere not a bande of Seinte George"; and it appears that all the English soldiers were bound, under severe penalties, to carry this distinguishing badge. Compare *Amulet*. It is curious that the same Ordinances, which were promulgated by Henry V. in 1415, served the same purpose in 1513, when Henry VIII. made his expedition to Boulogne, *mutatis mutandis*. In Coates's "History of Reading," p. 221, under Churchwardens' Accounts in the year 1536, are the following entries:

"Charg' of Saynt George.
"Ffirst payd for iii caffes-skynes, and ii horse-skynnes, iii^s. vi^d.
Payd for makeyng the loft that Saynt George standeth upon, vi^d.
Payd for ii plonks for the same loft, viij^d.
Payd for iiij pesses of clowt lether, ij^s ij^d.
Payd for makeyng the yron that the hors resteth vpon, vj^d.
Payd for makeyng of Saynt George's cote, viij^d.
Payd to John Paynter for his labour, xlv^s.
Payd for roses, bells, gyrdle, sword, and dager, iij^s. iiij^d.
Payd for settyng on the bells and roses, iij^d.
Payd for naylls necessarye thereto, x^d. ob."

In the hamlet of Y Faerdref, in the commote of Isdulas, in Denbighshire, is a small village called St. George, on the churchyard-wall of which it was formerly believed that the print of the shoes of St. George's horse could be seen. The neighbouring woods were supposed to be haunted by fairies and other spirits. *Denbigh and its Lordship*, by John Williams, 1860, pp. 217-18. Machyn the Diarist notes that, on St. George's Day, 1559, the Knights of the Garter went about the Hall singing in procession in the morning, and in the afternoon was the election of new knights. Machyn appears, in one place, to insinuate, a sort of dissatisfaction at the occasional departure from the old usage of holding the chapter of the order of the garter at Westminster instead of Windsor, as was the case once or twice in the early part of Elizabeth's reign. Comp. Evelyn's *Diary*, April 23, 1667.

It seems to be the case that at ceremonial observances in St. George's Chapel at Windsor in the case of installations or otherwise the choristers demanded as a fee the King's spurs, which were redeemed by a pecuniary payment. In the Privy Purse Expenses of Henry VII., under 1495, we find : "To the children for the King's spoures, 4s.," and there are similar entries in the Expenses of Henry VIII. under 1530.

It appears that blue coats were formerly worn by people of fashion on St. George's Day. Hazlitt's *Dodsley*, x., 349. Among the Fins, whoever makes a riot on St. George's Day is in danger of suffering from storms and tempests.

Germanus, St., Bishop of Auxerre.—Pennant remarks that the Church of Llanarmon in Denbighshire is dedicated to this personage, who with St. Lupus, says he, "contributed to gain the famous *Victoria Alleluiatica* over the Picts and Saxons near Mold." *Tours in Wales*, 1810, ii., 17. Owing to this circumstance it doubtless was that Bishop Germanus was a favourite in Wales, and had many churches dedicated to him. There were apparently two or three sainted persons of this name, nor is it clear to which Woodes refers where in his *Conflict of Conscience*, 1581, he makes one of the characters say :

"Sent Iob heale the pore, the agew
    Sent Germayne."

Ghosts.—"A ghost," according to Grose, "is supposed to be the spirit of a person deceased, who is either commissioned to return for some especial errand, such as the discovery of a murder, to procure restitution of land or money unjustly withheld from an orphan or widow, or, having committed some injustice whilst living, cannot rest, till that is redressed. Sometimes the occasion of spirits revisiting this world is to inform their heir in what secret place, or private drawer in an old trunk, they had hidden the title deeds of the estate; or where, in troublesome times, they buried their money or plate. Some ghosts of murdered persons, whose bodies have been secretly buried, cannot be at ease till their bones have been taken up, and deposited in consecrated ground, with all the rites of Christian burial. This idea is the remain of a very old piece of heathen superstition : the ancients believed that Charon was not permitted to ferry over the ghosts of unburied persons, but that they wandered up and down the banks of the river Styx for a hundred years, after which they were admitted to a passage. This is mentioned by Virgil :

' Hæc omnis quam cernis, inops inhumataque turba est :
Portitor ille, Charon ; hi quos vehit unda, sepulti.
Nec ripas datur horrendas, et rauca, fluenta,
Transportare prius quam sedibus ossa quierunt.
Centum errant annos, volitantque hæc littora circum :
Tum, demum admissi, stagna exoptata revisunt.'

Sometimes ghosts appear in consequence of an agreement made, whilst living, with some particular friend, that he who first died should appear to the survivor. Glanvil tells us of a ghost of a person who had lived but a disorderly kind of life, for which it was condemned to wander up and down the earth, in the company of evil spirits, till the Day of Judgment. In most of the relations of ghosts they are supposed to be mere aërial beings, without substance, and that they can pass through walls and other solid bodies at pleasure. A particular instance of this is given in Relation the 27th in Glanvil's Collection, where one David Hunter, neat-herd to the Bishop of Down and Connor, was for a long time haunted by the apparition of an old woman, whom he was by a secret impulse obliged to follow whenever she appeared, which he says he did for a considerable time, even if in bed with his wife ; and because his wife could not hold him in his bed, she would go too, and walk after him till day, though she saw nothing ; but his little dog was so well acquainted with the apparition, that he would follow it as well as his master. If a tree stood in her walk, he observed her always to go through it. Notwithstanding this seeming immateriality, this very ghost was not without some substance ; for, having performed her errand, she desired Hunter to lift her from the ground, in the doing of which, he says, she felt just like a bag of feathers. We sometimes also read of ghosts striking violent blows; and that, if not made way for, they overturn all impediments, like a furious whirlwind. Glanvil mentions an instance of this, in Relation 17th of a Dutch lieutenant, who had the faculty of seeing ghosts ; and who, being prevented making way for one which he mentioned to some friends as coming towards them, was, with his companions, violently thrown down, and sorely bruised. We further learn, by Relation 16th, that the hand of a ghost is 'as cold as a clod.'

"The usual time at which ghosts make their appearance is midnight, and seldom before it is dark; though some audacious spirits have been said to appear even by day-light: but of this there are few instances, and those mostly ghosts who have been laid, perhaps in the Red Sea (of which more hereafter), and whose times of confinement were expired: these, like felons confined to the lighters, are said to return more troublesome and daring than before. No Ghosts can appear on Christmas Eve; this Shakespear has put into the mouth of one of his characters in Hamlet." "Ghosts," Grose adds, "commonly appear in the same dress they usually wore whilst living; though they are sometimes cloathed all in white; but that is chiefly the churchyard ghosts, who have no particular business, but seem to appear *pro bono publico*, or to scare drunken rustics from tumbling over their graves. I cannot learn that ghosts carry tapers in their hands, as they are sometimes depicted, though the room in which they appear, if without fire or candle, is frequently said to be as light as day. Dragging chains is not the fashion of English ghosts; chains and black vestments being chiefly the accoutrements of foreign spectres, seen in arbitrary governments; dead or alive, English spirits are free. If, during the time of an apparition, there is a lighted candle in the room, it will burn extremely blue: this is so universally acknowledged, that many eminent philosophers have busied themselves in accounting for it, without once doubting the truth of the fact. Dogs too have the faculty of seeing spirits, as is instanced in David Hunter's relation, above quoted; but in that case they usually shew signs of terror, by whining and creeping to their master for protection: and it is generally supposed that they often see things of this nature when their owner cannot; there being some persons, particularly those born on a Christmas Eve, who cannot see spirits. The coming of a spirit is announced some time before its appearance, by a variety of loud and dreadful noises; sometimes rattling in the old hall like a coach and six, and rumbling up and down the staircase like the trundling of bowls or cannon balls. At length the door flies open, and the spectre stalks slowly up to the bed's foot, and opening the curtains, looks steadfastly at the person in bed by whom it is seen; a ghost being very rarely visible to more than one person, although there are several in company. It is here necessary to observe that it has been universally found by experience, as well as affirmed by divers apparitions themselves, that a ghost has not the power to speak till it has been first spoken to; so, that, notwithstanding the urgency of the business on which it may come, every thing must stand still till the person visited can find sufficient courage to speak to it; an event that sometimes does not take place for many years. It has not been found that female ghosts are more loquacious than those of the male sex, both being equally restrained by this law.

The mode of addressing a ghost is, by commanding it, in the name of the three persons of the Trinity, to tell you who it is, and what is its business; this it may be necessary to repeat three times; after which it will, in a low and hollow voice, declare its satisfaction at being spoken to, and desire the party addressing it not to be afraid, for it will do him no harm. This being premised, it commonly enters into its narrative, which being completed, and its request or commands given, with injunctions that they be immediately executed, it vanishes away, frequently in a flash of light; in which case some ghosts have been so considerate as to desire the party to whom they appear to shut their eyes: sometimes its departure is attended with delightful music. During the narration of its business, a ghost must by no means be interrupted by questions of any kind; so doing is extremely dangerous; if any doubts arise, they must be stated after the spirit has done its tale. Questions respecting its state, or the state of any of their former acquaintance, are offensive, and not often answered, spirits, perhaps, being restrained from divulging the secrets of their prison-house. Occasionally spirits will even condescend to talk on common occurrences, as is instanced by Glanvil in the apparition of Major George Sydenham to Captain William Dyke, Relation 10th. Wherein the Major reproved the Captain for suffering a sword he had given him to grow rusty, saying, 'Captain, Captain, this sword did not used to be kept after this manner when it was mine.' This attention to the state of the weapon was a remnant of the Major's professional duty when living.

It is somewhat remarkable that ghosts do not go about their business like the persons of this world. In cases of murder, a ghost, instead of going to the next Justice of the Peace, and laying its information, or to the nearest relation of the person murdered, appears to some poor labourer who knows none of the parties, draws the curtains of some decrepit nurse or almswoman, or hovers about the place where his body is deposited. The same circuitous mode is pursued with respect to redressing injured orphans or widows : when it seems as if the shortest and most certain way would be, to go to the person guilty of the injustice, and haunt him continually till he be terrified into a restitution. Nor are the pointing out lost writings generally managed in a more summary way, the ghost commonly applying to a third person, ignorant of the whole affair, and a stranger to all concerned. But it is presumptuous to scrutinize too far into these matters : Ghosts have undoubtedly forms and customs peculiar to themselves. If, after the first appearance, the persons employed neglect, or are prevented from, performing the message or business committed to their management, the ghost appears continually to them, at first with a discontented, next an angry, and at length with a furious countenance, threatening to tear them in pieces if the matter is not forthwith executed : sometimes terrifying them, as in Glanvil's Relation 26th, by appearing in many formidable shapes, and sometimes even striking them a violent blow. Of blows given by ghosts there are many instances, and some wherein they have been followed by an incurable lameness. It should have been observed that ghosts, in delivering their commissions, in order to ensure belief, communicate to the persons employed some secret, known only to the parties concerned and themselves, the relation of which always produces the effect intended. The business being completed, ghosts appear with a cheerful countenance, saying they shall now be at rest, and will never more disturb any one ; and, thanking their agents, by way of reward communicate to them something relative to themselves, which they will never reveal. Sometimes ghosts appear, and disturb a house, without deigning to give any reason for so doing : with these the shortest and only way is to exorcise and eject them, or, as the vulgar term is, lay them. For this purpose there must be two or three clergymen, and the ceremony must be performed in Latin ; a language that strikes the most audacious ghost with terror. A ghost may be laid for any term less than a hundred years, and in any place or body, full or empty ; as, a solid oak—the pommel of a sword—a barrel of beer, if a yeoman or simple gentleman, or a pipe of wine, if an esquire or justice. But of all places the most common, and what a ghost least likes, is the Red Sea : it being related in many instances, that ghosts have most earnestly besought the exorcists not to confine them in that place. It is nevertheless considered as an indisputable fact,

that there are an infinite number laid there, perhaps from it being a safer prison than any other nearer at hand ; though neither history nor tradition gives us any instance of ghosts escaping or returning from this kind of transportation before their time."

It is to be suspected that the ancient ideas of a ghost were as indefinite and loose as those now prevalent among us. *St. John's Manners and Customs of Ancient Greece*, 1842, i., 364, *et seqq.* The vulgar superstition, that ghosts walk about in white sheets or clothes seems to have had existence at an early date : for in the story of the Miller and the Tailor in "A C. Mery Talys," 1526, the sexton mistakes the miller in his white coat for the dead farmer's troubled spirit risen from the grave. But in the " Awntyrs of Arthur at the Ternewathelyn " there is a description of an apparition, which proceeds on a somewhat more intelligent theory, so to speak :

" Bare was hir body, and blak to the bane,
Vnbeclosut in a cloude, in clethyng evyl clad ;
Hit zaulut, hit zamurt, lyke a woman,
Nauthyr of hyde, nyf of heue, no hyllyng hit had.
. . . .
Alle gloet as the gledes, the gost qwere hit glidus,
Was vnbyclosut in a cloude, in clething vn-clere,
Was sette aure with serpentes, that sate to the sydus ;
To telle the todus ther opon with tung were to tere."

Shakespear's ghosts excel all others. The terrible indeed is his forte. How awful is that description of the dead time of night, the season of their perambulation !

" 'Tis now the very witching time of night,
When churchyards yawn, and hell itself breathes out
Contagion to this world."

I append two other early notices :

" I know thee well, I heare the watchfull dogs,
With hollow howling tell of thy approach,
The lights burne dim, affrighted with thy presence :
And this distemper'd and tempestuous night
Tells me the ayre is troubled with some devill."
Merry Devil of Edmonton, 1608.

" Ghosts never walk till after midnight,
If I may believe my Grannam."
Beaumont and Fletcher, *Lovers Progress*, act iv.

"Various ways," says a writer in the *Gentleman's Magazine*, 1732, "have been proposed by the learned for laying of ghosts. Those of the artificial sort are easily quieted. Thus when a fryer, personating an apparition, haunted the chambers of the late Emperor Josephus, the present King Augustus, then at the Imperial Court, flung him out of the window, and laid him effectually. The late Dr. Fowler, Bishop of Gloucester, and the late Mr. Justice Powell, had frequent altercations upon this subject. The Bishop was a zealous defender of ghosts; the Justice somewhat sceptical, and distrustful of their being. In a visit the Bishop one day made his friend, the Justice told him, that since their last disputation he had had ocular demonstration to convince him of the existence of ghosts. How, says the Bishop, what! ocular demonstration? I am glad, Mr. Justice, you are become a convert; I beseech you let me know the whole story at large. 'My Lord,' answers the Justice, 'as I lay one night in my bed, about the hour of twelve, I was wak'd by an uncommon noise, and heard something coming upstairs, and stalking directly towards my room. I drew the curtain, and saw a faint glimmering of light enter my chamber.'—'Of a blue colour, no doubt,' (says the Bishop),—'Of a pale blue' (answers the Justice): the light was follow'd by a tall, meagre, and stern personage, who seemed about 70, in a long dangling rugg gown, bound round with a broad leathern girdle; his beard thick and grizly; a large furr-cap on his head, and a long staff in his hand; his face wrinkled and of a dark sable hue. I was struck with the appearance, and felt some unusual shocks; for you know the old saying I made use of in Court, when part of the lanthorn upon Westminster Hall fell down in the midst of our proceedings, to the no small terror of one or two of my brethren,

　　Si fractus illabatur Orbis,
　　Impavidum ferient Ruinæ.

But, to go on: it drew near and stared me full in the face.' 'And did you not speak to it?' (interrupted the Bishop); there was money hid or murder committed, to be sure.' 'My Lord, I did speak to it '—'And what answer, Mr. Justice?' 'My Lord, the answer was, (not without a thump of the staff and a shake of the lanthorn), that he was the watchman of the night, and came to give me notice that he had found the street-door open; and that unless I rose and shut it, I might chance to be robbed before break of day.' The Judge had no sooner ended, but the Bishop disappear'd." The same author adds: "The cheat is begun by nurses with stories of bug-bears, &c. from whence we are gradually led to the traditionary accounts of local ghosts, which, like the genii of the ancients, have been reported to haunt certain family seats and cities, famous for their antiquities and decays. Of this sort are the apparitions at Verulam, Silchester, Reculver, and Rochester: the Dæmon of Tidworth, the Black Dog of Winchester, and the Bar-guest of York. The story of Madam Veal has been of singular use to the editors of Drelincourt on Death." And he afterward ironically observes: "When we read of the ghost of Sir George Villiers, of the Piper of Hamelm, the Dæmon of Moscow, or the German Colonel mentioned by Ponti, and see the names of Clarendon, Boyle, &c. to these accounts, we find reason for our credulity; till, at last, we are convinc'd by a whole conclave of ghosts met in the works of Glanvil and Moreton." The Madame Veal above-mentioned was the same as the person of whom Defoe wrote. Mr. Locke assures us we have as clear an idea of spirit as of body."

In the "Antiquarian Repertory" is a singular narrative of a man named Richard Clarke, a farming-labourer at Hamington, in Northamptonshire, who was haunted by the ghost of another man, name apparently unknown, who declared to Clarke once, through a large hole in the wall of one of the rooms of his (Clarke's) house, that he had been murdered near his own house 267 years, 9 months, and 2 days ago, (this was in 1675), and buried in the orchard. He added that his wife and children, who had lived in Southwark, never knew what became of him; that he had some treasures and paper buried in the cellar of a house near London, and that Clarke must seek for it, and that he (the ghost) would meet him in the cellar, to assist him in the search. Clarke asked time to consider; but the ghost was peremptory. He told him that, as soon as the money and the writings were found, and duly delivered to certain relatives of his in Southwark at such an address, removed from him in the fourth generation, he (the ghost) would cease to visit him, and would leave him in peace; at present he said "that he rece'd much hurt in his cattele by him, yᵗ he shooke the house when his first wife lay in, and frighted her so, she dyed of it." Hereupon Clarke went to town, and on London Bridge the ghost passed him, and conducted him to the house, where his wife had lived four generations before. Clarke found everything answerable to the account which the ghost had given him; the money and the documents were discovered, the writings on vellum found, but those on paper decayed. Clarke divided the money, and acted exactly as the ghost of the murdered man directed him to do, and the latter "lookt chearfully upon him, and gave him thankes, and said now he should be at rest, and spoke to those other persons which were of his generation, relations, but they had not courage to answer; but Clarke talked for them." Morgan, the writer of the letter, in which this story appears, quite believed in the account, and he says, alluding to the money: "It must be coyne of Hen. 4 time and will come amongst the goldsmiths one time or other, if care be taken in it; methinks it should make some noise in Southwarke, and might be found out there. He (Clarke) hath several brothers in London whom he was w^th; perhaps some discovery may be made from them of the place. . . . . I had this story from Mr. Clarke himself." Original letter from Fr. Morgan at Kingsthorpe near Northton (Northampton) to a correspondent at Garraway's Coffee-house, printed in A. R. ed. 1808, vol. iv. p. 635-7. "Tout est prodige pour l'ignorance, qui, dans le cercle étroit de ses habitudes, voit le cercle ou se meut l'univers. Pour le philosophe, il n'y a pas de prodiges: une naissance monstrueuse, l'eboulement subit de la roche la plus dure, resultent, il le sait, de causes aussi naturelles, aussi necessaires, que le retour alternatif du jour et de la nuit."—Salverte, *Des Sciences Occultes*, p. 7.

Gifts.—See *Nails*.

Giles's, St., Day.—(September 1.) An account of this Saint and of the origin of the consecration of the 1st of September to his memory in our calendar, may be found in the "Book of Days." Many churches bear his name. There is the following description in Machyn's "Diary," of the procession in the city of London in 1556, round the parish of St. Giles, Cripplegate: "The furst day of September was Sant Gylles day, and ther was a goodly processyon abowt the parryche with the whettes (waits), and the canepe borne, and the sacrament, and ther was a goodly masse songe as has bene hard; and master Thomas Greuelle, waxchandler, mad a grett dener for master Garter (lord mayor) and my lade, and master Machylle the shreyffe and ys wyff, and boyth the chamburlayns, and mony worshefull men and women at dener, and the whettes playng and dyver odur mynstrelles, for ther was a grett dener." Brand has observed silence respecting St. Giles's Bowl, the flagon or jug of ale, which was in the old times presented to the condemned convict at St. Giles's Hospital, on the road to Tyburn. It appears to be established with tolerable

certainty, that the gallows stood on the site of a portion of Connaught Square; but I am not aware that the precise spot has been settled beyond dispute. A correspondent of "Current Notes" for August 1856, quotes Burton the Leicestershire historian's account of this ceremony. "At the Hospital of St. Giles in the Fields, without the bar of the old Temple, London, and the *Domus Conversorum* (now the Rolls), the prisoners conveyed from the City of London towards Teybourne, there to be executed for treasons, felonies, or other trespasses, were presented with a great bowle of ale thereof to drinke at their pleasure, as to be their last refreshing in this life." The writer goes on to say that Parton, in his account of St. Giles's Hospital and Parish, 1822, refers to this as a peculiar custom; but he points out that "the custom was not so peculiar, but appears to have been an observance of Popish times." He seems rather to mean Catholic countries, for the period, of which he had been before speaking, was antecedent, of course, to the Reformation, and he just afterwards cites some examples of a similar usage among the French in the XVth century. Churchyard also refers to it in his "Mirror and Manners of Men," 1594:

"Trusting in friendship makes some be trust up,
Or ride in a cart to kis Saint Giles his cup."

There is a Yorkshire proverb: "He will be hanged for leaving his liquor, like the saddler of Bawtrey," which refers to a similar usage. A saddler from Bawtrey, on his way to execution declined the proffered bowl of ale, and was consequently turned off, just before a reprieve arrived.

In Lyndsay's time, and long before, the inhabitants of Edinburgh used to carry about the town, on St. Giles's Day, what the poet calls "an auld stock image," and likens to the image of Bell, which they bore in procession at Babylon. The passage is in the "Monarke," first printed about 1554:

"On thare feist day, all creature may se:
Thay beir an auld stock image throuch ye toun,
With talbrone, trompet, schalme, and clarioun,
Quhilk hes bene vsit mony one zeir bigone;
With priestis and freris, in to processioun,
Siclyke as bell wes borne throuch Babilone.' '

"The arm-bone of St. Giles," observes Mr. D. Laing, " was regarded as a relique of inestimable value, when brought to this country by William Prestoun of Gourtoun, who bequeathed it to 'our mother kirk of Sant Gele of Edynburgh,' 11th of January, 1454-5." Notes to reprint of "Dundee Psalms," 1868, p. 257. Mr. Laing refers us to the "Charters of the Collegiate Church of St. Giles." Bann. Club, 1859.

Giles's, St., Fair. — One of the chief fairs was that of St. Giles's Hill or Down, near Winchester : the Conqueror instituted it and gave it as a kind of revenue to the Bishop of Winchester. It was at first for three days, but afterwards, by Henry III., prolonged to sixteen days. Its jurisdiction extended seven miles round, and comprehended even Southampton, then a capital and trading town. Merchants who sold wares at that time within that circuit forfeited them to the bishop. Officers were placed at a considerable distance, at bridges and other avenues of access to the fair, to exact toll of all merchandize passing that way. In the meantime, all shops in the city of Winchester were shut. A court, called the Pavilion, composed of the bishop's justiciaries and other officers, had power to try causes of various sorts for seven miles round. The bishop had a toll of every load or parcel of goods passing through the gates of the city. On St. Giles's Eve the Mayor, bailiffs, and citizens of Winchester delivered the keys of the four gates to the bishop's officers. Many and extraordinary were the privileges granted to the bishop on this occasion, all tending to obstruct trade and to oppress the people. Numerous foreign merchants frequented this fair; and several streets were formed in it, assigned to the sale of different commodities. The surrounding monasteries had shops or houses in these streets, used only at the fair; which they held under the bishop, and often let by lease for a term of years. Different counties had their different stations. In the Revenue Roll of William of Waynflete, An. 1471, this fair appears to have greatly decayed; in which, among other proofs, a district of the fair is mentioned as being unoccupied : "Ubi Homines Cornubiæ stare solebant."

Gilligate, Durham. — The septennial Capital Court of the Marquess of Londonderry for the borough and manor of "Gilligate" — the ancient name for that part of Durham city now called Gilesgate—was held May 8, 1902. After the officials had been chosen, and local differences righted, the steward and his suite, with a crowd of the inhabitants, proceeded to perambulate the boundaries, in the course of which many curious gifts have to be provided by his lordship's re-tainers. Sports and a dinner wound up the day's proceedings.

Gimmal Ring. — See *Rings* and compare Nares, *Glossary*, 1859, in v.

Ginger.—See *Nuptial Usages*.

Girdle.—See *Lying-In*.

Gisborough, co. York.—In an old account of the Lordship of Gisborough, Yorkshire, and the adjoining coast, speaking of the fishermen, it is stated, that "upon St. Peters Daye they invite their friends and kinsfolk to a festyvall kept after their fashion with a free hearte and noe shew of nigardnesse : that daye their boates are dressed curiously for the shewe, their mastes are painted, and certain rytes observed amongste them, with sprinkling their prowes with good liquor, sold with them at a groate the quarte, which custome or superstition suckt from their auncestors, even contynueth down unto this present time." *Antiq. Repertory*, iii., 304.

Glass, Looking.—Potter says : "When divination by water was performed with a looking-glass, it was called catoptromancy : sometimes they (the Greeks) dipped a looking glass into the water, when they desired to know what would become of a sick person : for as he looked well or ill in the glass, accordingly they presumed of his future condition. Sometimes, also, glasses were used and the images of what should happen, without water. *Greek Antiquities*, i., 350. Douce's MSS. notes add that "washing hands in the same water is said to forbode a quarrell." "Some magicians," writes an old author, " being curious to find out by help of a looking-glass, or a glasse-viall full of water, a thiefe that lies hidden, make choyce of young maides, or boyes unpolluted, to discerne therein those images or sights which a person defiled cannot see. Bodin, in the third book of his " Dæmonomachia," chap. 3, reporteth that in his time there was at Thoulouse a certain Portugais, who shewed within a boyes naile things that were hidden. And he added that God hath expressly forbidden that none should worship the Stone of Imagination. His opinion is that this Imagination or Adoration (for so expoundeth he the first verse of the 26th chapter of Leviticus, where he speaketh of the idoll, the graven image, and the painted stone) was smooth and cleare as a looking-glasse, wherein they saw certaine images or sights of which they enquired after the things hidden. In our time conjurers use christall, calling the divination chrystallomantia, or onychomantia, in which, after they have rubbed one of the nayles of their fingers, or a piece of chrystall, they utter I know not what words, and they call a boy that is pure and no way corrupted, to see therein that which they require, as the same Bodin doth also make mention." Molle's *Living Librarie,* 1621, p. 2.

In the " Marriage of the Arts," by Barten Holiday, 1618, is this : " I have often heard them say, 'tis ill luck to see one's face in a glass by candle-light." Among unlucky portents must also be noticed the strong objection which persons even of enlightened views and good position in society still have to allow a young baby to see itself in the glass. The reason is not particularly obvious; but in such a case perhaps a lady's reason ought to be accounted sufficient. When a looking glass is broken, it is an omen that the party to whom it belongs will lose his best friend. See the Greek Scholia on the *Nubes* of Aristophanes, p. 169. Grose tells us that " Breaking a looking glass betokens a mortality in the family, commonly the master."

Glastonbury Thorn.—Collinson, speaking of Glastonbury, says : " South-west from the town is Wearyall Hill, an eminence so-called (if we will believe the monkish writers) from St. Joseph and his companions sitting down here, all weary with their journey. Here St. Joseph struck his stick into the earth, which, although a dry hawthorn stick, thenceforth grew, and constantly budded on Christmas-Day. It had two trunks or bodies till the time of Queen Elizabeth, when a Puritan exterminated one, and left the other, which was the size of a common man, to be viewed in wonder by strangers; and the blossoms thereof were esteemed such curiosities by people of all nations, that the Bristol merchants made a traffick of them, and exported them into foreign parts. In the Great Rebellion, during the time of King Charles I., the remaining trunk of this tree was also cut down : but other trees from its branches are still growing in many gardens of Glastonbury and in the different nurseries of this kingdom. It is probable that the monks of Glastonbury procured this tree from Palestine, where abundance of the same sort grew, and flower about the same time. Where this thorn grew is said to have been a nunnery dedicated to St. Peter, without the Pale of Weriel Park, belonging to the Abbey. It is strange to say how much this tree was sought after by the credulous; and though a common thorn, Queen Anne, King James, and many of the nobility of the realm, even when the times of monkish superstition had ceased, gave large sums of money for small cuttings from the original." *Somersetshire,* ii., 265.

I have no doubt but that the early blossoming of the Glastonbury Thorn was owing to a natural cause. It is mentioned by Gerard and Parkinson in their herbals. Camden also notices it. Ashmole tells us that he had often heard it spoken of, " and by some who have seen it whilst it flourished at Glastonbury." He adds : " Upon St. Stephen's Day, Anno 1672, Mr. Stainsby (an ingenious enquirer after things worthy memorial) brought me a branch of hawthorne having green leaves, faire buds, and full flowers, all thick and very beautifull, and (which is more notable) many of the hawes and berries upon it red and plump, some of which branch is yet preserved in the plant booke of my collection. This he had from a hawthorne tree now growing at Sir Lancelote Lake's house, near Edgworth (Edgeware) in Middlesex, concerning which, falling after into the company of the said knight, 7 July, 1673, he told me that the tree, whence this branch was plucked, grew from a slip taken from the Glastonbury Thorn about sixty years since, which is now a bigg tree, and flowers every winter about Christmas." Appendix to Hearne's *Antiquities of Glastonbury,* p. 303. Sir Thomas Browne remarks : " Certainly many precocious trees, and such as spring in the winter, may be found in England. Most trees sprout in the fall of the leaf or autumn, and if not kept back by cold and outward causes, would leaf about the solstice. Now if it happen that any be so strongly constituted as to make this good against the power of winter, they may produce their leaves or blossoms at that season, and perform that in some singles which is observable in whole kinds: as in ivy, which blossoms and bears at least twice a year, and once in the winter: as also in Furze, which flowereth in that season." " This tree," says Worlidge, " flourished many years in Wilton Garden, near Salisbury, and, I suppose, is there yet; but is not altogether so exact to a day as its original from whence it came was reported to be; it's probable the faith of our ancestors might contribute much towards its certainty of time. For imagination doth operate on inanimate things, as some have observed." *Systema Horticulturæ,* 1677, p. 88.

In the metrical life of Joseph of Arimathea, probably written in the reign of Henry VII., three hawthorns are mentioned :

" Thre hawthornes also that groweth in werall
Do burge and bere grene leaves at Christmas
As fresshe as other in May whan ye nightyngale

Wrestes out her notes musicall as pure
    as glas
Of al wodes and forestes she is yᵉ chefe
    chauntres
In wynter to synge yf it were her
    nature
In werall she might haue a playne place
On those hawthornes to shewe her notes
    clere."

Lyfe of Joseph of Arimathea, 1520, sig.
B 2. Dr. Leighton, writing to Cromwell
about 1537, says : " Pleesith it your worship to understand that yester night we
came from Glastonbury to Bristow ? I here
send you for relicks two flowers wrapped
up in black sarcenet, that on Christmas
even will spring and burgen, and bear
flowers." Manningham, in his *Diary*,
May 2, 1602, records, apparently as something of which he had heard, that " At
Glastenbury there are certaine bushes
which beare May flowers at Christmas and
in January."

A writer in the " World " has
the following irony on the alteration
of the stile in 1752 : " It is well known
that the correction of the Calendar was
enacted by Pope Gregory the thirteenth,
and that the Reformed Churches have,
with a proper spirit of opposition, adhered to the old calculation of the Emperor Julius Cæsar, who was by no means
a Papist. Nearly two years ago the
Popish Calendar was brought in (I hope
by persons well affected). Certain it is
that the Glastonbury Thorn has preserved
its inflexibility, and observed its old anniversary. Many thousand spectators
visited it on the parliamentary Christmas
Day—not a bud was to be seen !—on the
true nativity it was covered with blos-
some. One must be an infidel indeed to
spurn at such authority." *Paper of*
March 8, 1753. The following account
was communicated to the " Gentleman's
Magazine " for January, 1753, by a correspondent at Quainton, in Buckinghamshire : " Above two thousand people came
here this night with lanthorns and
candles, to view a black thorn which
grows in this neighbourhood, and which
was remembered (this year only) to be a
slip from the famous Glastonbury Thorn,
that always budded on the 24th, was full
blown the next day, and went all off at
night; but the people finding no appearance of a bud, 'twas agreed by all, that
Dec. 25th, N.S. could not be the right
Christmas Day, and accordingly refused
going to church, and treating their friends
on that day as usual : at length the affair
became so serious, that the ministers
of the neighbouring villages, in order to
appease the people, thought it prudent
to give notice, that the old Christmas
Day should be kept holy as before.   A

vast concourse of people attended the
noted thorns at Glastonbury on Christmas
Eve, new style ; but to their great disappointment, there was no appearance of
its blowing, which made them watch it
narrowly the 5th of January, the Christmas Day old style, when it blowed as
usual."

Gleek.—A game at cards, played by
three persons with 44 cards. See Halliwell in v. The game of *cleke*, for which
in the *Privy Purse Expenses of Henry
VII.*, under September 15, 1503, one Weston receives £2 on the King's account,
was apparently our gleek. In Gayton's
" Notes on Don Quixote," 1654, is the
following : " A lady once requesting a
gentleman to play at gleeke, was refused,
but civilly, and upon three reasons : the
first whereof, madam, said the gentleman,
is I have no money. Her ladyship knew
that was so nateriall and sufficient, that
she desired him to keep the other two
reasons to himself." Under date of Jan.
13, 1661-2, Pepys wrote : " My aunt
Wright and my wife and I to cards, she
teaching us to play at Gleeke, which is a
pretty game ; but I love not my aunt so
far as to be troubled with it." However,
on the 17th of the following month the
Diarist was sufficiently composed to play
at it, and won 9s. 6d. clear—" the most
that ever I won in my life. I pray God
it may not tempt me to play again."
There is no farther reference to it. We
are told that the Lord Keeper Guildford was fond of this and other similar
amusements. The best account of this
amusement is in Cotgrave's *Wits Interpreter*, 1655.

Gloves.—Felix, in his Anglo-Saxon
Life of St. Guthlac, Hermit of Crowland, circâ A.D. 749, mentions the use of
gloves as a covering for the hand in chap.
xi., and it is related of the consort of
Domenigo Selvo, Doge of Venice (1071-84)
that she always wore gloves. Hazlitt's
Venetian Republic, 1900, ii., 767-8. Gloves
were in use in France in the beginning
of the ninth century. Johannes de Gar-
landia in his *Dictionary*, (13th century),
speaks of the glovers of Paris as cheating
the scholars by selling them gloves of inferior material. He describes them as of
lambskin, fox-fur, and rabbit's-skin ; and
he refers to leathern mittens. Wright's
Vocabularies, 1857, p. 124 ; see also Fairholt's *Costume in England*, 1860, p. 460-
463 ; and Hazlitt's *Livery Companies*,1892,
pp. 520-3. In the " Year Book of Edw.
I." 1302, it is laid down that, in cases of
acquittal of a charge of manslaughter, the
prisoner was obliged to pay a fee to the
justices' clerk in the form of a pair of
gloves, besides the fees to the marshal. A
good deal of interesting and authentic in-

formation under this head may be found in Pegge's "Curialia," 1818, to which, the work being so accessible, it would be useless to do more than refer the reader. A custom still prevails at maiden assizes, i.e., when no prisoner is capitally con-victed, to present the judges, &c., with white gloves. It should seem, by the dedi-cation of Clavell's "Recantation of an ill-led life," 1628, to some of the judges, that anciently this present was made by such prisoners as received pardon after condemnation. Fuller says: "It passeth for a general report of what was custom-ary in former times, that the sheriff of the county used to present the judge with a pair of white gloves, at those which we call mayden-assizes, viz., when no male-factor is put to death therein." Among the lots in "A Lottery presented before the late Queenes Maiesty at the Lord Chancellor's (Keeper's) house, 1601," is A Pair of Gloues with a posy. Davison's "Poetical Rapsodie," 1611, p. 44. Also at p. 44, of ed. 1621, and in Nicolas's, ed. vol. i. p. 7. This lottery is given rather differently in "Early Poetical Miscellanies" (Percy Soc.) The Lord Keeper was Sir T. Eger-ton. There is some pleasantry in the very common notion, and not exclusively vulgar one, as Brand alleged, that if a woman surprizes a man sleeping, and can steal a kiss without waking him, she has a right to demand a pair of gloves. Thus Gay in his Sixth Pastoral:

> "Cic'ly, brisk maid, steps forth before the rout,
> And kiss'd with smacking lip the sno-ring lout :
> For custom says, whoe'er this venture proves,
> For such a kiss demands a pair of gloves."

It was customary in Tusser's day to give the reapers gloves when the wheat was thistly, and Hilman, the author of "Tus-ser Redivivus," 1710, observes that the largess, which seems to have been usual in the old writer's time, was still a matter of course, of which the reapers did not require to be reminded. Can the custom of dropping or sending the glove, as the signal of a challenge, have been derived from the circumstance of it being the cover of the hand, and therefore put for the hand itself? The giving of the hand is well known to intimate that the person who does so will not deceive, but stand to his agreement. To "shake hands upon it" would not, it should seem, be very delicate in an agreement to fight, and therefore gloves may possibly have been deputed as substitutes. We may, perhaps, trace the same idea in wedding gloves.

But there was equally a custom in former times to wear a glove in the hat as a signal of challenge as well as in token of the favour of a mistress or of the loss of a friend. Fairholt's *Costume in England*, 1860, p. 461. But Edgar, in *Lear*, is made to say that he wore them in his cap, when he was a serving-man. A pair of gloves used to be both a Shrovetide and a Christmas gift. See Whitelocke's *Liber Famelicus*, 1858, p. 49, under date of 1615.

Gloves at Funerals. — Gloves were not less common at funerals than at weddings. In some cases, where the family was rich, or at least in good cir-cumstances, as many as an hundred pairs were given away. In our time, the un-dertaker provides gloves for the mourners, and the friends of the departed usually get kid gloves, the servants worsted. But only those who are present, or are un-avoidably absent, receive any. At the funeral of John Wilson, a Sussex gentle-man, in 1640, there were one hundred and fifty pairs of gloves. *Sussex Arch. Coll.*, xi., 147. I may call attention to a very serviceable paper by Mr. Henry John Feasey on Bishops' gloves in the *Antiquary* for 1898, with general remarks on the subject and an engraving of a mediæval pontifical glove.

Gloves at Weddings.—It ap-pears from Selden, that the Belgic cus-tom at marriages was for the priest to ask of the bridegroom the ring, and, if they could be had, a pair of red gloves, with three pieces of silver money in them (arrhæ loco)—then putting the gloves into the bridegroom's right hand, and joining it with that of the bride, and the gloves were left, on loosing their right hands, in that of the bride. "Uxor Hebraica," Opera, tom. iii. p. 673 : "De More Veterum mit-tendi Chirothecam in rei fidem cum Nun-tio, quem quopiam ablegabant alibi agetur vocabatur id genus Symbolum Jertekn." Ihre's "Glossarium," v. Handske. Du Cange says : "Chirothecam in signum Consensus dare." "Etiam Rex in signum sui Consensus, suam ad hoc mittere debet Chirothecam." In Ar-nold's Chronicle, 1502, among "the artycles upon whiche is to inquyre in the visitacyons of ordynaryes of churches," we read : "Item, whether the curat refuse to do the solemnysacyon of lawfull matrymonye before he have gyftes of money, hoses, or gloves." Mr. Halliwell prints a posy supposed to ac-company the present of a pair of gloves from a gentleman to his mistress, and notices the incident in "Much Ado About Nothing," where the Count sends Hero a pair of perfumed gloves. The posy runs as follows :

" Love, to thee I send these gloves ;
　　If you love me,
　　Leave out the G,
And make a pair of loves."

Popular Rhymes and Nursery Tales, 1849,
p. 250.   The custom occurs in " The
Miseries of inforced Marriage" (by George
Wilkins the Elder, 1607), and in Herrick.
White gloves still continue to be presented
to the guests on this occasion.   Sir Dudley Carleton, describing to Winwood, in
a letter of January, 1604-5, the marriage
between Sir Philip Herbert and the Lady
Susan, says : " No ceremony was omitted
of   bride-cakes,   points,   garters,   and
gloves."   In Jonson's " Silent Woman,"
Lady Haughty observes to Morose : "We
see no ensigns of a wedding here, no
character of a bridale ; where be our
scarves and our gloves ? "   The bride's
gloves are noticed by Stephens : " She
hath no rarity worth observance, if her
gloves be not miraculous and singular :
those be the trophy of some forlorne sutor
who contents himself with a large offering, or this glorious sentence, that she
should have been his bed-fellow."   *Essays
and Characters*, 1615.   At Wrexham in
Flintshire," says Dr. Lort, in his copy
of Bourne and Brand, 1777, " on occasion
of the marriage of the surgeon and apo-
thecary of the place, August 1785, I saw
at the doors of his own and neighbours'
houses, throughout the street where he
lived, large boughs and posts of trees,
that had been cut down and fixed there,
filled with white paper, cut in the shape
of women's gloves, and of white ribbons."

Goat.—There is a popular superstition relative to goats : they are supposed
never to be seen for twenty-four hours together ; and that, once in that space, they
pay a visit to the Devil in order to have
their beards combed.   This is common
both in England and Scotland.   The Rev.
Donald McQueen, in the " Gentleman's
Magazine " for February, 1795, speaking
of the Isle of Skye, says : " In this hyper-
borean country, in every district, there is
to be met with a rude stone consecrated
to Gruagach or Apollo.   The first who
is done with his reaping, sends a man or
a maiden with a bundle of corn to his
next neighbour, who hath not yet reaped
down his harvest, who when he has finished, dispatches to his own next neighbour, who is behind in his work, and so
on, until the whole corns are cut down.
This sheaf is called the Cripple Goat, an
Gaobbir Bhacagh, and is at present meant
as a brag or affront to the farmer, for
being more remiss, or later than others
in reaping the harvest, for which reason
the bearer of it must make as good a pair
of heels, for fear of being ill-used for his
indiscretion, as he can.   Whether the ap-

pelation of cripple goat may have any
the least reference to the Apollonian Altar
of Goats' Horns, I shall not pretend to determine."

Godfathers and Godmothers.
—This was probably an ancient secular
custom and form of suretyship spiritua-
lized by the Church in the same way as
the rite of marriage itself.   Ralph Sadler,
in a letter to Cromwell, without date,
but about 1532-3, asking him to stand
sponsor for his newly-born child, says :
" I wold also be right glad to have Mr.
Richards wyf, or my lady Weston to be
the godmother.   Ther is a certen supersty-
cious opynyon and vsage amongst women,
which is, that in case a woman go with
childe she may chrysten no other mannes
childe as long as she is in that case : and
therfore not knowing whether Mr. Richards wyf be with childe or not, I do name
my lady Weston."   Queen Elizabeth stood
sponsor in person or by proxy for a great
number of the children of her courtiers
and favourites, and some of her predecessors had done the same to a certain extent.   In the Privy Purse Expenses of
our early kings are many entries, shewing
that where they did not honour the ceremony with their presence, they sent a
suitable person to represent them, and a
gift.   Strype, in his " Annals," A.D. 1559,
informs us that " on the 27th of October
of that year, the Prince of Sweden, the
Lord Robert and the Lady Marchioness
of Northampton, stood sureties at the
christening of Sir Thomas Chamberlaynes
son, who was baptized at St. Benet's
Church, at Paul's Wharf.   The church
was hung with cloth of arras ; and, after
the christening, were brought wafers,
comfits, and divers banquetting dishes,
and hypocras and Muscadine wine, to entertain the guests."   On the 17th of
December, 1566, James, the son of Mary,
Queen of Scots, was baptized according to
the rites of the Popish Church, at Edinburgh.   Queen Elizabeth had been asked
to become one of the sponsors, and sent
the Earl of Bedford with a gold font as a
present.   The prince was held up by the
Countess of Argyll in the behalf of the
English queen ; after the baptism had
been solemnized, the names and the titles
of the royal infant were proclaimed to the
sound of trumpets. In Stow's "Chronicle"
by Howes, 1631, speaking of the life and
reign of King James, he observes : " At
this time, and for many yeares before, it
was not the use and custome (as now it is)
for godfathers and godmothers generally
to give plate at the baptisme of children (as spoones, cupps, and such like),
but onely to give christening shirts, with
little bands and cuffs, wrought either with
silke or blew threed, the best of them,

for chiefe persons weare, edged with a small lace of blacke silke and gold, the highest price of which for great men's children was seldom above a noble, and the common sort, two, three, or foure, and five shillings a piece." At the christening of Prince Charles, afterwards Charles I., in 1630, the Duchess of Richmond, who stood proxy for the queen-mother of France, presented a jewel valued at £7000 or £8000, and gave the melch, or wet-nurse, a chain of rubies of the estimated worth of £200. Cowell says: "It was a good old custom for godfathers and godmothers, every time their godchildren asked them blessing, to give them a cake, which was a gods-kichell; it is still a proverbial saying in some countries, ' Ask me a blessing, and I will give you some plum-cake." *Law Dictionary, v. Kichell.* In a tract of the 18th century it is said: "The godmother, hearing when the child's to be coated, brings it a gilt coral, a silver spoon, and porringer, and a brave new tankard of the same metal. The godfather comes too, the one with a whole piece of flower'd silk, the other with a set of gilt spoons, the gifts of Lord Mayors at several times." *Fifteen Comforts of Wooing,* p. 162. At ordinary christenings, at least, it appears to have been the custom in Pepys's day (*Diary,* August 25th, 1667), for the godfather to give the name in the case of a boy, and the godmother otherwise. At the baptism of Bamfylde Moore Carew in 1693, his godfathers being the Hon. Hugh Bamfylde and Major Moore, these two gentlemen tossed up whose name should stand first, and Bamfylde won the precedence. *Life and Adventures of B. M. Carew,* 1745, p. 2.

God's Penny.—In the story of the *Heir of Linne,* John o' the Scales exclaims, when the hero has engaged to sell his patrimony : "I draw you to record, lords, and a God's penny, lo ! I cast to the Heir of Linne." Hazlitt's *Tales and Legends,* 1892, p. 381. Percy notes : "Godspennie, i.e., earnest-money ; from the French ' Denier á Dieu.' " The bishop adds : " At this day, (1794) when application is made to the Dean and Chapter of Carlisle to accept an exchange of the tenant under one of their leases, a piece of silver is presented by the new tenant, which is still called a God's Penny." Mr. Atkinson, " Cleveland Glossary," 1868, p. 225, says: " God's penny. Earnest money, given to a servant on concluding the hiring compact : customarily half-a-crown." It is still customary in the West of England, when the conditions of a bargain are agreed upon, for the parties to ratify it by joining their hands, and at the same time for the purchaser to give an earnest.

Gog and Magog.—Bishop Hall, in his " Satires," 1597-8, speaks of the old figures as then in their places in Guildhall. Stow mentions the older figures as representations of a Briton and a Saxon. In Smith's " De Urbis Londini Incendio," 1667, the carrying about of pageants once a year is confirmed ; and in Marston's " Dutch Courtezan," we read : " Yet all will scarce make me so high as one of the giant's stilts that stalks before my Lord Maiors Pageants." Sir H. Ellis refers to Hatton's " New View of London," 1708, as an authority for believing that Gog and Magog were restored in 1707. Bragg says, " I was hemmed in like a wrestler in Moorfields ; the cits begged the colours taken at Ramilies, to put up in Guildhall. When I entered the Hall, I protest, Master, I never saw so much joy in the countenances of the people in my life, as in the cits on this occasion ; nay, the very giants stared at the colours with all the eyes they had, and smiled as well as they could." In Grosley's Tour to London, translated by Nugent, 1772, vol. ii. p. 88, we find the following passage :

" The English have, in general, a rambling taste for the several objects of the polite arts, which does not even exclude the Gothic : it still prevails, not only in ornaments of fancy, but even in some modern buildings. To this taste they are indebted for the preservation of the two giants in Guildhall. These giants, in comparison of which the Jacquemard of St. Paul's at Paris is a bauble, seem placed there for no other end but to frighten children : the better to answer this purpose, care has frequently been taken to renew the daubing on their faces and arms. There might be some reason for retaining those monstrous figures, if they were of great antiquity, or if, like the stone which served as the first throne to the Kings of Scotland, and is carefully preserved at Westminster, the people looked upon them as the palladium of the nation ; but they have nothing to recommend them, and they only raise, at first view, a surprise in foreigners, who must consider them as a production, in which both Danish and Saxon barbarism are happily combined." Hone devotes the 11th section of his " Ancient Mysteries Described," 1823, to this subject, and gives representations of the giants. He refers us to a small tract entitled The *Gigantick History of the two famous Giants in Guildhall,* 1741, and points out the error of Noorthouck in his account of London, 1773, in stating the figures to be formed of pasteboard, like the giant at Salisbury.

The latter is still preserved in the Museum there.

Goitre.—A correspondent of "Notes and Queries" for May 24, 1851, furnishes two remedies then in use at Withyam, Sussex, for goitre, which is common to all regions, where the water is unduly charged with lime: "A common snake, held by its head and tail, is slowly drawn by someone standing by nine times across the front part of the neck of the person affected, the reptile being allowed, after every third time, to crawl about for a while. Afterwards the snake is put alive into a bottle, which is corked tightly, and then buried in the ground. The tradition is, that as the snake decays, the swelling vanishes. The second mode of treatment is just the same as the above, with the exception of the snake's doom. In this case it is killed, and its skin, sewn in a piece of silk, is worn round the diseased neck. By degrees the swelling in this case also disappears." But Dr. Bell has shown that the belief in the efficacy of sacrifice as a charm was not confined to Sussex or to reptiles. *Shakespear's Puck,* i., 117-19.

Golf, Goff, or **Gouf.** (*Dutch Kolef* or *Kolf.*)—Strutt considers this as one of the most ancient games played with the ball that require the assistance of a club or bat. A ball, let us bear in mind, is the basis of some of our own, and other nations' and ages,' most permanent and favourite pastimes. Ball, pure and simple, foot-ball, club-ball, golf, hockey, rounders, cricket, fives, tennis, hurling, and croquet. "In the reign of Edward the third, the Latin name *Cambuca* was applied to this pastime, and it derived the denomination, no doubt, from the crooked club or bat with which it was played; that bat was also called a bandy from it being bent, and hence the game itself is frequently written in English bandy-ball. Jamieson derives golf from the Dutch kolf a club. Wachter derives it from klopp-en to strike, from Keltic goll, the hand, which, curiously enough, degenerated in the course of time into a mere vulgarism, like our modern phrase paw.

I find the following description of this sport in an ancient church writer, which evinces its high antiquity: "Pueros videmus certatim gestientes, testarum in mare jaculationibus ludere. Is lusus est, testam teretem, jactatione Fluctuum lævigatam, legere de litore: eam testem plano situ digitis comprehensam, inclinem ipsum atque humilem, quantum potest, super undas irrotare: ut illud jaculum vel dorsum maris raderet, vel enataret, dum leni impetu labitur: vel summis fluctibus tonsis emicaret, emergeret, dum assiduo saltu sublevatur. Is se in pueris victorem ferebat, cujus testa et procurreret longius, et frequentius exsiliret." *Minucius Felix,* 1712, p. 28. St. Cuthbert, Bishop of Durham, a North-country man, who died in 687, is said to have been acquainted with the game. Why not? The idea is simple and obvious enough. Golf and foot-ball appear to have been prohibited in Scotland by James II. in 1457; and again in 1491 by James IV. The ball used at this game was stuffed very hard with feathers. Northbrooke, a native of Devonshire, speaks of it as a favourite amusement in that county in the reign of Elizabeth. His treatise against dicing and other profanities appeared in 1577. Strutt says that this game is much practiced in the north of England; and Jamieson, that it is a common game in Scotland. In the *North American Review* for July, 1899, Mr. Andrew Lang has an interesting paper, entitled: "Golf from a St. Andrew's point of view," where it is suggested that the game probably came to Scotland from Holland, as the terms are Dutch, and where the writer enumerates the eminent personages, from Mary Stuart downward, who have taken pleasure in this sport. The patronage of golf by the Stuarts was not continued in England after their fall by their successors; but it has now been introduced again with full honours, having always survived in North Britain, and having had many distinguished historical characters of the eighteenth century among its votaries. There is proof that the ancient Dutch method of playing the game was not dissimilar from ours. There are Dutch prints of the 17th century, displaying the method then used, and an etching by Rembrandt, where the amusement is called *Kolef.* But in an account of the voyage of the Hollanders in 1596-7, which was signalized by the discovery of Spitzbergen, the crew of one of the vessels made a staff to play at Colfe, thereby to stretch their joints. Prince Henry, eldest son of James I., who died in 1612, is said by Sir Simonds D'Ewes to have been "rather addicted to martial studies and exercises than to goff, tennis, or other boys' play." "At any rate, it should seem that golf was a fashionable game among the nobility at the commencement of the seventeenth century, and it was one of the exercises with which even Prince Henry occasionally amused himself, as we learn from the following anecdote recorded by a person who was present: 'At another time playing at goff, a play not unlike to pale-maille, whilst his schoolmaster stood talking with another and marked not his highness warning him to stand further off, the prince thinking he had gone aside, lifted up his goff-club to strike the ball; mean tyme one standing by said to him, Beware that you hit not master Newton, wherewith he, drawing back his hand, said, Had I done so, I had but paid my debts.'"

There was in the 18th century a Society of Golfers at Blackheath, and we have a large portrait of a member by Abbott, 1792, accompanied by his servant, carrying his sticks. Of this painting there is a print.

At the end of Ferrier's *Guide to North Berwick*, 1881, are "Rules for the game of golf, as it is played on the Links" there. A writer in the "Book of Days" ascribes to this sport, of which he gives a very good account, the origin of the common phrase, getting into a scrape.

This etymology may be correct; the expression itself was used at least as far back as the time of George III. in its present sense. M. Berjeau, who refers to two curious works on the game, both published in the last century, seems to consider that golf resembled "the present fashionable game of croquet." *Bookworm*, iii., 173-4. The fact is, that the game was susceptible of modifications, according to circumstances, or the opportunity of those playing at it. In the French rules printed at Paris in 1717, it is said that the club and ball were both to be made of the root of the box-tree. The caddie, who follows the players with the sticks and reserve balls, is the same as the Edinburgh *cadie* or running stationer of the eighteenth century.

Good Friday.—"The Festival," 1511, fol. 36, says: "This day is called, in many places, Goddes Sondaye: ye knowe well that it is the maner at this daye to do the fyre out of the hall, and the blacke wynter brondes, and all thynges that is foule with fume and smoke shall be done awaye, and there the fyre was shall be gayly arayed with fayre floures, and strewed with grene rysshes all aboute." It may have been termed Good Friday to distinguish it from the other Fridays of the year, as it was considered an unlucky day. It was customary in the popish times to erect on Good Friday a small building to represent the Sepulchre of our Saviour. In this was placed the host, and a person set to watch it both that night and the next; and the following morning very early, the host being taken out, Christ was said to have arisen. Hospinian tells us that the Kings of England had a custom of hallowing rings with much ceremony on Good Friday, the wearers of which will not be afflicted with the falling sickness. He adds, that the custom took its rise from a ring, which had

been long preserved with great veneration in Westminster Abbey, and was supposed to have great efficacy against the cramp and falling sickness, when touched by those who were afflicted with either of those disorders. This ring is reported to have been brought to King Edward by some persons coming from Jerusalem, and which he himself had long before given privately to a poor person who had asked alms of him for the love he bare to St. John the Evangelist. In his "Curialia Miscellanea," 1818, Appendix 3, Pegge has printed the formulary at length. It was usual, at this season, to eschew ordinary butter, and to substitute almond butter, which formed an element in English cookery from a very remote date. In a collection of culinary recipes, attributed to the reign of Richard II., there is one for making this article of diet. It is mentioned in the printed Wardrobe Accounts of Edward IV., 1480, and elsewhere. In the List of Church Plate, Vestments, &c., in the Churchwardens' Accounts of St. Mary at Hill, 10 Hen. VI., occurs also: "an olde Vestment of red silke lyned with yelow for Good Friday." On Good Friday the Roman Catholics offered unto Christ Eggs and Bacon to be in his favour till Easter Day was past; from which we may at least gather with certainty that eggs and bacon composed a usual dish on that day.—Keth's *Sermon*, 1570, p. 18. In Braithwaite's "Whimzies," 1631, p. 196, we have this trait of "a zealous brother": "he is an antipos to all Church-government: when she feasts he fasts; when she fasts he feasts: Good Friday is his Shrove Tuesday: he commends this notable carnall caveat to his family — eate flesh upon dayes prohibited, it is good against Popery." "To holde forth the crosse for egges on Good Friday" occurs among the Roman Catholic customs censured by John Bale, in his "Declaration of Bonner's Articles," 1554, Signat. D 3, as is ibid D 4, verso, "to creape to the Crosse on Good Friday featly." Compare *Creeping to the Cross.*

Among Good Friday customs still observed, may be enumerated that of laying one-and-twenty sixpences on the spot in the churchyard of St. Bartholomew the Great, Smithfield, in London, supposed to be the resting-place of a lady who left the fund for as many aged widows, on condition that each recipient should be able to stoop, and pick up the coin without help. A small sum is also payable from the same source for a sermon on this day. At All Hallows, Lombard Street, after the service, sixty of the younger scholars from Christ's Hospital were presented by the incumbent, under the will of Peter Symonds (1687), with a new penny and a packet of raisins. In Langbourne Ward, such of the school-children as assisted in the choir received hot-cross buns and trifling gratuities in money. At Tenby there was the old custom of walking to church barefoot on this day, and the people about the same time collected long reeds from the river to make Christ's bed."

It was an ancient belief in Flanders, that children born on Good Friday possessed the power of curing themselves, without aid, of fevers and other ailments. It used to be thought that eggs laid on this day were capable of extinguishing fires, and that three loaves baked then, and buried in corn, were safe from the depredation of all vermin. There is a curious usage still in vogue among the Spanish and Portuguese sailors who happen to be in the English Docks at this time, of flogging an effigy, which they called Judas Iscariot (in commemoration of Judas's share in Christ's death). The author of the "Popish Kingdom" describes the worship of the Cross on Good Friday, and the absurd burlesque on the burial of the Saviour. The opening lines are too ludicrous to be omitted :

"Two priestes, the next day following, vpon their shoulders beare
The image of the Crucifixe, about the altar neare,
Being clad in coape of crimozen die, and dolefully they sing :
At length, before the steps, his coate pluckt off, they straight him bring :
And upon Turkey carpettes lay him down full tenderly !"

The *Globe* newspaper of April 24, 1897, published the following account : "Yesterday was the Greek Good Friday, and in view of the particular circumstances of the occasion the celebration was marked by much emotion on the part of the inhabitants. Unusually large crowds assembled in the streets in the evening to witness the customary processions, and Constitution-square, where all the processions meet about 10 o'clock, was densely packed with thousands of people, all holding lighted candles. Viewed from the balconies and windows overlooking the square, the spectacle was an extremely striking one. The procession to the Cathedral, where the King and Queen attended Mass, included the whole of the officials of the capital, and was headed by the Metropolitan wearing his gold embroidered robes and a glittering tiara on his head. As the procession passed, choirs chanted the prayers for the day, set to melodious and extremely impressive

music. In the middle of the square the procession stopped, while the Metropolitan, in a loud, clear voice, offered prayers invoking the protection of God for the soldiers who had gone to defend the national honour and to fight for the glory of the Cross. At this moment the emotion of the people reached its height, the silence of the multitude, standing bareheaded in the light of the flickering candles, being only broken by the occasional sound of uncontrollable sobs. The different processions afterwards returned to their respective churches."

Good Friday Bun.—Hutchinson, in his "History of Northumberland," following Mr. Bryant's "Analysis," derives the Good Friday Bun from the sacred cakes which were offered at the Arkite Temples, styled boun, and presented every seventh day. Bryant has the following passage on this subject : "The offerings which people in ancient times used to present to the gods, were generally purchased at the entrance of the Temple ; especially every species of consecrated bread, which was denominated accordingly. One species of sacred bread which used to be offered to the gods was of great antiquity, and called boun. The Greeks who changed the *nu* final into a *sigma*, expressed it in the nominative, but in the accusative more truly, Boun. Hesychius speaks of the boun, and describes it a kind of cake with a representation of two horns. Julius Pollux mentions it after the same manner, a sort of cake with horns. Diogenes Laertius, speaking of the same offering being made by Empedocles, describes the chief ingredients of which it was composed : "He offered one of the sacred Liba, called a bouse, which was made of fine flour and honey." It is said of Cecrops that he first offered up this sort of sweet bread. Hence we may judge of the antiquity of the custom, from the times to which Cecrops is referred. The prophet Jeremiah takes notice of this kind of offering, when he is speaking of the Jewish women at Pathros, in Egypt, and of their base idolatry ; in all which their husbands had encouraged them. The women, in their expostulation upon his rebuke, tell him : "Did we make her cakes to worship her ?" Jerem. xilv. 18, 19 ; vii. 18. Hutchinson concludes : "We only retain the name and form of the boun ; the sacred uses are no more."

A writer in *Once a Week* observes : "Do our Ritualists eat hot cross-buns on Good Friday ? Perhaps they do not, but consider the consumption of such cakes to be a weak concession to the childish appetites of those who would not duly observe their Lenten fastings ; and who,.

had they lived in the days of George III., would have been among the crowds who clustered beneath the wooden porticoes of the two royal and rival bun-houses at Chelsea. But there is the cross-mark on the surface of the bun to commend it to the minds which are favourably disposed to symbolism; and there is the history of the cross-bun itself, which goes back to the time of Cecrops, and to the *liba* offered to Astarte, and to the Jewish passover cakes, and to the eucharistic bread, or cross-marked wafers, mentioned in St. Chrysostom's Liturgy, and thence adopted by the early Christians. So that the Good Friday bun has antiquity and tradition to recommend it; and indeed its very name of bun is but the oblique boun, from bous, the sacred ox, the semblance of whose horns was stamped upon the cake. There, too, they also did duty for the horns of Astarte, in which word some philologists would affect to trace a connection with Easter. The substitution by Greeks of the cross-mark in place of the horn-mark would seem to have chiefly been for the easier division of the round bun into four equal parts. Such cross-marked buns were found at Herculaneum."

Hazlitt, in his *Livery Companies*, 1892, p. 104, quotes Maitland's *Account of London*, 1739, for the origin of this usage: "The bakers, probably perceiving that great profits arose to the clergy by the use of the symbols of the cross, *Agnus Deis*, and name of Jesus, to oblige their customers (for their own interest) began to imprint upon their bread the like representations." This practice seems to have been interdicted by a royal mandate of 1252, but it has been more or less continued ever since. The people in the North of England and elsewhere make with a knife many little cross-marks on their cakes before they put them into the oven. It is still a common belief that one cross-bun should be kept for luck's sake from Good Friday to Good Friday. It seems that, in Dorsetshire, a loaf baked on the day, and hung over the chimney-piece, will have the effect, in the popular estimation, of preventing the bread baked in the house during the year from going reamy or stringy. The small loaf of bread, not unusually baked on Good Friday morning by many country folks, is carefully preserved as a medicine for diarrhœa. It is considered that a little of the Good-Friday loaf, grated into a proper proportion of water, is an infallible remedy for this complaint. A relative of the present writer had a loaf of this description, baked on the Good Friday after her marriage in 1856; and it was long kept with this view. The lower classes of society do not monopolize these superstitions.

Good Man's Croft.—Andrews tells us, on the authority of Arnot, that "In 1594, the Elders of the Scotish Church exerted their utmost influence to abolish an irrational custom among the husbandmen, which with some reason gave great offence. The farmers were apt to leave a portion of their land untilled and uncropt year after year. This spot was supposed to be dedicated to Satan, and was styled 'the Good Man's Croft,' viz. the Landlord's Acre. It seems probable that some Pagan ceremony had given rise to so strange a superstition": no doubt as a charm or peace-offering, that the rest might be fertile. Cont. of *Henry's History of Great Britain*, p. 502 Note.

Gooding on St. Thomas's Day.—I find some faint traces of a custom of going a gooding (as it is called) on St. Thomas's Day, which seems to have been done by women only, who, in return for the alms they received, appear to have presented their benefactors with sprigs of evergreens, probably to deck their houses with at the ensuing festival. Perhaps this is only another name for the Northern custom to be presently noticed, of going about and crying Hagmena. In the "Gentleman's Magazine" for April, 1794, where the writer is speaking of the preceding mild winter, he says: "The women who went a gooding (as they call it in these parts) on St. Thomas's Day, might, in return for alms, have presented their benefactors with sprigs of palm and bunches of primroses." Ellis was informed that this practice was still kept up in 1813 in Kent, in the neighbourhood of Maidstone. Miss Baker, in the "Northamptonshire Glossary," 1854, says: "In some villages in the county, I am informed, they formerly went about with a two-handled pad or gossiping-pot, begging furmety, or wheat, for making it. My good old grandfather always, on this day, gave a bowl of wheat to any of the poor in the village who chose to come for it. . . Going a gooding is, I understand, still continued at Peterborough, and in some few villages, but it is going fast into desuetude." In some places they speak of these days as "goodish days." The subjoined is from "Notes and Queries" for December 19, 1857: "In the Staffordshire parish, from which I write, St. Thomas's Day is observed thus: not only do the old women and widows, but representatives also from each poorer family in the parish, come round for alms. The clergyman is expected to give one shilling to each person. . . Some of the parishioners give alms in money, others in kind. Thus some of the farmers give corn, which the miller grinds gratis. The day's custom is termed 'Gooding.' In neighbouring parishes no corn is given, the farmers giving money instead; and in some places the money collected is placed in the hands of the clergyman and churchwardens, who, on the Sunday nearest to St. Thomas's Day, distribute it at the vestry. The fund is called St. Thomas's Dole, and the day itself is termed Doleing Day." The custom which children have of going about before Christmas, to collect fruit, or anything which people choose to bestow on them, has always been common to this country, and to its continental neighbours. Comp. *Corning.*

It is thus described by Naogeorgus:

"Three weekes before the day whereon was borne the Lorde of Grace,
And on the Thursdaye boyes and girls do runne in every place,
And bounce and beate at every doore, with blowes and lustie snaps,
And crie, the Advent of the Lord not borne as yet perhaps.
And wishing to the neighbours all, that in the houses dwell,
A happie yeare, and every thing to spring and prosper well:
Here have they peares, and plumbs, and pence, ech man gives willinglie,
For these three nights are alwayes thought vnfortunate to bee:
Wherein they are afrayde of sprites and cankred witches spight,
And dreadfull devils blacke and grim, that then have chiefest might."

Goose.—An early author, speaking of the goose, says: "She is no witch, or astrologer, to divine by the starres, but yet hath a shrewd guesse of rainie weather, being as good as an almanack to some that beleeve in her." *Strange Metamorphosis of Man*, 1634. There is a proverbial phrase in Skelton's *Garland of Laurel*, 1523:

"When the rain raineth, and the goose winketh,
Little wots the gosling, what the goose thinketh."

A German writer cited by Mr. Atkinson in his "Cleveland Glossary," 1868, says: "From the breast-bone of a goose eaten at Martinmas Eve (old style), it is possible to ascertain what the winter is likely to be. When picked, it must be held up to the light, and the white marks then discernible betoken snow, the darker ones, frost and cold weather. It should also be remarked, that the front part of the bone foretells the weather before Christmas, the hinder part the weather after Christmas."

Goose.—A game mentioned in the Stationers' Register under 1597, and described as "new and most pleasant." It does not seem to be otherwise known, but that it was popular, and long continued in vogue seems to be shown by an advertisement as late as 1670, at the end of Robert Pricke's translation of Le Muet's Architecture, of this pastime as a publication then in print.

Goose-Grass.—See *Whittlegait.*

Goose Intentos.—Corrupted into *goose in ten toes*, the goose popularly regarded by the husbandmen in Lancashire as due to them for a dinner on the sixteenth Sunday after Pentecost, when the old prayer for the day concluded with *præstet esse intentos.* Blount and Halliwell in v.

Goose, Winchester.—The venereal disease, from the stews at Southwark, formerly under the jurisdiction of the see of Winchester. It is one of the species of *goose* enumerated and described by Taylor the Water-poet, in his cognominal tract, 1621. In a tract printed under Edward VI.'s reign, called the *Upchering of the Mass*, it is referred to as the "Winchester gosling."

Goose Riding.—A goose, whose neck is greased, being suspended by the legs to a cord tied to two trees or high posts, a number of men on horseback riding at full-speed attempt to pull off the head, which if they accomplish they win the goose. This has been practised in Derbyshire within the memory of persons lately living. Douce says, his worthy friend Mr. Lumisden informed him that when young he remembered the sport of "riding the goose" at Edinburgh. A bar was placed across the road, to which a goose, whose neck had been previously greased, was tied. At this the candidates, as before mentioned, plucked.

Gooseberry Fair.—See *Running for the Smock*. In Paulinus "de Candore," p. 264, we read: "In Dania, tempore quadragesimali Belgæ rustici in Insula Amack, Anserem (candidum ego vidi), fune alligatum, inque sublimi pendentem, habent, ad quem citatis Equis certatim properant, quique caput ei prius abruperit, victor evasit." Concerning the practice of swarming up a pole after a goose placed at top, see Sauval, "Antiquités de Paris," tom. ii. p. 696.

At the present day a leg of mutton or a pig is frequently scrambled for in the same manner at fairs and regattas.

Gospel Oak.—The place called Gospel Oak, near Kentish Town, doubtless derived its name from the same custom as the Gospel Trees mentioned elsewhere. Comp. *Parochial Perambulations.*

Gossiping-Pot.—See *Gooding*.

Gossip's Cake.—In his *Twelve Months*, 1661, Stevenson, speaking of the month of August, observes: "The new wheat make the Gossips Cake, and the Bride-Cup is carryed above the heads of the whole parish."

Govor's, St., Well.—St. Govor's Well, in Kensington Gardens, London, is still visited by persons who have faith in the virtues of the water. It is, I believe, an artesian spring. The name of this saint, who does not belong to the English series, and is consequently unnoticed by Butler, has been corrupted into Go'or, whence Kensington Gore, in the immediate vicinity, seems to have been derived.

Graal, or **Grail.**—A dish supposed to have held the paschal lamb at the Last Supper, and which, after being brought (as it was said) to England by Joseph of Arimathea, was lost, and formed the object of quest for knights-errant. See a rather long note in Nares, *Glossary* in v. In the common translation of "Don Quixote," the holy Graal is called Saint Graal, a very unauthorized accession to the Romish Calendar; and an eminent historian of our own day has discovered a new saint in the Holy Vial, of which he speaks as Saint Ampoule.

Grace-Cup. — Milner, on an ancient cup ("Archæologia," vol. xi. p. 240), informs us that the introduction of Christianity amongst our ancestors did not at all contribute to the abolition of the practice of wassailing. On the contrary, it began to assume a kind of religious aspect; and the wassail bowl itself, which in the great monasteries was placed on the Abbot's table, at the upper end of the refectory or eating hall, to be circulated among the community at his discretion, received the honourable appellation of 'Poculum Charitatis.' This in our Universities is called the Grace-cup."

Grail. — An abbreviated form of *Graduale*, one of the ancient musical service books of the Church in Romish times. There is one for the use of Salisbury.

Graves. — Graves were anciently called pyttes, and in large towns and cities in and after the middle ages a common pit for the dead was provided in some retired spot. See Strutt's "Manners and Customs," vol. iii., p. 172. But the converse was and remains true; for in Lincolnshire the potato-mounds raised above the ground and covered with earth are known as graves, although they are not dug. I find in Durandus, lib. vii. De Officio Mortuorum, cap. 35-39, the following: "Debet autem quis sic sepeliri, ut capite ad occidentem posito, pedes dirigat ad Orientem, in quâ quasi ipsa positione orat : et innuit quod promptus est, ut de occasu festinet ad ortum : de Mundo ad Seculum." Cullum says : "There is a great partiality here, to burying on the south and east sides of the church yard. About twenty years ago, when I first became rector, and observed how those sides (particularly the south), were crowded with graves, I prevailed upon a few persons to bury their friends on the north, which was entirely vacant; but the example was not followed as I hoped it would : and they continue to bury on the south, where a corpse is rarely interred without disturbing the bones of its ancestors. This partiality may perhaps at first have partly arisen from the antient custom of praying for the dead; for as the usual approach to this and most country churches is by the south, it was natural for burials to be on that side, that those who were going to divine service might, in their way, by the sight of the graves of their friends, be put in mind to offer up a prayer for the welfare of their souls; and even now, since the custom of praying for the dead is abolished, the same obvious situation of graves may excite some tender recollection in those who view them, and silently implore 'the passing tribute of a sigh.' That this motive has its influence, may be concluded from the graves that appear on the north side of the church yard, when the approach to the church happens to be that way; of this there are some few instances in this neighbourhood." *Hist. and Antiq. of Hawsted, Suffolk.* 1784, apud *Bibl. Top. Brit.*, xxiii. "As to the position in the grave, though we decline," says Browne in his "Urne-burial," "the religious consideration, yet in cœmeterial and narrower burying-places, to avoid confusion and cross-position, a certain posture were to be admitted. The Persians lay north and south; the Megarians and Phœnicians placed their heads to the east : the Athenians, some think, towards the west, which Christians still retain : and Bede will have it to be the posture of our Saviour. That Christians bury their dead on their backs, or in a supine position, seems agreeable to profound sleep and the common posture of dying; contrary also to the most natural way of birth; not unlike our pendulous posture in the doubtful state of the womb. Diogenes was singular, who preferred a prone position in the grave; and some Christians like neither, (Russians, &c.) who decline the figure of rest, and make choice of an erect posture." In the Ely Articles of Enquiry, (with some directions intermingled), 1662, it is asked, "When graves are digged, are they made six foot deep, (at the least), and east and west?" In the position of the graves the common and honourable direction is from east to west, the dishonourable one from north to south. Hearne had such correct notions on this head, that he left orders for his grave to be made straight by a compass, due east and west: in consequence of which his monument, which I have often seen, is placed in a direction not parallel with any of the other graves. Its being placed seemingly awry, gives it a very remarkable appearance.

In the Cambrian Register is the following very apposite passage respecting church-yards in Wales. "In country church yards the relations of the deceased crowd them into that part which is south of the church; the north side, in their opinion, being unhallowed ground, fit only to be the dormitory of stillborn infants and suicides. For an example to his neighbours, and as well to escape the barbarities of the sexton, the writer of the above account ordered himself to be buried on the north side of the church yard. But as he was accounted an infidel when alive, his neighbours could not think it creditable to associate with him when dead. His dust, therefore, is likely to pass a solitary retirement, and for ages to remain undisturbed by the hands of men." 1796, p. 374, *Notes.* In "Cymbeline," act iv. sc. 2, Guiderius, speaking of the disguised and (supposed) dead Imogen, says: "Nay, Cadwal, we must lay his head to the east; my father has a reason for't." And in *Guy Mannering* we similarly have: "Na, na! Not that way: the feet to the east." Moresin says that in Popish burying grounds, those who were reputed good Christians lay towards the south and east; others, who had suffered capital punishment, laid violent hands on themselves, or the like, were buried towards the north: a custom that had formerly been of frequent use in Scotland. In "Martins Months Mind," 1589, we read: "He died excommunicate, and they might not therefore burie him in Christian buriall, and his will was not to come there in any wise. His bodie should not be buried in any church, (especiallye cathedrall, whichever he detested), chappell, nor church yard; for they have been profaned with superstition. He would not be laid east and west, (for he ever went against the haire), but north and south: I think because 'Ab Aquilone omne malum,' and the south wind ever brings corruption with it." In the trial of Robert Fitzgerald Esq., and others, for the murder of Patrick Randal M'Donnel, Esq. (in Ireland in 1786), we read: "The body of Mr. Fitzgerald, immediately after exe-

cution, was carried to the ruins of Turlagh House, and was waked in a stable adjoining, with a few candles placed about it. On the next day it was carried to the church yard of Turlagh, where he was buried on what is generally termed the wrong side of the church, in his cloaths, without a coffin." Craven Ord, Esq. informed Brand that "at the east end of the chancel, in the church yard, of Fornham All Saints, near Bury, Suffolk, is the coffin-shaped monument of Henrietta Maria Cornwallis, who died in 1707. It stands north and south, and the parish tradition says that she ordered that position of it as a mark of penitence and humiliation." Pennant, in allusion to Whiteford Church, says: "I step into the churchyard and sigh over the number of departed which fill the inevitable retreat. In no distant time the north side, like those of all other Welsh Churches, was through some superstition to be occupied only by persons executed, or by suicides. It is now nearly as much crowded as the other parts." He adds, that, in North Wales none but excommunicated or very poor and friendless people, are buried on the north side of the church yard. *Hist. of Whiteford*, p. 102. Gilbert White, speaking of Selborne church yard, observes: "Considering the size of the church, and the extent of the parish, the church yard is very scanty; and especially as all wish to be buried in the south side, which is become such a mass of mortality, that no person can be there interred without disturbing or displacing the bones of his ancestors. There is reason to suppose that it once was larger, and extended to what is now the Vicarage Court and garden. At the east end are a few graves; yet none, till very lately, on the north side; but as two or three families of best repute have begun to bury in that quarter, prejudice may wear out by degrees, and their example be followed by the rest of the neighbourhood." In "Paradoxical Assertions," &c., by R. H., 1664, we read:

"Cœlo tegitur, qui non habet urnam." "Doubtless that man's bones in the north church yard rest in more quiet than his that lies entomb'd in the chancel." Benjamin Rhodes, steward to one of the earls of Elgin, requested, it seems, "to be interred in the open church yard, on the north side (to crosse the received superstition, as he thought, of the constant choice of the south side), near the new chapel." Rhodes was interred in Malden Church in Bedfordshire. "Life and Death of Mr. Benjamin Rhodes," &c., by P. Samwaies, his lordship's chaplain, 1657, p. 27. One of Mr. Brand's lady correspondents seems to have thought that if she died an old maid, she would have to lie in her grave with her face downwards.

In the poet Mason's time, it appears to have been usual to whiten the head and footstones of graves at Christmas, Easter, and Whitsuntide; but of course the custom was one which would vary exceedingly. I do not exactly know the origin of the phrase, to mark with a white stone, employed in allusion to a lucky or auspicious day in one of Hazlitt's Essays.

Gray's-Inn.—See *Antients, Pension,* and *Lord of Misrule.*

Greengoose or **Goose Fair.**— A fair formerly held at Stratford-le-Bow on Thursday in Whitsun week, when green geese were the chief features in the entertainment. See Nares, *Glossary* in v. The fair seems to have flourished in 1694, when a popular tract made its appearance with the title of *The Three Merry Wives of Greengoose Fair,* including a story similar to that of the *Crucified Priest,* in La Fontaine. Hazlitt's *Bibl. Coll.,* i., 455.

Green Men or **Wild Men.**—See Halliwell in v., and Hazlitt's *Livery Companies,* 1892, p. 311.

Greenock Fair.—A correspondent of "Notes and Queries" describes the pompous ceremonial which attended the opening of this fair. A Greenock correspondent informs the Editor that it is still kept up on the first Thursday in July and the fourth Tuesday in November, and with more than questionable advantage to the locality and neighbourhood. Formerly at least the offices and other places of business were closed for the day, and he recollects going as a lad, like all the rest, to see the show. *Letter from Allan Park Paton,* April 30, 1897.

Greenwich Fair.—The rolling of young couples down Greenwich-hill, at Easter and Whitsuntide, while the fair was held there, appears by the following extract from R. Fletcher's "Ex Otio Negotium," 1656, p. 210, in a poem called "May Day," to be the vestige of a May game:

"The game at best, the girls now rould must bee,
Where Coryden and Mopsa, he and shee,
Each happy pair make one Hermophrodite,
And tumbling, bounce together, black and white."

This custom, which many still among us must remember, has died with the abolition of Greenwich Fair.

Gregory's, St., Day. — Gregory mentions a singular superstition: "Some are so superstitiously given, as upon the night of St. Gregory's Day, to have their children ask the question in their sleep, whether they have anie minde to book or no; and if they saie yes, they count it a very good presage: but if the children answer nothing, or nothing to that purpose, they put them over to the plough." *Posthuma,* 1649, 113. In Hazlitts' *Handbook,* 1867, p. 244, there is a notice of an unique life of this saint's mother in verse, published about 1540.

Grimp.—St. Evremond, in a letter to Henry Jermyn, Earl of St. Albans, speaks of playing at *ombre* and *grimpe* as an agreeable way of passing a man's last moments. It was probably a game of cards, perhaps only a French game.

Groaning Chair.—An essayist in the "Gentleman's Magazine' 'for May, 1732, observes: "Among the women there is the groaning chair, in which the matron sits to receive visits of congratulation. This is a kind of female ovation due to every good woman who goes through such eminent perils in the service of her country."

"For a nurse, the child to dandle
Sugar, sope, spic'd pots, and candle,
A groaning chair, and eke a cradle.—
Blanckets of a several scantling
Therein for to wrap the bantling:
Sweetmeats from comfit-maker's trade
When the child's a Christian made—
Pincushions and other such knacks
A child-bed woman always lacks,
Caudles, grewels, costly jellies, &c."
—*Poor Robin* for 1676.

Groaning Cheese.—Against the time of the good wife's delivery, it used to be everywhere the custom for the husband to provide a large cheese and a cake. These, from time immemorial, have been the objects of ancient superstition. It is customary at Oxford to cut the cheese (called in the North of England, in allusion to the mother's complaints at her delivery, the Groaning Cheese) in the middle when the child is born, and so by degrees form it into a large kind of ring, through which the child must be passed on the day of the christening. It was not unusual to preserve for many years, I know not for what superstitious intent, pieces of the groaning cake. Thus I read in Gayton: "And hath a piece of the groaning cake (as they call it) which she kept religiously with her Good Friday bun, full forty years un-mouldy and un-mouse-eaten." *Festivous Notes on Don Quixote,* 1654, p. 17. In other places the first cut of the sick wife's cheese (so also they call the groaning cheese) is to be divided into little pieces and tossed in the midwife's smock, to cause young women to dream of their lovers. Slices of the first cut of the groaning cheese are in the North of England laid under the pillows of young persons for the above purpose. In "The Vow-Breaker," by W. Sampson, 1636, in a scene where is discovered "a bed covered with white; enter Prattle, Magpy, Long-tongue, Barren with a childe, Anne in bed " : Boote says, "Neece, bring the groaning cheece, and all requisites, I must supply the father's place, and bid god-fathers."

Guinea Game.—A sport or amusement, so-called, is mentioned in the Stationers' Register under 1587-8.

Gule of August, or **Lammas Day.**—Pettingal derives "Gule" from the Celtic or British "Wyl," or "Gwyl," signifying a festival or holyday, and explains "Gule of August" to mean no more than the holyday of St. Peter ad Vincula in August, when the people of England under popery paid their Peter pence. This is confirmed by Blount, who tells us that Lammas Day, the first of August, otherwise called the Gule or Yule of August, may be a corruption of the British word "Gwyl Awst, signifying the feast of August." Vallancey says that *Cul* and *Gul* in the Irish implies a complete wheel, a belt, a whul, an anniversary. It may be synonymous with *Yule*. Spelman, in his Glossary, under the Gules of August, observes : "It often occurs in ancient parchments (especially legal ones) for the Feast of St. Peter ad Vincula, which is celebrated on the same calends of August. Durandus, in his Rationale, suggests, as a reason for this among others that, the Tribune Quirinus having a daughter whose throat was diseased, the girl was ordered by the Pope to kiss the chains wherewith St. Peter had been shackled, which wrought her complete cure, and led to the institution of the festival, as well as the erection of a memorial church." Vallancey cites Cormac, Archbishop of Cashel in the tenth century, in his Irish Glossary, as telling us that, "in his time, four great fires were lighted up on the four great festivals of the Druids; viz., in February, May, August, and November." Vallancey also tells us that "this day was dedicated to the sacrifice of the fruits of the soil. La-ith-mas was the day of oblation of grain. It is pronounced La-ee-mas, a word readily corrupted to Lammas. *Ith* is all kinds of grain, particularly wheat and mas, fruit of all kinds, especially the acorn, whence mast." Mr. Way, in a note to the word Lammas, in his edition of the "Promptorium Parvulorum," 1865, observes : "On the calends, or first of August, the festival of

St. Peter *ad vincula*, it was customary in Anglo-Saxon times to make a votive offering of the first fruits of the harvest, and thence the feast was termed hlaf mæsse, Lammas, from hlaf, panis, and mæsse, missa, festum." Lammas day is called in the "Red Book of Derby hlaɼ mæɼɼe ꝺæᵹ." But in the "Saxon Chronicle" it is hlam mæɼɼe. Mass was a word for festival ; hence our way of naming the festivals of Christmass, Candlemass, Martinmass, &c . The remark in the Calendar of the Romish Church, under the first of August, is :

"Chains are worshipped," &c.

"Catenæ coluntur ad Aram in Exquiliis Ad Vicum Cyprium juxta Titi thermas."

Comp. *Lammas.*

Gwindy or **Wine-House.**—A curious institution in Wales in former days, where friends, neighbours, &c., assembled, *ymgampio*, or to perform feats of strength and activity, as archery, wrestling, throwing the sledge, and afterward the company called for wine, which the master supplied at a profit. This practice became an abuse, as criminals were sheltered at these places. Pennant's *Tours in Wales*, 1810, ii., 129-30. This gwindy was different from the summer-house surmounting a cellar which the same writer notes as having at his own residence, and to which the gentlemen of a party withdrew after dinner to take their wine and converse more freely. *Hist. of Whiteford and Holywell*, 1796, p. 28.

Gypsies.—The history and migration of the gipsies, says Professor Sayce, have been traced step by step by means of an examination of their lexicon. The grammar and dictionary of the Romany prove that they started from their kindred, the Játs, on the north-western coast of India, near the mouths of the Indus, not earlier than the tenth century of the Christian era ; that they slowly made their way through Persia, Armenia and Greece, until, after a sojourn in Hungary, they finally spread themselves through western Europe into Spain on the one side and England on the other. The views of the old writers on this subject, cited below, are rather uncritical. Ralph Volaterranus affirms that they first proceeded, or strolled, from among the Uxi, a people of Persia. Sir Thomas Browne cites Polydore Vergil as accounting them originally Syrians : Philip Bergoinas as deriving them from Chaldea ; Æneas Sylvius as from some part of Tartary ; Bellonius, as from Wallachia and Bulgaria ; and Aventinus as fetching them from the confines of Hungary. He adds that "they have been banished by most Christian Princes. The great Turk at least tolerates them near the Imperial City: he is said to employ them as spies: they were banished as such by the Emperor Charles the fifth." Sir Thomas Browne gives this general account of the gipsies: "They are a kind of counterfeit Moors, to be found in many parts of Europe, Asia, and Africa. They are commonly supposed to have come from Egypt, whence they derive themselves. Munster discovered in the Letters and Pass, which they obtained from Sigismund the Emperor, that they first came out of Lesser Egypt, that having turned apostates from Christianity and relapsed into Pagan rites, some of every family were enjoined this penance, to wander about the world. Aventinus tells us, that they pretend, for this vagabond course, a judgment of God upon their forefathers who refused to entertain the Virgin Mary and Jesus, when she fled into their country." *Vulgar Errors*, p. 280. He adds: "Their first appearance was in Germany since the year 1400. Nor were they observed before in other parts of Europe, as is deducible from Munster, Genebrard, Crantsius, and Ortelius." *Ibid.* p. 287. Yet Bellonius, who met great droves of gipsies in Egypt, in villages on the banks of the Nile, where they were accounted strangers and wanderers from foreign parts, as with us, affirms that they are no Egyptians. *Observat.* lib. ii. Blackstone, in his "Commentaries," has the following account of them: "They are a strange kind of commonwealth among themselves of wandering impostors and juglers, who first made their appearance in Germany about the beginning of the sixteenth century. Munster, it is true, who is followed and relied upon by Spelman, fixes the time of their first appearance to the year 1417: but as he owns that the first he ever saw were in 1529, it was probably an error of the press for 1517, especially as other historians inform us, that when Sultan Selim conquered Egypt in 1517 several of the natives refused to submit to the Turkish yoke, and revolted under one Zinganeus, whence the Turks call them Zinganees; but being at length surrounded and banished, they agreed to disperse in small parties all over the world, where their supposed skill in the black art gave them an universal reception in that age of superstition and credulity. In the compass of a very few years they gained such a number of idle proselytes, (who imitated their language and complexion, and betook themselves to the same arts of chiromancy, begging, and pilfering), that they became troublesome and even formidable to most of the States of Europe.

Hence they were expelled from France in the year 1560, and from Spain 1591, and the Government of England took the alarm much earlier, for in 1530 they are described, Stat. 22 Hen. VIII. c. x., as an 'outlandish people calling themselves Egyptians, using no craft, nor feat of merchandize, who have come into this realm and gone from shire to shire, and place to place, in great company, and used great, subtle, and crafty means to deceive the people, and also have committed many heinous felonies and robberies.' Wherefore they are directed to avoid the realm, and not to return under pain of imprisonment and forfeiture of their goods and chattells; and upon their trials for any felony which they may have committed, they shall not be intitled to a jury *de medietate linguæ*. And afterwards it was enacted by Statutes 1 and 2 Ph. and Mary, c. iv., and 5 Eliz. c. xx., that if any such persons shall be imported into the kingdom, the importers shall forfeit forty pounds. And if the Egyptians themselves remain one month in the kingdom, or if any person, being fourteen years old, whether natural-born subject or stranger, which hath been seen or found in the fellowship of such Egyptians, or which hath disguised him or herself like them, shall remain in the same one month at one or several times, it is felony without benefit of clergy. And Sir Matthew Hale informs us that at one Suffolk Assize no less than thirteen persons were executed upon these Statutes a few years before the Restoration. But to the honour of our national humanity, there are no instances more modern than this of carrying these laws into practice."

The subsequent passage, from the "British Critic," exhibits a proof of the same tendency. "In a late meeting of the Royal Society of Gottingen, Professor Blumenbach laid before the members a second Decad of the crania of persons of different nations contrasted with each other, in the same manner as in the first, and ranged according to the order observed by him in his other works. In the first variety was the cranium of a real gipsey, who died in prison at Clausenburg, communicated by Dr. Patacki of that place. The resemblance between this and that of the Egyptian mummy in the first decad was very striking. Both differed essentially from the sixty-four crania of other persons belonging to foreign nations, in the possession of the author: a circumstance which, among others, tends to confirm the opinion of Profess. Meiners, that the Hindoos, from whom Grielman derives the gipsies, came themselves originally from Egypt." The gipsies, as it should thus seem, came originally from Hindostan, where they are supposed to have been of the lowest class of Indians, namely Parias, or, as they are called in Hindostan, Suders. They are thought to have migrated about A.D. 1408 or 1409,when Timur Beg ravaged India for the purpose of spreading the Mahometan religion. On this occasion so many thousands were made slaves and put to death, that an universal panic took place, and a very great number of terrified inhabitants endeavoured to save themselves by flight. As every part towards the north and east was beset by the enemy, it is most probable that the country below Multan, to the mouth of the Indus, was the first asylum and rendezvous of the fugitive Suders. This is called the country of Zinganen. Here they were safe, and remained so till Timur returned from his victories on the Ganges. Then it was that they first entirely quitted the country, and probably with them a considerable number of the natives, which will explain the meaning of their original name. By what track they came to us cannot be ascertained. If they went straight through the southern Persian deserts of Sigistan, Makran, and Kirman, along the Persian Gulf to the mouth of the Euphrates, from thence they might get, by Bassora, into the great deserts of Arabia, afterwards into Arabia Petræa and so arrive in Egypt by the Isthmus of Suez. They must certainly have been in Egypt before they reached us, otherwise it is incomprehensible how the report arose that they were Egyptians. Pasquier, in his "Recherches de la France," has the following: "On August 17, 1427, came to Paris twelve Penitents (penanciers) as they call themselves, viz., a duke, an earl, and ten men, all on horseback, and calling themselves good Christians. They were of lower Egypt, and gave out that not long before the Christians had subdued their country, and obliged them to embrace Christianity, or put them to death. Those who were baptized were great lords in their own country, and had a King and Queen there. Some time after their conversion, the Saracens overran their country and obliged them to renounce Christianity. When the Emperor of Germany, the King of Poland, and other Christian Princes heard this, they fell upon them and obliged them all, both great and small, to quit their country, and go to the Pope at Rome, who enjoined them seven years penance to wander over the world without lying in a bed; every bishop and abbot to give them once 10 livres tournois; and he gave them letters to this purpose, and his blessing. They had been wandering five years when they came to Paris. They were lodged by the police out of the City, at Chapel St. Denis. Almost all had their ears bored, and one or two silver rings in each, which they said was esteemed an ornament in their country. The men were very black, their hair curled; the women remarkably ugly and black, all their faces scarred (deplayez), their hair black, like a horse's tail, their only habit was an old shaggy garment (flossoye) tied over their shoulders with a cloth or cord-sash, and under it a poor petticoat or shift. In short they were the poorest wretches that had ever been seen in France; and, notwithstanding their poverty, there were among them women who, by looking into people's hands, told their fortunes *et meirent contens en plusieurs mariages;* for they said, thy wife has played thee false (Ta femme t'a fait coup) and what was worse, they picked people's pockets of their money and got it into their own by telling these things by art, magic, or the intervention of the Devil or by a certain knack." It is added that they were expelled from France in 1561.

At a comparatively early date the terms *Œgyptian* and *Bohemian* were rather wrongly applied to them. For in Grielman's *Dissertation on the Gypsies,* translated by Raper, 1787, we read that, in 1418, the gipsies first arrived in Switzerland near Zürich and other places, to the number, men, women, and children, of fourteen thousand. In a provincial council, held at Tarragona in 1591 there was the subjoined decree promulgated against them: "Curandum etiam est ut publici Magistratus eos coerceant qui se Ægyptiacos vel Bohemianos vocant, quos vix constat esse Christianos, nisi ex eorum relatione; cum tamen sint mendaces, fures, et deceptores, et aliis sceleribus multi eorum assueti." "Ægyptiaci," says Ducange, "vagi homines, harioli ac fatidici, qui hac & illac errantes ex manus inspectione futura præsagire se fingunt, ut de marsupiis incautorum nummos corrogent."

In Grielman a very copious catalogue is given of gipsy and Hindostan words collated, by which it appears that every third gipsy word is likewise an Hindostan one, or still more, that out of every thirty gipsy words eleven or twelve are common to Hindostan. This agreement will appear uncommonly great if we recollect that the above words have only been learned from the gipsies within these very few years, consequently after a separation of near four complete centuries from Hindostan, their supposed native country, among people who talked languages totally different, and in which the gipsies themselves conversed; for under the constant and so long continued influx of these languages, their own must necessarily have suffered great alteration. In this learned work there is also a comparison of the gipsies with the above cast of Suders: but I lay the greatest stress upon those proofs which are deduced from the similarity of the languages. In the supplement it is mentioned that Marsden had obtained as many words as he could get, and that by a correspondence from Constantinople he procured a collection of words used by the Cingaris thereabouts; and these, together with the words given by Ludolph in his "Historia Æthiopica," compared with Hindostan vulgar language, show it to be the same that is spoken by the gipsies and in Hindostan.

Harrison, in his "Description of England," describing the various sorts of cheats practised by the voluntary poor, after enumerating those who maim or disfigure their bodies by sores, or counterfeit the guise of labourers or serving men, or mariners seeking for ships which they have not lost, to extort charity, adds: "It is not yet full threescore years since this trade began: but how it hath prospered since that time it is easie to judge, for they are now supposed of one sex and another to amount vnto aboue 10,000 persons, as I haue heard reported. Moreouer, in counterfeiting the Egyptian roges, they haue deuised a language among themselues which they name Canting, but others Pedlers French, a speach compact thirtie yeares since of English and a great number of od words of their owne deuising, without all order or reason: and yet such is it as none but themselues are able to vnderstand. The first deuiser thereof was hanged by the necke, a iust reward no doubt for his deceits and a common end to all of that profession." *Holinshed*, 1587, p. 183. In Rid's *Art of Jugling*, 1612, sign.B b, is the following account:— "These kind of people about an hundred years agoe, about the twentieth yeare of King Henry the eight, began to gather an head, at the first heere about the Southerne parts, and this (as I am informed) and as I can gather, was their beginning. Certaine Egiptians, banished their cuntry, (belike not for their good conditions), arrived heere in England, who being excellent in quaint tricks and devises, not known heere at that time among us, were esteemed and had in great admiration, for what with strangeness of their attire and garments, together with their sleights and legerdemaines, they were spoke of farre and neere, insomuch that many of our English loyterers joyned with them, and in time learned their crafte and cosening. The speach which they used was

the right Egyptian language, with whome our Englishmen conversing with, at least learned their language. These people continuing about the country in this fashion, practicing their cosening art of fast and loose legerdemaine, purchased themselves great credit among the cuntry people, and got much by palmistry and telling of fortunes, insomuch they pitifully cosened the poore contry girles, both of money, silver spones, and the best of their apparrell, or any good thing they could make, onely to hear their fortunes." "This Giles Hather (for so was his name) together with his whore, Kit Calot, in short space had following them a pretty traine, he terming himself the King of the Egiptians, and she the quene, ryding about the cuntry at their pleasure uncontrolld." He then mentions the statute against them of the 1st and 2d of Philip and Mary, on which he observes— "But what a number were executed presently upon this statute, you would wonder: yet, notwithstanding, all would not prevaile: but still they wandred, as before, up and downe, and meeting once in a yeare at a place appointed: sometime at the Devil's A—— in Peake in Darbishire, and otherwhiles at Ketbrooke by Blackheath, or elsewhere, as they agreed still at their meeting." Speaking of his own time, he adds: "These fellowes seeing that no profit comes by wandring, but hazard of their lives, do daily decrease and breake off their wonted society, and betake themselves, many of them, some to be pedlers, some tinkers, some juglers, and some to one kinde of life or other." William Bullein, in his Treatise "of Simples and Surgery," accompanying his *Bulwarke of Defence*, 1562, in which the author speaks of dog-leeches and Egyptians, and Jews: all pretending to the telling of fortunes and curing by charms. "They" (dog-leeches) "buy some gross stuff, with a box of salve and cases of tools to set forth their slender market withal, &c. Then fall they to palmistry and telling of fortunes, daily deceiving the simple. Like unto the swarms of vagabonds, Egyptians, and some that call themselves Jews: whose eyes were so sharp as lynx. For they see all the people with their knacks, pricks, domifying, and figuring, with such like fantasies. Faining that they have familiers and glasses, whereby they may find things that be lost. And, besides them, are infinite of old doltish witches with blessings for the fair and conjuring of cattel." Strype's *Annals*, ii., 611. In Dekker's *Lanthorne and Candlelight*, 1608, Sign. G 2, the gipsies are called Moone-men, and a section is devoted to an account of "a strange wild people, very dangerous to townes and country villages," as they are called; and Dekker draws a picture of them, which closely corresponds with our experience of their modern descendants or representatives. I am sorry that his account is too long for transfer hither. "In "Witt's Recreations," a long piece called "The gipsies" occurs, which is curious, as it contains a good deal of phraseology evidently supposed by the writer to be peculiar to the class, but then, as now, common to all the mendicant fraternity. In Harman's time (1566) many of the terms were current among thieves and beggars, which are familiar to modern ears. Spelman's portrait of the gipsy fraternity in his time, which seems to have been taken *ad vivum*, is as follows: "Egyptiani. Errorum Impostorumque genus nequissimum: in Continente ortum, sed ad Britannias nostras et Europam reliquam pervolans:—nigredine deformes, excocti sole, immundi veste, et usu rerum omnium fœdi.—Fœminæ cum stratis et parvulis, jumento invehuntur. Literas circumferunt Principum, ut innoxius illis permittatur transitus.—Oriuntur quippe et in nostra et in omni Regione, spurci hujusmodi nebulones, qui sui similes in Gymnasium sceleris adsciscentes; vultum, cultum, moresque supradictos sibi inducunt. Linguam (ut exotici magis videantur) fictitiam blaterant, provinciasque vicatim pervagantes, auguriis et furtis, imposturis & technarum millibus plebeculam rodunt et illudunt, linguam, hanc Germani Rotwelch, quasi rubrum Wallicum, id est Barbarismum; Angli Canting nuncupant." In "The Character of a Quack Astrologer," 1673, sign. A 3 verso, our wise man, "a gypsey of the upper form," is called "a three-penny prophet that undertakes the telling of other folks fortunes, meerly to supply the pinching necessities of his own." At sign. B 3 our cunning man is said to "begin with theft, and to help people to what they have lost, picks their pockets afresh; not a ring or spoon is nim'd away, but pays him twelvepence toll, and the ale-drapers' often-straying tankard yields him a constant revenue: for that purpose he maintains as strict a correspondence with gilts and lifters, as a mountebank with applauding midwives and recommending nurses: and if at any time, to keep up his credit with the rabble, he discovers anything, 'tis done by the same occult Hermetic learning, heretofore profest by the renowned Mall-Cut-Purse." These used still, in Brand's time, to be called "Wise Men" in the villages of Durham and Northumberland. Gay, in his "Pastorals," speaking of a girl who is slighted by her lover, thus describes the gipsies:

"Last Friday's eve, when as the sun was set,
I, near yon stile, three sallow gipsies met;
Upon my hand they cast a poring look,
Bid me beware, and thrice their heads they shook:
They said that many crosses I must prove,
Some in my worldly gain, but most in love.
Next morn I miss'd three hens and our old cock,
And, off the hedge, two pinners and a smock."

In the North of England and Scotland they seem to have enjoyed some share of indulgence. Before the middle of the sixteenth century we meet with " ' Letters of Defence and Concurrence to John Fall, Lord and Earl of Little Egypt, for assisting him in the execution of Justice upon his Company, conform to the Laws of Egypt, February 15th, 1540-1.' These are supposed to have been a gang of gypsies associated together in defiance of the State under Fall, as their head or king, and these the articles of association for their internal government, mutual defence and security, the embroil'd and infirm state of the Scotish nation at that time not permitting them to repress or restrain a combination of vagrants, who had got above the laws, and erected themselves into a separate community as a set of banditti." There is a curious letter of the justices of Durham to the Earl of Shrewsbury, Lord President of the North, dated at Durham, Jan. 19, 1549-50, concerning the gipsies and Faws. A writ of Privy Seal, dated 1549, supports John Faw, Lord and Earl of Little Egypt, in the execution of justice on his company and folk, conform to the laws of Egypt, and in punishing certain persons there named, who rebelled against him, left him, robbed him, and refused to return home with him. James's subjects are commanded to assist in apprehending them, and in assisting Faw and his adherents to return home. There is a like writ in his favour from Mary Queen of Scots, 1553; and in 1554 he obtained a pardon for the murder of Nunan Small. So that it appears he had staid long in Scotland, and perhaps some time in England, and from him this kind of strolling people might receive the name of Faw Gang, which they still retain. "Privy Seal Book of Edinburgh," no. xiv. fol. 59, quoted in "Gent. Mag." for Oct. 1785. This document is noticed by Ellis in his first series of "Original Letters," 1825. Lodge's "Illust. of British History," vol. i. p. 135. Mr. Hampton has pointed out, in his most interesting " Origines Patriciæ," 1846, that Johnny Faw, the familiar name for the old gipsy chiefs, was corrupted from Fowde or Faad, the Danish name for a governor, and the same writer mentions that, in the Acts of James VI. of Scotland, 1581, the term is used in the sense of bailiff.

In Scotland, in the eighteenth century, the gipsies appear to have been tolerably abundant. A person writing from Eaglesham, Co. Renfrew, about 1795, says: "There is no magistrate nearer than within four miles; and the place is oppressed with gangs of gipsies, commonly called tinkers or randy-beggars, because there is nobody to take the smallest account of them." *Stat. Acc.* ii., 124. There is a well-known Scotish song entitled "Johnny Faa, the Gypsie Laddie." An advertisement in the "Newcastle Courant," July 27, 1754, offers a reward for the apprehending of John Fall and Margaret his wife, William Fall and Jane, otherwise Ann his wife, &c. "commonly called or known by the name of Fawe," &c. Gipsies still continue to be called "Faws" in the North of England. Since the repeal of the Act against this people in 1788 they are said to have declined in numbers. In May, 1797, their settlement at Norwood was broken up, and they were treated as vagrants. The number of genuine gipsies in England is not large; but there are thousands of women fortune-tellers, who pretend to be gipsies, and affect to understand palmistry and divination. The gipsies are universally considered in the same light, i.e., of cheats and pilferers. Witness the definition of them in Ducange and the curious etchings of them by Callot. The engraver does not represent them in a more favourable light than the lexicographer, for, besides his inimitable delineations of their dissolute manner of living, he has accompanied his plates with verses, which are very far from celebrating their honesty. It appears from many preceding allusions that the modern artifices in practice among this class of persons date somewhat far back. We find in the old ballad of "The brave English Gipsey," that the still familiar trick of dyeing the face with walnut-juice was in vogue in the time of Charles I. :

"Our dye is not in vaine;
For we do dye in graine:
The walnut-tree supplies our lacke;
What was made faire, we can make
blacke."

The whole piece is curious, and worthy of perusal, as it shews that the gipsy has always led a pretty similar kind of existence in this country, employing the same shifts, and known by the same characteristics. The ballad was an imitation of one written on the same plan under the title of "The Spanish Gipsy."

The late Dr. Diamond, of Twickenham, told me that when he was a boy, a gipsy chief died in his neighbourhood, and over the place of interment his followers laid a black coffin-shaped stone of peculiar appearance; and it was their practice every year to come and sit in a circle round the stone, as a mark of homage to the departed. So lately as September, 1894, in the Chapelry of Withernsea, in the East Riding of Yorkshire, after the death of "Fiddler Jack," his clothes and effects were burnt, to prevent any dispute among his relatives, who had to begin again, and buy their own belongings; and a second motive was that the widow might not be wooed for the sake of her property. *Antiquary,* November, 1894.

The subjoined paragraph in a newspaper of the 19th Nov. 1903, seems barely credible:—The effects of the Queen of the Boswell tribe of Gipsies, who died and was buried in Falkirk last week, have been destroyed at the gipsy encampment in accordance with a native custom of the tribe, which is invariably followed. The goods destroyed were of the value of £150, including five bags full of valuable costumes, a solid silver George III. tea set, antique china, silver teaspoons and forks. The caravan of the deceased, which cost £130, is also to be destroyed by fire.

In the present editor's boyhood there was a song in common use, of which he remembers one stanza:

"Hark, hark, the dogs do bark;
The gipsies are coming to town;
Some in rags, and some in jags,
And some in velvet gown."

Twiss, in his "Travels," gives the following account of them in Spain: "They are very numerous about and in Murcia, Cordova, Cadiz, and Ronda. The race of these vagabonds is found in every part of Europe; the French call them Bohemiens, the Italians Zingari, the Germans Zigeunen, the Dutch Heydenen (Pagans), the Portuguese Siganos, and the Spaniards Gitanos, in Latin Cingari. Their language, which is peculiar to themselves, is everywhere so similar, that they undoubtedly are all derived from the same source. They began to appear in Europe in the 15th century, and are probably a mixture of Egyptians and Ethiopians. The men are all thieves, and the women libertines. They follow no certain trade, and have no fixed religion. They do not enter into the order of society, wherein they are only tolerated. It is supposed there are upwards of 40,000 of them in Spain, great numbers of whom are inn-keepers in the villages and small towns, and are everywhere fortune-tellers. In Spain they are not allowed to possess any lands, or even to serve as soldiers. They marry among themselves, stroll in troops about the country, and bury their dead under water. They are contented if they can procure food by showing feats of dexterity, and only pilfer to supply themselves with the trifles they want; so that they never render themselves liable to any severer chastisement than whipping for having stolen chickens, linen, &c. Most of the men have a smattering of physic and surgery, and are skilled in tricks performed by sleight of hand. The foregoing account is partly extracted from le Voyageur François, vol. xvi. but the assertion that they are all so abandoned as that author says, is too general." In the "Pall Mall Gazette," 1869, it was stated that the Pope went out of Rome to bless some Bohemians, encamped on the outskirts of the city, and inspected their quarters.

See upon the subject Pasquier, "Recherches de la France," p. 392; "Dictionnaire des Origines, v. Bohemiens"; De Pauw, "Recherches sur les Egyptiens," tom. i. p. 169; Camerarius, "Horæ Subsecivæ"; "Gent. Mag.", vol. liii. p. 1009; ibid. vol. lvii. p. 897. "Antiquarian Repertory," ed. 1807, vol. iii. p. 375-9; Borrow's "Bible in Spain" and "Gipsies in Spain," &c.

Hab-Nab.—The exposition offered by Isaac Reed seems most consonant with truth. It occurs in a note upon that passage in "Twelfth Night," where a character speaking of a duellist says, "His incensement at this moment is so implacable that satisfaction can be none but by pangs of death, and sepulchre; hob, nob, is his word; give't or take't." In Anglo-Saxon, habban is to have, and næbban to want. May it not therefore be explained in this sense, as signifying, "Do you chuse a glass of wine, or would you rather let it alone?" An even earlier author has the following passage:

"Where wooers hoppe in and out, long time may bryng
Him that hoppeth best, at last to have the ryng.
I hoppyng without for a ringe of a rush,
And while I at length debate and beate the bushe,
There shall steppe in other men, and catch the burdes,
And by long time lost in many vaine wurdes.
Betwene these two wives, make slouth speede confounde
While betweene two stooles my tayle goe to the ground.

By this, sens we see slouth must breede a scab,
Best sticke to the tone out of hand, hab or nab."

The phrase occurs in Ben Jonson's 'Tale of a Tub':

' I put it
Even to your Worship's bitterment hab nab
I shall have a chance o' the dice for't, I hope.' "

And Malone adds a passage from Holinshed: "The citizens in their rage shot habbe or nabbe, at random." In Harington's "Epigrams," book iv., ep. 91, we read:

" Not of Jack Straw, with his rebellious crew,
That set King, realme, and lawes at hab or nab,
Whom London's worthy Maior so bravely slew
With dudgeon dagger's honourable stab."

In "The New Courtier," a ballad, preserved in "Le Prince 'Amour," 1660, we find hab nab thus introduced:

"I write not of religion
For (to tell you truly) we have none.
If any me to question call,
With pen or sword, hab nab's the word,
Have at all."

It is said of the quack astrologer: "He writes of the weather hab nab, and as the toy takes him, chequers the year with foul and fair." So we perceive that the true sense of the expression was gradually forgotten. On the other hand, in *Appius and Virginia*, 1575 (Hazlitt's Dodsley, IV., 127), we have:

"There is no more ways, but *hap or hap not*"—

Hackin. — Hackin, a large sort of sausage, being a portion of the cheer provided for Christmas festivities, from to hack or chop, hackstock being still a chopping-block in the Scotish dialect." Nares *Gloss.*, 1859, in v. In "Round about our Coal-Fire" (circâ 1730) I find the following account of the usual diet and drink of this season, with other curious particulars: "An English gentleman at the opening of the great day, i.e., on Christmas Day in the morning, had all his tenants and neighbours enter his hall by day-break. The strong beer was broached, and the black-jacks went plentifully about with toast, sugar, nutmegg, and good Cheshire cheese. The Hackin (the great sausage) must be boiled by day-break, or else two young men must take the maiden (i.e., the cook), by the arms, and run her round the market-place till she is ashamed or her laziness.''

Haddock.—Pennant tells us that, '' On each side beyond the gills of a haddock is a large black spot. Superstition assigns this mark to the impression St. Peter left with his finger and thumb, when he took the tribute out of the mouth of a fish of this species, which has been continued to the whole race of haddocks ever since that miracle.'' '' Zoology,'' vol. iii., p. 182, edit. 1776.

'' But superstitious haddock, which appear
With marks of Rome, St. Peter's finger here.''

Haddock has spots on either side, which are said to be marks of St. Peter's fingers, when he catched that fish for the tribute.'' —'' Metellus his dialogues,'' &c., 1693, p. 57 :

'' O superstitious dainty, Peter's fish,
How com'st thou here to make so godly dish? ''
Ibid.

Haddon or Hardwicke, Co. Derby, Headless Steeds of.— The superstitious notion that a coach drawn by headless steeds, and driven by a headless coachman, haunted this locality, appears to have been common to Parsloes in Essex, and several other places. The late Mr. Thoms, under the *nom de plume* of Ambrose Merton, wrote a letter to the *Athenæum* about 1857 on the subject. A correspondent of the same paper, replying to Thoms, enquired whether the neighbourhood of Haddon or of Hardwicke was still visited by the phantom coach. Comp. Allies' *Antiquities of Worcestershire,* 1856, p. 462.

Haggs.—There is sometimes an appearance of phosphorus upon the manes of horses or men's hair (*flammæ lambentes*), called '' Haggs.'' Blount says, '' Hags are said to be made of sweat or other some vapour issuing out of the head : a not unusual sight among us when we ride by night in summer time. They are extinguished like flames by shaking the horses' manes; but I believe rather it is only a vapour reflecting light, but fat and sturdy, compacted about the manes of horses, or men's hair.'' Hyll, in his *Contemplation of Mysteries* (1568), sign. E 2, speaking of '' the fire cleaving and hanging on the parts of men and beasts,'' observes : '' This impression for troth is prodigious without any phisicke cause expressing the same when as the flame or fire compasseth about anye persons heade. And this straunge wonder and sight doth signifie the royal assaultes of mightie monarchies, and kinges, the governments at the Emperie, and other matters wor-

thie memory, of which the Phisicke Causes sufficient cannot be demonstrated. Seeing then such fyers or lightes are, as they wer, counterfets or figures of matters to come, it sufficiently appeareth, that those not rashely do appeare or showe but by Gods holy will and pleasure sent, that they maye signifie some rare matter to men. This light doth Virgill write of in the seconde Booke of Æneados of Ascanius, which had a like flame burning without harme on his heade. Also Livius in his first Book, and Valerius Maximus reporte of Servius Tullius, a childe who, sleeping on bedde, such a flame appeared on his heade and burned rounde about the heade without harme, to the wonder of the beholders : which sight pronounced after his ripe age the comming unto royall Estate.'' He devotes another section to the consideration of the question : '' What is to be thought of the flame of fyre, which cleaveth to the heares of the heade and to the heares of beastes?'' He says here : '' Experience witnesseth, that the fyre do cleave manye times to the heades and eares of beastes, and often times also to the heades and shoulders of men ryding and going on foote. For the exhalations dispearsed by the ayre, cleave to the heares of horses, and garments of men : which of the lightnesse doe so ascend, and by the heate kindled. Also this is often caused when men and other beastes by a vehement and swift motion wax very hote, that the sweate, fattie and clammye, is sent forth, which kindled yeldeth this forme. And the like maner in all places, (as afore uttered), as eyther in moyst and clammie places, and marishes, in churchyards, cloysters, kitchins, under galosses, valleys, and other places, where many deade bodies are laide, doe such burning lightes often appeare. The reason is that, in these places the earth continually breatheth forth fatte fumes, grosse and clammy, which come forth of dead bodyes : and when the fume doth continually issue forth, then is the same kindled by the labouring heate, or by the smiting togither : even as out of two flint stones smitten togither fyre is gotten. To conclude, it appeareth that such fyres are seene in moyst kitchins, sinckes, or guttours, and where the orfall of beastes killed are thrown : or in such places most commonly are woont to be seene. Such fires cleaving, doe marveylously amase the fearfull. Yet not all fires which are seene in the night are perfite fiers in that many have a kinde without a substaunce and heate, as those which are the delusions of the devill, well knowne to be the Prince of the World, and flyeth about in the ayre.'' In a work already cited, occurs an account '' of flames that appear upon the hairs of men and beasts, their cause. These are sometimes clammy exhalations scattered in the air in small parts, which, in the night, by the resistance of the cold, are kindled, by cleaving to horse's ears and men's heades and shoulders, riding or walking; and that they cleave to hair or garments, it is by the same reason the dew cleaves to them, they being dry and attractive, and so more proper to receive them. Another kind of these flames are when the bodies of men and beasts are chafed and heated, they send forth a fat clammy sweat, which in like manner kindles, as is seen by sparkles of fire that fly about when a black horse is very hard curried in the dark, or as the blue fire on the shells of oysters, caused by the nitrous salt. Livy also tells us of one Marius, a knight of Rome who, as he was making an oration to his soldiers in Spain with such vehemency as heated him, his head appeared to them all in a flame, though himself was not aware of it." *Account of Storms*, 1704, p. 79.

Hagmena.—The word "Hagmena" is by some supposed of an antiquity prior to the introduction of the Christian Faith. On the Norman *Hoquinanno* Douce observes: "This comes nearer to our word, which was probably imported with the Normans. It was also by the French called Haguillennes and Haguimento, and I have likewise found it corrupted into Haguirenleux," (and he refers to Carpentier, Menage, and other authorities). He says also: "I am further informed that the words used upon this occasion are 'Hagmena, Hagmena, gives us cakes and cheese, and let us go away.' Cheese and oaten-cakes, which are called farls, are distributed on this occasion among the cryers." Subjoined is all that appears to have survived of the Yorkshire Hagmena Song:

"To-night it is the New Year's night, to-morrow is the day,
And we are come for our right and for our ray,
As we used to do in old King Henry's Day:
Sing fellows, sing, hag-man, ha!
If you go to the bacon-flick cut me a good bit;
Cut, cut and low, beware of your maw.
Cut, cut, and round, beware of your thumb,
That me and my merry men may have some:
Sing, fellows, sing, hag-man, ha!
If you go to the black ark, bring me ten mark;
Ten mark ten pound, throw it down upon the ground,
That me and my merry men may have some;
Sing, fellows, sing, hag-man, ha!"

For the following lines, which the common people repeat upon this occasion, on New Year's Day, in some parts of France, I am indebted to M. Olivier:

"Aguilaneuf de céans
On le voit a sa fenêtre,
Avec son petit bonnet blanc,
Il dit qu'il sera le Maître,
Mettera le Pot au feu;
Donnez nous, ma bonne dame,
Donnez nous Aguilaneuf."

A writer in the "Gentleman's Magazine" for July, 1790, tells us: "In Scotland, till very lately (if not in the present time), there was a custom of distributing sweet cakes and a particular kind of sugared bread, for several days before and after the New Year; and on the last night of the old year (peculiarly called Hagmenai), the visitors and company made a point of not separating till after the clock struck twelve, when they rose, and, mutually kissing, wished each other a happy New Year. Children and others, for several nights, went about from house to house as guisarts, that is, disguised, or in masquerade dresses, singing:

"'Rise up, good wife, and be no swier
To deal your bread as long's your here,
The time will come when you'll be dead,
And neither want nor meal nor bread.'

"Some of those masquerades had a fiddle, and, when admitted into a house, entertained the company with a dramatic dialogue, partly extempore."

We read in the "Scotch Presbyterian Eloquence Displayed" that "it is ordinary among some plebians in the South of Scotland, to go about from door to door upon New Year's Eve, crying Hagmena, a corrupted word from the Greek for *holy month*. John Dixon, holding forth against this custom once, in a sermon at Kelso, says: 'Sirs, do you know what Hagmane signifies? It is, the Devil be in the house! that's the meaning of its Hebrew original.'" Page 102. Comp. *Tappy Tousie*.

Hair (i.) Customs.—The Countess of Dorset, Pembroke, and Montgomery, in her *Day-Book*, 1676, notes the visits of one Richard Goodgeon to Brougham Castle to cut her ladyship's hair. The custom of wearing the hair down the back loose, and a coif between the crown and the head, seems to have been preserved for a long time, and to have been in vogue on the Continent. The Princess Catherine of Aragon is described as wearing her hair so arranged in the contemporary narrative of her journey to England, previously to her espousal to Prince Arthur, son of Henry VII., and her ladies-in-waiting appear to have followed the same fashion. *Antiq. Repert.*, 1807, ii., p. 278. At the coronation of Elizabeth of York, in November, 1487, the Queen is described as wearing her fair yellow hair plain behind her back, with a caul of pipes over it, somewhat, perhaps, in the later Roman style, as we see it on coins. Compare *Marriage*, infrâ. This habit was not confined, however, to women, for the younger portraits of Henry VII. on his coins represent him with long unkempt hair, somewhat like that worn by Lorenzo dé Medici in the paintings or prints of him, by members of the Della Rovera, Visconti, Este, and other families on coins of nearly the same period, and by Louis XII. of France on his Franco-Italian money, as well as in fact the fashion followed in the 15th and 16th centuries by all male personages of rank on the Continent. On the title of an edition of Donatus the Grammarian, printed by Wynkyn de Worde about 1496, are four figures with their hair similarly left to fall over the neck and shoulders, and numerous illustrations of the fashion occur in Fairholt and Planché. The mode may be taken to have been borrowed from Italy.

Hair (ii.) Superstitions.—There is a vulgar notion that men's hair will sometimes turn grey upon a sudden and violent fright, to which Shakespear alludes in a speech of Falstaff to Prince Henry : " Thy father's beard is turned white with the news." Grey remarks : " This whimsical opinion was humorously bantered by a wag in a coffee-house ; who, upon hearing a young gentleman giving the same reason for the change of his hair from black to grey, observed that there was no great matter in it, and told the company that he had a friend, who wore a coal-black wig, which was turned grey by a fright in an instant." Of late years the large sums offered by the trade for hair of a particular hue and length have overcome in many instances the old repugnance to part with this ornament, not only on the ground of pride or vanity, but on that of superstitious fear ; for it was anciently a current vulgar belief, that if any portion of hair was left about, the birds would steal it to build their nests with, a fatal consequence to the owner, especially if the bird was a pie. Going still farther back, we arrive at the barbarous idea, of which Scott has availed himself in the " Pirate," that hair thrown into the sea had the power of kindling a storm, or (as Scott has it) of appeasing the waters. The hair from a calf's tail, inserted in the cow's ear, is supposed, or was formerly, to be efficacious in making the mother forget the loss of its young one ; and the hair of a dog, which has bitten you, is held to be an antidote against any evil consequences, if given by the owner to the person bitten. But compare Hazlitt's *Proverbs*, 1882, p. 19.

Halcyon or **Kingfisher.**—See, as to the superstition about this bird, Nares, *Glossary*, 1859, in v., *Halcyon.*

Hallow Eve at Oxford. — See *Christmas Prince.*

Hallow E'en.—In North Wales, according to Pennant, there was a custom upon all Saints' Eve of making a great fire called Coel Coeth, when every family about an hour in the night makes a great bonfire in the most conspicuous place near the house, and when the fire is almost extinguished, every one throws a white stone into the ashes, having first marked it ; then having said their prayers turning round the fire, they go to bed. In the morning, as soon as they are up, they come to search out the stones, and if any one of them is found wanting they have a notion that the person who threw it in, will die before he sees another All Saints' Eve. They have a custom also of distributing Soul Cakes on All Souls' Day, at the receiving of which poor people pray to God to bless the next crop of wheat. But many of these customs, even in Pennant's time, had fallen into disuse. In Owen's account of the Bards we read : " The autumnal fire is still kindled in North Wales, being on the eve of the first day of November, and is attended by many ceremonies ; such as running through the fire and smoke, each casting a stone into the fire, and all running off at the conclusion to escape from the black short-tailed sow ; then supping upon parsneps, nuts, and apples : catching at an apple suspended by a string with the mouth alone, and the same by an apple in a tub of water : each throwing a nut into the fire ; and those that burn bright, betoken prosperity to the owners through the following year, but those that burn black and crackle, denote misfortune. On the following morning the stones are searched for in the fire, and if any be missing, they betide ill to those who threw them in." Owen has prefaced these curious particulars by the following observations : " Amongst the first aberrations may be traced that of the knowledge of the great Huon, or the Supreme Being, which was obscured by the hieroglyphics or emblems of his different attributes, so that the grovelling minds of the multitude often sought not beyond those representations for the objects of worship and adoration. This opened an inlet for numerous errors more minute ; and many superstitions became attached to their periodical solemnities, and more particularly to their rejoicing fires, on the appearance of vegetation in spring, and on the completion of harvest in autumn."

Hallow E'en in Scotland.—

Shaw, in his *Account of Moray*, seems to consider the festivity of this night as a kind of harvest home rejoicing: "A solemnity was kept," says he, "on the eve of the first of November as a thanksgiving for the safe in-gathering of the produce of the fields. This I am told, but have not seen it, is observed in Buchan and other counties, by having Hallow Eve fire kindled on some rising ground." Martin tells us that the inhabitants of St. Kilda, on the festival of All Saints, baked "a large cake, in the form of a triangle, furrowed round, and which was to be all eaten that night." "The passion of prying into futurity," says Burns, in the notes to his poem, "makes a striking part of the history of human nature, in its rude state, in all ages and nations; and it may be some entertainment to a philosophic mind to see the remains of it among the more unenlightened in our own." He gives therefore the principal charms and spells of this night, so big with prophecy to the peasantry in the West of Scotland. One of these by young women is by pulling stalks of corn: another by the blue clue: a third by eating the apple at the glass. Burns goes on to enumerate several other very observable customs of divination on this even of Allhallows. The first is "Sowing Hemp seed." The second is: "To winn three wechts o'naethings." Others are: "to fathom the stack three times," "to dip your left shirt sleeve in a burn where three Lairds' lands meet"; and the last is a singular species of divination "with three luggies or dishes." The minister of Logierait, in Perthshire, says: "On the evening of the 31st of October, O.S. among many others, one remarkable ceremony is observed. Heath, broom, and dressings of flax are tied upon a pole. This faggot is then kindled. One takes it upon his shoulders, and, running, bears it round the village. A crowd attend. When the first faggot is burnt out, a second is bound to the pole, and kindled in the same manner as before. Numbers of these blazing faggots are often carried about together, and when the night happens to be dark they form a splendid illumination." The minister of Callander says: "On All Saints' Even they set up bonfires in every village. When the bonfire is consumed, the ashes are carefully collected into the form of a circle. There is a stone put in near the circumference, for every person of the several families interested in the bonfire; and whatever stone is moved out of its place, or injured next morning, the person represented by that stone is de-

voted or fey, and is supposed not to live twelve months from that day. The people received the consecrated fire from the Druid priests next morning, the virtues of which were supposed to continue for a year." The minister of Kirkmichael, in Perthshire, says: "The practice of lighting bonfires on the first night of winter, accompanied with various ceremonies, still prevails in this and the neighbouring highland parishes. Formerly the Hallow Even fire, a relic of Druidism, was kindled in Buchan. Various magic ceremonies were then celebrated to counteract the influence of witches and demons, and to prognosticate to the young their success or disappointment in the matrimonial lottery. These being devoutly finished, the hallow fire was kindled, and guarded by the male part of the family. Societies were formed, either by pique or humour, to scatter certain fires, and the attack and defence were often conducted with art and fury."—"But now the hallow fire, when kindled, is attended by children only : and the country girl, renouncing the rites of magic, endeavours to enchant her swain by the charms of dress and of industry." Pennant tells us, in his "Tour in Scotland," that the young women there determine the figure and size of their husbands by drawing cabbages blind-fold on Allhallow Even. "The first ceremony of Hallow-e'en is pulling each a stock or plant of kail. They must go out, hand-in-hand, with eyes shut, and pull the first they meet with. Its being big or little, straight or crooked, is prophetic of the size and shape of the grand object of all their spells—the husband or wife. If any yird or earth stick to the root, that is tocher or fortune; and the taste of the custoc, that is the heart of the stem, is indicative of the natural temper and disposition. Lastly, the stems, or to give them their ordinary appellation, the runts, are placed somewhere above the head of the door; and the christian names of the people whom chance brings into the house, are, according to the priority of placing the runts, the names in question."

Of the scanty particulars known to us of the great Watt one is that his grandfather, Thomas Watt, was a baillie at Greenock, till his death in 1734, and in this capacity fined evil-doers on Hallow E'en night. The *Dundee Advertiser*, reporting the celebration of the old Scotish festival of "Hallowe'en" at Balmoral Castle in 1871, says :—"The demonstration has come to be known in Balmoral and throughout the district as 'The Queen's Hallowe'en;' and in accordance with the royal desire, and following the custom of past years, most of the people, both on the Balmoral and Abergeldie estates, turned out on Tuesday night, and formed a torchlight procession, which had a picturesque and imposing appearance. There were altogether from 180 to 200 torch-bearers; and her Majesty, with several members of the Royal family, viewed the scene with evident pleasure and satisfaction. Her Majesty remained for fully an hour an interested spectator of the proceedings. After the torch-bearers had promenaded for some time, the torches were heaped in a pile on the roadway a litle to the west, and in full view from the windows of the Castle. Empty boxes and other materials were soon added, and in a short time a splendid bonfire blazed famously, a gentle breeze helping to fan the flames. Her Majesty, the Prince and Princess Louise, the Princess Beatrice, and the ladies and gentlemen of the suite, then retired indoors, and took up positions at the windows to see the rest of the merry-making. Dancing was begun with great vigour round the bonfire. The demonstration culminated in a vehicle containing a well got-up effigy of the Hallowe'en witch being drawn to the fire by a band of sturdy Highlanders. The witch had a number of boys for a guard of honour, headed by the piper, and in the rear came Mr. Cowley, her Majesty's yager, whose workmanship the effigy was. The fire was kept up for a long time with fresh fuel, and when all had danced till they could almost dance no longer, the health of her Majesty was proposed by Mr. Cowley, and responded to with the utmost enthusiasm, accompanied by three times three rounds of vociferous cheering. Later in the evening the servants and others about the Castle enjoyed a dance in the ghillie hall. The ball broke up at an early hour on Wednesday morning." In a newspaper of 1877, this custom is described as still existing in Perthshire.

Hallowmass. — In the "Festyvall," 1511, is the following passage: "We rede in olde tyme good people wolde on All halowen daye bake brade and dele it for all crysten soules." On Allhallows' Day, or Hallowmass, it was an ancient English custom for poor persons and beggars to go a-souling, which signified to go round asking for money, to fast for the souls of the donors of alms or their kinsfolk. In the "Two Gentlemen of Verona," Shakespear makes Speed speak of some one puling, "like a beggar at Hallowmass." But the usage is referred to by Scot in his "Discovery of Witchcraft," 1584. In Shropshire (and perhaps elsewhere) the children still go souling, as they did in Aubrey's day, on Hallowmass, and they sing the following verses, for which I am indebted to a correspondent of "Notes and Queries":

"Soul! soul! for a soul-cake;
Pray, good mistress, for a soul-cake.
One for Peter, two for Paul,
Three for them that made us all.
Soul! soul! for an apple or two;
If you've got no apples, pears will do.
Up with your kettle, and down with your pan :
Give me a good big one, and I'll be gone.
　　　　Soul! soul! &c.
An apple or pear, a plum or a cherry,
Is a very good thing to make us merry.
　　　　Soul! soul! &c.

Some of the richer sorts of persons in Lancashire and Herefordshire (among the papists there) used to give cakes of oaten bread to the poor on this day: and they, in retribution of their charity, hold themselves obliged to say this old couplet:

—"God have your Saul,
Beens and all."

In the Cleveland country these loaves are called similarly Sau'mas Loaves. In the Whitby Glossary, they are described as "sets of square farthing cakes with currants in the centre, commonly given by bakers to their customers; and it was usual to keep them in the house for good luck." In this last respect they resembled the Good Friday bread and cross-buns. Mr. Brand's servant, who was a native of Warwickshire, told him that seedcakes at Allhallows were also usual in that country. Harvey, the Dublin conjurer, states that, on this Eve, which he characterizes as an "anile, chimerical solemnity," his servants demanded apples, ale, and nuts, and left him alone, while they went to enjoy themselves.

In the Churchwardens' Accounts of Heybridge, Essex, under 1517, are the following items: "Payed to Andrew Elyott, of Maldon, for newe mendynge of the bell knappelle agenste Hallowmasse, £0 1s. 8d. Item, payed to John Gidney, of Maldon, for a new bell-rope agenste Hallowmasse, £0 0s. 8d." In the time of Henry VIII. "the Vigil and ringing of bells all the night long upon Allhallow day at night," was abolished. In the appendix also to Strype's "Annals," the following injunction, made early in the reign of Elizabeth, occurs: "that the superfluous ringing of bels, and the superstitious ringing of bels at Alhallown tide, and at All Souls' Day with the two nights next before and after, be prohibited." It is stated in Kethe's Sermon preached at Blandford, 1570, that "there was a custom, in the papal times, to ring bells at Allhallow-tide for all Christian souls." No. 130 of "Mery Tales and Quicke Answers," 1567, however, is "Of the gentilman that checked his seruant for talke of ryngyng." "A Gentilman, brought vp at London in an In of court, was maryed, and kepte an house in the countrey : and as he sate at supper with his neyghbours aboute hym, vpon an alhalow daie at night, amonge other communication, he talked of the solemne ringyng of the belles (as was the vsage than)." The feast of Allhallows is said to drive the Finns almost out of their wits.

Hallowmass in Scotland.—

Martin, speaking of the Isle of Lewis, says that it was long before the minister there could persuade the people to relinquish a ridiculous custom they had of going by night on Hallow-tide to the Church of St. Mulvay, whence one of their number went into the sea up to his waist, with a cup of ale brewed for the occasion with malt contributed by the inhabitants (each family giving a peck), and pouring the liquid into the water, addressed a propitiatory allocution to a sea-god called Shony, who was supposed to have an influence over the crops. They then returned to church, observed a moment's dead silence, then extinguished at a given signal the candle on the altar, and proceeded to the fields, where the rest of the night was spent in revelry.

Hand, The.—

It is probable that if an exhaustive research into the subject were undertaken, the folk-lore of the Hand would occupy a considerable space, and develop many curious particulars.

The practice of holding up the right hand as a mark of submission or assent is extremely ancient and very widely spread. A small silver coin of Udalric, Duke of Bohemia (1012-37), bears on one side an open hand, which might have stood as a symbol of the Deity, or as a signification of allegiance to his suzerain ; and the same type occurs in pennies of Edward the Elder, (901-57) and Ethelred II. of England, who began to reign in 979. In a coin of the former the third and fourth fingers are closed in token of the bestowal of the Latin benediction. Barrington says that it was anciently the custom for a person swearing fealty "to hold his hands joined together between those of his lord; the reason for which seems to have been that some Lord had been assassinated under pretence of paying homage ; but, while the tenant's hands continued in this attitude, it was impossible for him to make such an attempt." *Observations on the Statutes*, 1775, p. 206. In the *Squire of Low Degree*, where the King of Hungary takes the hero out of prison, and makes him swear to keep his counsel, it is said :

" The squyer there helde vp his hande, His byddyng neuer he should withstande."

In the old story of *Adam Bel*, printed before 1536, and reproducing far earlier notions, we find the hand introduced where the outlaws come into the presence of the king :

" And when they came before our kyng, As it was the lawe of the lande, They kneled down without lettynge, And eche held vp his hande."

Cetewayo held up his hand to our Queen, but he stood erect.

It may be suggested that the custom of elevating the right hand—the hand which usually held the weapon—may have been designed, on the same principle as that indicated by Barrington, at the outset as a guarantee of good faith and an assurance of security. In some Popish countries, and in our Canadian possessions, which include the old Colony of New France, the usage of holding up the right hand in making oath is supplemented by the obligation of doing so before a crucifix, which is suspended in the Court for that purpose. Where there is a search for weapons, the person concerned usually raises both his arms. Bingham has a quotation from St. Austin on superstitious observations, among which, he says, " You are told in a fit of convulsion or shortness of breath, to hold your left thumb with your right hand." Cited by Bourne, *Antiq. Vulg.*, c. 18. There is a superstition that the forefinger of the right hand is venomous, and is therefore not fit to touch any wound or sore. "That a yellow death-mould may never appear upon your hand, or any part of your body," occurs among the omens introduced in Holiday's " Marriage of the Arts," 1618. It is still usual in parts of the country to tap the back of the hand or the forearm thrice to avert a bad omen (*absit omen!*)when a person has been speaking of his or her good health or good fortune. This I saw done at Bowdon, near Manchester, in 1870, by the late Mrs. Alexander Ireland. Gaule ridicules the popular belief that " a great thick hand denotes one not only strong but stout : a little slender one a person weak but timorous : a long hand and long fingers betoken a man not only apt for mechanical artifice, but liberally ingenious ; but those short, on the contrary, note a foole and fit for nothing : an hard brawny hand signes dull and rude ; a soft hand, witty but effeminate ; an hairy hand, luxurious ; longe joynts signe generous, yet if they be thick withal, not so ingenious ; the often clapping and folding of the hands note covetous ; and their much moving in speech, loquacious; an ambidexter is noted for ireful, crafty, injurious; short and fat fingers mark a man out for intemperate and silly; but long and leane, for witty; if his fingers crook upward, that shewes long nailes and crooked, signe one brutish, ravenous, unchaste; very short nails, pale, and sharp, shew him false, subtile, beguiling; and so round nails, libidinous; but nails broad, plain, white, thin and reddish, are the token of a very good wit." *Mag-Astromancer posed*, 187. It is not unusual in a family to see some of the children follow the father in possessing long slender hands and fingers, and others the mother in having short and thick, or *vice versâ*. A moist hand is vulgarly accounted a sign of an amorous constitution. The Chief Justice, in "Henry IV., Part IV." enumerates a dry hand among the characteristics of age and debility.

The Cagots, a persecuted race in the Pyrenees, have been said to possess the power of making an apple decay by holding it within the hand, their hands being remarkable for moist heat. Hence I heard a lady from Penrith say gravely that her mother was thought to have Cagot blood in her, because her hand was unusually hot and moist.

According to Grose, the Hand of Glory at one time formed a staple article of belief among housebreakers in many parts of France, Germany, and Spain. From *Les Secrets du petit Albert*, 1751, he translates the following passage: "I acknowledge that I never tried the Secret of the Hand of Glory, but I have thrice assisted at the definitive judgement of certain criminals, who under the torture confessed having used it. Being asked what it was, how they procured it, and what were its uses and properties? they answered, first, that the use of the Hand of Glory was to stupefy those to whom it was presented, and to render them motionless insomuch that they could not stir any more than if they were dead; secondly that it was the hand of a hanged man; and thirdly, that it must be prepared in the manner following:—Take the hand, right or left, of a person hanged and exposed on the highway; wrap it up in a piece of a shroud or winding-sheet, in which let it be well squeezed, to get out any small quantity of blood that may have remain'd in it: then put it into an earthen vessel, with zimat, salt-petre, salt, and long pepper, the whole well powdered; leave it fifteen days in that vessel; afterwards take it out, and expose it to the noon-tide sun in the dog-days, till it is thoroughly dry; and if the sun is not sufficient, put it into an oven heated with fern and vervain: then compose a kind of candle with the fat of a hanged man, vir-

gin wax, and sisame of Lapland. The Hand of Glory is used as a candlestick to hold this candle, when lighted. Its properties are that wheresoever any one goes with this dreadful instrument, the persons to whom it is presented will be deprived of all power of motion. On being asked if there was no remedy or antidote to counteract this charm, they said the Hand of Glory would cease to take effect, and thieves could not make use of it, if the threshold of the door of the house, and other places by which they might enter, were anointed with an unguent composed of the gall of a black cat, the fat of a white hen, and the blood of a screech-owl; which mixture must necessarily be prepared during the dog-days." Grose adds that the mode of preparation appears to have been given by a judge. In the latter there is a striking resemblance to the charm in Macbeth. Grose says that "a dead man's hand is supposed to have the quality of dispelling tumours, such as wens, or swelled glands, by striking with it nine times the place affected. It seems as if the hand of a person dying a violent death was deemed particularly efficacious, as it very frequently happens that nurses bring children to be stroked with the hands of executed criminals, even whilst they are hanging on the gallows." He adds: "Moss growing on a human skull, if dried, powdered, and taken as snuff, will cure the head-ach." "The chips or cuttings of a gibbet or gallows, on which one or more persons have been executed or exposed, if worn next the skin, or round the neck in a bag, will cure the ague, or prevent it." Brand relates that he saw about 1790 some saw-dust, in which blood was absorbed, taken for the purpose of charming away some disease or other from off the scaffold on the beheading of one of the rebel lords in 1746. In a newspaper, 1777, it is said: "After he (Doctor Dodd) had hung about ten minutes, a very decently dressed young woman went up to the gallows in order to have a wen in her face stroked by the Doctor's hand, it being a received opinion among the vulgar that it is a certain cure for such a disorder. The executioner, having untied the doctor's hand, stroked the part affected several times therewith." But at the execution of Crowley the murderer at Warwick in 1845 a similar scene is described in the newspapers: "At least five thousand persons were mustered on this occasion to witness the dying moments of the unhappy culprit. . . . As is usual in such cases, a number of females were present, and scarcely had the soul of the deceased taken its farewell flight from its earthly tabernacle, than the scaffold was crowded by members of the 'gentler sex' afflicted with wens in the neck, with white swellings in the knees, &c., upon whose afflictions the cold clammy hand of the sufferer was passed to and fro for the benefit of his executioner."

I have somewhere read, that the custom of kissing the hand by way of salutation is derived from the manner in which the ancient Persians worshipped the sun: which was by first laying their hands upon their mouths, and then lifting them up by way of adoration. A practice which receives illustration from a passage in the Book of Job, a work replete with allusions to ancient manners—"If I beheld the sun, when it shined, or the moon walking in brightness; and my heart hath been secretly enticed, or my mouth hath kissed my hand." *Archæologia*, xxxi., 26-7. In a paper in the *Antiquary* for 1891, on Handprints and Footprints on Stones, Margaret Stokes instances cases of hand-markings or impressions of hands or fingers associated in the popular mind abroad or in the East with miraculous properties.

Handball or Jeu de Paume.—

One of the most ancient games, perhaps, in the world, which was known to the Greeks under the name of Sphairisis, and to the Romans as Pila. It is introduced on some of the coins of Larissa in Thessaly (Head's *Historia Numorum*, 1887, p. 254). It was originally, even among the modern nations, played with the hand, which was protected by a thick glove; hence came the French jeu de paume; and the racket was a comparatively recent improvement. Fitzstephen seems to allude to this sport, where he says: "After dinner, all the youths go into the fields, to play at the ball. The scholars of every school have their ball, or bastion, in their hands. The antient and wealthy men of the city come forth on horseback, to see the sport of the young men, and to take part of the pleasure, in beholding their agility. See Halliwell in v., where Stowe's *Survey*, 1720, is cited for the custom of playing at this on Easter-day for a tansy cake. The following beautiful description in the "Mons Catharinæ" may almost equally be applied to hand-ball:

" His datur orbiculum
Præcipiti—levem per gramina mittere lapsu :
Ast aliis, quorum pedibus fiducia major
Sectari, et jam jam salienti insistere prædæ ;
Aut volitantem altè longéque per aëra pulsum
Suspiciunt, pronosque inhiant, captanque volatus,

Sortiti fortunam oculis ; manibusque paratis
Expectant propriorem, intercipiuntque caducum."—p. 6.

Compare what has been said under *Golf*.

Hand-Fasting.—

There was a remarkable kind of marriage-contract among the ancient Danes called Hand-festing. It is mentioned in Ray's "Glossarium Northanhymbricum" in his collection of local words. " Hand-fæstning, promissio, quæ sit stipulata manu, sive cives fidem suam principi spondeant, sive mutuum inter se matrimonium inituri, a phrasi *fœsta* hand, quæ notat dextram dextræ jungere." Ihre "Glossar, Suio-Gothicum," in v.; Ibid. in v. Bröllop. Brudkaup. In "The Christian State of Matrimony," 1543, p. 43 verso, we read : " Yet in thys thynge also must I warne everye reasonable and honest parson, to beware that in contractyng of maryage they dyssemble not, ner set forthe any lye. Every man lykewyse must esteme the parson to whom he is handfasted, none otherwyse than for his owne spouse, though as yet it be not done in the church ner in the streate.—After the handfastynge and makyng of the contracte ye churchgoyng and weddyng shuld not be differed to longe, lest the wickedde sowe hys ungracious sede in the meane season. Into this dysh hath the Dyvell put his foote and mengled it wythe many wycked uses and coustumes. For in some places ther is such a maner, wel worthy to be rebuked, that at the handefasting ther is made a greate feaste and superfluous bancket, and even the same night are the two handfasted personnes brought and layed together, yea, certan wekes afore they go to the chyrch."

In 1794, the Minister of Eskdalemuir, Dumfries, mentioning an annual fair held time out of mind at the meeting of the Black and White Esks, now entirely laid aside, reported: " At that fair it was the custom for the unmarried persons of both sexes to choose a companion according to their liking, with whom they were to live till that time next year. This was called hand-fasting, or hand in fist. If they were pleased with each other at that time, then they continued together for life: if not they separated, and were free to make another choice as at the first. The fruit of the connection (if there were any) was always attached to the disaffected person. In later times, when this part of the country belonged to the Abbacy of Melrose, a priest, to whom they gave the name of Book i'bosom (either because he carried in his bosom a Bible, or perhaps a register of the marriages), came from time to time to confirm the marriages. This place is only a small distance from the Roman encampment of Castle-o'er. May not the fair have been first instituted when the Romans resided there? And may not the 'hand-fasting' have taken its rise from their manner of celebrating marriage, ex usu, by which, if a woman, with the consent of her parents or guardians, lived with a man for a year, without being absent three nights, she became his wife? Perhaps, when Christianity was introduced the form of marriage may have been looked upon as imperfect, without confirmation by a priest, and therefore, one may have been sent from time to time for this purpose." Compare *Betrothal, Trothplight*, &c., and Hazlitt's Monograph on Shakespear, 2nd edit. 1903, p. 9, where the case of the poet and his wife is treated.

Handicap.—Under September 18, 1660, Pepys notes, that some of his party, at the Mitre in Wood Street, "fell to handicap, a sport that I never knew before, which was very good"; but unfortunately he has furnished no particulars. Was it an early anticipation of a table game of race-horses?

Hand in and Hand Out.—Halliwell thus describes this amusement: "A company of young people are drawn up in a circle, when one of them, pitched upon by lot, walks round the band, and, if a boy, hits a girl, or if a girl, she strikes a boy whom she chooses, on which the party striking and the party struck run in pursuit of each other, till the latter is caught, whose lot it then becomes to perform the same part." It seems equally impossible to determine whether this was identical with the hand-out mentioned by Sir John Harington or with the Hand-in-Hand-out prohibited by 17 Edw. IV. c. 2. If the latter were the case, some licentious outgrowth from the original game has to be supposed, and it seems more logical to infer that the Edward statute had a different pastime in view, though Harington's Hand-out may very well have been the one objected to by the law, and still more or less pursued.

Handkerchief.—We gather from Howes's Additions to Stow's Chronicle that, in the reign of Queen Elizabeth, "it was the custome for maydes and gentilwomen to give their favorites, as tokens of their love, little handkerchiefs of about three or four inches square, wrought round about, and with a button or a tassel at each corner, and a little one in the middle, with silk and threed : the best edged with a small gold lace or twist, which being foulded up in foure crosse foldes, so as the middle might be seene,

gentlemen and others did usually weare them in their hatts, as favours of their loves and mistresses. Some cost six pence apiece, some twelve pence, and the richest sixteene pence." It appears, from a passage in Heywood's "Fayre Mayde of the Exchange," 1607, that it was not unusual to furnish these handkerchiefs with amorous devices worked in the corners. It is where Phillis brings the handkerchief to the Cripple of Fanchurch to be so embroidered. She says :

"Only this handkercher, a young gentlewoman
Wish'd me to acquaint you with her mind herein :
In one corner of the same, place wanton Love,
Drawing his bow, shooting an amorous dart—
Opposite against him an arrow in an heart :
In a third corner picture forth Disdain,
A cruel fate unto a loving vein ;
In the fourth draw a springing laurel-tree,
Circled about with a ring of poesy."

In Sampson's play of "The Vow-Breaker," 1636, act i. sc. 1, Miles, a miller, is introduced telling his sweetheart, on going away to the wars : "Mistress Ursula, 'tis not unknowne that I have lov'd you; if I die, it shall be for your sake, and it shall be valiantly : I leave an hand-kercher with you : 'tis wrought with blew Coventry : let me not, at my returne, fall to my old song, she had a clowte of mine sowde with blew Coventry, and so hang myself at your infidelity." In an account of Dunton Church, in Barnstable Hundred, Essex, is the following remark : "Here has been a custom, time out of mind at the churching of a woman, for her to give a white Cambrick Handkerchief to the minister as an offering. Morant's *Essex*, i., 219. This is observed by Mr. Lewis in his 'History of the Isle of Thanet,' where the same custom is kept up."

Handsel.—The first money taken at a market or fair. It is still usual, both here and abroad, to spit on it, and in Italy and Portugal, in the case of an ordinary gift to the poor, the recipient will spit on it, press it to his forehead, and cross himself with the benefaction. Lemon's *Dictionary*, 1783, explains "Handsell," "the first money received at market, which many superstitious people will spit on, either to render it tenacious that it may remain with them, and not vanish away like a fairy gift, or else to render it propitious and lucky, that it may draw more money to it." It is quoted in the "Pedlar's Lamentation," an old ballad (circâ 1640):

> "Come, pretty fair maids, then make
> no delay,
> But give me your handsel, and pack
> me away."

Handsel Monday and Tuesday.

"The minister of Moulin, in Perthshire, informs us, that 'beside the stated fees, the master (of the parochial school there) receives some small gratuity, generally two-pence or three-pence, from each scholar, on Handsel-Monday or Shrove-Tuesday. It is worth mentioning that one William Hunter, a collier, was cured in the year 1758 of an inveterate rheumatism or gout, by drinking freely of new ale, full of barm or yest. The poor man had been confined to his bed for a year and a half, having almost entirely lost the use of his limbs. On the evening of Handsel Monday, as it is called, (i.e., the first Monday of the New Year, O.S.) some of his neighbours came to make merry with him. Though he could not rise, yet he always took his share of the ale, as it passed round the company, and, in the end, became much intoxicated. The consequence was, that he had the use of his limbs the next morning, and was able to walk about. He lived more than twenty years after this, and never had the smallest return of his old complaint."

Handy-Dandy.

By far the most copious and satisfactory account of this ancient English game is to be found in Mr. Halliwell's "Popular Rhymes and Nursery Tales," 1849, to which I must beg to refer the reader. The earliest allusion to it yet discovered is the passage in "Piers Ploughman," cited by Mr. Halliwell. Browne, in the fifth song of "Britannia's Pastorals," 1614, describes it as a boy's game:

> "Who so hath seene young lads (to
> sport themselues),
> Run in a low ebbe to the sandy shelues :
> Where seriously they worke in digging
> wels,
> Or building childish forts of cockle-
> shels ;
> Or liquid water each to other bandy ;
> Or with the pibbles play at handy-
> dandy—"

This game is mentioned in the dedication to Mr. William Lilly, by Democritus Pseudomantis, of Pantagruel's Prognostication, about 1645. But Halliwell (*Archaic Dictionary*, in v.) cites the Nomenclator of Adrianus Junius for some description of handy-dandy different from the ordinary game, "the play called handie dandie or the casting or pitching of the barre." Perhaps this was some foreign variety.

Cornelius Scriblerus, in forbidding certain sports to his son Martin till he is better informed of their antiquity, says : "Neither cross and pile, nor ducks and drakes, are quite so ancient as handy-dandy, tho' Macrobius and St. Augustine take notice of the first, and Minutius Foelix describes the latter ; but handy-dandy is mentioned by Aristotle, Plato, and Aristophanes."

Hanging out the Besom.

The appearance of a besom on the top of a ship's mast is certainly not always an indication of the vessel being for sale, as it is also usual to place it there, when the craft is in port being cleaned or under repair. To hang out a besom from a house is in some places received as a sign that the master is from home. Comp. *Broom.*

Hangman's Wages.

In a letter to Edward King, Esq., President of the Society of Antiquaries, Dr. Pegge has entered with some minuteness and care into this question, and into the origin of the old, but now obsolete, practice of presenting the public executioner with thirteen pence halfpenny (the Scotish merk, minus two placks), as his wages for performing the unenviable task. Pegge's paper ought to be read as it stands without curtailment. But it is certainly strange that Brand and his editor should, both of them, have overlooked this point, which was worth at least a reference to the place, where it is discussed. It is generally known, that the hangman is ex-officio the sheriff's deputy, and that, in default of a person to execute the office, the sheriff himself would even now be obliged to act. It is observable, as regards the wages of the executioner, that by Halifax Law no man could be punished capitally for a theft not exceeding thirteenpence halfpenny : the coincidence is curious ; but it may be nothing more than a coincidence. The earliest example of the grant of a prisoner's clothes to anyone is not to the executioner, but to the person whom the authorities chose to dig the grave. Thus in *Adam Bel*, 1536 :—

> The Justice called to hym a ladde,
> Cloudesles clothes sholde he haue,
> To take the mesure of that yeman,
> And therafter to make hys graue.

It reads as if the Justice himself performed the office in this particular case ; yet the sheriff was present.

Happy Foot.

In a statistical account of the parish of Forglen, co. Banff, drawn up about 1795, it is said : "There are happy and unhappy feet. Thus they wish bridegrooms and brides a happy foot, and to prevent any bad effect, they salute those they meet on the road with a kiss. It is hard, however, if any misfortune happens when you are passing, that you should be blamed, when neither you nor your feet ever thought of the matter." *Stat. Acc.* xiv., 541.

Hare.—The ancient Romans made use of hares for the purposes of divination. They were never killed for the table. Borlase tells us of "a remarkable way of divining related of Bonduca or Boadicea Queen of the Iceni—when she had harangued her soldiers to spirit them up against the Romans, she opened her bosom and let go a hare, which she had there concealed, that the augurs might thence proceed to divine. The frighted animal made such turnings and windings in her course, as, according to the then rules of judging, prognosticated happy success. The joyful multitude made loud huzzas, Boadicea seized the opportunity, approved their ardour, led them straight to their enemies, and gained the victory." *Antiq. of Cornwall*, p. 135. 'Tis perhaps hence that they have been accounted ominous by the vulgar. *Cæsar's Comment.*, p. 89. An opinion was formerly entertained both in England and abroad, that a hare crossing the path of any one was a portent of misfortune, and a warning to return, or retrace one's steps; and of this almost universal superstition our own early writers, and those of the Continent, abound in confirmations. Sir Thomas Browne tells us, "if an hare cross the highway, there are a few above three score years that are not perplexed thereat, which, notwithstanding, is but an augurial terror, according to that received expression Inauspicatum dat iter oblatus lepus. And the ground of the conceit was probably no greater than this, that a fearful animal, passing by us, portended unto us something to be feared : as, upon the like consideration, the meeting of a fox presaged some future imposture. These good or bad signs sometimes succeeding according to fears or desires, have left impressions and timorous expectations in credulous minds for ever." Home adds: ". . . In so much as some in company with a woman great with childe have upon the crossing of such creatures, cut or torn some of the clothes off that woman with childe, to prevent (as they imagined) the ill luck that might befall her. I know I tell you most true; and I hope in such a subject as this, touching these superstitions, I shall not offend in acquainting you with these particulars." *Demonologie*, 1650, p. 50. Among the Forfarshire fishermen, the portent of the hare crossing the path, which in many other places is regarded as unlucky, has sufficient influence to deter any one from going out. See Machin's "Dumb Knight," 1608, Hazlitt's Dodsley, x; Hall's "Characters of Vertues and Vices,"

1608; Melton's "Astrologaster," 1620, p. 45; Burton's "Anatomy of Melancholy," 1621, p. 214; Ellison's "Trip to Benwel," p. lx.; Mason's "Anatomie of Sorcery," 1612, p. 85; Gaule's "Mag-Astromancer Posed," etc., p. 181; Ramsey's "Elminthologia," 1668, p. 271. Alexander ab Alexandro, "Geniales Dies," vol. v. p. 13; Bebelius, "Facetiæ," 1516, sign. E 3; Townson's "Travels in Hungary." Pepys seems to have believed in the virtues of a hare's foot as a preservative against the colic; but he did not at first apply it properly; for in the *Diary*, January 20, 1664-5, there is this odd entry: "Homeward, in my way buying a hare, and taking it home, which arose upon my discourse to-day with Mr. Batten, in Westminster Hall, who showed me my mistake, that my hare's foot hath not the joynt to it, and assures me he never had his cholique since he carried it about with him; and it is a strange thing how fancy works for I no sooner handled his foot, but I became very well, and so continue."

Hare and Hounds.—An out-door sport, where a youth (the hare) starts in advance, and traverses a line of country, dropping, as he proceeds, something to indicate his route, and is followed by the others—the hounds, who have to get up to him, and capture him. All are dressed in jerseys, and the amusement seems to have nothing to recommend it, as the exercise is too violent to suit many boys or young men. Saturday afternoons during all seasons of the year are occupied in this way by seekers of active recreation.

Harper. — Puttenham speaks of "blind harpers or such like tauerne minstrels that give a fit of mirth for a groat, and their matters being for the most part stories of old time, as the Tale of Sir Topas, the Reportes of Bevis of Southampton, Guy of Warwicke, Adam Bell, and Clymme of the Clough, and such other old romances, or historicall rimes, made purposely for recreation of the common people at Christmasse diners and Brideales, and in tauernes and ale-houses, and such other places of base resort." There is the tract by Martin Parker, 1641, entitled *The Poet's Blind Man's Bough; or, Have among You, my Blind Harpers.* Possibly the blindness, real or supposed, was found remunerative.

Harvest.—Macrobius tells us that, among the ancients, the masters of families, when they had got in their harvest, were wont to feast with their servants, who had laboured for them in tilling the ground. In exact conformity to this, it is common among us, when the fruits of the earth are gathered in and laid in their proper repositories, to provide a plentiful supper for the harvest men and the servants of the family. At this entertainment all are in the modern revolutionary idea of the word perfectly equal. Here is no distinction of persons; but master and servant sit at the same table, converse freely together, and spend the remainder of the night in dancing, singing, &c., in the most easy familiarity. *Saturn. Conviv*, cap. 10. Durandus mentions that it was formerly usual among the Gentiles for the servants, both male and female, to take their masters' or employers' places after the gathering-in of the harvest, and usurp their authority for a time. *Rationale*. vi., 86. Bourne thinks the original of both these customs is Jewish, and cites Hospinian, who tells us that the heathens copied this custom of the Jews, and at the end of their harvest, offered up their first fruits to the gods. For the Jews rejoiced and feasted at the getting in of the harvest. This festivity is undoubtedly of the most remote antiquity. In the "Roman Calendar" I find the following observation on the eleventh of June: (the harvests in Italy are much earlier than with us). "The season of reapers, and their custom with rustic pomp." Theophylact mentions "Sceno-pegia, quod celebrant in gratiarum actionem propter convectas Fruges in Mense Septembri. Tunc enim gratias agebant Deo, convectis omnibus fructibus, &c."— Theoph. in 7 cap. Joan. Vacuna, so called, as it is said, *à vacando*, among the ancients, was the name of the goddess to whom rustics sacrificed at the conclusion of harvest.

That men in all nations where agriculture flourished should have expressed their joy on this occasion by some outward ceremonies, has its foundation in the nature of things. Sowing is hope; reaping, fruition of the expected good. To the husbandman, whom the fear of wet, blights, &c., had harrassed with great anxiety, the completion of his wishes could not fail of imparting an enviable feeling of delight. Festivity is but the reflex of inward joy, and it could hardly fail of being produced on this occasion, which is a temporary suspension of every care. The respect shown to servants at this season seems to have sprung from a grateful sense of their good services. Every thing depends at this juncture on their labour and dispatch. In Carew's "Survey of Cornwall," p. 20, verso, "an ill kerned or saved harvest" occurs. We do not recognise among more modern European societies any analogue to the Roman *Fornacalia* or rites to the goddess Fornax for the happy taking of the corn, which concluded, with the harvest itself and other early local institu-

tions, with a period of licence, known as *Stultorum Feriæ*. The *Fornacalia*, traditionally established by Numa, was held on the 18th of February.

Harvest in Scotland.—Moresin tells us that Popery, in imitation of this, brings home her chaplets of corn, which she suspends on poles, that offerings are made on the altars of her tutelar gods, while thanks are returned for the collected stores, and prayers are made for future ease and rest. Images too of straw or stubble, he adds, are wont to be carried about on this occasion; and that in England he himself saw the rustics bringing home in a cart a figure made of corn, round which men and women were singing promiscuously, preceded by a drum or piper. *Papatus*, p. 173, v. *Vacona*. Johnson tells us, in his "Tour to the Hebrides," that he saw the harvest of a small field in one of the Western Islands. The strokes of the sickle were timed by the modulation of the harvest song, in which all their voices were united. They accompany, in the Highlands, every action which can be done in equal time with an appropriate strain, which has, they say, not much meaning, but its effects are regularity and cheerfulness. The ancient proceleusmatic song, by which the rowers of gallies were animated, may be supposed to have been of this kind. There is now an oar song used by Hebridians. In the "Statistical Account of Scotland," it is said, "There is one family on the Cupar-Grange Estate, which has been there a century. The former tenant in that family kept a piper to play to his shearers all the time of harvest, and gave him his harvest-fee. The slowest shearer had always the drone behind him. In Henry IV.'s time, the French peasants were accustomed to regale after the getting in of the harvest, on what was called a harvest Gosling. Armstrong says: "Their harvests are generally gathered by the middle of June: and, as the corn ripens, a number of boys and girls station themselves at the edges of the fields, and on the tops of the fence walls, to fright away the small birds with their shouts and cries. This puts one in mind of Virgil's precept in the first book of his Georgicks,

'Et sonitu terrebis aves'——

and was a custom, I doubt not, among the Roman farmers, from whom the ancient Minorquins learned it. They also use, for the same purpose, a split reed; which makes a horrid rattling, as they shake it with their hands. *Hist. of Minorca*, 177. A personal friend of the writer saw a farmer near Edinburgh, about ten years ago, personally superintending the inning process, assisted by his daughter; and he was a man of large fortune.

Harvest Doll.—An old woman,

who in a case of this nature is respectable authority, at a village in Northumberland, informed Mr. Brand, that in the first half of the 18th century, they used every where to dress up something similar to the figure above described, at the end of harvest, which was caled a Harvest Doll or Kern Baby. This northern word is plainly a corruption of corn baby or image, as is the Kern Supper or Corn Supper. Comp. *Harvest.*

Harvest Home. — In Tusser's "Husbandry," 1580, under August, are the following lines alluding to this festivity:

"In harvest time, harvest folke, servants and all,
Should make, alltogither, good cheere in the hall,
And fill out the black bol of bleith to their song,
And let them be merie al harvest time long.
Once ended thy harvest, let none be begilde,
Please such as did please thee, man, woman, and child.
Thus doing, with alway suche helpe as they can,
Thou winnist the praise of the labouring man."

On which is this note in Hilman: "This, the poor labourer thinks, crowns all, a good supper must be provided, and every one that did any thing towards the inning must now have some reward, as ribbons, laces, rows of pins to boys and girls, if never so small, for their encouragement; and, to be sure, plumb-pudding. The men must now have some better than best drink, which, with a little tobacco and their screaming for their largesses, their business will soon be done." *Tusser Redivivus,* 1710, ed. 1749, 104. In another part of Tusser's work under "The Ploughman's Feast Days," are these lines:

"For all this good feasting, yet art thou not loose,
Til ploughman thou givest his harvest home goose;
Though goose go in stubble, I passe not for that,
Let goose have a goose, be she lean, be she fat."

On which Hilman remarks: "The goose is forfeited, if they overthrow during harvest." In his "Travels," in England and elsewhere, temp. Elizabeth, speaking of Windsor, Hentzner says, "As we were returning to our inn we happened to meet some country people celebrating their harvest home; their last load of corn they crown with flowers, having besides an image richly dressed, by which perhaps they would signify Ceres: this they keep moving about, while men and women, men and maid-servants, riding through the streets in the cart, shout as loud as they can till they arrive at the barn." In Cornwall, it should seem, they have "Harvest Dinners"; and these, too, not given immediately at the end of the harvest. "The harvest dinners," says Carew, "are held by every wealthy man, or, as we term it, every good liver, between Michaelmas and Candlemas, whereto he inviteth his next neighbours and kindred. And, though it beare only the name of a dinner, yet the ghests take their supper also with them, and consume a great part of the night after in Christmas rule. Neither doth the good cheere wholly expire (though it somewhat decrease) but with the end of the weeke." *Survey,* 1602, 68. Stevenson thus glances at the customs of harvest home. "The furmenty pot welcomes home the harvest cart, and the garland of flowers crowns the captain of the reapers; the battle of the field is now stoutly fought. The pipe and the tabor are now busily set a-work, and the lad and the lass will have no lead on their heels. O, 'tis the merry time wherein honest neighbours make good cheer and God is glorified in his blessings on the earth." *Twelve Moneths,* 1661, p. 37 (August).

"Hoacky is brought
Home with hallowin,
Boys with Plumb-cake,
The cart following."

Poor Robin for 1676. A newspaper for 1773 says: "A few days ago a melancholy accident happened near Worcester at a harvest home. As near thirty persons were coming from the field in a waggon, it overturned, whereby great part of the company had one or other of their limbs broken, or were dangerously bruised, and one young woman was killed on the spot." Thomson, in his "Seasons," (Autumn), has left us a beautiful description of this annual festivity of harvest home. Other terms for it are the *Mell, Kern,* or *Chern Supper,* and the *Ingathering* or *Inning.* Cuthbert Bede, in *Notes and Queries,* October 12, 1875, gives the following account of a Rutland custom:—"On Wednesday evening, Sep. 18, 1875, I was at a farm-house in the county of Rutland, and saw "the last load" brought in. As marking the conclusion of harvest, and, as they termed it, "harvest home," the load (of beans) was decorated with green boughs; and on the top of the load were several children, who were lustily cheering as the waggon came lumbering along the road. It was eight o'clock, and a resplendent harvest-moon was just rising over the trees that girdled the old church hard by the farmer's stackyard. A company of us stood at his gate to watch the scene. Near to us, but concealed by the hedge, were the female and other servants, ready prepared with buckets of water and pitchers, and also with baskets of apples. As the last load passed us, with its drivers and occupants shouting "Harvest home!" and cheering, the liers-in-wait behind the hedge suddenly rose up to view and pelted the waggon-load with a shower of apples, and also dashed pitchers full of water over men, horses, children and beans. This had to be done quickly, while the waggon was moving by; so they who ran the gauntlet were not much damaged, and the children on top of the load got more apples than water, and were proportionately thankful and applausive. But the waggon had to go to the bean-stack in the well-filled stack-yard, whither it was followed by those who had already received it with the salute of apples and water, and where also all the labourers on the farm were waiting for it. A liberal supply of buckets of water was there at hand for the reception of the last load and its attendants; and we followed to see the fun. As the waggon drew up at the appointed spot, and the ladder was reared against its side to assist the children from the top of the load, the signal was given for a species of free fight with buckets and pails of water. The children evidently did not relish their douche bath, and were helped down from the top of the bean-load, sobbing bitterly, and bewailing their soaked condition. Friend and foe seemed to be treated with equal impartiality, and the water was scooped out of the buckets and dashed indiscriminately over male and female. A reverend gentleman, who was making off round the stack, was not recognized (let us hope!) in the semi-darkness, and, falling between two fires, received a ducking. I had just left him, in order to follow the sobbing children and administer to them pecuniary comfort; so I escaped with dry clothes, being, I think, the only one on the spot who did so."

Harvest Home Song.—Formerly, it should seem, there was a harvest home song. Kennett tells us: "Homines de Hedyngton ad curiam Domini singulis annis inter festum S. Michaelis et festum S. Martini venient cum toto et pleno Dyteno, sicut hactenus consueverunt." This, he adds, is singing harvest home. *Gloss. to Paroch. Antiq. v. Dytenum.* Mr. Brand notes: "I have often observed at Newcastle-upon-Tyne (and I suppose it is the same in other sea-port towns) that the sailors, in heaving their anchors, made use of a similar kind of song. In ploughing with oxen in Devonshire, I observed a song of the same kind."

Harvest Lord and Lady.—The two principal reapers are known in the eastern counties as the Harvest Lord and Lady. The former, says Forby, used to be addressed as "My Lord." He directs the operations of his companions. There is no other dignity attached to the rank, unless it be the first and second place respectively at the harvest home. In the *Penny Magazine* for November, 1835, is a representation of the Hop Queen, who appears to be the same as the harvest lady above mentioned. Possibly she, with a male associate, *Lord* or *King*, presided over the festivities at the conclusion of the work. Comp. *Harvest Queen* below.

Harvest Queen. — Hutchinson, speaking of the parish of Easington, in Durham, observes, "In this part of the country are retained some ancient customs evidently derived from the Romans, particularly that of dressing up a figure of Ceres, during harvest, which is placed in the field while the reapers are labouring, and brought home on the last evening of reaping, with musick and great acclamation. After this a feast is made, called the mell-supper, from the ancient sacrifice of mingling the new meal." *Hist. of Durham*, ii., 583. "I have seen," he elsewhere says, "in some places an image apparelled in great finery, crowned with flowers, a sheaf of corn placed under her arm, and a scycle in her hand, carried out of the village in the morning of the conclusive reaping day, with musick and much clamour of the reapers, into the field, where it stands fixed on a pole all day, and when the reaping is done, is brought home in like manner. This they call the Harvest Queen, and it represents the Roman Ceres." *Hist. of North.*, ii., 17. Clarke in his "Travels," incidentally observes: "At the Hawkie (at Cambridge), as it is called, I have seen a clown dressed in woman's clothes, having his face painted, his head decorated with ears of corn, and bearing about him other symbols of Ceres, carried in a waggon, with great pomp and loud shouts, through the streets, the horses being covered with white sheets; and when I enquired the meaning of the ceremony, was answered by the people that they were drawing the Harvest Queen."

Hawkie.—The name of a place at Cambridge, formerly dedicated to the holding of the fair, and apparently a corruption of the Breton *Hourquie*, Latin *Furcia*. See Hazlitt's *Coins of Europe*, 1893, p. 134; and see above.

Head.—Gaule mentions as a notion current in his day (in which he by no means concurred : "That a great head is an omen, or a sign of a sluggish fool"—this reminds one of the old saying, "Great head and little wit ")—"A little head of a subtile knave. A middle head, of a liberal wit. A round head, of a senselesse irrational fellow. A sharp head, of an impudent sot," &c. Our author's remarks, or rather citation of the remarks, upon round heads above, seem not to have been over-well timed, for this book was printed in 1652, and is dedicated to Cromwell. *Mag-Astromancer posed*, p. 183.

Head-Ache.—John London, writing to Cromwell, about 1536, mentions a recipe for the head-ache, which was supposed at that time to have great virtue. He writes: "In the body of the Churche at Tellisford Cross (or Crutched) Friars, Somersetshire, wasse an image at an awters end callid Mayden Cutbrogh, and vnder her feete wasse a trowgh of wodde descending vnder the awter wich wasse hollow. Thyder resortyd such as wer trobely with the hedde ache, or hadde any slottiche wydowes lockes, viz. here growen to gether in a tufte. Ther must they putt in to the trowgh a pecke of oots, and when they wer oons slydyd vndre the awter, the Crosse Fryers schuld behynd the awter pryvily stele them owt, and the sykk person must geve to the Fryer a peny for a pynte of these Mayden Cutbrogh owts, and then ther heds schuld ak no more till the next tyme."

Head-Penny.—A payment in former times to a parson for burying a poor parishioner or otherwise; but it was the old silver coin. The money was also applicable to the purchase of bread and wine. Comp. *Easter Offering.*

Heads and Points.—A child's game, played with pins. It seems to have been popular in Scotland in 1724. Chambers, *Dom. Annals*, iii., 491.

Heads or Tails.—This is the modern game of toss, and corresponds to the *Capita aut Navia* of the Romans. It was known, it appears, in Edward II.'s time, and formed a favourite diversion of that prince, who won and lost money at it, as is to be collected from entries among his privy purse expenses: "Item paid to the King himself to play at Cross and Pile by the hands of Richard de Mereworth, the receiver of the Treasury, 12 pence. Item paid there to Henry, the King's barber, for money which he lent to the King to play at cross and pile. . . 5s. Item paid there to Peres Barnard Usher of the King's Chamber money which he lent to the King, and which he lost at cross and pile to monsieur Robert Wattewylle. . . eightpence." In the preface to *Plantagruel's Prognostication* (about 1645) it is called Cross or Pile.

Healths.—The Greeks and Romans used at their meals to make libations, pour out, and even drink wine, in honour of the gods. The classical writings abound with proofs of this. The Greeks had the practice of toasting the nine Muses as Three times Three, of which the origin and antiquity may not be generally known, and which is yet followed both in England and abroad.

The Greek and Roman writers have also transmitted to us accounts of the graceful custom of drinking to the health of our benefactors and of our acquaintances:

"Pro te, fortissime, vota
Publica suscipimus: Bacchi tibi sumimus haustus."

It appears that the men of gallantry among the Romans used to take off as many glasses to their respective mistresses as there were letters in the name of each. Thus Martial:

"Six cups to Nævia's health go quickly round,
And be with seven the fair Justina's crown'd."

How exceedingly similar to our modern custom of saying to each of the company in turn ,"Give us a lady to toast," is the following:

"Da puere ab summo, age tu interibi ab infimo da suavium."

Plauti *Asinaria*, v. 2. In the "Maner of the tryumphes at Caleys & Bullen," 1532, Henry VIII. and the French king are described as drinking to each other: " And than they dyd lyght of theyr horses & dranke eche to other/the frenshe kyng dranke fyrst to our kynge/ & whan they had dronke/ they embraced eche other agayn with great loue/" Francis I. drank before his guest in this case, perhaps, in order to prove that there was no foul play. Pasquier, in his " Recherches," p. 501, mentions that Mary, Queen of Scots, previously to her execution, drank to all her attendants, desiring them to pledge her. See what the same author has said in p. 785 of his work concerning this custom. In Decker's *Lanthorne and Candle-light*, 1608, sign. H 2, we have: "The third man squires her to a play, which being ended, and the wine offered and taken (for she's no Recusant, to refuse anything) him she leanes too; and being set vpon by a fourth, him she answers at his own weapon, sups with him, and drincks Vpsie Freeze. . . ." In the second part of Dekker's " Honest Whore," 1630, signat. 1 verso, is the following: "Will you fall on your maribones and pledge this health, 'tis to my mistris?" So in Marmion's " Antiquary," act ii. :

" Drank to your health whole nights in
    Hippocrase,
Upon my knees, with more religion
Than e'er I said my prayers, which
    Heaven forgive me."
Pledging is again mentioned in act iv. :
" To our noble Duke's health, I can drink
no lesse, not a drop lesse; and you his
servants will pledge me, I am sure."
Braithwaite says: " These cups proceed
either in order or out of order. In order,
when no person transgresseth or drinkes
out of course, but the cup goes round according to their manner of sitting: and
this we call an health cup, because in our
wishing or confirming of any one's health,
bare-headed and standing, it is performed
by all the company. It is drunke without
order, when the course or method of order
is not observed, and that the cup passeth
on whomsoever we shall appoint."Again :
" Some joyne two cups one upon another
and drinke them together." *Laws of
Drinking*, 1617, p. 9. It seems to have
been formerly usual for a man in company,
not contented with taking what he chooses,
to bind another to drink the same quantity that he does. In the following passage one proposes a health which another
pledges to honour by drinking to it an
equal quantity with him that proposed
it :
" Oh, how they'll wind men in, do what
    they can,
By drinking healths, first unto such a
    man,
Then unto such a woman. Then they'll
    send
An health to each man's mistresse or his
    friend ;
Then to their kindreds or their parents
    deare,
They needs must have the other jug of
    beere.
Then to their captains and commanders
    stout,
Who for to pledge they think none shall
    stand out,
Last to the King and Queen, they'll
    have a cruse,
Whom for to pledge they think none
    dare refuse."

Ward of Ipswich, in his *Woe to Drunkards*, 1622, strenuously, but vainly exhorted his countrymen to abandon " that
foolish and vicious custome, as Ambrose
and Basil call it, of drinking healths, and
making that a sacrifice to God for the
health of others, which is rather a sacrifice to the Devill, and a bane of their
owne." It appears from the same writer,
that it was a custom to drink healths at
that time upon their bare knees. The
author is speaking of pot-wits and spirits
of the buttery, " who never bared their
knees to drink healthes, nor ever needed

to whet thir wits with wine, or arme their
courage with pot-harnesse." In Braithwaite's " Times Curtaine drawne," 1621,
is the subsequent passage :

" I was conjured by my kissing friend
To pledge him but an health, and then
    depart,
Which if I did I'de ever have his heart.
I gave assent; the health five senses
    were,
(Though scarce one sense did 'twixt us
    both appeare)
Which as he drunk I pledg'd; both
    pledg'd and drunk,
Seeing him now full charg'd, behinde I
    shrunke," &c.

In Marmion's " Antiquary," 1641, act iv.,
is the following passage : " Why they are
as jovial as twenty beggars, drink their
whole cups, sixe glasses at a health."
Douce's MSS. Notes say : " It was the
custom in Beaumont and Fletcher's time,
for the young gallants to stab themselves
in the arms or elsewhere, in order to drink
the healths of their mistresses, or to write
their names in their own blood." So, in
a song to a Scotish tune, the following
lines occur :

" I stab'd mine arm to drink her health,
    The more the fool I, the more the fool
      I," &c.

And
" I will no more her servant be
    The wiser I, the wiser I,
Nor pledge her health upon my
    knee," &c.

At Christmas, 1623, the gentlemen of the
Middle Temple, according to one of the
Harleian MSS., quoted in the " Life of
Sir Simonds D'Ewes," drank a health to
Princess Elizabeth who, with her husband
the King of Bohemia, was then in great
straits, and stood up, one after the other,
their cup in one hand, and their sword in
the other, and pledged her, swearing to
die in her service, which is said to have
greatly offended James I. Herrick writes :

" Remember us in cups full crown'd,
And let our Citie-health go round,
Quite through the young maids and the
    men,
To the ninth number, if not tenne ;
Untill the fired chestnuts leape
For Joy to see the Fruits ye reape.
From the plumpe Challice and the Cup
That tempts till it be tossed up."

Hesperides, 1648, pp. 146, 87. The following is a curious epigram of Owen on
this subject :

" Quo tibi potarum plus est in ventre
    Salutum,
    Hoc minus epotis, hisce Salutis habes.
Una salus sanis, nullam potare Salutem,
    Non est in potâ vera Salute salus."
Part I. lib. ii. Ep. 42.

561. HEALTH.

"Even from my heart much health I
    wish,
No health I'll wash with drink,
Health wish'd, not wash'd, in words,
    not wine,
To be the best I think."

Witts Recreat., 1667. Evelyn, speaking
of taverns, says, "Your L. will not believe me that the ladies of greatest quality
suffer themselves to be treated in one of
these taverns, but you will be more as-
tonisht when I assure you that they
drink their crowned cups roundly, strain
healths through their smocks, daunce after
the fiddle, kiss freely, and term it an honourable treat. There is a sort of perfect
debauchees, who stile themselves Hectors,
that in their mad and unheard of revels,
pierce their veins to quaff their own blood,
which some of them have drank to that
excess, that they died of intemperance. . .
I don't remember, my Lord, ever to have
known (or very rarely), a health drank in
France, no, not the King's; and if we
say *a vôtre Santé, Monsieur*, it neither
expects pledge or ceremony. 'Tis here so
the custome to drink to every one at the
table, that by the time a gentleman has
done his duty to the whole company, he
is ready to fall asleep, whereas with us,
we salute the whole table with a single
glass onely. *Character of England*,
1659, pp. 34-6-7. In his *Diary*, June 19,
1663, Pepys observes: "To the Rhenish
wine-house, where Mr. Moore showed us
the French manner, when a health is
drunk, to bow to him that drunk to you,
and then apply yourself to him, whose
lady's health is drunk, and then to the
person that you drink to, which I never
knew before; but it seems it is now the
fashion." In 1666, at the Bear Garden,
on a thanks-giving day, the Diarist drank
Mercer's health with his hat off. But in
1668, at Sir George Carteret's at Cran-
bourne, the party drank to the Duke of
York's health on their knees in turn, the
King included. *Pepys*, 23rd Sept. 1668.
M. Jorevin, who was here in Charles
II.'s time, speaking of Worcester and the
Stag Inn there, observes: "According to
the custom of the country, the landladies
sup with strangers and passengers, and if
they have daughters, they are also of the
company, to entertain the guests at table
with pleasant conceits, where they drink
as much as the men. But what is to me
the most disgusting in all this is, that
when one drinks the health of any person
in company, the custom of the country
does not permit you to drink more than
half the cup, which is filled up, and presented to him or her whose health you
have drank." *Antiq. Repert*, 1808, iv.,

563. In "Folly in Print," 1667, in a
catch made before the King's coming to
Worcester with the Scotish army, is something to the purpose:

"Each man upon his back
Shall swallow his sack,
    This health will endure no shrink-
        ing;
The rest shall dance round
Him that lyes on the ground;
    Fore me this is excellent drinking."

Misson has some curious remarks on the
manner of drinking healths in England
in his time. An author who wrote at
about the same period, alludes to a custom at the Old Crown Inn, at Ware, by
which every one coming to see the great
bed there preserved, was expected to
drink "a small can of beer," and to repeat some health, but the gentleman un-
luckily forgot what this was. *A Journey
from London to Scarborough*, 1734, p. 4.

Healths in Scotland.—Ramsay
mentions as in use among the Scots, "Hy
jinks," "a drunken game, or new project
to drink and be rich; thus, the quaff or
cup is filled to the brim, then one of the
company takes a pair of dice, and after
crying Hy-jinks, he throws them out:
the number he casts up points out the
person must drink, he who threw, beginning at himself number one, and so round
till the number of the persons agree with
that of the dice, (which may fall upon himself if the number be within twelve); then
he sets the dice to him, or bids him take
them: he on whom they fall is obliged to
drink, or pay a small forfeiture in money;
then throws, and so on: but if he forgets
to cry Hy-jinks he pays a forfeiture into
the bank. Now he on whom it falls to
drink, if there be anything in bank worth
drawing, gets it all if he drinks. Then,
with a great deal of caution he empties
his cup, sweeps up the money, and orders
the cup to be filled again, and then
throws; for, if he err in the articles, he
loses the privilege of drawing the money,
The articles are (1) drink. (2) draw. (3)
fill. (4) cry Hy-jinks. (5) Count just.
(6) Chuse your doublet man, viz. when two
equal numbers of the dice are thrown, the
person whom you chuse must pay a double
of the common forfeiture, and so must you
when the dice is in his hand. A rare project this," adds honest Allan, "and no
bubble, I can assure you; for a covetous
fellow may save money, and get himself
as drunk as he can desire in less than an
hour's time." The following passage is
curious: "Now to drink all out every
man: (Drinking and Carrowsing) which
is a fashion as little in use amongst us, as
ye terme itselfe is barbarous and strange:
I meane, Ick bring you, is sure a foule

thing of itselfe, and in our countrie so coldly accepted yet, that we must not go about to bring it in for a fashion. If a man doe quaffe or carrouse unto you, you may honestly say nay to pledge him, and geveing him thankes, confesse your weaknesse, that you are not able to beare it: or else to doe him a pleasure, you may for curtesie sake taste it: and then set downe the cup to them that will, and charge yourselfe no further. And although this, Ick bring you, as I have heard many learned men say, hath beene an auncient custome in Greece: and that the Grecians doe much commend a good man of that time, Socrates by name, for that hee sat out one whole night long, drinking a *Vie* with another good man, Aristophanes; and yet the next morning, in the breake of the daye, without any rest uppon his drinking, made such a cunning geometrical instrument, that there was no maner of faulte to be found in the same: bycause the drinking of wine after this sorte in a *Vie*, in such excesse and waste, is a shrewde assault to trie the strength of him that quaffes so lustily." Della Casa's *Galateo*, 1576, transl. by Peterson, sign. Q 2.

"Healths and Toasts," says Lord Cockburn, in his *Memorials*, were special torments—oppressions which cannot now be conceived. Every glass during dinner required to be dedicated to the health of some one. It was thought sottish and rude to take wine without this, as if forsooth there was nobody present worth drinking with. I was present about 1803, when the late Duke of Buccleuch took a glass of sherry by himself at the table of Charles Hope, then Lord Advocate, and this was noticed afterwards as a piece of direct contempt." Cockburn refers to the period, when he and Sir Walter Scott were young men; and he proceeds to describe the ceremonious manner in which the healths were proposed and drunk. The master or the landlord, as the case might be, was privileged to include several persons in the same health. Among the modern Germans offence is apt to be taken if a stranger, invited to drink wine with them, declines the compliment. It is a method of qualifying the person for companionship, a sort of credentials.

Heam.—Waller, in his *Advice to a Painter*, 1681, has the following passage:

" barking bear-ward—
Whom pray'e dont forget to paint with's Staff,
Just at this green bear's tail,——
Watching (as carefull neat-herds do their kine)
Lest he should eat her nauseous secundine.

Then draw a haw-thorn bush, and let him place
The Heam upon't, with faith, that the next race
May females prove "—

with this explanation at p. 13:—"This alludes to a little piece of superstition which the country people use, carefully attending their calving cows, lest they should eat their after-burthen, which they commonly throw upon a hawthorn bush, with steadfast belief they shall have a cow-calf the next year after." Heam is explained to mean "the same in beasts as the secundine or skin that the young is wrapped in." It is apparently akin to *halm*, *heaulme*, and *helm*.

Heaving.—"The counties of Shropshire, Cheshire, and Lancashire, boast a custom which they call heaving, and perform with the following ceremonies, on the Monday and Tuesday in the Easter week. On the first day, a party of men go with a chair into every house to which they can get admission, force every female to be seated in their vehicle, and lift them up three times, with loud huzzas. For this they claim the reward of a chaste salute, which those who are too coy to submit to may get exempted from by a fine of one shilling, and receive a written testimony, which secures them from a repetition of the ceremony of that day. On the Tuesday the women claim the same privilege, and pursue their business in the same manner, with this addition—that they guard every avenue to the town, and stop every passenger, pedestrian, equestrian, or vehicular."—*Public Advertiser*, April 13, 1787. See also on this subject "Gent. Mag." for 1783, p. 378; the same for 1798, p. 325; and comp. *Hoke-Tide* and *Lifting*.

Hedgehog. — Philip de Thaun, in his Anglo-Norman Bestiary, circâ 1120, has this odd fallacy: "Hear," says he, " of the hedgehog, what we understand by it. Physiologus says of it in his writings, 'It is made like a little pig, prickles in its skin—in the time of wine-harvest it mounts the tree, when the cluster of grapes is; it knows which is the ripest, and knocks down the grapes: it is a very bad neighbour to it (the tree): then it descends from the tree, spreads itself out upon the grapes, then folds itself up upon them, round like a ball; when it is well charged, and has stuck its prickles into the grapes, thus by kind it carries its food to its children." *Wright's Popular Treatises on Science*, 1841, p. 103.

Helen's, St., or **Eline's Day.**— (May 2). "The 2nd of May, St. Helen's Day," says Mr. Atkinson, 1868, "is Rowan-tree (mountain-ash) day, or

Rowan-tree Witch-day, and on that day, even yet with some, the method of proceeding is for some member of the household or family to go the first thing in the morning, with no thought of any particular rowan-tree. From this tree a sufficient supply of branches is taken and (a different path home having been taken, by the strict observers, from that by which they went) on reaching home twigs are stuck over every door of every house in the homestead, and scrupulously left there, till they fall out of themselves. A piece is also always borne about by many in their pockets or purses, as a prophylactie against witching. Not so very long since, either, the farmers used to have whipstocks of rowan-tree wood—rowan-tree gads they were called—and it was held that, thus supplied, they were safe against having their draught fixed, or their horses made restive by a witch." In the "Plumpton Correspondence," under the date of 1489-90 circiter, is a letter from Edward Plumpton, in which he says that he has made an appointment to meet a person at Knaresborough "the Wednesday next after Saynt Eline Day." This was also called the Invention of the Holy Cross, in commemoration of the discovery of that sacred relic by the Empress Helena. A sufficiently ample account of this legend is given in "The Book of Days." And the Holy Cross or Holy Rood Day will be noticed elsewhere, the Emperor Heraclius having also been the fortunate finder of a portion of the cross, and the founder of a festival in honour of the incident on the 14th September. "Two pieces off the holye crosse," occur in an inventory of Reading Abbey in 1537, and probably there was not a religious house in the kingdom without a similar curiosity in its possession ; so that to assume all these relics genuine, we must also assume the cross itself to have been of considerable dimensions. In the *Northumberland Household Book* mention occurs of Saint Elyn Day as a day when certain servants were to receive their yearly allowance for horse-meat ; but the editor supposes (I do not know why) that the reference is to dies Helenæ regis, viz., May 21 ; and I see that Nicolas, in the *Chronology of History,* makes only one saint of this name fall in May, namely, Queen Helena, on the 21st. See *Castor and Pollux.*

Hen and Chickens.—This is a Devonshire legend. I cannot resist the temptation of transcribing the account of it I find in "Notes and Queries" : "The vicar of a certain Devonshire parish was a distinguished student of the black art, and possessed a large collection of mysterious books and MSS. During his absence

at church one of his servants entered his study, and, finding a large volume open on the desk, imprudently began to read it aloud. He had scarcely read half a page, when the sky became dark and a great wind shook the house violently ; still he read on, and in the midst of the storm the doors flew open, and a black hen and chickens came into the room. They were of the ordinary size, when they first appeared, but gradually became larger and larger, until the hen was of the bigness of a good-sized ox. At this point the Vicar (in the church) suddenly closed his discourse, and dismissed his congregation, saying he was wanted at home, and hoped he might arrive there in time. When he entered the chamber, the hen was already touching the ceiling. But he threw down a bag of rice, which stood ready in the corner ; and whilst the hen and chickens were busily picking up the grains, the vicar had time to reverse the spell." The same writer adds : "I believe a hen and chickens is sometimes found on the bosses of early church roofs : a sow and pigs certainly are. A black sow and pigs haunt many cross-roads in Devonshire."

Hens.—
"At Shroftide to shroving, go thresh the fat hen,
If blindfold can kill her, then give it thy men."

These lines from Tusser, in "Tusser Redivivus" (by Daniel Hilman), 1710, p. 80, are explained in a note : "The hen is hung at a fellow's back, who has also some horse-bells about him, the rest of the fellows are blinded, and have boughs in their hands, with which they chase this fellow and his hen about some large court or small enclosure. The fellow with his hen and bells shifting as well as he can, they follow the sound, and sometimes hit him and his hen ; other times, if he can get behind one of them, they thresh one another well favouredly ; but the jest is, the maids are to blind the fellows, which they do with their aprons, and the cunning baggages will endear their sweethearts with a peeping-hole, while the others look out as sharp to hinder it. After this the hen is boiled with bacon, and store of pancakes and fritters are made. In Baron's "Cyprian Academy," 1648, p. 53, a clown is speaking. "By the maskins I would give the best cow in my yard to find out this raskall. And I would thrash him as I did the henne last Shrove Tuesday." Mr. Jones informed Mr. Brand that, in Wales, such hens as did not lay eggs before Shrove Tuesday were, when he was a boy, destined to be threshed on that day by a man with a flail, as being no longer good for anything. If the man hit the hen, and consequently killed her, he got her for his pains.

Herne the Hunter.—Of this legendary character, mentioned in the *Merry Wives of Windsor*, and introduced into Ainsworth's *Windsor Castle*, there appear to be no authentic memorials. We merely hear in a vague manner that he was at some remote period a keeper in the Forest. The story may be a graft from one of the numerous Teutonic myths of the same class.

Hiccius Doctius.—"A common term among our modern sleight of hand men. The origin of this is probably to be found among the old Roman Catholics. When the good people of this Island were under their thraldom, their priests were looked up to with the greatest veneration, and their presence announced in the assemblies with the terms hic est doctus! hic est doctus! and this probably is the origin of the modern corruption Hiccius doctius. M.F." Note in ed. of Brand, 1813.

Hide Fox and All After.—Supposed to be an old form and name of the modern children's sport of *Hide and seek*, *Whoop and hide*, &c. The idea of the fox may correspond with the present amusement among young lads of fox and hounds. Comp. *All-Hid*.

High Wycombe.—The old ceremony of weighing the Mayor and Corporation on November 9 is still observed here. The origin of the custom has not been ascertained. It is not mentioned by Lysons.

Hob.—Mr. Atkinson, in his "Cleveland Glossary, 1868," observes: "Probably, like the nisses of popular faith in Denmark, there were many hobs, each with a 'local' habitation and a 'local' name. Thus there is a Hob Hole at Runswick, a Hob Hole near Kempswithen, a Hob's Cave at Mulgrave, Hobt'rush Rook on the Farndale Moors, and so on."

Hobby-Horse.—The sport which Plot describes as having been performed within his memory at Abbot's or Paget's Bromley, under the name of the Hobby-horse dance, is nothing more than the common rustic diversion, not disused till of late years, in which a man, carrying the image of a horse between his legs, and in his hands holding a bow and arrow, plays the horse. "The latter," says Douce, "passing through a hole in the bow, and stopping on a shoulder, made a snapping noise when drawn to and fro, keeping time with music. With this man danced six others, carrying on their shoulders as many reindeer heads, with the arms of the chief families to whom the revenues of the town belonged. They danced the heys and other country dance. To the above hobby-horse dance there belonged a pot, which was kept by turns by the reeves of the town, who provided cakes and ale to put into this pot; all people who had any kindness for the good intent of the institution of the sport giving pence a-piece for themselves and families. Foreigners also that came to see it contributed; and the money, after defraying the expense of the cakes and ale, went to repair the church and support the poor : which charges, adds Plot, are not now perhaps so cheerfully borne." Tollett is induced to think the famous hobby horse to be the King of the May, thogh he now appear as a juggler and a buffoon, from the crimson foot-cloth fretted with gold, the golden bit, the purple bridle, with a golden tassel, and studded with gold, the man's purple mantle with a golden border, which is latticed with purple, his golden crown, purple cap, with a red feather and with a golden knop. The foot-cloth, however, was used by the Fool. In Braithwaite's "Strappado for the Divell," 1615, p. 30, we read :

"Erect our aged fortunes make them shine
(Not like the Foole in's foot-cloath but) like Time
Adorn'd with true experiments," &c.

"Our hobby," Tollett adds, " is a spirited horse of pasteboard, in which the master dances and displays tricks of legerdemain, such as the threading of the needle, the mimicking of the whigh-hie, and the daggers in the nose, &c., as Ben Jonson acquaints us, and thereby explains the swords in the man's cheeks. What is stuck in the horse's mouth I apprehend to be a ladle, ornamented with a ribbon. Its use was to receive the spectator's pecuniary donations." " The colour of the hobby horse is a reddish white, like the beautiful blossom of the peach-tree. The man's coat or doublet is the only one upon the window that has buttons upon it, and the right side of it is yellow, and the left red." In a tract of 1601, speaking of Weston the Jesuit, the writer says: " He lifted up his countenance, as if a new spirit had been put into him, and tooke upon him to controll, and finde fault with this and that: (as the comming into the hall of the hobby-horse in Christmas:) affirming that he would no longer tolerate these and those so grosse abuses, but would have them reformed." There is a passage in Kemp's " Nine Daies Wonder," 1600: " On Munday morning, very early, I rid the 3 myles that I daunst the Satterday before; where alighting, my taberer struck up, and lightly I tript forward, but I had the heauiest way that euer mad Morrice-dancer trod; yet

With hey and ho, through thicke and
thin,
The Hobby-horse quite forgotten,
I followed, as I did begin,
Although the way were rotten."

See Mr. Hunter's "New Illustrations of
Shakespear," vol. ii. p. 248. Shakespear,
in "Hamlet," acted in 1602, makes his
Anglo-Danish hero complain of the oblivion into which the hobby-horse had then
fallen. And in the ballad introduced into
Weelkes's "Ayres," 1608, there is the
same allusion:—

"Since Robin Hood, Maid Marian,
And Little John are gone—a;
The hobby-horse was quite forgot,
When Kempe did daunce alone a."

This character is introduced into several
of the old comedies. In "Patient Gris-
sil," 1603, there is the following:

"*Urc.* No more of these jadish tricks:
here comes the hobby-horse.
Far. Oh, he would dance a morrice
rarely, if he were hung with bells.
Urc. He would jangle villainously."

And again:

"*Gelas.*—Dost thou know where
Are any wodden horses to be sould,
That neede noe spurre nor haye? Ile
aske this stranger.
Pæd. H'st, master, what say to a hobby
horse?—'"

Timon, a Play, i. 4. In "The Vow-
Breaker," 1636, by William Sampson, is
the following dialogue between Miles, the
Miller of Ruddington, and Ball, which
throws great light upon this now obsolete
character:

"*Ball.* But who shall play the hobby
horse? Master Major?
"*Miles.* I hope I looke as like a hobby
horse as Master Major. I have not liv'd
to these yeares, but a man woo'd thinke
I should be old enough and wise enough to
play the hobby horse as well as ever a
Major on 'em all. Let the Major play the
hobby horse among his brethren, and he
will; I hope our towne ladds cannot want
a hobby horse. Have I practic'd my
reines, my carree'res, my pranckers, my
ambles, my false trotts, my smooth ambles,
and Canterbury paces, and shall Master
Major put me besides the hobby horse?
Have I borrow'd the fore horse-bells, his
plumes, and braveries, nay, had his mane
new shorne and frizl'd and shall the Major
put me besides the hobby-horse? Let him
hobby-horse at home, and he will. Am I
not going to buy ribbons and toyes of
sweet Ursula for the Marian, and shall I
not play the hobby horse?
"*Ball.* What shall Joshua doe?
"*Miles.* Not know of it, by any meanes;
hee'l keepe more stir with the hobby horse

then he did with the pipers at Tedbury
Bull-running: provide thou for the
Dragon, and leave me for a hobby horse.
"*Ball.* Feare not, I'le be a fiery Dra-
gon."

And afterwards, when Boote askes him:
"Miles, the Miller of Ruddington,
gentleman and souldier, what make you
here?
"*Miles.* Alas, Sir, to borrow a few rib-
bandes, bracelets, eare-rings, wyertyers,
and silke girdles and hand-kerchers for a
Morice, and a show before the Queene.
"*Boote.* Miles, you came to steale my
Neece.
"*Miles.* Oh Lord! Sir, I came to fur-
nish the hobby horse.
"*Boote.* Get into your hobby horse,
gallop, and be gon then, or I'le Moris-
dance you—Mistris, waite you on me.
Exit.
"*Ursula.* Farewell, good hobby horse.
—*Weehee. Exit.*"

We perhaps owe to the hobby horse not
only the familiar expression, "to ride a
hobby," that is to say, to indulge a crot-
chet, but "to ride the great horse," which
is mentioned in a paper inserted by Gutch
in his "Collectanea Curiosa," 1781, in
apparent reference to Sir Balthazar Gerbier's project for a Royal Academy or
College of Honour, conceived by him in
the reign of James I. This great horse
was, so far as one can collect, the new
system or curriculum, which Gerbier was
then endeavouring to institute. In the
later literature of the seventeenth century, if not in that of Shakespear's own
day, hobby-horse evidently stands very
often for a children's horse, the toy which
has been elaborated by modern art into
a rocking-horse. Thus, in "Musarum Deliciæ," 1656:

"Another sware, that I no more did
ride,
Then children, that a hobby-horse be-
stride."

But Bayes's Troop in the Duke of Buckingham's *Rehearsal* is said by Douce to
afford a fair idea of the hobby horse in the
Morris. Comp. *Irish Hobby.*

Hobgoblin.—As to this term, I find
it difficult to concur with Wedgwood (*Dict.*
in v.); I think a more rational solution of
the word to be a clownish spirit, or supernatural Hob, who might be supposed to
partake of the awkwardness of the mortal
rustic.

Hock-Cart or **Hockey-Cart.**—
That which brings the last corn and the
children rejoicing with boughs in their
hands, with which the horses also are attired. Herrick addressed to the poet-earl
of Westmoreland, author of "Otia Sacra,"
1648, a copy of verses, in which he pleasantly describes the usages of the harvest

home. He alludes to the crowning of the hock-cart, and the other ceremonies observed after the gathering-in of the crop. Lord Westmoreland himself tells us:

> "How the hock-cart with all its gear
> Should be trick'd up, and what good chear."

Hockey.—This is a game played with a ball and sticks. Several persons may partake in the recreation, and the sport consists in driving the ball in different directions, each player being provided with a stick, with which, by the exercise of a good deal of agility and quickness of eye, he may succeed in outstripping his competitors, and bringing the ball to the appointed goal. Hockey has, of late years, rather increased in popularity; like other diversions, the interest fluctuates from period to period.

Hockey Cake.—That distributed to the people at *Harvest-home*.

Hocus-pocus or **Hoax.**—Vallancey, speaking of hocus pocus, derives it from the Irish "*Coic* an omen, a mystery; and *bais*, the palm of the hand: whence is formed *Coiche-bais*, legerdemain; Persicé *choko-baz*: whence the vulgar English hocus pocus." He is noticing the communication in former days between Ireland and the East. *Collect.* xiii., 93. Ady, speaking of common jugglers, that go up and down to play their tricks in fairs and markets, says: "I will speak of one man more excelling in that craft than others, that went about in King James his time, and long since, who called himself the Kings Majesties most excellent Hocus Pocus, and so was he called, because that at the playing of every trick, he used to say 'Hocus pocus, tontus, talontus, vade celeriter jubeo,' a dark composure of words, to blinde the eyes of the beholders." *Candle in the Dark*, 1659, p. 29. Archbishop Tillotson tells us that "in all probability those common jugling words of hocus pocus are nothing else but a corruption of *hoc est Corpus*, by way of ridiculous imitation of the priests of the Church of Rome in their trick of Transubstantiation," &c. *Discourse on Transubstantiation*. With due submission to his Grace, this appears rather a fanciful etymology. In 1634 was published a tract entitled *Hocus Pocus Junior, the Anatomy of Legerdemain*, which passed through about ten impressions, and is illustrated with wood-cuts of the various tricks. Butler has these lines:

> "With a slight
> Convey men's interest, and right,
> From Stiles's pocket into Nokes's
> As easily as hocus pocus."

Hodening.—Busby, in his "Concert-Room Anecdotes," gives an account of this usage, which is merely another form of the "Mari Llwyd" hereafter described.

Hognell or **Hogling Money.**—See *Hoke-Tide*.

Hoisting.—A process to which soldiers were subjected on returning to barracks for the first time after being married.

Hoke-Tide or **Hoc-Tide.**—This festival was celebrated, according to ancient writers, on the Quindena Paschæ, by which, Mr. Denne informs us, the second Sunday after Easter cannot be meant, but some day in the ensuing week: and Matthew Paris and other writers have expressly named Tuesday. There are strong evidences remaining to shew that more days were kept than one. As it is observed in the "Glossary" of Nares, Hoke Day cannot be the anniversary of any fixed event, as it is a movable feast, varying with Easter-tide. Matthew Paris (who is the oldest authority for the word), has the following passages concerning Hoc-tide. "Post diem Martis quæ vulgariter Hokedaie appellatur, factum est Parliamentum Londini," p. 963. "Die videlicet Lunæ quæ ipsum diem præcedit proximò quem Hokedaie vulgariter appellamus," p. 834. "In quindena Paschæ quæ vulgariter Hokedaie appellatur," p. 908. On these passages Watts, in his Glossary, observes, "adhuc in ea die solent mulieres jocose vias Oppidorum funibus impedire, et transeuntes ad se attrahere, ut ab eis munusculum aliquod extorqueant, in pios usus aliquos erogandum"; and then refers to Spelman. But there can be no doubt that the term is derived from hoch-zeit, the high tide, a festival, which in modern German signifies marriage. I find that Easter is called "Hye-tyde" in Robert of Gloucester, vol. i. p. 156. Colonel Vallancey communicated to Mr. Brand a curious paper in his own hand-writing, to the following effect: "Hoc-Tide. In Erse and Irish oach or oac is rent, tribute. The time of paying rents was twice in the year, at La Samham, the day of Saman (2nd Nov.) and La Oac, the day of Hock (April). See La Saman, 'Collectanea,' No. 12. "Hoguera (Spanish) el fuego que se haze con hacina de lennos que levanta llama; y assi se enciende siempre en lugar descubierto. Hazian hogueras los antiguos para quemar los cuerpos de los difuntos, y en ciertas fiestas que llamavam lustros; y en tiempo de peste se han usado para purificar el aire. Por regoziio se hazen hogueras en la fiesta de san Juan Baptista, y otros Santos, y en las alegrias por nacimientos de principes, y por otras causas. El saltar por encima de las hogueras se haze agora con simplicidad; pero

antiguamente tenia cierto genero de su-
persticion ; y tuvo origen de los Caldeos,
segun escriven autores graves. Llevadme
cavallera, y sea a la hoguera. Esto dixo
una hechizera, llevandola a quemar. Acos-
tumbran en muchas partes llevar a losque
han de justiciar por su pie : y pienso que
la costumbre de llevarlos en Castilla ca-
valleros es pia y llegada a razon ; porque
el que va a padecer va debilitado, tem-
blando con todo su cuerpo : y con esta fa-
tiga puede ser, que no vaya tan atento, ni
los religiosos que le van confortando. Vltra
desto, como va levantado en alto, venle
todos, para exemplo, y para comisera-
cion.''—Tesoro de la Lingua Castellana
por Don Seb. de Cobarruvias Orosco, fol.
Madr. 1611.

Blount, in his edition of Cowell's
Glossary, says, that Hoc Tuesday money
was a duty given to the landlord,
that his tenants and bondsmen might sol-
emnize that day on which the English mas-
tered the Danes, being the second Tuesday
after Easter week. Neither Alfred of
Beverley, Hardyng, nor the anonymous
writer of the Chronicle usually called Caxton's, mentions the massacre. Higden
says it happened on St. Brice's night, fol.
244 b. Fabyan says it happened on St.
Brice's day, and began at Welwyn in Hertfordshire, p. 259. Grafton follows him in
the same words. Holinshed makes it to
have taken place on St. Brice's day in the
year 1012 ; and adds, that the place where
it began is uncertain, some saying at Welwyn, and others at Howahil, in Staffordshire, 1st edit. fol. 242. Matthew of
Westminster gives more particulars of the
massacre than any other historian, and
makes it to have happened in 1012, but
says nothing of Hoctide in that place.
Stowe very briefly mentions the fact as
having happened on St. Brice's day, 1002.
Mr. Brand himself observed, that the
strongest testimony against the hypothesis that the festival was instituted to commemorate the destruction of the Danes by
Ethelred in 1002, is that of Henry, Archdeacon of Huntingdon, who expressly says
that the massacre of the Danes happened
on the feast of St. Brice, which is well
known to be on the thirteenth of November. Other ancient authorities for the
mention of Hoctide are, 1. "Monast. An-
glic." vol. i., p. 104, "A die quæ dicitur
Hokedai usque ad festum S. Michaelis."
2. An instrument in Kennett's "Paroch.
Antiq." dated 1363, which speaks of a
period between Hoke Day and St. Martin's Day. 3. A Chartulary at Caen, cited
by Du Cange, p. 1150, in which a period between "Hocedei usque ad Au-
gustum" is mentioned. 4. An Inspexi-
mus in Madox's "Formulare," p. 225,
dated 42 Ed. III. in which mention is
made of "die Martis proximo post Quin-

denam Paschæ qui vocatur Hokeday.'' In
"an indenture constituting John att
Hyde steward of the Priory of Poghley,"
among many other things granted him,
are two oxen for the larder on Hoke-day.
"Item ii. Boves pro lardario apud Hocco-
day." It is dated on the feast of the An-
nunciation, in the 49th of Edward the
Third.

By a proclamation of Henry IV. in
1409, this sport was to be permitted as
for that year on Hock-Monday and Tuesday in the City of London and suburbs,
without hinderance or exception, within
doors and without. Riley's *Memorials*,
1868, p. 571. There is preserved in the
fifth volume of Leland's "Collectanea,"
1770, p. 298, a curious inhibition of John,
Bishop of Worcester, against the abuses of
the "Hoc-days," dated 6th April, 1450.
The expression Hock, or Hoketyde, com-
prizes both days. Hoke-Monday was for
the women, and Hock Tuesday for the
men. On both days the men and women,
alternately, with great merriment inter-
cepted the public roads with ropes, and
pulled passengers to them, from whom
they exacted money to be laid out in pious
uses. So that Hoketyde began on the
Monday immediately following the second
Sunday after Easter, in the same manner
as several feasts of the dedications of
churches, and other holidays, commenced
on the day or the vigil before, and was a
sort of preparation for, or introduction
to, the principal feast. In Coates's Extracts from the Accounts of St. Laurence's
parish, Reading, under 1499, 14 Hen. VII.
are the following entries : "It. rec. of Hok
money gaderyd of women, xxs." "It. rec.
of Hok money gadyeryd of men iiijs.'"—
History of Reading, p. 214. Among the
"Privy Purse Expenses of Henry VII."
many of which shew that prince's kindness
of heart and generosity of character, is
one to this point : "To Lendesay for the
wyffs at Grenewiche upon Hockmonday,
3s. 4d.'" The date is March 9, 1505-6.
It appears clearly, from these and other
extracts, that the women made their collection on the Monday : and it is likewise
shown that the women always collected
more than the men. Plot expressly mentions that in his time they had two Hoc-
days, viz., "The Monday for the women,"
which, says he, "is the more solemn, and
the Tuesday for the men, which is very inconsiderable." Blount, in his own "Law
Dictionary," v. Hokeday, says he has seen
a lease, without date, reserving so much
rent payable "ad duos anni terminos, scil.
ad le Hokeday, et ad festum S. Mich." He
adds, that in the accounts of Magdalen
College, in Oxford, there is yearly an allowance pro mulieribus hocantibus, in
some manors of theirs in Hampshire,
where the men hoc the women on the Mon-

day, and contra on Tuesday. In some Churchwardens' Accounts, appertaining to the parochial affairs of Bletchingley, in Surrey, printed in the "Loseley MSS.," 1836, occurs an item called Hognell money —presumably connected with this occasion. In the Churchwardens' Accounts of Cheddar, co. Somerset, under 1612 and 1631, are two entries of amounts received as hogling money, namely, £9 13s. 4d. and £9 3s. 4d. I conclude this to be connected with Hoc or Hoke Tide; yet the amounts collected are far in excess of what seems to have been usual. *Notes and Queries*, 3rd Ser., iii., 423. The custom of men and women heaving each other alternately on Easter Monday and Easter Tuesday in North Wales (mentioned by Pennant) must have been derived from this hocking each other on Hok-days, after the keeping of the original days had been set aside. I find this, amongst other sports, exhibited at Kenilworth Castle by the Earl of Leicester, for the entertainment of Queen Elizabeth, A.D. 1575, under the superintendence of Captain Cox. "And that there might be nothing wanting that these parts could afford, hither came the Coventre men, and acted the ancient play, long since used in that city, called Hocks-Tuesday, setting forth the destruction of the Danes in King Ethelred's time, with which the Queen was so pleas'd, that she gave them a brace of bucks, and five marks in money, to bear the charges of a feast." The play was an annual event here.

Plot says that one of the uses of the money collected at Hoketyde was the reparation of the several parish churches where it was gathered. This is confirmed by extracts from the Lambeth Book:

"1556—1557. Item, of Godman Rundells wife, Godman Jacksons wife, and Godwife Tegg, for Hoxce money by them received to the use of the Church, xijs."

"1518—1519. Item, of William Elyot and John Chamberlayne, for Hoke money gyderid in the pareys, iijs. ixd."

"Item of the gaderyng of the Churchwardens wyffes on Hoke Monday, viijs. iijd."

In "Peshall's History of the City of Oxford," under St. Mary's parish, are the following curious extracts from old records:

P. 67. "1510, sub tit. Recepts. Recd. atte Hoctyde of the wyves gaderynge, xvs. ijd. From 1522 to 3, sub tit. Rec. for the wyfes gatheryng at Hoctyde de claro, xvis. xd."

P. 83. Parish of St. Peter in the East. "1662. About that time it was customary for a parish that wanted to raise money to do any repairs towards the church to keep a Hocktyde, the benefit of which was often very great: as, for instance, this parish of St. Peter in the

East gained by the Hocktide and Whitsuntide, anno 1664, the sum of £14.

"1663. Hocktide brought in this year £6.

"1667. £4 10s. gained by Hocktide." *Archæologia*, vii., 252. In the Churchwardens' Accounts of St. Mary at Hill, London, under the year 1496, is the following article: "Spent on the wyves that gaderyd money on Hob Monday, 10d." Ibid. 1518, there is an order for several sums of money gathered on Hob Monday, &c. to go towards the organs, but crossed out with a pen afterwards. Ibid. 1497. "Gatherd by the women on Hob Monday, 13s. 3d. By the men on the Tuesday, 5s." There are many other entries to the same effect. See Nichols' "Illust." 1797. In Lysons' extracts from the Churchwardens' and Chamberlain's Books at Kingston-upon-Thames are the following concerning Hocktide:

"1 Hen. VIII. Recd. for the gaderyng at Hocktyde, 14s.

2 Hen. VIII. Payd for mete and drink at Hoc-tyde, 12d."

The last time that the celebration of Hocktyde appears is in 1578:

"Recd. of the women upon Hoc Monday, 5s. 2d."

Ibid. vol. ii. p. 145. Parish of Chelsea. "Of the women that went a hocking, 13 April, 1607, 45s." There is a passage in Wither's "Abuses stript and whipt," 1613, which seems to imply that Hock-tide was then still generally observed. It declined soon after the Restoration, yet as late as 1667 there is a trace of it in Parish Books.

Holed or **Pierced Stones.**—See *Stones*.

Holling.—The Eve of the Epiphany is so called at Brough in Westmoreland, where there is an annual procession of an ash-tree, lighted on the tops of its branches, to which combustible matter has been tied. This custom is in commemoration of the star of the Wise Men of the East. Halliwell's *Dict.*, 1860, in v.

Holly.—"Mary," says Gascoigne, in the *Pleasures at Kenilworth*, 1576, "there are two kinds of holly, that is to say, he holly and she holly. Nowe some will say that the she holly hath no prickes, but thereof I entermeddle not." Poems by Hazlitt, ii., 139. From a carol in praise of the holly, temp. Hen. VI. in Harl. MS. 5396, it should seem that holly was used only to deck the inside of houses at Christmas: while ivy was used not only as a vintner's sign, but also among the evergreens at funerals.

Holly-Boy and Ivy-Girl. — A sport formerly practised in East Kent. A writer in the *Gentleman's Magazine* for 1779 says: "Mr. Urban being on a visit on

Tuesday last in a little obscure village in this county, I found an odd kind of sport going forward : the girls, from eighteen to five or six years old, were assembled in a crowd, and burning an uncouth effigy, which they called an Holly-Boy, and which it seems they had stolen from the boys, who, in another part of the village were assembled together, and burning what they called an Ivy-Girl, which they had stolen from the girls : all this ceremony was accompanied with loud huzzas, noise, and acclamations. What it all means I cannot tell, although I inquired of several of the oldest people in the place, who could only answer that it had always been a sport at this season of the year." A correspondent of Mr. Brand described the Ivy Girl to him somewhat differently, namely, as a figure composed of some of the best corn the field produces, and made, as well as they can, into a human shape ; this is afterwards curiously dressed by the women, and adorned with paper trimmings, cut to resemble a cap, ruffles, handkerchief, &c. of the finest lace. It is brought home with the last load of corn from the field upon the waggon, and they suppose entitles them to a supper at the expense of their employers. Naogeorgus or Kirchemair seems to allude to a similar practice in his *Popish Kingdom*, translated by Googe, 1570 :

" Now when at length the pleasant time
    of Shrove-tide comes in place,
And cruell fasting dayes at hand approch with solemne grace :
Then olde and yong are both as mad, as
    ghestes of Bacchus feast,
And foure dayes long they tipple square,
    and feede and never reast.
Downe goes the hogges in every place,
    and puddings every wheare
Do swarme : the dice are shakte and
    tost, and cardes apace they teare :
In every house are showtes and cryes,
    and mirth, and revell route,
And daintie tables spred, and all be set
    with ghestes about :
With sundrie playes and Christmas
    games, and feare and shame away,
The tongue is set at libertie, and hath
    no kinde of stay.
All thinges are lawfull then and done,
    no pleasure passed by,
That in their mindes they can deuise, as
    if they then should die."

Purchas, speaking of the Peruvian superstitions, mentions an usage rather analogous to the English one : " In the sixt moneth they offered a hundred sheepe of all colours, and then made a feast, bringing mayz from the fields into the house, which they yet vse. This feast is made, comming from the farme to the house, saying certaine songs, and praying that the mayz may long continue. They put a quantitie of the mayz (the best that groweth in their farmes) in a thing which they call Pirua, with certaine ceremonies watching three nights. Then doe they put it in the richest garment they haue, and, being thus wrapped and dressed, they worship this Pirua, holding it in great veneration, and saying, It is the mother of the mayz of their inheritances, and that by this meanes the mayz augments and is preserued. In this moneth they make a particular sacrifice, and the witches demand of this Pirua if it hath strength enough to continue vntill the next yeere. And if it answeres no, then they carrie this maiz to the farme whence it was taken, to burne and make another Pirua as before : and this foolish vanitie still continueth." " Pilgrimes," vol. v., lib. ix., c. 12. He cites Acosta, lib. vi. c. 3.

Holly Bussing.—The "Newcastle Express," quoted by "Notes and Queries," May 2, 1857, thus describes the local practice of holly bussing. "On Easter Tuesday, the lads and lasses of the village and vicinity (of Netherwitton, Northumberland) meet, and accompanied by our worthy parish clerk, who plays an excellent fiddle, . . . proceed to the wood to get holly, with which some decorate a stone cross that stands in the village, while others are ' bobbing around ' to ' Speed the Plough ' or ' Birnie Bouzle.' Accordingly, on Tuesday last, a merry party assembled, and after going through the usual routine, dancing was kept up on the green till the shades of evening were closing on them."

Holydays.—Philip de Thaun, in his "Livre des Creatures," circâ A.D. 1121, says, respecting the Latin term *Feriæ :*

" Mais ço truvum lisant en cel compot
    Gerlant,
Que li bers Sainz Silvestre, qui de Rume
    fud mestre,
Feries les apelat, e lur nuns tresturnat,
Pur ço que cristiens ne cresisant paiens
De fole entenciun ne de male raisun."

Wright's *Popular Treatises on Science,* 1841, p. 28.

There is an order from the Bishop of Worcester, given in April, 1450, to the Almoner of Worcester Cathedral and others, that all persons within the jurisdiction of the diocese should cease woodcutting and dishonest sports on the days vulgarly called holy-days, under pain of excommunication. Hooker says : "Holydays were set apart to be the landmarks to distinguish times." In " Barten Holiday to the Puritan in his Technogamia," in " Witts Recreations," 1640, the writer says :

" 'Tis not my person, nor my play,
But my sirname, Holiday,
That does offend thee, thy complaints
Are not against me, but the Saints."

Holy Dust.—Among the Britons and early Saxons the idea of sanctity was not limited to those who had received canonization or to gods. Bede apprises us that the dust of Oswald, King of Northumbria, was preserved as a cure for sickness, and narrates an anecdote of a countryman who had travelled far to collect this precious medicine, which he carried home, wrapped up in a linen cloth. Barnes, *Notes on Ancient Britain*, 1858, p. 22.

Holy Hand.—A communication to *Notes and Queries* (August 31, 1872), intimates the survival of the belief at Lancaster and the vicinity that the touch of Father Arrowsmith's right hand was efficacious in curing various complaints. It will be better to append the account itself:—" At last week's meeting of the Wigan Board of Guardians, a case was brought forward relating to an extraordinary superstition in Lancaster. The assistant-overseer of Ashton-in-Makerfield had sent to the Wigan workhouse a woman who gave the name of Catherine Collins, and who had been sitting all day on a doorstep, and was wholly destitute. She stated that she had come out of Salford Workhouse, on leave, to have the holy hand applied to her paralysed side. Mr. Clarke, one of the Guardians for Ashton, stated to the Board that hundreds of persons visited the township for similar purposes. The holy hand is kept by the Roman Catholic priest at Garswood, in Ashton township, and is preserved with great care in a white silk bag. Many wonderful cures were said to have been wrought by this saintly relic, which is alleged to be the hand of Father Arrowsmith, a priest who was put to death for his religion at Lancaster. When about to suffer he desired his spiritual attendant to cut off his right hand, which should then have the power to work miraculous cures on those who had faith to believe in its efficacy."

Holy Name of Jesus.—(August 7.) In the " Plumpton Correspondence " occurs a letter to Sir Richard Plumpton from John Pullen, under the supposed date of 1499, in which the writer says: " Sir, as hartylie as I can, I commaund me unto you ; and within a box to my lady . . . is the fest of Nomen Jesu with Utas.". . . The Editor conjectures, and doubtless properly, that what Pullen sent to Lady Plumpton was the book or MS. containing the service used on this particular day, with the octave or Utas. Of this, however, Pynson printed at least two editions, and one of these may have been the book above mentioned. Hone, in his *Every-Day Book*, gives an account of the anniversary.

Holy-Rood Day.—(Sept. 14). This festival, called also Holy Cross Day, was instituted on account of the recovery of a large piece of the Cross by the Emperor Heraclius, after it had been taken away, on the plundering of Jerusalem by Chosroes, King of Persia, about 615. Churchwardens' Accounts, previous to the Reformation, are usually full of entries relating to the Rood-loft. In the accounts of St. Mary at Hill, 5 Hen. VI. we have : " Also for makynge of a peire endentors betwene William Serle, carpenter, and us, for the Rode lofte and the under clerks. chambre, ijs. viijd. Also refs. of certeyn men for the Rod loft; fyrst of Ric. Goslyn, £10 ; also of Thomas Raynwall, £10 ; also of Rook 26s. 7d."; and eighteen others. " Summa totalis £95 11s. 9d." Sir H. Ellis remarks that the carpenters on this occasion appear to have had what in modern language is called " their drinks" allowed them over and above their wages. " Also the day after St. Dunstan, the 19 day of May, two carpenters with her nonsiens (nuncheons or luncheons)." Other entries respecting the Rood-loft occur in the above-cited accounts :

" Also payd for a rolle and 2 gojons of iron and a rope, xiiijd.

Also payd to 3 carpenters removing the stallis of the quer, xxd.

Also payd for 6 peny nail and 5 peny nail, xjd.

Also for crochats, and 3 iron pynnes and a staple, xiijd.

Also for 5 yardis and a halfe of grene Bokeram, iijs. iijd. ob.

Also for lengthyng of 2 cheynes and 6 zerdes of gret wyer, xiiijd.

Also payd for eleven dozen pavyng tyles, iijs. iijd."

Ellis points out that, in Howes' edition of Stow, 2 Edw. VI. 1547, we read : "The 17 of Nov. was begun to be pulled down the Roode in Paules Church, with Mary and John, and all other images in the church, and then the like was done in all the Churches in London, and so throughout England, and texts of Scripture were written upon the walls of those churches against images, &c." He adds: "Many of our Rood-lofts, however, were not taken down till late in the reign of Queen Elizabeth."

It appears to have been the custom to go a nutting upon this day, from the following passage in " Grim the Collier of Croydon," 1662 :

"This day, they say, is called Holy-
rood Day,
And all the youth are now a nutting
gone."
Hazlitt's Dodsley, vii., 443.

Holy Saturday.—See *Easter Eve.*

Holy Thursday.—Various rites
appear to have been performed on Holy
Thursday at wells, in different parts of
the kingdom: such as decorating them
with boughs of trees, garlands of tulips,
and other flowers, placed in various fancied devices. In some places indeed it
was the custom, after prayers for the day
at the church, for the clergyman and singers even to pray and sing psalms at the
wells. At the village of Tissington, in the
county of Derby, a place remarkable for
fine springs of water, it has been the custom from time immemorial. *Gents. Mag.*,
Feb., 1794. This usage is still in force,
and was observed in 1903. I subjoin the
acount of it in the *Daily Mail* of May 22:
"After service in the parish church the
clergy led a procession round the wells,
which were attractively decorated with
flowers. The designs included representations of a lighthouse, castles, and St.
George's encounter with the dragon. At
one the hymn, "Rock of Ages," was flor-
ally illustrated. Over each well was an
appropriate inscription. It is said that
the custom originated in 1615 as a form of
thanksgiving for a bounteous supply of
water during a season of exceptional
drought." A writer in the "Gentleman's
Magazine" for March, 1794, says: "The
same custom was observed of late years, if
not at the present time, at Brewood and
Bilbrook, two places in the county of
Stafford." Plot tells us: "They have a
custom in this county, which I observed
on Holy Thursday at Brewood and Bilbrook, of adorning their wells with boughs
and flowers. This, it seems, they doe too
at all gospell-places, whether wells, trees,
or hills: which being now observed only
for decency and custom sake, is innocent
enough. Heretofore, too, it was usual to
pay this respect to such wells as were eminent for cureing distempers, on the Saint's
Day whose name the well bore, diverting
themselves with cakes and ale, and a little
musicke and dancing; which, whilst within these bounds, was also an innocent recreation. But whenever they began to
place sanctity in them, to bring alms and
offerings, or make vows at them, as the
antient Germans and Britons did, and the
Saxons and English were too much inclined to, for which St. Edmund's Well,
without Saint Clements near Oxford, and
St. Laurence's at Peterborough, were famous heretofore: I doe not find but they
were forbid in those times, as well as now,
this superstitious devotion being called

ƿilþeorðunᵹa, which Somner rightly translates Well-worship, and was strictly
prohibited by our Anglican Councils as
long agoe as King Edgar; and in the reign
of Canutus; not long after again in a
Council at London under S. Anselm, Archbishop of Canterbury, A.D. 1102, as it was
also particularly at these two wells near
Oxford and Peterborough, by Oliver Sutton, Bishop of Lincoln." *Staffordshire*,
p. 318.

A writer in *Notes and Queries* (Mr.
A. P. Allsopp) says:—"The belief
that rain-water, caught on Holy Thursday and put into a bottle and corked
will keep good for any length of time is
not confined to Surrey, but is also prevalent in some parts of Worcestershire, e.g.,
in the parishes of Martley and Hindlip,
especially among the old women. The
daughter of one of our servants was
troubled with sore eyes whilst she was living at Harrow some years ago, but by the
application of some rain-water, which
had been caught on Holy Thursday and
carefully preserved in a bottle by an old
friend in Buckinghamshire, the sore eyes
were cured. The water was quite fresh,
and as clear as crystal, although many
years had elapsed since it was first caught.
Aubrey, who wrote about 1670, says in
his "Remains of Gentilism and Judaism": "The fellows of New College have,
time out of mind, every Holy Thursday,
betwixt the hours of eight and nine, gonne
to the hospitall called Bart'lemews neer
Oxford, when they retire into the chapell,
and certaine prayers are read, and an an-
theme sung: from thence they goe to the
upper end of the grove adjoyning to the
chapell (the way being beforehand strewed
with flowers by the poor people of the
hospitall), they place themselves round
about the well there, where they warble
forth melodiously a song of three, four,
or five parts; which being performed, they
refresh themselves with a morning's
draught there, and retire to Oxford before
sermon." Hearne notes in his *Diary*,
Jan. 19, 1725: "They have a custom in
St. Aldgate's parish, Oxford, for people of
the parish to eat sugar sopps out of the
font in the church every holy Thursday,
and this is done in the morning." Mr.
Brand's servant B. Jelkes, who lived several years at Evesham in Worcestershire,
informed him of an ancient custom in that
place for the master-gardeners to give
their workpeople a treat of baked peas,
both white and grey (and pork) every year
on Holy Thursday. Compare *Rogation
Week.*

Holy Water.—The ancient Greeks
were perfectly acquainted with the
use and supposed virtue of holy water.
St. John's *Manners and Customs of*

w

Ancient Greece, 1842, 1., 367. All the Romish service books contain the *Benedictio Salis et Aquæ*. But the sanctification of water for medical and sanitary purposes was carried on to some considerable extent. The "Durham Ritual" contains a benedictio for cases of sore eyes, bodily infirmity, &c. There seems to have been scarcely an article of use or consumption, which was not brought within the operation of holy water. Pennant communicated to Brand a MS. account of customs in North Wales, in which occurred the following passage: "If there be a Fynnon Vair, Well of our Lady or other Saint in the parish, the water that is used for baptism in the font is fetched thence. Old women are very fond of washing their eyes with the water after baptism. It is still a common article of popular belief in North Wales, even among educated people that the holy water used in baptism should never be thrown away afterwards, but should be employed to moisten some tree or shrub, to whose growth it is held to be propitious. The nurses and gossips in the same part of the country also maintain that a child should cry at the baptismal font, or it is a sign that it will not live. They will even pinch it, rather than the lucky omen should be wanting. Rose, in a note to his translation of "Amadis of Gaul, 1803, mentions that in the romance of "Petit Jean de Saintres," the king's chamber is "sprinkled at night with holy water as a protection against evil spirits." In the "Life of Henrietta Maria," 1669, p. 3, we read: "On the 25th of June, 1610, she was carried with her brother to perform the Ceremony of casting Holy-water on the corps of her dead father (Henry the Fourth of France), who was buried the 28th following." Comp. *Orkneys*.

Mungo Park, in his "Travels," tells us, "At Baniseribe—a Slatee having seated himself upon a mat by the threshold of his door, a young woman (his intended bride) brought a little water in a calabash, and kneeling down before him, desired him to wash his hands: when he had done this, the girl, with a tear of joy sparkling in her eye, drank the water; this being considered as the greatest proof of her fidelity and love."

Holy Wells and Fountains.—
The custom of giving names to wells and fountains is of the most remote antiquity. In giving particular names to inanimate things it is obviously the principal intention to secure or distinguish the property of them. A well was a most valuable treasure in those dry and parched countries which composed the scene of the Patriarchal History, and therefore we find in one of the earliest of human writ-

ings, the Book of Genesis, that it was a frequent subject of contention (*Genesis*, xxi., 31, also xxvi.), and so it continued to be down to modern days, and even in Western Europe as frequently the sole source of water supply to a village or district. The association of a holy name with such spots was actuated, no doubt, by a desire to protect them from injury and pollution. At Rome Fontinalia was a religious feast, celebrated on the 13th of October, in honour of the nymphs of wells and fountains. The ceremony consisted in throwing nosegays into the fountains, and putting crowns of flowers upon the wells. We judge that the ancients discerned some supernatural influence behind these gifts of Nature. "Horace, in one of his odes, made a solemn promise that he would make a present of a very fine kid, some sweet wine, and flowers, to a noble fountain in his own Sabine villa. See Ovid's "Fasti," lib. iii., 300 :

"—Fonti rex Numa mactat ovem."

Comp. *Holy Thursday*. In the Papal times there was a custom in this country, if a well had an awful situation, if its waters were bright and clear, or if it was considered as having a medicinal quality, to dedicate it to some saint, by honouring it with his name. We find that the superstitious adoration of fountains is forbidden so early as in the 16th of the canons made in the reign of Edgar, A.D. 960: as also in the canons of St. Anselm made in 1102. There are interdictions of this superstition in the laws of Canute, also preserved in Wheloc's edition of Lambarde's "Archaionomia," 1644.

Fitzstephen, in his account of London in the time of Henry II., writes: "There are also about London, on the north of the suburbs, choice fountains of water, sweet, wholesome and clear, streaming forth among the glistering pebble-stones: in this number, Holy-well, Clerken-well, and Saint Clement's-well, are of most note, and frequented above the rest, when scholars and the youths of the city take the air abroad in the summer evenings." Our British topography abounds with accounts of holy wells, or such as had assigned them, by ancient superstition, most extraordinary properties. These ideas, so far from being worn out in a more enlightened age, were long retained by the vulgar, not only in the distant provinces, but also close to the metropolis itself. The custom of affixing ladles of iron, &c. by a chain to wells, is of great antiquity. Strutt, in his "Anglo-Saxon Æra," tells us, that Edwine caused ladles or cups of brass to be fastened to the clear springs and wells, for the refreshment of the passengers. Venerable Bede is his authority, Eccles. Hist. ii. 16. The passage is as follows: "Tantum quoque rex idem utilitati suæ gentis consuluit, ut plerisque in locis ubi fontes lucidos juxta publicos viarum transitus conspexit, ibi ob refrigerium viantium erectis stipitibus et æneos caucos suspendi juberet, neque hos quisquam nisi ad usum necessarium contingere præ magnitudine vel timoris ejus auderet, vel amoris vellet."

The present class of superstition appears to have been very prevalent in this island till the age before the Reformation, and is not even yet entirely extinguished among the Roman Catholics and the common people. In the parish of Ilam, Staffordshire, there used to be the tomb, well, and ash of St. Bertram, who was a worker of miracles in the county. The ash grew over the spring, and was regarded as inviolable. *England's Gazetteer*, 1751, v. *Ilam.*

Borlase observes: "A very singular manner of curing madness, mentioned by Carew in the parish of Altarnun—was to place the disordered in mind on the brink of a square pool, filled with water from St. Nun's Well. The patient, having no intimation of what was intended, was, by a sudden blow on the breast, tumbled into the pool, where he was tossed up and down by some persons of superior strength, till, being quite debilitated, his fury forsook him; he was then carried to Church, and certain masses sung over him. The Cornish call this immersion Boossenning, from beuzi or bidhyzi in the Cornu-British and Armoric, signifying to dip or drown." *Antiq. of Cornwall*, 138. *Nat. Hist. of Cornwall*, 302; Carew's *Survey*, 1602, p. 123.

"In thys estate rode lamentabillye,
Tyll he approched, certes, sodenlye,
The fontayn and well of Thursty Gladnesse
(As said is, it came of the fayrie)."
Romance of Partenay (or Melusine), circâ 1500, ed. Skeat, 18.

"For to that holy wood is consecrate
A virtuous well, about whose flowery banks
The nimble-footed fairies dance their rounds
By the pale moonshine, dipping oftentimes
Their stolen children, so to make them free
From dying flesh and dull mortality—"
Fletcher's *Faithful Shepherdess* (1610). I find the following recipe for making a holy well: "Let them finde out some strange water, some unheard of spring. It is an easie matter to discolour or alter the taste of it in some measure (it makes no matter how little). Report strange cures that it hath done. Beget a superstitious opinion of it. Good fellowship shall uphold it, and the neighbouring townes shall all sweare for it." Powell's *Tom of all Trades*, 1631, p. 31. Compare *Bromfield.*

Holy Wells and Fountains in Scotland.

—Shaw, in his "History of the Province of Moray," tells us "that true rational Christian knowledge, which was almost quite lost under Popery, made very slow progress after the Reformation. That the prevailing ignorance was attended with much superstition and credulity; heathenish and Romish customs were much practised: Pilgrimages to wells and chapels were frequent." Henry Adamson says, in the "Muses Threnodie," St. Conil's Well, in Scotland. "This well, dedicated to St. Conwall, whose anniversary was celebrated on the 18th of May, is near to Ruthven Castle or Hunting Tower. It is sufficient to serve the town of Perth with pure, wholesome water, if it were brought down by pipes. In the days of superstition this well was much resorted to." *Repr. of Ed.* 1638, 175. We find that in the last century there was at Balmanno "a fine spring-well, called St. John's Well, which in antient times was held in great estimation. Numbers, who thought its waters of a sanative quality, brought their rickety children to be washed in its stream. Its water was likewise thought a sovereign remedy for sore eyes, which, by frequent washing, was supposed to cure them. To shew their gratitude to the Saint, and that he might be propitious to continue the virtues of the waters, they put into the well presents, not indeed of any great value, or such as would have been of the least service to him, if he had stood in need of money, but such as they conceived the good and merciful apostle, who did not delight in costly oblations, could not fail to accept. The presents generally given were pins, needles, and rags taken from their cloaths. This may point out the superstition of those times. "Stat. Acc. of Scotl." vol. xviii., p. 630, Parish of Mary-kirk, co. Kincardine. Comp. *Blessing of Clouts.*

It appears, that in the last century, it was usual at Nigg, co. Kincardine, in the month of May, for many of the lower ranks from around the adjacent city (Aberdeen) to come to drink of a well in the Bay of Nigg, called Downey Well; and, proceeding a little farther, to go over a narrow pass, the Brigge of ae Hair, to Downy-Hill, a green island in the sea, where young people cut their favourites' names in the sward. It seems to have been the remains of some superstitious respect to the fountain and retreat of a reputed saint gone into an innocent amusement. *Stat. Acc. of Scotland*, vii., 213. The minister of Kirkmichael, Banffshire, about the same time, made these general remarks on the subject: "The same credulity that gives hair-formed inhabitants to green hillocks and solitary groves, has given their portion of genii to rivers and fountains. The presiding spirit of that element, in Celtic mythology, was called Neithe. The primitive of this word signifies to wash or purify with water. To this day fountains are regarded with particular veneration over every part of the Highlands. The sick, who resort to them for health, address their vows to the presiding powers, and offer presents to conciliate their favour. These presents generally consist of a small piece of money, or a few fragrant flowers. The vulgar in many parts of the Highlands, even at present, not only pay a sacred regard to particular fountains, but are firmly persuaded that certain lakes are inhabited by spirits. In Strathspey there is a lake called Lochnan Spioradan, the Lake of Spirits. Two frequently make their appearance — the Horse, and the Bull of the Water. The Mermaid is another. Before the rivers are swelled by heavy rains, she is frequently seen, and is always considered as a sure prognostication of drowning. In Celtic mythology to the above-named is a fourth spirit added. When the waters are agitated by a violent current of wind, and streams are swept from their surface and driven before the blast, or whirled in circling eddies aloft in the air, the vulgar, to this day, consider this phenomenon as the effect of the angry spirit operating upon that element. They call it by a very expressive name, the Mariach shine, or the Rider of the Storm." It is added: "Near the kirk of this parish there is (1794) a fountain, once highly celebrated, and antiently dedicated to St. Michael. Many a patient have its waters restored to health, and many more have attested the efficacy of their virtues. But, as the presiding power is sometimes capricious, and apt to desert his charge, it now lies neglected, choked with weeds, unhonoured and unfrequented. In better days it was not so; for the winged guardian, under the semblance of a fly, was never absent from his duty. If the sober matron wished to know the issue of her husband's ailment, or the love-sick nymph that of her languishing swain, they visited the Well of St. Michael. Every movement of the sympathetic fly was regarded in silent awe; and as he appeared cheerful or dejected, the anxious votaries drew their presages; their breasts vibrated with correspondent emotions. Like the Delai Lama of Thibet, or the King of Great Britain, whom a fiction of the English law supposes never to die, the Guardian Fly of the Well of St. Michael was believed to be exempted from the laws of mortality.

To the eye of ignorance he might sometimes appear dead, but agreeably to the Druidic system, it was only a transmigration into a similar form, which made little alteration on the real identity." "Not later than a fortnight ago," (it is added) "the writer of this account was much entertained to hear an old man lamenting with regret the degeneracy of the times; particularly the contempt in which objects of former veneration were held by the unthinking crowd. If the infirmities of years and the distance of his residence did not prevent him, he would still pay his devotional visits to the Well of St. Michael. He would clear the bed of its ouze, open a passage for the streamlet, plant the borders with fragrant flowers, and once more, as in the days of youth, enjoy the pleasure of seeing the Guardian Fly skim in sportive circles over the bubbling wave, and with its little proboscis imbibe the panacean dews." Ordiquhill, Banffshire. The Mineral Well, "dedicated to the Virgin Mary, was formerly, at certain seasons, much resorted to by the superstitious as well as the sick." "There are in Perthshire several wells and springs dedicated to St. Fillan, which are still places of pilgrimage and offerings, even among the Protestants. They are held powerful in cases of madness, and in cases of very late occurrence lunatics have been left all night bound to the holy stone, in confidence that the saint would cure and unloose them before morning." *Stat. Acc.*, xvii., 377. Again: Parish of Little Dunkeld, Perthshire. "Here there are a fountain and the ruins of a chapel, both dedicated by antient superstition to St. Laurence": and again: "Near Tarbat, (Synod of Ross), there is a plentiful spring of water, which continues to bear the name of Tobair Mhuir, or Mary's Well." Glenorchay and Inishail, Argyleshire. "Near the parish school, is the well of St. Connon," the tutelar saint of the county, "memorable for the lightness and salubrity of its water." Trinity Gask, Perthshire. "The most noted well in the parish is at Trinity Gask. It is remarkable for the purity and lightness of its water; the spring is copious and perennial. Superstitions, aided by the interested artifices of Popish priests, raised, in times of ignorance and bigotry, this well to no small degree of celebrity. It was affirmed that every person who was baptized with the water would never be seized with the plague. The extraordinary virtue of Trinity Gask Well has perished with the downfall of superstition." *Stat. Acc. of Scotl.*, vi., 384, 431; viii., 351; xii., 464; xvi., xviii., 487.

Martin observes, "Loch-siant Well in Skie is much frequented by strangers as well as by the inhabitants of the Isle, who generally believe it to be a specifick for several diseases; such as stitches, headaches, stone, consumptions, megrim. Several of the common people oblige themselves by a vow to come to this Well and make the ordinary tour about it, called dessil, which is performed thus: They move thrice round the well, proceeding sun-ways, from east to west, and so on. This is done after drinking of the water; and when one goes away from the well, it's a never failing custom to leave some small offering on the stone which covers the well. There is a small coppice near it, of which none of the natives dare venture to cut the least branch, for fear of some signal judgement to follow upon it." He also speaks of a well of similar quality, at which, after drinking, they make a tour and then leave an offering of some small token, such as a pin, needle, farthing, or the like, on the stone cover which is above the well.

In the *Antiquary* for 1890, Mr. Hope printed a long series of notices of wells and fountains of reputed sanctity in different parts of the kingdom. It has been shown (ibid. 1884) that the practice of well-dressing, or decking the wells with garlands and flowers, inherited from the Roman *Fontinalia*, yet lingered in some parts of the country down to about 1830. It is to be regarded as one of the numberless vestiges and survivals of Paganism. See *St. Andrew's Well, Bede's Well, Stones,* and *Waking the Well.*

Camerarius gives us a minute account of presaging fountains: "I have heard a Prince say, that there is in his territories a fountaine that yeelds a current of water which runs continually; and ever when it decreaseth, it presageth dearnesse of victuals: but when it groweth drie, it signifieth a dearth. There is a fountaine in Glomutz, a citie of Misnia, a league from the river Elbis, which of itself making a pond, produceth oftentimes certaine strange effects, as the inhabitants of the country say, and many that have seene the same witnesse. When there was like to be a good and fruitful peace in all the places about, this fountaine would appeare covered with wheat, oats, and akornes, to the great joy of the countrey people that flock thether from all parts to see the same. If any cruell war doe threaten the countrey, the water is all thick with blood and with ashes, a certaine presage of miserie and ruine to come. In old times the Vandals Sorabes came everie yeare in great troupes to this wonderfull fountaine, where they sacrificed to their idols and enquired after the fruitfulnesse of the yeare following. And myselfe know some gentlemen that confesse, if a certaine fountaine (being otherwise very cleane and cleare), be suddenly troubled by meanes of a worme unknowne, that the same is a personall summons for some of them to depart out of the world." Dallaway, speaking of the Bosphorus, tells us "Frequent fountains are seen on the shore, of the purest water, to which is attached one of the strongest and most antient superstitions of the Greek Church. They are called 'ayasmà,' and to repeat certain prayers at stated seasons, and to drink deeply of them, is held to be a most salutary act of their religion. *Constantinople,* 1797, 144. Commander Cameron, in his well-known *Narrative of a Journey across Africa,* mentions several instances of the idolatrous veneration of the natives for springs, which they imagine to be the abiding-places of spirits, and into which they cast a bead or so for the purpose of propitiation.

Honey Fair.—At Wrexham, in North Wales, this used, before the introduction of railways, to be held four times a year, and March Honey Fair lasted a fortnight. There were squares of shops, where the produce from various parts was on sale: The Birmingham Square, the Yorkshire Square, &c. All the shop-keepers in North Wales, as well as private persons, attended to make purchases. Honey was almost exclusively the article offered; but Irish lace and Belfast linen were other specialities. At present the trade in honey is chiefly conducted on the two last Thursdays in September in the General Market as part of the business; the old Squares have been pulled down or converted to other purposes. *Mr. John Bury of Wrexham's Letter to the Editor,* 20 Feb., 1897.

Honeymoon.—The honeymoon does not seem to have been observed of old, and no stated time was understood to elapse between the nuptials and the reception of friends at home by the married couple. Thomas Copley, Esq., of Gatton, county Surrey, in a letter to Sir Thomas Cawarden, July 18th, 1558, says that he was going to be married on the Sunday following, and that on the Wednesday he should be happy to see Sir Thomas at Gatton, "at wch daie I thynke we shall come home." In the "Wright's Chast Wife," a poem supposed by Mr. Furnivall to have been written about 1462, it is said of the Wright and his magical rose garland:

> "Of thys chaplett hym was fulle fayne,
> And of hys wyfe, was nott to layne;
> He weddyd her fulle sone,
> And ladde her home wyth solempnite,
> And hyld her brydlle dayes thre,
> Whan they home come."

This poem is laid in a humble sphere of life; and even now it is not usual for working folks to remain more than a few days away after the marriage.

The French have the equivalent, which they know as *Lune de Miel*.

Hoodman-Blind or **Hooper's Hide.** — Variant names for blindman's buff. Nares, *Gloss.* in v. cites a passage, where the second name is figuratively applied.

Hoop.—A boy's game from very ancient days. See St. John's *Manners and Customs of Ancient Greece*, 1842, i., 147-8. It probably evolved from the improved wheel, as that may have done from the mathematical circle. Hoop occurs among the puerile sports delineated in the Missal seen by Strutt in the possesion of Mr. Ives. It is also noticed by Charlotte Smith in her "Rural Walks":

"Sweet age of blest delusion ! blooming boys,
Ah ! revel long in childhood's thoughtless joys;
With light and pliant spirits, that can stoop
To follow sportively the rolling hoop;
To watch the sleeping top with gay delight,
Or mark with raptur'd gaze the sailing kite :
Or eagerly pursuing pleasure's call,
Can find it centred in the bounding ball !"

and Gray recalls in his verses his youthful experiences in this direction at Eton. Some of the Latin poets allude to *plectrum*, or hoop-stick. Both hoop and conductor were originally of wood.

Hopping is derived from the A.-S. *hoppan*, to leap, or dance. Dancings in the North of England, and I believe (colloquially) in other parts, are called Hops. The word in its original meaning is preserved in grass-hopper. The word "hoppe" occurs in Chaucer, in the beginning of the "Cokes Tale." In many villages in the North of England these meetings are still kept up, under the name of Hoppings. We shall hope that the rejoicings on them are still restrained in general within the bounds of innocent festivity; though it is to be feared they sometimes prove fatal to the morals of our swains, and corrupt the innocence of our rustic maids. In "A Joco-serious Discourse between a Northumberland Gentleman and his Tenant" (by George Stuart), 1686, p. 32, we read :

"To horse-race, fair, or hoppin go,
There play our casts among the whipsters,
Throw for the hammer, lowp for flippers,
And see the maids dance for the ring,
Or any other pleasant thing;
——for the Pigg, lye for the Whetstone,
Or chuse what side to lay our betts on."

Hop Queen.—See *Harvest Lord and Lady.*

Hopscotch.—A common children's game. See Halliwell in v.

Horn. — It is well known that the word horn in the sacred writings denotes fortitude and vigour of mind; and that in the classics personal courage (metaphorically from the pushing of horned animals) is intimated by horns. Horn is used vulgarly to signify the virile symbol : "His horn shall be exalted"; "The horn of my salvation," &c. Comp. *Horns.*

Horn, Tenure by the.—Compare Hazlitt's ed. of Blount's *Tenures*, 1874, pp. 248, 346. It may be added that at Queen's College, Oxford, there is a drinking horn, presented by the foundress, Philippa, queen of Edward III., holding two quarts Winchester measure, and securing the ownership of a manor in Dorsetshire.

Horn-Book or **Battledore.**—See Halliwell in v., and the late Mr. A. W. Tuer's monograph.

Horn Dance.—An amusement pursued at Abbot's Bromley, a village on the borders of Needwood Forest, in Staffordshire, since ancient times, and described and illustrated in the *Strand Magazine* for November, 1896.

Horn Fair.—Grose mentions a fair called Horn-Fair, held at Charlton, in Kent, on St. Luke's Day, the 18th October. It consisted of a riotous mob, who, after a printed summons dispersed through the adjacent towns, met at Cuckold's Point, near Deptford, and marched from thence in procession through that town and Greenwich to Charlton, with horns of different kinds upon their heads; and at the fair there were sold rams' horns and every sort of toy made of horn; even the ginger-bread figures had horns. A sermon used to be preached at Charlton Church on the fair day. Tradition attributes the origin of this licentious fair to King John, who being detected in an adulterous amour, compounded for his crime by granting to the injured husband all the land from Charlton to Cuckold's Point, and established the fair as a tenure. It appears that it was the fashion in William Fuller's time to go to Horn Fair dressed in women's clothes. "I remember being there upon Horn Fair day, I was dressed in my land-lady's best gown, and other women's attire, and to Horn Fair we went, and as we were coming back by water, all the cloaths were spoiled by dirty water, &c., that was flung on us in an inundation, for which I was obliged to present her with two guineas, to make atonement for the damage sustained." &c. *Life of W. Fuller*, 1703, p. 122. In an extract from an old newspaper, I find it was formerly a custom for a procession to go from some of the inns in Bishopsgate Street, in which were a king. a queen, a miller, a councillor, &c., and a great number of others, with horns in their hats, to Charlton, where they went round the church three times, &c. So many indecencies were committed upon this occasion on Blackheath (as the whipping of females with furze, &c.), that it gave rise to the proverb of "all is fair at Horn Fair." This account is perhaps connected with that given in a tract of 1711, which is a letter announcing a meeting of the most Ancient Company of Fumblers at the annual festival at Horn Fair, October 14th, when it appears that they wore horns on their head and carried pickaxes, shovels. &c., in their hands. Lysons in his "Environs," says, the burlesque procession has been discontinued since the year 1768.

Horning.—A Scotish method of proclaiming an offender. There is a warrant under the date 1680 for imprisoning and putting to the horn one Roderick Mackenzie. Under the old Scotish law a witness might be debarred from deposing or giving his evidence, and tendering his oath, by horning, and in the same way he was bound to compear and respond on a future occasion at the horn under pain of contumacy. Spotiswood's *Form of Process*, 1711, p. 78.

Hornpipe.—Henry Spelman, in his *Relation of Virginia*, 1609., says, under the head of *Pastimes*, "When they meet at feasts or otherwise, "they vse sports much like to ours heare in England, as ther daunsinge, wch is like our darbysher Hornepipe, a man first and then a woman, and so through them all, hanging all in a round ; ther is one wch stands in the midest wth a pipe and a rattell, wth wh. when he beginns to make a noyse all the rest gigetts about, wriinge ther neckes and scrapinge on ye ground." Humphrey King, in his *Halfe-Pennyworth of Wit*, 1613, refers to "a harsh Lancashire Horn-pipe."

Horns (i.).—Hearne, in his Preface to "Robert of Gloucester," p. xviii., speaking of the old custom of drinking out of horns, observes : "'Tis no wonder, therefore, that, upon the Jollities on the first of May formerly, the custom of blowing with, and drinking in, horns so much prevailed, which, though it be now generally disus'd, yet the custom of blowing them prevails at this season, even to this day, at Oxford, to remind people of the pleasantness of that part of the year, which ought to create mirth and gayety, such as is sketch'd out in some old books of Offices, such as the ' Prymer of Salisbury,' printed at Rouen, 1551, 8vo." That the twofold use of the horn for drinking and blowing purposes is very ancient seems to be shown

by the poem entitled "The Cokwolds Daunce" ("Remains of E. P. Poetry of Eng." i.). Aubrey, in his "Remains of Gentilisme and Judaisme," MS. Lansd. 226, fol. 5 b. says : "Memorandum, at Oxford the boys do blow cow horns and hollow canes all night ; and on May Day the young maids of every parish carry about garlands of flowers, which afterwards they hang up in their churches."

Horns (ii.).—There used to be a vulgar saying that "a husband wears horns," or is a Cornute, when his wife proves false to him ; as also that of the meaning of the word cuckold, which has for many ages been the popular indication of the same kind of infamy. The following is extracted from the "Gentleman's Magazine" for December, 1786 : "I know not how far back the idea of giving his head this ornament may be traced, but it may be met with in Artemidorus (Lib. ii.) and I believe we must have recourse to a Greek epigram for an illustration :

Οστις εσω πυροος καταλαμβανει ουκ αγοραζων,

Κεινον Αμαλθειας ή γυνη εστι κερq.

"—— Namque in malos asperrimus Parata tollo Cornua."—Horat. *Epod.*
"Jam feror in pugnas & nondum Cornua sumpsi."

Ovid *De Ebrietate*. It is said to have been a custom of the Emperor Andronicus to hang up in a frolic, in the porticoes of the Forum, the stag's horns he had taken in hunting, intending, as he says, by this new kind of insignia, to denote at once the manners of the city, the lasciviousness of the wives he had debauched, and the size of the animals he had made his prey, and that from hence the sarcasm spread abroad that the husband of an adulterous wife bare horns. The twofold application of the horn is suggested in a passage in the *Boke of Mayd Emlyn* (about 1540) :

"She wude byte and whyne
Whan she saw her tyme,
   And with a prety gynne
Gyue her husbande an horne,
To blow with on the morne :
   Beshrewe her whyte skynne."

Hazlitt's *Popular Poetry*, iv., 84. There is a singular passage upon this subject, which I shall give, and leave, too, without comment, as I find it. The historians are speaking of the monument of Thomas the first Lord Wharton, in the church of Kirby Stephen in Westmoreland, the crest of whose arms was a bull's head : "The consideration of horns, generally used upon the crest, seemeth to account for what hath hitherto by no author or other person ever been accounted for ; namely the connexion betwixt horns and cuckolds. The notion of cuckolds wearing horns prevails through all the modern European languages, and is of four or five hundred years standing. The particular estimation of badges and distinction of arms began in the time of the Crusades, being then more especially necessary to distinguish the several nations of which the armies were composed. Horns upon the crest, according to that of Silius Italicus,

' Casside cornigera dependens Insula ' were erected in terrorem; and after the husband had been absent three or four years, and came home in his regimental accoutrements, it might be no impossible supposition that the man who wore the horns was a cuckold. And this accounts, also, why no author at that time, when the droll notion was started, hath ventured to explain the connexion : for, woe be to the man in those days that should have made a joke of the Holy War ; which indeed, in consideration of the expence of blood and treasure attending it, was a very serious affair." Nicolson and Burn's " History of Westmoreland and Cumberland," vol. i., p. 540. Bulwer, in his *Chironomia*, says : " To present the index and eare-finger (i.e. the fore and little finger) wagging, with the thumb applied unto the temples is their expression who would scornfully reprove any. The same gesture, if you take away the motion, is used, in our nimble-fingered times, to call one cuckold, and to present the Badge of Cuckoldry, that mentall and imaginary horn ; seeming to cry, ' O man of happy note, whom Fortune meaning highly to promote, hath stucke on thy forehead the earnest penny of succeeding good lucke."

In Greene's *Disputation between a He Conycatcher and a She Conycatcher*, 1592, is the following witticism on this head : " Hee that was hit with the horne was pincht at the heart." Again : " Let him dub her husband Knight of the forked Order." In "Titus Andronicus," 1594, act ii., sc. 3, the following occurs :

" Under your patience, gentle Emperess,
'Tis thought you have a goodly gift in horning.
Jove shield your husband from his hounds to day !
'Tis pity, they should take him for a stag."

Shakespear and Ben Jonson seem both to have considered the horns in this light : " Well, he may sleep in security, for he hath the horn of abundance, and the lightness of his wife shines through it : and yet he cannot see, though he has his own lanthorn to light him."

" What ! never sigh,
Be of good cheer, man, for thou art a cuckold.
'Tis done, 'tis done ! nay, when such flowing store,
Plenty itself, falls in my wife's lap,
The Cornu Copiæ will be mine, I know."

So in *Othello*, 1622 :

" O curse of marriage !
—'Tis Destiny, unshunnable like Death.
Even then this forked plague is fated to us,
When we do quicken."—Act iii., sc. 3.

There is the following curious epigram in " Witts Recreations," 1640 :

" *To Festus.*
" Festus th' art old, and yet wouldst maryed be :
Ere thou do so, this counsel take of me :
Look into Lillies Grammar, there thou'lt find,
Cornu a horn, a word still undeclin'd."

The following passage occurs in " The Horne exalted," 1661 : " Horns are signified by the throwing out the little and fore-finger when we point at such whom we tacitly call cuckolds." In " The English Fortune Teller," by Philips, 1703, the author, speaking of a wanton's husband, says : " He is the wanton wenches game amongst themselves, and Wagges sport to poynt at with two fingers."

Armstrong says, the inhabitants of Minorca bear hatred to the sight and name of a horn : " for they never mention it but in anger, and then they curse with it, saying *Guerno*, as they would *Diablo*." *Hist. of Minorca*, 2nd ed., 1756, p. 170. In Spain it is a crime as much punishable by the laws to put up horns against a neighbour's house, as to have written a libel against him. It was an offence also in the eye of the law among the Venetians, and a doge's son was severely punished on this account in the fourteenth century. Hazlitt's *Venice*, 1900, ii., 742. We are told that even among the Indians it was the highest indignity that could be offered them even to point at a horn. Comp. *Cuckoldom and Skimmington*.

Horns at Highgate, to Swear on the. — A sufficient account of this usage may be found in Hone and other readily accessible authorities. The Green Dragon at Highgate, demolished in 1899, was one of the houses where the burlesque oath was administered in the coaching days. The Old Red Lion was another. See Hazlitt's *Proverbs*, 1882, p. 167.

Hornage.—A quantity of corn formerly given yearly to the lord of the manor for every ox worked in the plough on lands within his jurisdiction. *Halliwell.*

Horoscopes.—Sheridan says: "To give some little notion of the ancients concerning horoscopes. The Ascendant was understood by them, to be that part of Heaven which arises in the East the moment of the child's birth. This, containing thirty degrees, was called the first house. In this point the astrologers observed the position of the celestial constellations, the planets, and the fixed stars, placing the planets and the signs of the zodiac in a figure, which they divided into twelve houses, representing the whole circumference of Heaven. The first was Angulus Orientis, (by some called the Horoscope), shewing the form and complexion of the child then born: and likewise the rest had their several significations, too tedious to be inserted here, because of no use in the least. The heathen astrologers, in casting nativities, held that every man's genius was the companion of his horoscope, and that the horoscope was tempered by it: hence proceeded that union of minds and friendship which was observed among some. This appears from Plutarch in his Life of Anthony, concerning the Genii of Anthony and C. Octavius. Those who have the curiosity of being farther informed in these astrological traditions, let them consult Ptolemy, Alcabitius, Albo Hali, Guido Bonat, &c." *Notes on Persius*, p. 79, ed. 1739.

Horse.—Brand says:—"Perhaps it will be thought no uninteresting article in this little Code of Vulgar Antiquities to mention a well-known interjection used by the country people to their horses, when yoked to a cart, &c. Heit or Heck! I find this used in the days of Chaucer:

'Thay seigh a cart, that chargid was with hay,
Which that a carter drop forth in his way,
Deep was the way, for which the carte stood:
This carter smoot and cryde as he wer wood,
'Hayt, brok; hayt, scot;' what, spare ye for the stoones!'

The name of Brok is still in common use amongst farmers' draught oxen. A learned friend says, "the exclamation 'Geho, Geho,' which carmen use to their horses is not peculiar to this country, as I have heard it used in France." In the "Mactatio Abel," one of the Towneley series of Mysteries, there are some curious interjectional forms of this class. But in "John Bon and Mast Person," 1548, we get the form 'ree who' instead of 'gee

wo.' Hobs the tanner, in Heywood's Edward IV. 1600, says of his mare, "Why, man, Brock my mare knows ha and ree, and will stand when I cry ho." As to the meaning of the term brock, see Halliwell's "Archaic Dictionary," 1847, *ad vocem.* Forby, in his "Vocabulary," says that ge-ho means go-stop, and ge-wo go-go. In fact, when a driver wishes his horse to stop, he should say ho! and when he desires him to proceed, wo! The two words are at present confused. Ge—go seems to present itself in a reduplicated form in ge-ge, the nursery name for a horse. In "The Cold Yeare, 1614. A Deepe Snow, &c." printed in 1615, we find: "After the collier they (the team) ran, who cryed, hey, and hoe, and ree, and gee; but none of his carterly rethoricke was able to stay them." "In olde time," (it is said in the *Man in the Moon*, telling fortunes to Englishmen, 1609, sign. G 3), "such as solde horses were wont to put flowers or boughes upon their heads, to reveale that they were vendible." But the following passage from Flecknoe's Epigrams shews that ribbons were, as at present, also usual:

"As horse-coursers their horses set to sale,
With ribonds on their foreheads and their tail;
So all our poets' gallantry now-a-days
Is in the prologues and epilogues of their plays."

In the *Character of a Quack Astrologer*, 1673, speaking of "Itch of picture in the Front," the author says: "This sets off the pamphlet in a country fair, as the horse sells the better for the ribbon, wherewith a jockey tyes up his tail."

As regards the names of horses, one of the earliest English Lists seems to be that of certain horses destined to accompany the forces engaged in the French war at the time of the battle of Agincourt in 1415, where a very interesting entry presents itself in the mention of Thomas Chaucer, Butler of England, and of a horse, probably his, described as Bayard Chaucer. Other equine designations are Lyard, Grey, Morell, and Sorell. See Hunter's *Agincourt*, 1850, pp. 43, 54. Morel, Moriel, or Morrell became a favourite designation for a horse. In the *fabliau* of Eustace the Monk that daring adventurer makes off with Moriel, the horse of the Count of Boulogne, an animal of matchless swiftness. Among the Plumpton Correspondence, under 1466, there is a mention of "good morrel and his felow." *Pl. Corr.*, p. 17. In *John Bon and Mast Person* (1548) the concluding lines seem to point to contemporary terms for horses employed at the plough:

" Ha ! browne done ! forth, that horson crabbe ! ...
haight, blake hab !
Have agayne, bald before, hayght, ree who !—"

—Hazlitt's *Popular Poetry*, 1864-6, iv., 16. In the Diary of the first Earl of Bristol (1665-1751) a series of equine appellations will be found. The list has been recently (1904) communicated by the present writer to the *Connoisseur*. Morel continued to be a common term for a dark-coloured horse in the time of Elizabeth, and occurs in the familiar story of the *Wife lapped in Morel's Skin*. In *Twelfth Night*, iii., 4, Sir Andrew Aguecheek is made to propose the gift of his horse Grey Capilet to the man, whose anger he is desirous of averting.

The horse ridden by Charles VIII. of France at the battle of Fornovo in 1495 was called Savoy, and was remarkable for his swiftness. Hazlitt's *Venetian Republic*, 1900, ii., 137. Presents of horses were frequently made to Henry VIII. by foreign potentates with a view to propitiating him. Ibid., ii, 408.

In Homeric times the Greeks prided themselves on their breeds of horses; but some of the most celebrated came from the East. As it was with the Romans they employed the swiftest and most enduring, not in the way that the modern nations do, but in their chariot races. St. John's *Manners and Customs of Ancient Greece*, 1842, ii., 280-2. The tradition of the winged steed Pegasus was of course founded on his speed; the Hellenic thorough-breds were said to have the velocity of birds. The horse of Alexander, called *Bucephalus*, suggests an animal with a short, thick neck, and in the mediæval MSS., where horses are portrayed, this type is conspicuous. Equine nomenclature, as we know, dates very far back into antiquity. Aristotle mentions a mare named *Dicæa*. Amongst the better classes at Rome and in the Roman colonies the names of horses were placed over the stall which each animal occupied, and these memorials have in some cases been preserved in the remains of buildings. Comp. *May-Day* and *Omens* infrâ, and Hazlitt's *Proverbs*, 1882, pp. 37, 108.

Horse and Hattock.—Aubrey, in his " Miscellanies," gives us the following most important piece of information respecting fairies: " When fairies remove from place to place they are said to use the words Horse and Hattock."

Horse-block.—A familiar object outside doors in country-houses and inns, to enable persons, especially ladies, to mount. They were in use at Pompeii, and go back to an era, when riders had no stirrups. Fosbrooke's *Encyclopædia*, 1843, p. 314.

Horse, Dr. Story's Wooden, of Troy.—The executioner's cart. See Halliwell's *Books of Characters*, 22. Dr. Story was hanged in 1571. See Hazlitt's *Bibl. Coll.*, General Index in v.

Horse-Races.—The earliest appear to have been instituted in England in Hyde Park about 1637, when Shirley's *Hyde Park* was published. Before 1646 Charles I. established the races at Newmarket, and we have the name of a horse which won the cup there in Shirley's *Poems*, 1646.—Bay Tarrall. The resort to Epsom Downs does not seem to have been anterior to the closing years of the reign of Anne; but under Charles II. there were races at Leith under the control of the Lord Provost of Edinburgh, as we learn from the Rules or Articles drawn up for their management, and printed as a folio broadside. Compare Haydn's *Dict. v. Races* for a very fair outline of the subject, and Hazlitt's *Manual of Old Plays*, 1892, v. *Hyde Park*. In 1654 and 1658 proclamations appeared forbidding for a certain term the usual horse-races throughout England and Wales. But Scotland and Ireland are not indicated.

Horse-Shoe.—Nailing of horseshoes seems to have been practised as well to keep witches in, as to keep them out. Douce's notes say: " The practice of nailing horse-shoes to thresholds resembles that of driving nails into the walls of cottages among the Romans, which they believed to be an antidote against the plague : for this purpose L. Manlius, A. U. C. 390, was named Dictator, to drive the nail." " That the horse-shoe may never be pul'd from your threshold," occurs among the good wishes introduced by Holiday in " The Marriage of the Arts," 1618. Aubrey tells us that " it is a thing very common to nail horseshoes on the thresholds of doors : which is to hinder the power of witches that enter into the house. Most houses of the West end of London have the horse-shoe on the threshold. It should be a horse-shoe that one finds." But the horse-shoe, as it has been elsewhere explained, was used for other purposes. " In the Bermudas they use to put an iron into the fire when a witch comes in. Mars is enemy to Saturn." Aubrey adds: " under the porch of Staninfield Church in Suffolk, I saw a tile with a horse-shoe upon it, placed there for this purpose, though one would imagine that holy water would alone have been sufficient. I am told there are many other similar instances." *Miscellanies*, p. 148. In Gay's fable of "The Old Woman and her Cats," the supposed witch complains as follows:

—"Crouds of boys
Worry me with eternal noise;
Straws laid across my pace retard,
The horse-shoe's nailed, (each thresh-
    old's guard),
The stunted broom the wenches hide,
For fear that I should up and ride;
They stick with pins my bleeding seat,
And bid me show my secret teat."

Misson, speaking on the subject of the horse-shoe nailed on the door, tells us: "Ayant souvent remarqué un fer de Cheval cloüe au Seuils des portes (chez les Gens de petite etoffe) j'ai demandé a plusieurs ce que cela vouloit dire? On m'a repondu diverses choses differentes; mais la plus generale Reponse a eté, que ces fers se mettoient pour empêcher, les Sorciers d'entrer. Ils rient en disant cela, mais ils ne le disent pourtant pas tout-a-fait en riant; car ils croyent qu'il y a là dedans, ou du moins qu'il peut y avoir quelque vertu secrete: et s'ils n'av-oient pas cette opinion, ils ne s'amuse-roient pas a clouer ce fer à leur porte." *Travels in England*, p. 192. In Mon-mouth-street, says Brand, "many horse-shoes nailed to the thresholds are still to be seen (1797). There used to be one at the corner of Little Queen-street, Hol-born. Sir H. Ellis, on the 26th of April, 1813, counted no fewer than seventeen horse-shoes in Monmouth-street nailed against the steps of doors. There was one in 1869 over the door of a private dwelling in Fulham, near the Bishop's Palace. There is a saying: "When a fool finds a horse-shoe, he thinks aye the like to do." The Editor was driv-ing with the late Mr. Henry Stopes, an East Anglian, in a hansom cab in the Borough in 1887, when the horse slipped its shoe, and Mr. Stopes at once leapt out of the cab and secured it, to place it over the door of his office. It is a piece of Scotish folk-lore, that a horse-shoe nailed to the mast of a fishing-smack will pro-tect it against the weather.

The bawds of Amsterdam believed (in 1687) that a horse-shoe which had either been found or stolen, placed on the chim-ney-hearth, would bring good luck to their houses. They also believed that horse's dung dropped before the house, and put fresh behind the door, would produce the same effect. *Putanisme d'Amsterdam*, pp. 56-7.

Horse-Trick.—A nuptial scene is introduced into Heywood's "Woman Kilde with Kindnesse," 1607. Among the steps in dancing mentioned there, I observe the horse-trick and the cross-point. These two terpsichorean accomplishments

are unnoticed by Strutt, Halliwell, Nares, and others.

Hot Cockles or **Hautes Co-quilles.**—Aubrey says that at funerals in parts of Yorkshire one of the pastimes was Hot Cockles, and what follows illus-trates this observation to a certain ex-tent, although Aubrey does not notice the connection. "Young wenches," says he, "have a wanton sport, which they call moulding of cockle-bread, viz., they gett upon a table-board, and then gather up their knees and their coates with their hands as high as they can, and then they wabble to and fro and say these words, viz.:

My dame is sick and gonne to bed,
And I'll go mowld my cockle-bread.

In Oxfordshire the maids, when they have put themselves into the fit posture, say thus:

My granny is sick, and now is dead,
    And wee'l goe mould some cockle-
        bread.
Up wth my heels and down with my
    head,
And this is the way to mould cockle-
    bread.

I did imagine nothing to have been in this but mere wantonness of youth. (Here he misquotes Juvenal, vi., 129.) But I find in Burchardus, in his *Methodus Con-fitendi*, on the VII. Commandment, one of ye Articles of interrogating a young woman is, if she did ever *subigere panem clunibus*, and then bake it, and give it to one that she loved to eate, *ut in majo-rem modum exardesceret amor?* So here I find it to be a relique of Naturall Mag-ick, an unlawfull philtrum." The full question put to the woman was, accord-ing to Grimm's citation of Burchardus, "Fecisti quod quædam mulieres facere solent, prosternunt se in faciem, et disco-opertis natibus jubent, ut supra nudas nates conficiatur panis, et eo decocto tradunt maritis suis ad comedendum. Hoc ideo faciunt ut plus exardescant in amo-rem illarum." Cockle seems to be, in fact, a corruption of the French coquille, which Le Roux (*Dictionnaire Comique*, 1786, v. *Coquille*) says, "Dans le sens libre signifie á mots couverts la nature d'une femme," for which he quotes a passage from the *History of Francion*. Hot Cockles is therefore Hautes Coquilles; and the custom is very likely to have been introduced hither from France. We know that cockle-bread was the term applied to bread of a coarse brand, made partly of cockle, and it seems very likely that in England the two phrases were confused, and at an early period the distinction lost between the thing supposed to be made and the part, on which it was to be kneaded, our cockle and the French co-quille being so near in sound. The quotation from Burchardus is important, because it demonstrates that the practice was not confined to the young, but was a general usage among females. The late Mr. Coote had heard part of the rhyme given above employed in his time by a nurse to a baby, as she tossed it in her lap:

Up with your heels, and down with your head,
That is the way to make cockle-bread,

which is a singular instance not only of survival, but of distortion. Taking this usage of cockle-bread and its sundry outgrowths as a whole, it has merely to be predicated of it, I think, that we owe our knowledge of such practices to the casual removal of the veil, and by men working on totally different lines, like Aubrey and Burchardt, from the darker phases of the human character and the hidden impurities of life. That libidinous impulses are capable of these and similar excesses, no one required to be told; but the Apostles of Folk-lore, Aubrey, and Burchardt, the publisher of real or supposed scenes in the Confessional, have, each from his own point of view, disclosed here a touch of the less divine part of their own physiology and ours. They have given a few paragraphs where they might have given volumes. After all, I entertain a conviction that, with respect to these hot cockles and likewise to leap-candle, we are merely on the threshold of the inquiry; there is more than Aubrey says, or than appears on the surface, pretty clearly; and the question stands at present much as if one had picked up by accident the husk of some lost substance. Speaking conjecturally, but with certain sidelights to encourage me, this seems a case of the insensible degradation of rite into custom.

Wright furnishes an account of this sport, as practised both here and abroad, tending to shew that its character was modified, and possibly its original incidence forgotten, at a later period, unless there were different types. For the description and accompanying illustrations seem to go no farther than to portray a variety of blindman's buff or hoodman blind, while the one above given represents something infinitely less innocent, and is not even suggested by Mr. Wright. In the following passage from Stevenson's *Twelve Moneths*, 1661, under October, (which work, let us recollect, was originally a reissue of a 1626 book), a different recreation seems to be intended: — "It is now not amisse

to play at hot-cockles hot, unlesse coals be the cheaper." Possibly it is the same as is described in the *Vindication of Christmas*, 1651, as "a harmless sport." Compare Nares, *Gloss.*, 1859, in v. We have here probably the transition successively from a rite to what Nares makes of it, and to a meaningless nursery rhyme. But, again, Mr. Ditchfield *(Old English Customs)*, 1896, p. 64, informs us independently that at Norwich on Shrove Tuesday they sell at the bakers' and confectioners' shops a small currant-loaf called a *coquille*, and that in the shop-windows a notice is set up, that "hot coquilles" are to be had at eight in the morning and four in the afternoon. This is survival with a difference, and another type of coquille, and the form is curious in connection with the Lowestoft *largie*.

House, Haunted.—Pliny tells us that houses were anciently hallowed against evil spirits with brimstone! Gay gives us a fine description of a haunted house:

"Now there spreaden a rumour that everich night
The rooms ihaunted been by many a sprite,
The miller avoucheth, and all thereabout,
That they full oft hearen the hellish rout;
Some saine they hear the gingling of chains,
And some hath heard the Psautries straines,
At midnight some the headless horse imeet,
And some espien a corse in a white sheet,
And oother things, faye, elfin, and elfe,
And shapes that fear createn to itself."

Bourne has preserved the form of exorcising a haunted house, a truly tedious process for the expulsion of demons, who, it should seem, have not been easily ferreted out of their quarters, if one may judge of their unwillingness to depart by the prolixity of this removal-warrant. *Antiq. Vulg.*, 1725, ch. ii.

House-Warming.—This is to the present day a well-understood expression for the entertainment which it is usual to give on removal to a new house, or establishment of a household. The phrase occurs in a letter from Fleetwood, Recorder of London, to Lord Burleigh, July 30, 1577: "Upon Tuesday we had little or no business, saving that the Shoemakers of London [the Cordwainers' Gild], having builded a faire and a newe Hall, made a royalle feast for theire friends, which they call their house-warming." It would not be difficult to accumulate instances of the use of the term in later correspondence; but I do not happen to have met with any earlier example. Pepys, in his *Diary*, Nov. 1, 1666, notes having received a noble cake as a gift, and going the same day with his wife and others, and the addition of some wine, to house-warm Betty Michell. The ceremony has long been exclusively performed at the cost of the householder himself.

Houseleek.—It was thought formerly (and the idea is not perhaps entirely extinct) "that if the herb houseleek, or syngreen, do grow on the house-top, the same house is never stricken with lightning or thunder." It is still common in many parts of England, to plant the herb house-leek upon the tops of cottage houses.

Hove-Dance. — The Court-dance. *Halliwell.*

Huers.—Persons employed to watch on the Cornish coasts, and to give the alarm through a long trumpet, which they carry, of the approach of the shoals of pilchards.

Hugh's St., Day.—The best popular account of St. Hugh, Bishop of Lincoln, may be read in Hone's "Every-Day Book," under Nov. 17. This was also the Shoemakers' feast, St. Hugh being the patron of the "gentle craft," and from a notice in "The Christmas Prince," 1607, the fraternity are to be suspected of having sometimes overstepped the bounds of strict decorum and sobriety on the great professional holiday:

"Bouzer I am not, but mild, sober Tuesday,
    As catt in cap case, if I light not on St. Hewsday."

Compare *Queen Elizabeth's Accession.*

Hunt the Slipper.—This game is noticed by Rogers in the "Pleasures of Memory," 1. 35:

"Twas here we chas'd the slipper by its sound."

It is a holiday game which was till lately in vogue, and is played by children of various growths, sitting on the carpet in a circle.

Hunting of the Ram.—See *Eton School.*

Hunting the Fox.—An early boy's game. See Halliwell in v.

Huntingdon. — The whole of the freemen of the borough assemble in the market-place on the morning of September 15th. The skull of an ox, borne on two poles, is placed at the head of a pro-

cession composed of the freemen and their sons, a certain number of them bearing spades and sticks. Three cheers having been given, the procession moves out of the town, and proceeds to the nearest point of the borough boundary, where the skull is lowered. The procession then moves along the boundary line of the borough, the skull being dragged along the line as if it were a plough. The boundary-holes are dug afresh, and a boy thrown into the hole and struck with a spade. At a particular point called Blackstone Leys refreshments are provided, and the boys compete for prizes. The skull is then raised aloft, and the procession returns to the market-place, and then disperses after three more cheers have been given. *Antiquary*, 1892.

Hunt's Up.—A tune played on the horn to awaken the huntsmen on the morning of the chase. See Halliwell in v.

Hurling.—A game at ball, played with two sides, and a favourite pastime in Cornwall, where at present it is exclusively pursued. A description of it may be found in the *Antiquary*, January, 1888. The rocks called the Hurlers, near Liskeard, are traditionally said to have owed their origin to the conversion into stone of certain players at this game on a Sunday. As early as 1654 a hurling match was played in Hyde Park before the Protector and his council between fifty Cornishmen wearing red caps and fifty others wearing white.

Hurly-Hacket.—An early school boy's diversion in Scotland, which appears to have consisted in sliding down a sharp incline. It is mentioned by Sir David Lyndsay as common to adults in a passage quoted in Southey's *Commonplace Book*, 2nd Series, p. 310.

Hyde Park Fair.—A cant expression for Tyburn. See Hazlitt's *Handbook*, 1867, under *T. R.*

Hydromancy.—Very anciently a species of hydromancy appears to have been practised at wells. "The Druids," says Borlase, "(as we have great reason to think) pretended to predict future events, not only from holy wells and running streams, but from the rain and snow water, which, when settled, and afterwards stirr'd either by oak-leaf, or branch or magic wand, might exhibit appearances of great information to the quick-sighted Druid, or seem so to do to the credulous enquirer, when the priest was at full liberty to represent the appearances as he thought most for his purpose." *Antiq. of Cornwall*, 137. To the divination by water also must be referred the following passage in a list of superstitious practices preserved in the "Life of Harvey the

Conjuror," 1728, p. 58. "Immersion of wooden bowls in water, sinking incharmed and inchanted amulets under water, or burying them under a stone in a grave in a churchyard." I suppose the following species of divination must be considered as a vestige of the ancient hydromancy. An essayist introduces "a person surprising a lady and her company in close cabal over their coffee; the rest very intent upon one, who by her dress and intelligence he guessed was a tire-woman; to which she added the secret of divining by coffee-grounds: she was then in full inspiration, and with much solemnity observing the atoms round the cup: on one hand sat a widow, on the other a maiden lady, both attentive to the predictions to be given of their future fate. The lady (his acquaintance), tho' marryed, was no less earnest in contemplating her cup than the other two. They assured him that every cast of the cup is a picture of all one's life to come: and every transaction and circumstance is delineated with the exactest certainty." *Gents. Mag.*, March, 1731. The same practice is noticed in the "Connoisseur," No. 56, where a girl is represented divining to find out of what rank her husband shall be: "I have seen him several times in coffee grounds with a sword by his side; and he was once at the bottom of a tea cup in a coach and six with two footmen behind."

Hynny-Pynny. — A game played with marbles in Devon and Somerset. See Halliwell in v.